Berlin

THE DOWNFALL 1945

BERLIN

THE DOWNFALL 1945

Antony Beevor

VIKING
an imprint of
PENGUIN BOOKS

VIKING

Published by the Penguin Group
Penguin Books Ltd, 80 Strand, London WC2R 0RL, England
Penguin Putnam Inc., 375 Hudson Street, New York, New York 10014, USA
Penguin Books Australia Ltd, 250 Camberwell Road, Camberwell, Victoria 3124, Australia
Penguin Books Canada Ltd, 10 Alcorn Avenue, Toronto, Ontario, Canada M4V 3B2
Penguin Books India (P) Ltd, 11 Community Centre, Panchsheel Park, New Delhi – 110 017, India
Penguin Books (NZ) Ltd, Cnr Rosedale and Airborne Roads, Albany, Auckland, New Zealand
Penguin Books (South Africa) (Pty) Ltd, 24 Sturdee Avenue, Rosebank 2196, South Africa

Penguin Books Ltd, Registered Offices: 80 Strand, London WC2R 0RL, England

www.penguin.com

First published 2002

6

Copyright © Antony Beevor, 2002
Maps copyright © Raymond Turvey, 2002

The moral right of the author has been asserted

Set in 11.75/14.5pt Monotype Ehrhardt
Typeset by Rowland Phototypesetting Ltd,
Bury St Edmunds, Suffolk
Printed in Great Britain by Clays Ltd, St Ives plc

A CIP catalogue record for this book is available from the British Library

ISBN 0-670-88695-5

Contents

Contents

List of Illustrations

*

43. The end of the battle for Hans-Georg Henke, a teenage conscript.
44. A wounded Soviet soldier tended by a female medical assistant.
45. General Stumpff, Field Marshal Keitel and Admiral von Friedeburg arrive at Karlshorst to sign the final surrender.
46. A Red Army soldier tries to seize a Berliner's bicycle.
47. Marshal Zhukov takes the victory parade on the horse which had thrown Stalin.
48. Zhukov watched by General K. F. Telegin, head of the political department, and General Ivan Serov, the NKVD chief.
49. Visiting the battleground inside the Reichstag.

PHOTOGRAPHIC ACKNOWLEDGEMENTS

AKG London: 3, 6, 7, 8, 9, 13, 17, 22, 24, 26, 28, 34, 37, 40, 42
Alexander Ustinov/Bildarchiv Preußischer Kulturbesitz, Berlin: 27
Bildarchiv Preußischer Kulturbesitz, Berlin: 16, 21, 39, 43
Bundesarchiv Bild, Koblenz: 2 (146/85/22/20), 47 (183/K0907/310)
Chronos, Berlin: 18, 19, 36
Hilmar Pabel/Bildarchiv Preußischer Kulturbesitz, Berlin: 15
Hulton Getty: 46
Imperial War Museum, London: 10 (FLM 3345), 29 (FLM 3351), 30 (FLM 3349), 31 (FLM 3348), 32 (FLM 3346), 33 (FLM 3350)
Jürgen Stumpff/Bildarchiv Preußischer Kulturbesitz, Berlin: 45
National Archives and Records Administration, Maryland: 20 (111-SC-205221), 41 (111-SC-205367), 49 (306-NT-885-C2)
PK-Benno Wundshammer/Bildarchiv Preußischer Kulturbesitz, Berlin: 1
Private Collection/Novosti/Bridgeman Art Library: 23, 25
Ullstein Bild, Berlin: 4, 5, 11, 12, 14, 38, 44
Victor Tiomin: Endpapers, 35

Every effort has been made to contact all copyright holders. The publishers will be glad to make good in future editions any errors or omissions brought to their attention.

Maps

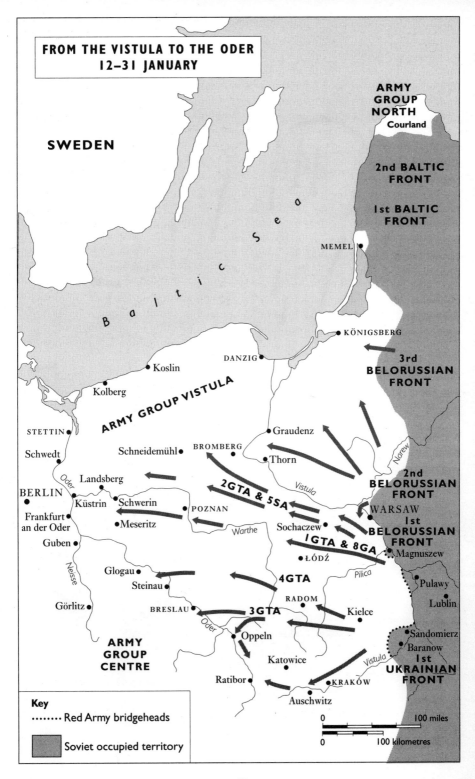

**FROM THE VISTULA TO THE ODER
12–31 JANUARY**

SWEDEN

Baltic Sea

ARMY GROUP NORTH
Courland

2nd BALTIC FRONT

1st BALTIC FRONT

MEMEL

KÖNIGSBERG

3rd BELORUSSIAN FRONT

DANZIG

ARMY GROUP VISTULA

Koslin

Kolberg

STETTIN

Schwedt

Graudenz

Schneidemühl

BROMBERG

Thorn

Narew

Landsberg

2GTA & 5SA

Vistula

2nd BELORUSSIAN FRONT

BERLIN

Küstrin

Schwerin

POZNAN

Sochaczew

WARSAW

1st BELORUSSIAN FRONT

Oder

Frankfurt an der Oder

Meseritz

Warthe

1GTA & 8GA

Guben

ŁÓDŹ

Magnuszew

Pilica

Glogau

4GTA

Pulawy

Neisse

Steinau

RADOM

Lublin

Görlitz

BRESLAU

3GTA

Kielce

Oder

Oppeln

Sandomierz

Baranow

ARMY GROUP CENTRE

Katowice

Vistula

1st UKRAINIAN FRONT

Ratibor

KRAKÓW

Auschwitz

Key

········· Red Army bridgeheads

▇ Soviet occupied territory

0 ——— 100 miles

0 ——— 100 kilometres

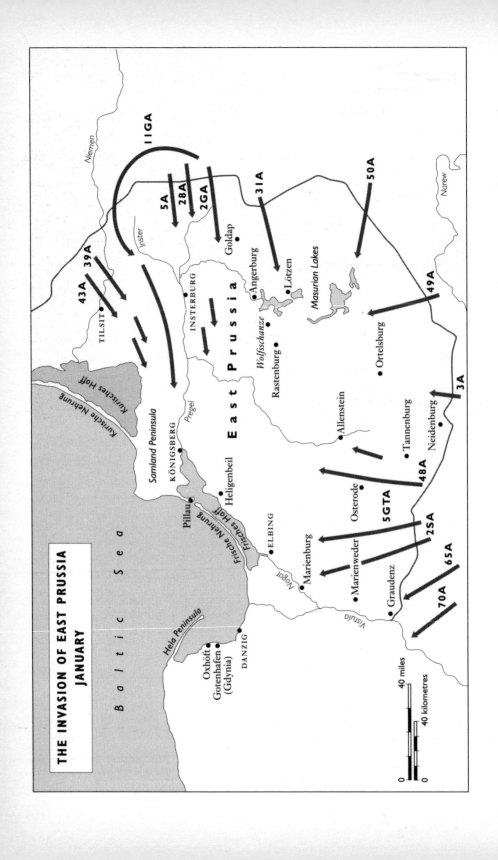

THE INVASION OF EAST PRUSSIA
JANUARY

Baltic Sea

Niemen

11GA

5A 28A 2GA

31A

50A

Narew

39A

43A

Inster

Goldap

Angerburg

Lötzen

Masurian Lakes

49A

TILSIT

INSTERBURG

East Prussia

Wolfsschanze

Rastenburg

Ortelsburg

3A

Kurische Nehrung

Kurisches Haff

Samland Peninsula

Pregel

KÖNIGSBERG

Heligenbeil

Allenstein

Tannenburg

Neidenburg

48A

Pillau

Frische Nehrung

Frisches Haff

ELBING

Ostrode

Osterode

5GTA

Marienburg

Marienweder

2SA

65A

Hela Peninsula

Nogat

Graudenz

70A

Oxhöft
Gotenhafen
(Gdynia)

DANZIG

Vistula

40 miles

40 kilometres

0

0

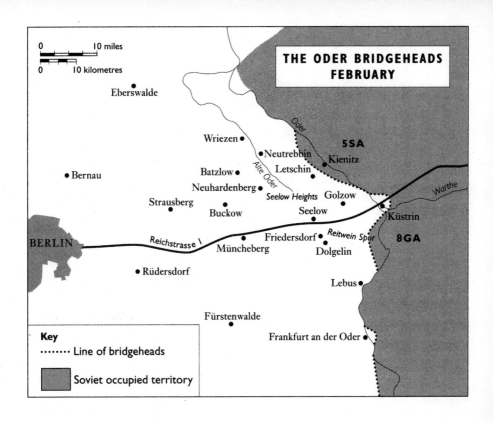

THE ODER BRIDGEHEADS FEBRUARY

0   10 miles
0   10 kilometres

Eberswalde

Wriezen •
•Neutrebbin
Kienitz
5SA
Oder
Batzlow •
Letschin
Alte Oder
Neuhardenberg •
Seelow Heights
Golzow
Bernau •
Strausberg •
Buckow •
Seelow
Worthe
Küstrin
BERLIN
Reichstrasse 1
Friedersdorf •
Reitwein Spur
8GA
Müncheberg
Dolgelin
Rüdersdorf •
Lebus •

Fürstenwalde •

Frankfurt an der Oder •

Key
········ Line of bridgeheads
▨ Soviet occupied territory

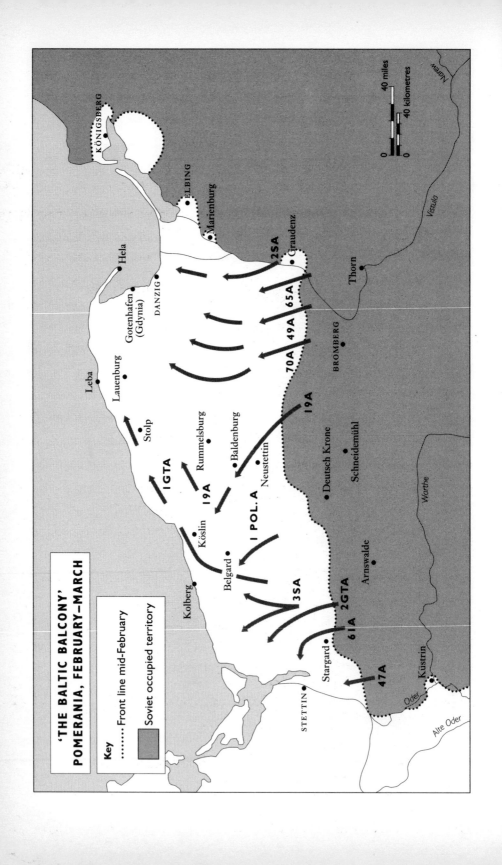

'THE BALTIC BALCONY'
POMERANIA, FEBRUARY–MARCH

Key
.... Front line mid-February
Soviet occupied territory

KÖNIGSBERG

ELBING
Marienburg
Graudenz
Thorn
BROMBERG
Deutsch Krone
Schneidemühl
Arnswalde
Küstrin
Stargard
STETTIN
Kolberg
Belgard
Köslin
Baldenburg
Neustettin
Rummelsburg
Stolp
Lauenburg
Leba
Hela
DANZIG
Gotenhafen
(Gdynia)

Narew
Vistula
Worthe
Oder
Alte Oder

2SA
65A
49A
70A
19A
1GTA
19A
I POL.A
3SA
2GTA
61A
47A

40 miles
40 kilometres
0

Allied and liberated territories

North Sea

HOLLAND

HANOVER ●

Rotterdam ●   ● Arnhem

Waal

GERMANY

Maas

**CAN.
FIRST**

Eindhoven ●   **BR.
SECOND**

● KREFELD

● ANTWERP   **US NINTH**

Ruhr

KASSEL ●

Rhine

BRUSSELS   ●   Hurtgen ●   ● COLOGNE

BELGIUM   ● AACHEN   ● BONN

Remagen ●

US FIRST   ● KOBLENZ

Ardennes

Moselle   FRANKFURT AM MAIN ●

**US
THIRD**   ● MAINZ

LUXEMBOURG

**US
SEVENTH**   ● MANNHEIM

Verdun ●   ● METZ

● KARLSRUHE

● NANCY   STUTTGART ●

STRASBOURG ●

FRANCE   **FR. FIRST**

Black Forest

COLMAR ●

0   100 miles

0   100 kilometres

MULHOUSE ●

Belfort ●

**THE WESTERN FRONT
MARCH–APRIL**

SWITZERLAND

xvii

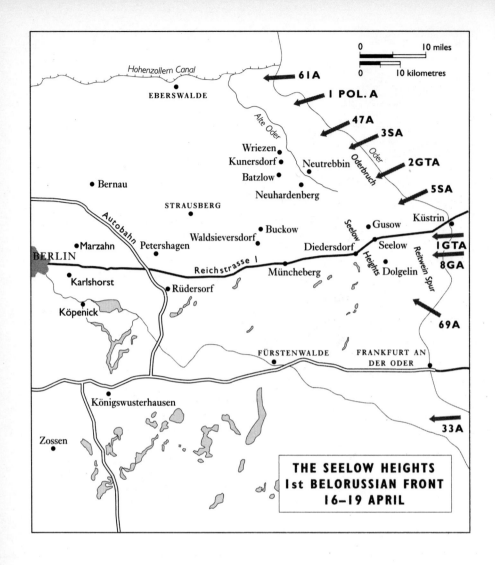

THE SEELOW HEIGHTS
1st BELORUSSIAN FRONT
16–19 APRIL

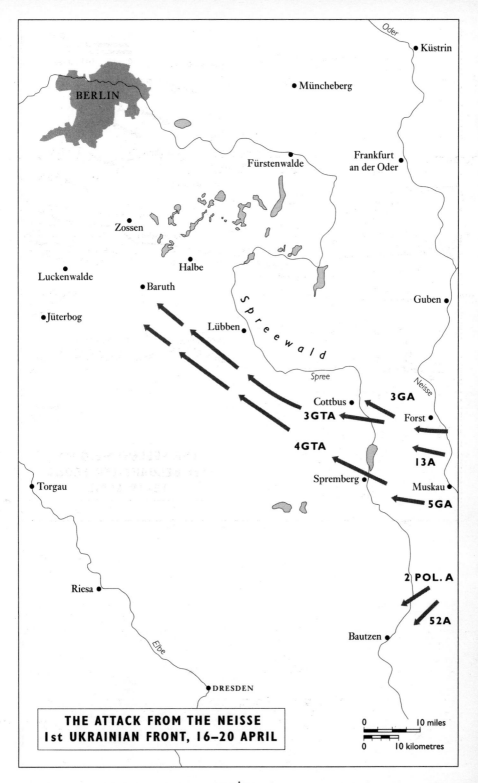

Oder

● Küstrin

● Müncheberg

BERLIN

Frankfurt
an der Oder

Fürstenwalde ●

Zossen ●

Halbe ●

Luckenwalde ●

● Baruth

Lübben ●

Guben ●

● Jüterbog

S p r e e w a l d

Spree

Neisse

Cottbus ●   **3GA**

3GTA   Forst ●

4GTA

13A

Torgau ●

Spremberg ●   Muskau ●

5GA

Riesa ●

2 POL. A

52A

Bautzen ●

Elbe

● DRESDEN

THE ATTACK FROM THE NEISSE
1st UKRAINIAN FRONT, 16–20 APRIL

0   10 miles

0   10 kilometres

xix

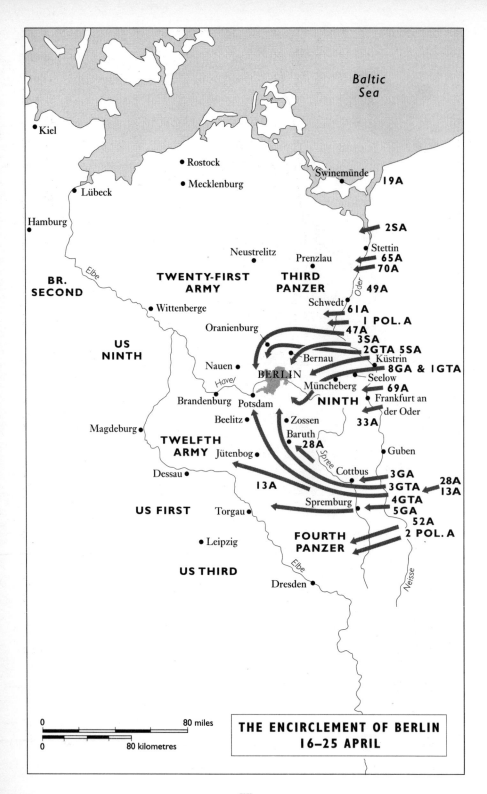

Baltic
Sea

Kiel

Rostock

Mecklenburg

Swinemünde   **19A**

Lübeck

Hamburg

2SA

Neustrelitz   Prenzlau   Stettin

65A

70A

BR.   **TWENTY-FIRST**   **THIRD**   **49A**
SECOND   **ARMY**   **PANZER**

Wittenberge   Schwedt **61A**

US   Oranienburg   **I POL. A**
NINTH   **47A**
                                                3SA
                        Nauen   Bernau   **2GTA 5SA**
                              BERLIN   Küstrin
                                                8GA & IGTA
                                      Müncheberg   Seelow
                        Brandenburg Potsdam **NINTH** **69A**
                                                Frankfurt an
                                                der Oder
Magdeburg   Beelitz   Zossen   **33A**
                                   Baruth
              TWELFTH   **28A**
                ARMY Jütenbog   Guben
                                        Spree Cottbus **3GA** **28A**
Dessau   **13A**   **3GTA** **13A**
US FIRST   Torgau   Spremburg **4GTA**
                                                5GA
                                                52A
                                                2 POL. A
              Leipzig   **FOURTH**
                                   PANZER

US THIRD   Elbe

                        Dresden   Neisse

0   80 miles

0   80 kilometres

THE ENCIRCLEMENT OF BERLIN
16–25 APRIL

XX

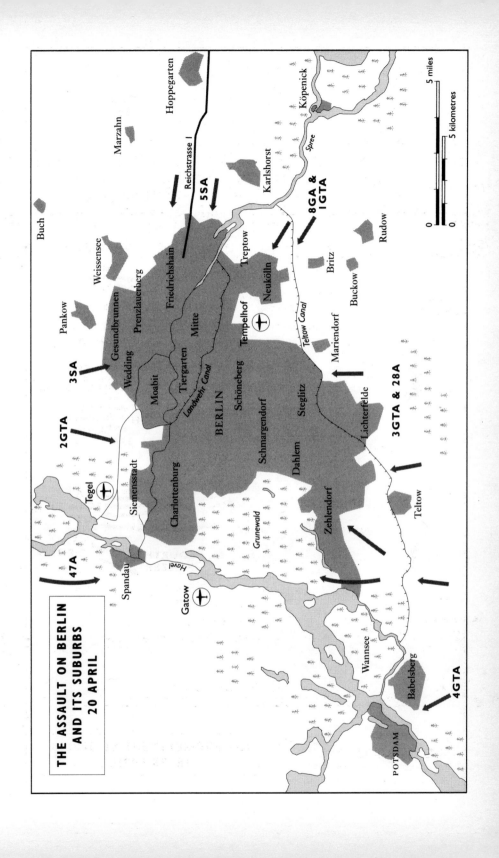

THE ASSAULT ON BERLIN
AND ITS SUBURBS
20 APRIL

5 miles
5 kilometres

47A

2GTA

3SA

Buch

Hoppegarten

Marzahn

Reichstrasse I

5SA

Köpenick

Karlshorst

Spree

8GA &
1GTA

Weissensee

Pankow

Gesundbrunnen

Prenzlauerberg

Friedrichshain

Treptow

Neuköllln

Britz

Buckow

Rudow

Wedding

Moabit

Tiergarten

Mitte

Landwehr Canal

BERLIN

Schöneberg

Tempelhof

Teltow Canal

Mariendorf

Tegel

Siemensstadt

Charlottenburg

Schmargendorf

Dahlem

Steglitz

Lichterfelde

3GTA & 28A

Spandau

Havel

Gatow

Grunewald

Zehlendorf

Teltow

Wannsee

Babelsberg

POTSDAM

4GTA

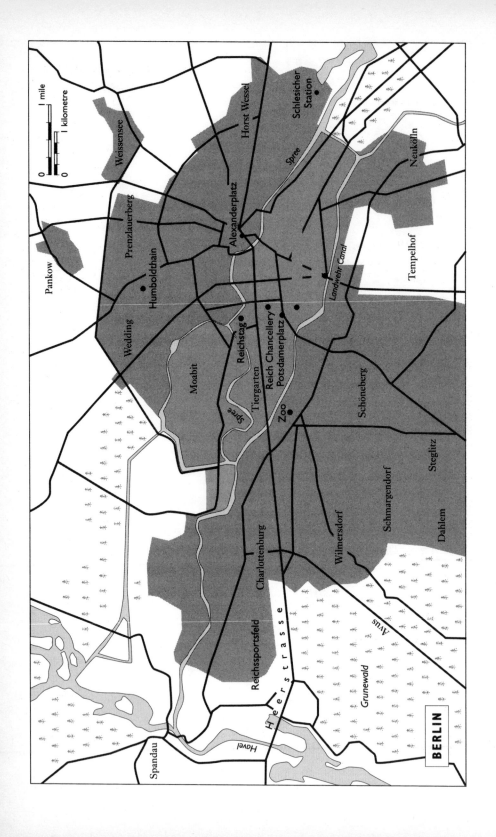

BERLIN

Spandau

Havel

Reichssportsfeld

H e e r s t r a s s e

Charlottenburg

Grunewald

Avus

Wilmersdorf

Schmargendorf

Dahlem

Steglitz

Schöneberg

Moabit

Spree

Tiergarten

Reichstag

Reich Chancellery
Potsdamerplatz

Zoo

Wedding

Prenzlauerberg

Humboldthain

Pankow

Weissensee

Alexanderplatz

Spree

Horst Wessel

Schlesischer
Station

Neukölln

Tempelhof

Landwehr Canal

1 mile

1 kilometre

0   0

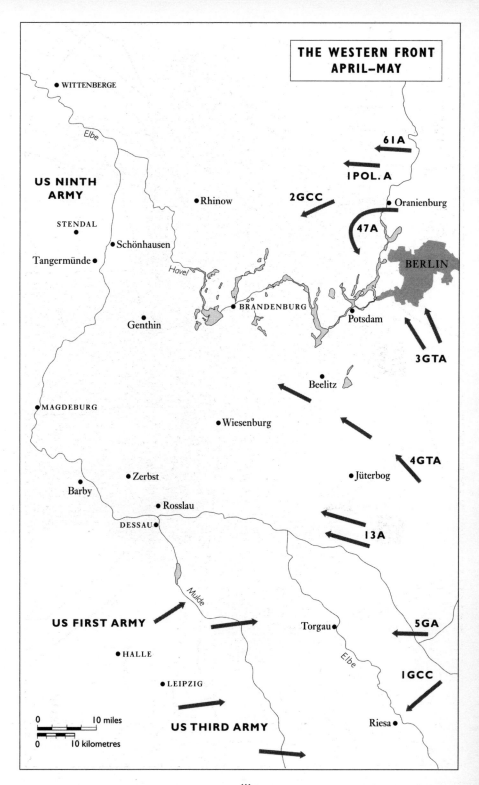

THE WESTERN FRONT
APRIL–MAY

● WITTENBERGE

Elbe

US NINTH
ARMY

STENDAL ●

Tangermünde ●

Schönhausen ●

● Rhinow

Havel

61A

1 POL. A

2GCC

47A

● Oranienburg

BERLIN

BRANDENBURG

Potsdam ●

Genthin ●

3GTA

●MAGDEBURG

● Beelitz

● Wiesenburg

4GTA

● Zerbst

Barby ●

● Jüterbog

● Rosslau

DESSAU ●

13A

Mulde

US FIRST ARMY

Torgau ●

5GA

● HALLE

Elbe

1GCC

● LEIPZIG

0   10 miles

0   10 kilometres

US THIRD ARMY

Riesa ●

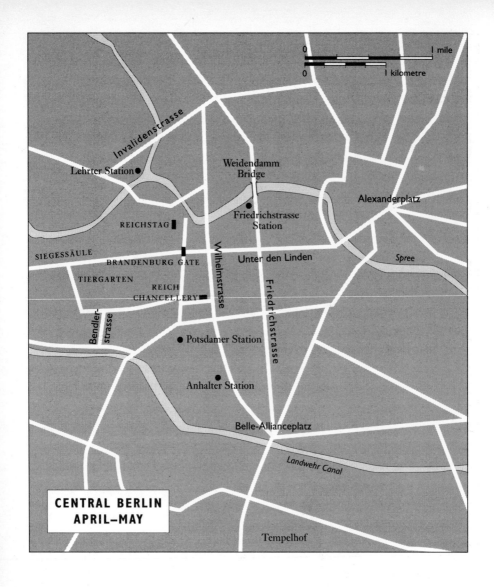

0 _____ 1 mile
0 _____ 1 kilometre

Invalidenstrasse

Lehrter Station ●

Weidendamm
Bridge

Alexanderplatz

REICHSTAG ■

● Friedrichstrasse
Station

SIEGESSÄULE

Wilhelmstrasse

Unter den Linden

Spree

BRANDENBURG GATE ■

Friedrichstrasse

TIERGARTEN

REICH
CHANCELLERY ■

Bendler-strasse

● Potsdamer Station

Anhalter Station ●

Belle-Allianceplatz

Landwehr Canal

**CENTRAL BERLIN
APRIL–MAY**

Tempelhof

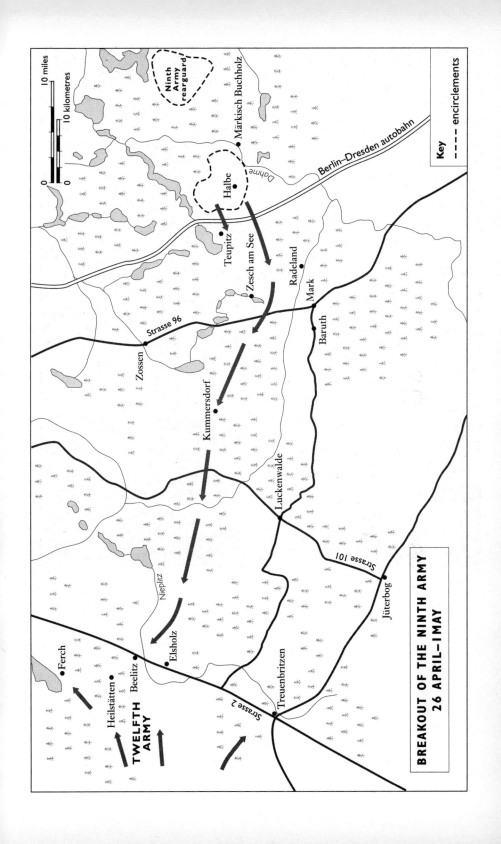

Ninth
Army
rearguard

Märkisch Buchholz

10 miles

10 kilometres

Berlin–Dresden autobahn

Key

– – – – encirclements

Halbe

Dahme

Teupitz

Zesch am See

Radeland

Mark

Strasse 96

Baruth

Zossen

Kummersdorf

Luckenwalde

Strasse 101

Nieplitz

Jüterbog

Ferch

Elsholz

Heilstätten

Beelitz

Treuenbritzen

Strasse 2

TWELFTH
ARMY

BREAKOUT OF THE NINTH ARMY
26 APRIL–1 MAY

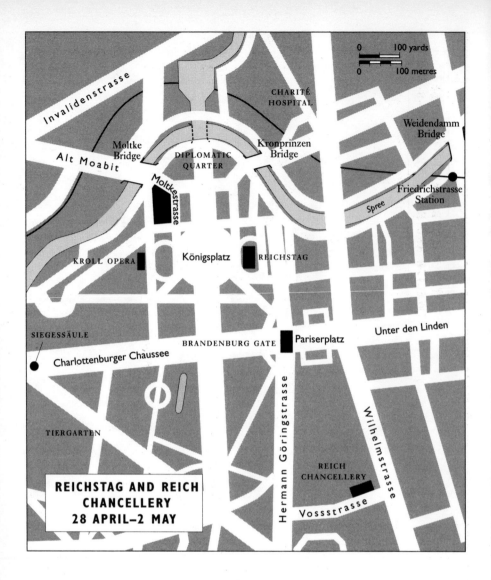

REICHSTAG AND REICH
CHANCELLERY
28 APRIL–2 MAY

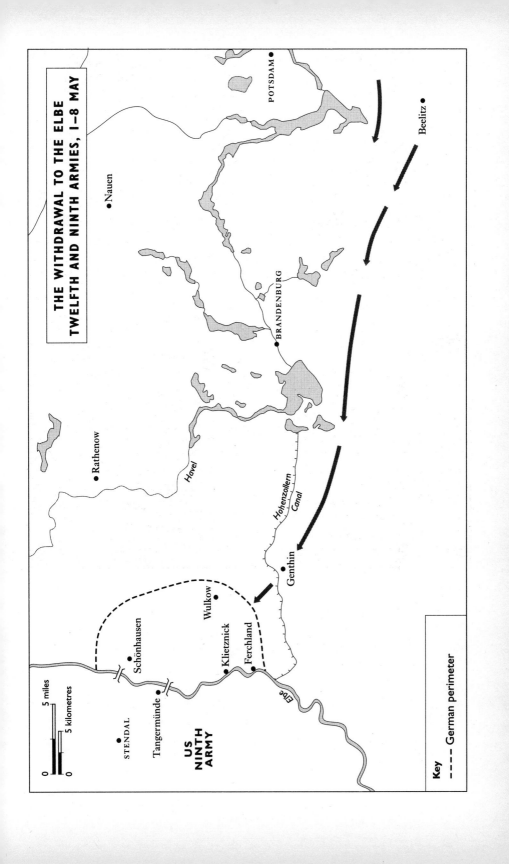

THE WITHDRAWAL TO THE ELBE
TWELFTH AND NINTH ARMIES, 1–8 MAY

POTSDAM

Beelitz

Nauen

BRANDENBURG

Rathenow

Havel

Hohenzollern
Canal

Genthin

Wulkow

Schönhausen

Klietznick

Ferchland

Elbe

STENDAL

Tangermünde

US
NINTH
ARMY

5 miles

5 kilometres

0

0

Key

- - - - German perimeter

Glossary

All dates given in the book refer to 1945 unless otherwise stated.

BdM Bund deutscher Mädel, League of German Girls, female equivalent of Hitler Youth.

Fritz Russian name for a German soldier. The plural was used for Germans in general.

frontovik Red Army soldier with frontline experience.

Ivan (or Iwan in German), an ordinary Soviet soldier. Term used by Red Army as well as Germans.

Kessel (German for 'a cauldron') a group of forces encircled by the enemy.

Landser an ordinary German soldier with frontline experience. The equivalent of the Red Army *frontovik*.

NKVD Soviet secret police under control of Lavrenty Beria. Military NKVD units – NKVD rifle divisions made up mostly of NKVD frontier guards regiments – were attached to each Soviet Front command. The NKVD chief with each Front was answerable only to Beria and Stalin, not to the military chain of command in the Red Army.

OKH Oberkommando des Heeres, in theory the supreme headquarters of the German Army, but in the later stages of the war its most important role was operational command of the Eastern Front.

OKW Oberkommando der Wehrmacht, the supreme headquarters of all the armed forces, Army, Luftwaffe and Kriegsmarine, controlled by Hitler through Field Marshal Keitel and General Jodl. It directed operations on all fronts except for the Eastern Front.

political department a political officer (*politruk*) was responsible for the political education of all soldiers. The political department of each Soviet army and Front came under the Main Political Administration of the Red Army (GlavPURRKA).

S-Bahn city and suburban railway, mostly on the surface, but some of it underground.

7th Department an organization at each Soviet army headquarters whose main task was to demoralize the enemy. German Communists worked under Soviet officers, and also many German prisoners of war who had undergone 'anti-fascist' training in Soviet camps. They were known by the Germans as 'Seydlitz troops' after General von Seydlitz Kurzbach, who had surrendered at Stalingrad and helped form the so-called National Committee for a Free Germany, which was completely under NKVD control.

SHAEF Supreme Headquarters Allied Expeditionary Force Europe.

shtraf company or battalion, the Soviet copy of German *Straf* (penal) units. Disgraced officers, deserters and defaulters were condemned to these penal units, where they were in theory offered the chance to redeem 'their guilt with their blood'. This meant that they were used for the almost suicidal tasks, such as advancing first through a minefield. *Straf* units always had an escort ready to shoot any members who disobeyed orders.

SMERSH the acronym for *smert shpionam* (death to spies), a name allegedly chosen by Stalin himself for the counter-intelligence organization attached to Red Army units and formations. Until April 1943, when Viktor Abakumov became its chief, it had been known as the 'special department' of the NKVD.

Stavka the Soviet supreme headquarters of the armed forces, directly under Stalin's control. The chief of staff in 1945 was General Antonov.

U-Bahn underground railway.

Verkhovny commander-in-chief, the term which Zhukov and other senior commanders used to refer to Stalin.

MILITARY ORGANIZATION

Army Group and **Front** A German 'Army Group' or a Red Army 'Front' represented a collection of armies under a single commander-in-chief. Depending on circumstances, strengths could vary enormously – anything from 250,000 to over a million men.

Army Each German army, usually varying in strength between 40,000 and over 100,000 men, has its name written in full in the text: e.g. Ninth Army or Third Panzer Army. Soviet armies, generally smaller, are written thus: 47th Army or 2nd Guards Tank Army. Most armies usually consisted of two or three corps. A Soviet tank army had in theory 620 tanks and 188 self-propelled assault guns.

Corps A corps consisted of several divisions, usually between two and four. A Soviet tank corps, however, consisted of three tank brigades of sixty-five tanks each and was closer in size to a full-strength German panzer division.

Division Divisions varied greatly in size. A Soviet Rifle Division in theory should have mustered 11,780 men, but most had between 3,000 and 7,000 men. German Infantry Divisions were often even more understrength by 1945.

Brigade This formation, between a regiment and a division, was used more by the US Army and the British than by the Germans and Red Army, both of which had at least two or three regiments to a division. The Red Army, however, had three tank brigades to each tank corps.

Regiment This consisted of at least two or three battalions, with anything up to 700 men each, but often far fewer.

Battalion Each battalion consisted of at least three rifle companies – each one theoretically around eighty men strong – as well as support companies, with machine guns, mortars or anti-tank guns, and then transport and supply companies.

Military rank equivalents between the British Army, the US Army, the German Army and the Waffen SS can be found on antonybeevor.com in the annexe section to this book.

Preface

'History always emphasizes terminal events,' Albert Speer observed bitterly to his American interrogators just after the end of the war. He hated the idea that the early achievements of Hitler's regime would be obscured by its final collapse. Yet Speer, like other prominent Nazis, refused to recognize that few things reveal more about political leaders and their systems than the manner of their downfall. This is why the subject of National Socialism's final defeat is so fascinating, and also so important at a time when teenagers, especially in Germany, are finding much to admire in the Third Reich.

The Nazis' enemies had first been able to visualize their moment of vengeance just over two years before. On 1 February 1943, an angry Soviet colonel collared a group of emaciated German prisoners in the rubble of Stalingrad. 'That's how Berlin is going to look!' he yelled, pointing to the ruined buildings all around. When I read those words some six years ago, I sensed immediately what my next book had to be. Among the graffiti preserved on the Reichstag's walls in Berlin, one can still see the two cities linked by Russians exulting in their revenge, forcing the invaders from their furthest point of eastward advance right back to the heart of the Reich.

Hitler too remained obsessed with this decisive defeat. In November 1944, as the Red Army was grouping beyond the Reich's eastern frontiers, he pointed back to Stalingrad. Germany's reverses had all begun, he said in a major speech, 'with the breakthrough of Russian armies on the Romanian front on the Don in November 1942'. He blamed his hapless allies, under-armed and ignored on the vulnerable flanks either side of Stalingrad, not his own obsessive refusal to heed the warnings of danger. Hitler had learned nothing and had forgotten nothing.

That same speech demonstrated with terrible clarity the distorted logic in which the German people had allowed themselves to become ensnared. When published, it was entitled 'Capitulation Means Annihilation'. He warned that if the Bolshevists won, the fate of the German people was destruction, rape and slavery, with 'immense columns of men treading their way to the Siberian tundra'.

Hitler vehemently refused to acknowledge the consequences of his own actions, and the German people realized far too late that they were trapped by a terrifying confusion of cause and effect. Instead of eliminating Bolshevism, as he had claimed, Hitler had brought it to the very heart of Europe. His abominably cruel invasion of Russia had been carried out by a generation of German youth weaned on a demonically clever combination. Goebbels's propaganda did not simply dehumanize Jews, commissars and the whole Slav people, it made the German people fear and hate them. Hitler, in these gigantic crimes, had managed to manacle the nation to him and the approaching violence of the Red Army was the self-fulfilment of their leader's prophecy.

Stalin, while happy to make use of symbols when it suited him, was far more calculating. The Reich's capital was indeed the 'culmination of all the operations of our army in this war', but he had other vital interests. Not least of these was the plan formulated under Lavrenty Beria, Stalin's minister of state security, to strip atomic research establishments in Berlin of all their equipment and uranium before the Americans and British arrived. The work of the Manhattan Project carried out in Los Alamos was already well known in the Kremlin, thanks to the pro-Communist spy, Dr Klaus Fuchs. Soviet science was far behind, and Stalin and Beria were convinced that if they were to seize the German laboratories and scientists in Berlin before the Western Allies got there, then they too could produce an atom bomb like the Americans.

The scale of the human tragedy by the end of the war is beyond the imagination of everyone who did not live through it, but especially of those who have grown up in the demilitarized society of the post-Cold War age. Yet this moment of fate for millions of people still has much to teach us. One important lesson is that one should be extremely wary of any generalization concerning the conduct of individuals. Extremes of human suffering and even degradation can bring out the best as well as the worst in human nature. Human behaviour to a large extent mirrors the utter unpredictability of life or death. Many Soviet troops, especially in frontline formations, unlike those who came behind, often behaved with great kindness to German civilians. In a world of cruelty and horror where any conception of humanity had almost been destroyed by ideology, just a few acts of often unexpected kindness and self-sacrifice lighten what would otherwise be an almost unbearable story.

This book could not possibly have been researched without the help of many people. I am first of all deeply obliged to the directors and staff in numerous archives: Colonel Shuvashin and the staff of the Central Archive of the Ministry of Defence (TsAMO) at Podolsk; Dr Natalya Borisovna Volkova and her staff at the Russian State Archive for Literature and the Arts (RGALI); Dr Vladimir Kuzelenkov and Dr Vladimir Korotaev of the Russian State Military Archive (RGVA); Professor Kyrill Mikhailovich Andersen and Dr Oleg Vladimirovich Naumov at the Russian State Archive for Social-Political History (RGASPI); Dr Manfred Kehrig, Director of the Bundesarchiv-Militärarchiv, Freiburg, and Frau Weibl; Dr Rolf-Dieter Müller and Hauptmann Luckszat at the MGFA in Potsdam; Professor Dr Eckhart Henning of the Archiv zur Geschichte der Max-Planck-Gesellschaft; Dr Wulf-Ekkehard Lucke at the Landesarchiv-Berlin; Frau Irina Renz of the Bibliothek für Zeitgeschichte in Stuttgart; Dr Lars Ericson and Per Clason at the Krigsarkivet in Stockholm; John E. Taylor, Wilbert Mahoney and Robin Cookson at National Archives II, College Park, Maryland; Dr Jeffrey Clarke at the United States Army Center of Military History.

Bengt von zur Mühlen, the founder of Chronos-Film, has been particularly generous with archival footage and taped interviews of participants. I am also greatly obliged to Gerald Ramm and to Dietmar Arnold of Berliner Unterwelten for their help.

I am truly grateful to all those who aided me so much during my travels with advice, introductions and hospitality: in Russia, Dr Galya and Dr Luba Vinogradova, Professor Anatoly Aleksandrovich Chernobayev, and Simon Smith and Sian Stickings; in Germany, William

Durie, Staatssekretar a.D. Karl-Günther and Frau von Hase, and Andrew and Sally Gimson; in the United States, Susan Mary Alsop, Major General and Mrs Charles Vyvyan, Bruce Lee, Mr and Mrs Charles von Luttichau and Martin Blumenson.

It has been a great pleasure for me, as well as extremely useful for the book, to work in partnership with BBC Timewatch. I am deeply grateful to Laurence Rees, whose idea it was, to Dr Tilman Remme, in whose company I have most enjoyably learned a great deal, and to Detlef Siebert, who generously helped so much at an early stage with advice and interviewees. Others who have also provided introductions, information, help and advice include Anne Applebaum, Christopher Arkell, Claudia Bismarck, Leopold Graf von Bismarck, Sir Rodric Braithwaite, Professor Christopher Dandeker, Dr Engel of the Archiv der Freien Universität, Professor John Erickson, Wolf Gebhardt, Jon Halliday, Nina Lobanov-Rostovsky, Dr Catherine Merridale, Professor Oleg Aleksandrovich Rzheshevsky, Professor Moshe Schein of the New York Methodist Hospital, Karl Schwarz, Simon Sebag-Montefiore, Gia Sulkhanishvili, Dr Galya Vinogradova and Ian Weston-Smith.

This book, quite literally, would never have been possible in the form it takes without the wonderful help I have had from Dr Luba Vinogradova in Russia and Angelica von Hase in Germany. It has been a privilege and a pleasure to work with them. I am also extremely grateful to Sarah Jackson for all her work on photographic research, to Bettina von Hase for supplementary archival research in Germany and to David List in England. Charlotte Salford very kindly translated the documents from the Krigsarkivet in Stockholm for me.

I am profoundly grateful to Professor Michael Burleigh, Professor Norman Davies and Dr Catherine Merridale for reading all or parts of the typescript and making very useful criticisms. Any mistakes which remain are, of course, entirely my responsibility.

I cannot thank Mark Le Fanu and the Society of Authors enough for recovering the websites antonybeevor.com, antonybeevor.org and antonybeevor.net from a cybersquatter. These can now be used to provide an 'author's cut' – a writer's answer to the director's cut – thus making available archival and other material for which there was no room in the published version of the book.

I owe, as always, a huge debt to my agent Andrew Nurnberg and to

Eleo Gordon, my editor at Penguin, both of whom pushed an initially reluctant author down this route. Once again my wife, writing partner and editor of first resort, Artemis Cooper, has had to put up with constant absences and many extra burdens. I am eternally grateful.

I

Berlin in the New Year

Berliners, gaunt from short rations and stress, had little to celebrate at Christmas in 1944. Much of the capital of the Reich had been reduced to rubble by bombing raids. The Berlin talent for black jokes had turned to gallows humour. The quip of that unfestive season was, 'Be practical: give a coffin.'

The mood in Germany had changed exactly two years before. Rumours had begun to circulate just before Christmas 1942 that General Paulus's Sixth Army had been encircled on the Volga by the Red Army. The Nazi regime found it hard to admit that the largest formation in the whole of the Wehrmacht was doomed to annihilation in the ruins of Stalingrad and in the frozen steppe outside. To prepare the country for bad news, Joseph Goebbels, the Reichsminister for Propaganda and Enlightenment, had announced a 'German Christmas', which in National Socialist terms meant austerity and ideological determination, not candles and pine wreathes and singing '*Heilige Nacht*'. By 1944, the traditional roast goose had become a distant memory.

In streets where the façade of a house had collapsed, pictures could still be seen hanging on the walls of what had been a sitting room or bedroom. The actress Hildegard Knef gazed at a piano left exposed on the remnants of a floor. Nobody could get to it, and she wondered how long it would be before it tumbled down to join the rubble below. Messages from families were scrawled on gutted buildings to tell a son returning from the front that they were all right and staying elsewhere. Nazi Party notices warned, 'Looters will be punished with death!'

Air raids were so frequent, with the British by night and the Americans by day, that Berliners felt that they spent more time in cellars and air-raid shelters than in their own beds. The lack of sleep contributed to the strange mixture of suppressed hysteria and fatalism. Far fewer people seemed to worry about being denounced to the Gestapo for defeatism, as the rash of jokes indicated. The ubiquitous initials LSR for *Luftschutzraum*, or air-raid shelter, were said to stand for '*Lernt schnell Russisch*': 'Learn Russian quickly'. Most Berliners had entirely dropped the '*Heil Hitler!*' greeting. When Lothar Loewe, a Hitler Youth who had been away from the city, used it on entering a shop, everyone turned and stared at him. It was the last time he uttered the words when not on duty. Loewe found that the most common greeting had become '*Bleib übrig!*' – 'Survive!'

The humour also reflected the grotesque, sometimes surreal, images of the time. The largest air-raid construction in Berlin was the Zoo bunker, a vast ferro-concrete fortress of the totalitarian age, with flak batteries on the roof and huge shelters below, into which crowds of Berliners packed when the sirens sounded. The diarist Ursula von Kardorff described it as 'like a stage-set for the prison scene in *Fidelio*'. Meanwhile, loving couples embraced on concrete spiral staircases as if taking part in a 'travesty of a fancy-dress ball'.

There was a pervasive atmosphere of impending downfall in personal lives as much as in the nation's existence. People spent their money recklessly, half-assuming that it would soon be worthless. And there were stories, although hard to confirm, of girls and young women coupling with strangers in dark corners around the Zoo station and in the Tiergarten. The desire to dispense with innocence is said to have become even more desperate later as the Red Army approached Berlin.

The air-raid shelters themselves, lit with blue lights, could indeed provide a foretaste of claustrophobic hell, as people pushed in bundled in their warmest clothes and carrying small cardboard suitcases containing sandwiches and thermos. In theory, all basic needs were catered for in the shelters. There was a *Sanitätsraum* with a nurse, where women could go into labour. Childbirth seemed to be accelerated by the vibrations from bomb explosions, which felt as if they came as much from the centre of the earth as from ground level. The ceilings were painted with luminous paint for the frequent occasions during the air raids when the lights failed, first dimming then flickering off. Water supplies ceased when mains were hit, and the *Aborte*, or lavatories, soon became disgusting, a real distress for a nation preoccupied with hygiene. Often the lavatories were sealed off by the authorities because there were so many cases of depressed people who, having locked the door, committed suicide.

For a population of around 3 million, Berlin did not have enough shelters, so they were usually overcrowded. In the main corridors, seating halls and bunk rooms, the air was foul from over-use and condensation dripped from the ceilings. The complex of shelters under the Gesundbrunnen U-Bahn station had been designed to take 1,500 people, yet often more than three times that number packed in. Candles were used to measure the diminishing levels of oxygen. When a candle placed on the floor went out, children were picked up and held at shoulder height. When a candle on a chair went out, then the evacuation of the level began. And if a third candle, positioned at about chin level, began to sputter, then the whole bunker was evacuated, however heavy the attack above.

The foreign workers in Berlin, 300,000 strong and identifiable by a letter painted on their clothes to denote their country of origin, were simply forbidden entry to underground bunkers and cellars. This was partly an extension of the Nazi policy to stop them mingling intimately with the German race, but the overriding concern of the authorities was to save the lives of Germans. A forced labourer, particularly an '*Ostarbeiter*', or eastern worker, most of whom had been rounded up in the Ukraine and Belorussia, was regarded as expendable. Yet many foreign workers, conscripted as well as volunteers, enjoyed a far greater degree of freedom than the unfortunates consigned to camps. Those who worked in armaments factories around the capital, for example, had created their own refuge and Bohemian subculture with newssheets and plays in the depths of the Friedrichstrasse station. Their spirits were rising visibly as the Red Army advanced, while those of their exploiters fell. Most Germans looked on foreign workers with trepidation. They saw them as a Trojan Horse garrison ready to attack and revenge themselves as soon as the enemy armies approached the city.

Berliners suffered from an atavistic and visceral fear of the Slav invader from the east. Fear was easily turned to hate. As the Red Army approached, Goebbels's propaganda harked on again and again about the atrocities at Nemmersdorf, when Red Army troops had invaded the south-eastern corner of East Prussia the previous autumn and raped and murdered inhabitants of this village.

Some people had their own reasons for refusing to take shelter during a bombing raid. A married man who used to visit his mistress regularly in the district of Prenzlauerberg could not go down to the communal cellar because that would have aroused suspicions. One evening, the building received a direct hit, and the luckless adulterer, who had been sitting on a sofa, was buried up to his neck in rubble. After the raid, a boy called Erich Schmidtke and a Czech labourer whose illegal presence in the cellar had been tolerated heard his screams of pain and ran upstairs towards the sound. After he had been dug out and carried off for treatment, the fourteen-year-old Erich then had to go to tell the injured man's wife that her husband had been badly injured in this other woman's flat. She started screaming in anger. The fact that he had been with this woman agitated her far more than his fate. Children in those times received a harsh introduction to the realities of the adult world.

General Günther Blumentritt, like most of those in authority, was convinced that the bombing raids on Germany produced a real '*Volksgenossenschaft*' or 'patriotic comradeship'. This may well have been true in 1942 and 1943, but by late 1944 the effect tended to polarize opinion between the hardliners and the war-weary. Berlin had been the city with the highest proportion of opponents to the Nazi regime, as its voting records before 1933 indicate. But with the exception of a very small and courageous minority, opposition to the Nazis had generally been limited to gibes and grumbles. The majority had been genuinely horrified by the assassination attempt against Hitler on 20 July 1944. And as the Reich's frontiers became threatened both in the east and in the west, they drank in Goebbels's stream of lies that the Führer would unleash new 'wonder weapons' against their enemies, as if he were about to assume the role of a wrathful Jupiter flinging thunderbolts as a symbol of his power.

A letter written by a wife to her husband in a French prison camp reveals the embattled mentality and the readiness to believe the regime's propaganda. 'I have such faith in our destiny,' she wrote, 'that nothing can shake a confidence which is born from our long history, from our glorious past, as Dr Goebbels says. It's impossible that things turn out differently. We may have reached a very low point at this moment, but we have men who are decisive. The whole country is ready to march, weapons in hand. We have secret weapons which will be used at the chosen moment, and we have above all a Führer whom we can follow with our eyes closed. Don't allow yourself to be beaten down, you must not at any price.'

The Ardennes offensive, launched on 16 December 1944, intoxicated Hitler loyalists with revived morale. The tables had at last turned. Belief in the Führer and in the *Wunderwaffen*, the miracle weapons such as the V-2, blinded them to reality. Rumours spread that the US First Army had been completely surrounded and taken prisoner due to an anaesthetic gas. They thought that they could hold the world to ransom and take revenge for all that Germany had suffered. Veteran NCOs appear to have been among the most embittered. Paris was about to be recaptured, they told each other with fierce glee. Many regretted that the French capital should have been spared from destruction the year before while Berlin was bombed to ruins. They exulted at the idea that history might now be corrected.

The German Army's high command did not share this enthusiasm for the offensive in the west. General staff officers feared that Hitler's strategic coup against the Americans in the Ardennes would weaken the Eastern Front at a decisive moment. The plan was in any case vastly over-ambitious. The operation was spearheaded by the Sixth SS Panzer Army of Oberstgruppenführer Sepp Dietrich and the Fifth Panzer Army of General Hasso von Manteuffel. Yet the lack of fuel made it extremely unlikely that they would ever reach their objective of Antwerp, the Western Allies' main supply base.

Hitler was fixated by dreams of dramatically reversing the fortunes of war and forcing Roosevelt and Churchill to come to terms. He had decisively rejected any suggestion of overtures to the Soviet Union, partly for the sound reason that Stalin was interested only in the destruction of Nazi Germany, but there was also a fundamental impediment. Hitler suffered from an atrocious personal vanity. He could not be seen to sue for peace when Germany was losing. A victory in the Ardennes was therefore vital for every reason. But American doggedness in defence, especially at Bastogne, and the massive deployment of Allied air power once the weather cleared, broke the momentum of attack within a week.

On Christmas Eve, General Heinz Guderian, the chief of the army supreme command, OKH, drove in his large Mercedes staff car to Führer headquarters in the west. After abandoning the *Wolfsschanze*, or 'Wolf's Lair', in East Prussia on 20 November 1944, Hitler had moved to Berlin for a minor operation on his throat. He had then left the capital on the evening of 10 December in his personal armoured train. His destination was another secret and camouflaged complex in woods near Ziegenberg, less than forty kilometres from Frankfurt am Main. Designated the *Adlerhorst*, or 'Eagle's Eyrie', it was the last of his field headquarters to be known by codenames which reeked of puerile fantasy.

Guderian, the great theorist of tank warfare, had known the dangers of such an operation from the start, but he had little say in the matter. Although the OKH was responsible for the Eastern Front it was never allowed a free hand. The OKW, the high command of the Wehrmacht (all the armed forces), was responsible for operations outside the Eastern Front. Both organizations were based just south of Berlin in neighbouring underground complexes at Zossen.

Despite having as quick a temper as Hitler, Guderian was very different in outlook. He had little time for an entirely speculative international strategy when the country was under attack from both sides. Instead, he relied on a soldier's instinct for the point of maximum danger. There was no doubt where that lay. His briefcase contained the intelligence analysis of General Reinhard Gehlen, the head of Fremde Heere Ost, the military intelligence department for the Eastern Front. Gehlen calculated that around 12 January the Red Army would launch a massive attack from the line of the River Vistula. His department estimated that the enemy had a superiority of eleven to one in infantry, seven to one in tanks and twenty to one in artillery and also in aviation.

Guderian entered the conference room at the *Adlerhorst* to find himself facing Hitler and his military staff, and also Heinrich Himmler, the Reichsführer SS who, after the July plot, had also been made commander of the Replacement Army. Every member of Hitler's military staff had been selected for his unquestioning loyalty. Field Marshal Keitel, the chief of staff of the OKW, was famous for his pompous servility to

Hitler. Exasperated army officers referred to him either as the 'Reich's garage attendant' or the 'nodding donkey'. Colonel General Jodl, who had a cold, hard face, was far more competent than Keitel, yet he hardly ever opposed the Führer's disastrous attempts to control every battalion. He had very nearly been dismissed in the autumn of 1942 for having dared to contradict his master. General Burgdorf, Hitler's chief military adjutant and chief of the army personnel department controlling all appointments, had replaced the devoted General Schmundt, mortally wounded by Stauffenberg's bomb at the *Wolfsschanze*. Burgdorf was the man who had delivered the poison to Field Marshal Rommel, with the ultimatum to commit suicide.

Using the findings of Gehlen's intelligence department, Guderian outlined the Red Army's build-up for a huge offensive in the east. He warned that the attack would take place within three weeks and requested that, since the Ardennes offensive had now ground to a halt, as many divisions as possible should be withdrawn for redeployment on the Vistula front. Hitler stopped him. He declared that such estimates of enemy strength were preposterous. Soviet rifle divisions never had more than 7,000 men each. Their tank corps had hardly any tanks. 'It's the greatest imposture since Genghis Khan,' he shouted, working himself up. 'Who is responsible for producing all this rubbish?'

Guderian resisted the temptation to reply that it was Hitler himself who talked of German 'armies' when they were the size of a single corps, and of 'infantry divisions' reduced to battalion strength. Instead, he defended Gehlen's figures. To his horror, General Jodl argued that the offensive in the west should continue with further attacks. Since this was exactly what Hitler wanted, Guderian was thwarted. It was even more provoking for him to have to listen at dinner to the verdict of Himmler, who revelled in his new role of military leader. He had recently been made army group commander on the upper Rhine in addition to his other appointments. 'You know, my dear Colonel General,' he said to Guderian, 'I don't really believe that the Russians will attack at all. It's all an enormous bluff.'

Guderian had no alternative but to return to OKH headquarters at Zossen. In the meantime, the losses in the west mounted. The Ardennes offensive and its ancillary operations cost 80,000 German casualties. In addition, it had used up a large proportion of Germany's rapidly dwindling fuel reserves. Hitler refused to accept that the Ardennes battle was his equivalent of the *Kaiserschlacht*, the last great German attack of the First World War. He obsessively rejected any parallels with 1918. For him, 1918 symbolized only the revolutionary 'stab in the back' which brought down the Kaiser and reduced Germany to a humiliating defeat. Yet Hitler had moments of clarity during those days. 'I know the war is lost,' he said late one evening to Colonel Nicolaus von Below, his Luftwaffe aide. 'The enemy's superiority is too great.' But he continued to lay all the blame on others for the sequence of disasters. They were all 'traitors', especially army officers. He suspected that many more had sympathized with the failed assassins, yet they had been pleased enough to accept medals and decorations from him. 'We will never surrender,' he said. 'We may go down, but we will take a world with us.'

Horrified by the new disaster looming on the Vistula, Guderian returned to the *Adlerhorst* at Ziegenberg twice more in rapid succession. To make matters worse, he heard that Hitler, without warning him, was transferring SS panzer troops from the Vistula front to Hungary. Hitler, convinced as usual that only he could see the strategic issues, had suddenly decided to launch a counter-attack there on the grounds that the oilfields must be retaken. In fact he wanted to break through to Budapest, which had been surrounded by the Red Army on Christmas Eve.

Guderian's visit on New Year's Day coincided with the annual procession of the regime's grandees and the chiefs of staff, to transmit in person to the Führer their 'wishes for a successful New Year'. That same morning Operation North Wind, the main subsidiary action to prolong the Ardennes offensive, was launched in Alsace. The day turned out to be a catastrophe for the Luftwaffe. Göring, in a grand gesture of characteristic irresponsibility, committed almost 1,000 planes to attack ground targets on the Western Front. This attempt to impress Hitler led to the final destruction of the Luftwaffe as an effective force. It gave the Allies total air supremacy.

The Grossdeutscher Rundfunk broadcast Hitler's New Year speech that day. No mention was made of the fighting in the west, which suggested failure there, and surprisingly little was said of the *Wunderwaffen*. A number of people believed that the speech had been pre-recorded or even faked. Hitler had not been seen in public for so long that wild rumours were circulating. Some asserted that he had gone completely mad and that Göring was in a secret prison because he had tried to escape to Sweden.

Some Berliners, fearful of what the year would bring, had not quite dared to clink glasses when it came to the toast '*Prosit Neujahr!*' The Goebbels family entertained Colonel Hans-Ulrich Rudel, the Stuka ace and the most decorated officer in the Luftwaffe. They sat down to a dinner of potato soup as a symbol of austerity.

The New Year holiday ended on the morning of 3 January. The German devotion to work and duty remained unquestioned, however improbable the circumstances. Many had little to do in their offices and factories, owing to shortages of raw materials and parts, but they still set out on foot through the rubble or on public transport. Once again, miracles had been achieved repairing the U-Bahn and the S-Bahn tracks, even though few of the carriages had unbroken windows. Factories and offices were also freezing due to smashed windows and so little fuel for heating. Those with colds or flu had to struggle on. There was no point attempting to see a doctor unless you were seriously ill. Almost all the German doctors had been sent to the army. Local surgeries and hospitals depended almost entirely on foreigners. Even Berlin's main teaching hospital, the Charité, included doctors from over half a dozen countries on its staff, including Dutch, Peruvians, Romanians, Ukrainians and Hungarians.

The only industry which appeared to be flourishing was armaments production, directed by Hitler's personal architect and *Wunderkind*, Albert Speer. On 13 January, Speer gave a presentation to army corps commanders in the camp at Krampnitz just outside Berlin. He emphasized the importance of contact between front commanders and the war industries. Speer, unlike other Nazi ministers, did not insult his audience's intelligence. He disdained euphemisms about the situation and did not shrink from mentioning the 'catastrophic losses' sustained by the Wehrmacht over the last eight months.

The Allied bombing campaign was not the problem, he argued. German industry had produced 218,000 rifles in December alone. This was nearly double the average monthly output achieved in 1941, the year the Wehrmacht had invaded the Soviet Union. The manufacture of automatic weapons had risen by nearly four times and tank production nearly fivefold. In December 1944, they had produced 1,840 armoured vehicles in a single month, over half what they had made in the whole of 1941. This also included far heavier tanks. 'The trickiest problem', he warned them, was the shortage of fuel. Surprisingly, he said little of ammunition reserves. There was little point producing all these weapons if munitions production failed to keep pace.

Speer spoke for over forty minutes, reeling off his statistics with quiet professionalism. He did not rub in the fact that it was the massive defeats on the eastern and western fronts over the last eight months which had reduced the Wehrmacht to such shortages in all types of weapons. He voiced the hope that German factories might reach a production level of 100,000 machine pistols a month by the spring of 1946. The fact that these enterprises relied largely on slave labourers dragooned by the SS was not, of course, mentioned. Speer also failed to remark upon their wastage – thousands of deaths a day. And the territories from which they came were about to diminish further. At that very moment, Soviet armies numbering over 4 million men were massed in Poland along the River Vistula and just south of the East Prussian border. They were starting the offensive which Hitler had dismissed as an imposture.

2

The 'House of Cards' on the Vistula

General Gehlen's estimates of Soviet strength were certainly not exaggerated. If anything, they were well short of the mark on the threatened sectors. The Red Army had 6.7 million men along a front which stretched from the Baltic to the Adriatic. This was over twice the strength of the Wehrmacht and its allies when they invaded the Soviet Union in June 1941. Hitler's conviction that summer that the Red Army was about to collapse had proved to be one of the most catastrophic miscalculations in history.

'We are lost,' a German sergeant acknowledged in January 1945, 'but we will fight to the last man.' Battle-hardened combatants of the Eastern Front had come to believe that it must all end in death. Any other outcome appeared unthinkable after everything that had gone before. They knew what had been done in the occupied territories and that the Red Army intended to exact revenge. Surrender meant being worked to death in Siberian labour camps as a '*Stalinpferd*', a 'Stalin horse'. 'We no longer fought for Hitler, or for National Socialism, or for the Third Reich,' wrote an Alsatian veteran of the *Grossdeutschland* Division, 'or even for our fiancées or mothers or families trapped in bomb-ravaged towns. We fought from simple fear . . . We fought for ourselves, so that we wouldn't die in holes filled with mud and snow; we fought like rats.'

The disasters of the previous year, above all the encirclement and destruction of Army Group Centre, were hard to forget. National Socialist leadership officers, the Nazi imitation of the Soviet commissar, tried to raise the fighting morale of the ordinary German soldier, the

Landser, with promises as well as threats of execution for anyone who deserted or retreated without orders. 'You do not need to fear the Russian offensive,' they told them. 'If the enemy start to attack, our tanks will be here in four hours.' But the more experienced soldiers knew what they were up against.

Although Guderian's staff officers at Zossen had formed an accurate idea of the date of attack, the information does not seem to have filtered down to the front line. Corporal Alois K., of the 304th Infantry Division, seized as a 'tongue' by a Soviet raiding party, told intelligence officers of the 1st Ukrainian Front that they had expected an attack before Christmas, then they were told to expect one on 10 January because it was supposed to be Stalin's birthday.

On 9 January, after an urgent tour of the three main eastern fronts – Hungary, the Vistula and East Prussia – General Guderian, accompanied by his aide, Major Baron Freytag von Loringhoven, had again gone to see Hitler at Ziegenberg. He presented the latest estimates of enemy strengths, both Gehlen's compilation and also those of the Luftwaffe commander, General Seidemann. Air reconnaissance indicated that there were 8,000 Soviet planes concentrated on the Vistula and East Prussian fronts. Göring interrupted the army chief of staff. 'Mein Führer, don't believe that,' he said to Hitler. 'Those are not real planes. Those are just decoys.' Keitel, in a sycophantic show of resolution, smashed his fist down on the table. 'The Reichsmarschall is right,' he declared.

The meeting continued as a black farce. Hitler repeated his view that the intelligence figures were 'completely idiotic' and added that the man who compiled them should be locked in a lunatic asylum. Guderian retorted angrily that since he supported them completely, he had better be certified as well. Hitler refused out of hand the requests of General Harpe on the Vistula front and General Reinhardt in East Prussia to withdraw their most exposed troops to more defensible positions. He also insisted that the 200,000 German troops trapped on the Courland peninsula in Latvia should remain there and not be evacuated by sea to defend the Reich's borders. Guderian, disgusted with the 'ostrich strategy' of Führer headquarters, prepared to take his leave.

'The Eastern Front,' said Hitler, suddenly trying to charm him, 'has never before possessed such a strong reserve as now. That is your doing. I thank you for it.'

'The Eastern Front,' Guderian retorted, 'is like a house of cards. If the front is broken through at one point all the rest will collapse.' Ironically, Goebbels had used exactly the same simile in 1941 about the Red Army.

Guderian returned to Zossen in 'a very grave mood'. He wondered whether Hitler and Jodl's lack of imagination had something to do with the fact that they both came from parts of the Reich – Austria and Bavaria – which were not threatened. Guderian was a Prussian. His homeland was about to be ravaged, and probably lost for ever. Hitler, to reward his great panzer leader for his successes early in the war, had presented him with the expropriated estate of Deipenhof in the Warthegau, the region of western Poland which the Nazis had seized and incorporated into the Reich. But now the imminent offensive across the Vistula threatened that too. His wife was still there. Watched closely by the local Nazi Party chiefs, she would not be able to leave until the very last moment.

Just over twenty-four hours later, Guderian's staff at Zossen received confirmation that the attack was now hours rather than days away. Red Army sappers were clearing minefields at night and tank corps were being brought forward into the bridgeheads. Hitler ordered that the panzer reserves on the Vistula front should be moved forward, despite warnings that this would bring them within range of Soviet artillery. Some senior officers began to wonder whether Hitler subconsciously wanted to lose the war.

The Red Army seemed to make a habit of attacking in atrocious weather conditions. German veterans, accustomed to this pattern, used to call it 'weather for Russians'. Soviet troops were convinced that they had a distinct advantage in winter warfare, whether through frost or mud. Their comparatively low rates of frostbite and trench foot were attributed to the traditional Russian army use of rough linen foot bandages instead of socks. Weather forecasts had foretold a 'strange winter'. After the hard cold of January, 'heavy rain and wet snow' were predicted. An order went out: 'Leather boots must be mended.'

The Red Army had improved in so many ways – its heavy weaponry, the professionalism of its planning, the camouflage and control of operations which had frequently caught the Germans off balance – yet some weaknesses remained. The worst was the chaotic lack of discipline, which seems astonishing in a totalitarian state. Part of the problem came from the terrible attrition among young officers.

It was a hard school indeed for seventeen- and eighteen-year-old junior lieutenants in the infantry. 'At that time,' wrote the novelist and war correspondent Konstantin Simonov, 'young people were becoming adult in a year, a month or even in the course of one battle.' Many, of course, never survived that first battle. Determined to prove themselves worthy of commanding veterans, some of whom were old enough to be their fathers, they showed reckless courage and suffered for it.

Indiscipline came also from the dehumanized way in which Red Army soldiers were treated by their own authorities. And, of course, the strengths and weaknesses of the complex national character played its part too. 'The Russian infantryman,' as one writer put it, 'is hardy, undemanding, careless and a convinced fatalist . . . It is these character-istics which make him incomparable.' An ordinary soldier in a rifle division provided a summary in his diary of the changing moods of his comrades. 'First state: soldier with no chiefs around. He is a grumbler. He threatens and shows off. He is keen to pocket something or grab someone in a stupid argument. One can see from this irritability that the soldier's life is hard for him. Second state: soldier in the presence of chiefs: submissive and inarticulate. Readily agrees with what he is told. Easily believes promises. Blossoms when praised and is eager to admire the strictness of officers whom he makes fun of behind their backs. Third state: working together or in battle: here he is a hero. He won't leave his comrade in danger. He dies quietly, as if it is still part of his work.'

Tank troops in the Red Army were in particularly good heart. Having been as demoralized as Soviet aviation in the early part of the war, they were starting to enjoy heroic status. Vasily Grossman, another novelist and war correspondent, now found 'tankists' almost as fascinating as he had found snipers at Stalingrad. He described them admiringly as 'cavalrymen, artillerymen and mechanics all rolled in one'. But the greatest strength of the Red Army was the burning idea that they were finally within striking distance of the Reich. The violators of the Soviet Motherland were about to discover the true meaning of the proverb, 'You will harvest what you have sown.'

*

The basic concept of the campaign had been decided in outline by the end of October 1944. The *Stavka*, the Soviet supreme headquarters, was headed by Marshal Stalin, as he had promoted himself after the battle of Stalingrad. Stalin intended to keep full control. He allowed commanders a latitude of action which their German counterparts envied, and, unlike Hitler, he would listen carefully to counter-arguments. Nevertheless, he had no intention of allowing Red Army commanders to get above themselves as the moment of victory approached. He stopped the usual practice of appointing 'representatives of the *Stavka*' to oversee operations. Instead, he took on this role himself, even though he still had no intention of going anywhere near the front.

Stalin also decided to shake up the key commands. If this resulted in jealousies and 'disconcertedness', then he was far from displeased. The main change was to replace Marshal Konstantin Rokossovsky, the commander-in-chief of the 1st Belorussian Front, the main group of armies on the axis of advance to Berlin. Rokossovsky, a tall, elegant and good-looking cavalryman, presented a striking contrast to most Russian commanders, many of whom were squat, thick-necked and shaven-headed. He was also different in another way. Born Konstanty Rokosowski, he was half-Polish, the grandson and great-grandson of Polish cavalry officers. This made him dangerous in the eyes of Stalin. Stalin's hatred of the country had started during the Soviet-Polish war of 1920, when he had been partly blamed for the disastrous defeat of the Red Army attacking Warsaw.

Rokossovsky was outraged when he heard that he was to be transferred to command the 2nd Belorussian Front army group to attack East Prussia. Marshal Georgy Zhukov, the stocky and immensely tough commander who directed the defence of Moscow in December 1941, was to take his place. 'Why this disgrace?' Rokossovsky demanded. 'Why am I being moved from the main axis to one of secondary importance?' Rokossovsky suspected that Zhukov, whom he had con-sidered a friend, had undermined him, but in fact Stalin did not want a Pole to enjoy the glory of taking Berlin. It was natural that Rokossovsky should be suspicious. He had been arrested during the purge of the Red Army in 1937. The beatings from Beria's henchmen demanding confessions of treason were enough to make even the most balanced person slightly paranoid. And Rokossovsky knew that Lavrenty Beria, the head of the NKVD secret police, and Viktor Abakumov, the chief of SMERSH counter-intelligence, watched him closely. Stalin had left Rokossovsky in no doubt that the 1937 accusations still hung over him. He had simply been released conditionally. Any blunder as a commander would put him straight back into NKVD custody. 'I know very well what Beria is capable of,' Rokossovsky said to Zhukov during the changeover. 'I have been in his prisons.' It would take Soviet generals eight years to get their revenge on Beria.

The forces of the 1st Belorussian Front and the 1st Ukrainian Front lining up against the German front line along the Vistula were not simply superior, they were overwhelming. To Zhukov's south, Marshal Konev's 1st Ukrainian Front would attack due east towards Breslau. Its main thrust would be launched from the Sandomierz bridgehead, the largest salient of all on the west bank of the Vistula. Unlike Zhukov, however, Konev intended to use his two tank armies to smash the enemy line on the very first day.

Konev, according to Beria's son, had 'wicked little eyes, a shaven head that looked like a pumpkin, and an expression full of self-conceit'. He was probably Stalin's favourite general and one of the very few senior commanders whom even Stalin admired for his ruthlessness. Stalin had promoted him to marshal of the Soviet Union after his crushing of the Korsun pocket, south of Kiev, just under a year before. It had been one of the most pitiless engagements in a very cruel war. Konev ordered his aircraft to drop incendiaries on the small town of Shanderovka to force the Germans sheltering there out into the blizzard. As they struggled to break out of the encirclement on 17 February 1944, Konev sprang his trap. His tank crews charged straight for the column, firing machine guns and running men down to crush them under their tracks. As the Germans scattered, trying to flee through the heavy snow, Konev's three divisions of cavalry set off in pursuit. The Cossacks cut them down mercilessly with their sabres, apparently hacking even at arms raised in surrender. Some 20,000 Germans died that day.

On 12 January, the Vistula offensive began at 5 a.m. Moscow time, when Konev's 1st Ukrainian Front attacked out of the Sandomierz bridgehead. The snow was quite heavy and visibility almost nil. After *shtraf* companies of prisoners were forced through the minefields, rifle battalions secured the front line. The full artillery bombardment then began, using up to 300 guns per kilometre, which meant one every three to four metres. The German defenders were shattered. Most of them surrendered, grey-faced and trembling. A panzergrenadier officer watching from the rear described the spectacle on the horizon as a 'fire-storm' and added that it was 'like the heavens falling down on earth'. Prisoners from the 16th Panzer Division captured late that day claimed that once the bombardment started, their commander, Major General Müller, drove off towards the town of Kielce, abandoning his men.

Soviet tank crews had painted slogans on their turrets: 'Forward into the fascist lair!' and 'Revenge and death to the German occupiers!' They faced little resistance as their T–34 and heavy Stalin tanks moved forward at 2 p.m. Their hulls coated in frost were well camouflaged for the snowy landscape ahead, even if all was brown in the middle distance from shell-churned mud.

Along with Breslau, the main objectives of General Rybalko's 3rd Guards Tank Army and General Lelyushenko's 4th Guards Tank Army were the industrial regions of Silesia. When Stalin had briefed Konev in Moscow, he had pointed at the map and circled the area with his finger. He mouthed a single word: 'Gold'. No further comment was needed. Konev knew that Stalin wanted the factories and mines to be taken intact.

On the morning after Konev's attack from the Sandomierz bridgehead, the assault on East Prussia began with General Chernyakhovsky's 3rd Belorussian Front. On the following day, 14 January, Rokossovsky's forces attacked East Prussia from the River Narew bridgeheads. Zhukov's 1st Belorussian Front went into action on its two bridgeheads on the Vistula at Magnuszew and Pulawy. A thin layer of snow covered the ground and dense mist lasted until noon. At 8.30 a.m., Zhukov's 1st Belorussian Front opened up with twenty-five minutes of 'rolling fire'. The advanced rifle battalions, supported by self-propelled assault guns, seized the front lines in the Magnuszew bridgehead. The 8th Guards Army and the 5th Shock Army, with heavy artillery support, then broke open the third line. The main barrier beyond was the River Pilica. Zhukov's plan was for rifle divisions to seize crossing places for the guards tank brigades following on behind.

The right-hand tank brigade of Bogdanov's 2nd Guards Tank Army was one of the first to cross the Pilica. As a lead unit, the 47th Guards Tank Brigade had a variety of support attached, including sappers, self-propelled artillery, motorized anti-aircraft guns, and a battalion of sub-machine gunners mounted in trucks. Its objective was an airfield just south of the town of Sochaczew, an important junction due west of Warsaw. Over the next two days, the brigade charged northwards, destroying columns of fleeing Germans on the way and crushing staff cars 'with their tracks'.

It took much longer for the 1st Guards Tank Army on the left to break through. Colonel Gusakovsky, a Hero of the Soviet Union twice over, was so impatient after the long wait that when his 44th Guards Tank Brigade reached the Pilica, he refused to wait for the bridging equipment. It appeared to be a shallow stretch of the river, so to save 'two or three hours' he ordered his tank commanders first to smash the ice with gunfire, then to drive their vehicles across the river bed. The tanks, acting like icebreakers, pushed the broken ice aside 'with a terrible thundering noise'. It must have been terrifying for the tank drivers, but Gusakovsky did not seem concerned by such problems. Zhukov too was interested only in getting the tank brigades across so that they could deal with the 25th and the 19th Panzer Divisions. After that, the country lay open ahead.

Things had gone just as well for him at the Pulawy bridgehead on 14 January. The plan was not to bombard the whole line, but simply to blast corridors through it. By that evening they were well on the way to the city of Radom. Meanwhile on the 1st Belorussian Front's extreme right, the 47th Army began to encircle Warsaw from the north and the 1st Polish Army fought into the suburbs.

In the late afternoon of Monday 15 January, 'because of the big advance in the east', Hitler left the *Adlerhorst* at Ziegenberg to return to Berlin on his special train. Guderian had been forcefully requesting his return for the last three days. At first, Hitler had said that the Eastern Front must sort itself out, but finally he agreed to halt all activity in the west and return. Without consulting Guderian or the two army groups involved, he had just issued orders for the *Grossdeutschland* Corps to be moved from East Prussia to Kielce to shore up the Vistula front, even though this meant taking it out of the battle for at least a week.

Hitler's journey by rail to Berlin took nineteen hours. He did not entirely neglect domestic matters. He told Martin Bormann to stay at the Obersalzburg for the time being, where he and his wife kept Eva Braun and her sister Gretl Fegelein company.

Stalin, meanwhile, was in excellent spirits. That same evening, he welcomed General Eisenhower's chief of staff, Air Chief Marshal Tedder, who had finally arrived in Moscow after long delays in Cairo due to bad flying conditions. Tedder had come to discuss future developments, but Stalin observed smugly that the Ardennes offensive had been 'very stupid' of the Germans. He was also particularly pleased that the Germans had retained thirty divisions as 'a prestige garrison' in Courland – the remains of Army Group North, which Guderian wanted to bring back to Germany.

The Soviet leader made an effort to charm Tedder. He clearly wanted to convince Eisenhower's deputy that he had done everything possible by the timing of the Red Army's great offensive to help them out over the Ardennes. It is impossible to tell whether or not he foresaw that this would help exacerbate the rift between the Americans and the much more sceptical Churchill.

Soviet historians always tried to maintain that Stalin was planning to launch the attack on 20 January, but then, when he received a letter from Churchill on 6 January begging for help, he gave the order the next day to advance the attack to 12 January, even though the weather conditions were unfavourable. This was a gross misrepresentation of Churchill's letter. It was not a begging letter to save the Allies in the Ardennes. He had already written to say that the Allies were now 'masters of the situation' and Stalin knew perfectly well from his liaison officers in the west that the German threat there had collapsed by Christmas. Churchill was simply asking for information on when the Red Army was going to launch its great winter offensive, because the Kremlin had resolutely refused to reply to such requests, even when Soviet liaison officers were kept abreast of Eisenhower's plans.

The Vistula offensive, planned since October, had been prepared well ahead: one Soviet source even says that it had been possible 'to start the advance on 8–10 January'. Stalin was therefore more than happy to give the impression that he was saving his allies from a difficult situation, especially when he had reasons of his own for pushing forward the date.

Churchill was becoming increasingly concerned at Stalin's intention to impose on Poland its puppet 'Lublin government' made up of exiled Polish Communists controlled by Beria's NKVD. The Crimean conference at Yalta was imminent and Stalin wanted to make sure that his armies controlled the whole of Poland by the time he sat down with the American and British leaders. His law could be imposed ruthlessly on Polish territory purely because it constituted the immediate rear area to his operational troops. Anyone who objected could be classified as a saboteur or fascist agent. Finally, there was a much more down-to-earth reason for bringing the great offensive forward. Stalin was worried that the predicted change in the weather for the beginning of February would turn hard ground to mud and therefore slow up his tanks.

One aspect of the meeting with Tedder is most revealing. 'Stalin emphasized,' the American report states, 'that one of the difficulties [of the Vistula offensive] was the large number of trained German agents among the Poles, Latvians, Lithuanians, Ukrainians and German-speaking Russians. He said that they were all equipped with radios and, as a result, the element of surprise was practically eliminated. However the Russians have succeeded in eliminating this menace to a large measure. He said that he considers the clearance of the rear areas to be just as important as bringing up supplies.' This gross exaggeration of German-trained stay-behind groups was Stalin's pre-emptive justification of Soviet ruthlessness in Poland. Beria was also trying to brand the non-Communist resistance, the Armia Krajowa, as 'fascist' despite its suicidal bravery in the Warsaw uprising.

The next twenty-four hours proved that the Soviet armies which had broken through the Vistula front were indeed advancing at full speed. Each seemed to outbid the other.

The rapid advances of Zhukov's tank armies were partly due to the simplicity and robust construction of the T-34 tank and its broad tracks, which could cope with snow, ice and mud. Even so, the mechanic's skills proved at least as important as cavalry dash, because field workshops could not keep up. 'Ah, what a life it was before the war,' a driver remarked to Grossman. 'There were plenty of spare parts then.' Once the weather cleared, Shturmovik fighter bombers, known to the Germans as 'Jabos' for *Jagdbomber*, were able to support the headlong advance, as

Zhukov had promised his tank commanders. 'Our tanks move faster than the trains to Berlin,' boasted the ebullient Colonel Gusakovsky, who had blasted his way across the Pilica.

The small German garrison in Warsaw did not stand a chance. It consisted of engineer detachments and four fortress battalions – one of them was an 'ear battalion' made up of hearing casualties recycled back into service. The thrust of the 47th Guards Tank Brigade up to Sochaczew from the south and the encirclement of Warsaw from the north by the 47th Army meant that the garrison lost contact with its parent formation, the Ninth Army.

General Harpe's staff at Army Group 'A' warned OKH in Zossen on the evening of 16 January that they would not be able to hold the city. Colonel Bogislaw von Bonin, the head of the operations department, discussed the situation with Guderian. They decided to give army group headquarters a free hand in the decision, and Guderian signed the signals log with his usual 'G' in green ink. But in the *Nachtlage*, Hitler's midnight situation conference, the proposal to abandon Warsaw was reported to Hitler by one of his own staff before Guderian's deputy, General Walther Wenck, brought the subject up. Hitler exploded. 'You must stop everything!' he shouted. 'Fortress Warsaw must be held!' But it was already too late and radio communications had broken down. A few days later Hitler issued an order that every instruction sent to an army group had to be submitted to him first.

The fall of Warsaw led to another bitter row between Hitler and Guderian, who were still arguing over Hitler's decision to move the *Grossdeutschland* Corps. Guderian was even more furious to hear that Hitler was transferring the Sixth SS Panzer Army not to the Vistula front, but to Hungary. Hitler, however, refused to discuss it. The withdrawal from Warsaw was, in his eyes, a far more burning issue.

At the noon conference next day, 18 January, Guderian was given a public dressing-down, but worse was to follow. 'That evening,' recounted Colonel Baron von Humboldt of the OKH staff, 'it was Bonin's birthday. We were all standing round the map table with a glass of Sekt to congratulate him, when [General] Meisel, the second-in-command of the personnel department, arrived with two Oberleutnants armed with machine pistols. "Herr von Bonin," he said. "I must ask you to come with me."' Two others were arrested with Bonin, Lieutenant Colonel von Christen and Lieutenant Colonel von dem Knesebeck. They were taken off to the Prinz-Albrechtstrasse on Hitler's direct orders to be interrogated by the Gestapo.

Hitler saw the incident as yet another act of betrayal by the army. As well as sacking General Harpe, he also removed General von Luttwitz from command of the Ninth Army. But the truth was that his monstrous vanity could not allow him to lose a foreign capital, even one which he had totally destroyed. Guderian stood up for his three staff officers, insisting that he be interrogated too since the responsibility for the decision was entirely his. Hitler, longing to indict the general staff, took him at his word. At this most critical stage of the Vistula campaign, Guderian was subjected to hours of interrogation by Ernst Kaltenbrunner of the Reich Security Head Office, and Heinrich Müller, the chief of the Gestapo. The two more junior officers were released after two weeks, but Bonin remained in a concentration camp until the end of the war.

The day after Bonin's arrest, Martin Bormann reached Berlin. The next day, Saturday 20 January, he recorded in his diary: 'the situation in the east is becoming more and more threatening. We are abandoning the region of Warthegau. The leading tank units of the enemy are approaching Katowice.' It was the day that Soviet forces crossed the Reich border east of Hohensalza.

Guderian's wife abandoned Schloss Deipenhof 'half an hour before the first shells began to fall'. The chief of staff wrote that the estate workers (they were probably resettled Baltic Germans) 'stood in tears beside her car and many would willingly have accompanied her'. Although there can be little doubt about their desperation to leave, this may not have been due entirely to loyalty to their chatelaine. Rumours of what was happening in East Prussia had already started to circulate.

Soldiers of the Red Army, and its Polish formations especially, were unlikely to feel any more merciful after what they had witnessed in the Polish capital. 'We saw the destruction of Warsaw when we entered its empty streets on that memorable day, 17 January 1945,' wrote Captain Klochkov of the 3rd Shock Army. 'Nothing was left but ruins and ashes covered by snow. Badly starved and exhausted residents were making their way home.' Only 162,000 remained out of a pre-war population of

1,310,000. After the unbelievably brutal suppression of the Warsaw uprising in October 1944, the Germans had systematically destroyed all the historic monuments of the city, even though none had been used by the rebels. Vasily Grossman made his way through the ruined city to the ghetto. All that remained were the three-and-a-half-metre-high wall topped with broken glass and barbed wire and the Judenrat, the Jewish administrative building. The rest of the ghetto was 'a single undulating red sea of broken bricks'. Grossman wondered how many thousands of bodies were buried underneath. It was hard to imagine anyone escaping, but a Pole led him to where four Jews had just emerged from their hiding place high above the girders of a tall skeleton of a building.

3

Fire and Sword and 'Noble Fury'

When General Chernyakhovsky launched his offensive against East Prussia on 13 January, political officers erected signs to arouse the troops: 'Soldier, remember you are now entering the lair of the fascist beast!'

Chernyakhovsky's attack did not get off to a good start. The commander of the Third Panzer Army, on the basis of good intelligence, withdrew his troops from the front line of trenches at the last moment. This meant that the massive bombardment was wasted. The Germans then launched some very effective counter-attacks. And in the course of the following week, Chernyakhovsky found, as he had feared, that German defence works on the Insterburg gap cost his armies very heavy casualties.

Chernyakhovsky, however, soon spotted an opportunity. He was one of the most decisive and intelligent of senior Soviet commanders. The 39th Army was making better progress on the extreme right, so he suddenly moved the 11th Guards Army round behind and switched the weight of the attack to that flank. This unexpected thrust between the River Pregel and the River Niemen caused panic in the Volkssturm militia units. It was accompanied by another attack across the Niemen in the area of Tilsit by the 43rd Army. Chaos mounted in the German rear, largely because the Nazi Party officials had forbidden the evacuation of civilians. By 24 January, Chernyakhovsky's 3rd Belorussian Front was within striking distance of Königsberg, the capital of East Prussia.

As well as ignoring *Stavka* instructions when it was necessary, Chernyakhovsky, a tank commander and a 'master of military science', was also willing to change approved battle tactics. 'Self-propelled guns became an integral part of the infantry after the crossing of the Niemen,' Vasily Grossman noted. At thirty-seven years old, Ivan Danilovich Chernyakhovsky was much younger than most other Soviet commanders-in-chief. He was also something of an intellectual and used to recite romantic poetry with humorous panache to the writer Ilya Ehrenburg. Chernyakhovsky was intrigued by contradictions. He described Stalin as a living example of a dialectical process. 'It's impossible to understand him. All you can do is to have faith.' Chernyakhovsky was clearly not destined to survive into the post-war Stalinist petrification. He was perhaps fortunate to die soon in battle, his faith intact.

Ilya Ehrenburg's own mesmerizing calls for revenge on Germany in his articles in the Red Army newspaper *Krasnaya Zvezda* (*Red Star*) had created a huge following among the *frontoviki*, or frontline troops. Goebbels responded with loathing against 'the Jew Ilya Ehrenburg, Stalin's favourite rabble-rouser'. The propaganda ministry accused Ehrenburg of inciting the rape of German women. Yet while Ehrenburg never shrank from the most bloodthirsty harangues, the most notorious statement, which is still attributed to him by western historians, was a Nazi invention. He is accused of having urged Red Army soldiers to take German women as their 'lawful booty' and to 'break their racial pride'. 'There was a time,' Ehrenburg retorted in *Krasnaya Zvezda*, 'when Germans used to fake important documents of state. Now they have fallen so low as to fake my articles.' But Ehrenburg's assertion that the soldiers of the Red Army were 'not interested in Gretchens, but in those Fritzes who had insulted our women' proved to be wide of the mark, as the savage behaviour of the Red Army soon showed. And his frequent references to Germany as 'the Blonde Witch' certainly did not encourage a humane treatment of German and even Polish women.

Marshal Rokossovsky's 2nd Belorussian Front attacked north and north-westwards from the Narew bridgeheads on 14 January, the day after Chernyakhovsky. His main task was to cut off East Prussia by heading for the mouth of the Vistula and Danzig. Rokossovsky was uneasy about the *Stavka* plan. His armies would become detached from both Chernyakhovsky's attack on Königsberg and Zhukov's charge westwards from the Vistula.

The offensive against the German Second Army began 'in weather which was perfect for the attack', as the corps commander on the receiving end noted regretfully. A thin layer of snow covered the ground and the River Narew was frozen. The fog cleared at noon, and Rokossovsky's armies were soon supported by constant air sorties. Progress was still slow for the first two days, but once again it was the Soviet heavy artillery and the katyusha rocket launchers which made the first breakthroughs possible. Iron-hard ground also made the shells much more lethal, with surface explosions. The snowy landscape was rapidly scarred with craters and black and yellow scorch marks.

On that first evening, General Reinhardt, the commander-in-chief of the army group, telephoned Hitler, then still at the *Adlerhorst*. He tried to warn him of the danger to the whole of East Prussia if he were not allowed to withdraw. The Führer refused to listen. The next thing Reinhardt's headquarters received, at 3 a.m., was the order to transfer the *Grossdeutschland* Corps, the only effective reserve in the region, to the Vistula front.

Reinhardt was not the only field commander to fulminate against his superiors. On 20 January, the *Stavka* suddenly ordered Rokossovsky to alter the axis of his advance because Chernyakhovsky had been held up. He was now to attack north-eastwards into the centre of East Prussia, not simply seal the region off along the Vistula. Rokossovsky was concerned by the vast gap opening on his left as Zhukov's armies headed westwards for Berlin, but in East Prussia, this change of direction took German commanders by surprise. On Rokossovsky's right flank, the 3rd Guards Cavalry Corps moved rapidly over the frozen landscape and entered Allenstein at 3 a.m. on 22 January. On his left, Volsky's 5th Guards Tank Army advanced rapidly towards the city of Elbing beside the estuary of the Vistula. Part of the leading tank brigade entered the city on 23 January, having been mistaken for German panzers. A violent and chaotic skirmish broke out in the city centre, and they were forced out. The main body of the army bypassed the city and carried on to the shore of the great lagoon, the Frisches Haff. East Prussia was virtually cut off from the Reich.

Although the German armed forces had expected the assault on East Prussia for several months, disorganization and uncertainty reigned in towns and villages. In rear areas the hated military police, the Feldgend-armerie, exerted a harsh order. The *Landsers* called them 'chain-hounds' because the metal gorgette which they wore on a chain round the neck looked like a dog collar.

On the morning of Chernyakhovsky's attack, 13 January, a leave train bound for Berlin was halted in a station by Feldgendarmerie. They bellowed orders that all soldiers belonging to divisions whose numbers they were about to call were to get out and form up immediately. The soldiers departing on leave, many of whom had not seen their families for two years at least, sat clenched, praying that their division would not be called. But almost all had to descend and line up in ranks on the platform. Anyone who failed to report faced execution. A young soldier, Walter Beier, was one of the few to be spared. Barely daring to believe his luck, he continued on the journey to his family near Frankfurt an der Oder. But he was to find himself facing the Red Army closer to home than he had ever imagined.

The man most to blame for the chaos was Gauleiter Erich Koch, a Nazi leader already infamous for his rule as Reich's Commissar for the Ukraine. Koch was so proud of his brutality that he does not appear to have objected to his nickname, 'the second Stalin'. Completely imbued with the Hitlerian obstinacy of fixed defence, Koch had forced tens of thousands of civilians into digging earthworks. Unfortunately, he failed to consult army commanders on where they wanted them. He had also been the first to dragoon boys and old men into the Volkssturm militia, the Nazi Party's most flagrant example of useless sacrifice. But worst of all, Koch had refused to countenance evacuation of the civil population.

He and his local Nazi Party chiefs, having forbidden the evacuation of civilians as defeatist, then slipped away themselves without warning anybody when the attack came. The consequences were appalling for the wives, daughters and children who tried to escape too late across a landscape a metre deep in snow and temperatures down to minus twenty Celsius. A number of women farm workers, however, remained voluntarily, convinced that they would just be working under new masters and that little would change.

The distant thunder of artillery when the offensives began created terrible fear in the isolated farms and villages of the mainly flat and forested East Prussian landscape. Women in East Prussia had heard of the atrocities at Nemmersdorf the previous autumn, when some of Chernyakhovsky's troops invaded East Prussia at the end of the headlong advance in the summer of 1944. They may well have seen in a local town's *Kino* the terrible newsreel footage of sixty-two raped and murdered women and young girls. Goebbels's propaganda ministry had rushed cameramen to the front to record the atrocity and exploit it to the maximum. Yet there still seemed to be little idea of the degree of horrors in store for them. The most prevalent for girls and women of all ages was gang rape.

'Red Army soldiers don't believe in "individual liaisons" with German women,' wrote the playwright Zakhar Agranenko in his diary when serving as an officer of marine infantry in East Prussia. 'Nine, ten, twelve men at a time – they rape them on a collective basis.' He later described how German women in Elbing, in a desperate attempt to seek protection, offered themselves instead to Soviet marine infantrymen.

The Soviet armies advancing in huge, long columns were an extraordinary mixture of modern and medieval: tank troops in padded black helmets, their T-34s churning up the earth as they dipped and rolled with the ground, Cossack cavalrymen on shaggy mounts with loot strapped to the saddle, Lend-Lease Studebakers and Dodges towing light field guns, open Chevrolets with tarpaulin-covered mortars in the back and tractors hauling great howitzers, all eventually followed by a second echelon in horse-drawn carts. The variety of characters among the soldiers was almost as great as their military equipment. There were those who saw even young German boys as embryo SS men and believed that they should all be killed before they grew up and invaded Russia again, and there were those who spared children and gave them something to eat. There were freebooters who drank and raped quite shamelessly, and there were idealistic, austere Communists and members of the intelligentsia genuinely appalled by such behaviour. The writer Lev Kopelev, then a political officer, was arrested by SMERSH counter-intelligence for having 'engaged in the propaganda of bourgeois humanism, of pity for the enemy'. Kopelev had also dared to criticize the ferocity of Ilya Ehrenburg's articles.

The initial advances of Rokossovsky's armies were so rapid that the German authorities in Königsberg sent several refugee trains to Allenstein unaware that it had been captured by the 3rd Guards Cavalry

Corps. For the Cossacks, the refugee trains were ideal concentrations of women and booty falling into their hands.

Beria and Stalin back in Moscow knew perfectly well what was going on. In one report they were told that 'many Germans declare that all German women in East Prussia who stayed behind were raped by Red Army soldiers'. Numerous examples of gang rape were given – 'girls under eighteen and old women included'. In fact victims could be as young as twelve years old. 'The NKVD group attached to the 43rd Army discovered that German women who had stayed behind in Schpaleiten had tried to commit suicide', the report continued. 'They interrogated one of them called Emma Korn. "On 3 February," she told them, "frontline troops of the Red Army entered the town. They came into the cellar where we were hiding and pointed their weapons at me and the other two women and ordered us into the yard. In the yard twelve soldiers in turn raped me. Other soldiers did the same to my two neighbours. The following night six drunken soldiers broke into our cellar and raped us in front of the children. On 5 February, three soldiers came, and on 6 February eight drunken soldiers also raped and beat us."' Three days later the women tried to kill the children and themselves by cutting all their wrists, but evidently they had not known how to do it properly.

The Red Army attitude towards women had become openly proprietorial, especially since Stalin himself had stepped in to allow Red Army officers to keep a 'campaign wife'. (She was known as a PPZh, because the full term, '*pokhodno-polevaya zhena*', was so similar to PPSh, the standard Red Army sub-machine gun.) These young women, selected as mistresses by senior officers, were usually headquarters signallers, clerks or medics – young women soldiers who wore a beret on the back of the head instead of a fore-and-aft *pilotka*.

The lot of a campaign wife was not an easy one when male lust was both intense and indiscriminate. 'There you are, Vera,' a young woman soldier called Musya Annenkova in the 19th Army wrote to her friend. 'See what their "love" is like! They seem to be tender to you but it's difficult to know what's inside their souls. They've got no sincere feelings, only short-lived passion or love with animal feelings. How difficult it is here to find a really faithful man.'

*

Marshal Rokossovsky issued order No. 006 in an attempt to direct 'the feelings of hatred at fighting the enemy on the battlefield' and to underline the punishment for 'looting, violence, robbing, unnecessary arson and destruction'. It seems to have had little effect. There were also a few arbitrary attempts to exert authority. The commander of one rifle division is said to have 'personally shot a lieutenant who was lining up a group of his men before a German woman spread-eagled on the ground'. But either officers were involved themselves, or the lack of discipline made it too dangerous to restore order over drunken soldiers armed with sub-machine guns.

Even General Okorokov, the chief of the political department of the 2nd Belorussian Front, opposed at a meeting on 6 February what he saw as a 'refusal to take revenge on the enemy'. In Moscow, the authorities were less worried about rape and murder than about the senseless destruction. On 9 February, *Krasnaya Zvezda* declared in an editorial that 'every breach of military discipline only weakens the victorious Red Army . . . Our revenge is not blind. Our anger is not irrational. In a moment of blind rage one is apt to destroy a factory in conquered enemy territory – a factory that would be of value to us.'

Political officers hoped to adapt this approach to the question of rape as well. 'When we breed a true feeling of hatred in a soldier,' the political department of the 19th Army declared, 'the soldier will not try to have sex with a German woman, because he will be repulsed.' But this inept sophistry only serves to underline the failure of the authorities to understand the problem. Even young women soldiers and medics in the Red Army did not disapprove. 'Our soldiers' behaviour towards Germans, particularly German women, is absolutely correct!' said a twenty-one-year-old from Agranenko's reconnaissance detachment. Some seemed to find it amusing. Kopelev was angry when one of his women assistants in the political department made jokes about it.

German crimes in the Soviet Union and the regime's relentless propaganda certainly contributed to the terrible violence against German women in East Prussia. But vengeance can be only part of the expla-nation, even if it later became the justification for what happened. Once soldiers had alcohol inside them, the nationality of their prey made little difference. Lev Kopelev described hearing a 'frenzied scream' in Allenstein. He saw a girl, 'her long, braided blonde hair dishevelled, her

dress torn, shouting piercingly: "I'm Polish! Jesus Mary, I'm Polish!"'
She was pursued by two inebriated 'tankists' in full view of everyone.

The subject has been so repressed in Russia that even today veterans
refuse to acknowledge what really happened during the onslaught on
German territory. They will admit to hearing of a few excesses, and
then dismiss the subject as an inevitable result of war. Only a few are
prepared to acknowledge that they witnessed such scenes. The tiny
handful prepared to speak openly, however, are totally unrepentant.
'They all lifted their skirts for us and lay on the bed,' said the Komsomol
leader in a tank company. He even went on to boast that '2 million of
our children were born' in Germany.

The capacity of Soviet officers and soldiers to convince themselves
that most of the victims were either happy with their fate, or at least
accepted that it was their turn to suffer after what the Wehrmacht had
done in Russia, is remarkable. 'Our fellows were so sex-starved,' a Soviet
major told a British journalist at the time, 'that they often raped old
women of sixty, seventy or even eighty – much to these grandmothers'
surprise, if not downright delight.'

Drink of every variety, including dangerous chemicals seized from
laboratories and workshops, was a major factor. In fact, compulsive
drinking gravely damaged the fighting capacity of the Red Army. The
situation became so bad that the NKVD reported back to Moscow that
'mass poisoning from captured alcohol is taking place in occupied
German territory'. It seems as if Soviet soldiers needed alcoholic courage
to attack a woman. But then, all too often, they drank too much and,
unable to complete the act of rape, used the bottle instead with appalling
effect. A number of victims were mutilated obscenely.

One can only scratch at the surface of the bewildering psychological
contradictions. When gang-raped women in Königsberg begged their
attackers afterwards to put them out of their misery, the Red Army men
appear to have felt insulted. 'Russian soldiers do not shoot women,' they
replied. 'Only German soldiers do that.' The Red Army had managed
to convince itself that because it had assumed the moral mission to
liberate Europe from fascism, it could behave entirely as it liked, both
personally and politically.

Domination and humiliation permeated most soldiers' treatment of
women in East Prussia. The victims bore the brunt of revenge for the

Wehrmacht's crimes during the invasion of the Soviet Union. After the initial fury dissipated, this characteristic of sadistic humiliation became noticeably less marked. By the time the Red Army reached Berlin three months later, its soldiers tended to regard German women more as a casual right of conquest than a target of hate. The sense of domination certainly continued, but this was perhaps partly an indirect product of the humiliations which they themselves had suffered at the hands of their commanders and the Soviet authorities as a whole. 'The extreme violence of totalitarian systems,' wrote Vasily Grossman in his great novel *Life and Fate*, 'proved able to paralyse the human spirit throughout whole continents.'

There were, of course, a number of other forces or influences at work. Sexual freedom was a subject for lively debate within Communist Party circles during the 1920s, but during the following decade, Stalin ensured that Soviet society depicted itself as virtually asexual. This had nothing to do with genuine puritanism: it was because love and sex did not fit in with dogma designed to 'deindividualize' the individual. Human urges and emotions had to be suppressed. Freud's work was banned, divorce and adultery were matters for strong Party disapproval. Criminal sanctions against homosexuality were reintroduced. The new doctrine extended even to the complete suppression of sex education. In graphic art, the clothed outline of a woman's breasts was regarded as dangerously erotic. They had to be disguised under boiler suits. The regime clearly wanted any form of desire to be converted into love for the Party and, above all, the Great Leader.

Most ill-educated Red Army soldiers suffered from sexual ignorance and utterly unenlightened attitudes towards women. So the Soviet state's attempts to suppress the libido of its people created what one Russian writer described as a sort of 'barracks eroticism' which was far more primitive and violent than 'the most sordid foreign pornography'. And all this was combined with the dehumanizing influence of modern propaganda and the atavistic, warring impulses of men marked by fear and suffering.

Just as non-German nationality failed to save women from rape, so left-wing credentials provided little protection to men. German Communists who emerged from twelve years of clandestine belief to welcome their fraternal liberators usually found themselves handed over to SMERSH for investigation. The smiles of joy at the arrival of the Red Army soon froze on their faces in disbelief. The twisted logic of SMERSH could always turn a story, however genuine, into a conspiracy of calculated treachery. And there was always the killer question, formulated in advance in Moscow, to be posed to every prisoner or noncombatant who professed allegiance to Stalin: 'Why are you not with the partisans?' The fact that there were no partisan groups in Germany was not regarded as a valid excuse. This pitilessly Manichaean line drummed in during the years of war naturally tended to compound the generic hatred of many Soviet soldiers. They asked their political officers why the German working class had not fought Hitler and never received a direct answer. It is not surprising, therefore, that when the Party line changed abruptly in mid-April to say that you should not hate all Germans, only Nazis, many soldiers took little notice.

The hate propaganda had fallen on receptive ears and the degree of loathing for anything German had become truly visceral. 'Even the trees were enemy,' said a soldier of the 3rd Belorussian Front. The Red Army was shocked and disbelieving when General Chernyakhovsky was killed by a stray shell outside Königsberg. His soldiers buried him in a makeshift grave. Branches were cut from trees. They were the only available substitute for the flowers thrown in on top of the coffin according to tradition. But suddenly a young soldier jumped down into the grave, straddled the coffin and frantically threw all the branches back out again. They came from enemy trees. They were defiling their hero's resting place.

After Chernyakhovsky's death, Marshal Vasilevsky, the former chief of the general staff, took over command of the 3rd Belorussian Front on Stalin's order. Vasilevsky's approach to the problem of discipline appears to have been little different from that of other senior commanders. According to one account, his chief of staff reported to him on looting and damage. 'Comrade Marshal,' he said, 'the soldiers are not behaving themselves. They break furniture, mirrors and dishes. What are your instructions in this connection?' Vasilevsky, perhaps the most intelligent and cultivated of all Soviet commanders, was apparently silent for a few moments. 'I don't give a fuck,' he said eventually. 'It is now time for our soldiers to issue their own justice.'

The destructive urge of Soviet soldiers in East Prussia was truly alarming. It went far beyond the chopping up of furniture to make a fire. Without thinking, they torched houses which could have given them warmth and shelter for the night when all was frozen hard outside. They were also furious to find a standard of living among peasant farmers far higher than anything that they had ever imagined. This provoked outrage at the idea that Germans, who had already been living so well, should have invaded the Soviet Union to loot and destroy.

Agranenko recorded in his diary what an old sapper felt about Germans. 'How should one treat them, Comrade Captain? Just think of it. They were well off, well fed, had livestock, vegetable gardens and apple trees. And they invaded us. They went as far as my oblast of Voronezh. For this, Comrade Captain, we should strangle them.' He paused. 'I'm sorry for the children, Comrade Captain. Even though they are Fritz kids.'

The Soviet authorities, no doubt to save Stalin from blame for the disaster of 1941, had managed to inculcate a sense of collective guilt in the Soviet people that they had allowed the Motherland to be invaded. There can be little doubt that the expiation of suppressed guilt increases the violence of revenge. But many motives for violence were much more straightforward. Dmitry Shcheglov, a political officer with the 3rd Army, admitted that on seeing German larders they were 'disgusted by the plenty' which they found everywhere. They also hated the orderly arrangement of German domestic life. 'I'd just love to smash my fist into all those neat rows of tins and bottles,' he wrote. Red Army soldiers were astonished to see wirelesses in so many houses. The evidence of their eyes strongly implied that the Soviet Union was perhaps not quite the workers' and peasants' paradise they had been told. East Prussian farms produced a mixture of bewilderment, jealousy, admiration and anger which alarmed political officers.

The fears of army political departments were confirmed by reports from NKVD postal censors, who underlined negative comments in blue and positive comments in red. The NKVD drastically increased the censorship of letters home, hoping to control the way soldiers described the style of living of ordinary Germans and the 'politically incorrect conclusions' formed as a result. The NKVD was also horrified to find that soldiers were sending German postcards home. Some even had 'anti-Soviet quotations from Hitler's speeches'. This at least forced political departments to provide clean writing paper.

Clocks, china, mirrors and pianos were smashed in middle-class houses which Red Army soldiers assumed were those of German barons. A woman military doctor wrote home from near Königsberg, 'You cannot imagine how many valuable things have been destroyed by the Ivans, how many beautiful and comfortable houses have been burned down. At the same time, the soldiers are right. They can't take everything with them in this world or the other. And when a soldier breaks a wall-sized mirror, he somehow feels better. It's a kind of distraction loosening the general tension of the body and the mind.' In village streets there were snow storms from eviscerated pillows and feather mattresses. Much was also bewilderingly new to soldiers brought up in the provinces of the Soviet Union, especially Uzbeks and Turkmenians from Central Asia. They were apparently bemused on discovering hollow toothpicks for the first time: 'We thought they were straws for drinking wine,' one soldier said to Agranenko. Others, including officers, tried to smoke looted cigars, inhaling as if they were one of their newspaper roll-ups filled with black *makhorka* tobacco.

Objects taken as plunder were often discarded and trampled a few moments later. Nobody wanted to leave anything for a '*shtabnaya krysa*' – a 'staff rat' – or especially for a '*tylovaya krysa*' – a 'rear rat' from the second echelon. Solzhenitsyn described scenes resembling a 'tumultuous market', with soldiers trying on Prussian women's outsize drawers. Some fitted on so many layers of clothing under their overalls that they could hardly move, and tank crews stuffed so much plunder into their vehicles that it is amazing the turret could still traverse. The supply of artillery shells was also reduced because so many vehicles were loaded with indiscriminate loot. Officers shook their heads in despair at their men's choice of booty, such as dinner jackets, to send home in the monthly parcel. The idealistic Kopelev disapproved strongly. He regarded the specially permitted five-kilo parcel as a 'direct and unmistakable incitement to plunder'. Officers were allowed twice as much. For generals and SMERSH officers there was scarcely a limit, but generals did not really need to stoop to looting. Their officers brought select offerings. Even Kopelev chose an elaborate hunting rifle and a set of Dürer engravings for General Okorokov, his boss in the 2nd Belorussian Front political department.

A small group of pro-Soviet German officers was taken to visit East

Prussia. They were appalled by what they saw. One of them, Count von Einsiedel, vice-president of the NKVD-controlled National Committee for a Free Germany, told fellow members on his return, 'Russians are absolutely crazy about vodka and all alcoholic drinks. They rape women, drink themselves into unconsciousness and set houses on fire.' This was rapidly reported to Beria. Ilya Ehrenburg, the fieriest of all propagandists, was also deeply shaken on a visit, but it did not make him moderate his ferocity in print.

Red Army soldiers had never been well fed during the war. Most of the time they had been permanently hungry. If it had not been for the huge shipments of American Spam and wheat, many of them would have been close to starvation. They had inevitably resorted to living off the land, although it was never an official policy in the Red Army as it had been with the Wehrmacht. In Poland, they had stolen the seed corn of farmers and slaughtered for meat the few remaining animals missed by the Germans. In Lithuania the desperate urge for sugar had led to soldiers raiding beehives: in their ranks the previous autumn, many were conspicuous with faces and hands dramatically swollen by bee stings. But the well-ordered and well-stocked farms of East Prussia offered a bounty beyond their dreams. Cows mooing in agony from swollen udders because those who milked them had fled were frequently shot down with rifles and machine guns to be turned into improvised steaks. 'They ran away and left everything behind,' wrote one soldier, 'and now we have lots of pork, food and sugar. We have so much food now that we won't eat just anything.'

Although the Soviet authorities were well aware of the terrible retribution being exacted in East Prussia, they seemed angered, in fact almost offended, to find that German civilians were fleeing. Countryside and towns were virtually depopulated. The NKVD chief of the 2nd Belorussian Front reported to G. F. Aleksandrov, the chief ideologist on the central committee, that there were 'very few Germans left . . . many settlements are completely abandoned'. He gave examples of villages where half a dozen people remained and small towns with fifteen people or so, almost all over forty-five years of age. The 'noble fury' was triggering the largest panic migration in history. Between 12 January and mid-February 1945, almost 8.5 million Germans fled their homes in the eastern provinces of the Reich.

In East Prussia, a number went to hide in the forests, especially Volkssturm men and vulnerable women, praying for the fury to pass. The vast majority, on the other hand, had started to flee just ahead of the invasion. Some left messages for their menfolk. 'Dear Papa!' Dmitri Shcheglov found hurriedly chalked in a childish hand on one door. 'We must escape to Alt-P. by cart. From there on to the Reich by ship.' Hardly any were to see their homes again. It was the abrupt and total destruction of a whole region, with its own marked character and culture, emphasized perhaps because it had always been at the extremity of Germany on the Slav frontier. Stalin had already planned to take the northern half with Königsberg as part of the Soviet Union. The rest would be given to a satellite Poland as partial compensation for the annexation of all of its eastern territories as 'western Belorussia' and 'western Ukraine'. East Prussia itself was to be wiped from the map.

Once Rokossovsky's 5th Guards Tank Army had cut through to the Frisches Haff, the only routes out were by sea from Pillau at the south-west tip of the Samland Peninsula, or over the ice to the Frische Nehrung, the long sandbar enclosing the lagoon from the Danzig end. Perhaps the most unfortunate fugitives were the ones who fled into Königsberg, which was soon cut off on the landward side. Escape from the city proved far from easy, mainly because the Nazi authorities had made no preparations for the evacuation of civilians, and it took some time before the first ships appeared at Pillau. Meanwhile, the siege of the East Prussian capital became one of the most terrible of the war.

The refugees who reached the Frische Nehrung, the sandbar of the lagoon, the only route still open to the west, received little pity from Wehrmacht officers. They forced them off the road, insisting that it was for military use only. Trekkers had to abandon their carts and belongings and stagger through the dunes. Many never even reached the Frische Nehrung. On the mainland, Soviet tank columns simply crushed any refugee farm carts in the way and raked convoys with machine-gun fire. When a detachment of tank troops overtook a refugee column on 19 January, 'the passengers on the carts and vehicles were butchered'.

Even though East Prussia contained none of the Nazis' most notorious concentration camps, an NKVD detachment checking an area of forest near the village of Kumennen found 100 civilian corpses in three groups in the snow. They were presumably victims of a death march. Himmler had ordered the evacuation of camps when the Red Army approached. 'The majority are women aged 18–35,' the report stated, 'and clad in torn clothes with numbers and a six-pointed star on the left sleeve and on the front of their clothes. Some of them wore clogs. Mugs and spoons were fastened to their belts. Their pockets contained food – small potatoes, swede, grains of wheat etc. A special commission of investigation formed by doctors and officers established that they were shot at close range and all the executed women were half-starved.' Significantly, they were not identified by the Soviet authorities as Jews, despite the mention of six-pointed stars sewn on their clothing, but as 'citizens of the USSR, France and Romania'. The Nazis killed around 1.5 million Soviet Jews simply because they were Jewish, but Stalin did not want anything to divert attention from the suffering of the Motherland.

4

The Great Winter Offensive

When German generals addressed their men in familiar tones they called them '*Kinder*' – children. This came from a Prussian sense of paternalism which extended to the whole state. 'The soldier is the child of the people,' said General von Blumentritt at the end of the war, but any idea of a family tie between military and civilian society was by then wishful thinking.

Anger was rising at the futile sacrifices. People were now prepared to shelter deserters. A Polish farmer who had been in Berlin on 24 January witnessed women shouting at the officers and NCOs marching a column of German soldiers through the streets, 'Let our husbands come home! Make the Golden Pheasants [senior Nazis] fight instead!' General staff officers in their uniforms with thick red stripes down their trousers started to attract cries of 'Vampire!' when spotted by civilians. But this did not mean that revolution was in the air, as in 1918, the year which so obsessed the Nazis. The Swedish military attaché observed that there would be no revolt before the food ran out. This was acknowledged in a popular Berlin saying, 'The fighting will not stop until Göring fits into Goebbels's trousers.'

Few had any illusions about what lay ahead. The Berlin health department ordered hospitals to provide another 10,000 bed spaces for civilians and another 10,000 for military use as 'catastrophe beds'. This decree was typical of Nazi bureaucracy: it made no allowance for the effects of bombing and the scarcity of resources and trained medical staff. It was one thing to provide bed spaces, but doctors and nurses

39

were already desperately overstretched, and they simply did not have the personnel to move patients down into cellars during the nightly air raids. Meanwhile, hospital administrators were having to waste time negotiating with different Nazi Party departments to allow their staff to be excused call-up for the Volkssturm militia.

The Volkssturm itself had been born the previous autumn out of Nazi ideology and petty power struggles. Hitler's suspicions that the army's leadership was both treacherous and defeatist made him determined that control of this mass militia should be kept out of its hands. Himmler, head of the Waffen SS and commander-in-chief of the Replacement Army since the July plot, was an obvious candidate, but the ambitious Martin Bormann was determined that the Volkssturm should be organized locally by the Nazi Party Gauleiters who came under him. Since almost all German males between seventeen and forty-five had already been called up, the Volkssturm was an amalgam of teenagers and the elderly.

Goebbels, now also Reich Defence Commissar for Berlin, whipped up a propaganda campaign with slogans such as 'The Führer's call is our sacred order!' and 'Believe! Fight! Win!' Cinemas showed newsreels of marching men, elderly and young shoulder to shoulder, Volkssturm detachments receiving panzerfaust rocket-propelled grenades, then swearing the oath of allegiance to the Führer in massed ranks. The camera lingered on the faces of those listening to Goebbels's speech. There were many believers, ignorant of military reality, who were convinced by this show of determination. 'All the peoples of the world have hatched a plot against us, but we will show them what we are capable of,' a wife wrote to her soldier husband. 'Yesterday there took place here the swearing of the oath for everyone from the district. You should have seen it. I will never forget the impression of strength and pride. We don't yet know when they will be sent into battle.'

The morale of soldiers at the front was not, however, raised by all this. Many were appalled to hear in letters from home that their father, in some cases grandfather, or young brother was being drilled and given weapon training every Sunday. In fact most Germans, with their innate respect for professional specialization, were deeply sceptical. 'The people were predominantly of the opinion,' General Hans Kissel later told his captors, 'that if the Wehrmacht was unable to cope with the situation, then the Volkssturm would not be able to do so either.'

Most members of the Volkssturm guessed that they were to be thrown senselessly into battle for symbolic purposes and had no hope of making any impression on the Soviet onslaught. Some forty Volkssturm battalions raised in Silesia were allocated to defend their eastern and north-eastern frontiers. A few concrete emplacements were built, but since they had almost no anti-tank weapons, Soviet tank forces went straight through them.

In the industrial areas of Upper Silesia, the centre of 'gold' indicated by Stalin, German company directors became increasingly anxious. They feared a revolt among the 300,000 foreign workers, mainly Poles and forced labour from the Soviet Union, and insisted on 'security measures against enemy alien workers' before the Red Army's advance encouraged them to rise in revolt. But Marshal Konev's tanks were even closer than they thought.

The Soviet advances also prompted the evacuation of prisoner-of-war camps as well as concentration camps. Guards and prisoners trudged through bleak, snow-covered landscapes without any idea of direction or purpose. Late one afternoon, a column of British prisoners of war passed a large group of Soviet prisoners with rags wrapped round their bare feet. 'Their white starved faces,' wrote Robert Kee, 'contrasted horribly with the black unshaven growth of beard which covered them. Only their eyes shone out as something human, distressed and furtive but human all the same, flashing out a last desperate SOS from the person trapped inside.' The British took what they had in their pockets, whether soap or cigarettes, and threw it across. One of the packets of cigarettes fell short. As a Russian prisoner bent to pick it up, a Volkssturm guard ran up to stamp on his outstretched fingers. He then kicked the man and began to strike him with his rifle butt. This provoked 'a wild roar of rage' from the British column. 'The guard stopped beating the Russian and looked up astonished. He had obviously become so hardened to brutality that it no longer occurred to him that human beings had any right to protest.' He then began to bellow and wave his gun threateningly, but they roared and jeered all the more. Their own guards came pounding up to restore order and push the Volkssturm man back towards his own prisoners. 'My God!' said one of Kee's companions. 'I'll forgive the Russians absolutely anything they do to this country when they arrive. Absolutely anything.'

With Göring utterly discredited, the main struggle for power within the Nazi leadership was principally between Bormann and Himmler. The July plot had greatly increased Himmler's power. He was in charge of the only organizations – the Waffen SS and the Gestapo – which could control the army. With Hitler's physical and mental state gravely shaken by the same event, he was in a strong position to succeed as Führer, but whether he had the qualities to play Stalin to Hitler's Lenin, as some feared, was a different matter.

Himmler hardly looked the part. His 'chief physical characteristics were a receding chin, heavy jowls, and eyes which appeared not so much bespectacled as glazed in'. For so cold a man, so alien to any sort of humanity, the Reichsführer SS could be astonishingly naïve and complacent. Himmler, certain that he was next in line to the throne, gravely underestimated Martin Bormann, the bull-necked and round-faced secretary who had schemed his way into Hitler's confidence and now controlled access to him. Bormann secretly despised Himmler, and referred to him sarcastically as 'Uncle Heinrich'.

Bormann had long suspected that Himmler, the improbable creator of the Waffen SS, secretly longed to be a military commander in his own right. Offering the means to satisfy this fantasy was a good way of getting him out of Berlin and away from the centre of power. In early December, almost certainly on Bormann's suggestion, Hitler appointed Himmler commander-in-chief of a small army group on the upper Rhine. The Reichsführer SS refused to acknowledge that Field Marshal von Rundstedt, the commander-in-chief West, was his superior. But buried in south-west Germany in the Black Forest, Himmler did not realize that he was rapidly losing power back in Berlin. Kaltenbrunner, the head of the Reich Security Head Office, whom he himself had raised up after Heydrich's assassination in Prague, had been won over by Bormann, who gave him direct access to Hitler to receive his instructions in person. Himmler also did not realize that his liaison officer at Führer headquarters, SS Gruppenführer Hermann Fegelein, had also secretly joined Bormann's camp.

*

While Nazi leaders were scheming among themselves, the Vistula front had completely collapsed, as Guderian had predicted. The Soviet tank brigades did not stop at dusk. They pushed on through the hours of darkness, one commander explained, because they were 'less vulnerable in the dark, and our tanks are terrifying at night'.

Soviet point units were sometimes advancing by sixty to seventy kilometres a day. 'A German general,' claimed Colonel Gusakovsky, 'having checked enemy positions on the map, would take his trousers off and go to bed peacefully. We would hit this general at midnight.' Even allowing for a degree of boastful exaggeration, there can be no doubt that the momentum of the Soviet advance upset the German staff system. Reports on enemy positions at last light, passed back up the chain of command, reached army group headquarters at 8 a.m. Then OKH had to prepare its digest and situation map in time for Hitler's noontime conference. This might go on for some time. Freytag von Loringhoven, Guderian's military assistant, remembered one which lasted for seven hours. So orders issued on the basis of Hitler's instructions did not reach frontline units until twenty-four hours after their reports on the situation.

In this theatre of power politics, outsiders' contributions to operational discussions were seldom constructive. They were usually self-serving, especially if there was a chance to score a point over a rival at court. Göring now seemed devoid of Machiavellian finesse. He had no idea of military strategy yet would hold forth at length, his vast bulk bent across the map table, rendering it invisible to everyone else. Then, having made a fool of himself, he would retire to a chair nearby. An astonishingly long-suffering Hitler did not reprimand him when he went to sleep in full view of everyone present. On one occasion, Freytag von Loringhoven observed Göring fall asleep in a chair. The spare map folded over his face made him look like a pre-war commercial traveller snoozing on a train.

Soviet tank drivers were so exhausted that they too frequently fell asleep, but a T-34 or Stalin tank could clearly withstand rather more than an ordinary vehicle if it blundered into something. The padded leather or canvas tank helmets were certainly needed inside the lurching steel monsters. The crews were kept going to a large degree by the exhilaration of pursuit. The sight of German equipment abandoned brought fierce pleasure. 'He's not going to be allowed a chance to rest,' they swore. They revelled above all in the surprise they were achieving in the German rear.

At the slightest sign of determined resistance, Soviet commanders brought up their heavy artillery. Vasily Grossman observed 'disciplined German prisoners' marching themselves to the rear, some still shell-shocked from the massive artillery bombardments. 'One of them straightens his jacket and salutes every time a car passes,' he jotted in his notebook.

Zhukov's armies continued their virtually unopposed thrust north-westwards during the third week of January. The 2nd Guards Tank Army and the 5th Shock Army continued their partnership on the right, while the 1st Guards Tank Army and the 8th Guards Army cooperated closely on the left. Even the 1st Belorussian Front headquarters could not keep up with their progress, sometimes issuing orders for objectives which had already been seized. When General Vasily Chuikov's 8th Guards Army sighted the industrial city of Łódź on 18 January, five days ahead of schedule, he decided to attack without consulting Front headquarters. But as his rifle divisions deployed for their attack in the morning, they were very nearly bombed by Red Army aviation. The city was in their hands by evening. German soldiers lying dead in the streets had in many cases been killed by Polish patriots, carrying out 'their merciless but just executions'.

On 24 January, Chuikov, considered the best general for city fighting as a result of his Stalingrad experience, received orders to seize Poznan (Posen). On receiving the signal, he wondered whether Zhukov's head-quarters knew anything about this massive Silesian fortress.

Konev's 1st Ukrainian Front to the south had a much shorter advance to the frontier of the Reich. First of all, they managed to surprise the Germans in Kraków and liberate the city undamaged. But the rapidity of the advance produced unexpected complications as well. Zhukov and Konev's armies had overtaken tens of thousands of German troops, many of whom had evaded capture and were desperately trying to make their way westwards, hiding up by day in forests. Some of them ambushed passing Red Army men just to seize their bread bags. Meshik, the NKVD chief with Konev's 1st Ukrainian Front, informed Beria that his rifle regiments in charge of rear security were finding themselves in fire-fights with groups of stragglers up to 200 strong.

Large columns of mainly motorized formations also withdrew towards the Reich, trying to find a way through the mass of Soviet armies. They were known as 'roving cauldrons', fighting their way or slipping from one encirclement to another, cannibalizing vehicles to keep going and ruthlessly destroying guns and equipment which could no longer be used. The strongest and best known of these was based on General Nehring's Panzer Corps. They absorbed stragglers and units, and destroyed vehicles which broke down or ran out of fuel. They even sacrificed two tanks to prop up a bridge over which the lighter vehicles rushed before it collapsed. Nehring, helped by the unwitting choice of a route which ran roughly along the boundary between Zhukov's armies and Konev's, managed to avoid major engagements. In a brief radio message, Nehring heard that General von Saucken's *Grossdeutschland* Corps would try to link up with them. This they managed to do in heavy fog on 21 January. The combined group then withdrew to eventual safety beyond the Oder on 27 January.

On the same day as Nehring crossed the Oder, the barely believable criminality of the Nazi regime was revealed 200 kilometres to the south-east. Konev's 60th Army discovered the network of camps round Auschwitz. Reconnaissance troops from the 107th Rifle Division, some on horseback, with sub-machine guns slung across their backs, emerged from snow-laden forests to discover the grimmest symbol of modern history.

Soviet officers, on realizing what they had found, called forward all available medical teams to care for the 3,000 sick prisoners, many too close to death to save. They had been too weak to walk when the SS began to evacuate the camps nine days before. Soviet officers started to question some of the inmates. Adam Kurilowicz, the ex-chairman of the Polish railway workers' union, who had been in the camp since June 1941, told them how the first tests of the newly built gas chambers had been carried out on 15 September 1941, with eighty Red Army and 600 Polish prisoners. Professor Mansfeld, a Hungarian scientist, told them of the 'medical experiments', including injections of carbolic acid, a method used to kill 140 Polish boys. The Red Army authorities estimated that more than 4 million people were killed, although this was later shown to be a considerable over-estimate. An army photographer was summoned to take pictures of the Arbeit-Macht-Frei gateway covered in snow, dead children with swollen bellies, bundles of human hair, open-mouthed corpses and numbers tattooed on the arms of living skeletons. These were all sent back to Aleksandrov, the chief of Red Army propaganda in Moscow. But apart from a report published on 9 February in the Red Army newspaper *Stalinskoe Znamya* (*Stalin's Banner*), the Soviet Union suppressed all news of Auschwitz until 8 May, when the war had finished.

A Soviet officer also discovered an order from Himmler agreeing 'to delay the execution of those Russian prisoners sent to the camps who are physically fit enough for stone-breaking'. That winter, Russian prisoners, 'many dressed in army shirts or just underwear, and without any hats', were driven out with sticks and whips in temperatures of minus thirty-five Celsius. The very few who returned alive suffered from extreme frostbite. They could not have survived without medical help, of which there was none. The fact that the Wehrmacht had been handing over prisoners of war, their responsibility, to the SS for extermination could only harden the hearts of the avenging Red Army even more. They even discovered from a German staff interpreter that in at least one camp for Red Army soldiers, 'all prisoners on arrival were ordered to undress: those declared Jews were shot on the spot'. Once again, the Soviet authorities were interested only in crimes against Soviet citizens and soldiers. For Red Army soldiers, however, the evidence before their eyes sent a clear message. They would take no prisoners.

If those January days were disastrous for the Wehrmacht, they were far more terrible for the several million civilians who had fled their homes in East Prussia, Silesia and Pomerania. Farming families who for centuries had survived the harshest of winters now realized with horror how vulnerable they were. They faced merciless weather, with homesteads burned and foodstocks looted or destroyed in the retreat. Few acknowledged, however, that this had recently been the fate of Polish, Russian and Ukrainian peasants at the hands of their own brothers, sons and fathers.

The 'treks' from the regions along the Baltic coast – East and West

Prussia and Pomerania – headed for the Oder and Berlin. Those from further south – Silesia and the Wartheland – aimed for the Neisse, south of Berlin. The vast majority of the refugees were women and children, since almost all the remaining men had been drafted into the Volkssturm. The variety of transport ranged from handcarts and prams for those on foot to every sort of farm cart, pony trap and even the odd landau, exhumed from the stables of some schloss. There were hardly any motor vehicles because the Wehrmacht and the Nazi Party had requisitioned them already, as well as all fuel. Progress was pitifully slow, and not just because of the snow and ice. Columns kept halting because carts were overloaded and axles broke. Hay carts, filled with household objects, hams, kegs and jars of food, were turned into covered wagons with a crude superstructure and carpets draped over the outside. Mattresses inside provided some relief to heavily pregnant women and nursing mothers. On icy surfaces, undernourished horses found it hard work. Some carts were hauled by oxen whose unshod hooves were worn raw by the roads, leaving bloodstains in the snow. And when an animal died, as was all too often the case, there was seldom time to butcher it for food. Fear of the enemy drove the refugees on.

At night the columns were directed into wayside villages, where they were often allowed to camp in the barns and stables of manor houses. The owners would welcome in fellow aristocrats fleeing from East Prussia as if they were extra guests arriving for a shooting party. Near Stolp, in East Pomerania, Baron Jesko von Puttkamer slaughtered a pig to help feed hungry refugees on a trek. A 'short-legged, pot-bellied' local Nazi official turned up to warn him that slaughtering an animal without permission was 'a serious offence'. The baron bellowed at him to get off his property, otherwise he would slaughter him too.

Those who had escaped from East Prussia in trains were no better off. On 20 January, a freight train overloaded with people pulled slowly into the station in Stolp. 'Huddled shapes, rigid with cold, barely able to stand up any more and climb out; thin clothing, mostly in tatters, a few blankets over bowed shoulders; grey, hollow faces'. Nobody spoke. Stiff little bundles were removed from the cars and laid on the platform. They were children who had frozen to death. 'Out of the silence came the cries of a mother who did not want to surrender what she had lost,' recorded a woman witness. 'Horror and panic overcame me. Never had

I seen such misery. And behind this sight, a terrifying and powerful vision loomed up: we were these people; this was what was in store for us.'

The weather was about to get much worse a week later, with temperatures at night dropping from minus ten Celsius to minus thirty. Also another half a metre of snow fell in the last week of January, creating snowdrifts that were sometimes impassable even for tanks. Yet the panic-stricken migration increased. As Soviet forces headed for the Silesian capital of Breslau, which Hitler had designated a fortress to be defended to the last man and the last bullet, loudspeaker vans ordered civilians to leave the city as quickly as possible. Refugees were trampled to death in the rush for the trains. There was no question of evacuating the wounded or sick. They were given a grenade each to use on themselves and any Russians. Trains were not always the most certain means of transport. Journeys which usually took three hours 'in normal times', a report on the refugees noted, were taking twenty-one hours.

Eva Braun's sister Ilse, who lived in Breslau, was one of those to flee by train. An official car collected her from the Schlesischer Bahnhof in Berlin on the morning of 21 January and brought her to the Adlon Hotel, where Eva was living. They had dinner together that evening in the library of the Reich Chancellery. Eva, who had no inkling of the scale of the disaster in the east, chatted as though her sister could return to Breslau after a short holiday. Ilse could not restrain herself. She described the refugees fleeing through the snow out of fear of the enemy. She was so angry, she told Eva that Hitler was dragging the whole country into an abyss. Eva was deeply shocked and furious. How could she say such things about the Führer, who had been so generous and even offered to put her up at the Berghof? She deserved to be put against a wall and shot.

By 29 January the Nazi authorities calculated that 'around 4 million people from the evacuated areas' were heading for the centre of the Reich. This was clearly an underestimate. The figure rose to 7 million within a fortnight and to 8.35 million by 19 February. At the end of January, between 40,000 and 50,000 refugees were arriving in Berlin each day, mainly by train. The capital of the Reich did not welcome its victims. 'The Friedrichstrasse Bahnhof has become the transit point of Germany's fate,' an eyewitness wrote. 'Each new train that comes in unloads a mass of amorphous suffering on to the platform.' In their misery, they may not have noticed the sign there which proclaimed, 'Dogs and Jews are not allowed to use the escalator!' Soon energetic measures were taken by the German Red Cross to push refugees on from the Anhalter Bahnhof as quickly as possible, or to force trains to go round Berlin. The authorities were afraid of 'infectious diseases such as typhus' and an epidemic in the capital. Other illnesses that they feared the refugees would spread were dysentery, paratyphus, diphtheria and scarlet fever.

A good example of the chaos was shown by the figures for Danzig. On 8 February it was estimated that Danzig had 35,000–40,000 refugees, but should expect 400,000. Two days later it was decided that the figure of 400,000 had in fact already been reached. Having made no preparations for the disaster which Hitler had refused to acknowledge, the Nazi authorities now had to be seen to be making up for lost time if they were to retain any authority. They made a great show of using Junkers 88s from the Luftwaffe to drop supplies to snowbound and starving columns, but privately complained that it was 'a terrible strain' on their fuel reserves.

Food depots were set up for refugees round Danzig, but these were soon looted by German soldiers on short rations. Yet the area in most urgent need of help was still East Prussia, where the first ship to evacuate refugees did not arrive until 27 January, fourteen days after Chernyakhovsky's attack. Other vessels with supplies of bread and condensed milk for civilians did not leave until early February. Inevitably, a proportion of the relief never got through. An aircraft with 2,000 tins of condensed milk was shot down in one of the first attempts to fly in supplies.

Chernyakhovsky's and Rokossovsky's two groups of armies had forced the remnants of the three German armies defending East Prussia into pockets with their backs to the sea. Rokossovsky's left-flank armies had captured the Teutonic Knights' fortress towns on the east bank of the Vistula and Marienburg on the Nogat. This forced the German Second Army back into the Vistula estuary, but it still retained the Frische Nehrung sandbar. And with a third of a metre of ice on the Frisches Haff lagoon, refugees could still cross by foot from the mainland and then on to Danzig. Rokossovsky's right flank meanwhile had to redeploy rapidly to face a German attempt to break out to the west.

Hitler was obsessed with the idea of holding on to the defence line of the Masurian Lakes. He became incandescent with rage when he heard that General Hossbach, the Fourth Army commander, had abandoned its corner stone, the fortress of Lötzen, on 24 January. Even Guderian was shaken by the news. But both Hossbach and his superior, General Reinhardt, were determined to break Rokossovsky's encirclement and avoid another Stalingrad. Their attack, a battering ram to allow civilians to escape too, began on the clear, freezing night of 26 January. The sudden offensive smashed the Soviet 48th Army and almost reached Elbing, which the German Second Army had managed to hold after the first tank skirmish in its streets. But within three days of fighting in fierce cold and deep snow, Rokossovsky's armies had fought back the thrust. Hitler sacked both Reinhardt and Hossbach, whose divisions were now forced backwards into what became known as the Heiligenbeil *Kessel* or cauldron, an awkward quadrilateral with its back to the Frisches Haff. Over 600,000 civilians were also trapped in it.

The 3rd Belorussian Front had meanwhile surrounded Königsberg entirely on the landward side. The city's large garrison from the Third Panzer Army was thus cut off from the Samland Peninsula, which led to the small Baltic port of Pillau at the mouth of the lagoon. Close to 200,000 civilians were also trapped in the city with little to eat. This policy forced over 2,000 women and children a day to undertake the hazardous journey on foot, over the ice, to an already desperately overcrowded Pillau. Hundreds even walked out into the snow towards the Soviet troops to beg for food and throw themselves on their dubious mercy. The first steamer from Pillau taking 1,800 civilians and 1,200 wounded did not reach safety until 29 January. Gauleiter Koch, having condemned Generals Reinhardt and Hossbach for attempting to break out of East Prussia and having ordered the defenders of Königsberg to fight to the last man, fled his own capital. After a visit to Berlin, he then returned to the far safer Pillau, where he made a great show of organizing the marine evacuation using Kriegsmarine radio communications, before once more getting away himself.

Pillau could not handle very large ships, so the chief seaport for evacuations from the Baltic coast was Gdynia (or Gotenhafen), just north of Danzig. Grand Admiral Dönitz gave the order only on 21 January for Operation Hannibal, a mass evacuation of refugees using four large ships. On 30 January, Germany's largest 'Strength through Joy' sea-cruise liner, the *Wilhelm Gustloff*, which had been designed to take 2,000 passengers, left with around 6,600 people aboard. The next evening, escorted by a single motor torpedo boat, it was stalked by a Soviet submarine of the Baltic Fleet. Captain A. I. Marinesco fired three torpedoes. All hit their target. Exhausted refugees, shaken from their sleep, panicked. There was a desperate rush to reach the lifeboats. Many were cut off below as the icy sea rushed in: the air temperature outside was minus eighteen Celsius. The lifeboats which had been launched were upset by desperate refugees leaping from the ship's side. The ship sank in less than an hour. At least 5,300 people lost their lives. The 1,300 survivors were rescued by vessels, led by the heavy cruiser *Admiral Hipper*. It was the worst single maritime disaster to date, but was soon superseded by a greater one.

Russian historians, even today, still stick to the official Soviet line and claim that the ship carried 'over 6,000 Hitlerites on board, of which 3,700 were submariners'. The main interest in Russia seems to be not in the fate of the victims, but in that of the triumphant submarine commander A. I. Marinesco. The recommendation to make him a Hero of the Soviet Union was refused by the NKVD, because he had had an affair with a foreign citizen, a crime for which he narrowly escaped a tribunal and an automatic sentence to the Gulag. Only in 1990, 'on the eve of the forty-fifth anniversary of the victory', was he finally and posthumously made a Hero of the Soviet Union.

One of the side effects of the mass migration was a fuel and transport crisis in Germany. Coal supplies had been interrupted by the need for wagons to bring refugees through Pomerania. In some places bakers were unable to bake their bread. The general situation was now so desperate that, 'in order to save the Reich', full priority on goods trains was taken back from refugees and returned to the Wehrmacht and fuel distribution. This decision was made on 30 January, the twelfth anniversary of the Nazi Party's arrival in power.

Some generals regarded civilian refugees, not with pity as the chief victims of Soviet revenge for the Wehrmacht's invasion, but simply as a severe nuisance. One of Hitler's most favoured commanders, General Schörner, had given orders that a thirty-kilometre zone on the east bank of the upper Oder should be reserved for military operations. He also complained loudly that refugees were hindering military activity, and requested an order from Field Marshal Keitel that 'evacuations must now cease'. This presumably meant that he was prepared to take punitive measures against civilians fleeing from the Red Army.

National Socialist authorities at times treated German refugees almost as badly as concentration camp prisoners. Local administrators, the Kreisleiters, evaded responsibility for them, especially if they were sick. Three goods trains took refugees crammed in open wagons to Schleswig-Holstein. One train alone carried 3,500 people, mainly women and children. 'These people were in a dreadful state,' a report stated. 'They were riddled with lice and had many diseases such as scabies. After the long journey there were still many dead lying in the wagons. Often the contents of the trains were not offloaded at their destination but sent on to another Gau. Apart from that everything is in order in Schleswig-Holstein.'

Hitler himself decided that it would be a good idea to fill the 'Protectorate' of occupied Czechoslovakia with German refugees. 'He is of the opinion,' explained an official, 'that if the Czechs see the misery, they will not be tilted into a resistance movement.' This turned out to be yet another miscalculation of intention and effect. A report came back less than three weeks later warning that the Czechs, on seeing this proof of German defeat, were wasting no time in preparing their own administration, to be led by Beneš.

The crisis of National Socialism did not fail to affect the army. Hitler convinced himself that all would be well if a sufficiently ruthless and ideological military leader were appointed to defend the Reich in the east. General Guderian could scarcely believe his ears when Hitler decided on 24 January that Himmler, the Reichsführer SS, was to command the new Army Group Vistula between East Prussia and the remnants of Reinhardt's shattered army group in Silesia. Hitler's decision was also no doubt influenced by his threat to Guderian of a few days before to smash 'the general staff system', and revenge himself on a 'group of intellectuals' who presumed 'to press their views on their superiors'.

That afternoon, Colonel Hans Georg Eismann of the general staff received orders to proceed to Schneidemühl. He was to be the chief operations officer at the headquarters of Army Group Vistula. Eismann had never heard of such an army group. The general in charge of staff officer postings explained to him that it had just been constituted. Eismann heard with just as much astonishment as Guderian that Himmler was to be its commander-in-chief.

Eismann had no choice but to set off eastwards that evening by Kübelwagen, the hefty German equivalent of the jeep. As they drove through the freezing night out along Reichsstrasse 1, 'the whole extent of the chaos and misery' became clear to him. 'Along all roads could be seen endless convoys of refugees from the east.' Most gave an impression of exhausted aimlessness.

Eismann hoped to be able to form a clearer picture of the situation once he reached his destination but, as he soon found, Army Group Vistula headquarters was unlike any other. In Schneidemühl he asked a military traffic controller the way, but evidently its location was a closely guarded secret. He fortunately spotted Major von Hase, whom he knew, and finally received directions.

The headquarters was established aboard Himmler's special train, the Sonderzug *Steiermark*, a sleek black line of sleeping cars with anti-aircraft wagons attached. Armed SS sentries stood along the platform at regular intervals. In a 'very elegant dining car' Eismann found a young Untersturmführer who took him down the train to meet the Reichsführer SS and commander-in-chief.

Himmler was seated at a writing table in his saloon. When he stood up to welcome his visitor with a handshake, Eismann found that his hand was 'soft like a woman's'. Eismann, who had seen him only in pictures or at a distance, studied him carefully. The bespectacled Reichsführer SS was wearing not his usual black SS uniform, but field grey, presumably to emphasize his military role. He was slightly flabby, with an upper body that was too long. His receding chin and narrowed eyes gave him a 'slightly Mongolian' look. He led Eismann over to a larger table to study the operations map. Eismann saw that it was at least twenty-four hours out of date.

'What have we got to close this gap and establish a new front?' Eismann asked. He was not new to crises exacerbated, if not created, by

Führer headquarters. In December 1942, he had been the officer flown into the Stalingrad encirclement on Field Marshal von Manstein's orders to discuss the situation with General Paulus.

Himmler answered with all the thoughtless clichés of his master: 'immediate counter-attack', 'smash in their flank' and so on. His replies were devoid of any basic military knowledge. Eismann had the impression 'that a blind man was speaking about colour'. He then asked what battle-worthy formations they had at their disposal. Himmler had no idea. He seemed unaware of the fact that the Ninth Army virtually existed in name only. Only one thing was clear. The Reichsführer SS did not appreciate direct questions in general staff style.

Army Group Vistula headquarters, it turned out, not only lacked trained staff officers, it also had no supply or transport organization and no signals detachment. The sole means of communication was the chief of staff's telephone. And apart from the road map which Eismann had brought on his journey from Berlin, the headquarters possessed no more than one map. Even those general staff officers who had experienced earlier disasters still found it hard to fathom the degree of incompetence and irresponsibility of 'Hitler's *Kamarilla*'.

Himmler, still determined on a counter-attack, wanted to throw together odd regiments and battalions. Eismann suggested a divisional commander, who at least had a staff and communications, to organize it, but Himmler insisted on a corps commander to make it sound impressive. He chose Obergruppenführer Demmlhuber. (Army officers had given Demmlhuber the nickname of 'Tosca' after a well-known scent of that name which he was suspected of using.) A makeshift corps staff was assembled and the following day Demmlhuber took over. Demmlhuber, who had more experience than Himmler, was not overjoyed at the task given him. The operation, if it deserved such a name, proved a complete failure, and he became one of the very few Waffen SS generals to be dismissed. This perhaps provoked jokes among opera-lovers on the army general staff that 'Tosca' may have been pushed out, but at least he had not had to jump.

Another Waffen SS officer arrived to take over as chief of staff of the army group. This was Brigadeführer Lammerding, a former commander of the SS *Das Reich* Panzer Division. Although a respected commander, he had little staff experience and no taste for compromise. Meanwhile,

the Soviet advance on Schneidemühl forced Army Group Vistula headquarters to withdraw northwards to Falkenburg. Schneidemühl, designated a fortress by Hitler along with Poznan, was left to its fate,
with eight battalions of Volkssturm, a few engineers and some fortress
artillery. Hitler's dogma, 'Where the German soldier has once stood, he
will never retreat', remained the watchword.

A Pomeranian Volkssturm battalion on its way to Schneidemühl by
train from Stolp passed Himmler's *Steiermark* train. This so-called
'battalion' was commanded by Baron Jesko von Puttkamer, the landowner who had threatened the pot-bellied Nazi official. He and his
officers, dressed in their uniforms from the First World War, had
brought their old service pistols. Their men, mostly farmers and shop-
keepers, had no weapons at all, only Volkssturm armbands. They were
supposed to receive weapons in Schneidemühl. Suddenly, the train
came under fire from Soviet tanks. The driver managed to stop and then
reverse with remarkable promptness.

Once they were well away from danger, Puttkamer ordered his men
out of the train. He then marched them back to Stolp through the
knee-deep snow, with the strongest placed at the front to trample a
route for the rest. He refused to allow them to be killed for nothing. On
their return, the townspeople greeted him as a hero in the Stephansplatz
outside the town hall. But Baron von Puttkamer retired to his house, sick
at heart, and put away the old uniform, which had become dishonoured
'under these Hitlers and Himmlers'.

5

The Charge to the Oder

By the fourth week in January, Berlin appeared to be in a state of 'hysteria and disintegration'. There were two air-raid warnings a night, one at 8 and the next at 11. Refugees from the eastern territories passed on terrible accounts of the fate of those caught by the Red Army. Hungary, Germany's last ally in the Balkans, was now siding openly with the Soviet Union and rumours of the rapid advance of Soviet tank armies led to predictions that the whole Eastern Front was disintegrating. Ordinary soldiers hoped that the enemy would shoot only officers and the SS, and workers and minor officials tried to convince themselves that the Russians would do them no harm.

The most accurate news of the situation on the Eastern Front filtered back through railway workers. They often knew how far the enemy had advanced before the general staff. More and more Germans took the risk of listening to the BBC to find out what was really happening. If denounced to the Gestapo by a neighbour, they faced a spell in a concentration camp. Yet many Hitler and Goebbels loyalists still passionately believed every word of the news according to the 'Promi', the Propaganda Ministerium.

Public transport was still repaired and people continued their struggle to work each day through the ruins. But more and more arranged to sleep in apartments closer to their work. A sleeping-bag had become one of the most essential items of equipment. Camp beds were also needed for relatives and friends fleeing from the east or who had been bombed out in Berlin. The well connected discussed different ways to escape the capital. Rumours of landowners shot out of hand by Soviet troops in East Prussia convinced them that the upper classes as a whole would be targets. Soviet propaganda was aimed almost as much at the eradication of 'Junker militarism' as at National Socialism.

Those attempting to get out had to be careful, because Goebbels had declared that leaving Berlin without permission was tantamount to desertion. First of all, they needed a travel permit, which could be obtained only with some story of essential work outside the capital. Many of those who really did have an official trip to make away from Berlin received murmured advice from envious colleagues, 'Don't come back. Stay there.' Almost everyone dreamed of seeking sanctuary in a quiet corner of the countryside where farms still had food. Some even investigated the possibility of purchasing false passports, and foreign diplomats suddenly found themselves extremely popular. Members of ministries were fortunate. They were evacuated to the south over the next few weeks.

Most menacing of all was the wave of executions carried out by the SS on Himmler's orders. On 23 January, with the Red Army now breaching the old frontiers of the Reich, several members of the German resistance linked to the July plot were put to death in Plötzensee prison. The victims included Count Helmuth James von Moltke, Eugen Bolz and Erwin Planck, the son of the Nobel Prize-winning physicist Max Planck.

Goebbels's new slogan, 'We shall win, because we must win', provoked contempt and despair among non-Nazis, but the majority of Germans did not yet think to question it. Even though only fanatics now believed in 'final victory', most still held on because they could not imagine anything else. The strategy of Goebbels's relentless propaganda, ever since the war in the east turned against Germany, had been to undermine any notion of choice or alternative.

Goebbels, as both Reich Commissar for the Defence of Berlin and minister for propaganda, appeared in his element as chief advocate of total warfare: visiting troops, making speeches, reviewing Volkssturm parades and haranguing them. The population at large saw nothing of Hitler. He had disappeared from the newsreels, and they heard only Hitler's very last broadcast on 30 January, marking twelve years of Nazi government. His voice had lost all its strength and sounded completely different. It was hardly surprising that so many rumours circulated about his death or confinement. The public was not told whether he was at Berchtesgaden or in Berlin. And while Goebbels visited the victims of bombing, gaining considerable popularity as a result, Hitler refused even to look at his severely damaged capital.

The Führer's invisibility was due partly to his own withdrawal from public life and partly to the difficulty of concealing the dramatic changes in his appearance. Staff officers visiting the Reich Chancellery bunker who had not seen him since before the 20 July bomb explosion were shaken. 'He was sometimes hunched over so much,' said Guderian's aide, Major Freytag von Loringhoven, 'that he almost had a hump.' The once glittering eyes were dull, the pale skin now had a grey tinge. He dragged his left leg behind him on entering the conference room and his handshake was limp. Hitler often held his left hand with his right in an attempt to conceal its trembling. Still just short of his fifty-sixth birthday, the Führer had the air and appearance of a senile old man. He had also lost his astonishing grasp of detail and statistics, with which he used to batter doubters into submission. And he no longer received any pleasure from playing followers off against each other. Now, he saw treason all around him.

Officers of the general staff were all too aware of the anti-army atmosphere when they visited the Reich Chancellery bunker each day from Zossen. Guderian's arrival in his large staff Mercedes was greeted by SS sentries presenting arms, but once inside, he and his aides had to offer up their briefcases to be searched. Their pistols were taken from them and they had to stand while SS guards examined the line of their uniform with a practised eye, searching for suspicious bulges.

Army officers also had to remind themselves before entering the Reich Chancellery that saluting in the traditional manner had now been banned. All members of the Wehrmacht had to use the 'German greeting', as the Nazi salute was known. Many found themselves raising their hand to the cap, then suddenly having to shoot the whole arm outwards. Freytag von Loringhoven, for example, was not in the most comfortable of positions in such surroundings. His predecessor had been hanged as part of the July plot, and his cousin Colonel Baron Freytag von Loringhoven, another conspirator, had committed suicide.

The Reich Chancellery was almost bare. Paintings, tapestries and furniture had been removed. There were huge cracks in the ceilings, smashed windows were boarded up and plywood partitions concealed the worst of the bomb damage. Not long before, in one of the huge marble corridors leading to the situation room, Freytag had been surprised to see two expensively dressed young women with permed hair. Such elegant frivolity seemed so out of place in the surroundings that he had turned to his companion, Keitel's adjutant, to ask who they were.

'That was Eva Braun.'

'Who's Eva Braun?' he asked.

'She's the Führer's mistress.' Keitel's adjutant smiled at his amazement. 'And that was her sister, who's married to Fegelein.' The Wehrmacht officers attached to the Reich Chancellery had remained completely discreet. Hardly anyone outside had ever heard of her, even those who visited the place regularly from the army high command headquarters at Zossen.

Freytag certainly knew Fegelein, Himmler's liaison officer. He thought him 'a dreadful vulgarian with a terrible Munich accent, an arrogant air and bad manners'. Fegelein used to interrupt generals in mid-conversation, trying to involve himself in everything. But despite his intense dislike, Freytag summoned up his courage to ask a favour. A friend of his had been one of the many arrested in the wake of the July plot and was still held in the cellars of Gestapo headquarters. He told Fegelein that he was virtually certain that his friend had had nothing to do with the conspiracy, and asked if he could at least find out what charges were being laid against him. To his surprise, Fegelein agreed to look into it and his friend was released shortly afterwards.

Fegelein, an SS cavalry commander who had won the Knight's Cross fighting partisans in Yugoslavia, was enamoured of his own rather louche good looks. He clearly enjoyed using his massive influence, which came partly from his position as Himmler's representative and partly from his proximity to the Führer. He had become very close to Eva Braun, with whom he danced and rode. Some suspected an affair between them, but this was unlikely. She was genuinely devoted to Hitler, while he was probably too ambitious to risk a dalliance with the Führer's mistress. On 3 June 1944, on the eve of the Allied invasion, Hitler had been chief witness at Fegelein's marriage to Eva's youngest sister, Gretl. It was the closest anyone could get to a dynastic marriage under National Socialism.

Hitler's ostensibly military court managed to be both superficially austere and profoundly corrupt at the same time, a contradiction which the rhetoric of self-sacrifice failed to conceal. Incompetence and chaos between competing warlords and party functionaries were cloaked by a false unity of loyalty to their ideological godhead. The mentality of such an assembly, despite all its military uniforms, saluting and twice-daily situation conferences, could not have been further from the reality of the front. And while Hitler's health visibly deteriorated, intrigues and jockeying for position increased as the Reich crumbled. Göring, Goebbels, Himmler and Bormann all visualized themselves as the Führer's successor. Perhaps the true measure of the fantasy of Nazi leaders was the very notion that the world might accept any form of succession within the Third Reich, assuming that it had any territory left.

At the end of the third week in January, Marshal Konev's 1st Ukrainian Front surged into Silesia after the capture of Kraków and Radom. Konev, to preserve the mines and factories of Upper Silesia, as Stalin had instructed, decided to commence a semi-encirclement of the industrial and mining region from Katowice to Ratibor while leaving a route of escape for the German forces left in the area. The 3rd Guards Tank Army had been heading for Breslau but, on Konev's order, wheeled hard left on the march and came back up along the eastern bank of the Oder towards Oppeln. As if organizing a great shoot, Konev brought up the 21st, 59th and 60th Armies to flush the Germans out.

On the night of 27 January, the German divisions of the Seventeenth Army pulled out and fled for the Oder. General Rybalko's 3rd Guards Tank Army then acted as the guns, catching large numbers of them in the snow-covered landscape. Rybalko's tanks were camouflaged, rather improbably, with white tulle from a large supply captured in a Silesian textile factory supposedly devoted to total war.

Stalin's 'gold' was secured intact over the next two days. It was a disaster for Germany, as Guderian had warned. Speer's forecasts for armaments production, presented to the corps commanders at Krampnitz only two weeks before, lay in ruins. He recognized this himself, predicting that Germany could now hold out for a matter of weeks at best. The loss of the mines as well as the steelworks and factories was probably a greater blow for German production than all the Allied bombing of the Ruhr industrial region over the last two years.

Perhaps the most surprising part of the operation was the fact that the German withdrawal was authorized by Führer headquarters. Hitler had sacked General Harpe and replaced him with his favourite commander, General Schörner, a convinced Nazi whose motto was 'Strength through fear'. Schörner was only satisfied when his soldiers were more afraid of his punishment than they were of the enemy.

The Seventeenth Army managed to withdraw, but relatively few women and children escaped from Upper Silesia. Many, especially the old, stayed out of choice. Sometimes widows refused to leave the grave of a husband, while others could not face leaving farms which had been in their family for generations. They sensed that if they left, they would never return. A Swedish woman who managed to make her way through Soviet lines in a farm cart told the Swedish embassy that although Soviet troops 'had acted in a correct manner' in some places, German propaganda stories seemed to be mostly true. She added that this did not surprise her after the way that the Germans had behaved in Russia. Soviet troops were equally ruthless whenever they suspected 'partisan' activity. The officers of a rifle company, on finding a Russian soldier from a patrol lying dead in a village street, 'ordered their men to liquidate the whole population of the village'.

The rapidity of the 1st Ukrainian Front's advance created its own problems for the Soviet authorities. NKVD rifle regiments for the repression of rear areas were sometimes thrown into battle against by-passed German units. They had to reorganize rapidly, in some cases even having to refer to the Red Army instruction book. In the headlong advance, General Karpov, the commander of the NKVD rifle division following the fighting troops, complained on 26 January to Meshik, the Front's NKVD chief, that their three regiments were 'clearly not sufficient for this area which has difficult terrain and is covered with large areas of forest'. They would need even more troops and vehicles to guard their lines of communications and depots when they crossed the Oder.

In Konev's centre, meanwhile, the 5th Guards, helped by German chaos when faced with Rybalko's sweeping manoeuvre, managed to seize a bridgehead across the Oder around Ohlau, between Breslau and

Oppeln. And Lelyushenko's 4th Guards Tank Army on the right seized another bridgehead on the west bank of the Oder round Steinau, northeast of Breslau, even though Steinau itself was fiercely defended by NCOs from a nearby training school. His tank crews appear to have made good use of their time before the Vistula offensive began. Lelyushenko had given them intensive target practice on Tiger tanks captured the previous autumn, and their gunnery, seldom a strong point in Red Army tank formations, had improved. They now began target practice on German steamers heading downstream from Breslau.

The Germans, meanwhile, were rushing the 169th Infantry Division to stiffen the defences of the Silesian capital, which Führer headquarters had declared to be 'Fortress Breslau'. Hitler, on hearing that Soviet troops had established the Steinau bridgehead, ordered General von Saucken and General Nehring to counter-attack immediately, even though their troops had not had a chance to recover and replenish since their hazardous escape from Poland.

Whether or not German refugees from Breslau went down with the steamers sunk by Lelyushenko's tanks, the fate of women and children who had left the city on foot during the panic-stricken evacuation was terrible. All husbands not already serving in the Wehrmacht were called up for the Volkssturm to defend the city. Wives were therefore left to fend for themselves entirely. All they heard were the loudspeaker vans telling civilians to flee the city. Although frightened, the mothers who did not manage to obtain places on the overcrowded trains took the normal precautions to look after infant children, such as filling a thermos with hot milk and bundling them up as warmly as possible. They took rucksacks containing powdered milk and food for themselves. In any case, they expected after the announcements that the Nazi Party social welfare organization, the NSV, would have prepared some form of help along the way.

Outside Breslau, however, the women found that they were on their own. Very few motor vehicles were leaving the city, so only a lucky few received lifts. The snow was deep on the roads and eventually most women had to abandon their prams and carry the youngest children. In the icy wind they also found that their thermoses had cooled. There was only one way to feed a hungry infant, but they could not find any shelter in which to breast-feed. All the houses were locked, either abandoned already or owned by people who refused to open their door to anyone. In despair, some mothers offered their baby a breast in the lea of a shed or some other windbreak, but it was no good. The child would not feed and the mother's body temperature dropped dangerously. Some even suffered a frostbitten breast. One young wife, in a letter to her mother explaining the death from cold of her own child, also described the fate of other mothers, some crying over a bundle which contained a baby frozen to death, others sitting in the snow, propped against a tree by the side of the road, with older children standing nearby whimpering in fear, not knowing whether their mother was unconscious or dead. In that cold it made little difference.

Zhukov's 1st Belorussian Front, meanwhile, had been progressing even more rapidly in its drive to the north-west. He told his two tank armies to avoid areas of resistance and to advance between seventy and 100 kilometres a day. Yet on 25 January, Stalin rang Zhukov in the afternoon to tell him to rein in. 'When you reach the Oder,' he said, 'you'll be more than 150 kilometres from the flank of the 2nd Belorussian Front. You can't do this now. You must wait until [Rokossovsky] finishes operations in East Prussia and deploys across the Vistula.' Stalin was concerned about a German counter-attack on Zhukov's right flank from German troops along the Pomeranian coastline, what became known as the 'Baltic balcony'. Zhukov begged Stalin to let him continue. If he waited another ten days for Rokossovsky to finish in East Prussia, that would give the Germans time to man the Meseritz fortified line. Stalin agreed with great reluctance.

Zhukov's armies were crossing the region the Nazis had called the Wartheland, the area of western Poland which they had seized after their invasion in 1939. Its Gauleiter, Arthur Greiser, was an unspeakable racist even by Nazi standards. His Warthegau province had been the scene of the most brutal evictions imaginable. Over 700,000 Poles lost everything, their possessions as well as their homes, which were handed over to Volksdeutsch settlers brought in from all over central and south-eastern Europe. The dispossessed Poles had been dumped in the General Gouvernement without shelter, food or hope of work. The treatment of Jews had been even worse. Over 160,000 had been forced into the tiny ghetto in Łódź. Those who did not die of starvation ended up in concentration camps. Just 850 remained alive when the Soviet tanks entered the city.

The Polish desire for revenge was so fierce that Serov, the chief of NKVD of the 1st Belorussian Front, complained to Beria that it interfered with intelligence-gathering. 'Troops of the 1st Polish Army treat Germans especially severely,' he wrote. 'Often captured German officers and soldiers do not reach the prisoner assembly areas. They are shot en route. For example, on the sector of the 2nd Infantry Regiment of the 1st Infantry Division, eighty Germans were captured. Just two prisoners reached the assembly area. All the others had been executed. The two survivors were questioned by the regimental commander, but when he sent them to be interrogated by his intelligence officer, the pair were shot on the way.'

Zhukov's decision to force forward with his two tank armies paid off. The Germans never had a chance to organize a line of defence. On the right, the 3rd Shock Army, the 47th, the 61st and the 1st Polish Armies advanced parallel to the Vistula and headed between Bromberg and Schneidemühl to protect the exposed flank. In the middle, Bogdanov's 2nd Guards Tank Army pushed on, followed by Berzarin's 5th Shock Army. And on the left Katukov's 1st Guards Tank Army charged ahead to Poznan. But Poznan was not like Łódź. On reaching Poznan on 25 January, Katukov saw that it could not be captured off the march, and pushed straight on as Zhukov had instructed. Poznan was left to Chuikov, following closely with the 8th Guards Army, to sort out. He was not pleased, and it seems only to have increased his dislike for Zhukov.

Gauleiter Greiser, like Koch in East Prussia, had fled his capital, having ordered everyone else to hold fast. He had refused to allow the evacuation of any civilians until 20 January, and as a result it seems that in many areas more than half of the population failed to get away. Vasily Grossman, who had attached himself again to Chuikov's 8th Guards Army, became increasingly conscious of 'the German civilian, secretly watching us from behind curtains'.

There was plenty to watch outside. 'The infantry is moving in a whole variety of horse-drawn vehicles,' Grossman jotted in his notebook. 'The boys are smoking *makhorka*, eating and drinking, and playing cards. A convoy of carts decorated with carpets passes by. The drivers are sitting on feather mattresses. Soldiers no longer eat military rations.

They eat pork, turkey and chicken. Rosy and well-fed faces are to be seen for the first time.' 'German civilians, already overtaken by our leading tank detachments, have turned round and are now moving back. They receive a good beating and their horses are stolen from them by Poles who take every opportunity to rob them.' Grossman, like most Soviet citizens, had little idea of what had really happened in 1939 and 1940, and therefore of the reasons why Poles hated the Germans as much as they did. Stalin's secret treaty with Hitler, dividing the country between them, had been veiled by a news blackout in the Soviet Union.

Grossman did not hide unpalatable truths from himself, however, even if he could never publish them. 'There were 250 of our girls whom the Germans had brought from the oblasts of Voroshilovgrad, Kharkov and Kiev. The chief of the army political department said that these girls had been left almost without clothes. They were covered in lice and their bellies swollen from hunger. But a man from the army newspaper told me that these girls had been quite neat and well dressed, until our soldiers arrived and took everything from them.'

Grossman soon discovered how much the Red Army men took. 'Liberated Soviet girls quite often complain that our soldiers rape them,' he noted. 'One girl said to me in tears, "He was an old man, older than my father."' But Grossman refused to believe the worst of the true *frontoviki*. 'Frontline soldiers are advancing day and night under fire, with pure and saintly hearts. The rear echelon men who follow along behind are raping, drinking and looting.'

The street battles in Poznan provided a foretaste of what lay ahead in Berlin. Grossman, who had spent so much time in Stalingrad during the battle, was interested to see what Chuikov, who had coined the phrase the 'Stalingrad Academy of street-fighting', was going to do. 'The main principle in Stalingrad,' Grossman observed, 'was that we upset the balance between the power of machinery and the vulnerability of infantry. But now Academician Chuikov is forced by circumstances into the same sort of situation as at Stalingrad, only with roles reversed. He is attacking the Germans violently in the streets of Poznan, using huge mechanical power and little infantry.'

He spent some time with Chuikov during the battle for Poznan. 'Chuikov is sitting in a cold, brightly lit room on the second floor of a requisitioned villa. The telephone rings constantly. Unit commanders are reporting on the street fighting in Poznan.' Between calls, Chuikov was boasting how he had 'smashed the German defences round Warsaw'.

'Chuikov listens to the telephone, reaches for the map, and says, "Sorry, I've just got to put my glasses on."' The reading glasses looked strange on his tough face. 'He reads the report, chuckles and taps his adjutant on the nose with a pencil.' (When angry with an officer, Chuikov more often used his fist, and it was not a tap, according to one of his staff.) 'He then shouts into the telephone, "If they try to break through to the west, let them out into the open and we'll squash them like bugs. Now it's death to the Germans. They won't escape."'

'It really is amazing,' Chuikov remarked sarcastically in one of his gibes against Zhukov, 'when you consider our battle experience and our wonderful intelligence, that we failed to notice one little detail. We didn't know that there's a first-class fortress at Poznan. One of the strongest in Europe. We thought it was just a town which we could take off the march, and now we're really in for it.'

While Chuikov remained behind to deal with the fortress of Poznan, the rest of his army and the 1st Guards Tank Army pushed forward to the Meseritz line east of the Oder. Their main problem was not German resistance but their supply lines. Railroads had been smashed by the retreating Germans, but also Poland had a different gauge of track from the Soviet Union. As a result, the movement of supplies depended on trucks, mostly American Studebakers. Significantly, there has been little acknowledgement by Russian historians that if it had not been for American Lend-Lease trucks, the Red Army's advance would have taken far longer and the Western Allies might well have reached Berlin first.

Almost every Soviet soldier remembered vividly the moment of crossing the pre-1939 frontier into Germany. 'We marched out of a forest,' Senior Lieutenant Klochkov with the 3rd Shock Army recalled, 'and we saw a board nailed to a post. On it was written, "Here it is – the accursed Germany." We were entering the territory of Hitler's Reich. Soldiers began looking around curiously. German villages are in many ways different from Polish villages. Most houses are built from brick and stone. They have tidily trimmed fruit trees in their little gardens. The roads are good.' Klochkov, like so many of his fellow countrymen, could not understand why Germans, 'who were not thoughtless people', should have risked prosperous and comfortable lives to invade the Soviet Union.

Further along the road to the Reich capital, Vasily Grossman accompanied part of the 8th Guards Army sent on ahead from Poznan. Its political department had erected placards by the side of the road on which was written, 'Tremble with fear, fascist Germany, the day of reckoning has come!'

Grossman was with them when they sacked the town of Schwerin. He jotted down in pencil in a small notebook whatever he saw: 'Everything is on fire . . . An old woman jumps from a window in a burning building . . . Looting is going on . . . It's light during the night because everything is ablaze . . . At the [town] commandant's office, a German woman dressed in black and with dead lips, is speaking in a weak, whispering voice. There is a girl with her who has black bruises on her neck and face, a swollen eye and terrible bruises on her hands. The girl was raped by a soldier from the headquarters signals company. He is also present. He has a full, red face and looks sleepy. The commandant is questioning them all together.'

Grossman noted the 'horror in the eyes of women and girls . . . Terrible things are happening to German women. A cultivated German man explains with expressive gestures and broken Russian words that his wife has been raped by ten men that day . . . Soviet girls who have been liberated from camps are suffering greatly too. Last night some of them hid in the room provided for the war correspondents. Screams wake us up in the night. One of the correspondents could not restrain himself. An animated discussion takes place, and order is restored.' Grossman then noted what he had evidently heard about a young mother. She was being raped continuously in a farm shed. Her relatives came to the shed and asked the soldiers to allow her a break to breast-feed the baby because it would not stop crying. All this was taking place next to a headquarters and in the full sight of officers supposedly responsible for discipline.

On Tuesday 30 January, the day that Hitler addressed the German people for the last time, the German army suddenly realized that the threat to Berlin was even greater than they had feared. Zhukov's leading units had not only penetrated the Meseritz defence zone with ease, they were within striking distance of the Oder. At 7.30 a.m., the headquarters of Army Group Vistula heard that the Landsberg road was 'full of enemy tanks'. Air reconnaissance flights were scrambled.

Himmler insisted on sending a battalion of Tiger tanks all on its own by train to restore the situation. His staff 's protests had no effect because the Reichsführer SS was firmly convinced that a battalion of Tigers could defeat a whole Soviet tank army. The fifty-ton monsters were still fastened to their railway flat cars when they came under fire from three or four Soviet tanks. The battalion suffered heavy losses before the train managed to withdraw urgently towards Küstrin. Himmler wanted the battalion commander court-martialled until he was eventually persuaded that a Tiger tank fastened to a railway wagon was not in the best position to fight.

During this time of extreme crisis, Himmler imitated Stalin's 'Not one step back' order of 1942, even if his version did not have the same ring. It was entitled '*Tod und Strafe für Pflichtvergessenheit*' – 'Death and punishment for failure to carry out one's duty'. It tried to end on an uplifting note. 'After hard trials lasting several weeks the day will come,' he claimed, 'when German territories will be free again.' Another order forbade women on pain of severe punishment to give any food to retreating troops. And in an order of the day to Army Group Vistula he declared, 'The Lord God has never forsaken our people and he has always helped the brave in their hour of greatest need.' Both historically and theologically, this was an extremely dubious assertion.

Himmler, aware that word was spreading fast of the flight of senior Nazi officials, especially Gauleiters Koch and Greiser, decided to make an example at a lower level. On the same day as his other orders, he announced the execution of the police director of Bromberg for abandoning his post. A bürgermeister who had 'left his town without giving an evacuation order' was hanged at 3 p.m. at Schwedt on the Oder a few days later.

This twelfth anniversary of Hitler's regime was also the second anniversary of the defeat at Stalingrad. Beria was informed of a conversation picked up by microphones hidden in a prison cell between Field Marshal Paulus, General Strecker, the commander who held out for longest in the factory district, and General von Seydlitz.

'Captured German generals are in very bad spirits', Beria was informed. They had been horrified by Churchill's speech in the House of Commons six weeks earlier, supporting Stalin's proposal that Poland should be compensated with East Prussia and other areas. The German generals felt that their position in the Soviet-controlled Free Germany movement had become impossible. 'The Nazis in this matter are more positive than we are,' Field Marshal Paulus acknowledged, 'because they are holding on to German territory, trying to preserve its integrity.'

Even General von Seydlitz, who had proposed the airlift of anti-Nazi German prisoners of war to start a revolution within the Reich, thought that 'the ripping away of German lands to create a safety barrier will not be fair'. All the captured generals now realized that the anti-Nazi League of German Officers had just been exploited by the Soviet Union for its own ends. 'I am tormented by a terrible anxiety,' said Seydlitz, 'whether we have chosen the right course.' The Nazi regime had labelled him 'the traitor Seydlitz' and condemned him to death *in absentia*.

'All Hitler thinks about,' said Paulus, 'is how to force the German people into new sacrifices. Never before in history has lying been such a powerful weapon in diplomacy and policy. We Germans have been cunningly deceived by a man who usurped power.'

'Why has God become so angry with Germany,' replied Strecker, 'that he sent us Hitler! Are the German people so ignoble? Have they deserved such a punishment?'

'It is two years since the Stalingrad catastrophe,' said Paulus. 'And now the whole of Germany is becoming a gigantic Stalingrad.'

Himmler's threats and exhortations did nothing to save the situation. That very night Soviet rifle battalions led by Colonel Esipenko, the deputy commander of the 89th Guards Rifle Division, reached the Oder and crossed the ice during darkness. They fanned out, forming a small bridgehead just north of Küstrin.

Berzarin's men from the 5th Shock Army achieved what Zhukov described as 'a stunning surprise' late in the morning of Sunday 31 January, when they entered the town of Kienitz. 'German soldiers were walking around its streets calmly and the restaurant was full of officers. The trains to Berlin were still running on time, and the telephone lines were all working.' The Reich Chancellery lay just over sixty-five kilometres away. The station master approached Colonel Esipenko and asked whether he would allow the Berlin train to depart. With equal gravity, Esipenko replied that services would be interrupted for a short period, which was to say until the end of the war.

On the same day, just south of Küstrin, the ebullient Colonel Gusakovsky crossed the Oder with his 44th Guards Tank Brigade, forming another bridgehead. He thus won his second gold star of Hero of the Soviet Union. Soviet troops on both bridgeheads immediately began digging trenches in the frozen marshy ground of the Oderbruch, the Oder flood plain between the river and the Seelow Heights. Artillery regiments were rushed forward to give them support. They expected a rapid and furious counter-attack, but the Germans were so shaken by what had happened – Goebbels was still trying to pretend that fighting was going on close to Warsaw – that it took them time to rush in sufficient ground forces. Focke-Wulf fighters, however, were in action over the Oder the following morning, strafing the freshly dug trenches and anti-tank gun positions. The Soviet anti-aircraft division which had been promised did not turn up for three more days, so Chuikov's men, laying ice tracks across the thinly frozen river, were extremely vulnerable. They managed nevertheless to pull anti-tank guns across on skis to defend their positions.

The news of Soviet bridgeheads across the Oder was just as much of a shock to soldiers as to local civilians. Walter Beier, who had been spared from the Feldgendarmerie's trawl of leave-takers on the train from East Prussia, was enjoying his last days at home in the small village of Buchsmühlenweg, between Küstrin and Frankfurt an der Oder. 'Happiness in the bosom of the family did not last long,' he recorded. On the evening of 2 February an agitated neighbour came running to the house to say that about 800 Russians had taken up position in an oak wood only 500 metres away.

There were no troops in the area except for a few Volkssturm companies armed with nothing more than rifles and a couple of panzerfausts. Commanded by an old headmaster, they kept their distance. They found that Soviet snipers had climbed into the oak trees. An alarm battalion of anti-Soviet Caucasians, stiffened with some Germans from the 6th

Fortress Regiment, was hurried to the spot from Frankfurt. Beier, as a frontline soldier, was put in charge of a group by an officer.

While Beier was observing the wood with them from a ditch, one of the Caucasians pointed at it and said in broken German, 'You no shoot, we no shoot there. We no shoot at comrades.' Beier reported this and the Caucasians were disarmed and sent back from the front line to dig trenches instead. Their fate, when captured later by the Red Army, would not have been softened by this refusal to fire at their own countrymen.

The scratch German force was joined by a group of very young trainee soldiers of the SS Panzergrenadier Division *Feldherrnhalle*. Most of them were between sixteen and eighteen years old. They began to mortar the oak wood, one of the few patches of deciduous woodland in the area. There were around 350 of them in a chaotic array of uniforms. Some had steel helmets, some had *Käppis*, or sidehats, others wore peaked caps. Many had nothing more than their Hitler Youth uniforms. They were intensely proud of their task, yet many of them could hardly pick up a full ammunition box, and they could not hold the rifles properly into the shoulder, because the butts were too long for their arms. On their first attack, the Soviet sharpshooters picked them off with deliberate aim. The unit commander fell with a bullet through the head. Only a handful of the soldiers returned alive.

Beier managed to slip back to his parents' house. He found that a dressing station had been set up in the cellar and all their sheets were being torn up for bandages.

More weighty reinforcements arrived to attack the bridgehead as Chuikov's men pushed forward to seize the Reitwein Spur, a command-ing feature which looked up the whole Oderbruch and across to the Seelow Heights on its western edge. On 2 February the 506th SS Heavy Mortar Battalion moved north to the edge of the bridgehead and in three days and nights it fired 14,000 rounds. A battalion of the *Kurmark* Panzer Regiment was also brought up. On 4 February the battalion, recently re-equipped with Panther tanks, was sent in to attack the Reitwein Spur from its southern end. The tanks, however, failed disas-trously because the thaw predicted by meteorologists had started, and they slipped and slithered on the muddy hillsides.

*

News of Red Army troops crossing the Oder shocked Berlin. '*Stalin ante portas!*' wrote Wilfred von Oven, Goebbels's press attaché, in his diary on 1 February. 'This cry of alarm runs like the wind through the Reich capital.'

National Socialist rhetoric became fanatical, if not hysterical. The guard regiment of the *Grossdeutschland* Division was paraded. They were told that the Oder bridgeheads must be recaptured for the Führer. Berlin city buses drove up and they were taken out to Seelow, overlooking the Oderbruch.

A new SS Division was also formed. It was to be called the *30. Januar* in honour of the twelfth anniversary of the Nazis taking power. This division was given a core of SS veterans, but many of them were convalescent wounded. Eberhard Baumgart, a former member of the SS *Leibstandarte* at a recuperation camp, received orders to parade along with the other SS invalids. An Obersturmführer told them of the new division. Its task was to defend the Reich's capital. The new division needed battle-hardened veterans. He called on them to volunteer and yelled the SS motto devised by Himmler at them: '*Unsere Ehre heisst Treue, Kameraden!*' – 'Our honour is called loyalty.'

Such fanaticism was becoming rare, as senior members of the SS recognized with alarm. On 12 February, Obergruppenführer Berger reported to Himmler that the organization was becoming thoroughly disliked both by the civil population and by the army, which strongly resented its 'marked uncomradely attitude'. The army, he concluded, was 'no longer on speaking terms with the SS'.

Even SS volunteers felt enthusiasm dissolving when they reached the Oderbruch, a dreary expanse of waterlogged fields and dykes. 'We're at the end of the world!' one of the group earmarked for the *30. Januar* announced. They were even more dispirited to find that this new formation had no tanks or assault guns. 'This is no division,' the same man remarked, 'it's a heap that's just been scraped together.' Because of his unhealed wounds, Baumgart was attached as a clerk to divisional headquarters, which was established in a requisitioned farmhouse. The young wife of a farmer, who was serving somewhere else, watched in a daze as their furniture was manhandled out of the parlour and field telephones and typewriters were installed. The new inhabitants soon discovered, however, that the tile-roof of the farmhouse provided a clearly visible target for Soviet artillery.

Baumgart found himself hunched over one of the typewriters, bashing out reports of interviews with three Red Army deserters. They had apparently decided to cross to the German lines after being made to wade through the icy waters of the Oder, carrying their divisional commander on their shoulders to keep him dry. The Volga German interpreters at divisional headquarters later read out articles from captured copies of *Pravda*. The communiqué published at the end of the Yalta conference described what the allies intended to do with Germany. The idea of defeat appalled Baumgart and his comrades. 'We simply have to win in the end!' they said to themselves.

On 9 February 1945, the anti-Soviet renegade General Andrey Vlasov, with Himmler's encouragement, threw his headquarters security battalion into the bridgehead battle. This Russian battalion, as part of the *Döberitz* Division, attacked the Soviet 230th Rifle Division in the bridgehead just north of Küstrin. Vlasov's guard battalion fought well, even though the attempt was unsuccessful. The German propaganda account described them as fighting with 'enthusiasm and fanaticism', proving themselves as close-quarter combat specialists. They were supposedly given the nickname '*Panzerknacker*' by admiring German units, but this may well have been the touch of a popular journalist turned propagandist. Their commander, Colonel Zakharov, and four men received the Iron Cross second class, and the Reichsführer SS himself sent a message to congratulate Vlasov 'with comradely greetings' on the fact that his guard battalion had 'fought quite outstandingly well'.

Such marks of favour to those who had previously been categorized and treated as *Untermenschen* was a good indication of Nazi desperation, even if Hitler himself still disapproved. On 12 February, Goebbels received a delegation of Cossacks 'as the first volunteers on our side in the battle against Bolshevism'. They were even treated to a bottle of '*Weissbier*' in his offices. Goebbels praised the Cossacks, calling them 'a freedom-loving people of warrior-farmers'. Unfortunately, their freedom-loving ways in north Italy brought to Berlin bitter complaints about their treatment of the population in the Friuli district from the German adviser for civil affairs. The Cossacks, however, refused to have anything to do with Vlasov and his ideas of old Russian supremacy, as did most of the SS volunteers from national minorities.

The Führer's response to the onrush of Soviet tank brigades towards Berlin had been to order the establishment of a *Panzerjagd* Division, but in typical Nazi style, this impressive-sounding organization for destroying tanks failed to live up to its title. It consisted of bicycle companies mainly from the Hitler Youth. Each bicyclist was to carry two panzerfaust anti-tank launchers clamped upright either side of the front wheel and attached to the handlebars. The bicyclist was supposed to be able to dismount in a moment and be ready for action against a T-34 or Stalin tank. Even the Japanese did not expect their kamikazes to ride into battle on a bicycle.

Himmler talked about the panzerfaust as if it were another miracle weapon, akin to the V-2. He enthused about how wonderful it was for close-quarter fighting against tanks, but any sane soldier given the choice would have preferred an 88mm gun to take on Soviet tanks at a distance of half a kilometre. Himmler was almost apoplectic about rumours that the panzerfaust could not penetrate enemy armour. Such a story, he asserted, was '*ein absoluter Schwindel*'.

With the enemy so close, it appears that the Nazi leadership had started to consider the possibility of suicide. The headquarters of Gau Berlin issued an order that 'political leaders' were to receive top priority for firearms certificates. And a senior executive in a pharmaceutical company told Ursula von Kardorff and a friend of hers that a 'Golden Pheasant' had appeared in his laboratory demanding a supply of poison for the Reich Chancellery.

Hitler and his associates now finally found themselves closer to the very violence of war which they had unleashed. Revenge for the recent executions of men associated with the July plot arrived in unexpected form less than two weeks after the event. On the morning of 3 February, there were exceptionally heavy US Air Force raids on Berlin. Some 3,000 Berliners died. The newspaper district, as well as other areas, was almost totally destroyed. Allied bombs also found Nazi targets. The Reich Chancellery and the Party Chancellery were hit and both Gestapo headquarters in the Prinz-Albrechtstrasse and the People's Court were badly damaged. Roland Freisler, the President of the People's Court, who had screamed at the accused July plotters, was crushed to death sheltering in its cellars. The news briefly cheered dejected resistance circles, but rumours that concentration camps and prisons had been mined made them even more alarmed for relatives and friends in detention. Their only hope was that Himmler might keep them as bargaining counters. Martin Bormann in his diary wrote of the day's air raid: 'Suffered from bombing: new Reich Chancellery, the hell of Hitler's apartments, the dining room, the winter garden and the Party Chancellery.' He seems to have been concerned only with the monuments of Nazism. No mention was made of civilian casualties.

The most important event on Tuesday 6 February, according to Bormann's diary, was Eva Braun's birthday. Hitler, apparently, was 'in a radiant mood', watching her dance with others. As usual, Bormann was conferring privately with Kaltenbrunner. On 7 February, Gauleiter Koch, apparently forgiven for having abandoned Königsberg after all his orders to shoot those who left their place of duty, had discussions with Hitler. That evening, Bormann dined at the Fegeleins. One of the guests was Heinrich Himmler, whom he, Fegelein and Kaltenbrunner were seeking to undermine. The situation at the front was disastrous, yet Himmler, although commander-in-chief of Army Group Vistula, felt able to relax away from his headquarters. After supper Bormann and Fegelein talked with Eva Braun. The subject was probably her departure from Berlin, for Hitler wanted her out of danger. The next night she held a small farewell party for Hitler, Bormann and the Fegeleins. She left for Berchtesgaden the following evening, Friday 9 February, with her sister Gretl Fegelein. Hitler made sure that Bormann escorted them to the train.

Bormann, the Reichsleiter of the National Socialist Party, whose Gauleiters had in most cases stopped the evacuation of women and children until it was too late, never mentions in his diary those fleeing in panic from the eastern regions. The incompetence with which they handled the refugee crisis was chilling, yet in the case of the Nazi hierarchy it is often hard to tell where irresponsibility ended and inhumanity began. In an 'Evacuation Situation' report of 10 February, they suddenly realized that with 800,000 civilians still to be rescued from the Baltic coast, and with trains and ships taking an average of 1,000 people each, 'There are neither enough vessels, rolling stock nor vehicles at our disposal.' Yet there was no question of Nazi leaders giving up their luxurious 'special trains'.

6

East and West

On the morning of 2 February, just as the first German counter-attacks were launched against the Oder bridgeheads, the USS *Quincy* reached Malta. 'The cruiser which bore the President,' wrote Churchill, 'steamed majestically into the battle-scarred' Grand Harbour of Valetta. He went on board to greet Roosevelt. Although Churchill did not acknowledge that the President was ill, his colleagues were shaken to see how exhausted he looked.

The reunion between the two men was friendly, if not affectionate, yet Churchill's foreign secretary, Anthony Eden, was worried. Tension had continued to grow between the Western Allies over the invasion of Germany from the west. Now they were about to fly to Yalta in the Crimea to decide the post-war map of central Europe with Stalin. They were divided on this too, while the Soviet leader knew exactly what he wanted. Churchill and Eden were most concerned about the independence of Poland. Roosevelt's main priority was the establishment of the United Nations for the post-war world.

In separate aircraft, the President and the Prime Minister took off in the early hours of 3 February. Escorted by long-range Mustang fighters, and with no cabin lights showing, they flew east towards the Black Sea, following a fleet of transport aeroplanes carrying the two delegations. They arrived after a flight of seven and a half hours at Saki near Eupatoria. There, they were met by Molotov and Vyshinsky, the former prosecutor at the show trials and now deputy foreign minister. Stalin, who suffered from a terrible fear of flying, did not arrive until the next morning, Sunday 4 February. He had travelled down from Moscow in his green railway carriage, still with some of its Art Nouveau decoration from Tsarist days.

The American chiefs of staff were housed in the Tsar's former palace. General George C. Marshall found himself in the Tsarina's bedroom, with a secret staircase allegedly used by Rasputin. Their British counterparts were in Prince Vorontsov's Castle of Alupka, an extravagant mid-nineteenth-century mixture of Moorish and Scottish baronial. President Roosevelt, to save him any more journeys, was installed in the Livadia Palace, where the main discussions were to take place. So much had been wrecked during the fighting in the Crimea and the German withdrawal that major works, including complete replumbing, had been carried out at great speed by the Soviet authorities to make these palaces habitable. Amid the terrible war damage, no efforts were spared to entertain their guests with banquets of caviare and Caucasian champagne. Churchill could not resist calling this coast of ghostly summer palaces the 'Riviera of Hades'. Not even he suspected that all their rooms had been bugged. The NKVD had also positioned directional microphones to cover the gardens.

Stalin visited Churchill that afternoon, keen to convey the impression that the Red Army could be in Berlin in no time. He then paid his respects to President Roosevelt. With Roosevelt, his manner became almost deferential and his version of events changed completely. Stalin now emphasized the strength of German resistance and the difficulty of crossing the River Oder. Roosevelt was certain that he, not Churchill, knew how to handle the Soviet leader and Stalin played up to this. Roosevelt believed that it was just a matter of winning Stalin's trust, something which Churchill could never do. He even admitted openly his disagreements with the British over the strategy for the invasion of Germany. When he suggested that Eisenhower should have direct contact with the *Stavka*, Stalin encouraged the idea warmly. The Soviet leader saw the advantages of American frankness, while giving away little in return.

American leaders had another reason for not opposing Stalin. They did not yet know whether the atomic bomb would work, so they desperately wanted to bring Stalin into the war against Japan. It did not seem to occur to them that it was also very much to Stalin's advantage to come in as a victor to the spoils after the fighting was virtually over.

At the first session, which began shortly afterwards, Stalin graciously proposed that President Roosevelt should chair the meetings. The Soviet leader was wearing the medal of Hero of the Soviet Union with his uniform of Marshal of the Soviet Union. The striped trousers were tucked into boots of soft Caucasian leather. These boots had built-up heels because he was extremely conscious of his short stature. Stalin also avoided bright lights wherever possible because they showed up the pockmarks on his face. All official portraits were heavily retouched to conceal such imperfections.

General Antonov, the Soviet chief of staff, gave an impressive-sounding account of the situation, but both American and British chiefs of staff sensed that it was short on detail. The British especially felt that information between allies appeared to be a one-way traffic. Antonov also claimed that the date of their great offensive had been brought forward to assist the Americans and British. General Marshall, for his part, underlined the effect of Allied bombing on German war industry, rail communications and fuel supplies, all of which had greatly assisted the Soviet Union in its recent successes. The mood of the meeting became almost ugly when Stalin deliberately twisted things said by Churchill, and Roosevelt had to intervene.

That evening at dinner, the generally amicable mood was again threatened by Soviet remarks demonstrating total contempt for the rights of small nations. Roosevelt, hoping to lighten the atmosphere, told Stalin that he was popularly known as 'Uncle Joe'. Stalin, who had clearly never been informed of this by his own diplomats, was insulted by what he regarded as a vulgar and disrespectful nickname. This time, Churchill stepped in to rescue the situation with a toast to the Big Three – an expression of self-congratulation to which Stalin could not fail to respond. But he took this as another opportunity to re-emphasize the point that the Big Three would decide the fate of the world and that smaller nations should have no veto. Both Roosevelt and Churchill failed to see the implication.

The next morning, Monday 5 February, the American and British combined chiefs of staff met with the *Stavka* team led by General Antonov. The *Stavka* particularly wanted pressure to be exerted in Italy to prevent German divisions being withdrawn for use in Hungary. This was perfectly reasonable and logical in itself, but it may have also been part of the Soviet attempt to persuade the Americans and British to concentrate their efforts more to the south, well away from Berlin. But both General Marshall, the American army chief of staff, and Field Marshal Sir Alan Brooke, the Chief of the Imperial General Staff, warned the *Stavka* quite openly that they could not prevent the movement of German formations from one front to another, apart from stepping up air raids on railways and communications centres.

The crux of the whole conference became apparent that afternoon and on the following day. The discussion began with the immediate post-war period and the treatment of defeated Germany. Victory was estimated to take place at any time from the summer onwards. Roosevelt talked about the European Advisory Commission and future zones of occupation. Stalin made it clear that he wanted Germany to be completely dismembered. Then Roosevelt announced without warning that United States forces would not remain in Europe for more than two years after Germany's surrender. Churchill was privately appalled. This would only encourage Stalin to be more obdurate, and a war-ravaged Europe might well be too weak to resist Communist unrest.

Stalin also made clear that he intended to strip German industry as a down payment in kind towards the Soviet Union's claim for $10 billion in reparations. He did not mention it at the conference, but government commissions composed of Soviet accountants looking very awkward in new colonels' uniforms were closely following each army in its advance. Their task was 'the systematic confiscation of German industry and wealth'. In addition, the NKVD group at each army headquarters had a team specialized in opening safes, preferably before a Soviet soldier tried to blast the door off with a captured panzerfaust, destroying everything inside. Stalin was determined to extract every ounce of gold he could.

The one issue which both Stalin and Churchill felt passionately about was Poland. The debate was not so much over the future frontiers of the country, but over the composition of its government. Churchill declared that a fully independent Poland, the very reason for which Great Britain had gone to war in September 1939, was a question of honour.

Stalin in his reply referred very obliquely to the secret clauses of the 1939 Nazi-Soviet pact, which had allowed the Soviet Union to invade and occupy the eastern part of Poland and the Baltic states while the Nazis seized the western half. 'It is a question of honour,' Stalin said, standing up, 'because the Russians have committed many sins against the Poles in the past, and the Soviet government wishes to make amends.' After this shameless opening, considering the Soviet oppression in Poland already under way, Stalin went to the heart of the matter. 'It is also a question of security, because Poland presents the gravest of strategic problems for the Soviet Union. Throughout history, Poland has served as a corridor for enemies coming to attack Russia.' He then argued that to prevent this, Poland had to be strong. 'That is why the Soviet Union is interested in the creation of a mighty, free and independent Poland. The Polish question is a question of life and death for the Soviet state.' The flagrant mutual contradiction of the last two sentences was obvious. Although it was never stated openly, the Soviet Union would accept nothing less than a totally subservient Poland as a buffer zone. Neither Churchill nor Roosevelt could fully appreciate the shock of the German invasion in 1941 and Stalin's determination never to be surprised by another enemy. One could well argue that the origins of the Cold War lay in that traumatic experience.

Churchill nevertheless realized that he stood no chance when Stalin invoked the necessity of securing the Red Army's lines of communications in the approaching battle for Berlin. The Soviet leader played his cards very cleverly. The provisional 'Warsaw government', as he insisted on calling it – the Americans and British still referred to these NKVD-controlled Communists as the 'Lublin government' – was in place and, he claimed, highly popular. As for democracy, he argued, the Polish government in exile in London possessed no more democratic support than De Gaulle enjoyed in France. One cannot know for sure whether Churchill properly decoded the unspoken message: you must not thwart me over Poland, because I have kept the French Communist Party under control. Your lines of communication have not been disturbed by revolutionary activity in France by the Communist-dominated resistance movement.

To rub in the point about respective spheres of influence, Stalin asked disingenuously how things were in Greece. The Soviet leader, on the basis of the so-called 'percentage' agreement of the previous October, apportioning spheres of influence in the Balkans, had undertaken not to cause trouble in Greece and to respect British control there. At Yalta, Stalin appears to have been signalling that both Poland and France should be considered as an extension of the percentage agreement, but the British Prime Minister failed to decipher the text. Field Marshal Sir Alan Brooke suspected at the time that there was much that Churchill did not take in.

Stalin did not relax the pressure. He claimed that 212 Soviet soldiers had been killed by Poles. Churchill was forced to agree that attacks on the Red Army by the Polish non-Communist resistance, the Armia Krajowa, were utterly unacceptable. The Prime Minister did not know that the NKVD regiments in charge of rear area security were in most cases the aggressors, arresting any members of the underground and sometimes using torture to force them to reveal other names and the locations of their arms dumps. Roosevelt, clearly too ill and exhausted to intervene, could insist only on free elections in Poland, but that was a pious hope with the machinery entirely in Soviet hands. His chief aide, Harry Hopkins, estimated that Roosevelt had probably not taken in more than half of what was said.

Stalin was convinced that he had won. As soon as the Soviet delegates felt that there was no further challenge to their control of Poland, they suddenly dropped their opposition to the voting system proposed by the Americans for the United Nations. The other principal American concern, that Stalin would commit himself to the war against Japan within a short time of the defeat of Germany, was achieved at a private meeting on 8 February.

The Soviet leader was not gracious in victory. When Churchill expressed his fears at another meeting that such a massive change in Poland's frontiers at Germany's expense would cause an enormous shift in population, Stalin retorted that it would not be a problem. He spoke triumphantly of the huge wave of German refugees running away from the Red Army.

On 13 February, two days after the Yalta conference ended, Soviet might was reconfirmed with the fall of Budapest. The end of this terrible battle for the city was marked by an orgy of killing, looting, destruction and rape. Yet Hitler still wanted to counter-attack in Hungary with the Sixth SS Panzer Army. He hoped to smash Marshal Tolbukhin's 3rd

Ukrainian Front, but this was the compulsive gambler throwing on to the table the last few chips left over from the Ardennes.

That night, the British bombed Dresden. The following morning, which happened to be Ash Wednesday, the US Air Force followed in their path and also attacked several lesser targets. It was intended as a rapid fulfilment of the promise to the *Stavka* to hinder German troop movements by smashing rail communications. The fact that there were 180 V-bomb rocket attacks on England that week, the highest number so far, did little to soften the planners' hearts. Dresden, the exquisitely beautiful capital of Saxony, had never been seriously bombed before. Dresdeners used to joke, half-believing it, that Churchill had an aunt living in the city and that was why they had been spared. But the raids on 13 and 14 February were merciless. The effect was in some ways comparable to the Hamburg fire-storm raid. But Dresden's population was swollen by up to 300,000 refugees from the east. Several trains full of them were stuck in the main station. The tragedy was that instead of troops passing through Dresden to the front, as Soviet military intelligence had asserted, the traffic was civilian and going in the opposite direction.

Goebbels apparently shook with fury on hearing the news. He wanted to execute as many prisoners of war as the number of civilians killed in the attack. The idea appealed to Hitler. Such an extreme measure would tear up the Geneva Convention in the face of the Western Allies and force his own troops to fight to the end. But General Jodl, supported by Ribbentrop, Field Marshal Keitel and Grand Admiral Dönitz finally persuaded him that such an escalation of terror would turn out worse for Germany. Goebbels nevertheless extracted all he could from this 'terror attack'. Soldiers with relatives in the city were promised compassionate leave. Hans-Dietrich Genscher remembers some of them returning from their visit. They were reluctant to talk about what they had seen.

On the Western Front, the Americans and the British had not been advancing anything like as rapidly as the Red Army. The battle for the Rhineland, which began during the talks at Yalta, was also slow and deliberate. Eisenhower was in no hurry. He thought that spring floodwater would make the Rhine impassable until the beginning of

May. It was to take another six weeks before all Eisenhower's armies were ready on the west bank of the Rhine. Only the miracle of capturing intact the Rhine bridge at Remagen allowed an acceleration of the programme.

Eisenhower was deeply irritated by the continuing British criticism of his methodical broad-front strategy. Churchill, Brooke and Field Marshal Montgomery all wanted a reinforced breakthrough to head for Berlin. Their reasons were mainly political. The capture of Berlin before the Red Army arrived would help to restore the balance of power with Stalin. Yet they also felt on military grounds that to seize the capital of the Reich would deal the greatest psychological blow to German resistance and shorten the war. British arguments for the single thrust into the heart of Germany, however, had not been helped by the insufferable Field Marshal Montgomery. At the end of the first week of January, he had tried to take far more credit for the defeat of the German offensive in the Ardennes than was his due. This crass and unpleasant blunder naturally infuriated American generals and deeply embarrassed Churchill. It certainly did not help persuade Eisenhower to allow Montgomery to lead a major push through northern Germany to Berlin.

Eisenhower, as supreme commander, continued to insist that it was not his job to look towards the post-war world. His task was to finish the war effectively with as few casualties as possible. He felt that the British were allowing post-war politics to rule military strategy. Eisenhower was genuinely grateful to Stalin for the effort made to advance the date of the January offensive, even if he was unaware of Stalin's ulterior motive of securing Poland before the Yalta conference.

United States policy-makers simply did not wish to provoke Stalin in any way. John G. Winant, the United States ambassador in London, when discussing zones of occupation on the European Advisory Commission, even refused to raise the issue of a land corridor to Berlin in case it spoiled his relationship with his Soviet opposite number. The policy of appeasing Stalin came from the top and was widely accepted. Eisenhower's political adviser, Robert Murphy, had been told by Roosevelt that 'the most important thing was to persuade the Russians to trust us'. This could not have suited Stalin better. Roosevelt's claim, 'I can handle Stalin', was part of what Robert Murphy acknowledged to be 'the all-too-prevalent American theory' that individual friendships can determine national policy. 'Soviet policy-makers and diplomats never operate on that theory,' he added. The American longing to be trusted by Stalin blinded them to the question of how far they should trust him. And this was a man whose lack of respect for international law had led him to suggest quite calmly that they should invade Germany via neutral Switzerland, thus 'outflanking the West Wall'.

Soviet resentment was based on the fact that the United States and Britain had suffered so little in comparison. Nazi Germany also treated Allied prisoners in a totally different way from Red Army prisoners. A 1st Belorussian Front report on the liberation of a prisoner-of-war camp near Torn underlined the contrast in fates. The appearance of the Americans, British and French inmates was healthy. 'They looked more like people on holiday than prisoners of war,' the report stated, 'while Soviet prisoners were emaciated, wrapped in blankets.' Prisoners from the Western Allied countries did not have to work, they were allowed to play football and they received food parcels from the Red Cross. Meanwhile, in the other part of the camp, '17,000 Soviet prisoners had been killed or died from starvation or illness. The "special regime" for Soviet prisoners consisted of 300 grams of ersatz bread and 1 litre of soup made from rotten mangelwurzels per day. Healthy prisoners were made to dig trenches, the weak ones were killed or buried alive.'

They were guarded by 'traitors' from the Red Army, recruited with the promise of better rations. These volunteers treated 'Soviet prisoners of war with more cruelty than the Germans'. Some of the guards were said to have been Volga Germans. They ordered prisoners to strip and set dogs on them. The Germans had apparently carried out 'a massive propaganda' attempt to persuade prisoners to join the ROA, General Vlasov's army of former Soviet soldiers in Wehrmacht uniform. 'Many Ukrainians and Uzbeks sold themselves to the Germans,' stated a prisoner. He was described as an 'ex-Party member' and 'former senior lieutenant'. This was because members of the Red Army were stripped of all status simply for having allowed themselves to be taken prisoner.

The punishments inflicted on Soviet prisoners included forcing them to do knee-bends for up to seven hours, 'which completely crippled the victim'. They were also made to run up and down stairs past guards armed with rubber truncheons on every landing. In another camp, wounded officers were placed under cold showers in winter and left to die of hypothermia. Soviet soldiers were subjected to the 'saw-horse', the eighteenth-century torture of strapping a prisoner astride a huge trestle. Some were made to run as live targets for shooting practice by SS guards. Another punishment was known as '*Achtung!*' A Soviet prisoner was made to strip and kneel in the open. Handlers with attack dogs waited on either side. The moment he stopped shouting, '*Achtung! Achtung! Achtung!*' the dogs were set on him. Dogs were also used when prisoners collapsed after being forced to do 'sport marches', goose-stepping in rapid time. It may have been news of these sorts of punishment which inspired similar practices against German prisoners taken by Soviet troops in their recent advances. An escaped British prisoner of war, a fighter pilot, picked up by a unit of the 1st Ukrainian Front and taken along, saw a young SS soldier forced to play a piano for his Russian captors. They made it clear in sign language that he would be executed the moment he stopped. He managed to play for sixteen hours before he collapsed sobbing on the keyboard. They slapped him on the back, then dragged him out and shot him.

The Red Army advanced into German territory with a turbulent mixture of anger and exultation. 'Everybody seems to have German harmonicas,' noted Grossman, 'a soldier's instrument because it is the only one possible to play on a rattling vehicle or cart.' They also mourned their comrades. Yakov Zinovievich Aronov, an artilleryman, was killed near Königsberg on 19 February. Shortly before his death he wrote a typical soldier's letter home: 'We are beating and destroying the enemy, who is running back to his lair like a wounded beast. I live very well and I'm alive and I'm healthy. All my thoughts are about beating the enemy and coming home to you all.' Another of his letters was much more revealing, because it was to a fellow soldier who would understand. 'I love life so much, I have not yet lived. I am only nineteen. I often see death in front of me and I struggle with it. I fight and so far I am winning. I am an artillery reconnaissance man, and you can imagine what it is like. To make a long story short, I very often correct the fire of my battery and only when shells hit the target, I feel joy.'

Aronov was killed 'one foggy Prussian morning', wrote his closest friend to the dead boy's sister Irina. The two of them had fought together all the way from Vitebsk to Königsberg. 'So, Ira, the war has separated many friends and a lot of blood has been shed, but we comrades in arms are taking vengeance on Hitler's serpents for our brothers and friends, for their blood.' Aronov's body was buried by his comrades 'on the edge of the forest'. Presumably its site was marked like others by a stick with a small bit of red rag tied to it. If refound by the pioneers responsible, it would be replaced by a small wooden plaque. There were too many bodies spread too widely for reburying in cemeteries.

Red Army soldiers were also marked by their encounters with slave workers, attempting to return home. Many were peasant women with knotted headkerchiefs covering their foreheads and wearing improvised puttees for warmth. Captain Agranenko, the dramatist, encountered a cart full of women in East Prussia. He asked who they were. 'We are Russian. Russian,' they answered, overjoyed to hear a friendly voice. He shook hands with each one of them. An old woman suddenly began to cry. 'It is the first time in three years that someone has shaken my hand,' she explained.

Agranenko also encountered 'a beauty from the region of Orel called Tatyana Khilchakova'. She was returning home with a two-month-old baby. In the German camp for slave labourers she had met a Czech and fallen in love with him. They had exchanged marriage vows, but when the Red Army arrived, her Czech had immediately volunteered to fight the Germans. 'Tatyana does not know his address. He does not know hers. And it is unlikely that the war will ever throw them together again.' Perhaps, even more unfortunately, she would probably be made to suffer on her return home to Orel for having had relations with a foreigner.

The chief concern for the *Stavka* at this time continued to be the wide gap across the 'Baltic balcony' between Zhukov's 1st Belorussian Front and the left flank of Rokossovsky's 2nd Belorussian Front. On 6 February, Stalin had rung Zhukov from Yalta. He asked what he was doing. Zhukov replied that he was in a meeting of army commanders to discuss the advance on Berlin from the new Oder bridgeheads. Stalin retorted that he was wasting his time. They should consolidate on the Oder, and then turn north to join up with Rokossovsky.

Chuikov, the commander of the 8th Guards Army, who appears to have resented Zhukov since Stalingrad, was contemptuous that Zhukov did not argue forcefully for a push on Berlin. The bitter debate continued well into the post-war years. Chuikov argued that a rapid push at the beginning of February would have caught Berlin undefended. But Zhukov and others felt that with exhausted troops and serious supply shortages, to say nothing of the threat of a counter-attack from the north on their exposed right flank, the risk was far too great.

In East Prussia, meanwhile, German forces were contained but not yet defeated. The remains of the Fourth Army, having failed to break out at the end of January, was squeezed in the Heiligenbeil *Kessel*, with its back to the Frisches Haff. Its main artillery support came from the heavy guns of the cruisers *Admiral Scheer* and *Lützow*, firing from out in the Baltic across the sandbar of the Frische Nehrung and the frozen lagoon.

The remnants of the Third Panzer Army in Königsberg had been cut off from the Samland Peninsula, but on 19 February, a joint attack from both sides created a land corridor which was then bitterly defended. The evacuation of civilians and wounded from the small port of Pillau at the tip of the Samland Peninsula was intensified, but many civilians feared to leave by ship after the torpedo attacks on the *Wilhelm Gustloff* and other refugee ships. In the early hours of 12 February, the hospital ship *General von Steuben* was torpedoed after leaving Pillau with 2,680 wounded. Almost all were drowned.

The Second Army, meanwhile, had been forced back towards the lower Vistula and its estuary, defending Danzig and the port of Gdynia. It formed the left flank of Himmler's Army Group Vistula. In the centre, in eastern Pomerania, a new Eleventh SS Panzer Army was being formed. Himmler's right flank on the Oder consisted of the remnants of General Busse's Ninth Army, which had been so badly mauled in western Poland.

Himmler seldom ventured out of his luxurious special train, the *Steiermark*, which he had designated his 'field headquarters'. The Reichsführer SS now realized that the responsibilities of military command were rather greater than he had imagined. His 'insecurity as a military leader,' wrote Colonel Eismann, 'made him incapable of a determined presentation of the operational situation to Hitler, let alone of asserting himself '. Himmler used to return from the Führer situation conference a nervous wreck. Staff officers received little pleasure from the paradox that the feared Himmler should be so fearful. His 'servile attitude' towards Hitler and his fear of admitting the disastrous state of his forces, 'caused great damage and cost a vast amount of unnecessary blood'.

Himmler, seeking refuge in the Führer's own aggressive clichés, talked of more counter-attacks. Following the Demmlhuber débâcle, Himmler set his mind on establishing the so-called Eleventh SS Panzer Army. In fact the whole of Army Group Vistula in the early days contained only three under-strength panzer divisions. At best, the formations available constituted a corps, 'but panzer army', observed Eismann, 'has a better ring to it'. Himmler had another motive, however. It was to promote Waffen SS officers on the staff and in field command. Obergruppenführer Steiner was named as its commander. Steiner, an experienced soldier, was certainly a much better choice than other senior Waffen SS officers. But he did not have an easy task.

General Guderian, determined to keep a corridor open to the edge of East Prussia, argued at a situation conference in the first week of February that an ambitious operation was needed. He was even more outspoken than usual that day, having drunk a certain amount at an early lunch with the Japanese ambassador. Guderian wanted a pincer movement from the Oder south of Berlin and an attack down from Pomerania to cut off Zhukov's leading armies. To assemble enough troops, more of the divisions trapped uselessly in Courland and else-where needed to be brought back by sea and the offensive in Hungary postponed. Hitler refused yet again.

'You must believe me,' Guderian persisted, 'when I say it is not just pig-headedness on my part that makes me keep on proposing the evacuation of Courland. I can see no other way left to us of accumulating reserves, and without reserves we cannot hope to defend the capital. I assure you I am acting solely in Germany's interests.' Hitler began trembling in anger as he jumped to his feet. 'How dare you speak to me like that?' he shouted. 'Don't you think I'm fighting for Germany? My whole life has been one long struggle for Germany!' Colonel de Maizière, the new operations officer at Zossen, had never seen such a row and stood there shocked and afraid for the chief of staff. To bring an end to Hitler's frenzy, Göring led Guderian out of the room to find some coffee while everyone calmed down.

Guderian's main fear was that the Second Army, trying to maintain a link between East Prussia and Pomerania, was in danger of being cut off. He therefore argued instead for a single attack southwards from the 'Baltic balcony'. This attack on Zhukov's right flank would also deter the Soviets from trying to attack Berlin immediately. On 13 February, a final conference on the operation was held in the Reich Chancellery. Himmler, as commander-in-chief of Army Group Vistula, was present, and so was Oberstgruppenführer Sepp Dietrich. Guderian also brought his extremely capable deputy, General Wenck. Guderian made plain right from the start that he wanted the operation to start in two days' time. Himmler objected, saying that not all the fuel and ammunition had arrived. Hitler supported him and soon the Führer and his army chief of staff were having another row. Guderian insisted that Wenck should direct the operation.

'The Reichsführer SS is man enough to carry out the attack on his own,' Hitler said.

'The Reichsführer SS has neither the requisite experience nor a sufficiently competent staff to control the attack single-handed. The presence of General Wenck is therefore essential.'

'I don't permit you,' Hitler shouted, 'to tell me that the Reichsführer SS is incapable of performing his duties.'

The argument raged for a long time. Hitler was literally raving in anger and screaming. Guderian claims to have glanced up at a helmeted portrait of Bismarck, the Iron Chancellor, and wondered what he thought of what was happening in the country he had helped to create. To Guderian's surprise, Hitler suddenly stopped his pacing up and down and told Himmler that General Wenck would join his headquarters that night and direct the offensive. He then sat down again abruptly and smiled at Guderian. 'Now please continue with the conference. The general staff has won a battle this day.' Guderian ignored Keitel's remonstrances later in the anteroom that he might have caused the Führer to suffer a stroke. He feared that his limited triumph might be short-lived.

On 16 February, the Pomeranian offensive, known as the Stargard tank battle, began under Wenck's direction. Over 1,200 tanks had been allocated, but the trains to transport them were lacking. Even an under-strength panzer division needed fifty trains to move its men and

1. (*Previous page*) Hitler Youth during the fighting in Lauban in Silesia, 30 March.
2. Part of the *Grossdeutschland* Corps being inspected in an East Prussian forest before the Soviet onslaught of 14 January.

3. Volkssturm captured in Insterburg, East Prussia, 22 January.

4. Berliners after a heavy air raid.

5. A 'trek' of German refugees from Silesia fleeing before the Red Army.

6. Red Army troops march into an East Prussian town, January.

7. Soviet mechanized troops enter the East Prussian town of Mühlhausen.

8. Red Army troops occupy Tilsit.

9. A Soviet self-propelled assault gun breaks into Danzig, 23 March.

10. A Hitler Youth at a Volkssturm parade taken by Goebbels.

11. Two German soldiers in the defence of the besieged
Silesian capital, Breslau.

12. SS Panzergrenadiers before a counter-attack in southern Pomerania.

13. Goebbels decorates a Hitler Youth after the recapture of Lauban, 9 March.
14. (*Overleaf*) German women and children trying to escape westwards by rail.

vehicles. Far more serious was the shortage of ammunition and fuel, of which there were enough for only three days of operations. The lesson of the Ardennes offensive had not been learned.

Army staff officers had intended to give the offensive the codename '*Husarenritt*', or Hussar ride, which in itself seemed to acknowledge that this could be no more than a raid. But the SS insisted on a much more dramatic name: '*Sonnenwende*', or solstice. In the event it was neither a Hussar ride – a sudden thaw meant that the armoured vehicles were soon bogged down in the mud – nor a solstice, since it changed very little. The Wehrmacht could ill afford the heavy loss of tanks when the 2nd Guards Tank Army counter-attacked.

The highest-ranking casualty was General Wenck, who, driving back to his headquarters from briefing thc Führer on the night of 17 February, fell asleep at the wheel and was badly hurt. He was replaced by General Krebs, a clever staff officer who had been military attaché in Moscow before Operation Barbarossa. The attempt to force back the Soviet counter-attack, however, had to be abandoned after two days. All that can be said in favour of the offensive is that it bought time. The Kremlin became convinced that a quick dash to Berlin was out of the question until the Pomeranian coastline was secured.

Hitler's attempts to designate 'fortress' towns and to refuse to allow the evacuation of encircled troops, were part of a suicidal pattern of enforced sacrifice and useless suffering. He knew that they were doomed because the Luftwaffe lacked the fuel and aircraft to supply them, and yet his policy deprived Army Group Vistula of experienced troops.

Königsberg and Breslau held out, but other towns designated as fortresses or breakwaters by Hitler soon fell. In southern Pomerania, Schneidemühl, the smallest and the least well defended, fell on 14 February after a desperate defence. For once, even Hitler had no complaints and awarded Knight's Crosses to both the commander and the second-in-command. Four days later, on 18 February, just as Operation *Sonnenwende* became bogged down in the mud, General Chuikov gave the signal for the storming of the fortress of Poznan. His 7th Department, as at Stalingrad, had preceded the bombardment with loudspeaker programmes of lugubrious music interspersed with messages that surrender was the only way to save your life and return home. The Germans were told that they had no hope of escape because they were now over 200 kilometres behind the front line.

Siege artillery had begun the softening-up process nine days before, but by the morning of 18 February, 1,400 guns, mortars and katyusha launchers were ready for the four-hour bombardment. Storm groups fought into the fortress, whose superstructure had been crushed by explosive fire. When resistance from a building continued, a 203mm howitzer was brought up and blasted the walls over open sights. Flame-throwers were used and explosive charges dropped down ventilation shafts. German soldiers who tried to surrender were shot by their own officers. But the end was imminent. On the night of 22–23 February, the commandant, Major General Ernst Gomell, spread out the swastika flag on the floor of his room, lay down on it and shot himself. The remnants of the garrison capitulated.

The siege of Breslau was to be even more prolonged: the city held out even after Berlin had fallen. As a result it was one of the most terrible of the war. The fanatical Gauleiter Hanke was determined that the capital of Silesia should remain unconquered. It was he who used loudspeaker vans to order women and children to flee the city in late January. Those who froze to death were entirely his responsibility.

The city had good stocks of food but little ammunition. The attempts to drop ammunition by parachute were a terrible waste of Luftwaffe resources. Colonel General Schörner, the commander-in-chief of Army Group Centre, then decided to send part of the 25th Parachute Regiment at the end of February to strengthen the garrison. The regimental commander protested strenuously that there was no landing zone, but on 22 February the battalion boarded Junkers 52 transports at Jüterbog, south of Berlin. At midnight the aircraft approached Breslau. 'Over the city,' one of the paratroopers wrote later, 'we could see extensive fires and we encountered heavy anti-aircraft fire.' A hit on the radio left them out of contact with ground control and they landed at an airfield near Dresden. Another attempt was made two nights later. The Soviet flak was even more intense as they circled the burning city for twenty minutes, trying to find a landing place. Three of the aircraft were lost: one of them crashed into a factory chimney.

Hanke's disciplinary measures, backed by General Schörner's policy of 'strength through fear', were terrible. Execution was arbitrary. Even ten-year-old children were put to work under Soviet air and artillery attack to clear an air strip within the city. Any attempt to surrender by those who sought to 'preserve their pitiful lives' would be met by a death sentence instantly carried out. 'Decisive measures' would also be taken against their families. Schörner argued that 'almost four years of an Asiatic war' had changed the soldier at the front completely: 'It has hardened him and fanaticized him in the struggle against the Bolsheviks . . . The campaign in the east has developed the political soldier.'

Stalin's boast at Yalta that the populations of East Prussia and Silesia had fled was not yet true. All too many were still trapped in besieged cities. German civilians in East Prussia also continued to suffer wherever they were, whether in Königsberg and the Heiligenbeil *Kessel*, attempting to leave the port of Pillau by ship, escaping on foot to the west or remaining at home. The February thaw meant that the ice of the Frisches Haff could be crossed only on foot and not by cart. The exit to Danzig, Pomerania and the west still remained open, but everyone realized that it was only a matter of time before the 1st Belorussian Front cut through to the Baltic.

Beria was informed by a senior SMERSH officer that the 'significant part of the population of East Prussia' which had fled into Königsberg had found that there was little room for them and even less food. They were lucky if they received 180 grams of bread a day. 'Starved women with children are dragging themselves along the road' in the hope that the Red Army might feed them. From these civilians, Red Army intelligence heard that 'the morale of the Königsberg garrison is severely shaken. New general orders have been issued that any German male who does not report for frontline service will be shot on the spot . . . Soldiers put on civilian clothes and desert. On 6 and 7 February, the bodies of eighty German soldiers were piled up at the northern railway station. A placard was erected above them: "They were cowards but died just the same."'

After the failure of Operation *Sonnenwende*, Danzig was increasingly threatened. The Kriegsmarine made great efforts to rescue as many wounded and civilians as possible. In the course of a single day, 21

February, 51,000 were brought out. The Nazi authorities estimated that only 150,000 remained to be evacuated, but a week later they found that Danzig now had a population of 1.2 million, of whom 530,000 were refugees. Greater efforts were made. On 8 March thirty-four trains of cattle trucks full of civilians left Pomerania for Mecklenburg, west of the Oder. Hitler wanted to move 150,000 refugees into Denmark. Two days later instructions were issued: 'The Führer has ordered that from now on Copenhagen is to become a target sanctuary.' Also on 10 March, the estimated running total of German refugees from the eastern provinces rose to 11 million people.

Yet even while the city of Danzig swarmed with frightened refugees desperate to escape, vile work continued in the Danzig Anatomical Medical Institute. After the Red Army captured the city a special commission was sent there to investigate the manufacture of soap and leather from 'corpses of citizens of the USSR, Poland and other countries killed in German concentration camps'. In 1943 Professor Spanner and Assistant Professor Volman had begun to experiment. They then built special facilities for production. 'The examination of the premises of the Anatomical Institute revealed 148 human corpses which were stored for the production of soap of which 126 were male corpses, eighteen female and four children. Eighty male corpses and two female corpses were without heads. Eighty-nine human heads were also found.' All corpses and heads were stored in metal containers in an alcohol-carbolic solution. It appears that most of the corpses came from Stutthof concentration camp, near the city. 'The executed people whose corpses were made for using soap were of different nationalities, but mostly Poles, Russians and Uzbeks.' The work evidently received official approval, considering the high rank of its visitors. 'The Anatomical Institute was visited by the Minister of Education Rust and Minister of Health Care Konti. Gauleiter of Danzig Albert Förster visited the institute in 1944, when soap was already being produced. He examined all the premises of the Anatomical Institute and I think that he knew about the production of soap from human corpses.' The most astonishing aspects of this appalling story are that nothing was destroyed before the Red Army arrived and that Professor Spanner and his associates never faced charges after the war. The processing of corpses was not a crime.

Stutthof camp contained mainly Soviet prisoners and a number of

Poles, a mixture of soldiers and Jews. Some 16,000 prisoners died in the camp from typhoid in six weeks. As the Red Army approached, prisoners were ordered to eliminate all traces. The crematorium was blown up and ten barrack blocks in which Jews had been kept were burned down. Apparently ordinary German soldiers were made to take part in the executions of Red Army prisoners of war and Soviet civilians.

Whether prompted by fear of retribution for war crimes or fear of the Bolsheviks and slave labour in Siberia, the exhausted Wehrmacht still marched and fought. 'The Germans have not yet lost hope,' stated a French intelligence analysis that February, 'they don't dare to.' Soviet officers put it slightly differently: 'Morale is low but discipline is strong.'

7

Clearing the Rear Areas

On 14 February, in East Prussia, a convoy of military vehicles with Red Army markings turned off the main route from Rastenburg to Angeburg. This side road led into dense pine forest. The whole region was imbued with an atmosphere of melancholy.

A tall barbed-wire fence surmounted by concertina wire became visible from the road. The vehicles soon reached a barrier with a sign in German: 'Halt. Military Site. Entrance Forbidden to Civilians.' This was the entrance to Hitler's former headquarters, the *Wolfsschanze*.

The trucks carried frontier guard troops from the 57th NKVD Rifle Division. The officers in command of the convoy wore Red Army uniforms, yet they owed no allegiance to its chain of command. As members of SMERSH counter-intelligence, they were in theory answerable only to Stalin. Their feelings towards the Red Army at that time were not comradely. The dilapidated vehicles which they had been given came from army units who had taken the opportunity to rid themselves of their worst equipment. Although this was common practice, SMERSH and the NKVD did not appreciate it.

Their leader wore the uniform of a Red Army general. This was Commissar of State Security of the Second Rank, Viktor Semyonovich Abakumov. Beria had appointed him the first chief of SMERSH in April 1943, soon after the victory at Stalingrad. Abakumov occasionally followed his leader's habit of arresting young women in order to rape them, but his chief speciality was taking part in the beatings of prisoners with a rubber truncheon. In order not to spoil the Persian carpet in his office, 'a dirty runner bespattered with blood was rolled out' before the unfortunate was brought in.

Abakumov, although still chief of SMERSH, had been sent by Beria 'to carry out the necessary Chekist measures' behind the advance of the 3rd Belorussian Front into East Prussia. Abakumov had ensured that the 12,000-strong NKVD forces directly under his command were the largest of all those attached to army groups invading Germany. They were larger even than those with Marshal Zhukov's armies.

Wet snow lay all around. To judge from Abakumov's report to Beria, the NKVD troops dismounted and blocked the road, while he and the SMERSH officers began their inspection. Since German booby traps had been reported in the Rastenburg area, they were no doubt cautious. To the right of the entrance barrier stood several stone blockhouses which contained mines and camouflage material. On the left-hand side there were barrack blocks where the guards had lived. The SMERSH officers found epaulettes and uniforms from the *Führerbegleit* battalion. Hitler's fear the previous year of being captured by a surprise Soviet parachute drop had led 'the Führer's guard battalion to be increased to a mixed brigade'.

Following the road deeper into the forest, Abakumov saw signs on either side of the road. These were translated for him by his interpreter: 'It is forbidden to step off the road' and 'Beware mines!' Abakumov was clearly taking notes the whole time for his report to Beria, which he knew would be passed to Stalin. The Boss was obsessively interested in all details of Hitler's life.

The most striking aspect of Abakumov's report, however, is the degree of Soviet ignorance it reveals about the place. This is especially surprising when one considers how many German generals they had captured and interrogated between the surrender at Stalingrad and the beginning of 1945. They appear to have taken almost two weeks to find this complex, four kilometres square. Concealment from the air was indeed impressive. Every road and alley was covered with green camouflage nets. Straight lines were broken with artificial trees and bushes. All the exterior lights had dark blue bulbs. Even the observation posts, up to thirty-five metres high in the forest, had been made to look like pine trees.

When they entered the first inner perimeter, Abakumov observed the 'ferro-concrete defences, barbed wire, minefields and large numbers of fire positions and barracks for guards'. At Gate No. 1 all the bunkers had been blown up after the Führer's final departure on 20 November 1944, less than three months before, but Abakumov clearly had no idea when the complex had been abandoned. They came to a second perimeter fence of barbed wire, then a third. Within the central compound, they found bunkers with armoured shutters linked to an underground garage capable of taking eighteen cars.

'We entered with great care,' Abakumov wrote. They found a safe but it was empty. The rooms, he noted, were 'very simply furnished'. (The place had once been described as a cross between a monastery and a concentration camp.) The SMERSH officers were only certain that they had found the right place when they discovered a sign on a door which read, 'Führer's Wehrmacht Adjutant'. Hitler's room was identified by a photograph of him with Mussolini.

Abakumov did not reveal any emotion over the fact that they were standing at last in the place from where Hitler had directed his merciless onslaught against the Soviet Union. He seemed far more preoccupied by the ferro-concrete constructions and their dimensions. Deeply impressed, he appears to have wondered whether Beria and Stalin might like something similar constructed: 'I think it would be interesting for our specialists to inspect Hitler's headquarters and see all these well-organized bunkers,' he wrote. Despite their imminent victory, Soviet leaders did not appear to feel so very much more secure than their arch-enemy.

The SMERSH detachments and NKVD divisions attached to the Fronts were, in Stalin's own words, 'indispensable' to deal with 'all unreliable elements encountered in occupied territories'. 'The divisions have no artillery,' Stalin had told General Bull of the US Army during the meeting with Air Marshal Tedder, 'but they are strong in automatic weapons, armoured cars and light armoured vehicles. They must also have well developed investigation and interrogation facilities.'

In German territories, such as East Prussia and Silesia, the first priority of the NKVD rifle regiments was to round up or hunt down German stragglers bypassed in the advance. Soviet authorities defined each Volkssturm man as a member of the Wehrmacht, but since almost

every male between fifteen and fifty-five was called up, that included a
large majority of local men. Those Volkssturm members who remained
at home, rather than fleeing on the treks, were thus in many cases
marked down as stay-behind sabotage groups, however elderly. Over
200 German 'saboteurs and terrorists' were reported 'shot on the spot'
by NKVD forces, but the true figure was likely to have been far higher.

In Poland, Stalin's description of 'unreliable elements' did not refer
to the tiny minority of Poles who had collaborated with the Germans.
It applied to all those who supported the Polish government in exile and
the Armia Krajowa, which had launched the Warsaw Uprising the
previous year. Stalin regarded the Warsaw revolt against the Germans
as a 'criminal act of an anti-Soviet policy'. In his eyes, it was clearly an
attempt to seize the Polish capital for the 'émigré government in London'
just before the arrival of the Red Army, which had done all the fighting
and dying. His shameful betrayal of Poland to the Nazis in 1939 and
Beria's massacre of Polish officers at Katyn were evidently not worth
considering. He also ignored the fact that the Poles had proportionately
suffered even more than the Soviet Union, losing over 20 per cent of
their population. Stalin was convinced that Poland and its government
was his by right of conquest, and this proprietorial sentiment was widely
shared within the Red Army. When Soviet forces crossed the German
frontier from Poland, many 'felt that we had at last cleansed our own
territory', instinctively assuming that Poland was an integral part of the
Soviet Union.

Stalin's claim at Yalta that the Communist provisional government
enjoyed great popularity in Poland was, of course, a totally subjective
statement. Zhukov's memoirs were rather more revealing when he
referred to the Poles in general, then added, 'some of whom were
loyal to us'. Opponents to Soviet rule were designated 'enemy agents',
whatever their record of resistance to the Germans. The fact that the
Armia Krajowa was an Allied force was ignored. In another interesting
sentence, Zhukov referred to the need to control his own troops: 'We
had to make the educational work even more developed among all troops
of the Front so that there would not be any thoughtless acts from the
start of our stay.' Their 'stay' was to last over forty-five years.

The degree of Beria's control over the Polish provisional government
was indicated by the appointment of General Serov himself as 'adviser'

at Poland's ministry of security on 20 March under the name 'Ivanov'. Advisers do not come much higher than Commissar of State Security of the Second Rank. Serov was particularly well qualified for the post. He had overseen the mass deportations from the Caucasus and previously had been in charge of the repression in Lvov in 1939, when the Soviet Union seized eastern Poland and arrested and killed officers, landowners, priests and teachers who might oppose their rule. Some 2 million Poles were deported to the Gulag and a campaign of forced collectivization began.

Stalin's deliberate policy was to confuse the Armia Krajowa with the Ukrainian nationalist force, the UPA, or at least imply that they were closely linked. Goebbels, meanwhile, seized upon every example of partisan resistance to Soviet occupation. He claimed that there were 40,000 men in the Estonian resistance, 10,000 in Lithuania and 50,000 in the Ukraine. He even quoted *Pravda* of 7 October 1944, claiming that there were 'Ukrainian-German nationalists'. All this gave even more excuse to the NKVD regiments in their 'cleansing of the rear areas'. It was a good example of both sides feeding profitably on each other's propaganda.

Another Polish potential enemy was also investigated in early March. Almost as soon as SMERSH was established in Poland, it launched an 'inquiry into Rokossovsky's relatives', presumably to see whether any of them could be defined as 'enemy elements'. Marshal Rokossovsky was half-Polish, and this investigation was almost certainly carried out on Beria's instructions. He had not forgotten that Rokossovsky had escaped his grasp. Nikolai Bulganin, the political member of Rokossovsky's military council of the 2nd Belorussian Front, was Stalin's watchdog.

Stalin's determination to stamp out the Armia Krajowa later turned a minor incident into a major contretemps between the Soviet Union and the United States. On 5 February, just as the Yalta conference was getting under way, Lieutenant Myron King of the US Air Force made an emergency landing in his B-17 at Kuflevo. A young Pole appeared and asked to leave with them. They took him on board and flew on to the Soviet airbase at Shchuchin, where they could repair the aircraft properly. The crew lent him articles of uniform, and when they landed 'the civilian pretended to be Jack Smith, a member of the crew', General Antonov wrote in his official complaint. 'Only after intervention by the Soviet command,' Antonov continued, 'Lieutenant King announced that this was not a member of the crew, but a stranger whom they did not know and took on board the airplane to take him away to England.' 'According to our information,' Antonov concluded, 'he was a terrorist-saboteur brought into Poland from London.' The United States government apologized profusely. It even organized King's court martial in the Soviet Union at their borrowed air base near Poltava and requested Antonov to provide prosecution witnesses. Stalin played this incident up to the hilt. He told Averell Harriman that this proved that the United States was supplying the White Poles to attack the Red Army.

Another incident occurred on 22 March at the Soviet aviation base of Mielec, where an American Liberator landed due to lack of fuel. The Soviet commander, aware of the dangers after the King incident, put a guard on the plane and forced the crew to spend the night in a hut nearby. But the ten-man crew under Lieutenant Donald Bridge, after being held for two days, requested permission to fetch personal belongings from the aircraft. As soon as they were on board, they started the engines and took off, ignoring all signals to halt. 'Soviet Engineer-Captain Melamedev, who accepted Donald Bridge's crew,' wrote Antonov to General Reade in Moscow, 'was so indignant and put out by this instance [*sic*] that on the very same day he shot himself.' His death, however, may well have had more to do with the outrage of SMERSH officers at the 'negligence of the officer and guards who had been detailed to watch the plane'. This incident was also cited as 'proof' that 'enemy elements are using these landings to transport to Polish territory terrorists, saboteurs and agents of the Polish émigré government in London'.

It is hard to know whether the Soviet authorities were genuinely paranoid or had whipped themselves up into a self-perpetuating moral outrage. When an American lieutenant colonel who had been visiting released US prisoners of war in Lublin returned to Moscow after his pass had expired, General Antonov, no doubt on Stalin's instructions, grounded all US aircraft 'in the Soviet Union and in Red Army-controlled areas'.

*

In East Prussia, reports referred to 'German bands up to 1,000 strong' attacking the rear of Rokossovsky's 2nd Belorussian Front. NKVD units mounted 'sweeps through the forest to liquidate them'. In most cases, however, these bands consisted of a group of local Volkssturm men hiding in forests. Sometimes they ambushed trucks, motorcyclists and supply carts to get food. In Kreisburg, NKVD troops discovered two 'secret bakeries' making bread for soldiers out in the woods. Young women taking food out to them were captured by NKVD patrols.

On a sweep on 21 February, the 14th Cordon of the 127th Frontier Guards Regiment, led by Junior Lieutenant Khismatulin, was searching a patch of thick woodland when Sergeant Zavgorodny noticed woollen stockings hanging from a tree. 'This made him suspect the presence of unknown persons. They searched the area and found three well-camouflaged trenches leading to a bunker where they found three enemy soldiers with rifles.'

Mines and booby traps remained a major concern. To improve mine clearance, twenty-two dogs were allocated to each NKVD Frontier Guards Regiment. Sniffer dogs – 'special dogs for smelling bandits', as the report put it – were also brought in to round up more of the Germans hiding in East Prussian forests.

Many reports appear to have been dramatized and exaggerated by local commanders wanting to make their work sound more important. A report on captured 'terrorists handed over to SMERSH for interrogation' revealed that all these 'terrorists' were born before 1900. Tsanava, the NKVD chief of the 2nd Belorussian Front, reported the arrest of Ulrich Behr, a German born in 1906. 'He confessed under interrogation that in February 1945 he was engaged as a spy by a resident of German intelligence, Hauptmann Schrap. His mission was to stay in the rear of the Red Army to recruit agents and to carry out sabotage, intelligence and terroristic activities. Fulfilling this task, Behr recruited twelve agents.' On a number of occasions, stragglers or local Volkssturm soldiers were described as 'Left in the rear by German intelligence with the task of committing sabotage'. The most ridiculous incident was the 'sabotage of an electric power line near Hindenburg', in Silesia. After a fearsome search for culprits, this turned out to have been caused by Red Army artillery practice. Pieces of shrapnel had severed the cables.

On the other hand, when the chief of SMERSH with the 2nd

Belorussian Front claimed that his men had discovered 'a German sabotage school in the village of Kovalyowo', he may have been right. The names of those trained there were all Russian or Ukrainian. The Germans, in their desperation, had been resorting to the use of Soviet prisoners more and more. Many of these Russians and Ukrainians had probably volunteered in the hope of an easy way home, but even their prompt surrender to Soviet military authorities would not have saved them, to judge by other cases.

NKVD detachments seem to have spent more time searching houses and barns than combing the huge areas of forest. One detachment found a group of eight German women sitting in a hay stack. 'An attentive sergeant' found that they were not women, but 'German soldiers wearing women's dresses'. There were many reports of this nature.

It appears that East Prussian peasant families were often as naïve as their Russian counterparts. Patrols on house searches found that the inhabitants could not stop glancing at a particular object or leave it alone. In one house, the woman went to sit on a trunk. The NKVD soldiers pushed her aside and found a man hidden in the trunk. One patrol noted the worried glances of the owner of the house towards the bed. The NKVD soldiers pulled off the mattress and saw that the boards of the bed were very high. They removed the boards and found a man dressed in women's clothes. In another house they found a man hiding under the coats on a coat-stand. The man's feet were off the ground because he had strung himself up with a strap under his armpits. Usually, the most obvious hiding places were used, such as sheds, barns and hay ricks. Sniffer dogs soon found them. Only a few constructed underground refuges. Sometimes the NKVD patrols did not bother to search a house. They set it on fire, and those who were not burned to death were shot as they jumped from the windows.

While many Volkssturm men wanted to stay near their farms, stragglers from the Wehrmacht were trying to slip back through the lines to Germany. In many cases they dressed themselves in Red Army uniforms taken from soldiers they had killed. If caught, they were mostly shot on the spot. Any prisoners taken, whether German, Russian or Polish, were put in a 'preliminary prison'. These buildings were usually just a commandeered house with barbed wire nailed over the windows and the sign 'Jail: NKVD of the USSR' chalked up on a wall outside. They were then interrogated by SMERSH, and, depending on the confession obtained, were sent off to a camp or to forced labour battalions.

NKVD chiefs also kept a sharp eye on their business affairs. Major General Rogatin, the commander of NKVD troops with the 2nd Belorussian Front and formerly the NKVD commander at Stalingrad, discovered 'that in some [NKVD] units a majority of officers and soldiers are not engaged in their duty, but are active in the collection of looted property . . . It was established that looted property was shared out within the regiments without the knowledge of division staff. In the regiments there are cases of selling and bartering looted products, sugar, tobacco, wine and gasoline taken from drivers with the advancing units of the Red Army, and motorcycles. Such a situation in the [NKVD] regiments and absence of discipline has led to a sharp increase in extraordinary events. There are soldiers who do their duty, and then there are the others who are doing nothing but loot. The looters should now be put to work along with those who do their duty.' It appears that there was no question of punishing them, and the phrase 'without the knowledge of division staff' is most revealing. Divisional headquarters was outraged presumably because it had discovered that it was not receiving its share of the proceeds.

There can be little doubt that the Red Army resented the 'rear rats' in the NKVD, but the feeling ran both ways. The NKVD did not appreciate having to deal with ammunition and weapons abandoned by Germans and advancing units of Red Army. 'All this leads to massive stealing by bandits and the local population. It has been noticed that adolescents get hold of these weapons and organize armed groups and terrorize the population. This creates favourable conditions for the growth of banditry.' An order was also issued forbidding the use of grenades for fishing, a popular sport among Red Army men in the many lakes of East Prussia and Poland.

NKVD rifle regiments had to deal not only with German stragglers and Volkssturm living like outlaws in the forests, but also with groups of Red Army deserters. On 7 March, a group of 'fifteen armed deserters' ambushed an NKVD patrol of the 2nd Belorussian Front near the village of Dertz. Another group of eight was also living in the forest nearby. All had deserted at the end of December 1944. Two days later, the NKVD reported 'finding more deserters travelling away from the front in the rear areas'. Another 'bandit group' of deserters from the 3rd Army, led by a Ukrainian captain and Party member with the order of the Red Banner, who had deserted from hospital on 6 March, lived off the land round Ortelsburg. Their group, armed with sub-machine guns and pistols, was extremely mixed. It included men from Tula, Sverdlovsk, Voronezh and the Ukraine, as well as a Pole, three German women and another German man from the Ortelsburg district.

Most deserters, however, especially Belorussians and Ukrainians, many of whom were coopted Poles, tried to sneak home in ones and twos. Some dressed up as women. Others bandaged themselves up, then went to railheads and stole the documents of wounded men. A new special pass for wounded men had to be brought in to stop this. Sometimes men simply disappeared, and nobody knew whether they had deserted or been killed in battle. On 27 January, two T-34 tanks from the 6th Guards Tank Corps in East Prussia left on an operation and neither the tanks nor the sixteen tankists and infantrymen with them were ever seen again, dead or alive.

In spite of the large numbers of NKVD troops in the rear areas, there was astonishingly little control over Red Army personnel. 'The Soviet military leadership,' stated a German intelligence report of 9 February, 'is concerned about the growing lack of discipline as a result of their advance into what for Russians is a prosperous region.' Property was being looted and destroyed and civilians needed for forced labour were killed for little reason. Chaos was also caused by the number of civilian 'citizens of the USSR who come to East Prussia to collect captured property'.

The senseless death of a Hero of the Soviet Union, Colonel Gorelov, commander of a guards tank brigade, horrified many officers in the 1st Belorussian Front. At the beginning of February he was sorting out a traffic jam on the road a few kilometres from the German border and was shot by drunken soldiers. 'Such cases of bloody drunken violence are not isolated,' Grossman noted. A single NKVD regiment lost five dead and thirty-four men injured from being run down by drivers during the first ten weeks of the year.

The young women traffic controllers did not blow whistles when attempting to restore order in traffic jams, they fired their sub-machine guns in the air. On one occasion behind the 2nd Belorussian Front, a young woman traffic controller called Lydia ran up to the driver's window of a vehicle which had blocked the road. She began to yell obscenities at him. This had little effect. Obscenities were yelled back at her. But then she received unexpected reinforcements in the tall and impressive form of Marshal Rokossovsky, who had leaped from his staff car, drawing his pistol in anger. When the driver saw the marshal he was literally paralysed with fear. His officer lost his head completely. He jumped out of the cab and ran into the bushes to hide.

The entry of Soviet forces into German territory meant that Stalin's plans to force Germans to work for the Soviet Union could be put into action. On 6 February an order was issued to 'mobilize all Germans fit for work from seventeen to fifty years of age and to form labour battalions of 1,000 to 1,200 men each and send them to Belorussia and the Ukraine to repair war damage'. The Germans mobilized were told to report to assembly points wearing warm clothes and good boots. They were also to bring bedding, reserves of underwear and two weeks' food supply.

With Volkssturm members sent to prisoner-of-war camps, the NKVD managed to conscript only 68,680 German forced labourers by 9 March, the vast majority in the rear of Zhukov and Konev's armies. A large proportion were women. At first, many of the so-called labour battalions were used locally for rubble clearance and assisting the Red Army. The attitude of Soviet soldiers towards the conscripted civilians was one of intense *schadenfreude*. Agranenko watched a Red Army corporal form up a working party of German men and women in four lines. He barked out the word of command in pidgin-German, 'To Siberia, fuck you!'

By 10 April, the proportion sent back to the Soviet Union for forced labour increased rapidly, with 59,536 sent to western parts, mostly the Ukraine. Although still fewer than Stalin had planned, they suffered at least as much as their Soviet counterparts rounded up earlier by the Wehrmacht. It was naturally worst for the women. Many were forced to leave children behind with relatives or friends. In some cases they had even been forced to abandon them altogether. Their life ahead was not simply one of subjection to hard labour, but also to casual rape by guards, with venereal infections as a by-product. Another 20,000 men were put to 'demontage work', stripping the factories of Silesia.

Stalin may have described the NKVD rifle regiments to General Bull as 'a gendarmerie', but it is still striking how little they intervened to stop looting, rape and the random murder of civilians. There appears to be only one example of intervention in their reports. In April, a group from the NKVD 217th Frontier Guards Regiment arrested five soldiers who broke into a 'hostel of repatriated Polish women'.

Quite how little the NKVD troops were doing to protect civilians from violence of every sort is indirectly revealed in their own chiefs' reports to Beria. On 8 March, Serov, the NKVD representative with the 1st Belorussian Front, reported on the continuing wave of suicides. On 12 March, two months after Chernyakhovsky's offensive began, the NKVD chief in northern East Prussia reported to Beria that 'suicides of Germans, particularly women, are becoming more and more widespread'. For those who did not have a pistol or poison, most of the suicides consisted of people hanging themselves in attics with the rope tied to the rafters. A number of women, unable to bring themselves to hang a child, cut their children's wrists first and then their own.

NKVD rifle regiments did not punish their own soldiers for rape, they punished them only if they caught venereal disease from victims, who had usually caught it from a previous rapist. Rape itself, in a typically Stalinist euphemism, was referred to as an 'immoral event'. It is interesting that Russian historians today still produce evasive circumlocutions. 'Negative phenomena in the army of liberation,' writes one on the subject of mass rape, 'caused significant damage to the prestige of the Soviet Union and the armed forces and could have a negative influence in the future relations with the countries through which our troops were passing.'

This sentence also indirectly acknowledges that there were many cases of rape in Poland. But far more shocking from a Russian point of view is the fact that Red Army officers and soldiers also raped Ukrainian, Russian and Belorussian women and girls released from slave labour in Germany. Many of the girls were as young as sixteen when taken to the Reich; some were just fourteen. The widespread raping of women taken forcibly from the Soviet Union completely undermines any attempts at justifying Red Army behaviour on the grounds of revenge for German brutality in the Soviet Union. The evidence for this is certainly not restricted just to the unpublished notebooks of Vasily Grossman. A very detailed report goes much further.

On 29 March, the Central Committee of the Komsomol (Communist Youth) informed Stalin's associate Malenkov of a report from the 1st Ukrainian Front. 'This memorandum is about young people taken to Germany and liberated by the troops of the Red Army. Tsygankov [the deputy chief of the political department of the 1st Ukrainian Front] relates numerous extraordinary facts which affect the great happiness of Soviet citizens released from German slavery. Young people express their gratitude to Comrade Stalin and the Red Army for their salvation.'

'On the night of 24 February,' Tsygankov reported in the first of many examples, 'a group of thirty-five provisional lieutenants on a course and their battalion commander entered the women's dormitory in the village of Grutenberg, ten kilometres east of Els, and raped them.' Three days later, 'an unknown senior lieutenant of tank troops went by horse to where girls were gathering grain. He left his horse and spoke to a girl from the Dnepropetrovsk region called Gritsenko, Anna. "Where are you from?" he asked. She answered this senior lieutenant. He ordered her to come closer. She refused. So he took his gun and shot her, but she did not die. Many similar incidents took place.'

'In the town of Bunslau, there are over 100 women and girls in the headquarters. They live in a separate building not far from the kommandantur, but there is no security there and because of this, there are many offences and even rape of women who live in this dormitory by different soldiers who enter the dormitory at night and terrorize the women. On 5 March late at night, sixty officers and soldiers entered, mainly from the 3rd Guards Tank Army. Most of them were drunk, and they attacked and offended against women and girls. Even though they were ordered by the commandant to leave the dormitory, the group of tankists threatened him with their guns and caused a scuffle . . . This is not the only incident. It happens every night and because of this, those who stay in Bunslau are frightened and demoralized and there is much dissatisfaction among them. One of them, Maria Shapoval, said, "I waited for the Red Army for days and nights. I waited for my liberation, and now our soldiers treat us worse than the Germans did. I am not happy to be alive."' 'It was very hard to stay with Germans,' Klavdia Malaschenko said, 'but now it is very unhappy. This is not liberation. They treat us terribly. They do terrible things to us.'

'There are many cases of offences against them,' Tsygankov continued. 'On the night of 14–15 February in one of the villages where the cattle are herded a *shtraf* company under the command of a senior lieutenant surrounded the village and shot the Red Army soldiers who were on guard there. They went to the women's dormitory and started their organized mass rape of the women, who had just been liberated by the Red Army.'

'There are also many offences by officers against women. Three officers on 26 February entered the dormitory in the bread depot, and when Major Soloviev (the commandant) tried to stop them, one of them, a major, said, "I've just come from the front and I need a woman." After that he debauched himself in the dormitory.'

'Lantsova, Vera, born 1926, was raped twice – first when the vanguard troops came through the territory, and second on 14 February by a soldier. From 15–22 February Lieutenant Isaev A. A. made her sleep with him by beating her and frightening her with threats that he would shoot her. A number of officers, sergeants and soldiers tell the liberated women, "There is an order not to allow you back to the Soviet Union, and if they do allow some of you back, you will live in the north" [i.e. in Gulag camps]. Because of such attitudes to the women and girls, many women think that in the Red Army and in their country, they are not treated as Soviet citizens and that anything can be done to them – killed, raped, beaten and that they will not be allowed home.'

The notion that Soviet women and girls taken for slave labour in Germany 'had sold themselves to the Germans' was very widespread in the Red Army, which provides part of the explanation of why they were so badly treated. Young women who had somehow managed to stay alive under Wehrmacht occupation were known as 'German dolls'. There was even an airman's song about it:

> Young girls are smiling at Germans
> Having forgotten about their guys . . .
> When times became hard, you forgot your falcons,
> And sold yourselves to Germans for a crust of bread.

It is hard to pin down the origin of this assumption about women collaborating with the enemy. It cannot be traced to remarks made by political officers in late 1944 or early 1945, yet it appears that a general idea had earlier been fomented by the regime that any Soviet citizen taken to Germany, either as a prisoner of war or as a slave labourer, had tacitly consented because they had failed to kill themselves or 'join the partisans'. Any notion of 'the honour and dignity of the Soviet girl' was accorded only to young women serving in the Red Army or the war industries. But it is perhaps significant that, according to one woman officer, female soldiers in the Red Army started to be treated badly by their male counterparts from the time that Soviet troops moved on to foreign territory.

Official complaints of rape to a senior officer were worse than useless. 'For example, Eva Shtul, born 1926, said, "My father and two brothers joined the Red Army at the beginning of the war. Soon the Germans came and I was taken to Germany by force. I worked in a factory here. I cried and waited for the day of liberation. Soon the Red Army came and its soldiers dishonoured me. I cried and told the senior officer about my brothers in the Red Army and he beat me and raped me. It would have been better if he had killed me."'

'All this,' concluded Tsygankov, 'provides fertile ground for unhealthy, negative moods to grow among liberated Soviet citizens; it causes discontent and mistrust before their return to their mother country.' His recommendations, however, did not focus on tightening Red Army discipline. He suggested instead that the main political department of the Red Army and the Komsomol should concentrate on 'improving political and cultural work with repatriated Soviet citizens' so that they should not return home with negative ideas about the Red Army.

By 15 February, the 1st Ukrainian Front alone had liberated 49,500 Soviet citizens and 8,868 foreigners from German forced labour, mainly in Silesia. But this represented only a small percentage of the total. Just over a week later, the Soviet authorities in Moscow estimated that they should prepare to receive and process a total of 4 million former Red Army soldiers and civilian deportees.

The first priority was not medical care for those who had suffered so appallingly in German camps, it was a screening process to weed out traitors. The second priority was political re-education for those who had been subject to foreign contamination. Both the 1st Belorussian Front and the 1st Ukrainian Front were ordered to set up three assembly and transit camps well to their rear in Poland. The re-education teams each had a mobile film unit, a radio with a loudspeaker, two accordions, a library of 20,000 Communist Party booklets, forty metres of red fabric for decorating premises and a set of portraits of Comrade Stalin.

Solzhenitsyn wrote of liberated prisoners of war, with their heads down as they were marched along. They feared retribution simply for having surrendered. But the need for reinforcements was so great that the vast majority were sent to reserve regiments for re-education and retraining, in order to have them ready for the final offensive on Berlin. This, however, was just a temporary reprieve. Another screening would come later when the fighting was over, and even those who fought heroically in the battle for Berlin were not immune from being sent to the camps later.

The Red Army's urgent need of more 'meat for the cannon' meant that former slave labourers without any military training were also conscripted on the spot. And most of the 'western Belorussians' and 'western Ukrainians' from the regions seized by Stalin in 1939 still regarded themselves as Poles. But they were given little choice in the matter.

Once they reached the screening camp, the liberated Soviet prisoners had many questions. 'What will be their status? Will they have full citizens' rights on returning to Russia? Will they be deprived in some way? Will they be sent to the camps?' Once again the Soviet authorities did not acknowledge that these were pertinent questions. They were immediately attributed to 'fascist propaganda, because the Germans terrified our people in Germany and this false propaganda was intensified towards the end of the war'.

The political workers in the camps gave talks, mainly of Red Army successes and the achievements of the Soviet rear, and about the Party leaders, especially Comrade Stalin. 'They also show them Soviet movies,' reported the chief of the political department of the 1st Ukrainian Front. 'The people like them very much, they cry "Hooray!" very often, especially when Stalin appears, and "Long live the Red Army", and after the cinema show they go away crying in happiness. Among those who were liberated are only a few who betrayed the Motherland.' In the screening camp in Kraków, only four were arrested as traitors out of a total of forty suspects. Yet these figures were to rise greatly later.

There are stories, and it is very hard to know how true they are, that even forced labourers from the Soviet Union were executed shortly after liberation without any investigation. For example, the Swedish military attaché heard that after the occupation of Oppeln in Silesia, around 250 of them were summoned to a political meeting. Immediately afterwards, they were cornered by Red Army or NKVD troops. Somebody yelled a question at them demanding why they had not become partisans, then the soldiers opened fire.

The term 'Traitor of the Motherland' did not just cover soldiers recruited from prison camps by the Germans. It was to cover Red Army soldiers who had been captured in 1941, some of whom had been so badly wounded that they could not fight to the end. Solzhenitsyn argued in their case that the phrase 'Traitor *of* the Motherland', rather than 'Traitor *to* the Motherland' was a significant Freudian slip. 'They were not traitors *to her*. They were *her* traitors. It was not they, the unfortunates, who had betrayed the Motherland, but their calculating Motherland who had betrayed them.' The Soviet state had betrayed them through incompetence and lack of preparation in 1941. It had then refused to acknowledge their dreadful fate in German prison camps. And the final betrayal came when they were encouraged to believe that they had redeemed themselves by their bravery in the last weeks of the war, only to be arrested after the fighting was over. Solzhenitsyn felt that 'to betray one's own soldiers and proclaim them traitors' was the foulest deed in Russian history.

Few Red Army soldiers, whether prisoners of war or those fortunate enough never to have been captured, would ever forgive those who had put on German uniform whatever the circumstances. Members of Vlasov's ROA, known as *Vlasovtsy*, SS volunteers, Ukrainian and Caucasian camp guards, General von Pannwitz's Cossack cavalry corps, police teams, anti-partisan 'security detachments' and even the unfortunate 'Hiwis' (short for *Hilfsfreiwillige*, or volunteer helpers) were all tarred with the same brush.

Estimates for all categories range between 1 million and 1.5 millon men. Red Army authorities insisted that there had been over a million Hiwis serving in the Wehrmacht. Those taken, or who surrendered voluntarily, were frequently shot on the spot or soon afterwards. '*Vlasovtsy* and other accomplices of the Nazis were usually executed on the spot,' the latest Russian official history states. 'This is not surprising. The battle code of the Red Army infantry demanded that each soldier must "be ruthless to all turncoats and traitors of the Motherland".' It also appears to have been a matter of regional honour. Men from their area would be found to take revenge: 'A man from Orel kills a man from Orel and an Uzbek kills an Uzbek.'

The NKVD troops were understandably merciless in their search for Ukrainians and Caucasians who had worked as camp guards, where they had frequently proved themselves even more brutal than their German overseers. Yet the fact that Red Army prisoners of war could be treated in virtually the same way as those who had put on enemy uniform was part of a systematic attitude within the NKVD. 'There must be a single view of all the categories of prisoners,' the NKVD rifle regiments in the 2nd Belorussian Front were told. Deserters, robbers and former prisoners of war were to be treated in the same way as 'those who betrayed our state'.

While it is extremely hard to have any sympathy for camp guards, the vast majority of the Hiwis had been brutally press-ganged or starved into submission. Of the categories in between, many who served in SS or German army units were nationalists, whether Ukrainians, Balts, Cossacks or Caucasians, all of whom hated Soviet rule from Moscow. Some *Vlasovtsy* had had no compunction about joining their former enemy because they had not forgiven the arbitrary executions of friends by Red Army officers and blocking detachments during 1941 and 1942. Others were peasants who loathed forced collectivization. Yet many of the ordinary Vlasov soldiers and Hiwis were often extraordinarily naïve and ill-informed. A Russian interpreter in a German prisoner-of-war camp recounted how, at one propaganda meeting to recruit volunteers for Vlasov's army, a Russian prisoner put up his hand and said, 'Comrade President, we would like to know how many cigarettes one is given per day in the Vlasov army?' Evidently for many, an army was just an army. What difference did it make whose uniform you wore, especially if you were fed, instead of being starved and maltreated in a camp? All of those who followed that route were to suffer far more than they had ever imagined. Even those who survived fifteen or twenty years in the Gulag after the war remained marked men. Those thought to have cooperated with the enemy did not have their civic rights restored until the fiftieth anniversary of the victory in 1995.

Letters were found on Russian prisoners of war who had served in the German Army, almost certainly as Hiwis. One, barely literate, was written on a blank fly-leaf torn from a German book. 'Comrade soldiers,' it said, 'we give ourselves up to you begging a big favour. Tell us please why are you killing those Russian people from German prisons? We happened to be captured and then they took us to work for their regiments and we worked purely in order not to starve to death. Now these people happen to get to the Russian side, back to their own army, and you shoot them. What for, we ask. Is it because the Soviet command betrayed these people in 1941 and 1942?'

8

Pomerania and the Oder Bridgeheads

In February and March, while bitter fighting continued for the Oder bridgeheads opposite Berlin, Zhukov and Rokossovsky crushed the 'Baltic balcony' of Pomerania and West Prussia. In the second and third weeks of February, Rokossovsky's four armies across the Vistula pushed into the southern part of West Prussia. Then, on 24 February, Zhukov's right-flank armies and Rokossovsky's left flank forced northwards towards the Baltic to split Pomerania in two.

The most vulnerable German formation was the Second Army. It still just managed to keep open the last land route from East Prussia along the Frische Nehrung sandbar to the Vistula estuary. The Second Army, with its left flank just across the Nogat in Elbing and maintaining a foothold in the Teutonic Knights' castle of Marienburg, was the most overstretched of all Army Group Vistula.

Rokossovsky's attack began on 24 February. The 19th Army advanced north-westwards towards the area between Neustettin and Baldenburg, but its troops were shaken by the ferocity of the fighting and it faltered. Rokossovsky sacked the army commander, pushed a tank corps into the attack as well, and forced them on. The combination of the tank corps and the 2nd and 3rd Guards Cavalry Corps led to the rapid fall of Neustettin, the 'cornerstone' of the Pomeranian defence line.

Soviet cavalry played a successful part in the reduction of Pomerania. They captured several towns on their own, such as the seaside town of Leba, mainly by surprise. The 2nd Guards Cavalry Corps, which formed the extreme right of Zhukov's 1st Belorussian Front, was commanded by Lieutenant General Vladimir Viktorovich Kryukov, a resourceful leader married to Russia's favourite folk-singer, Lydia Ruslanova.

Zhukov's attack northwards some fifty kilometres east of Stettin began in earnest on 1 March. Combining the 3rd Shock Army and the 1st and 2nd Guards Tank Army, it was a far stronger force. The weak German divisions did not stand a chance. The leading tank brigades dashed ahead, charging through towns where unprepared civilians stared at them in horror. The 3rd Shock Army and the 1st Polish Army coming behind consolidated their gains. On 4 March, the 1st Guards Tank Army reached the Baltic near Kolberg. Colonel Morgunov, the commander of the 45th Guards Tank Brigade, the first to reach the sea, sent bottles of saltwater to Zhukov and to Katukov, his army commander. It proved Katukov's dictum. 'The success of the advance,' he had told Grossman, 'is determined by our huge mechanized power, which is now greater than it has ever been. A colossal rapidity of advance means small losses and the enemy is scattered.'

The whole of the German Second Army and part of the Third Panzer Army were now completely cut off from the Reich. And as if to emphasize the Baltic catastrophe, news arrived that Finland, albeit under heavy pressure from the Soviet Union, had declared war the day before on her former ally, Nazi Germany. Among those cut off to the east of Zhukov's thrust was the SS *Charlemagne* Division, already greatly reduced from its strength of 12,000 men. Along with three German divisions, they had been positioned near Belgard. General von Tettau ordered them to try to break out north-westwards towards the Baltic coast at the mouth of the Oder. The *Charlemagne* commander, SS Brigadeführer Gustav Krukenberg, accompanied 1,000 of his Frenchmen on silent compass marches through snow-laden pine forests. As things turned out, part of this ill-assorted group of right-wing intellectuals, workers and reactionary aristocrats, united only by their ferocious anti-Communism, was to form the last defence of Hitler's Chancellery in Berlin.

Hitler, however, demonstrated scant sympathy for the defenders of his Reich. When the commander of the Second Army, Colonel General Weiss, warned Führer headquarters that the Elbing pocket, which had cost so much blood already, could not be held much longer, Hitler simply retorted, 'Weiss is a liar, like all generals.'

The second phase of the Pomeranian campaign began almost immediately, only two days after the 1st Guards Tank Army reached the sea. The 1st Guards Tank Army was transferred temporarily to Rokossovsky. Zhukov telephoned him to say that he wanted Katukov's army 'returned in the same state as you received it'. The operation consisted of a large, left-flanking wheel to roll up eastern Pomerania and Danzig from the west, while Rokossovsky's strongest formation, the 2nd Shock Army, attacked up from the south, parallel to the Vistula.

The commander of the Soviet 2nd Shock Army, Colonel General Fedyuninsky, was keeping a close eye on the calendar. He had been wounded four times in the course of the war. Every time it happened on the 20th of the month, and so now he never moved from his headquarters on that day. Fedyuninsky did not believe that the looted resources of Prussia should be squandered. He made his army load livestock, bread, rice, sugar and cheese on to trains, which were sent to Leningrad to compensate its citizens for their suffering during the terrible siege.

Fedyuninsky's advance cut off the German defenders of Marienburg castle, who had been assisted in their defence by salvoes fired from the heavy cruiser *Prinz Eugen*, out in the Baltic. The castle was abandoned on the night of 8 March, and two days later Elbing fell, as Weiss had warned. The German Second Army, threatened from the west and the south, pulled in to defend Danzig and Gdynia to allow as many civilians and wounded as possible to be evacuated from the ports packed with refugees.

On 8 March, just two days after the start of the westward sweep on Danzig, Soviet forces occupied the town of Stolp unopposed, and two days later, the 1st Guards Tank Army and the 19th Army reached Lauenburg. A refugee column fleeing for the ports was overtaken by a tank brigade. Women and children fled, stumbling through the snow, to shelter in the forest while Soviet tanks crushed their carts under their tracks. They were more fortunate than other trek columns.

Not far from Lauenburg, Red Army troops discovered another concentration camp. This was a women's camp, and their doctors immediately set to work caring for the survivors.

The fate of Pomeranian families was similar to those in East Prussia. Himmler had forbidden the evacuation of civilians from eastern

Pomerania, so around 1.2 million were cut off by the thrust north to the Baltic on 4 March. They had also been deprived of news, just as in East Prussia. But most families had heard rumours and, refusing to trust the Nazi authorities, they prepared themselves.

Landowning families – 'the manor folk', as the villagers called them – knew that they were the most likely to be shot, and their tenants urged them to leave for their own good. Carriages and carts were prepared. Near Stolp, Libussa von Oldershausen, the stepdaughter of Baron Jesko von Puttkammer, who had refused to sacrifice the local Volkssturm at Schneidemühl, was nine months pregnant. The estate carpenter built a wagon frame over which the large carpet from the library was fastened to provide shelter from the snow. The expectant mother would lie inside on a mattress.

In the early hours of 8 March, Libussa was woken by a pounding on the door. 'Trek orders!' somebody shouted. 'Get up! Hurry! We're leaving as soon as possible.' She dressed as quickly as she could and packed her jewels. The manor house was already full of refugees and some of them began to loot the rooms even before the family had left.

As many Pomeranian and East Prussian families found, their French prisoner-of-war labourers insisted on coming with them rather than wait behind to be liberated by the Red Army. The rumble of artillery fire could be heard in the distance as they climbed into the converted cart and other horse-drawn vehicles. They headed east for Danzig. But even with a headstart, their horse-drawn carts were outpaced in a few days by Katukov's tank brigades.

Libussa awoke in the middle of the night after they had heard that they would not reach safety in time. By the light of a candle-stump, she saw that her stepfather had put on his uniform and medals. Her mother was also dressed. Since the Red Army was bound to cut them off, they had decided to commit suicide. Nemmersdorf and recent atrocity tales from East Prussia had convinced them that they should not be taken alive. 'It's time,' said Baron Jesko. 'The Russians will be here in an hour or two.' Libussa accompanied them outside, planning to do the same, but at the last moment she suddenly changed her mind. 'I want to go with you, but I can't. I'm carrying the baby, my baby. It's kicking so hard. It wants to live. I can't kill it.' Her mother understood and said that she would stay with her. The baron, bewildered and dismayed, was forced to get rid of his uniform and pistol. Their only hope of survival was to be indistinguishable from the other refugees when the Red Army arrived. They must not be spotted as 'lordships'.

The first sign that Soviet troops had arrived was a signal flare which shot out of a plantation of firs. It was rapidly followed by the roar of tank engines. Small trees were crushed flat as the tanks emerged like monsters from the forest. A couple of them fired their main armament to intimidate the villagers, then sub-machine gunners fanned out to search the houses. They fired short bursts on entering rooms to cow those inside. This brought down a shower of plaster. They were not the conquerors the Germans had expected. Their shabby brown uniforms, stained and ripped, their boots falling to pieces and lengths of string used instead of gun slings were so unlike images of the victorious Wehrmacht projected in newsreels earlier in the war.

Looting was carried out briskly with cries of '*Uri Uri!*' as the Soviet soldiers went round grabbing watches. Pierre, their French prisoner of war, protested in vain that he was an ally. He received a rifle butt in the stomach. They then searched the refugees' luggage and bundles until they heard orders yelled by their officers outside. The soldiers stuffed their booty down the fronts of their padded jackets and ran out to rejoin their armoured vehicles.

The civilians, shaking with a mixture of fear and relief that they had survived this first encounter with the dreaded enemy, suddenly faced the second wave, in this case a cavalry detachment. They had more time, which meant time to rape. The door was thrown open and a small group of Red Army soldiers came in to pick their victims.

Hitler had sacked General Weiss, the commander of the Second Army, for having warned Führer headquarters that Elbing could not be held. In his place, he had appointed General von Saucken, the former commander of the *Grossdeutschland* Corps.

On 12 March, General von Saucken was summoned to the Reich Chancellery to be briefed on his new appointment. This former cavalryman entered the room wearing a monocle and the Knight's Cross with Swords and Oak Leaves at his neck. Slim and elegant, Saucken was an ultra-conservative who openly despised the '*braune Bande*' of Nazis. Hitler asked Guderian to brief him on the situation in Danzig. Once that was completed, Hitler told Saucken that he must take his orders from the Gauleiter, Albert Förster. General von Saucken stared back at Hitler. 'I have no intention,' he replied, 'of placing myself under the orders of a Gauleiter.' Not only had Saucken flatly contradicted Hitler, he had failed to address him as '*Mein Führer*'. Even Guderian, who had been through more rows with Hitler than most people, was shaken. Yet onlookers were even more surprised by Hitler's acquiescence. 'All right, Saucken,' he replied weakly. 'Keep the command to yourself.'

Saucken flew to Danzig the next day. He was determined to hold the two ports to allow the escape of as many civilians as possible. It was estimated that Danzig's population was swollen to 1.5 million and that there were at least 100,000 wounded. Amid the chaos, the SS began seizing stragglers at random and hanging them from trees as deserters. Food was desperately short. A 21,000-ton supply ship hit a mine and sank with six days' supplies for Danzig and Gdynia.

The Kriegsmarine not only demonstrated extraordinary tenacity and bravery in the evacuation, it also continued to give offshore fire support despite constant air attacks and the threat of torpedoes from Soviet submarines of the Baltic Fleet. The cruisers *Prinz Eugen* and *Leipzig* and the old battleship *Schlesien* thundered away with their main armament at the encircling Red Army. But on 22 March, the Red Army smashed the Danzig–Gdynia defence perimeter in the middle, between the two ports. Soon both came under accurate artillery fire in addition to the never-ending raids by Soviet aviation.

Fighter bombers strafed the towns and the port areas. Soviet Shturmoviks treated civilian and military targets alike. A church was as good as a bunker, especially when it seemed as if the objective was to flatten every building which still protruded conspicuously above the ground. Wounded waiting on the quays to be embarked were riddled on their stretchers. Tens of thousands of women and children, terrified of losing their places in the queues to escape, provided unmissable targets. There was no time to help or pity the dead and injured. Only children, orphaned from one instant to the next, would be gathered up. And with the unremitting racket of the 88mm and light flak anti-aircraft batteries, nobody could hear their sobbing.

The scratch crews of the Kriegsmarine, using any craft available – tenders, barges, pinnaces, tugs and E-boats – returned in a constant shuttle to snatch the civilians and wounded to ferry them across to the small port of Hela at the tip of the nearby peninsula. Destroyers offshore gave the small boats as much anti-aircraft covering fire as possible. The sailors hardly ever faltered, even though a near miss was enough to overturn some of the smaller craft. On 25 March, a young woman from the Polish resistance brought General Katukov a plan of the Gdynia defence system. At first he thought it might be a trick, but it proved to be authentic. As the Soviet troops fought into the outskirts of Gdynia, the Kriegsmarine carried on, even accelerating its rhythm to grab as many refugees as possible before the end. Their boats now had to contend with another weapon. Katukov's tank crews had learned to adapt their gunnery to targets at sea, making it an even more dangerous task.

A fragment of a platoon from the *Grossdeutschland*, which had escaped amid nightmare scenes from the final evacuation of Memel at the most north-eastern point of East Prussia, found itself reliving a similar experience. Deciding to shelter in a vaulted cellar as Soviet troops fought towards the port, they found a doctor delivering a baby by the light of a couple of lanterns. 'If the birth of a child is usually a joyful event,' wrote one of the soldiers, 'this particular birth only seemed to add to the general tragedy. The mother's screams no longer had any meaning in a world made of screams, and the wailing child seemed to regret the beginning of its life.' The soldiers hoped for the child's sake, as they made their way down to the port, that it would die. The Soviet advance into Gdynia was marked by a horizon of red flames against thick black smoke. The final attack had begun, and by that evening of 26 March the Red Army was in possession of the town and port.

The sack of Gdynia and the treatment of the survivors appear to have shaken even the Soviet military authorities. 'The number of extraordinary events is growing,' the political department reported in its usual vocabulary of euphemisms, 'as well as immoral phenomena and military crimes. Among our troops there are disgraceful and politically harmful phenomena when, under the slogan of revenge, some officers and soldiers commit outrages and looting instead of honestly and selflessly fulfilling their duty to their Motherland.'

Just to the south, meanwhile, Danzig too was under heavy assault from the west. The defenders were forced back bit by bit, and by 28

March Danzig also fell, with appalling consequences for the remaining civilians. The remainder of Saucken's troops withdrew eastwards into the Vistula estuary, where they remained besieged until the end of the war.

For German officers, especially Pomeranians and Prussians, the loss of the Hanseatic city of Danzig, with its fine old buildings marked by distinctive stepped gables, was a disaster. It signified the end of German Baltic life for ever. Yet while mourning the loss of a long-established culture, they closed their eyes to the horrors of the regime which they had so effectively supported in its war aims. They may not have known about the manufacture of soap and leather from corpses in the Danzig Anatomical Medical Institute, but they certainly knew about Stutthof concentration camp in the Vistula estuary, because Wehrmacht troops, not just SS, had been involved in the massacre of its prisoners as the Red Army approached.

West Prussia and Pomerania may not have suffered quite as much as East Prussia, but the fate of civilians was still terrible. Their culture was also exterminated as churches and old buildings went up in flames.

The Soviet commandant of Lauenburg complained to Captain Agranenko that it was 'absolutely impossible to stop the violence'. Agranenko found that Red Army soldiers did not bother with official euphemisms for rape, such as 'violence against the civil population' or 'immorality'. They simply used the phrase 'to fuck'. A Cossack officer told him that German women were 'too proud'. You had to 'get astride' them. Others complained that German women looked 'like draught-horses'. In Glowitz, he noted that women were 'using children like a screen'. Soviet soldiers once again demonstrated an utterly bewildering mixture of irrational violence, drunken lust and spontaneous kindness to children.

Young women, desperate to escape the notice of soldiers, rubbed wood-ash and soot into their faces. They tied peasant headkerchiefs low over the brow, bundled themselves up to hide their figures and hobbled along the roadside like ancient crones. Yet this concealment of youth was no automatic safeguard. Many elderly women were raped as well.

German women developed their own verbal formulae for what they had been through. Many used to say, 'I had to concede.' One recounted that she had to concede thirteen times. 'Her horror seemed to contain a touch of pride at what she had endured,' Libussa von Oldershausen noted with surprise. But far more women were traumatized by their terrible experiences. Some became catatonic, others committed suicide. But as with Libussa von Oldershausen, pregnant women usually rejected this escape route. An instinctive duty to their unborn child became paramount.

A few women had the idea of dotting their faces with red to indicate spotted typhus. Others discovered the Russian word for typhus and its Cyrillic form in order to put up warning notices on their doors implying that the household was infected. In more remote areas, whole communities hid in farmsteads away from major routes. A lookout always remained close to the road, with a flashlight at night or a shirt to wave by day to warn of Soviet troops turning off towards their hiding place. Women then rushed to hide, and poultry and pigs were driven into pens concealed in the forest. Such precautions for survival must have been used in the Thirty Years War. They were probably as old as warfare itself.

Of all the signs of fighting which refugees found when forced to return home after the fall of Danzig, the worst were the 'gallows alleys' where SS and Feldgendarmerie had hanged deserters. Signs had been tied around their necks, such as, 'Here I hang because I did not believe in the Führer.' Libussa von Oldershausen and her family, forced to return home by the fall of the two ports, also saw a couple of Feldgendarmerie who had been caught and hanged by the Soviets. The route back was littered with wrecked wagons pushed into ditches by Soviet tanks, with looted baggage scattered all around, bedlinen, crockery, suitcases and toys. The carcasses of horses and cattle in roadside ditches had had strips of meat hacked from their flanks.

Many Pomeranians were murdered in the first week of occupation. Near the Puttkamers' village, an elderly couple were chased into the icy waters of a village pond, where they died. A man was harnessed to a plough, which he was forced to drag until he collapsed. His tormentors then finished him off with a burst of sub-machine-gun fire. Herr von Livonius, the owner of an estate at Grumbkow, was dismembered and his body thrown to the pigs. Even those landowners who had been part of the anti-Nazi resistance fared little better. Eberhard von Braunschweig and his family, assuming that they had little to fear, awaited the arrival of the Red Army in their manor house at Lübzow, near Karzin. But his reputation and numerous arrests by the Gestapo did him little good. The whole family was dragged outside and shot. Villagers and French prisoners of war sometimes bravely came to the defence of a well-liked landowner, but many others were left to their fate.

Nothing was predictable. In Karzin, the elderly Frau von Puttkamer retired to bed when the sounds of firing and tank engines could be heard. Not long afterwards, a young Soviet soldier opened her bedroom door, very drunk after the capture of the next-door village. He signalled for her to get out of bed to let him sleep there. She refused, saying that it was her bed, but that she would give him a pillow and he could sleep on the bedside rug. She then put her hands together and began to say her prayers. Too befuddled to argue, the young soldier lay down and slept where he had been told.

Just after the capture of Pomerania, Captain Agranenko, always the playwright collecting new material, travelled round taking notes. He observed that when he was scribbling away in his little notebook, people looked at him fearfully, thinking that he must be a member of the NKVD.

On 23 March, when in Kolberg, he exulted in the sudden arrival of spring weather. 'Birds are singing. Buds are opening. Nature does not care about war.' He watched Red Army soldiers trying to learn to ride their plundered bicycles. They were wobbling dangerously all over the place. In fact, Front commands issued an order forbidding them to ride bicycles on the road as so many of them were being knocked down and killed. The rapid invasion of Pomerania had liberated thousands of foreign workers and prisoners. At night, the roads were lined with their campfires. By day, they embarked on their long trudge home. Most of them had fashioned national flags to identify them as non-German. Agranenko and some other officers encountered some Lithuanians displaying their flag. 'We explained to them,' he wrote, 'that now their national flag is red.' Clearly Agranenko, like most Russians, regarded the Soviet Union's seizure of the Baltic states as quite natural, even if they did not realize that it was part of the secret protocol of the Nazi-Soviet pact.

While the liberated foreign labourers and prisoners carried their flags, Germans wore white armbands and hung white flags from their houses to emphasize their surrender. They knew that any sign of resistance or even resentment would do them no good. The Soviet-appointed bürgermeister in Köslin, a fifty-five-year-old Jewish jeweller named Usef Ludinsky, wore a bowler hat and a red armband when he read out proclamations from the military authorities from the town-hall steps. The German inhabitants listened in silence. In Leba, the cavalry which captured it had looted all the clocks and watches, so each morning the bürgermeister had to walk up and down the streets ringing a large handbell and shouting '*Nach Arbeit!*' to wake the townsfolk mobilized for labour by the Soviet authorities.

In Stargard, Agranenko observed a tankist in padded leather helmet approach the fresh graves in the square opposite the magistrate's court. The young soldier read the name on each grave, evidently searching. He stopped at one, took off his tank helmet and bowed his head. Then, he suddenly jerked his sub-machine gun up and fired a long burst. He was saluting his commander buried there at his feet.

Agranenko also chatted with young women traffic controllers. 'Our weddings won't happen soon,' they told him. 'We've already forgotten that we're girls. We're just soldiers.' They seemed to sense that they would be part of that generation condemned to post-war spinsterhood by the Red Army's 9 million casualties.

While Zhukov's armies had been destroying the 'Baltic balcony', Marshal Konev's 1st Ukrainian Front was still engaged in Silesia. His main obstacle was the fortress city of Breslau, astride the Oder, defended under the fanatical leadership of the Gauleiter, Karl Hanke. But Konev did not want to miss the Berlin operation, so he besieged the city, as Zhukov had done with Poznan, and pushed on across the Oder from the Steinau and Ohlau bridgeheads. His objective was the Neisse, the southern tributary of the Oder, from which he would launch his assault to the south of Berlin.

On 8 February, Konev's armies attacked from the two bridgeheads either side of Breslau. The main thrust came from the Steinau bridge-head against the so-called Fourth Panzer Army, whose defence line quickly crumbled. To speed the advance from the Ohlau bridgehead,

Konev then switched Rybalko's 3rd Guards Tank Army. By 12 February, Breslau was surrounded. Over 80,000 civilians were trapped in the
city.

Lelyushenko's 4th Guards Tank Army pushed forward to the Neisse,
which it reached in six days. During the advance, the tank troops found
that only a few inhabitants had remained behind. Sometimes the local
priest would come out to meet them with a letter from the village 'to
assure the Russians of their friendship', and the 1st Ukrainian Front
noted that on several occasions German civilian doctors 'offered assistance to our wounded'.

Lelyushenko then had a nasty surprise. He found that the remnants
of the *Grossdeutschland* Corps and Nehring's XXIV Panzer Corps were
attacking his lines of communication and rear echelon. After two days
of fighting, however, the Germans had to pull back. The result was that
Konev remained in firm control of over 100 kilometres of the Neisse.
His start-line for the Berlin operation was secured and Breslau was
surrounded. But fighting still continued south of the Ohlau bridgehead
throughout the rest of February and March against the German Seventeenth Army.

The Nazis had thought that the fact of fighting on German soil would
automatically fanaticize resistance, but this does not always appear to
have been the case. 'Morale is being completely destroyed by warfare
on German territory,' a prisoner from the 359th Infantry Division told
his Soviet interrogator. 'We are told to fight to the death, but it is a
complete blind alley.'

General Schörner had the idea of a counter-attack against the town
of Lauban, starting on 1 March. The 3rd Guards Tank Army was taken
by surprise and the town was reoccupied. Goebbels was ecstatic. On 8
March, he drove down to Görlitz, followed by photographers from the
propaganda ministry, where he met Schörner. Together, they drove to
Lauban, where they made speeches of mutual congratulation in the
market square to a parade of regular troops, Volkssturm and Hitler
Youth. Goebbels presented Iron Crosses to some Hitler Youth for the
cameras, and then went to visit the Soviet tanks destroyed in the
operation.

The following day, Schörner's next operation to recapture a town
was launched. This time it was the turn of Striegau, forty kilometres

west of Breslau. The German forces who retook the town claimed that they found the few surviving civilians wandering around, psychologically broken by the atrocities committed by Konev's troops. They swore that they would kill every Red Army soldier who fell into their hands. But the behaviour of German troops at this time was certainly not above reproach. The Nazi authorities were not disconcerted by reports of them killing Soviet prisoners with spades, but they were shocked by more and more reports of what Bormann termed 'looting by German soldiers in evacuated areas'. He issued orders through Field Marshal Keitel that officers were to address their soldiers at least once a week on their duty towards German civilians.

The fighting in Silesia was merciless, with both sides imposing a brutal battle discipline on their own men. General Schörner had declared war on malingerers and stragglers, who were hanged by the roadside without even the pretence of a summary court martial. According to soldiers from the 85th Pioneer Battalion taken prisoner, twenty-two death sentences were carried out in the town of Neisse alone during the second half of March. 'The number of death sentences for running away from the field of battle, desertion, self-inflicted wounds and so forth is increasing every week,' the 1st Ukrainian Front reported on prisoner interrogations. 'The death sentences are read out to all soldiers.'

Soviet propaganda specialists in the 7th Department of Front head-quarters soon discovered through the interrogation of prisoners that resentment in the ranks against commanders could be exploited. With bad communications and sudden withdrawals, it was quite easy to make German soldiers believe that their commander had run away and left them behind. For example, the 20th Panzer Division, when surrounded near Oppeln, began receiving leaflets which said, 'Colonel General Schörner leaves his troops in Oppeln in the lurch! He takes his armoured command vehicle and drives like hell for the Neisse.' German soldiers were also suffering badly from lice. They had not changed their under-clothes or visited a field bath unit since December. All they received was 'a completely useless louse powder'. They had also received no pay for the months of January, February and March and most soldiers had not received any letters from home since before Christmas.

Discipline became harsher on the Soviet side as well. Military reverses were regarded as a failure to observe Stalin's Order No. 5 on vigilance.

Colonel V., the Soviet commander at Striegau, was charged with 'criminal carelessness' because his regiment was caught off guard. Although his troops fought well, the town had been abandoned. 'This shameful event was thoroughly investigated by the military council of the Front and the guilty were strictly punished.' Colonel V.'s sentence was not given, but, to judge by another case, it must have been a longish spell in the Gulag. Lieutenant Colonel M. and Captain D. were both charged in front of a military tribunal after the captain left his battery of field guns near houses, without taking up proper position. He then 'went off to have a rest', which was often a Soviet euphemism for incapacity through alcohol. The Germans launched a surprise counter-attack, the guns could not be used and the enemy 'inflicted serious damage'. The captain was dismissed from the Party and sentenced to ten years in the Gulag.

For officers and soldiers alike, the angel of fear in the form of the SMERSH detachment hovered just behind their backs. After all their suffering, their wounds and their lost comrades, they felt great resentment against SMERSH operatives, who longed to accuse them of treason or cowardice without ever facing the dangers of the front themselves. There was a *samizdat* song about SMERSH, still often referred to by its pre-1943 name of the Special Department:

> The first piece of metal made a hole in the fuel tank.
> I jumped out of the T-34, I don't know how,
> And then they called me to the Special Department.
> 'Why aren't you burnt, along with the tank, you bastard?'
> 'I'll definitely burn in the next attack,' I answered.

The soldiers of the 1st Ukrainian Front were not only exhausted after all the battles and advances, they were also dirty, louse-infested and increasingly ill from dysentery. A large part of the problem was due to the fact that health and safety at work was not a high priority in the Red Army. Underclothes were never washed. Drinking water was seldom boiled and chlorine was not added, despite instructions. Above all, food was prepared in appallingly unsanitary conditions. 'Livestock was slaughtered incorrectly on dirty straw by the side of the road,' a report pointed out, 'then taken to the canteen. Sausages were made on a dirty table and the man making the sausages was wearing a filthy coat.'

By the second week in March, the authorities had woken to the danger of typhus, although three types of typhus had been identified in Poland during the winter. Even the NKVD troops were in a bad state. Between a third and two thirds were lice-ridden. The figure for frontline troops must have been much higher. Things started to improve only when the front line in Silesia became stabilized and each regiment set up its *banya*, or bathhouse, behind the lines. Three baths a month were regarded as perfectly adequate. Underwear had to be treated with a special liquid known as 'SK', which no doubt contained terrifying chemicals. An order was issued that all troops were to be vaccinated against typhus and polio, but there was probably not enough time. On 15 March, Konev, under pressure from Stalin, began his assault on southern Silesia.

The left flank of the 1st Ukrainian Front cut off the 30,000 German troops round Oppeln with a thrust southwards towards Neustadt out of the Ohlau bridgehead. This was combined with an attack across the Oder between Oppeln and Ratibor to complete the encirclement. In very little time, the 59th and 21st Armies encircled the Estonian 20th SS Division and the 168th Infantry Division. The Soviet armies' 7th Department propaganda specialists sent in 'anti-fascist' German prisoners of war in an attempt to convince the surrounded troops that Soviet prisons were not as bad as they had heard, but many of these envoys were shot on officers' orders.

The only thing which German soldiers found amusing at this time was the way that Estonians and Ukrainians in the SS picked up Soviet leaflets printed in German and showed them to *Landsers*, asking them what they said. The *Landsers* thought it funny because the mere possession of one of these leaflets, even to roll a cigarette or wipe your bottom, risked a death sentence. On 20 March, near the village of Rinkwitz, Red Army soldiers caught and shot down staff officers of the Estonian 20th SS Division who were hurriedly burning documents. Some half-burned papers, carried on the wind, were retrieved from peasants' back yards. These reports included orders and sentences carried out by SS military tribunals.

German attempts from outside to break the Soviet ring round the Oppeln *Kessel* were repulsed and half of the 30,000 Germans trapped there were killed. Konev was assisted by an attack further to the south-east by the neighbouring 4th Ukrainian Front. On 30 March, the 60th

Army and the 4th Guards Tank Army seized Ratibor. The 1st Ukrainian Front now controlled virtually all of Upper Silesia.

Despite the constant loss of German territory, the Nazi leadership still did not change its ways. The grandiose title of Army Group Vistula became not merely unconvincing, but ridiculous. Even this, however, was not quite as preposterous as its commander-in-chief's new field command post west of the Oder.

Himmler's headquarters were established ninety kilometres north of Berlin in a forest near Hassleben, a village to the south-east of Prenzlau. This distance from the capital reassured the Reichsführer SS that there was little risk from bombing raids. The camp consisted mainly of standard wooden barrack blocks surrounded by a high barbed-wire fence. The only exception was the 'Reichsführerbaracke', a specially built and much larger building, expensively furnished. 'The bedroom,' noted one of his staff officers, 'was very elegant in reddish wood, with a suite of furniture and carpet in pale green. It was more the boudoir of a great lady than of a man commanding troops in war.'

The entrance hall even had a huge imitation Gobelins wall tapestry with a 'Nordic' theme. Everything came from SS factories, even the expensive porcelain. So much, thought army officers, for the Nazi leadership's practice of 'total warfare', as vaunted by Goebbels. Himmler's routine was equally unimpressive for a field commander. After a bath, a massage from his personal masseur and breakfast, he was finally ready for work at 10.30 a.m. Whatever the crisis, Himmler's sleep was not to be disturbed, even if an urgent decision had to be made. All he really wanted to do was to present medals. He greatly enjoyed such ceremonies, which offered an effortless assertion of his own pre-eminence. According to Guderian, his one dream was to receive the Knight's Cross himself.

Himmler's performance at situation conferences in the Reich Chancellery, in contrast, remained pathetically inadequate. According to his operations officer, Colonel Eismann, Himmler increasingly repeated at the Reich Chancellery the words *Kriegsgericht* and *Standgericht*, court martial and drumhead court martial, as a sort of deadly mantra. Retreat meant lack of will and that could only be cured by the harshest measures. He also spoke constantly of 'incompetent and cowardly generals'. But whatever the faults of generals, they were sent home or transferred to another post. It was the retreating soldiers who were shot.

The *Standgericht*, or summary version, was naturally the method which Führer headquarters advocated. It had already been sketched out in principle. Just after the Red Army reached the Oder at the beginning of February, Hitler had copied Stalin's 'Not one step back' order of 1942, with the creation of blocking detachments. It included, as paragraph 5, the instruction, 'Military tribunals should take the strictest possible measures based on the principle that those who are afraid of an honest death in battle deserve the mean death of cowards.'

This was then elaborated in the Führer order of 9 March setting up the *Fliegende Standgericht*, the mobile drumhead court martial. Its establishment consisted of three senior officers, with two clerks and typewriters and office material, and, most essential of all, '*1 Unteroffizier und 8 Mann als Exekutionskommando*'. The guiding principle of its actions was simple: 'The justice of mercy is not applicable.' The organization was to start work the next day, ready to judge all members of the Wehrmacht and Waffen SS. Hitler's blitzkrieg against his own soldiers was extended to the Luftwaffe and Kriegsmarine in an instruction signed by General Burgdorf. He instructed them to make sure that the president in each case was 'firmly anchored in the ideology of our Reich'. Martin Bormann, not wanting the Nazi Party to be outdone, also issued an order to Gauleiters to suppress 'cowardice and defeatism' with death sentences by summary courts martial.

Four days after the Führer order on the *Fliegende Standgericht*, Hitler issued yet another order, probably drafted by Bormann, on National Socialist ideology in the army. 'The overriding priority in the duties of a leader of troops is to activate and fanaticize them politically and he is fully responsible to me for their National Socialist conduct.'

For Himmler, the man who preached pitilessness to waverers, the stress of command proved too much. Without warning Guderian, he retired with influenza to the sanatorium of Hohenlychen, some forty kilometres to the west of Hassleben, to be cared for by his personal physician. Guderian, on hearing of the chaotic situation at his head-quarters, drove up to Hassleben. Even Lammerding, Himmler's SS chief of staff, begged him to do something. Learning that the Reichs-führer SS was at Hohenlychen, Guderian went on to visit him there, having guessed the tactic to adopt. He said that Himmler was clearly overworked with all his responsibilities – Reichsführer SS, chief of the German Police, minister of the interior, commander-in-chief of the Replacement Army and commander-in-chief of Army Group Vistula. Guderian suggested that he should resign from Army Group Vistula. Since it was clear that Himmler wanted to, but did not dare tell Hitler himself, Guderian saw his chance. 'Then will you authorize me to say it for you?' he said. Himmler could not refuse. That night Guderian told Hitler and recommended Colonel General Gotthardt Heinrici as his replacement. Heinrici was the commander of the First Panzer Army, then involved in the fighting against Konev opposite Ratibor. Hitler, loath to admit that Himmler had been a disastrous choice, agreed with great reluctance.

Heinrici went to Hassleben to take up command. Himmler, hearing of his arrival, returned to hand over with a briefing on the situation which was full of pomposity and self-justification. Heinrici had to listen to this interminable speech until the telephone rang. Himmler answered. It was General Busse, the commander of the Ninth Army. A terrible blunder had taken place at Küstrin. The corridor to the fortress had been lost. Himmler promptly handed the telephone to Heinrici. 'You're the new commander-in-chief of the army group,' he said. 'You give the relevant orders.' And the Reichsführer SS took his leave with indecent haste.

The fighting in the Oder bridgeheads either side of Küstrin had been ferocious. If Soviet troops captured a village and found any Nazi SA uniforms or swastikas in a house, they often killed everyone inside. And yet the inhabitants of one village which had been occupied by the Red Army and then liberated by a German counter-attack 'had nothing negative to say about the Russian military'.

More and more German soldiers and young conscripts also showed that they did not want to die for a lost cause. A Swede coming by car from Küstrin to Berlin reported to the Swedish military attaché, Major Juhlin-Dannfel, that he had passed 'twenty Feldgendarmerie control points whose task was to capture deserters from the front'. Another Swede passing through the area reported that German troops appeared thin on the ground and the 'soldiers looked apathetic due to exhaustion'.

Conditions had been miserable. The Oderbruch was a semi-cultivated wetland, with a number of dykes. To dig in against artillery and air attack was a dispiriting experience, since in most places you reached water less than a metre down. February was not as cold as usual, but that did little to lessen the cases of trench foot. Apart from the lack of experienced troops, the German Army's main problems were shortages of ammunition and shortages of fuel for their vehicles. For example, in the SS *30. Januar* Division, the headquarters Kübelwagen could be used only in an emergency. And no artillery battery could fire without permission. The daily ration was two shells per gun.

The Red Army dug their fire trenches in a slightly rounded sausage shape, as well as individual foxholes. Their snipers took up position in patches of scrub woodland or in the rafters of a ruined house. Using well-developed camouflage techniques, they would stay in place for six to eight hours without moving. Their priority targets were first officers and then ration carriers. German soldiers could not move in daylight. And by restricting all movement to darkness, Soviet reconnaissance groups were able to penetrate the thinly held German line and snatch an unfortunate soldier on his own as a 'tongue' for their intelligence officers to interrogate. Artillery forward observation officers also concealed themselves like snipers; in fact they liked to think of themselves as snipers at one remove, but with bigger guns.

One of the most impressive Red Army specialities, which came in very useful for the Oder bridgeheads, was to build underwater bridges between twenty-five and thirty centimetres below the surface of the water. The Luftwaffe pilots, flying Focke-Wulfs and Stukas, found it very hard to spot these artificial fords on stilts.

While Goebbels the minister of propaganda still preached final victory, Goebbels the Gauleiter and Reich Defence Commissar for Berlin ordered obstacles to be constructed in and around the city. Tens of thousands of under-nourished civilians, mostly women, were marched out to expend what little energy they had on digging tank ditches. Rumours of resentment at Nazi bureaucracy, incompetence and the time wasted on useless defence preparations began to circulate, in spite of the penalties for defeatism. 'In the whole war,' one staff officer wrote scathingly, 'I have never seen a tank ditch, either one of ours or one of the enemy's, which managed to impede a tank attack.' The army opposed such senseless barriers constructed on Nazi Party orders, because they hindered military traffic going out towards the Seelow Heights and caused chaos with the stream of refugees now coming into the city from villages west of the Oder.

Brandenburger farmers who had to stay behind because they had been called up into the Volkssturm meanwhile found it increasingly difficult to farm. The local Nazi Party farm leader, the Ortsbauernführer, was ordered to requisition their carts and horses for the transport of wounded and ammunition. Even bicycles were being commandeered to equip the so-called tank-hunting division. But the most telling degree of the Wehrmacht's loss of equipment during the disastrous retreat from the Vistula was its need to take weapons from the Volkssturm.

Volkssturm battalion 16/69 was centred on Wriezen, at the edge of the Oderbruch, close to the front line. It mustered no more than 113 men, of whom thirty-two were on defence works in the rear and fourteen were ill or wounded. The rest guarded tank barricades and bridges. They had three sorts of machine gun, including several Russian ones, a flame-thrower lacking essential parts, three Spanish pistols and 228 rifles from six different nations. One must assume that this report on their weapon states is accurate since the district administration in Potsdam had issued a warning that to make a false report on this subject was 'tantamount to a war crime'. But in many cases even such useless arsenals were not handed over because Nazi Gauleiters told the Volkssturm to give up only weapons which had been lent by the Wehrmacht in the first place.

Nazi Party leaders had heard from Gestapo reports that the civilian population was expressing more and more contempt for the way they ordered others to die but did nothing themselves. The refugees in particular were apparently 'very harsh about the conduct of prominent personalities'. To counter this, a great deal of military posturing took place. The Gau leadership of Brandenburg issued calls to Party members for more volunteers to fight with the slogan, 'The fresh air of the front instead of overheated rooms!' Dr Ley, the chief of Nazi Party organization, appeared at Führer headquarters with a plan to raise a *Freikorps Adolf Hitler* with '40,000 fanatical volunteers'. He asked Guderian to make the army hand over 80,000 sub-machine guns at once. Guderian promised him the weapons once they were enrolled, knowing full well that this was pure bluster. Even Hitler did not look impressed.

Over the last few months, Goebbels had become alarmed at Hitler's withdrawal from public view. He finally persuaded him to agree to a visit to the Oder front, mainly for the benefit of the newsreel cameras. The Führer's visit, on 13 March, was kept very secret. SS patrols watched all the routes beforehand, then lined them just before the Führer's convoy arrived. In fact Hitler did not meet a single ordinary soldier. Formation commanders had been summoned without explanation to an old manor house near Wriezen which had once belonged to Blücher. They were astonished to see the decrepit Führer. One officer wrote of his 'chalk-white face' and 'his glittering eyes, which reminded me of the eyes of a snake'. General Busse, wearing field cap and spectacles, gave a formal presentation of the situation on his army's front. When Hitler spoke of the necessity of holding the Oder defence line, he made it clear, another officer recorded, 'that what we already had were the very last weapons and equipment available'.

The effort of talking must have drained Hitler. On the journey back to Berlin, he never said a word. According to his driver, he sat there 'lost in his thoughts'. It was his last journey. He was never to leave the Reich Chancellery again alive.

9

Objective Berlin

On 8 March, just when the Pomeranian operation was getting into full momentum, Stalin suddenly summoned Zhukov back to Moscow. It was a strange moment to drag a Front commander away from his headquarters. Zhukov drove straight from the central airport out to Stalin's dacha, where the Soviet leader was recuperating from exhaustion and stress.

After Zhukov had reported on the Pomeranian operation and the fighting in the Oder bridgeheads, Stalin led him outside for a walk in the grounds. He talked about his childhood. When they returned to the dacha for tea, Zhukov asked Stalin if anything had been heard of his son Yakov Djugashvili, who had been a prisoner of the Germans since 1941. Stalin had disowned his own son then for having allowed himself to be taken alive, but now his attitude seemed different. He did not answer Zhukov's question for some time. 'Yakov is never going to get out of prison alive,' he said eventually. 'The murderers will shoot him. According to our inquiries, they are keeping him isolated and are trying to persuade him to betray the Motherland.' He was silent for another long moment. 'No,' he said firmly. 'Yakov would prefer any kind of death to betraying the Motherland.'

When Stalin referred to 'our inquiries', they were of course Abakumov's inquiries. The most recent news of Yakov had come from General Stepanovic, a commander of the Yugoslav gendarmerie. Stepanovic had been released by Zhukov's own troops at the end of January, but then grabbed by SMERSH for interrogation. Stepanovic had earlier been in

Straflager X-C in Lübeck with Senior Lieutenant Djugashvili. According to Stepanovic, Yakov had conducted himself 'independently and proudly'. He refused to stand up if a German officer entered his room and turned his back if they spoke to him. The Germans had put him in a punishment cell. Despite an interview printed in the German press, Yakov Djugashvili insisted that he had never replied to any question from anyone. After an escape from the camp, he was taken away and flown to an unknown destination. To this day, the manner of his death is not clear, although the most common story is that he threw himself at the perimeter fence to force the guards to shoot him. Stalin may have changed his attitude towards his own son, but he remained pitiless towards the hundreds of thousands of other Soviet prisoners of war who had in most cases suffered an even worse fate than Yakov.

Stalin changed the subject. He said that he was 'very pleased' with the results of the Yalta conference. Roosevelt had been most friendly. Stalin's secretary, Poskrebyshev, then came in with papers for Stalin to sign. This was a signal for Zhukov to leave, yet it was also the moment for Stalin to explain the reason for the urgent summons to Moscow. 'Go to the *Stavka*,' he told Zhukov, 'and look at the calculations on the Berlin operation with Antonov. We will meet here tomorrow at 13.00.'

Antonov and Zhukov, who evidently sensed that there was a reason for the urgency, worked through the night. Next morning, Stalin changed both the time and the place. He came into Moscow, despite his weak state, so that a full-scale conference could take place at the *Stavka* with Malenkov, Molotov and other members of the State Defence Committee. Antonov made his presentation. When he had finished, Stalin gave his approval and told him to issue the orders for detailed planning.

Zhukov acknowledged in his memoirs that 'when we were working on the Berlin operation we took into account the action of our allies'. He even admitted their concern that 'the British command was still nursing the dream of capturing Berlin before the Red Army reached it'. What he does not mention, however, was that on 7 March, the day before Stalin summoned him so urgently to Moscow, the US Army had seized the bridge at Remagen. Stalin had immediately seen the implications of the Western Allies breaching the Rhine barrier so quickly.

*

The British desire to head for Berlin had never been concealed from Stalin. During Churchill's visit to Moscow in October 1944, Field Marshal Sir Alan Brooke told Stalin that after an encirclement of the Ruhr, 'the main axis of the Allied advance would then be directed on Berlin'. Churchill had re-emphasized the point. They hoped to cut off about 150,000 Germans in Holland, 'then drive steadily towards Berlin'. Stalin had made no comment.

There was a very strong reason for Stalin to want the Red Army to occupy Berlin first. In May 1942, three months before the start of the battle of Stalingrad, he had summoned Beria and the leading atomic physicists to his dacha. He was furious to have heard through spies that the United States and Britain were working on a uranium bomb. Stalin blamed Soviet scientists for not having taken the threat seriously, yet he was the one who had dismissed as a 'provocation' the first intelligence on the subject. This had come from the British traitor John Cairncross in November 1941. Stalin's angry dismissal of the information had been a curious repeat of his behaviour when warned of the German invasion six months before.

Over the next three years, the Soviet nuclear research programme, soon codenamed Operation Borodino, was dramatically accelerated with detailed research information from the Manhattan Project provided by Communist sympathizers, such as Klaus Fuchs. Beria himself took over supervision of the work and eventually brought Professor Igor Kurchatov's team of scientists under complete NKVD control.

The Soviet programme's main handicap, however, was a lack of uranium. No deposits had been identified yet in the Soviet Union. The main reserves in Europe lay in Saxony and Czechoslovakia, under Nazi control, but before the Red Army reached Berlin they appear to have had only the sketchiest information on the deposits there. On Beria's instructions, the Soviet Purchasing Committee in the United States asked the American War Production Board to sell it eight tons of uranium oxide. After consultation with Major General Groves, the head of the Manhattan Project, the US government authorized purely token supplies, mainly in the hope of finding out what the Soviet Union was up to.

Uranium deposits were discovered in Kazakhstan in 1945, but still in insufficient quantities. Stalin and Beria's greatest hope of getting the project moving ahead rapidly therefore lay in seizing German supplies of uranium before the Western Allies got to them. Beria had discovered from Soviet scientists who had worked there that the Kaiser Wilhelm Institute for Physics in Dahlem, a south-western suburb of Berlin, was the centre of German atomic research. Work was carried out there in a lead-lined bunker known as the 'Virus House', a codename designed to discourage outside interest. Next to this bunker stood the Blitzturm, or 'tower of lightning', which housed a cyclotron capable of creating 1.5 million volts. Beria, however, did not know that most of the Kaiser Wilhelm Institute's scientists, equipment and material, including seven tons of uranium oxide, had been evacuated to Haigerloch in the Black Forest. But a German bureaucratic mix-up had led to a further consignment being sent to Dahlem instead of Haigerloch. The rush for Dahlem was not to be entirely in vain.

There had never been any doubt in the minds of the Nazi leadership that the fight for Berlin would be the climax of the war. 'The National Socialists,' Goebbels had always insisted, 'will either win together in Berlin or die together in Berlin.' Perhaps unaware that he was paraphrasing Karl Marx, he used to declare that 'whoever possesses Berlin possesses Germany'. Stalin, on the other hand, undoubtedly knew the rest of Marx's quote: 'And whoever controls Germany, controls Europe.'

The American war leaders, however, were clearly unfamiliar with such European dicta. It was perhaps this ignorance of European power politics which provoked Brooke into his uncharitable opinion after a working breakfast with Eisenhower in London on 6 March: 'There is no doubt that he [Eisenhower] is a most attractive personality and at the same time [has] a very very limited brain from a strategic point of view.' The basic problem, which Brooke did not fully acknowledge, was that the Americans at that stage simply did not view Europe in strategic terms. They had a simple and limited objective: to win the war against Germany quickly, with as few casualties as possible, and then concentrate on Japan. Eisenhower – like his President, the chiefs of staff and other senior officials – failed to look ahead and completely misread Stalin's character. This exasperated British colleagues and led to the main rift in the western alliance. Some British officers even referred to

Eisenhower's deference to Stalin as 'Have a Go, Joe', a call used by London prostitutes when soliciting American soldiers.

On 2 March, Eisenhower signalled to Major General John R. Deane, the US liaison officer in Moscow, 'In view of the great progress of the Soviet offensive, is there likely to be any major change in Soviet plans from those explained to Tedder [on 15 January]?' He then asked whether there would be 'a lull in operations mid-March to mid-May'. But Deane found it impossible to obtain any reliable information from General Antonov. And when finally they did state their intentions, they deliberately misled Eisenhower to conceal their determination to seize Berlin first.

In the difference of views over strategy, personalities unavoidably played a large part. Eisenhower suspected that Montgomery's demands to be allowed to lead a single, full-blooded thrust towards Berlin were prompted solely by prima donna ambitions. Montgomery had done little to conceal his conviction that he should be the field commander while Eisenhower was left in a figurehead position. Above all, Montgomery's unforgivable boasting after the Ardennes battle had clearly entrenched Eisenhower's bad opinion of him. 'His relations with Monty are quite insoluble,' Field Marshal Sir Alan Brooke wrote in his diary after that breakfast meeting on 6 March. 'He only sees the worst side of Monty.' Yet the Americans, with some justification, felt that Montgomery would in any case be the worst choice to lead a rapid thrust. He was so notoriously pedantic about staff details that he took longer than any other general to mount an attack.

Montgomery's 21st Army Group in the north at Wesel faced the greatest concentration of German troops. He therefore planned a set-piece crossing of the Rhine with large-scale amphibious and airborne operations. But his minutely prepared performance was rather pre-empted by events further south. Hitler's frenzied reaction to the US First Army's rapidly reinforced bridgehead at Remagen was to order massive counter-attacks. This stripped other sectors of the Rhine. Soon, Patton's Third Army, which had been clearing the Palatinate with a panache reminiscent of that local cavalry leader Prince Rupert, was across the river at a number of points south of Koblenz.

Once Montgomery's 21st Army Group had also crossed the Rhine on the morning of 24 March, Eisenhower, Churchill and Brooke met on the banks of the river in euphoric mood. Montgomery believed that Eisenhower would allow him to charge north-eastwards towards the Baltic coast at Lübeck and perhaps even Berlin. He was soon disabused.

General Hodges had been building up the Remagen bridgehead and Patton, in a remarkably short time, had developed his main bridgehead south of Mainz. Eisenhower ordered them to converge their attacks eastwards before Hodges's First Army swung left to encircle the Ruhr from the south. He then, to Montgomery's utter dismay, detached Simpson's Ninth Army from his 21st Army Group and ordered Montgomery to head for Hamburg and Denmark, not for Berlin. The US Ninth Army was to form the northern part of the Ruhr operation to surround Field Marshal Model's Army Group defending Germany's last industrial region. The greatest blow to British hopes of a push north-eastwards towards Berlin was Eisenhower's decision on 30 March to concentrate efforts on central and southern Germany.

Bradley's 12th Army Group, augmented by the Ninth Army, was to cross the centre of Germany as soon as it had secured the Ruhr to head for Leipzig and Dresden. In the south, General Devers's 6th Army Group would head for Bavaria and northern Austria. Then, to the anger of the British chiefs of staff, who had not been consulted about the important change of emphasis in the overall plan, Eisenhower communicated its details to Stalin at the end of March without telling them or his British deputy, Air Chief Marshal Tedder. This signal, known as SCAF-252, became a bitter issue between the two allies.

Eisenhower weighted his attack southwards partly because he was convinced that Hitler would withdraw his armies to Bavaria and north-western Austria for a last-ditch defence of an Alpenfestung, or Alpine Fortress. He conceded later in his memoirs that Berlin was 'politically and psychologically important as the symbol of remaining German power', but he believed that 'it was not the logical nor the most desirable objective for the forces of the Western Allies'. He justified this decision on the grounds that the Red Army on the Oder was much closer and the logistic effort would have meant holding up his central and southern armies, and his objective of meeting up with the Red Army to split Germany in two.

On the banks of the Rhine only six days before Churchill had hoped that 'our armies will advance against little or no opposition and will reach the Elbe, or even Berlin, before the Bear'. He was now thoroughly dismayed. It seemed as if Eisenhower and Marshall were far too concerned with placating Stalin. The Soviet authorities were apparently furious about American fighters shooting down a number of their aircraft in a dogfight. Their reaction was in strong contrast to Stalin's remarks to Tedder in January that such accidents were bound to happen in war. The incident had taken place on 18 March between Berlin and Küstrin. The US Air Force fighter pilots thought that they had engaged eight German aircraft and claimed two Focke-Wulf 190s destroyed. Red Army aviation, on the other hand, asserted that the eight aircraft were Soviet and that six of them had been shot down, with two of their flyers killed and one seriously wounded. The mistake was blamed on the 'criminal action of individuals of the American air force'.

Ironically, it was the Americans, in the form of Allen Dulles of the OSS (Office of Strategic Services) in Berne, who provoked the biggest row with the Soviet Union at this time. Dulles had been approached by SS Obergruppenführer Karl Wolff about an armistice in north Italy. The Soviet leadership's demands to participate in the talks were rejected in case Wolff might break them off. This was a blunder. Churchill acknowledged that the Soviet Union was understandably alarmed. Stalin clearly feared a separate peace on the Western Front. His recurrent nightmare was a revived Wehrmacht supplied by the Americans, even if this was an illogical fear. The vast majority of Germany's most formidable formations had either been destroyed, captured or surrounded, and even if the Americans had provided all the weapons in the world, the Wehrmacht in 1945 bore little resemblance to the fighting machine of 1941.

Stalin also suspected that the huge numbers of Wehrmacht troops surrendering to the Americans and British in the west of Germany revealed not just their fear of becoming prisoners of the Red Army. He thought it was part of a deliberate attempt to open up the Western Front to allow the Americans and British to reach Berlin first. In fact, the reason for such large surrenders at that time was Hitler's refusal to allow any withdrawal. If he had brought his armies back to defend the Rhine after the Ardennes débâcle, the Allies would have faced a very hard task. But he did not, and this allowed them to trap so many divisions west of the Rhine. Similarly, Field Marshal Model's fixed defence of the Ruhr was equally doomed. 'We owed much to Hitler,' Eisenhower commented later.

In any case, Churchill felt strongly that until Stalin's post-war intentions in central Europe were clearer, then the West had to grab every good card available for bargaining with him. Recent reports of what was happening in Poland, with mass arrests of prominent figures who might not support Soviet rule, strongly suggested that Stalin had no intention of allowing an independent government to develop. Molotov had also become extremely aggressive. He was refusing to allow any western representatives into Poland. In fact, his general interpretation of their agreement at Yalta was very different from what both the British and the Americans had understood to be 'the letter and the spirit' of their accord.

Churchill's earlier confidence based on Stalin's lack of interference in Greece had now started to disintegrate. He suspected that both he and Roosevelt had been the victims of a massive confidence trick. Churchill still did not seem to realize that Stalin judged others by himself. It would appear that he had acted on the principle that Churchill, after all his comments at Yalta about having to face the House of Commons over the subject of Poland, had simply needed a bit of democratic gloss to keep any critics quiet until everything was irreversibly settled. Stalin now appeared to be angered by Churchill's renewed complaints over the Soviet Union's behaviour in Poland.

The Soviet authorities were well aware of the main political and military disagreements between the Western Allies, even if they did not know all the details immediately. The rift grew even greater after Eisenhower's SCAF-252 signal to Stalin. Eisenhower, stung by the furious British reaction, wrote later that the Combined Chiefs of Staff, after Tedder's visit to Moscow in January, had allowed him to communicate directly with Moscow 'on matters that were exclusively military in character'. 'Later in the campaign,' he wrote, 'my interpretation of this authorization was sharply challenged by Mr Churchill, the difficulty arising out of the age-old truth that politics and military activities are never completely separable.' In any case, Eisenhower's view that Berlin itself was 'no longer a particularly important objective' demonstrated an astonishing naïvety.

The irony, however, is that Eisenhower's decision to avoid Berlin was almost certainly the right one, albeit for totally the wrong reasons. For Stalin, the Red Army's capture of Berlin was not a matter of bargaining positions in the post-war game. He saw it as far too important for that. If any forces from the Western Allies had crossed the Elbe and headed for Berlin, they would almost certainly have found themselves warned off by the Soviet air force, and artillery if in range. Stalin would have had no compunction in condemning the Western Allies and accusing them of criminal adventurism. While Eisenhower gravely under-estimated the importance of Berlin, Churchill, on the other hand, underestimated both Stalin's determination to secure the city at any price and the genuine moral outrage which would have greeted any western attempt to seize the Red Army's prize from under its nose.

At the end of March, while the British and American chiefs of staff disagreed over Eisenhower's plans, the *Stavka* in Moscow put the finishing touches to the plan for 'the Berlin operation'. Zhukov left his headquarters on the morning of 29 March to fly back to Moscow, but bad weather forced him down in Minsk shortly after midday. He spent the afternoon talking with Ponomarenko, the secretary of the Communist Party of Belorussia, and, since the weather had still not improved, he took the train to Moscow.

The atmosphere in the Kremlin was extremely tense. Stalin was convinced that the Germans would do everything possible to make a deal with the Western Allies in order to hold off the Red Army in the east. The American talks in Berne with General Wolff about a possible cease-fire in northern Italy seemed to confirm his worst fears. Yet the Soviet leadership's intense suspicions failed to take into account Hitler's fanaticism. Figures around him might make peace overtures, but Hitler himself knew that surrender in any form, even to the Western Allies, offered him no future, save humiliation and the gallows. There could be no deal without some form of palace coup against the Führer.

Zhukov, who was to be responsible for seizing Berlin, also shared Stalin's fears that the Germans would open their front to the British and Americans. On 27 March, two days before he left for Moscow, the Reuters correspondent at 21st Army Group wrote that British and American troops heading for the heart of Germany were encountering no resistance. The Reuters report rang alarm bells in Moscow.

'The German front in the west has entirely collapsed,' was the first thing Stalin said to Zhukov when he finally reached Moscow. 'It seems that Hitler's men do not want to take any measures to stop the advance of the allies. At the same time they are strengthening their groups on the main axes against us.' Stalin gestured to the map, then knocked the ash from his pipe. 'I think we are going to have a serious fight.'

Zhukov produced his front intelligence map and Stalin studied it. 'When can our troops start to advance on the Berlin axis?' he asked.

'The 1st Belorussian Front will be able to advance in two weeks,' Zhukov replied. 'Apparently the 1st Ukrainian Front will be ready at the same time. And according to our information, the 2nd Belorussian Front will be held up liquidating the enemy at Danzig and Gdynia until the middle of April.'

'Well,' Stalin replied. 'We'll just have to start without waiting for Rokossovsky's Front.' He went to his desk and leafed through some papers, then passed Zhukov a letter. 'Here, read this,' Stalin said. According to Zhukov, the letter was from 'a foreign well-wisher' tipping off the Soviet leadership about secret negotiations between the Western Allies and the Nazis. It did, however, explain that the Americans and British had refused the German proposal of a separate peace, but the possibility of the Germans opening the route to Berlin 'could not be ruled out'.

'Well, what have you got to say?' said Stalin. Not waiting for a reply, he said, 'I think Roosevelt won't violate the Yalta agreement, but as for Churchill . . . that one's capable of anything.'

At 8 p.m. on 31 March, the United States ambassador, Averell Harriman, and his British counterpart, Sir Archibald Clerk Kerr, went to the Kremlin, accompanied by General Deane. They met Stalin, General Antonov and Molotov. 'Stalin was given an English and Russian text of the message contained in [Eisenhower's] SCAF-252,' Deane reported late that night. 'After Stalin had read Eisenhower's message, we pointed out the operations described in the message on the map. Stalin immediately reacted and said that the plan seemed to be a good one, but that he of course could not commit himself definitely until he had consulted his staff. He said that he would give us an answer tomorrow. He seemed to be favourably impressed with the direction of the attack in central

Germany and also of the secondary attack in the south. We emphasized the urgency of obtaining Stalin's views in order that the plans could be properly concerted . . . Stalin was much impressed with the number of prisoners that had been taken in the month of March and said certainly this will help finish the war very soon.' Stalin then talked about every front except the crucial Oder front. He estimated that 'only about a third of the Germans wanted to fight'. He again came back to Eisenhower's message. He said that the 'plan for Eisenhower's main effort was a good one in that it accomplished the most important objective of dividing Germany in half' . . . 'He felt that the Germans' last stand would probably be in the mountains of western Czechoslovakia and Bavaria.' The Soviet leader was clearly keen to encourage the idea of a German national redoubt in the south.

The very next morning, 1 April, Stalin received Marshals Zhukov and Konev in his large study in the Kremlin, with its long conference table and the portraits of Suvorov and Kutuzov on the wall. General Antonov, the chief of the general staff, and General Shtemenko, the chief of operations, were also present.

'Are you aware how the situation is shaping up?' Stalin asked the two marshals. Zhukov and Konev replied cautiously that they were, as far as the information which they had received.

'Read the telegram to them,' Stalin told General Shtemenko. This message, presumably from one of the Red Army liaison officers at SHAEF headquarters, claimed that Montgomery would head for Berlin and that Patton's Third Army would also divert from its drive towards Leipzig and Dresden to attack Berlin from the south. The *Stavka* had already heard of the contingency plan to drop parachute divisions on Berlin in the event of a sudden collapse of the Nazi regime. All this was evidently conflated into an Allied plot to seize Berlin first under the guise of assisting the Red Army. One cannot, of course, rule out the possibility that Stalin had the telegram faked to put pressure on both Zhukov and Konev.

'Well, then,' Stalin said, eyeing his two marshals. 'Who is going to take Berlin: are we or are the Allies?'

'It is we who shall take Berlin,' Konev replied immediately, 'and we will take it before the Allies.'

'So that's the sort of man you are,' Stalin replied with a faint smile. 'And how will you be able to organize forces for it? Your main force is on the southern flank [after the Silesian operation] and you'll have to do a good deal of regrouping.'

'You needn't worry, Comrade Stalin,' said Konev. 'The Front will carry out all the necessary measures.' Konev's desire to beat Zhukov to Berlin was unmistakable and Stalin, who liked to engender rivalry among his subordinates, was clearly satisfied.

Antonov presented the overall plan, then Zhukov and Konev presented theirs. Stalin made only one amendment. He did not agree with the *Stavka* demarcation line between the two Fronts. He leaned forward with his pencil and scribbled out the line west of Lübben, sixty kilometres south-east of Berlin. 'In the event,' he said, turning to Konev, 'of severe resistance on the eastern approaches to Berlin, which will definitely be the case . . . the 1st Ukrainian Front should be ready to attack with tank armies from the south.' Stalin approved the plans and gave orders for the operation to be ready 'in the shortest time possible and in any case no later than 16 April'.

'The *Stavka*', as the Russian official history puts it, 'worked in great haste, fearing that the Allies would be quicker than Soviet troops in taking Berlin.' They had much to coordinate. The operation to capture Berlin involved 2.5 million men, 41,600 guns and mortars, 6,250 tanks and self-propelled guns and 7,500 aircraft. No doubt Stalin took satisfaction in the fact he was concentrating a far more powerful mechanized force to seize the capital of the Reich than Hitler had deployed to invade the whole of the Soviet Union.

After the main conference on 1 April, Stalin replied to Eisenhower's message which had provided accurate details of forthcoming American and British operations. The Soviet leader informed the American supreme commander that his plan 'completely coincided' with the plans of the Red Army. Stalin then assured his trusting ally that 'Berlin has lost its former strategic importance' and that the Soviet command would send only second-rate forces against it. The Red Army would be delivering its main blow to the south, to join up with the Western Allies. The advance of the main forces would start approximately in the second half of May. 'However, this plan may undergo certain alterations, depending on circumstances.' It was the greatest April Fool in modern history.

10

The Kamarilla *and the General Staff*

During the final phase of the Soviet onslaught on Pomerania, General von Tippelskirch gave an evening reception for foreign military attachés out at Mellensee. They went mainly because it offered a good opportunity to hear something other than the official version of events, which hardly anybody believed. The capital was obsessed with rumours. Some were convinced that Hitler was dying from cancer and that the war would end soon. Many whispered, with rather more justification, that German Communists were rapidly stepping up their activities as the Red Army approached. There was also talk of a mutiny among the Volkssturm.

German officers present that evening were discussing the Pomeranian catastrophe. They blamed it on their lack of reserves. According to the Swedish military attaché, Major Juhlin-Dannfel, conversations ended with German officers saying how much they hoped that serious negotiations would start with the British. 'The British are partly responsible for the destiny of Europe,' he was told. 'And it is their duty to prevent German culture from being annihilated by a Red storm-flood.' German officers still seemed to believe that if Britain had not been so tiresome holding out in 1940 and the whole might of the Wehrmacht had been concentrated on the Soviet Union in 1941, the outcome would have been decisively different. 'Some of those present,' Juhlin-Dannfel concluded, 'became very sentimental and the whole thing seemed quite sad.'

The delusions of the German officer class, although different from those of Hitler's court circle, were no less deeply held. Their real regret about the invasion of the Soviet Union had been its lack of success. To the German Army's shame, no more than a small minority of officers had been genuinely outraged by the activities of the SS Einsatzgruppen and other paramilitary formations. In the course of the last nine months, anti-Nazi feelings had developed in army circles partly because of the cruel repression of the July plotters, but mainly as a result of Hitler's blatant ingratitude and prejudice against the army as a whole. His outright loathing of the general staff, and his attempts to shift the blame for his own catastrophic meddling on to the shoulders of field commanders were deeply resented. In addition, the preference given to the Waffen SS in weapons, manpower and promotion stirred strong feelings of resentment towards the Nazi praetorian guard.

A senior Kriegsmarine officer told Juhlin-Dannfel about a recent conference where senior military officers discussed the possibility of a last-ditch attack on the Eastern Front to force the Red Army back to the frontier of 1939. 'If the attempt were successful,' the naval officer said, 'then this would provide the right opportunity to open negotiations. In order to do this, Hitler must be removed. Himmler would take over and be the guarantor of maintaining order.' This idea revealed not just a stupendous lack of imagination. It also shows that Wehrmacht officers in Berlin seemed to have no understanding of the state of affairs at the front. The Vistula–Oder operation had smashed the German Army's capacity to launch another sustained offensive. The only question which remained was the number of days it would take the Red Army to reach Berlin from the front along the Oder, the line which – they now heard to their horror – might become the future frontier of Poland.

The events which brought the conflict between Hitler and Guderian to a head were linked to the rather grim fortress town of Küstrin, which stood between the two main Soviet bridgeheads across the Oder. Küstrin was known as the gateway to Berlin. It was situated on the confluence of the rivers Oder and Warthe, eighty kilometres east of Berlin and astride Reichsstrasse 1, the main road from the capital to Königsberg.

Küstrin was the focal point of operations for both sides. Zhukov wanted to merge the two bridgeheads – Berzarin's 5th Shock Army had the northern one and Chuikov's 8th Guards Army the southern one – to prepare a large forming-up area for the forthcoming Berlin offensive.

Hitler, meanwhile, had insisted on a counter-attack with five divisions from Frankfurt an der Oder, to encircle Chuikov's army from the south.

Guderian had tried to put a stop to Hitler's plan, knowing that they had neither the air and artillery support nor the tanks necessary for such an enterprise. The débâcle which happened on 22 March, the day Heinrici had been lectured by Himmler at the headquarters of Army Group Vistula, had taken place as divisions were redeployed for the offensive. The 25th Panzergrenadier Division withdrew from the Küstrin corridor before its replacement was ready. Berzarin's 5th Shock Army and Chuikov's 8th Guards Army reacted quickly and seized their chance. Küstrin was now isolated.

Guderian, however, still hoped that peace negotiations would save the Wehrmacht from total destruction. On 21 March, the day before the loss of the Küstrin corridor, he had approached Himmler in the Reich Chancellery garden, where he had been 'taking a stroll with Hitler among the rubble'. Hitler left the two men to talk. Guderian said straight out that the war could no longer be won. 'The only problem now is how most quickly to put an end to the senseless slaughter and bombing. Apart from Ribbentrop, you are the only man who still possesses contacts in neutral countries. Since the foreign minister has proved reluctant to propose to Hitler that negotiations be begun, I must ask you to make use of your contacts and go with me to Hitler and urge him to arrange an armistice.'

'My dear Colonel General,' Himmler replied. 'It is still too early for that.' Guderian persisted, but either Himmler was still afraid of Hitler, as Guderian thought, or he was playing his cards carefully. One of his confidants in the SS, Gruppenführer von Alvensleben, sounded out Colonel Eismann at Army Group Vistula, and told him in the strictest confidence that Himmler wanted to approach the Western Allies through Count Folke Bernadotte of the Swedish Red Cross. Eismann replied that first of all he thought it too late for any western leader to consider terms, and secondly Himmler struck him as 'the most unsuitable man in the whole of Germany for such negotiations'.

During the evening of 21 March, just after Guderian's approach to Himmler, Hitler told the army chief of staff that he should take sick leave, because of his heart trouble. Guderian replied that with General Wenck still recovering from his car crash, and General Krebs wounded in the heavy bombing raid on Zossen six days before, he could not abandon his post. Guderian states that while they were talking, an aide came in to tell Hitler that Speer wanted to see him. (He must have confused the date or the occasion, because Speer was not in Berlin at this time.) Hitler exploded and refused. 'Always when any man asks to see me alone,' he apparently complained to Guderian, 'it is because he has something unpleasant to say to me. I cannot stand any more of these Job's comforters. His memoranda begin with the words, "The war is lost!" And that's what he wants to tell me now. I always just lock his memoranda away in the safe, unread.' According to his aide, Nicolaus von Below, this was not true. Hitler did read them. But as Hitler's reaction to the loss of the bridge at Remagen had shown, he had only one reaction to disaster. It was to blame others. On that day, 8 March, Jodl had come in person to the conference to tell Hitler of the failure to blow the bridge. 'Hitler was very quiet then,' said a staff officer who had been present, 'but the next day he was raging.' He ordered the summary execution of five officers, a decision which horrified the Wehrmacht.

Even the Waffen SS soon found that it was not exempt from the Führer's rages. Hitler heard from either Bormann or Fegelein, both eager to undermine Himmler, that Waffen SS divisions in Hungary had been retreating without orders. As a humiliating punishment, Hitler decided to strip them, including his personal guard, the *Leibstandarte Adolf Hitler*, of their prized armband divisional titles. Himmler was forced to implement the order himself. 'This mission of his to Hungary,' Guderian noted with little regret, 'did not win him much affection from his Waffen SS.'

The attack from Frankfurt an der Oder, which Hitler still refused to give up, took place on 27 March. General Busse, the commander of the Ninth Army, was its reluctant orchestrator. The operation was a costly failure, even though it initially took the 8th Guards Army by surprise. German panzer and infantry troops in the open were massacred by Soviet artillery and aviation.

The next day, during the ninety-minute drive from Zossen into Berlin for the situation conference, Guderian made his intentions clear to his aide, Major Freytag von Loringhoven. 'Today I am really going to give it to him straight,' he said in the back of the huge Mercedes staff car.

The atmosphere in the Reich Chancellery bunker was tense even before General Burgdorf announced Hitler's arrival with his usual call – '*Meine Herren, der Führer kommt!*' This was the signal for everyone to come to attention and give the Nazi salute. Keitel and Jodl were there, and so was General Busse, whom Hitler had had summoned along with Guderian to explain the Küstrin fiasco.

While Jodl displayed his usual 'ice-cold lack of emotion', Guderian was clearly in a truculent frame of mind. Hitler's mood was evidently not improved by having just heard that General Patton's tanks had reached the outskirts of Frankfurt am Main. General Busse was told to present his report. As Busse spoke, Hitler demonstrated a mounting impatience. He suddenly demanded why the attack had failed. And before Busse or anyone else had the chance to reply, he began another tirade against the incompetence of the officer corps and the general staff. In this case he blamed Busse for not using his artillery.

Guderian stepped in to tell Hitler that General Busse had used all the artillery shells available to him. 'Then you should have arranged for him to have more!' Hitler screamed back at him. Freytag von Loringhoven observed Guderian's face turn red with rage as he defended Busse. The chief of staff turned the subject to Hitler's refusal to withdraw the divisions from Courland for the defence of Berlin. The row escalated rapidly to a terrifying intensity. 'Hitler became paler and paler,' noted Freytag von Loringhoven, 'while Guderian became redder and redder.'

The witnesses to this dispute were deeply alarmed. Freytag von Loringhoven slipped out of the conference room and put through an urgent call to General Krebs at Zossen. He explained the situation and suggested that he must interrupt the meeting with some excuse. Krebs agreed and Freytag von Loringhoven went back into the room to tell Guderian that Krebs needed to speak to him urgently. Krebs spoke to Guderian for ten minutes, during which time the chief of staff calmed down. When he went back into Hitler's presence, Jodl was reporting on developments in the west. Hitler insisted that everyone should leave the room except Field Marshal Keitel and General Guderian. He told Guderian that he must go away from Berlin to restore his health. 'In six weeks the situation will be very critical. Then I shall need you urgently.' Keitel asked him where he would go on leave. Guderian, suspicious of his motives, replied that he had made no plans.

Staff officers at Zossen and at Army Group Vistula headquarters were shocked by the day's events. Hitler's dismissal of Guderian threw them into a deep gloom. They were already suffering from what Colonel de Maizière described as 'a mixture of nervous energy and trance' and a feeling of 'having to do your duty while at the same time seeing that this duty was completely pointless'. Hitler's defiance of military logic reduced them to despair. The dictator's charisma, they had finally realized, was based on a '*kriminelle Energie*' and a complete disregard for good and evil. His severe personality disorder, even if it could not quite be defined as mental illness, had certainly made him deranged. Hitler had so utterly identified himself with the German people that he believed that anybody who opposed him was opposing the German people as a whole; and that if he were to die, the German people could not survive without him.

General Hans Krebs, Guderian's deputy, was appointed the new chief of staff. 'This short, bespectacled, somewhat bandy-legged man,' wrote one staff officer, 'had a perpetual smile and the air of a faun about him.' He had a sharp, often sarcastic, wit and always had the right joke or anecdote for any moment. Krebs, a staff officer and not a field commander, was the archetypal second-in-command, which was exactly what Hitler wanted. Krebs had been military attaché in Moscow in 1941 shortly before the German invasion of the Soviet Union. And for an officer of the Wehrmacht, he enjoyed the unusual distinction of having been slapped on the back by Stalin. 'We must always remain friends, whatever should happen,' the Soviet leader had then said to him, when saying farewell to the Japanese foreign minister on a Moscow railway platform early in 1941. 'I'm convinced of it,' Krebs had replied, quickly recovering from his astonishment. Field commanders, however, had little respect for Krebs's opportunism. He was known as 'the man who can make white out of black'.

On Guderian's departure, Freytag von Loringhoven asked to be sent to a frontline division, but Krebs insisted that he stayed on with him. 'The war's over anyway,' he said. 'I want you to help me in this last phase.' Freytag von Loringhoven felt obliged to agree. He thought that Krebs was 'no Nazi' and that he had refused to join the July plotters only because he was convinced that the attempt would fail. But others noticed how General Burgdorf, an old war academy classmate, persuaded Krebs to join the Bormann–Fegelein circle. Presumably in Bormann's scheme, a loyal Krebs would ensure the army's obedience. The bull-necked and rubber-faced Bormann appeared to be collecting supporters for the fast-approaching day when he hoped to slip into his master's shoes. He appears to have earmarked Fegelein, his favourite companion in the privacy of the sauna, where they almost certainly bragged to each other about their numerous affaires, as the future Reichsführer SS.

Staff officers from Zossen and Army Group Vistula observed the court of the Third Reich with a horrified fascination. They also watched Hitler's treatment of his entourage in case it signified a change in favour and therefore in the power struggle. Hitler addressed the discredited Göring as 'Herr Reichsmarschall' in an attempt to prop up what little dignity he had left. Although he remained on familiar '*du*' terms with Himmler, the Reichsführer SS had lost power since his moment of glory after the July plot. At that time, Himmler, as commander of the Waffen SS and the Gestapo, had appeared to be the only counterweight to the army.

Goebbels, although his propaganda talents were essential to the Nazi cause in its eclipse, had still not been accepted back to the same degree of intimacy he had enjoyed before his love affair with a Czech actress. Hitler, appalled that a leading member of the Nazi Party should consider divorce, had sided with Magda Goebbels. The Reichsminister for Propaganda was forced to uphold the family values of the regime.

Grand Admiral Dönitz was favoured because of his complete loyalty and because Hitler saw his new generation of U-boats as the most promising weapon of revenge. In German navy circles, Dönitz was known as 'Hitlerjunge Quex' – the devoted Nazi youth in a famous propaganda movie – because he was the 'mouthpiece of his Führer'. But Bormann appeared to be the best-placed member of the '*Kamarilla*'. Hitler called his indispensable assistant and chief administrator 'dear Martin'.

The officers also watched the deadly competition among the heirs apparent within the '*Kamarilla*'. Himmler and Bormann addressed each other as '*du*', but 'mutual respect was thin on the ground'. They also observed Fegelein, 'with his dirty finger sticking into everything', do his utmost to undermine Himmler, a man whose friendship he had sought and achieved. Himmler appears to have been oblivious of the treachery. He generously permitted his subordinate, no doubt as the Führer's brother-in-law presumptive, to address him as '*du*'.

Eva Braun had already returned to Berlin to stay by her adored Führer's side right to the end. The popular notion that her return from Bavaria was much later and totally unexpected is undermined by Bormann's diary entry of Wednesday 7 March: 'In the evening Eva Braun left for Berlin with a courier train.' If Bormann had known of her movements in advance then so, presumably, had Hitler.

On 13 March, a day in which 2,500 Berliners died in air raids and another 120,000 found themselves homeless, Bormann ordered 'on the grounds of security' that prisoners must be moved from areas close to the front to the interior of the Reich. It is not entirely clear whether this instruction also accelerated the existing SS programme for evacuating concentration camps threatened by advancing troops. The killing of sick prisoners and the death marches of concentration camp survivors were probably the most ghastly developments in the fall of the Third Reich. Those too weak to march and those regarded as politically dangerous were usually hanged or shot by the SS or Gestapo. On some occasions, even the local Volkssturm was used for execution squads. Yet men and women condemned for listening to a foreign radio station apparently constituted the largest group among those defined as 'dangerous'. The Gestapo and SS also reacted brutally to reports of looting, especially when it involved foreign workers. German citizens were usually spared. In this frenzy of reprisal and revenge, Italian forced labourers suffered more than almost any other national group. They suffered presumably because of a Nazi desire to take revenge on a former ally who had changed sides.

Soon after issuing his order for the evacuation of prisoners, Bormann flew to Salzburg on 15 March. Over the next three days he visited mines in the area. The purpose of this must have been to choose sites for concealing Nazi loot and Hitler's private possessions. He was back in Berlin on 19 March, after an overnight train journey. Later that day, Hitler issued what became known as the 'Nero' or 'scorched-earth' order. Everything which might be of use to the enemy should be destroyed on withdrawal. The timing, just after Bormann's journey to conceal Nazi loot, was an ironic coincidence.

It was Albert Speer's latest memorandum which had suddenly triggered Hitler's insistence on a scorched-earth policy to the end. When Speer tried to persuade Hitler in the early hours of that morning that bridges should not be blown up unnecessarily, because their destruction meant 'eliminating all further possibility for the German people to survive', Hitler's reply revealed his contempt for them all. 'This time you will receive a written reply to your memorandum,' Hitler told him. 'If the war is lost, the people will also be lost [and] it is not necessary to worry about their needs for elemental survival. On the contrary, it is best for us to destroy even these things. For the nation has proved to be weak, and the future belongs entirely to the strong people of the East. Whatever remains after this battle is in any case only the inadequates, because the good ones will be dead.'

Speer, who had travelled straight to Field Marshal Model's headquarters in the Ruhr to persuade him not to wreck the railway system, received Hitler's written reply on the morning of 20 March. 'All military, transport, communication and supply facilities, as well as all material assets in the territory of the Reich' were to be destroyed. Reichsminister Speer was relieved of all his responsibilities in this field and his orders for the preservation of factories were to be rescinded immediately. Speer had cleverly used an anti-defeatist argument, saying that factories and other structures should not be destroyed since they were bound to be recaptured in a counter-attack, but now Hitler had rumbled his tactic. One of the most striking aspects of this exchange was that Speer finally realized that Hitler was a 'criminal' only after receiving his patron's reply.

Speer, who had been touring the front from Field Marshal Model's headquarters, returned to Berlin on 26 March. He was summoned to the Reich Chancellery.

'I have reports that you are no longer in harmony with me,' Hitler said to his former protégé. 'It is apparent that you no longer believe that the war can be won.' He wanted to send Speer on leave. Speer suggested resignation instead, but Hitler refused.

Speer, although officially deposed, still managed to thwart those Gauleiters who wished to carry out Hitler's order, because he retained control over the supply of explosives. But on 27 March, Hitler issued yet another order, insisting on the 'total annihilation by explosives, fire or dismantlement' of the whole railway and other transport systems and all communications, including telephones, telegraph and broadcasting. Speer, who returned to Berlin in the early hours of 29 March, contacted various sympathetic generals, including the recently deposed Guderian, as well as the less fanatical Gauleiters, to see if they supported his plan to continue thwarting Hitler's mania for destruction. Guderian, with 'funereal laughter', warned him not to 'lose his head'.

That evening Hitler began by warning Speer that his conduct was treasonous. He asked Speer again whether he still believed that the war could be won. Speer said that he did not. Hitler claimed that it was 'impossible to deny the hope of final victory'. He talked about the disappointments of his own career, a favourite refrain which also confused his own fate with that of Germany. He demanded and advised Speer 'to repent and have faith'. Speer was given twenty-four hours to see whether he could bring himself to believe in victory. Hitler, clearly nervous of losing his most competent minister, did not wait for the ultimatum to expire. He rang him in his office at the armaments ministry on the Pariserplatz. Speer returned to the Reich Chancellery bunker.

'Well?' Hitler demanded.

'My Führer, I stand unconditionally behind you,' Speer replied, suddenly deciding to lie. Hitler became emotional. His eyes filled with tears and he shook Speer's hand warmly. 'But then it will help,' Speer continued, 'if you will immediately reconfirm my authority for the implementation of your 19 March decree.' Hitler agreed at once, and told him to draw up an authorization which he would sign. In the document, Speer reserved almost all demolition decisions for the minister of armaments and war production, that is to say for himself. Hitler must have sensed that he was being deceived, and yet his greatest need appears to have been to have his favourite minister back at his side.

Bormann, meanwhile, was issuing orders through the Gauleiters on a wide range of issues. It came to his attention, for example, that doctors were already carrying out abortions on many rape victims who arrived as refugees from the eastern provinces. On 28 March, he decided that the situation had to be regularized and issued an instruction classified 'Highly confidential!' Any woman requesting an abortion in these circumstances first had to be interrogated by an officer of the Kriminalpolizei to establish the probability that she had really been raped by a

Red Army soldier as she claimed. Only then would an abortion be permitted.

Speer, in his attempts to prevent needless destruction, was a frequent visitor to Army Group Vistula headquarters at Hassleben. He found that General Heinrici entirely agreed with his aims. Speer claimed when interrogated by the Americans after the defeat that he had suggested to Heinrici's chief of staff, General Kinzel, the possibility of withdrawing Army Group Vistula to the west of Berlin to save the city from more destruction.

Heinrici had now been given responsibility for the defence of Berlin, so he and Speer worked together on the best way to save as many bridges as possible from demolition. This was doubly important because water mains and sewage pipes were an integral part of their construction. The fifty-eight-year-old Heinrici, according to one of his many admirers on the general staff, was 'in our eyes the perfect example of a traditional Prussian officer'. He had recently been awarded the Knight's Cross with Swords and Oak-Leaves. This 'grizzled soldier' was a scruffy dresser who preferred a frontline sheepskin jacket and First World War leather leggings to the smart general staff uniform. His aide tried in vain to persuade him to order a new tunic at least.

General Helmuth Reymann, a not very imaginative officer who had been designated the commander of Berlin's defence, was planning to demolish all the city's bridges. So Speer, with Heinrici's support, played his defeatist card again and asked Reymann whether he believed in victory. Reymann could not, of course, say no. Speer then persuaded him to accept Heinrici's compromise formula: to restrict his demolition plans to the outermost bridges on the Red Army's line of advance and leave the bridges in the centre of the capital intact. After the meeting with Reymann, Heinrici told Speer that he had no intention of fighting a prolonged battle for Berlin. He just hoped that the Red Army would get there quickly and take Hitler and the Nazi leadership unawares.

The headquarters staff at Hassleben were interrupted by a constant stream of less welcome visitors. Gauleiter Greiser, who had claimed urgent duties in Berlin when abandoning the besieged population of Poznan to their fate, had turned up at Army Group Vistula headquarters and hung around listlessly. He said he wanted to work as an aide on the staff. Gauleiter Hildebrandt of Mecklenburg and Gauleiter Stürz of Brandenburg also turned up, demanding briefings on the situation. There was just one question which they really wanted to ask – '*Wann kommt der Russe?*' – but they did not quite dare, because it was defeatist.

Göring was also a frequent visitor to Army Group Vistula headquarters from his ostentatious mansion at Karinhall. He made much of the *Sonderstaffel* – the special planning group led by the famous Stuka ace Lieutenant Colonel Baumbach to target the Soviet bridges and crossing points to their Oder bridgeheads, dropping newly developed radio-controlled bombs. The Kriegsmarine also organized '*Sprengboote*', an explosive version of Elizabethan fireships, floating downriver. Attacks from neither the air nor the river achieved any lasting damage. Repairs were made with great sacrifice by Soviet engineers working in freezing water. Many of them lost their lives to the cold or the current. Colonel Baumbach admitted to army staff officers that it was pointless to continue. It would be better to distribute the aircraft fuel used to armoured units. Baumbach, who, according to Colonel Eismann, had none of the '*Primadonnallüren*' of many fighter aces, was a realist, unlike the Reichsmarschall.

Göring's vanity was as ludicrous as his irresponsibility. According to one staff officer at Army Group Vistula, his twinkling eyes and the fur trimming on his specially designed uniform gave him more the appearance of 'a cheerful market woman' than a Marshal of the Reich. Göring, wearing all his medals and thick gold-braid epaulettes, insisted on going on tours of inspection, and then spent his time sending messages to army commanders complaining that he had not been saluted properly by their men.

During one planning session at Hassleben, he described his two parachute divisions on the Oder front as '*Übermenschen*'. 'You must attack with both my paratroop divisions,' he declared, 'then you can send the whole Russian army to the devil.' Göring failed to acknowledge that even many of the officers were not paratroopers at all, but Luftwaffe personnel transferred to ground combat duties of which they had no experience. His cherished 9th Parachute Division would be the first to crack when the attack came.

Göring and Dönitz intended to raise at least 30,000 men from

Luftwaffe and Kriegsmarine base units to throw them into the battle. The fact that they had received virtually no training did not seem to concern them. A marine division was formed, with an admiral as divisional commander and only one army officer on the staff to advise them on tactics and staff procedures. Not to be outdone in the competitive bidding between the armed forces, the SS had formed more police battalions and a motorized brigade of Waffen SS headquarters staff. It was designated 'Thousand and One Nights'. SS codenames became curiously exotic as the end of the Third Reich approached: the brigade's tank-hunting detachment was codenamed *Suleika* and the reconnaissance battalion *Harem*.

On 2 April, one of Himmler's staff officers proposed from the special train of the Reichsführer SS that another 4,000 'front helpers' could be added to the figure of 25,000 men marked to come from the Reichspost. The Nazi leadership was trying to meet the target of '*Der 800,000 Mann-Plan*'. Army Group Vistula headquarters argued that if there were no weapons to give all these untrained men, then they would be worse than useless. Yet the Nazi authorities were quite prepared to distribute a few panzerfausts among them and give them a grenade each to take a few of the enemy with them. 'It was quite simply,' wrote Colonel Eismann, 'an order of organized mass murder, nothing less.'

The Nazi Party itself tried to keep alive the idea of the *Freikorps Adolf Hitler*. Bormann was still discussing it on Wednesday 28 March 'with Dr Kaltenbrunner'. Members of the SS were conspicuously punctilious about their academic qualifications. They were also keen to display their historical knowledge at a time when Dr Goebbels was dragging up every example of reversals of military fortune for his propaganda barrage. Frederick the Great and Blucher had been overused, so Kaltenbrunner recommended to the propaganda ministry the defeat of King Darius of Persia.

Army Group Vistula's two armies received largely unrealizable promises from the Nazi leadership. General Hasso von Manteuffel's so-called Third Panzer Army, on the Oder front north of the Ninth Army, had little more than a single panzer division. The bulk of his divisions were also composed of composite battalions and trainees. General Busse's Ninth Army was a similar hotch-potch. It even included an assault gun company wearing U-boat uniforms.

That sector of the Oderbruch front was almost entirely manned by training units sent forward with a small ration of bread, dry sausage and tobacco. Some soldiers were so young that they were given sweets instead of tobacco. Field kitchens were set up in the villages just behind the lines and the trainees were marched forward to start digging their trenches. A comrade, one of them wrote, was 'a companion in suffering'. They were not a unit in any usual military sense of the word. Nobody, not even their officers, knew what their duties were or what they were supposed to do. They just dug in and waited. Jokes reflected their mood. One of the current ones, a captured soldier told his Soviet interrogator, was, 'Life is like a child's shirt – short and shitty.'

German soldiers with enough experience of war to know that any fool could be uncomfortable took great pride in creating a '*gemütlich*' 'earth bunker', usually about two metres by three metres, with small tree trunks holding up the metre of earth cover above. 'My main dugout was really cosy,' wrote one soldier. 'I turned it into a little room with a wooden table and bench.' Mattresses and eiderdowns looted from nearby houses provided the final home comforts.

Since firelight or smoke attracted the attention of snipers, soldiers soon gave up shaving and washing. Rations started to get worse towards the end of March. On most days, each soldier received half a *Kommissbrot*, a rock-hard army loaf, and some stew or soup which reached the front at night, cold and congealed, from a field kitchen well to the rear. If the soldiers were lucky, they received a quarter-litre bottle of schnapps each and, very occasionally, '*Frontkämpferpäckchen*' – small packs for frontline combatants containing cake, sweets and chocolate. The main problem, however, was the lack of clean drinking water. As a result many soldiers suffered from dysentery and their trenches became squalid.

The faces of the young trainees were soon gaunt from tiredness and strain. Attacks by Shturmovik fighter-bombers in clear weather, the 'midday concert' of artillery and mortar fire, and random shelling at night took their toll. From time to time, the Soviet artillery ranged in on any buildings, in case they contained a command post, and then fired phosphorous shells. But for the young and inexperienced, the most frightening experience was a four-hour stint on sentry duty at night. Everyone feared a Soviet raiding party coming to grab them as 'a tongue'.

Nobody moved by day. A Soviet sniper shot Pohlmeyer, one of

Gerhard Tillery's comrades in the 'Potsdam' Regiment of officer cadets, straight through the head as he climbed out of his slit trench. Otterstedt, who tried to help him, was also picked off. They never spotted the muzzle flash, so they had no idea where the shot had come from. The Germans on that sector, however, had their own sniper. He was 'a really crazy type' who dressed up when off-duty in an undertaker's black top hat and tailcoat, to which he pinned his German Cross in Gold, a vulgar decoration known as 'the fried egg'. His eccentricities were presumably tolerated because of his 130 victories. This sniper used to take up position just behind the front line in a barn. Observers with binoculars in the trenches would then relay targets to him. One day when little was happening, the observer told him of a dog running around the Russian positions. The dog was killed with a single shot.

Ammunition was in such short supply that exact figures had to be reported every morning. Experienced company commanders were over-reporting expenditure to build up their own reserves for the big attack, which they knew must come soon. German formation commanders became increasingly uneasy during that last part of March. They felt that the Soviets were playing with them 'like a cat with a mouse', deliberately achieving two goals at once. The battle for the bridgeheads on the west side of the Oder was not only preparing the Red Army's springboard for Berlin, it was also grinding down the Ninth Army and forcing it to use up its dwindling supplies of ammunition before the big attack. German artillery guns, restricted to less than a couple of shells per gun per day, could not indulge in counter-battery fire, so the Soviet gunners were able to range at will on specified targets, ready for their opening bombardment. The major offensive against the Seelow Heights towards Berlin was only a matter of time.

Soldiers passed the day either catching up on sleep or writing home, even though little post had been getting through since the end of February. Officers felt that this collapse of the postal system at least had one advantage. There had been a number of suicides when soldiers received disastrous news from home, whether damage from bombing or members of the family killed. Captured German soldiers told their Soviet interrogators, and it is impossible to know whether they were speaking the truth or trying to curry favour, that their own artillery fired salvoes to explode behind their trenches as a warning not to retreat.

Soldiers knew that they were going to be overwhelmed and they waited only for one thing, the order to retreat. When a platoon commander rang back to company headquarters on the field telephone and received no reply, there was nearly always panic. Most jumped to the assumption that they had been abandoned by the very commanders who had ordered them to fight to the end, but they did not want to risk the Feldgendarmerie. The best solution was to bury themselves deep in a bunker and pray that Soviet attackers would give them a chance to surrender before chucking in a grenade. But even if their surrender was accepted, there was always the risk of an immediate German counter-attack. Any soldier found to have surrendered faced summary execution.

Despite all its weaknesses in trained men and ammunition, the German Army at bay could still prove itself a dangerous opponent. On 22 March, Chuikov's 8th Guards Army attacked at Gut Hathenow, on the treeless flood plain near the Reitwein Spur. The 920th Assault Gun Training Brigade with the 303rd *Döberitz* Infantry Division was alerted. They deployed rapidly on seeing T-34 tanks. Oberfeldwebel Weinheimer yelled his fire orders: 'Range – Armour-piercing – Target – Fire!' Gerhard Laudan reloaded as soon as the gun recoiled. The crew established a good rhythm of firing. They hit four T-34s in a matter of minutes, but then there was a blinding flash of light and they felt a huge blow as their armoured vehicle shuddered. Laudan's head struck the steel plate. He heard their commander scream, *'Raus!'* Laudan forced open the hatch to throw himself out, but was yanked back by his headset and microphone, which he had forgotten to detach. By the time he had extracted himself with only minor wounds, he found the rest of the crew outside sheltering in the lee of the vehicle. Amid the chaos of enemy tanks charging around, there seemed to be no chance of rescue or recovery. But then their driver, Soldat Klein, climbed back into the vehicle through a hatch. To their astonishment, they heard the engine restart. They scrambled back inside and the vehicle reversed slowly. They found that the enemy shell had struck the armour near the gun, but fortunately there was a gap there between the outer armour and the inner steel skin of the hull. This had saved them. 'For once "soldier's luck" was on our side,' Laudan commented. They were even able to drive the vehicle back to the brigade repair base at Rehfelde, south of Strausberg.

Both on the Oder front and on the Neisse opposite the 1st Ukrainian Front, officers suffered from mixed feelings. 'Officers have two opinions of the situation,' Soviet interrogators reported, 'the official version and their own views, which they share only with very close friends.' They firmly believed that they had to defend the Fatherland and their families, yet they were well aware that the situation was hopeless. 'One should distinguish between regiments,' a captured senior lieutenant told a 7th Department interrogator at 21st Army headquarters. 'The regular units are strong. The discipline and fighting spirit are good. But in the hastily thrown-together battle-groups, the situation is totally different. Discipline is terrible and as soon as Russian troops appear, the soldiers panic and run from their positions.'

'To be an officer,' another German lieutenant wrote to his fiancée, 'means always having to swing back and forth like a pendulum between a Knight's Cross, a birchwood cross and a court martial.'

11

Preparing the Coup de Grâce

On 3 April, Marshal Zhukov flew from Moscow's central airfield back to his headquarters. Konev took off in his aeroplane almost at the same time. The race was on. The plan was to launch the offensive on 16 April and to take Berlin on 22 April, Lenin's birthday. Zhukov was in constant touch with the *Stavka*, but all his communications with Moscow were controlled by the NKVD in the form of the 108th Special Communications Company attached to his headquarters.

'The Berlin operation . . . planned by the genius commander-in-chief, Comrade Stalin', as the political department of the 1st Ukrainian Front put it so diplomatically, was not a bad plan. The trouble was that the main bridgehead seized by the 1st Belorussian Front lay right under the best defensive feature in the whole region: the Seelow Heights. Zhukov admitted later that he underestimated the strength of this position.

The tasks facing the staffs of the two main Fronts involved in the operation were huge. Russian-gauge railways had been rapidly laid right across Poland and the temporary bridges over the Vistula to bring up the millions of tons of supplies required – including artillery shells and rockets, ammunition, fuel and food.

The Red Army's principal raw material, its manpower, also needed restocking and refashioning. Casualties in the Vistula–Oder and the Pomeranian operations had not been heavy by Red Army standards, especially when considering the huge advances made. But Zhukov and Konev's rifle divisions, averaging 4,000 men each, had never really had a chance to refill their ranks. By 5 September 1944, 1,030,494 criminals from the Gulag had been transferred to the Red Army. The term criminal also included those sentenced for failing to turn up at their place of work. Political prisoners, or *zeky*, accused of treason or anti-Soviet activities were deemed too dangerous for release even to *shtraf* companies.

Further transfers from the Gulag were made in the early spring of 1945, once again with the promise that a prisoner could expunge his crime with his blood. In fact, the need for reinforcements was deemed so great that at the end of March, just over two weeks from the offensive against Berlin, a decree of the State Defence Committee ordered a wide range of categories of prisoners to be produced from each oblast, NKVD department and from pending cases in front of procurators.

It is doubtful whether the idea of exchanging a Gulag death – 'a dog's death for dogs', as it was called – for a hero's death motivated a majority of these prisoners, even if five of them became Heroes of the Soviet Union, including one of the most famous heroes of the war, Aleksandr Matrosov, who reputedly threw himself against a German embrasure. Life in the camps had taught them to think no more than a day ahead. The only thing likely to inspire them was a complete change of routine and the chance of misbehaviour. Some of the ex-Gulag soldiers did indeed 'redeem their guilt with their blood', either with *shtraf* companies or in mine-clearing units. Those integrated with sapper companies appear, not surprisingly, to have fought much better than those sent to *shtraf* companies.

Liberated prisoners of war, those who had survived the appalling conditions of German camps, were treated little better. In October 1944, the State Defence Committee had decreed that, when liberated, they should be transferred to special reserve units of military districts for screening by NKVD and SMERSH. Those sent straight from reserve battalions to frontline units were often far from healthy after their ordeal. They were always treated as deeply suspect. Front commands did not hide their unease about reincorporating 'soldiers who were Soviet citizens released from fascist slavery'. Their 'morale' had been considerably lowered by 'false fascist propaganda' during their long imprisonment. Yet the methods of political officers were hardly likely to cure them of their worst impulses. They read them orders of Comrade Stalin, showed them films of the Soviet Union and the Great Patriotic War, and encouraged them to recount 'the terrible atrocities of the German bandits'.

'These men were important to the army,' the political department of the 1st Ukrainian Front wrote, 'because they were full of burning hatred for the enemy, and because they longed for revenge for all the atrocities and abuses they had suffered. At the same time they were not yet accustomed to strict military order.' This acknowledged that released prisoners tended to go in for rape, murder, looting, drunkenness and desertion. Like many of the Gulag criminals, they had been thoroughly brutalized by their experiences.

In the 5th Shock Army, the 94th Guards Rifle Division received a batch of forty-five former prisoners of war just five days before the Oder operation was due to take place. Political officers clearly did not trust them. 'Each day,' one of them wrote, 'I spent two hours talking to them about the Motherland, about the atrocities of Germans, and about the law concerning betrayal of the Motherland. We distributed them among different regiments to exclude the possibility of having two people in the same company who might have been in Germany together or who came from the same region. Every day and every hour we were informed of their morale and behaviour. To make them hate the Germans we used photographs of Germans abusing our civilian population, including children, and we showed them the mutilated corpse of one of our soldiers.'

The distrust of former prisoners of war was based on the Stalinist fear that anybody who had spent time outside the Soviet Union, whatever the circumstances, had been exposed to anti-Soviet influences. The fact of being in a German prison camp meant that they had been 'constantly influenced by Goebbels propaganda': 'They did not know the real situation in the Soviet Union and Red Army.' This suggests that the authorities feared that memories of the catastrophe of 1941 and any association of it with the leadership of Comrade Stalin had to be eliminated at all costs. Political officers were also appalled by a question apparently 'often asked' by former prisoners of war: 'Is it true that all the equipment used by the Red Army has been bought from the USA and England and that that's the job of Comrade Stalin?'

The NKVD was also concerned. 'Bad supervision and the unserious attitude of commanders' had failed to control cases of indiscipline, the breaking of state laws and 'immoral behaviour'. Even officers had been involved: 'The territory liberated by the Soviet Army is full of enemy elements, saboteurs and other agents.' The unserious attitude of commanders had extended to installing curtains which covered the side windows of staff cars. This presumably was done to conceal the presence of a senior officer's 'campaign wife', a mistress usually selected from the signals or medical unit attached to their headquarters. Even though Stalin had tacitly permitted the institution of 'campaign wives', the NKVD ordered that 'these [curtains] must be removed by checkpoints'.

Indoctrination was the highest priority, both for political officers and for the NKVD, which was in charge of 'Checking Fighting Fitness for Battle'. 'Political preparation', according to this criterion, was the most important of all categories. Special propaganda seminars were arranged for non-Russian-speaking nationalities in the 1st Belorussian Front, following the arrival at the end of March of a new draft. These included Poles from the 'western Ukraine' and 'western Belorussia' and Moldavians. Many of these conscripts, however, had seen the mass arrests and deportations of 1939–41 by the NKVD and resisted their indoctrination, which concentrated on the Communist-inspired self-sacrifice of Red Army soldiers. 'They regarded it quite sceptically,' one political department reported with alarm. 'After the conversation on the feat of Hero of the Soviet Union Sergeant Varlamov, who blocked the embrasure of an enemy firepoint with his body, there were comments that this cannot be possible.'

The quality of military training clearly left much to be desired. 'A large number of non-operational losses are due to the ignorance of officers and their bad training of soldiers,' an NKVD report stated. In one division alone, twenty-three soldiers were killed and sixty-seven wounded in a single month solely due to the mishandling of sub-machine guns: 'This happens because they are piled or hung up with loaded magazines still on.' Other soldiers were wounded when messing around with unfamiliar weapons and anti-tank grenades. Ill-informed soldiers put the wrong detonators into grenades, and some 'hit mines and shells with hard objects'.

Red Army sappers, on the other hand, needed to take risks, often to make up for the shortage of supplies. They took pride in recycling the contents of unexploded shells and German mines lifted by night. Their private motto remained 'One mistake and no more dinners.' They used to extract the explosive, then warm it up and roll it out on the inside of their thighs, like girls in a Cuban cigar factory, and finally feed it into one of their own wooden mine cases, which could not be picked up by German mine detectors. The degree of danger depended on the stability of the explosive which they extracted. Their courage and skills were highly respected by both rifle units and tankists, who never usually conceded anything to another arm or service.

The programme of hatred of the enemy had started in the late summer of 1942, at the time of the withdrawal to Stalingrad and Stalin's 'Not one step back' order. It had also been the time of Anna Akhmatova's poem 'The Hour of Courage has Struck'. But in February 1945, the Soviet authorities adapted her words: 'Red Army soldier: You are now on German soil. The hour of revenge has struck!' It was, in fact, Ilya Ehrenburg who first changed her words, he who had written in 1942, 'Do not count days; do not count miles. Count only the number of Germans you have killed. Kill the German – this is your mother's prayer. Kill the German – this is the cry of your Russian earth. Do not waver. Do not let up. Kill.'

Every opportunity had been taken to drum in the scale of German atrocities in the Soviet Union. According to a French informant, the Red Army authorities exhumed the bodies of some 65,000 Jews mass-acred near Nikolayev and Odessa, and ordered them to be placed alongside the road most used by troops. Every 200 metres a sign declared, 'Look how the Germans treat Soviet citizens.'

Liberated slave labourers were used as another example of German atrocities. The predominantly Ukrainian and Belorussian women were made to tell soldiers how badly they had been misused. 'Our soldiers got very angry,' a political officer remembered. But then he added, 'To be fair, some Germans treated their workers quite well, but they were a minority and in the mood of the time, the worst examples were the ones we remembered.'

'We were constantly trying to step up hatred towards Germans,' the political department of the 1st Ukrainian Front reported, 'and to stir up a passion for revenge.' Messages from forced labourers found in villages were printed and circulated to the troops. 'They put us in a camp,' one such letter read, 'in a grey dark barracks and force us to work from morning to night and feed us on turnip soup and a tiny piece of bread. They are constantly insulting us. This is how we have spent our youth. They took all the young people from the village – even the boys who were only thirteen years old – to their accursed Germany and we are all suffering here, barefoot and hungry. There are rumours that "our people" are getting close. We can hardly wait. Maybe we'll soon see our brothers and our suffering will end. The girls came to see me. We all sat down together to discuss it. Will we survive this terrible time? Will we ever see our families? We cannot stand it any more. It is terrible here in Germany. Zhenya Kovakchuk.' Another letter from her gave the words of what she called 'the song of the girl slaves'.

> Spring is over, summer has come
> Our flowers are blossoming in the garden
> And I, such a young girl,
> I spend my days in a German camp.

Another method for arousing hatred used by political officers was the 'revenge score'. 'In each regiment soldiers and officers were interviewed and facts of atrocities, "looting and violence by Hitler's beasts", were established. For example, in one battalion, a frightening revenge score was compiled and it was put on a poster: "We are now getting our revenge for 775 of our relatives who were killed, for 909 relatives who were taken away to slavery in Germany, for 478 burnt-down houses and for 303 destroyed farms" . . . In all regiments of the [1st Belorussian] Front "revenge meetings" were held and aroused great enthusiasm. Troops of our Front as well as soldiers of the whole Red Army are the noble avengers punishing fascist occupiers for all their monstrous atrocities and evil deeds.'

'There was a big slogan painted up in our canteen,' a cypherene with the headquarters of the 1st Belorussian Front remembered. '"Have you killed a German yet? Then kill him!" We were very strongly influenced by Ehrenburg's appeals and we had a lot to take revenge for.' Her own parents had been killed in Sevastopol. 'The hatred was so great that it was difficult to control the soldiers.'

While Soviet military authorities were cultivating their soldiers' anger ready for the final offensive, their 7th Department for propaganda was trying to persuade the German soldiers facing them that they would be well treated if they surrendered.

Occasionally raiding parties from reconnaissance companies would capture a Feldpost sack full of letters from home. These would be read and analysed by the German Communists or 'antifas' – anti-fascist prisoners of war attached to the department. Letters would also be taken from all prisoners for analysis. They were interested in the mood of the civilian population, the effects of American and British bombing and any references to shortages of food at home, especially the lack of milk for children. This information would be passed back upwards, but also put together for propaganda leaflets, printed on a mobile press attached to army headquarters.

One of the highest priorities for interrogation of captured 'tongues', deserters and other prisoners was the subject of chemical weapons. The Soviet military authorities were understandably concerned that Hitler might want to use chemical weapons as a last-ditch defence, especially after all the Nazi leadership's claims of 'miracle weapons'. Reports reached Sweden that chemical weapons had been distributed to special troops in long boxes, with the inscription 'Can only be used on the personal order of the Führer'. The Swedish military attaché heard that only fear of killing everyone in the vicinity prevented them from being used. If true, this would mean that supplies of Sarin and Tabun nerve gas from the Wehrmacht chemical weapons research centre in the massive citadel at Spandau had been distributed. Field Marshal Kesselring apparently told SS Obergruppenführer Wolff that Hitler's advisers were urging him to use the '*Verzweiflungswaffen*' – 'the weapons of despair'.

Albert Speer, when interrogated by the Americans a few weeks later, readily acknowledged that Nazi fanatics during this period had 'argued for chemical warfare'. But although Soviet sources allege that a gas attack using aircraft and mortar shells had been made against their troops in February near Gleiwitz, the lack of detail offered suggests that this was either a false scare or an attempt to provoke an interest in the threat. Soldiers were ordered to operate in gas masks for four hours a day and to sleep in them for at least one night. Paper garments and protective stockings were issued, and so were canvas masks for horses. Orders also went out to protect food and water sources, and to prepare basements and cellars in headquarters against gas attacks. But how much attention was paid to these instructions by the Red Army is very much open to question, especially since NKVD regiments were responsible for 'chemical discipline'.

Training in the German panzerfaust was taken much more seriously. Large quantities of the weapon had been captured and groups of 'trained fausters' were organized in each rifle battalion. Political officers coined the rather predictable slogan, 'Beat the enemy with his own weapons.' Training consisted of firing one of these rocket-propelled grenades at a burnt-out tank or wall at a range of about thirty metres. In the 3rd Shock Army, Komsomol instructors issued them out and taught the selected fausters how to aim. Sergeant Belyaev, in the 3rd Rifle Corps, fired at a wall fifty metres away. When the dust settled, he found that it had blasted a hole large enough to crawl through and smashed into the wall beyond. Most of those who tried them out were similarly impressed. They saw their advantage in the fighting which lay ahead in Berlin, not in the weapon's official anti-tank role, but to blast through walls to get from house to house.

12

Waiting for the Onslaught

During early April, as Berlin awaited the final Soviet onslaught along the Oder, the atmosphere in the city became a mixture of febrile exhaustion, terrible foreboding and despair.

'Yesterday,' the Swedish military attaché reported to Stockholm, 'the well-meaning von Tippelskirch invited us to another evening at Mellensee, and I went more out of curiosity than anything else. The expectation of hearing anything interesting was not high, since now everything happens from one moment to the next. The evening was quite tragic. The atmosphere was one of hopelessness. Most of them did not even pretend to keep up appearances, but showed the situation as it really was. Some became maudlin, seeking comfort in the bottle.'

Fanatical determination existed only among those Nazis who believed that surrender in any form meant execution. They, like Hitler, were determined to ensure that everyone else shared the same fate as themselves. In September 1944, when the Western Allies and the Red Army had been advancing towards the Reich with great speed, the Nazi leadership wanted to fight on against its sworn enemies even after defeat. It decided to set up a resistance movement to be known by the codename *Werwolf*.

The name *Werwolf* was inspired by a novel set in the Thirty Years War by Hermann Löns, an extreme nationalist killed in 1914 and revered by the Nazis. In October 1944, when the idea started to be put into effect, SS Obergruppenführer Hans Prützmann was appointed General-inspekteur für Spezialabwehr – General Inspector for Special Defence.

Prützmann, who had studied Soviet partisan tactics during his time in the Ukraine, was summoned back from Königsberg to establish a headquarters. But, as with many Nazi projects, rival factions wanted to create their own set-up or bring existing ones under their control. Even within the SS, there were to be two organizations, *Werwolf* and Otto Skorzeny's SS *Jagdverbände*. The figure rises to three if you include the unactivated Gestapo and SD version to be known by the codename *Bundschuh*.

In theory, the training programmes covered sabotage using tins of Heinz oxtail soup packed with plastic explosive and detonated with captured British time pencils. A whole range of items and even garments made of Nipolit explosive were designed, including raincoats with linings made of explosive. *Werwolf* recruits were taught to kill sentries with a slip-knotted garrotte about a metre long or a Walther pistol with silencer. Captured documents showed that their watchword was to be, 'Turn day into night, night into day! Hit the enemy wherever you meet him. Be sly! Steal weapons, ammunition and rations! Women helpers, support the battle of the *Werwolf* wherever you can.' They were to operate in groups of three to six men, and were to receive rations for sixty days. 'Special emphasis was put on gasoline and oil supplies' as targets. The Nazi authorities ordered 2,000 radios and 5,000 explosive kits, but few were ready in time. American incendiary bombs dropped in bombing raids were collected and concentration camp inmates were forced to check them and extract the material for re-use.

On 1 April at 8 p.m., an appeal was broadcast to the German people to join the *Werwolf*. 'Every Bolshevik, every Englishman, every American on our soil must be a target for our movement . . . Any German, whatever his profession or class, who puts himself at the service of the enemy and collaborates with him will feel the effect of our avenging hand . . . A single motto remains for us: "Conquer or die."' A few days later, Himmler issued a new order: 'Every male in a house where a white flag appears must be shot. Not a moment must be wasted in executing these measures. By male persons who must be considered responsible for their actions this means everyone aged fourteen years and upwards.'

The true objective of *Werwolf*, as a document of 4 April confirmed, came from the Nazi obsession with 1918. 'We know the plans of the enemy and we know that following a defeat there would be no chance

of Germany ever rising again like after 1918.' The threat of killing anyone
who collaborated with the allies was to prevent a 'Stresemann-Politik', a
reference to Gustav Stresemann's signature of the Treaty of Versailles
in 1919. The Nazi Party was rooted in the humiliation of that defeat and
it brought Germany back there again with terrible interest.

Hitler Youth boys were sent off to their selected areas, where they
were told to bury their explosive, then contact the local Nazi Kreisleiter
for accommodation and rations. They were all given single unspecified
missions, then told to go home as if nothing had happened. Towards
the end, the training became very hurried, so many of them were more
likely to blow themselves up rather than the enemy.

Ultimately, *Werwolf* achieved very little, apart from a couple of
assassinations – the mayors of Aachen and Krankenhagen – and the
intimidation of civilians. Hitler Youth chalked slogans on walls such
as, 'Traitor take care, the *Werwolf* is watching.' Both Skorzeny and
Prützmann seem to have become less enamoured of the project as the
allies closed in – if one is to believe Skorzeny's account in his interrogation. (Prützmann committed suicide after one brief interview.) In any
case, Himmler also had a change of heart in mid-April, just when
negotiations via Sweden were on his mind. He instructed Prützmann to
change *Werwolf* activity 'to that – exclusively – of propaganda'. The
only problem was that the *Werwolfsender* radio transmitter, under the
control of Goebbels, continued to order partisan action.

On the Eastern Front, the rapid advances of the Red Army from
January to March meant that hardly any groups were trained or equipped
in time, and the only stay-behind groups were usually Volkssturm
members, who had been cut off. The *Werwolf* propaganda simply lent
SMERSH and the NKVD rifle regiments an urgent focus to their
usual paranoia. In the west, the Allies found that *Werwolf* was a fiasco.
Bunkers prepared for *Werwolf* operations had supplies 'for 10–15 days
only' and the fanaticism of the Hitler Youth members they captured
had entirely disappeared. They were 'no more than frightened, unhappy
youths'. Few resorted to the suicide pills which they had been given 'to
escape the strain of interrogation and, above all, the inducement to
commit treason'. Many, when sent off by their controllers to prepare
terrorist acts, had sneaked home.

Some have pointed out that the whole *Werwolf* project did not fit with the national character. 'We Germans are not a nation of partisans,' wrote an anonymous woman diarist in Berlin. 'We wait for leadership, for orders.' She had travelled in the Soviet Union just before the Nazis came to power and, during long discussions on trains, Russians made jokes about the German lack of revolutionary spirit. 'German comrades would storm a railway station,' one said, 'only if they could first of all buy platform tickets!'

Reports also indicate that, although not part of the *Werwolf* programme, members of the Gestapo had been transferred to the Kriminalpolizei on the grounds that the Western Allies were sure to reinstate them later once military government was installed. As the reality of final collapse sank in, supposedly fanatical believers turned rapidly to self-preservation. Some SS members, to avoid prosecution, simply snaffled for themselves the false documents prepared for *Werwolf* members. Others procured Wehrmacht uniforms and the pay-books of dead men to provide themselves with new identities. German soldiers were furious that while the SS had been carrying out random executions for desertion, many of their officers were preparing their own escape. German prisoners of war told their American interrogators that tailors had been ordered to stitch a large P on jackets so that SS men trying to hide could masquerade as Polish workers.

The Nazi leadership did not just rely on the 'flying courts martial' and SS execution squads to terrorize soldiers into continuing the fight. The tales of atrocities from the propaganda ministry never ceased. Stories of women commissars castrating wounded soldiers, for example, were circulated. The ministry also had its own squads both in Berlin and close to the Oder front, painting slogans on walls as if they were the spontaneous expression of the civilian population, such as 'We believe in victory!', 'We will never surrender' and 'Protect our women and children from the Red beasts!' There was, however, one group who could demonstrate their feelings about the war without fear of reprisal. German wounded who had lost hands or arms would say '*Heil Hitler!*' and 'raise their stumps ostentatiously'.

The man with the least enviable task at this time was Lieutenant General Reymann, the officer appointed Commander of the Greater Berlin Defence Area. He faced the culmination of the Nazis' organizational chaos. General Halder, the army chief of staff sacked in 1942, was scathing on the subject. Both Hitler and Goebbels, the Reich Commissar for Defence of the capital, he wrote later, refused to give any 'thought to defending the city until it was much too late. Thus, the city's defence was characterized only by a mass of improvisations.'

Reymann was the third person to hold the post since Hitler had declared Berlin a fortress at the beginning of February. He found that he had to deal with Hitler, Goebbels, the Replacement Army commanded by Himmler, the Luftwaffe, Army Group Vistula head-quarters, the SS, the Hitler Youth and also the local Nazi Party organiz-ation, which controlled the Volkssturm. Hitler, having ordered that Berlin should be prepared for defence, then refused to allocate any troops to the task. He simply assured Reymann that sufficient forces would be provided if the enemy reached the capital. Neither Hitler nor Goebbels could face the reality of defeat. Goebbels in particular had convinced himself that the Red Army could be held on the Oder.

Berlin's population in early April stood at anything between 3 and 3.5 million people, including around 120,000 infants. When General Reymann raised the problem of feeding these children at a meeting in the Reich Chancellery bunker, Hitler stared at him. 'There are no children of that age left in Berlin,' he said. Reymann finally understood that his supreme commander had no contact with human reality. Goeb-bels, meanwhile, insisted that there were large reserves of tinned milk and that, if the city were encircled, cows could be brought into the centre. Reymann asked what the cows would be fed on. Goebbels had no idea. To make matters worse, the food depots were all situated on the outskirts of the city and were vulnerable to capture. Nothing was done to move either Wehrmacht or civilian supplies closer in.

Reymann and his chief of staff, Colonel Hans Refior, knew that Berlin had no hope of holding out with the forces at their disposal, so they recommended to Goebbels that civilians, especially women and children, should be allowed to leave. 'Evacuation,' replied Goebbels, 'is best organized by the SS and the police commander for the Spree region. I will give the order for evacuation at the right time.' It was quite clear that he had not for a moment seriously considered the logistic implications of evacuating such a mass of people by road and rail, to say nothing of feeding them on the way. There were not nearly enough trains still in service, and few vehicles with fuel capable of transporting the weak and the sick. The bulk of the population would have had to walk. One suspects that Goebbels, like Stalin at the start of the battle of Stalingrad, did not want to evacuate civilians in the hope that it would force the soldiers to defend the city more desperately.

From the regional headquarters for the Berlin district, a solid building on the Hohenzollerndamm, Reymann and his staff tried to find out how many soldiers and how many weapons could be counted on. Colonel Refior rapidly discovered that the 'Berlin Defence Area' carried no significance. It was just another phrase, like 'Fortress', coined in Führer headquarters which people were still supposed to defend to the death. He found that dealing with such 'short-sightedness, bureaucracy and bloody-mindedness, was enough to turn anybody's hair white'.

To defend the outer perimeter alone, ten divisions were needed. In fact, the Berlin Defence Area possessed in theory only a flak division, nine companies of the *Grossdeutschland* guard regiment, a couple of police battalions, a couple of pioneer battalions and twenty Volkssturm battalions which had been called up, but not trained. Another twenty would be called up if the city were surrounded. But although the Berlin Volkssturm amounted to 60,000 men on paper, it included both 'Volkssturm I', who had some weapons, and 'Volkssturm II', who had no weapons at all. In many cases, a former regular officer would send his unarmed Volkssturm soldiers home when the Red Army approached the city, but commanders who were Party functionaries seldom showed even the most basic humanity. One of the Nazi Kreisleiters was convinced that the only thing to do was to keep the men away from the influence of their wives, from the '*Muttis*', who might undermine their will to resist. But this was doomed to failure. No rations had been allocated for the Volkssturm, so they had to be fed by their families. In any case, commanders in charge of the defence soon found that only veterans of the First World War showed 'a sense of duty'. Most of the rest slipped away whenever the opportunity presented itself.

The most heavily armed force in Berlin was the 1st Flak Division, and yet it did not come under Reymann's command until the battle started. Based on the three vast concrete flak towers – the Zoobunker in the Tiergarten, the Humboldthain and the Friedrichshain – this Luftwaffe division had an impressive arsenal of 128mm, 88mm and 20mm guns, as well as the necessary ammunition to go with them. Reymann's artillery otherwise consisted of obsolete guns of various calibres taken earlier in the war from the French, Belgians and Yugoslavs. There were seldom more than half a dozen rounds per gun, often less. The only guideline on conducting a defence of the city was a pre-war instruction, which Refior described as a 'masterpiece of German bureaucratic art'.

The Nazi Party in Berlin talked of mobilizing armies of civilians to work on defences – both an 'obstacle ring' thirty kilometres out and a perimeter ring. But the maximum workforce ever achieved on one day was 70,000; it was usually no more than 30,000. Transport and a shortage of tools were the main problems, apart from the fact that most Berlin factories and offices continued to work as if nothing were amiss.

Reymann appointed Colonel Lohbeck, an engineer officer, to take over the Party-led chaos of defence works and he called on the school of military engineering at Karlshorst to provide demolition teams. Army officers were nervous about Speer's attempts to save the bridges within Berlin. They could not forget the execution of the officers over the bridge at Remagen. Reymann's sappers supervised the Todt Organization and the Reich Labour Service, both of which were far better equipped than the civilian corvée, but they found it impossible to obtain fuel and spare parts for the mechanical diggers. Most of the 17,000 French prisoners of war from Stalag III D were put to work in the city, creating barricades and digging foxholes in pavements at street corners. How much they achieved is open to question, however, especially since French prisoners round Berlin were those most regularly accused of being '*Arbeitsunlustig*' – reluctant to work – and of escaping from their camps, usually to visit German women.

Attempts to liaise with the field commanders, who were supposed to provide fighting troops for the defence of the city, were far from successful. When Refior went to visit Heinrici's chief of staff, Lieutenant General Kinzel, at Army Group Vistula headquarters, Kinzel simply glanced at the plans he presented for the defence of Berlin and said, 'Those madmen in Berlin should stew in their own juice.' The Ninth Army's chief of staff, Major General Hölz, regarded the plans as irrelevant for other reasons. 'The Ninth Army,' said Hölz, in a manner which Refior found rather too theatrical, 'stands and stays on the Oder. If it should be necessary, we will fall there, but we will not retreat.'

Neither Reymann nor Refior realized fully at the time that General Heinrici and his staff at Army Group Vistula had a very different plan from the Nazi leadership. They were hoping to prevent a last-ditch defence of the capital for the sake of the civil population. Albert Speer had suggested to Heinrici that the Ninth Army should withdraw from the Oder, bypassing Berlin entirely. Heinrici agreed in principle. In his view, the best way to avoid fighting in the city would be to order Reymann to send all his troops forward to the Oder at the last moment to strip Berlin of its defenders.

Another strong reason for avoiding a battle in the city was the Nazis' resort to boys as young as fourteen as cannon fodder. So many houses had a framed photograph on the wall of a son killed in Russia that a silent prayer arose that the regime would collapse before these children were sent into battle. Some did not shrink from openly calling it infanticide, whether it was exploiting the fanaticism of deluded Hitler Youth or forcing frightened boys into uniform through threat of execution. Older teachers in schools risked denunciation by advising their pupils on how to avoid being called up. The sense of bitterness was even greater after Goebbels's speech a few weeks before. 'The Führer once coined the phrase,' he reminded them, ' "Each mother who has given birth to a child has struck a blow for the future of our people." ' But it was now clear that Hitler and Goebbels were about to throw those children's lives away for a cause which had no possible future.

The fourteen-year-old Erich Schmidtke in Prenzlauerberg had been called up as a 'flak helper' to man anti-aircraft guns and ordered to report to the Hermann Göring barracks in Reinickendorf. His mother, whose husband was trapped with the army in Courland, was understandably upset and accompanied him to the barracks with his little suitcase. He felt more awed than afraid. After three days in the barracks, they were ordered to join the division being assembled at the Reichssportsfeld in the west of the city, next to the Olympic stadium. But on his way there, he thought of his father's words when on leave from the Eastern Front, telling him that he was now responsible for the family. He decided to desert and went into hiding until the war was over. Most of his contemporaries who joined the division were killed.

The so-called Hitler Youth Division raised by the Reich Youth

Leader, Artur Axmann, was also being trained at the Reichssportsfeld on the use of the panzerfaust. Axmann lectured them on the heroism of Sparta and tried to inspire an unwavering hatred of the enemy and an unwavering loyalty to Adolf Hitler. 'There is only victory or defeat,' he told them. Some of the young found their suicidal task ahead deeply stirring. Reinhard Appel thought of Rilke's *Cornet* charging out against the Turks, just as the lost generation of 1914 had when they volunteered. The fact that a detachment of '*Blitzmädel*' girls was also billeted on the Reichssportsfeld no doubt heightened the romantic appeal.

The Nazi leadership was also preparing at this time a *Wehrmachthelfer-innenkorps* of female military auxiliaries. Young women had to swear an oath of allegiance which began, 'I swear that I will be true and obedient to Adolf Hitler, the Führer and commander in chief of the Wehrmacht.' The words made it sound like a mass marriage. For somebody who had perhaps diverted his sexual drive into the pursuit of power, this may have provided its own form of *ersatz* fantasy.

In the Wilhelmstrasse district of ministries, government officials were trying to convince any diplomats who remained in the city that they were 'deciphering telegrams between Roosevelt and Churchill within two hours of their dispatch'. Meanwhile, rumours circulated of Communist shock troops being formed in the eastern 'Red' part of the city to liquidate Nazi Party members. 'There is an atmosphere of desperation at the top,' the Swedish military attaché reported to Stockholm. 'A determination to sell their lives dearly.' In fact, the only sabotage groups came from the other side of the lines, when members of the Soviet-controlled Freies Deutschland in Wehrmacht uniform slipped through German positions and moved towards Berlin. They cut cables, but little more. Freies Deutschland later claimed that its resistance group Osthafen had blown up a munitions dump in Berlin, but this is far from certain.

On 9 April, a number of well-known opponents of the regime were butchered by the SS in a variety of concentration camps. The order was given to ensure their deaths before the enemy could release them. In Dachau, Johann Georg Elser, the Communist who had tried to assassin-ate Hitler in the Burger Brau on 8 November 1939, was killed. Dietrich Bonhoeffer, Admiral Canaris and General Oster were executed in Flossenbürg and Hans von Dohnanyi in Sachsenhausen.

*

'Revenge is coming!' – '*Die Vergeltung kommt!*' – had been the Nazi propaganda slogan for the V-weapons. But this now had a hollow echo for officers on the Oder front as they awaited the onslaught. It was Soviet revenge which was coming and they knew that there were no more miracle weapons to save them. Many of them, under heavy pressure from above, lied to their men even more than before other similar defeats, with promises of miracle weapons, of rifts in the enemy coalition and of reinforcements. This was to contribute to the breakdown in discipline at the end of the battle.

Even the Waffen SS began to suffer from an unprecedented resentment between soldiers and officers. Eberhard Baumgart, the clerk with the SS Division *30. Januar*, went back to headquarters to deal with a report, but found that the sentries would not let him in. A look through the windows soon explained why. 'I thought I was dreaming,' he wrote later. 'Glittering dress uniforms swirled around with tarted-up women, music, noise, laughter, shrieking, cigarette smoke and clinking glasses.' Baumgart's mood next day was not helped when Georg, the Volga German interpreter, showed him a cartoon from *Pravda* of Hitler, Göring and Goebbels in an orgy in the Reich Chancellery. The caption read, 'Every day the German soldier holds on lengthens our lives.'

Instead of miracle weapons, many of the Volkssturm and other improvised units received weapons that were useless, such as the *Volks-handgranate 45*. This 'people's hand grenade' was simply a lump of concrete around a small explosive charge and a No. 8 detonator. It was more dangerous to the thrower than to the target. One detachment of officer cadets facing a Guards tank army received rifles captured from the French army in 1940 and just five rounds each. It was typical of Nazi corporate bluster that they continued to create impressive-sounding units – whether the *Sturmzug*, which lacked the weapons to storm anything, or the *Panzerjadgkompanie*, which was supposed to stalk tanks on foot.

Another formation, which had better reason than most to fear the consequences of capture, was the 1st Division of General Vlasov's Russian Army of Liberation. It had been Himmler's idea to bring the Vlasov division to the Oder front. He had trouble persuading Hitler, who still disliked the idea of using Slav troops. The German general staff had supported the idea earlier in the war of raising a Ukrainian army of a million men, but Hitler vetoed the plan, determined to maintain the separation of '*Herrenmensch und das Sklavenvolk*'. And then the terrible treatment of the Ukrainian people under Rosenberg and Gauleiter Koch in the Ukraine had put an end to Wehrmacht hopes.

Early in April, General Vlasov, accompanied by a liaison officer and an interpreter, came to Army Group Vistula headquarters to discuss matters with General Heinrici. Vlasov was a tall, rather gaunt man, with 'clever eyes' set in a colourless face, with one of those chins which looked grey even when freshly shaved. After a few optimistic expressions by Vlasov, Heinrici asked bluntly how such a recently formed division would perform in combat. German officers were concerned that these Russian volunteers would refuse to fight their fellow countrymen at the last moment. Now that the Third Reich was doomed to destruction, there was little incentive, save desperation, for the Vlasov volunteers.

Vlasov did not try to fool Heinrici. He explained that his plan had been to raise at least six divisions, hopefully ten, from prisoners of war in the camps. The problem was that the Nazi authorities had not come round to the idea until it was too late. He was aware of the risk of Soviet propaganda aimed at his men. Yet he felt that they should be allowed to prove themselves in an attack on one of the Oder bridgeheads.

General Busse chose for them an unimportant sector at Erlenhof, south of Frankfurt an der Oder. Soviet reconnaissance groups from the 33rd Army identified their presence almost immediately and a barrage of loudspeaker activity began. The advance of the *Vlasovtsy* started on 13 April. During two and a half hours' fighting, the 1st Division created a wedge 500 metres deep, but the Soviet artillery fire was so strong that they had to lie down. General Bunyachenko, their commander, seeing no sign of either air or artillery support which he thought that the Germans had promised, withdrew his men, disregarding Busse's order. The Vlasov division lost 370 men, including four officers. Busse was furious, and, on his recommendation, General Krebs ordered the division to be withdrawn from the front and stripped of its weapons, which would be used for 'better purposes'. The *Vlasovtsy* were deeply embittered. They blamed their reverse on the lack of artillery support, but perhaps nobody had warned them that German batteries were holding back their last rounds for the major attack.

*

During the first two weeks of April, sporadic fighting continued in the bridgeheads. Soviet attacks were aimed to deepen them. Behind the Oder, the activity was even more intense. Altogether, twenty-eight Soviet armies were involved in regrouping and redeploying in fifteen days. The commander of the 70th Army, Colonel General Popov, had to issue orders to corps commanders even before he received final instructions from above.

Several armies had large distances to cover and very little time. According to Soviet field regulations, a mechanized column was supposed to move 150 kilometres a day, but the 200th Rifle Division of the 49th Army managed to cover 358 kilometres in just twenty-five hours. In the 3rd Shock Army, which had been diverted for the Pomeranian operation, soldiers feared that they would never make it back in time and 'would only get to Berlin when everybody else would be picking up their hats [to go home]'. No true *frontovik* wanted to miss the climax of the war. He knew the jealousy which formations of the 1st Belorussian Front inspired in the rest of the Red Army.

Although the real *frontoviki* were determined to see victory in Berlin, desertions increased as the offensive came closer. Most of those who disappeared were conscripts from the recent drafts, especially Poles, Ukrainians and Romanians. An increase in desertions also meant a growing level of banditry, looting and violence towards the civilian population: 'Some deserters seize carts from local citizens, load them with different sorts of property and, pretending that they are carts belonging to the army, move from the front zone to the rear areas.'

NKVD rifle regiments behind the 1st Ukrainian Front arrested 355 deserters in the first part of April. The 1st Belorussian Front was even more concerned about discipline, as a report of 8 April reveals. 'Many soldiers are still hanging around in rear areas and describing themselves as separated from their units. They are in fact deserters. They carry out looting, robbery and violence. Recently up to 600 people were arrested in the sector of the 61st Army. All the roads are jammed with vehicles and carts used by military personnel on both legitimate missions and looting missions. They leave their vehicles and carts in the streets and in yards and wander around depots and apartments looking for things. Many officers, soldiers and NCOs are no longer looking like members of the Red Army. Some very serious deviations from standard uniform are being overlooked. It becomes difficult to distinguish between a soldier and an officer and between soldiers and civilians. Dangerous cases of disobedience to senior officers have taken place.'

NKVD rifle regiments and SMERSH were also continuing their work of rounding up suspects. They were, in Beria's view, both insufficiently selective and over-zealous. They had dispatched 148,540 prisoners to NKVD camps in the Soviet Union, yet 'barely one half were in a condition to perform physical labour'. They had simply packed off 'the people who were arrested as a result of clearing the rear areas of the Red Army'. Some priorities, however, did not change. Polish patriots were still considered as dangerous as Nazis. And NKVD regiments continued to encounter small groups of German stragglers trying to slip through Red Army lines after the fighting in Pomerania and Silesia. These small groups often ambushed the odd vehicle for food on the way, and the Soviet military authorities would respond, just as the Germans themselves had in the Soviet Union, by destroying the nearest village and shooting civilians.

The mood of Red Army officers and soldiers was tense but confident. Pyotr Mitrofanovich Sebelev, the second-in-command of an engineer brigade, had just been promoted to lieutenant colonel at the age of twenty-two. 'Hello Papa, Mama, Shura and Taya,' he wrote home on 10 April. 'At the moment, there is an unusual and therefore scaring quietness here. I was at a concert yesterday. Yes, don't be surprised, at a concert! given by artistes from Moscow. It cheered us up. We can't help thinking if only the war would finish as soon as possible, but I think it depends on us mainly. Two cases occurred yesterday which I must tell you about. I went to the front line with a man from the rear areas. We walked out of the forest and up a sandy mound, and lay down. The Oder was in front of us with a long spit of sand sticking out. The spit was occupied by Germans. Behind the Oder, the town of Küstrin, an ordinary town. Suddenly wet sand flew all around me and immediately I heard a shot: the Germans had spotted us and had begun shooting from this spit.

'Two hours ago, our recce men brought a captured German corporal to me who clicked his heels and immediately asked me through the interpreter, "Where am I, Mr Officer? Among Zhukov's troops, or in

Rokossovsky's band?" I laughed and said to the German, "You are with the troops of the 1st Belorussian Front, which is commanded by Marshal Zhukov. But why do you call Marshal Rokossovsky's troops a band?" The corporal answered, "They don't follow the rules when fighting. This is why German soldiers call them a band."

'Another piece of news. My adjutant, Kolya Kovalenko, was wounded in the arm but he escaped from hospital. I reprimanded him for this and he cursed and said, "You are depriving me of the honour of being one of the first to enter Berlin with our boys." . . . Goodbye, kisses to all of you. Your Pyotr.'

For the truly committed majority, the greatest concern was the rapid advance of the Western Allies. In the 69th Army, the political department reported the soldiers as saying, 'Our advance is too slow and the Germans will surrender their capital to the English and Americans.'

Komsomol members in the 4th Guards Tank Army prepared for the offensive by getting experienced soldiers to talk to the newcomers about the reality of battle. Komsomol members also helped the barely literate ones write letters home. They were particularly proud of having bought a T-34 tank with their own money. Their tank 'Komsomolets' had already 'destroyed a few enemy tanks and other armoured vehicles and crushed many Fritzes under its tracks'. At Party meetings members were reminded that 'all Communists have a duty to speak out against looting and drinking'.

Artillery regiments, meanwhile, paid 'special attention to the replacement of casualties'. They foresaw that losses would increase sharply once they reached Berlin, because gun crews would be firing over open sights. Crew members therefore had to train hard in each other's tasks. And each regiment prepared a reserve of trained gun layers, ready to replace casualties.

To preserve secrecy, 'the local population was sent twenty kilometres back from the front line'. Radio silence was imposed and signs were placed by every field telephone: 'Don't speak about things you should not speak about.'

German preparations, on the other hand, emphasized the reprisals that would be carried out against all those who failed in their duty and against their families, whatever their rank. An announcement was made that

General Lasch, the commander of Königsberg, had been condemned to death by hanging *in absentia* and his whole family arrested under the *Sippenhaft* law to persecute the closest relatives of traitors to the Nazi cause.

The final agony of East Prussia affected morale in Berlin almost as much as the threat from the Oder. On 2 April, Soviet artillery began its softening-up barrage on the centre of Königsberg. The Soviet artillery officer Senior Lieutenant Inozemstev recorded in his diary on 4 April that sixty shells from his battery had reduced one fortified building into 'a pile of stones'. The NKVD was concerned that nobody escaped. 'Encircled soldiers in Königsberg are putting on civilian clothes to get away. Documents must be checked more carefully in East Prussia.'

'The aviation is very effective,' Inozemstev wrote on 7 April. 'We are using flame-throwers on a massive scale. If there is only one German in a building he is chased out by the fire. There is no fighting for a storey or a staircase. It is already clear to everyone now that the storming of Königsberg will go down as a classic example of storming a big city.' The next day, when his comrade Safonov was killed, the regiment fired a salute of salvoes at the citadel.

The destruction was terrible. Thousands of soldiers and civilians were buried by the bombardments. There was a 'smell of death in the air', Inozemstev wrote, 'literally – because thousands of corpses are decomposing under the ruins'. As the wounded filled every usable cellar, General Lasch knew that there was no hope. The 11th Guards Army and the 43rd Army had fought their way right into the city. Even Koch's deputy Gauleiter urged the abandonment of the city, but all links with the Samland Peninsula had been severed. A counter-attack was mounted to force a way through, but it collapsed in chaos on the night of 8 April. The bombardment had blocked many of the routes leading to the start-line. The local Party leadership, without telling Lasch, had passed the word to civilians to assemble ready for the breakout, but their concentration attracted the attention of Soviet artillery observation officers and they were massacred.

The city was so enveloped in smoke the next day that only the fire-streaks of katyusha rockets were visible. Any civilians left alive hung sheets from windows in a signal of surrender and even tried to take rifles from German soldiers. Lasch knew that the end had come. He could expect no help from the Reich and did not want to impose any more useless suffering on the refugees and townsfolk. Only the SS wanted to fight on, but their attempts were useless. On the morning of 10 April, Lasch and other German officers acting as parliamentaries reached Marshal Vasilevsky's headquarters. The surviving garrison of just over 30,000 troops marched out to imprisonment. Their watches and any useful items were promptly grabbed by Red Army soldiers, who had managed to find stores of alcohol. The rape of women and girls went unchecked in the ruined city.

Inozemstev toured the smoking capital of East Prussia. 'A bronze Bismarck is gazing with one eye – part of his head had been knocked off by a shell – at the Soviet girl conducting the traffic, at the passing Red Army vehicles and at the mounted patrols. It looked as if he were asking, "Why are there Russians here? Who allowed that?"'

The end of East Prussia and Pomerania was underlined in a terrible fashion. On the night of 16 April, the hospital ship *Goya*, packed with over 7,000 refugees, was sunk by a Soviet submarine. It was the greatest disaster in maritime history. Only 165 people were saved.

The attack on Berlin was expected at any moment. On 6 April, Army Group Vistula headquarters noted in its war diary: 'On Ninth Army front, lively enemy activity – sounds of engines and tank tracks both on the Reitwein sector south-west of Küstrin and to the north-east near Kienitz.' They estimated that the attack would come in two days' time.

Five days later, however, they were still waiting. General Krebs at Zossen signalled to Heinrici on 11 April, 'Führer expects the Russian offensive against Army Group Vistula on 12 or 13 April.' Next day, Hitler told Krebs to telephone Heinrici to insist 'the Führer is instinctively convinced that the attack would really come in one to two days, that is to say on the 13 or 14 April'. Hitler had tried to predict the exact date of the Normandy invasion the year before, but failed. Now he again wanted to amaze his admirers with a show of uncanny foresight. It seemed to be one of the few ways left to him in which he could attempt to demonstrate some sort of control over events.

On the evening of 12 April, the Berlin Philharmonic gave its last performance. Albert Speer, who organized it, had invited Grand Admiral Dönitz and also Hitler's adjutant, Colonel von Below. The hall was properly lit for the occasion, despite the electricity cuts. 'The concert took us back to another world,' wrote Below. The programme included Beethoven's Violin Concerto, Bruckner's 8th Symphony – (Speer later claimed that this was his warning signal to the orchestra to escape Berlin immediately after the performance to avoid being drafted into the Volkssturm) – and the finale to Wagner's *Götterdämmerung*. Even if Wagner did not bring the audience back to present reality, the moment of escapism did not last long. It is said that, after the performance, the Nazi Party had organized Hitler Youth members to stand in uniform with baskets of cyanide capsules and offer them to members of the audience as they left.

On 14 April, when the attack had still not materialized, Hitler issued an 'Order of the Day' to Army Group Vistula. Predictably, it emphasized that 'whoever does not fulfil his duty will be treated as a traitor to our people'. It continued with a rambling distortion of history, and a reference to the repulse of the Turks before Vienna: 'The Bolshevik will this time experience the ancient fate of Asiatics.' Vienna had in fact just fallen to the eastern hordes and there was no hope of retaking it.

The following day, a sixteen-year-old Berliner called Dieter Borkovsky described what he witnessed in a crowded S-Bahn train from the Anhalter Bahnhof. 'There was terror on the faces of people. They were full of anger and despair. I had never heard such cursing before. Suddenly someone shouted above the noise, "Silence!" We saw a small dirty soldier with two Iron Crosses and the German Cross in Gold. On his sleeve he had a badge with four metal tanks, which meant that he had destroyed four tanks at close quarters. "I've got something to tell you," he shouted, and the carriage fell silent. "Even if you don't want to listen to me, stop whingeing. We have to win this war. We must not lose our courage. If others win the war, and if they do to us only a fraction of what we have done in the occupied territories, there won't be a single German left in a few weeks." It became so quiet in that carriage that one could have heard a pin drop.'

13

Americans on the Elbe

As the allied armies approached the heart of Germany from both directions, Berliners claimed that optimists were 'learning English and pessimists learning Russian'. The Nazi foreign minister, Joachim von Ribbentrop, who had no sense of humour, announced at a diplomatic dinner that 'Germany had lost the war but still had it in her power to decide to whom she lost'. It was this idea that disturbed Stalin so profoundly at the beginning of April.

Once Model's Army Group B with over 300,000 men was encircled in the Ruhr on 2 April, the divisions in Simpson's US Ninth Army began racing for the Elbe opposite Berlin. They and their army commander were convinced that their objective was the Nazis' capital. After the row with the British, Eisenhower had left open the capture of Berlin as a distinct possibility. In the second part of the orders to Simpson, the Ninth Army was told to 'exploit any opportunity for seizing a bridgehead over the Elbe and be prepared to continue the advance on Berlin or to the north-east'.

Its 2nd Armored Division – dubbed 'Hell on Wheels' – was the strongest in the US Army. It contained a large number of tough southerners who had joined during the Depression. Its commander, Major General Isaac D. White, had planned his route to Berlin well in advance. His idea was to cross the Elbe near Magdeburg. The US Ninth Army would use the autobahn to the capital as its centre-line. His closest rival in the race was the 83rd Infantry Division, known as the 'Rag-Tag Circus' because of its extraordinary assortment of captured vehicles and equipment sprayed olive green and given a white star. Both divisions reached the River Weser on 5 April.

To their north the 5th Armored Division headed for Tangermünde, and on the extreme left of Simpson's front, the 84th and 102nd Infantry Divisions pushed towards the Elbe on either side of its confluence with the Havel. The momentum of the advance was slowed momentarily by pockets of resistance, usually SS detachments, but most German troops surrendered in relief. The American crews stopped only to replenish or repair their vehicles. They remained dirty and unshaven. The adrenalin of the advance had almost replaced their need for sleep. The 84th Division was held up when ordered to take Hanover, but forty-eight hours later, it was ready to move on again. Eisenhower visited its commander, Major General Alexander Bolling, in Hanover on Sunday 8 April.

'Alex, where are you going next?' Eisenhower said to him.

'General, we're going to push on ahead. We have a clear go to Berlin and nothing can stop us.'

'Keep going,' the supreme commander told him, putting a hand on his shoulder. 'I wish you all the luck in the world and don't let anybody stop you.' Bolling took this as clear confirmation that their objective was Berlin.

On the US Ninth Army's left, the British Second Army of General Dempsey had reached Celle and was close to liberating Belsen concentration camp. Meanwhile, on Simpson's right, General Hodges's First Army headed for Dessau and Leipzig. General George Patton's Third Army forced its way ahead the furthest, into the Harz mountains, bypassing Leipzig to the south. On Thursday 5 April, Martin Bormann jotted in his diary, 'Bolsheviks near Vienna. Americans in the Thuringer-wald.' No further comment was needed on the disintegration of Greater Germany.

The speed of Patton's advance had an unintended side-effect. The SS, in many cases aided by the local Volkssturm, carried out a number of massacres of concentration camp prisoners and forced labourers. At the Thekla factory, which manufactured aircraft wings three kilometres north-east of Leipzig, 300 prisoners were forced into an isolated building by the SS and Volkssturm auxiliaries. All windows were fastened, then the SS threw in incendiary bombs. Those who managed to break out of the building were machine-gunned. Three Frenchmen survived. Over 100 allied prisoners – mainly French political prisoners – were executed in the courtyard of Leipzig prison. And a column of 6,500 women of many nationalities from the HASAG group of factories two kilometres north-east of Leipzig were marched towards Dresden. Allied air reconnaissance sighted them along their route. Prisoners too weak to march had been shot by SS guards and rolled into the ditch beside the road. Striped blue and white concentration camp garments 'marked the route and the Calvary of these unfortunate women'.

In southern Germany, meanwhile, General Devers's Sixth Army Group – consisting of General Patch's Seventh Army and the French First Army under General de Lattre de Tassigny – was pushing across the Black Forest. Its left flank advanced into Swabia. After the capture of Karlsruhe, they moved towards Stuttgart. Eisenhower, still concerned about an Alpine Fortress, wanted the two armies to head south-eastwards for the area of Salzburg and meet up with Soviet forces in the Danube valley.

German civilians used to gaze in amazement at American troops. GIs sprawled in jeeps, smoking or chewing gum, bore no resemblance to the German image of a soldier. Their olive-painted vehicles, even their tanks, were labelled with girls' names. But some soldierly habits proved universal. Wehrmacht troops when retreating had looted shamelessly, and now the liberators had arrived.

Looting by Allied forces appears to have begun even before the German frontier was crossed. 'On the basis of findings made,' an American report on the Ardennes stated, 'it may unequivocally be stated that pillage of Belgian civilian property by US troops did in fact take place on a considerable scale.' There had apparently been a good deal of safe-blowing with explosives. As US forces advanced into central and southern Germany, American military police erected signs at the entry to villages, 'No speeding, no looting, no fraternizing', but they had little effect on all counts.

Further north, an officer with the Scots Guards, and later a judge, wrote that the codename for the crossing of the Rhine, Operation Plunder, was most appropriate. He described how the smashed windows of shops provided 'a looter's paradise'. 'There was not very much one could do beyond restricting loot to small articles. The tanks came off best as they could carry everything from typewriters to wireless sets . . . I was cursing my platoon for looting rather than house clearing when I discovered that I was wearing two pairs of captured binoculars myself !'

Those acting independently, such as SAS teams, were able to be far more ambitious. One officer commented that 'Monty was very stuffy about looting'. Field Marshal Alexander had apparently been 'much more relaxed'. In one or two cases, some very fine jewellery was taken from German country houses at gunpoint in escapades which might even have shocked the legendary Raffles. One SAS troop later discovered a hoard of paintings accumulated by Göring's wife. The squadron commander insisted on having first pick himself, then let his officers make their choice. The canvases were removed from their stretchers, rolled up and slid into the mortar tubes.

Attitudes to the war varied between armies. Idealistic Americans and Canadians felt that they had a duty to rescue the old world, then return home as soon as possible. Their more cynical comrades took a close business interest in the black market. French regular officers in particular were focused on revenge for the humiliations of 1940 and on restoring national pride. In the British Army, however, a newly arrived officer might believe that he had come to take part in 'a life and death struggle for democracy and the freedom of the world', but found instead that the war was 'treated more as an incident in regimental history against a reasonably sporting opponent'. Nothing, needless to say, could have been further from the Russian view.

The sudden American advance in the centre aroused a mixture of suspicion and moral outrage in the Kremlin. The Soviet leadership, having complained so frequently of the Western Allies' slowness in starting a second front, was now appalled by the idea that they might reach Berlin first. The reality of Allied air power, with German troops fearing Typhoons and Mustangs far more than Shturmoviks, was completely overlooked in Moscow, perhaps deliberately. Stalin, never one to seek natural explanations, found it hard to swallow the fact that the Germans were bound to prefer to surrender to the Western Allies rather than to the Soviet Union, which promised and practised revenge on a huge scale.

'American tankists are enjoying excursions in the picturesque Harz mountains,' Ilya Ehrenburg wrote in *Krasnaya Zvezda*. The Germans were surrendering, he joked bitterly, 'with fanatical persistence'. They were behaving towards Americans, he claimed, as if they belonged to 'some neutral state'. The phrase which incensed Averell Harriman the most was his comment that the Americans were 'conquering with cameras'.

Stalin, perhaps judging others by himself, suspected that the Western Allies, hoping to reach Berlin first, would be tempted into a deal with Nazi factions. He seized on the contacts between Allen Dulles in Berne and SS-Obergruppenführer Wolff about a surrender in Italy as evidence of their double-dealing. Dulles had in fact also been contacted by a representative of Kaltenbrunner, who said that the SS wanted to launch a coup against the Nazi Party and the SS diehards who wished to continue the war. When this was done, the SS could 'arrange for an orderly transfer of administrative functions to the western powers'. Kaltenbrunner's man also talked of opening the Western Front to the Americans and British, while German troops there were switched to the east – the exact scenario that Stalin feared. Stalin fortunately did not learn of this until later, but he had heard that American and British airborne forces were ready to drop on Berlin if Nazi power suddenly collapsed. Indeed, the 101st Airborne Division had been allocated Tempelhof aerodrome as their dropping zone, the 82nd Airborne would drop on Gatow airfield and the British on Oranienburg, but ever since the decision to halt on the Elbe the whole operation was in abeyance. In any case, such contingency plans had nothing to do with any peace-feelers from the Germans. Since their declaration at the Casablanca conference insisting on Germany's unconditional surrender, neither Roosevelt nor even Churchill had seriously considered any backstairs deal with Nazi leaders.

All of Roosevelt and Eisenhower's optimism in February and March that they could win Stalin's trust was proved to be misplaced during the first week of April. As already mentioned, Eisenhower, in his controversial message to Stalin of 28 March, had given a detailed and accurate outline of his plans yet received nothing in return. In fact, on 1 April, Stalin had deliberately duped him when he said that Berlin had lost its former strategic importance. At that time, Stalin claimed that the Soviet offensive would probably come in the second half of May (instead of the middle of April), that the Red Army would concentrate its attack further south to meet up with him, and that only 'secondary forces' would be sent against Berlin.

Eisenhower, unaware that he had been tricked, curtly informed Montgomery that Berlin had become 'nothing but a geographical location'. He also continued, with General Marshall's strong support, to reject Churchill's arguments that the Americans and British 'should shake hands with the Russians as far to the east as possible'. He simply could not accept Churchill's point that Berlin, while it remained under the German flag, was bound to be 'the most decisive point in Germany'. Eisenhower obstinately believed that the Leipzig–Dresden axis, splitting Germany in two, was more important, and he was convinced that Stalin thought so too.

Eisenhower also refused to be influenced by Stalin's trickery over Poland. Churchill's worst fears were proved correct when sixteen leaders of Polish democratic parties who had been invited to confer with Zhukov under cover of a safe-conduct were arrested at the end of March by the NKVD and bundled off to Moscow. Yet even though Eisenhower had fallen for his lies, Stalin was far from relaxed. Perhaps he believed, with true Stalinian paranoia, that Eisenhower might be playing a double bluff. In any case, he was clearly determined to make the Americans feel guilty. In an aggressive signal to Roosevelt on 7 April, Stalin again made much of the German overtures through Dulles in Switzerland. He also emphasized that the Red Army was facing far more German divisions than the Western Allies. '[The Germans] continue to fight savagely against the Russians for some unknown junction in Czechoslovakia which they need as much as a dead man needs poultices,' Stalin wrote to the President, 'but [they] surrender without any resistance such important towns in central Germany as Osnabruck, Mannheim and Kassel. Don't you agree that such behaviour is more than strange and incomprehensible?'

Ironically, Hitler's ill-judged decision to keep the Sixth SS Panzer Army down near Vienna when Berlin was being threatened seemed to support the theory of the Alpine Fortress. SHAEF's joint intelligence committee acknowledged on 10 April that 'there is no evidence to show that the strategy of the German high command is being conducted with a view to occupying eventually the so-called National Redoubt'. But they then went on to say that the objective of the Redoubt was to drag the war into the next winter, in the hope that the Western Allies and the Soviet Union would fall out among themselves. Yet the same day, another report should have put paid to this extraordinarily deep-rooted idea. 'The interrogation of various German generals and senior officers recently captured reveals that none of them had heard of the National Redoubt. All of them consider such a plan to be "ridiculous and inapplicable".'

Neither Stalin nor Churchill realized that the American President was in no condition to read their telegrams, let alone answer them himself. On Good Friday, 30 March, Roosevelt had been taken down by train to Warm Springs, Georgia. It was his last journey alive. He had been carried to the waiting limousine barely conscious. Those who saw him were deeply shocked by his state. In less than two weeks Roosevelt would be dead and Harry Truman, his Vice-President, would become the next President of the United States.

On 11 April, the Americans reached Magdeburg. The next day they crossed the Elbe south of Dessau. Plans were drawn up on the projection that they could reach Berlin within forty-eight hours. This was not an improbable estimate. There were few SS units left on the western side of the capital.

On the same day, Germans were shaken by the ferocity of a French government radio station broadcasting from Cologne. '*Deutschland, dein Lebensraum ist jetzt dein Sterbensraum*' – 'Germany, your room to live is now your room to die.' It was the sort of remark which they would have expected of Ilya Ehrenburg.

Ehrenburg, on that day, published his last and most controversial article of the war in *Krasnaya Zvezda*. It was entitled '*Khvatit*' or 'Enough'. 'Germany is dying miserably, without pathos or dignity,' he wrote. 'Let us remember the pompous parades, the Sportpalast in Berlin, where Hitler used to roar that he was going to conquer the world. Where is he now? In what hole? He has led Germany to a precipice, and now he prefers not to show himself.' As far as Ehrenburg was concerned, 'Germany does not exist; there is only a colossal gang.'

This was the same article in which Ehrenburg bitterly compared

German resistance in the east and the surrenders in the west. He evoked 'the terrible wounds of Russia' which the Western Allies did not want to know about. He then mentioned the handful of German atrocities in France, such as the massacre of Oradour. 'There are four such villages in France. And how many are there in Belorussia? Let me remind you about villages in the region of Leningrad . . .'

Ehrenburg's inflammatory rhetoric often did not accord with his own views. In his article, he implicitly condoned looting – 'Well, German women are losing fur coats and spoons that had been stolen' – when in Red Army parlance looting often implicitly included rape. Yet he had recently lectured officers at the Frunze military academy, criticizing Red Army looting and destruction in East Prussia and blaming it on the troops' 'extremely low' level of culture. His only reference to rape, however, was to say that Soviet soldiers 'were not refusing "the compliments" of German women'. Abakumov, the head of SMERSH, reported Ehrenburg's 'incorrect opinions' to Stalin, who regarded them as 'politically harmful'. This, combined with the similar report on East Prussia by Count von Einsiedel of the NKVD-controlled National Committee for a Free Germany, set in motion a train of events and discussions which triggered a major reappraisal of Soviet policy.

The tone and content of Ehrenburg's article on 12 April were no more bloodthirsty than previous diatribes, but to the writer's shock it was attacked from on high to signal a change in the Party line. An embittered Ehrenburg later recognized that his role as the scourge of the Germans made him the obvious symbolic sacrifice in the circumstances. The Soviet leadership, rather late in the day, had finally realized that the horror inspired by the Red Army's onslaught on the civilian population was increasing enemy resistance and would complicate the post-war Soviet occupation of Germany. In Ehrenburg's words, they wanted to undermine the enemy's will to fight on 'by promising immunity to the rank and file of those who had carried out Hitler's orders'.

On 14 April, Georgy Aleksandrov, the main ideologist on the central committee and the chief of Soviet propaganda, replied in *Pravda* with an article entitled 'Comrade Ehrenburg Oversimplifies'. In a conspicuously important piece, which had no doubt been checked by Stalin if not virtually dictated by him, Aleksandrov rejected Ehrenburg's explanation of rapid surrender in the west and his depiction of Germany as 'only a colossal gang'. While some German officers 'fight for the cannibal regime, others throw bombs at Hitler and his clique [the July plotters] or persuade Germans to put down their weapons [General von Seydlitz and the League of German Officers]. The Gestapo hunt for opponents of the regime, and the appeals to Germans to denounce them proved that not all Germans were the same. It was the Nazi government which was desperate to call upon the idea of national unity. The very intensity of the appeals for national unity in fact proved how little unity there was.' Aleksandrov also quoted Stalin's remark, 'Hitlers come and go, but Germany and the German people remain' – a slogan first coined as early as 23 February 1942 but only really used in 1945.

Moscow radio broadcast Aleksandrov's article and *Krasnaya Zvezda* reprinted it. A devastated Ehrenburg found himself in a political limbo. His letter to Stalin appealing against the injustice was never answered. But Ehrenburg probably did not realize that he had been denounced for other criticisms of the Red Army and the inability of officers to control their men. He had reported how when a Soviet general reproved a soldier for cutting a patch of leather from a sofa, saying that it could be used by some family in the Soviet Union, the soldier had retorted, 'Your wife may get it, but definitely not mine', and carried on attacking the sofa. Abakumov's most serious charge, however, was that Ehrenburg had also said to the officers at the Frunze academy, 'Russians returning from "slavery" look well. Girls are well fed and dressed. Our articles in papers on the enslavement of persons who had been taken to Germany are not convincing.' If Ehrenburg had not enjoyed such a passionate following in the Red Army, he might easily have disappeared into a Gulag camp.

At the front, meanwhile, political departments were clearly uneasy about the situation. They reported how some officers supported Ehrenburg and still believed 'that we should be ruthless with the Germans and those Western Allies who start flirting with the Germans'. The Party line was, however, clear. 'We are no longer chasing Germans from our country, a situation in which the slogan, "Kill a German whenever you see one", seemed entirely fair. Instead, the time has now come to punish the enemy correctly for all his evil deeds.' Yet even though the political officers quoted Stalin's dictum that 'Hitlers come and go . . .', this did not seem to carry much weight with the soldiers. 'Many soldiers asked me,' one political officer reported, 'if Ehrenburg still continued to write and they told me that they are looking for his articles in every newspaper that they see.'

The change in policy just before the great offensive came far too late for soldiers imbued with the personal and propaganda hatreds of the last three years. One of the most unintentionally revealing remarks was made by one of Zhukov's divisional commanders, General Maslov. He described German children crying as they searched desperately for their parents in a blazing town. 'What was surprising,' wrote Maslov, 'was that they were crying in exactly the same way as our children cry.' Few Soviet soldiers or officers had imagined Germans as human beings. After Nazi propaganda had dehumanized the Slavs into *Untermenschen*, Soviet revenge propaganda had convinced its citizens that all Germans were ravening beasts.

The Soviet authorities had another reason for concern at the advance of the Western Allies. They were afraid that the majority of the 1st and 2nd Polish Armies would want to join the Polish forces which owed allegiance to the government in exile in London. On 14 April, Beria passed to Stalin the report from General Serov, the NKVD chief with Zhukov's 1st Belorussian Front. 'In connection with the rapid advance of the Allies on the Western Front,' Serov wrote, 'unhealthy moods developed among the soldiers and officers of the 1st Polish Army.' SMERSH had gone into action, carrying out mass arrests.

'Intelligence organs of the 1st Polish Army,' he reported, 'have discovered and taken under control [*sic*] nearly 2,000 ex-soldiers of the Anders army and members of the Armia Krajowa and soldiers who have close relatives in Anders's army.' The 'hostile attitude' of these Poles to the Soviet Union was underlined by the fact that they had concealed their real addresses from the Soviet authorities to prevent reprisals against their families. Serov also failed to mention the fact that since 43,000 members of the Polish Communist forces had been transferred straight from Gulag camps, their feelings towards the Soviet Union were unlikely to be entirely fraternal. And in Poland, members of the Armia Krajowa arrested by NKVD troops were given the choice of a labour camp in Siberia or the Communist army – '*W Sibir ili w Armiju?*'

SMERSH informers had warned their controllers that Polish soldiers were listening regularly to the 'London radio'. Informers also reported that Polish troops were convinced that 'Anders's army is coming to Berlin from the other side with the English army'. 'When the Polish troops meet up,' an officer unwittingly told an informer, 'the majority of our soldiers and officers will pass over to the Anders army. We've suffered enough from the Soviets in Siberia.' 'After the war, when Germany is finished,' a battalion chief of staff apparently told another informer, 'we'll still be fighting Russia. We have 3 million of Anders's men with the English.' 'They are pushing their "democracy" into our faces,' said a commander in the 2nd Artillery Brigade. 'As soon as our troops meet up with Anders's men, you can say goodbye to the [Soviet-controlled] provisional government. The London government will take power again and Poland will once more be what it was before 1939. England and America will help Poland get rid of the Russians.' Serov blamed commanders of the 1st Polish Army 'for not strengthening their political explanatory work'.

While the American Third and Ninth Armies were charging forward to the Elbe, Field Marshal Model's Army Group B in the Ruhr pocket was being ground down, largely by air attack. Model was one of the very few army commanders to be trusted completely by Hitler. His fellow generals, however, considered him to be 'extremely rude and unscrupulous'. Model was known to the troops as '*der Katastrophengeneral*' because of his habit of turning up in a sector when things were going very badly. The Ruhr, in any case, was Model's last catastrophe. He refused to fly out. On 21 April, when his troops began to surrender *en masse*, he shot himself, which was exactly what Hitler expected of his commanders.

Well before the end, Colonel Günther Reichhelm, the chief operations officer of Army Group B, was flown out of the Ruhr encirclement along with many other key personnel. Out of seventeen aircraft, only three reached Jüterbog, the airfield south of Berlin. Reichhelm was driven to OKH headquarters at Zossen, where he collapsed from exhaustion. He awoke only when Guderian's former deputy, General Wenck, sat on his bed. Wenck, brought back to operations before he had completely recovered from his car crash during Operation *Sonnenwende*, had just been appointed the commander-in-chief of the Twelfth Army. Wenck suspected that this new army existed more on paper than in reality, despite its task of holding the line of the Elbe against the Americans.

'You're coming as my chief of staff,' Wenck told him. But first of all Reichhelm had to report on the situation of Army Group B in the Ruhr pocket. Jodl ordered him to come to the Reich Chancellery bunker. There he found Hitler with Göring and Grand Admiral Dönitz. He told Hitler that Army Group B had no more ammunition, and its remaining tanks could not move because they had no more fuel. Hitler paused for a long time. 'Field Marshal Model was my best Field Marshal,' he said at last. Reichhelm thought that Hitler finally understood that it was all over, but he did not. Hitler said, 'You are to be chief of staff of the Twelfth Army. You must free yourself from the stupid guidelines of the general staff. You must learn from the Russians, who by sheer willpower overcame the Germans who stood before Moscow.'

Hitler then went on to say that the German Army must chop down trees in the Harz mountains to stop Patton's advance and launch a partisan war there. He demanded 1:25,000 scale maps, the sort which company commanders used, to prove his point. Jodl tried to disabuse him, but Hitler insisted that he knew the Harz well. Jodl, who was usually very controlled, replied sharply. 'I do not know the area at all,' he said, 'but I know the situation.' Göring, Reichhelm noticed, had meanwhile gone to sleep in a chair with a map over his face. He wondered whether he was full of drugs. Hitler finally told Reichhelm to join the Twelfth Army, but first he should go via the camp at Döberitz, where he could obtain 200 Volkswagen cross-country Kübelwagen jeeps for the Twelfth Army.

Reichhelm left with a sense of relief at escaping from a madhouse. At Döberitz he could lay his hands on only a dozen vehicles. Finding Wenck and the headquarters of the Twelfth Army was even harder. Eventually, he found Wenck in the sapper school at Rosslau on the opposite bank of the Elbe from Dessau. To his great pleasure, he saw that the chief operations officer was an old friend, Colonel Baron Hubertus von Humboldt-Dachroeden. Part of the Twelfth Army, he heard, was made up with 'astonishingly willing young soldiers trained for half a year in officers' schools', as well as many NCOs with front experience who had returned from hospital. Both officers greatly admired their army commander. Wenck was young, flexible and a good field commander who 'could look soldiers in the eye'.

Although the headquarters was improvised and had few radio sets, they found that they could use the local telephone network, which was still functioning well. The army was better supplied than most thanks to the army ammunition base at Altengrabow and the number of stranded barges and boats in the Havelsee. Wenck refused to follow Hitler's 'Nero' order, and he prevented the destruction of the electricity plant at Golpa, south-east of Dessau, one of the main electricity supply points for Berlin. On Wenck's orders, the Infantry Division *Hutten* provided guards to prevent any fanatics from trying to blow it up.

The Twelfth Army's principal task was to prepare for an attack by the American Ninth Army 'along and either side of the Hanover–Magdeburg autobahn'. The Americans were expected to develop a bridgehead on the east bank of the Elbe and then head for Berlin. The first attack took place sooner than expected. 'On 12 April, the first contact report arrived of the enemy attempt to cross near Schönebeck and Barby.' The *Scharnhorst* Infantry Division attempted to counter-attack with a battalion and a few assault guns on the following day. They put up fierce resistance on the first day, but they found the enemy, especially the US Air Force, far too strong.

Reichhelm realized that if the Americans were to cross the Elbe in force, there was 'no other possibility but to surrender'. The Twelfth Army could not have continued to fight 'for more than one or two days'. Humboldt was of exactly the same opinion. The Americans were across the Elbe in a number of places. By Saturday 14 April, SHAEF recorded, 'the Ninth Army has occupied Wittenberge, 100 kilometres north of Magdeburg. Three battalions of the 83rd Infantry Division have crossed the Elbe at Kameritz to the south-east of Magdeburg.' The 5th Armored Division, meanwhile, had reached the Elbe on a twenty-five kilometre front around Tangermünde. On 15 April, Wenck's Twelfth Army mounted a strong counter-attack against the 83rd Infantry Division near Zerbst, but this was repulsed.

The bridgeheads across the Elbe appeared to present more of a problem to Eisenhower than an opportunity. He spoke to General Bradley, the army group commander, to ask his view about pushing on to Berlin. He wanted to know his view of the casualties they would have to face taking the city. Bradley estimated that it might involve 100,000 casualties (a figure which, he later admitted, was far too high). He then added that it would be a stiff price to pay for a prestige objective when they would have to withdraw again once Germany surrendered. This clearly coincided with Eisenhower's thoughts, although he claimed later that the 'future division of Germany did not influence our military plans for the final conquest of the country'.

Eisenhower was also concerned about his extended lines of communication. The British Second Army was on the edge of Bremen, the US First Army was approaching Leipzig and Patton's lead units were close to the Czechoslovak border. The distances were so great that forward units had to be supplied by Dakotas. Large numbers of civilians, including prison and concentration camp inmates, also had to be fed. Considerable resources were required. Like many others, Eisenhower was totally unprepared for the full horror of the concentration camps. Seeing such unbelievable suffering at first hand affected many for years afterwards in a liberator's version of survivor guilt.

Commanders on the Western Front had little idea of the situation on the Eastern Front. They did not appreciate quite how keen the German Army was to allow the Americans in to Berlin before the Red Army reached it. 'Soldiers and officers,' observed Colonel de Maizière of the OKH, 'believed that it was far better to be beaten by the west. The exhausted Wehrmacht fought to the end purely to leave the Russians as little territory as possible.' The instincts of Simpson and his formation commanders in the Ninth Army proved much more accurate than those of the Supreme Commander. They estimated that there would be pockets of resistance but that these could be bypassed in a charge to the capital of the Reich, which lay less than 100 kilometres away.

The 83rd Infantry Division had already set up a bridge capable of taking the 2nd Armored Division's tanks, and during the night of Saturday 14 April, vehicles crossed in a steady stream. The forces in the bridgehead, which now stretched to Zerbst, started to build up rapidly. The excitement among the American troops was infectious. They longed for their orders to move out. But early on the Sunday morning, 15 April, their army commander, General Simpson, was summoned by General Bradley to his army group headquarters at Wiesbaden. Bradley met

Simpson at the airfield. They shook hands as he climbed out of the plane. Bradley, without any preamble, told him that the Ninth Army was to halt on the Elbe. It was not to advance any further in the direction of Berlin.

'Where in the hell did you get this?' Simpson asked.

'From Ike,' Bradley answered.

Simpson, feeling dazed and dejected, flew back to his headquarters, wondering how he was going to tell his commanders and his men.

These orders to stand fast on the Elbe, coming on top of the unexpected death of President Roosevelt, constituted a great blow to American morale. Roosevelt had died on 12 April, but the news was not released until the following day. Goebbels was ecstatic when told on his return from a visit to the front near Küstrin. He telephoned Hitler in the Reich Chancellery bunker immediately. 'My Führer, I congratulate you!' he said. 'Roosevelt is dead. It is written in the stars that the second half of April will be the turning point for us. This Friday, 13 April. It is the turning point!'

Just a few days before, Goebbels had been reading Carlyle's *History of Friedrich II of Prussia* aloud to Hitler to lift him from his depression. The passage had been the one where Frederick the Great, faced with disaster in the Seven Years War, thought of taking poison. But suddenly news of the death of the Tsarina Elizabeth arrived. 'The Miracle of the House of Brandenburg had come to pass.' Hitler's eyes had filled with tears at these words. Goebbels did not believe in astrological charts, but he was prepared to use anything to boost the Führer's flagging spirits and he worked Hitler up into a frenzy of optimism. The recluse in the bunker now gazed lovingly at the portrait of Frederick the Great, which had been brought down for him. On the next day, 14 April, in his order of the day to the army, Hitler became utterly carried away. 'At the moment when Fate has removed the greatest war criminal of all time from this earth, the turn of events in this war will be decisive.'

Another symbolic event involving Frederick the Great took place, but Hitler never mentioned it. In a massive air raid that night, Allied bombers attacked Potsdam. A Hitler Youth sheltering in a basement that night found the walls around him 'rocking like a ship'. The bombs destroyed much of the old town, including the Garnisonkirche, the spiritual home of the Prussian military caste and aristocracy. Ursula von Kardorff burst into tears in the street after hearing the news. 'A whole world was destroyed with it,' she wrote in her diary. But many officers still refused to acknowledge the responsibility of the German military leadership for supporting Hitler. Talk of the honour of a German officer when the liberation of concentration camps showed the nature of the regime they had fought for was unlikely to arouse sympathy, even among their most sporting opponents.

14

Eve of Battle

The Red Army, despite all its efforts and talent for camouflage, could not hope to conceal the huge attack about to be unleashed on the Oder and Neisse fronts. Zhukov's 1st Belorussian Front and Konev's 1st Ukrainian Front were to attack on 16 April. To the north, Rokossovsky's 2nd Belorussian Front would follow on soon afterwards across the lower Oder. Soviet forces amounted to 2.5 million men. They were backed by 41,600 guns and heavy mortars as well as 6,250 tanks and self-propelled guns and four air armies. It was the greatest concentration of firepower ever amassed.

On 14 April, a fighting reconnaissance from the Küstrin bridgehead proved most successful. Chuikov's 8th Guards Army managed to push the 20th Panzergrenadier Division back between two and five kilometres in places. Hitler is said to have been so angry that he gave orders to strip medals from all members of the division until they had been won back.

This extension of the bridgehead also helped the build-up of forces. That night the 1st Guards Tank Army began moving its brigades across the Oder under the cover of darkness. 'During the night there was a constant flow of tanks, guns, Studebakers loaded with ammunition, and columns of soldiers.' Young women traffic controllers waved their discs desperately, urging the tanks into the line marked by white tapes. Loud music and propaganda exhortations reverberated from 7th Department loudspeakers in an attempt to cover the noise of tank engines, but the Germans knew what was happening.

For the whole of 15 April, Red Army soldiers watched the German positions 'until our eyes ached', in case last-minute reinforcements were brought up or changes made. In the Oderbruch, April flowers had appeared on hillocks, but large chunks of ice still floated down the river, as well as branches and weed which caught on a wrecked railway bridge. In pine forests on the east bank, 'mysteriously quiet' by day, chopped branches camouflaged thousands of armoured vehicles and guns.

On the Neisse front, to the south, the 1st Ukrainian Front organized relentless political activity up to the last moment. 'Active Komsomol members were teaching young soldiers to love their tanks and to try to use the whole potential of this powerful weapon.' The Aleksandrov message had evidently not been digested, even by political departments. The message of revenge was clear in the latest slogan: 'There will be no pity. They have sown the wind and now they are harvesting the whirlwind.'

The 1st Ukrainian Front was more preoccupied by bad radio discipline. Even NKVD regiments had recently been 'transmitting in clear, using out-of-date codes and not answering signals'. No sub-units were allowed to use the radio: their sets had to be on receive and never on send. Concern about lapses of security was even greater on the night of 15 April, because the new wavelengths and codes up to the end of May 1945 were issued to headquarters.

Even though officers were told not to give out orders more than three hours before the attack, SMERSH was determined that there should be no last-minute desertions by Red Army soldiers who might warn the enemy. The SMERSH representative with the 1st Belorussian Front ordered all political officers to check every man in the front line and identify any who seemed suspicious or 'morally and politically unstable'. In an earlier round-up, SMERSH had arrested those denounced for making negative comments about collective farms. A special cordon was put in place 'so that our men will not manage to flee to the Germans' and to prevent the Germans from seizing 'tongues'. But all their efforts were in vain. On 15 April, a Red Army soldier south of Küstrin told his German captors that the great offensive was starting early the next morning.

Considering the proximity of defeat, the Germans had even stronger reasons to fear that their soldiers would desert or surrender at the first opportunity. Army Group Vistula issued orders signed by Heinrici that men from the same region should be split up, because they seldom did anything to prevent a comrade from home deserting. An officer of the *Grossdeutschland* guard regiment commanding a scratch battalion observed that his young soldiers had little intention of fighting for National Socialism. 'Many wanted to be wounded so that they could be sent back to the field hospital.' They stayed at their posts only out of a 'corpse-like obedience' inspired by fear of summary execution. After a Soviet loudspeaker broadcast across the lines, officers were appalled when soldiers began shouting back asking for details. Would they be sent to Siberia? How were civilians treated in the occupied areas of Germany?

Several German commanders in the Fourth Panzer Army facing Konev's 1st Ukrainian Front confiscated white handkerchiefs to prevent their men using them as a sign of surrender. Soldiers caught trying to desert were, in some cases, forced to dig trenches in the open in no man's land. Many longed to slip away into thick woodland to surrender out of sight to save their families from punishment decreed in Hitler's order.

German company commanders tried almost any means to persuade their soldiers to hold fast. Some informed them of Roosevelt's death on the evening of 14 April. This meant, they told them, that American tanks would no longer attack. In fact, they claimed, relations between the Western Allies and the Soviet Union had become so bad that the Americans and British would now join Germany in throwing back the Russians. Reservists in the 391st Security Division near Guben found SS troops from the *30. Januar* Division coming over to lecture them on the connection between the death of Roosevelt and the miracle that saved Frederick the Great as though this were holy scripture. They were not convinced at all, but many German soldiers still held on because they expected a massive counter-attack on the Führer's birthday, 20 April, with new secret 'wonder weapons'.

Some angry and embittered officers managed to remind veterans of the horrors of the Eastern Front and what it would mean if the Russians broke through to Berlin. 'You can't imagine,' a senior lieutenant wrote to his wife, 'what a terrible hatred is aroused here. I can promise you that we'll sort them out one day. The rapists of women and children will discover another experience. It is hard to believe what these beasts have done. We have sworn an oath that each man must kill ten Bolsheviks. God will help us achieve this.'

The bulk of the ill-trained young conscripts recently marched out to the front were far less likely to be persuaded. They just wanted to survive. In the 303rd *Döberitz* Infantry Division, a regimental commander gave one of his battalion commanders some advice. 'We have to hold the front at any cost. You're responsible. If a few soldiers start to run away, then you must shoot them. If you see many soldiers taking off, and you can't stop them and the situation is hopeless, then you'd better shoot yourself.'

On the Seelow Heights, apart from some strafing attacks, it was 'almost peaceful just before the storm'. German soldiers sent back from the front line checked and cleaned weapons, ate and washed. Some sat down to write home, just in case the Feldpost began to work again. For many, their homes were already occupied by the enemy, and others did not know where their families were.

Senior Lieutenant Wust sent his Luftwaffe trainee technicians back in batches to the field kitchen – or *'Gulaschkanone'* – in a village just behind their second line of trenches. He remained in a fire trench with his company sergeant major, gazing down over the trees to the Oderbruch and the Soviet positions from which the attack would come. Wust suddenly shivered. 'Tell me,' he said, turning to his Kompanie-truppführer. 'Are you also cold?'

'We're not cold, Herr Oberleutnant,' the man replied. 'We're afraid.'

Back in Berlin, safely behind the lines, Martin Bormann sent an eve of battle message to the Gauleiters. He ordered them to sort out the 'rabbit-hearted'. In the centre of the city, trams were manhandled across the street, then filled with brick and rubble as instant barricades. The Volkssturm was called out. Some of them had to wear blue-grey French helmets and even uniforms. It was the last of the booty from the great German victories in 1940 and 1941.

Hitler was not alone in looking back to the Seven Years War. *Pravda* had already published an article trumpeting the Russian entry into Berlin on 9 October 1760 with five Cossack regiments in the vanguard.

'The keys of the city were taken to St Petersburg for permanent keeping in the Kazansky Cathedral. We should remember this historic example and fulfil the order of the Motherland and Comrade Stalin.' General Chuikov's 8th Guards Army were given large key shapes cut out of cardboard to remind the troops of this moment as they prepared to go into the attack.

More modern symbols were also distributed in the form of red banners. These were issued to the attacking divisions. They were to be raised on significant buildings in Berlin and indicated on a large model of the city built by Front engineers. 'Socialist competition' was expected to push men forward to even greater sacrifice, and the greatest glory would go to those who stormed the Reichstag, the objective which Stalin had selected to represent the total conquest of the 'lair of the fascist beast'. That evening, in what amounted to a mass secular baptism, over 2,000 Red Army soldiers of the 1st Belorussian Front were received into the Communist Party.

Even though Soviet commanders did not doubt that they would break through, they were extremely nervous that the American and British armies might make it to Berlin first. Such an eventuality was seen as worse than a humiliation. Berlin belonged to the Soviet Union by right of suffering as well as by right of conquest. Each army commander had been left in no doubt of the feelings of the *Verkhovny*, their commander-in-chief, waiting impatiently in the Kremlin. They did not, however, know quite how disturbed Stalin was. Inaccurate newspaper reports in the western press claimed that American point units had reached Berlin on the evening of 13 April, but these detachments had then been withdrawn after protests from Moscow.

Only Zhukov and Konev and a few of their closest colleagues knew that the strategy of the whole Berlin operation was designed to surround the city first in order to warn off the Americans and British. But even the two Front commanders were unaware of the importance Stalin and Beria evidently attached to seizing the institutes of nuclear research, particularly the Kaiser Wilhelm Institute for Physics in Dahlem.

On the eve of battle, Stalin in Moscow maintained his shield of lies. General Deane reported on another session in the Kremlin in an 'Eyes only for Eisenhower' signal. At the end of a long meeting about the 'other matter' (the future deployment of Soviet forces in the Far East against the Japanese), 'Harriman mentioned that the Germans had announced that the Russians were planning an immediate renewal of their attack directed against Berlin. The Marshal [Stalin] stated that they were in fact going to begin an offensive; that he did not know how successful it would be, but the main blow would be in the direction of Dresden, as he had already told Eisenhower.'

Stalin and his entourage must have concealed their nervousness well. Neither Deane nor Harriman sensed that they were being lied to. The evening before, at a meeting with the *Stavka*, General Antonov seized upon a line in Eisenhower's latest message about the avoidance of confusion between western forces and the Red Army. He immediately wanted to know 'if this indicated any change in the zone of occupation previously agreed upon'. When he was assured that the reference was to tactical areas and that no change was implied in the zones of occupation, 'Antonov requested that confirmation be obtained from Eisenhower on this point.' The Soviet chief of staff then wanted to verify that 'upon completion of tactical operations the Anglo-American forces would withdraw from the previously agreed Soviet zone of occupation'. This was reconfirmed to him in a signal from Eisenhower on 16 April.

For Red Army soldiers, their first priority was a shave to make themselves presentable conquerors. While there was still enough daylight, those not on duty scraped away with cutthroat razors while squinting into a broken fragment of mirror. Few could sleep. 'Some of them shaded torches with their coats as they wrote letters home,' wrote an officer in the 3rd Shock Army. Their letters tended to be brief and uninformative. 'Greetings from the front,' ran a typical one. 'I am alive and healthy. We are not far from Berlin. Severe battles are going on, but soon the order will come, and we will advance to Berlin. We will have to storm it and I will see if I am still alive by then.'

Many wrote not to parents or to fiancées but to pen-pals. Thousands of lonely young women drafted to work in armaments factories out in the Urals or Siberia had been writing to soldiers at the front. Snapshots were exchanged at a certain stage in the relationship, but sex was not the driving force. For soldiers, a woman somewhere at home was the only thing left to remind them that a normal life could still exist.

Sergeant Vlasienko in the 1st Ukrainian Front wrote a pen-pal song in epistolary form. It was set to the haunting melody of '*Zemlyanka*', the great wartime song set in a frozen bunker 'just four steps from death'.

> The hurricane lamp is driving away darkness,
> Making a way for my pen.
> You and I are close through this letter.
> We are like a brother and a sister.
>
> I long for you from the front
> And I will find you when these days of fighting are over
> Deep in the homeland
> If only I survive.
>
> And if the worst happens
> If the days of my life are counted
> Remember me sometimes
> Remember me with a kind word.
>
> Well, goodbye for now.
> It is time for me to go to attack the Germans
> And I want to carry your name forward
> If only in my battle-cry '*Ura!*'

'Wait for Me', one of the most popular songs of the war, was based on the poem which made Konstantin Simonov famous in 1942. It evoked the Red Army's quasi-religious superstition that if a girlfriend remained faithful, the soldier would stay alive. It was permitted by the authorities only because it strengthened military patriotism. Many soldiers kept 'Wait for Me' written on a piece of paper in their left breast pocket, and read it silently to themselves like a prayer in the moments before they went into the attack.

The song 'Blue Shawl', about a faithful girl's farewell to her soldier lover, also produced such intense loyalty that many soldiers added it to the official battle-cry, making it '*Za Rodinu, za Stalina, za Siny Platochek!*' – 'For the Motherland, for Stalin, for the Blue Shawl!' A great number of Komsomol members still carried newspaper cuttings with a photograph of Zoya Kosmodemyanskaya, the young Komsomol partisan 'tortured to death by Germans'. Many wrote 'for Zoya' on their tanks and aircraft.

Another poem of Simonov's, on the other hand, was condemned as 'indecent', 'vulgar' and 'bad for morale'. It was ironically entitled '*Liricheskoe*', or 'Lyrical'.

> They remember names for an hour.
> Memories here do not last for long.
> Man says 'War . . .', and embraces a woman carelessly.
> He is grateful to those who had so easily,
> Without wanting to be called 'darling',
> Replaced for him another one who is far away.
> Here she was as compassionate as she could be to other women's
>   loved ones,
> And warmed them in bad times with the generosity of her
>   uncommitted body.
> And for those waiting to go into the attack,
> Those who may never live to see love,
> They find it easier when they remember that yesterday
> At least someone's arms were around them.

However much the authorities disapproved of songs or poems about unfaithful girlfriends, iconoclasts still thought up ribald versions of officially approved songs. The tear-jerker 'Dark Night', about a soldier's wife standing beside their child's cot 'secretly wiping her tears', was turned into 'secretly taking her streptocide', the Soviet wartime medicine for venereal disease.

Official patriotic songs never really took on. The only exception was the 'Song of the Artillerists', which came from the film *At Six o'clock in the Evening after the End of the War*. The film was screened for soldiers at the front just before the battle of Berlin. It showed an artillery officer who has survived to meet his true love in Moscow during the victory celebrations, but although this may have been good for morale in one way, it certainly did not help soldiers with the very natural fear of risking death when the fighting was almost over.

Other songs also looked beyond the end of the war. Soldiers of the 4th Guards Tank Army composed their own:

Soon we will return home.
The girls will meet us,
And the stars of the Urals will shine for us.
Some day we will remember these days.
Kamenets-Podolsk and the blue Carpathians.
The fighting thunder of the tanks.
Lvov and the steppe behind the Vistula.
You won't forget this year.
You'll tell your children of it.
Some day, we will remember these days.

Red Army soldiers experienced an irresistible urge to finish the war, but the closer they were to victory, the more they hoped to survive. And yet men desperately wanted a medal to take home. It would make a great difference to their standing in the community and especially within their own family. But there was one thing that they feared even more than being killed in the last days of the war after having survived so far against all odds. That was to lose legs and arms. A limbless veteran, known as a *samovar*, was treated like an outcast.

After sunset on the evening of 15 April, Colonel Kalashnik, the chief of the 47th Army's political department, sent Captain Vladimir Gall and the young Lieutenant Konrad Wolf to the front line, ready to interview the first prisoners brought back. Koni Wolf, a German, was the son of the Communist playwright Friedrich Wolf, who had become part of the 'Moscow emigration' in 1933 when the Nazis came to power. Koni's elder brother, Misha, became notorious in the Cold War as Markus Wolf, the chief of East German espionage.

It was virtually dark as the two friends, armed only with pistols, made their way forward through woods to the bank of the Oder. Tanks and men were camouflaged all around them. As the two young officers walked forward between the trees, they could sense that 'huge forces were concentrated there' all around them, even though they could hardly see anything because of the dark. 'It felt like a huge spring about to be released,' remarked Gall.

Others were engaged on much more dangerous work. Sappers had slipped out at nightfall into no man's land to clear mines. 'We warned all infantry people of what we were doing,' said Captain Shota Sulkhanishvili of the 3rd Shock Army, 'but when one of my sappers was returning, an infantry man threw a grenade at him. He was asleep and panicked when he heard steps. I was furious and beat him almost to death. For me, all my men were worth gold, especially the mine-clearers.'

Those who had already acquired watches longed to look at the time – to know how many more minutes remained before the attack. But no lights were allowed. It was hard to think of anything else.

15

Zhukov on the Reitwein Spur

General Chuikov, the commander of the 8th Guards Army, had the best view of the Oderbruch and the Seelow Escarpment from his forward command post on the Reitwein Spur. He was not pleased when Marshal Zhukov decided to join him there to watch the opening bombardment and the attack. Chuikov ordered Captain Merezhko, a staff officer who had been with him since Stalingrad, to go back across the Oder and lead the Front commander and his retinue to the position.

To Chuikov's fury, Zhukov's convoy of vehicles with their headlights on could be seen approaching from a great distance. Chuikov had almost certainly been prejudiced against Zhukov since the winter of 1942. He seems to have felt that the heroic role of his 62nd Army in Stalingrad was overlooked, and too much attention paid to Zhukov. Much more recently, he resented the remarks made about the length of time he had taken to capture the fortress of Poznan. And his own comments about the failure to have pushed straight on to Berlin at the beginning of February had clearly angered Zhukov.

Below them on the Oderbruch, an officer remembered, the trenches were alive with rattling pots. They could all smell the soup being ladled out by cooks to feed the men before the attack. In the forward trenches dug into the cold, sodden earth, troops took sips from their vodka ration. In command posts field telephones rang constantly and runners came and went.

Zhukov arrived, accompanied by a retinue including General Kazakov, his artillery commander, and General Telegin, the head of the

Front political department. They were led up a path round the side of the spur and reached the bunker dug by Chuikov's engineers in the side of the small cliff below the observation post. 'The hands of the clock had never gone round so slowly,' Zhukov recorded later. 'To fill the remaining minutes somehow, we decided to drink some hot, strong tea, which had been prepared in the same bunker by a girl soldier. I can remember for some reason that she had a non-Russian name, Margo. We drank the tea in silence, everyone occupied with his own thoughts.'

General Kazakov had 8,983 artillery pieces, with up to 270 guns per kilometre on the breakthrough sectors, which meant a field gun every four metres, including 152mm and 203mm howitzers, heavy mortars and regiments of katyusha rocket launchers. The 1st Belorussian Front had a stockpile of over 7 million shells, of which 1,236,000 rounds were fired on the first day. This artillery overkill and the overwhelming superiority of his forces had tempted Zhukov into underestimating the scale of the obstacle facing them.

Zhukov usually insisted on visiting the front line in person to study the terrain before a major offensive, but this time – mainly due to constant pressure from Stalin – he had relied largely on photo-reconnaissance. This vertical picture failed to reveal that the Seelow Heights, dominating his bridgehead on the Oderbruch, was a far more formidable feature than he had realized. Zhukov was also enamoured of a new idea. One hundred and forty-three searchlights had been brought forward, ready to blind the German defenders at the moment of attack.

Three minutes before the artillery preparation was due to start, the marshal and his generals filed out of the bunker. They went up the steep little path to the observation post, concealed by camouflage nets, on the top of the cliff. The Oderbruch below them was obscured by a pre-dawn mist. Zhukov looked at his watch. It was exactly 5 a.m. Moscow time, which was 3 a.m. Berlin time.

'Immediately the whole area was lit by many thousands of guns, mortars and our legendary katyushas.' No bombardment in the war had been so intense. General Kazakov's artillerymen worked in a frenzy. 'A terrible thunder shook everything around,' wrote a battery commander with the 3rd Shock Army. 'You would have thought that even us artillerists could not be scared by such a symphony, but this time, I too wanted to plug my ears. I had the feeling that my eardrums would burst.' Gunners had to remember to keep their mouths open to equalize the pressure on their ears.

At the first rumble, some German conscripts in their trenches awoke thinking that it was just another '*Morgenkonzert*', as the early-morning harassing fire was called. But soldiers with real experience of the Eastern Front had acquired a '*Landserinstinkt*' which told them that this was the great attack. NCOs screamed orders to take position immediately: '*Alarm! sofort Stellung beziehen!*' Survivors remember the feeling in their guts and their mouths going dry. 'Now we're in for it,' they muttered to themselves.

Those few trapped in trenches in the target area who somehow survived the terrifying bombardment could describe the experience afterwards only in terms of 'hell' or 'inferno', or an 'earthquake'. Many lost all sense of hearing. 'In a matter of a few seconds,' Gerd Wagner in the 27th Parachute Regiment recorded, 'all my ten comrades were dead.' When Wagner recovered consciousness, he found himself lying wounded in a smoking shell crater. He was only just able to struggle back to the second line. Few escaped alive from the artillery barrage which smashed trenches and buried their occupants, both alive and dead. Bodies are still being discovered well over half a century later.

Those to the rear who could feel the earth trembling grabbed their binoculars or trench periscopes. The commander of SS Heavy Panzer Battalion 502 gazed out through the periscope of his Tiger tank. 'In the field of view the eastern sky was in flames.' Another observer noted 'burning farmhouses, villages, banks of smoke as far as the eye could see'. A headquarters clerk could only mutter, 'Christ, the poor bastards up front.'

The days of the hearty German warrior – '*Krieg ist Krieg und Schnaps ist Schnaps*' – were well and truly past. Survivors were often not just completely disorientated, but shattered emotionally and psychologically. After the bombardment, a war correspondent with an SS propaganda company found a dazed soldier wandering in a wood, having thrown away his weapon. Apparently this was his first experience of the Eastern Front, having spent the best part of the war 'shaving officers in Paris'.

Yet even though almost every square metre of the German positions in front of the Seelow was churned up by shellfire, casualties were not nearly as high as they might have been. General Heinrici, helped by the

15. (*Previous page*) Famished refugees collecting beechnuts in a wood near Potsdam.
16. Eva Braun after the wedding of SS Gruppenführer Hermann Fegelein (*centre*) to her sister Gretl (*right*), Berchtesgaden, June 1944.

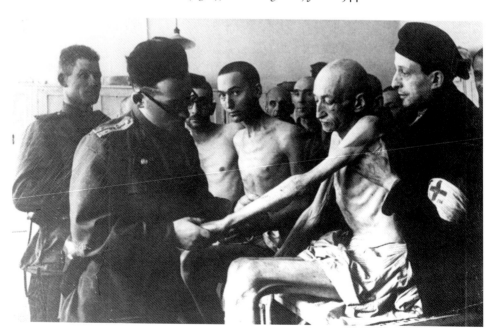

17. Red Army doctors care for Auschwitz survivors.

18–19. A German engineer (*left*) after commiting suicide with his family (*right*) before the arrival of the Red Army.

20. A German soldier hanged on the orders of General Schörner, whose motto was 'Strength through fear'. The placard reads, 'Whoever fights can die. Whoever betrays his fatherland must die! We <u>had</u> to <u>die</u>!'

21. Hitler Youth tank-hunting squad with panzerfausts clipped to their bicycles.

22. Reichsführer SS Heinrich Himmler, who seldom touched a gun yet dreamed of being a military leader.

23. Marshal Stalin and Winston Churchill at Yalta.

24. A T-34 of Marshal Zhukov's 1st Belorussian Front crosses the Oder.

25. (*Opposite*) Soviet sappers bridging the Oder to prepare the
assault on Berlin.
26. (*Above*) Red Army soldiers retrieving an anti-tank gun on the
waterlogged Oder flood plain.

27. Soviet women released from forced labour near Berlin by
the Red Army.

28. An improvised graveyard in the ruins of Berlin.

29. Hitler caresses one of his youngest defenders, watched by Artur Axmann, head of the Hitler Youth.

interrogation of the Red Army soldier south of Küstrin, had pulled the bulk of Ninth Army's troops back to the second line of trenches. On the sector south of Frankfurt an der Oder, facing the Soviet 33rd Army, some were less fortunate. Volkssturm and Hungarian detachments were sent to occupy the forward positions of the SS Division *30. Januar*. 'These men were sacrificed by headquarters as cannon fodder,' Obersturmführer Helmuth Schwarz wrote later, to preserve the regular units. Most of the Volkssturm were veterans of the First World War. Many of them had no uniforms and no weapons.

Zhukov was so encouraged by the lack of resistance shown that he assumed the Germans were crushed. 'It seemed that not a living soul was left on the enemy side after thirty minutes of bombardment,' he wrote later. He gave the order to start the general attack. 'Thousands of flares of many colours shot up into the air.' This was the signal to the young women soldiers operating the 143 searchlights – one every 200 metres.

'Along the whole length of the horizon it was as bright as daylight,' a Russian sapper colonel wrote home that night. 'On the German side, everything was covered with smoke and thick fountains of earth in clumps flying up. There were huge flocks of scared birds flying around in the sky, a constant humming, thunder, explosions. We had to cover our ears to prevent our eardrums breaking. Then tanks began roaring, searchlights were lit along all of the front line in order to blind the Germans. Then people started shouting everywhere, "*Na Berlin!*"'

Some German soldiers, no doubt over-influenced by *Wunderwaffen* propaganda, thought that the searchlights were a new weapon to blind them. On the Soviet side, attacking detachments may even have suspected for a moment that the lights were a new form of blocking detachment to prevent retreat. Captain Sulkhanishvili in the 3rd Shock Army found that 'the light was so blinding one couldn't turn around, one could only move forward'. Yet this invention, of which Zhukov was so proud, did more to disorientate the attackers than dazzle the defenders, because the light reflected back off the smoke and dust from the bombardment. Commanders with the forward troops passed back orders to turn off the lights, then a counter-order switched them back on, causing even more night blindness among the troops. Yet Zhukov had made a far greater mistake. His intensive bombardment against the first line had been pummelling mostly abandoned trenches. He does not admit this in his memoirs, nor that he was unpleasantly surprised by the intensity of German fire once the advance began in earnest. It must have been doubly galling for him, since during the main briefing conference several of his senior officers had recommended concentrating the fire on the second line.

The advance from the main Küstrin bridgehead began with Chuikov's 8th Guards Army on the left and Berzarin's 5th Shock Army on the right. Four days before, Zhukov had changed the *Stavka* plan, with Stalin's permission, to keep Katukov's 1st Guards Tank Army in support of Chuikov. They were then to force their way through to the southern suburbs of Berlin. On Berzarin's right was the 2nd Guards Tank Army, the 3rd Shock Army and the 47th Army.

On Zhukov's far right flank, the 1st Polish Army and the 61st Army had little in the way of bridgeheads. They had to cross the Oder under fire. Their leading battalions used amphibious vehicles – American DUKWs driven by young women soldiers, but most of the troops crossed in ordinary boats. Casualties were heavy in the crossing. Assault boats leaked and a number sank, 'producing losses'. The German resistance was also strong. When one battalion of the 12th Guards Rifle Division made the crossing, 'only eight men reached the west bank of the Oder'. One can deduce that there must have been a good deal of panic by the comment that 'some political officers showed indecisiveness when crossing the river'. The coded phrase implies that they should have used their pistols more.

On the extreme left flank, the 33rd Army, in its bridgehead south of Frankfurt an der Oder, and the 69th Army, north of it, were to advance to cut off the town with its fortress garrison.

Once the coloured signal flares streaked up into the overcast sky, the Soviet riflemen rose from the ground to move forward. Zhukov, the least sentimental of generals, sent the infantry through minefields which had to be cleared before he unleashed his tank armies. 'Oh, what a terrible sight it is to see a person blown up by an anti-tank mine,' a captain remembered. But the advance of the 8th Guards Army progressed well at first. The troops were encouraged by the lack of resistance. The ground-attack Shturmoviks of the 16th Air Army screamed in low over their heads to attack positions on the escarpment and heavier bomber regiments of the 18th Air Army flew to raid other targets and communications centres further back. There were 6,500 sorties that day on the 1st Belorussian Front sector, but the bad visibility, with river mist, thick smoke and dirt from explosions, concealed their targets. As a result, comparatively little damage to defensive positions was achieved by bombing and strafing. Unfortunately for the Ninth Army, whose ammunition situation was already disastrous, a main stockpile of shells at Alt Zeschdorf, west of Lebus, was hit and blown up.

Troops caught in the open were naturally the most vulnerable. The Volkssturm company of Erich Schröder, a forty-year-old called up only ten days before, was rushed to the front in trucks at 7 a.m. when they received the order 'Maximum Alert'. There was no time to dig in before the air attacks started. He remembered two almost simultaneous bomb explosions. One splinter took off a big toe, another penetrated his left calf and a third impaled him in the small of the back. He tried to limp to cover. Most of the vehicles in which they had just arrived were ablaze and the panzerfausts still on them began to explode. Eventually, he was taken in a surviving vehicle to a dressing station in Fürstenwalde, but that night a heavy Soviet bombing raid destroyed the whole building save the cellar in which they had been sheltered.

The young German conscripts and trainees had been panic-stricken by the bombardment and the searchlights. Only the seasoned soldiers prepared to open fire, but the problem was to identify a target in the virtually impenetrable mixture of river mist, smoke and dirt drifting in the air from the shellbursts. The defenders could hear the Russians calling to each other as they advanced, but it was impossible to see them. They could also hear in the distance the engines of Russian tanks straining. Even the broad tracks of the T-34 had trouble coping with the mud of the waterlogged flood plain. Survivors from forward positions who had abandoned their weapons fled back through the second line, yelling, '*Der Iwan kommt!*' One young soldier running back saw someone ahead and shouted the warning to him, but the figure who turned round proved to be a Red Army soldier. They both leaped for cover and began to fire at each other. The German boy, to his astonishment, killed the Russian.

*

The ground had been so broken up by the massive bombardment that Soviet anti-tank guns and divisional artillery found it very hard to follow the infantry. This was particularly true of the katyusha batteries mounted on the backs of trucks. Nevertheless, the Guards mortar regiments who fired the katyushas watched with satisfaction as the first German prisoners sent to the rear cringed on seeing the weapon which had struck more fear into the Wehrmacht than any other.

What the prisoners might also have seen were the huge traffic jams of vehicles in heavy mud, waiting for Chuikov's 8th Guards Army and Berzarin's 5th Shock Army to make a breakthrough. But progress that morning had been very slow. Zhukov, in the observation post on the Reitwein Spur, was losing his temper, swearing and threatening commanders with demotion and a *shtraf* company. He had a furious row with General Chuikov in front of staff officers, because the 8th Guards Army was bogged down on the Oderbruch below the escarpment.

By the middle of the day, an increasingly desperate Zhukov, no doubt dreading the next radio-telephone conversation with Stalin, decided to change his operational plan. The tank armies were not supposed to move forward until the infantry had broken open the German defence line and reached the Seelow Heights. But he could not wait. Chuikov was horrified, foreseeing the chaos this would cause, but Zhukov was adamant. At 3 p.m. he called the *Stavka* to speak to Stalin. Stalin listened to his report. 'So you've underestimated the enemy on the Berlin axis,' he said. 'I was thinking that you were already on the approaches to Berlin, but you're still on the Seelow Heights. Things have started more successfully for Konev.' He seemed to take Zhukov's change of plan in his stride, but Zhukov knew only too well that everything depended on results.

Katukov received orders in the afternoon to attack with the 1st Guards Tank Army in the direction of Seelow, while Bogdanov's 2nd Guards Tank Army was ordered to attack the Neuhardenberg sector. This premature movement of the tanks meant that the close-support artillery, which the rifle divisions had been demanding to deal with strongpoints, could not get forward, because of the state of the ground. There was indeed chaos, as Chuikov had predicted, with so many thousands of armoured vehicles packed into the bridgehead. Sorting out the different formations and units was a nightmare for the traffic controllers.

On the right, Bogdanov's tanks suffered badly from both the 88mm guns dug in below Neuhardenberg and fierce counter-attacks from small groups with panzerfausts. A platoon of assault guns led by Wachtmeister Gernert of the 111th Training Brigade suddenly appeared out of the smoke on the Oderbruch near Neutrebbin and engaged a mass of Soviet tanks. Gernert alone accounted for seven of them: his personal tally rose to forty-four enemy tanks the following day. 'His outstanding bravery and tactically clever leadership saved the flank of the brigade,' General Heinrici wrote, confirming the award of a Knight's Cross. But by the time he signed it on 28 April, the brigade, and indeed the Ninth Army as a recognizable formation, would have ceased to exist.

Eventually the leading brigades of the tank armies reached the bottom of the Seelow Heights and started the ascent. Engines began screaming with the effort. In many places the gradient was so steep that tank commanders had to find alternative routes. This often made them blunder into a German strongpoint.

Katukov's leading brigades on the left received their nastiest shock when advancing to the Dolgelin–Friedersdorf road south-east of Seelow. A murderous armoured engagement began there when they found Tiger tanks of SS Heavy Panzer Battalion 502 holding the line. The Soviet tank brigades were hampered by deep ditches and suffered heavy casualties.

In the centre, meanwhile, between Seelow and Neuhardenberg, Göring's vaunted 9th Parachute Division had buckled under the hammering. When the bombardment had begun that morning, the 27th Parachute Regiment had moved its headquarters from Schloss Gusow on the ridge back to a bunker in the woods behind. Hauptmann Finkler remained in the manor house connected by field telephone. He could see little through the smoke to report back, but the stream of young Luftwaffe personnel running from the front, having abandoned their weapons, indicated the collapse that was taking place. Eventually, a lieutenant arrived with the warning that the Soviet troops were already advancing towards the edge of the village. Colonel Menke, the regimental commander, ordered an immediate counter-attack. Finkler scraped together some ten men from the forward headquarters, charged out and ran almost straight into the enemy. Nearly all the paratroopers were shot down. Finkler and the lieutenant found an abandoned Hetzer tank-destroyer and sheltered in that.

*

In the headquarters for the defence of Berlin on the Hohenzollerndamm, Colonel Refior, General Reymann's chief of staff, was 'not surprised' when they were awoken that morning by 'a dull, continuous rolling thunder from the east'. The intensity of the bombardment was so great that in Berlin's eastern suburbs, sixty kilometres from the target area, the effect was like a small earthquake. Houses trembled, pictures fell off walls and telephone bells rang of their own accord. 'It's started,' people murmured anxiously to each other in the streets. Nobody had any illusions about what this signified. In the grey light of that overcast morning, 'women and girls stood around in huddled groups, listening in dread to the distant sounds of the front'. The most frequently asked question was whether the Americans would get to Berlin in time to save them.

The authorities' loudly stated confidence in the defence line on the Oder was rather undermined by the flurry of activity back in the capital, sealing barricades and manning defence points. Goebbels made a passion-ate but unconvincing speech about this new storm of Mongols breaking itself against their walls. The immediate preoccupation of Berliners, however, was to fill their larders before the siege of the city began. The queues outside bakeries and food shops were longer than ever.

Amid the frenzied denial of reality at the top, somebody that morning fortunately had the sense to order the children's clinic of the Potsdam hospital to move further away from the capital. The Potsdam hospital had been almost entirely destroyed in the Allied air raid on the night of 14 April. The devastation had been increased by an unlucky hit on an ammunition train standing in the station. The sick children in the infants' clinic were moved in a German Red Cross ambulance, towed very slowly by two emaciated horses through the rubble-filled streets to the Cecilienhof palace. The rather elderly crown prince had abandoned it only a few weeks before, but several ancient officers from the old Prussian army and their wives continued to shelter in the cellars. They had no idea that Potsdam was destined to be part of the Soviet zone of occupation.

On the morning of 16 April the nurses heard that they were to move the children south-westwards to Heilstätten near Beelitz. Almost all the Berlin hospitals, including the Charité, the Auguste-Viktoria and the

Robert-Koch clinic, were allocated accommodation there in a camouflaged stone-built barracks. This complex had also served as a hospital
during the First World War. Hitler had spent two months there at the
end of 1916, after being wounded. But the sick children were not yet
out of danger. As they were being unloaded from buses, there was a
cry of 'Take cover! Aircraft!' A Soviet biplane – the antiquated Po-2
crop-sprayer which the Germans called a 'coffee-grinder' – appeared at
tree height and opened fire.

In the underground headquarters in Zossen, telephones were ringing
continually. An exhausted General Krebs kept going on glasses of
vermouth from a bottle kept in his office safe. As the Soviet artillery and
aviation destroyed command posts and cut telephone cables, there were
soon many fewer headquarters to report in, but the calls from ministers
and General Burgdorf in the Reich Chancellery bunker increased. Everyone in Berlin's government quarter was demanding news. The thoughts
of staff officers, however, were with those at the front, imagining what
they were going through.

At the 11 a.m. conference, officers wanted to know what the evacuation
plans were. They all knew that Zossen, in its position south of Berlin,
was extremely vulnerable the moment that the 1st Ukrainian Front
broke through on the Neisse. One or two acid remarks were made about
Hitler's prediction that the attack on Berlin was a feint and that the Red
Army's real objective was Prague. To Heinrici's horror, Hitler had
even transferred three panzer divisions to the recently promoted Field
Marshal Schörner's command.

General Busse, the commander of the Ninth Army, needed them
desperately as a reserve for counter-attacks. His three corps – the CI
Army Corps on the left, General Helmuth Weidling's LVI Panzer
Corps in the centre and the XI SS Panzer Corps on the right – were
conspicuously short of tanks. They were doomed to a static defence
until they broke. The V SS Mountain Corps south of Frankfurt an der
Oder, although between the two main Soviet thrusts, faced the attack
of the 69th Army, which it managed to hold back.

On the Oderbruch and the Seelow Heights, the battle continued in
chaotic fashion. Because of the lack of visibility, much of the killing was

done at close range. One member of the *Grossdeutschland* guard regiment wrote later that the marshland was 'not a killing field but a slaughterhouse'.

'We moved across terrain cratered from shellfire,' the Soviet sapper officer Pyotr Sebelev wrote in his letter home that night. 'Everywhere lay smashed German guns, vehicles, burning tanks and many corpses, which our men dragged to a place to be buried. The weather is overcast. It is drizzling and our ground-attack aircraft are flying all over the German front line from time to time. Many of the Germans surrender. They don't want to fight and give their life for Hitler.'

Other Red Army officers were more exultant. Captain Klochkov in the 3rd Shock Army described the ground as 'covered with the corpses of Hitler's warriors who used to boast so much'. He then added, 'To the astonishment of our soldiers, some corpses would rise unsteadily to their feet from the bottom of trenches and raise their hands.' But this account overlooked their own casualties. The 1st Belorussian Front lost nearly three times as many men as the German defenders.

Subsequent inquests about that day of fighting established numerous shortcomings on the Soviet side. The 5th Shock Army apparently suffered from 'bad organization'. Radio discipline was lacking and communications were so bad that 'commanders did not know what was going on and gave false information'. To make matters worse, the excess of coded signals traffic meant that army headquarters could not cope with the deciphering. Many urgent signals were therefore delayed. Commanders were also claiming to have taken objectives they had not yet reached. It is hard to tell whether this was confusion or the terrible pressure for results from higher headquarters. This came from Zhukov bellowing into a field telephone at an army commander who, following standard Soviet alpha-male behaviour, would then stand up to bellow even more terrifyingly into his field telephone at the corps or divisional commander. The general commanding the 26th Guards Rifle Corps was badly caught out. He informed General Berzarin that his troops had taken one village and advanced two kilometres beyond it 'when this was not true'.

In the 248th Rifle Division, one commander lost his regiment. In another division, a battalion was sent in the wrong direction and as a result the whole regiment was late for the attack. And once the advance began, regiments lost touch with each other in the mist and smoke. They also failed to spot German gun emplacements, which 'continued to operate while the infantry moved forward and this led to heavy losses'. Commanders were also blamed for their mentality. They wanted only to move forward, when they should have been concentrating on the best way to destroy the enemy. This problem was attributed to a lack of motivated Party members rather than relentless pressure from higher command.

There were also, not for the first time, casualties from their own supporting artillery. On one occasion the problem was ascribed to the fact that 'quite often commanders are incapable of handling different technical devices', a description which perhaps included a prismatic compass and a radio set. On the first day, 16 April, the 266th Rifle Division was hit heavily by its own artillery as it reached the tree-line. On the next, both the 248th and the 301st Rifle Divisions suffered the same fate. The 5th Shock Army nevertheless claimed 33,000 prisoners, but did not state its own casualties.

The 8th Guards Army, meanwhile, suffered 'serious disadvantages', a standard euphemism for incompetence leading to near disaster. But the fault here was Zhukov's, not Chuikov's. 'The preparatory fire worked well on the enemy's front line, allowing the infantry to go through the first line, but our artillery could not destroy enemy fire positions, especially on the Seelow Heights, and even the use of aviation did not make up for this.' There were also cases of Soviet aircraft bombing and strafing their own men. This was partly due to the fact that the leading rifle battalions did not 'know the right signal flares to use to show our front line'. Since the signal was a white and a yellow flare and very few yellow flares had been issued, such mistakes were hardly surprising.

The report also mentions that the artillery failed to move forward to support the front line of infantry, but this was because the planners had failed to foresee that their massive bombardment would make the waterlogged ground almost impassable. The medical services were clearly overwhelmed and 'in some regiments the evacuation of the wounded from the battlefield was very badly organized'. One machine gunner lay for twenty hours without help. The wounded of the 27th Guards Rifle Division were left 'without any medical aid for four to five hours', and the casualty clearing station had only four operating tables.

South of Frankfurt an der Oder, the 33rd Army did not have an easy advance against the V SS Mountain Corps. They too seem to have been short of medical assistants to deal with their wounded. Officers were reduced to forcing German prisoners at gunpoint to carry the Soviet wounded to the rear and bring back ammunition. This appalled the army political department, which later criticized its own political officers for not having taken the German prisoners themselves, indoctrinated them 'and then sent them back to their comrades to demoralize them'. The priority awarded to their own wounded by Red Army authorities was indeed low. And whatever the pressure of work in a field hospital, SMERSH never shrank from pulling a doctor off an operation to examine suspected cases of self-inflicted wounds, because once the fighting began, they 'became much more frequent'.*

The battle for the Seelow Heights was certainly not Marshal Zhukov's finest hour, but even if the planning and command of the operation were faulty, the courage, stamina and self-sacrifice of most Red Army soldiers and junior officers cannot be doubted for a moment. This genuine heroism – as distinct from the lifeless propaganda version to be served up as a moral lesson for future generations – sadly did nothing to lessen the essential callousness of senior commanders and the Soviet political leadership. References to soldiers in veiled speech during telephone conversations were revealing. Commanders used to say, 'How many matches were burnt?' or 'How many pencils were broken?' when asking for casualty estimates.

On the German side, General Heinrici, the commander-in-chief of Army Group Vistula, and General Busse could not be expected to have done much better in the circumstances. German survivors of the battle still bless them for having saved countless lives by withdrawing the majority of troops from the forward positions just before the bombardment. But some senior officers still believed in Adolf Hitler. After nightfall on 16 April, Colonel Hans-Oscar Wöhlermann, the artillery commander in the LVI Panzer Corps, went to see his commander, General Weidling, at Waldsieversdorf, north-west of Müncheberg.

* Medical personnel had such a terrible time that a very large proportion gave up medicine at the end of the war.

Corps headquarters were established in the weekend house of a Berlin family. A single candle lit the room on the first floor. Weidling, who had no illusions about Hitler's conduct of the war, spoke his mind. The monocled Wöhlermann was shaken. 'I was deeply dismayed,' he wrote later, 'to find that even this dedicated soldier and daredevil, our old "Hard as Bones", as he had been known in the regiment, had lost faith in our highest leadership.'

Their conversation was brought to an abrupt halt by a bombing attack. Then reports came in indicating that a hole had opened up between them and the XI SS Panzer Corps on their right, and that another gap on their left was developing which threatened to break their link with General Berlin's CI Corps. Goebbels's notion of a wall against the Mongol hordes was disintegrating rapidly.

That night must have been one of the worst of Zhukov's life. The eyes of the army and, more crucially, the eyes of the Kremlin were fixed on the Seelow Heights, which he had failed to secure. His armies could not now perform their task of taking 'Berlin on the sixth day of the operation'. One of Chuikov's rifle regiments had reached the edge of the town of Seelow, and some of Katukov's tanks were nearly at the crest at one point, but this would certainly not satisfy Stalin.

The Soviet leader, who had sounded fairly relaxed during the afternoon, was clearly angry when Zhukov reported on the radio-telephone shortly before midnight that the heights were not occupied. Stalin blamed him for having changed the *Stavka* plan. 'Are you sure that you'll capture the Seelow line tomorrow?' he demanded.

'By the end of the day, tomorrow, 17 April,' Zhukov answered, trying to sound calm, 'the defence of Seelow Heights will be broken. I am convinced that the more troops the enemy sends against us here, the easier it will be to capture Berlin. It is much easier to destroy troops in open countryside than in a fortified city.'

Stalin did not sound convinced. Perhaps he was thinking of the Americans, who might come up from the south-west, rather than the German forces to the east of the capital. 'We are thinking,' Stalin said, 'of ordering Konev to send the tank armies of Rybalko and Lelyushenko towards Berlin from the south, and telling Rokossovsky to speed up the crossing and also attack from the north.' Stalin hung up with a curt '*do svidaniya*'. It was not long before Zhukov's chief of staff, General Malinin, discovered that Stalin had indeed told Konev to send his tank armies up against Berlin's southern flank.

Russian soldiers – in 1945 as in 1814 – despised the rivers of western Europe. They seemed miserable in comparison with the great rivers of the Motherland. Yet every river which they had crossed held a special significance, because it marked the advance in their relentless fight back against the invader. 'Even when I was wounded on the Volga near Stalingrad,' said Junior Lieutenant Maslov, 'I was convinced that I would return to the front and finally see the accursed Spree.'

The Neisse between Forst and Muskau was only about half the width of the Oder, but a river crossing against enemy troops in prepared positions was not a simple task. Marshal Konev decided that the best tactic for his 1st Ukrainian Front was to keep the enemy occupied and blind them while his point units crossed the river.

The artillery bombardment began at 6 a.m. Moscow time, 4 a.m. Berlin time. It boasted 249 guns per kilometre, their greatest concentration of the war, and was intensified by heavy carpet-bombing from the 2nd Air Army. 'The drone of aircraft and the thunder of guns and exploding bombs were so loud that one could not hear one's comrade shouting even a metre away,' one officer recorded. It was also a much longer barrage than Zhukov's, extending altogether to 145 minutes. 'The god of war is thundering very nicely today,' remarked a battery commander during a pause. The gun crews threw themselves into their work with the joy of vengeance, egged on by their commanders' orders: 'At the fascist lair – fire!', 'At the possessed Hitler – fire!', 'For the blood and suffering of our people – fire!'

Konev, to watch the battle open, had come from his Front headquarters near Breslau, where the bitter siege of the Silesian capital still continued. He went forward to the observation post of General Pukhov's 13th Army. This consisted of a dugout and trenches at the edge of a pine forest on a cliff which overlooked the river. Being within small-arms range of enemy positions on the west bank of the Neisse, they watched through trench telescopes. But their grand-circle view of events came to an end with the second phase of the bombardment when General Krasovsky's pilots in the 2nd Air Army flew fast at low level up the west bank of the river, dropping smoke bombs. This screen was laid along a frontage of 390 kilometres, which prevented the Fourth Panzer Army defenders from rapidly identifying the point of the main attack. Konev was fortunate. A breath of wind spread the screen without dispersing it too quickly.

The lead units dashed forward, carrying their assault boats, and launched themselves into the stream, paddling furiously. 'The assault boats were launched,' the 1st Ukrainian Front reported, 'before the guns fell silent. Communist Party activists and Komsomol members tried to be the first into the boats, and shouted encouraging slogans to their comrades: "For the Motherland! For Stalin!"' When the first landings were made on the western bank, little red flags were set up to encourage the next wave. Some battalions started to cross simply by swimming, an action that the veterans among them had performed several times before in the advance across the Ukraine. Other troops were able to make use of previously reconnoitred fords and waded across, their weapons held above their heads. Sappers responsible for preparing the first ferries and pontoon bridges jumped into the water and struck out for the far shore. Some 85mm anti-tank guns soon followed the first rifle battalions, and small bridgeheads were established.

The massive bombardment meant that few Germans in the forward positions were capable of effective resistance. Many were seriously shell-shocked. 'We had nowhere to hide,' Obergefreiter Karl Pafflik told his captors. 'The air was full of whistling and explosions. We suffered unimaginable losses. Those who survived were rushing around in trenches and bunkers like madmen trying to save themselves. We were speechless with terror.' Many took advantage of the smoke and chaos to surrender. No fewer than twenty-five men from the 500th Straf Regiment, who had better reasons to desert than most, gave themselves up in one group. German soldiers on their own or in batches would put up their hands, shouting in pidgin-Russian, 'Ivan, don't shoot, we are prison.' A deserter from the 500th Straf Regiment told his interrogators the well-known Berlin remark, 'The only promise Hitler has kept is the one he made before coming to power. Give me ten years and you will not be able to recognize Germany.' Other *Landsers* complained that they had been lied to by their officers, with promises of V-3 and V-4 rockets.

Once cables were secured over the river, ferries brought across the first T-34 tanks to support the infantry. The 1st Ukrainian Front engineer formations had planned no fewer than 133 crossing points in the main attack sectors. They were responsible for all the Neisse crossings. The engineers attached to the 3rd and 4th Guards Tank Armies had been ordered to keep all their equipment ready for the next river, the Spree. Soon after midday, with the first of the sixty-ton bridges in position in the area of the 5th Guards Army, the lead elements of Lelyushenko's 4th Guards Tank Army began to cross. During the afternoon, the remaining bulk of the fighting forces crossed the river and continued the advance. The tank brigades, ordered to push ahead with all speed, were ready to take on the Fourth Panzer Army's counterattack spearheaded by the 21st Panzer Division. On the southern part of the sector, the 2nd Polish Army and the 52nd Army had also crossed successfully and were pushing forward. Their orders were to make for Dresden.

Konev had good reason to be satisfied with the first day of the offensive. His lead units were halfway to the River Spree. The only fault established afterwards was that the evacuation of the wounded to hospitals was 'unbearably slow', but, like most other commanders, Konev did not seem unduly perturbed. At midnight, he reported to Stalin via radio-telephone that the 1st Ukrainian Front's advance was developing successfully. 'Zhukov is not getting on very well,' said Stalin, who had just spoken to him. 'Turn Rybalko [3rd Guards Tank Army] and Lelyushenko [4th Guards Tank Army] towards Zehlendorf [the most south-western suburb of Berlin]. You remember, like we arranged at the *Stavka*.' Konev remembered the meeting only too well, especially the moment when Stalin stopped the boundary between him and Zhukov at Lübben, thus leaving open the possibility that the 1st Ukrainian Front could attack Berlin from the south.

Stalin's choice of Zehlendorf as reference point is most interesting. He evidently wanted to spur Konev on to the furthest south-western part of Berlin as quickly as possible, since that would be the obvious line of approach from the American bridgehead at Zerbst. It was also perhaps no coincidence that just inside Zehlendorf lay Dahlem, where the Kaiser Wilhelm Institute had its nuclear research facilities.

Three hours earlier, at a 9 p.m. meeting at the *Stavka*, General Antonov, no doubt on Stalin's instructions, had yet again deliberately misled the Americans when they mentioned German reports of an all-out offensive against Berlin. '[Antonov] said,' stated the signal to the State Department in Washington, DC, 'that actually the Russians are undertaking a large-scale reconnaissance on the central sector of the front for the purpose of finding out details of the German defences.'

16

Seelow and the Spree

After Stalin's two midnight telephone conversations on 16 April, the race between Zhukov and Konev began in earnest. Konev, incited by Stalin, rose enthusiastically to the challenge. Zhukov, although rattled by the setback on the Seelow Heights, believed that Berlin was his by right.

The overcast sky and drizzle gave way to better weather on Tuesday 17 April. The Shturmoviks were able to attack the remaining German positions on the Seelow Heights with much greater accuracy. Down on the Oderbruch and up on the escarpment, small towns, hamlets and individual farmhouses still burned. The Soviet artillery and aviation had targeted any building in case it housed a command post. This resulted in an overpowering smell of charred flesh, mostly human in the villages and livestock on the farms. The shelling of farm buildings as likely depots and headquarters led to a terrible slaughter of animals unable to escape from being burned alive.

Behind the indistinct German lines, dressing stations were filled with wounded far beyond the capacity of the doctors. A stomach wound was as good as a death sentence under the system of triage, since the surgery it required took too long. The first priority for treatment were those capable of further combat. Specially detailed officers trawled the field hospitals for walking wounded capable of firing a gun.

The Feldgendarmerie at their improvised roadblocks were always on the lookout for stragglers, whether fit or lightly wounded, who could be forced back into scratch companies. As soon as a reasonable number had been assembled, they were marched into the line. Soldiers called the Feldgendarmerie not only 'chain-hounds', but also '*Heldenklauen*', or 'heroic talons', because they saw no fighting yet snatched anybody who retreated.

In their brutal zeal, the Feldgendarmerie often grabbed men who were genuinely trying to rejoin their battalions. They then found themselves mixed in with stragglers and fifteen- or sixteen-year-old Hitler Youth, some of whom were still in shorts. A smaller size of steel helmet had been manufactured for boy soldiers, but not nearly enough were produced. Their tense, pale faces could barely be seen under helmets that dropped over their ears. A group of Soviet sappers from the 3rd Shock Army called forward to clear a minefield were taken by surprise when a dozen Germans emerged from a trench to surrender. Suddenly a boy appeared from a bunker. 'He was wearing a long trench-coat and a cap,' recorded Captain Sulkhanishvili. 'He fired a burst with his sub-machine gun. But then, seeing that I didn't fall over, he dropped his sub-machine gun and started to sob. He tried to shout, "*Hitler kaputt, Stalin gut!*" I laughed. I hit him only once in the face. Poor boys, I felt sorry for them.'

The most dangerous of the Hitler Youth were often those whose homes and families had been ripped apart in the east by the Red Army. The only course for them seemed to be death in battle, taking as many hated Bolsheviks with them as possible.

The fighting qualities of the German Army had not yet collapsed, as Zhukov and his troops found to their cost. Another artillery and aviation bombardment on the morning of 17 April, followed by a renewed advance by Katukov and Bogdanov's tank armies, did not achieve the success which Zhukov had promised Stalin. The 88mm anti-aircraft guns and tank-hunting infantry with panzerfausts immobilized many of the tanks. At midday, almost as soon as Katukov's tank brigades moved into Dolgelin and Friedersdorf, they faced a counter-attack by the remaining Panther tanks of the *Kurmark* Panzer Division.

General Yushchuk's 11th Tank Corps, on the other hand, managed to surround Seelow itself astride the Reichsstrasse 1, the old Prussian highway which used to lead from Berlin all the way to the now destroyed East Prussian capital of Königsberg. But Yushchuk's tanks soon found themselves under fire from the artillery of the neighbouring 5th Shock Army. This led to a 'distinctly uncultured' row with Berzarin's head-quarters. It was not just the tank troops which suffered. 'In the opinion of the infantry,' a report on the fighting stated tactfully, 'the artillery is not firing at precise targets but at general area targets.'

In the confused fighting round Seelow, Yushchuk's tanks were repeat-edly attacked with panzerfausts fired at close range. His soldiers responded by grabbing wire-sprung mattresses from nearby houses and fastening them to their turrets and flanks. This improvised spaced armour made the hollow-charge of the panzerfaust detonate before hitting the hull or turret.

The T-34s and Stalin tanks of both Guards Tank Armies 'ironed' any trenches which they encountered, although most had by now been abandoned. In the more northerly part of the Oderbruch, the 3rd Shock Army, supported on its right by the 47th Army, pushed back the forward units of the CI Corps, many of whose regiments had been almost entirely composed of young trainees and officer candidates. The 'Potsdam' Regiment, which had reassembled near Neutrebbin, pulled back further behind the marshy banks of the Alte Oder, which was nearly ten metres wide at that point. There were only thirty-four boys left on their feet.

Again they heard the noise of tank engines. 'We infantry were once again the idiots. We were expected to halt the Russian advance when all the other arms were pulling back westwards.' Only a few self-propelled assault guns were left to take on Soviet tanks. The divisional artillery, having fired the last of their few rounds of ammunition, had blown up their guns and left. Not surprisingly, many of the infantry had slipped off with those withdrawing. Discipline was beginning to disintegrate, accelerated by feverish rumours that a cease-fire with the Western Allies had already begun.

In the centre, the 9th Parachute Division had completely collapsed. Its humiliated commander was General Bruno Bräuer, who had com-manded the airborne assault on Heraklion in Crete. Bräuer, an elegant man who used a cigarette holder, had later become the garrison com-mander on Crete. Yet despite all of Göring's preposterous boasts about his superhuman warriors, who had been kitted out to look the part with the paratrooper's rimless helmet, Bräuer was in fact commanding Luftwaffe ground personnel. Most had never jumped from an aircraft in their life, let alone seen action. When the bombardment and assault began, the officers were unable to control their panic-stricken men, especially when subjected to a katyusha rocket attack.

Colonel Menke, the commander of the 27th Parachute Regiment, had been killed when T-34s broke through near his headquarters. Only during the late morning of 17 April did the division rally a little, when armoured support arrived in the form of Panthers, Panzer Mark IVs and half-tracks. But the collapse started again soon afterwards. Wöhlermann, the artillery commander of LVI Corps, came upon Bräuer and found him 'completely shattered by the flight of his men'. The highly strung Bräuer suffered a nervous collapse and was relieved of his command. He was a truly unfortunate man. Shortly after the war he was tried and convicted in Athens for atrocities committed under another general on Crete and executed in 1947.

At 6.30 p.m., Ribbentrop arrived unannounced at Weidling's headquarters, demanding to be briefed on the situation. Wöhlermann happened to arrive at that moment. 'This is my artillery commander, who has just arrived from the front,' said Weidling. Wöhlermann received a flabby handshake from the foreign minister. 'He can report on the situation,' Weidling added. Then, having indicated that his subordinate should hold nothing back, Weidling sat down next to Ribbentrop to listen. Wöhlermann's 'report had a devastating effect on the foreign minister'. Ribbentrop asked one or two questions in a hoarse, barely audible voice. All he could do was make evasive references to a possible 'twelfth-hour' change in the situation and hint at negotiations with the Americans and the British. It was perhaps this assertion that prompted General Busse to send the signal, 'Hold on for two more days, then everything will be sorted out'. This suggestion of a deal with the Western Allies was the ultimate lie of the Nazi leadership.

Stragglers from the Oder flood plain pulled back into woods on the steep slope of the Seelow escarpment, often to find Soviet infantry and tank formations ahead of them. Groups of nervous soldiers often fired at their own side and both Soviet artillery and aviation continued to bombard their own men as much as the Germans. The Luftwaffe put up as many Focke-Wulf fighters that day as it could to oppose the onslaught and towards evening German aircraft attacked the pontoon bridges over the Oder, but in vain. A report from an unidentified source claimed that 'German pilots frequently death-dive into Russian bombers, causing both [to] plunge flaming groundwards'. If true, this would have signified a notable reversal of roles from 1941, when desperately brave Soviet pilots rammed their Luftwaffe attackers on the first day of Operation Barbarossa.

What is even more striking is the reported use of a kamikaze squadron against the Soviet bridges across the Oder. The Luftwaffe appears to have invented its own term – *Selbstopfereinsatz*, or 'self-sacrifice mission'. The pilots of the *Leonidas* squadron, based at Jüterbog and commanded by Lieutenant Colonel Heiner Lange, supposedly signed a declaration which ended with the words, 'I am above all clear that the mission will end in my death.' On the evening of 16 April, there was a farewell dance for the pilots on the base with young women from the Luftwaffe signals unit there. The dance ended with a final song. Major General Fuchs, the overall commander, was 'fighting back his tears'.

The next morning, the first of the so-called 'total missions' were flown against the thirty-two 'over-water and under-water bridges' repaired or built by Soviet engineers. The Germans used a variety of aircraft – Focke-Wulf 190, Messerschmitt 109 and Junkers 88 – whatever was available. One of the 'self-sacrifice pilots' flying the next day was Ernst Beichl, in a Focke-Wulf with a 500-kilogram bomb. His target was the pontoon bridge near Zellin. Air reconnaissance later reported it destroyed, but claims that a total of seventeen bridges were destroyed in the course of three days seem wildly exaggerated. The only other one that genuinely appears to have been hit was the railway bridge at Küstrin. Thirty-five pilots and aircraft were a high price to pay for such a limited and temporary success. This did not stop Major General Fuchs from sending their names in a special birthday message 'to the Führer on his imminent fifty-sixth birthday'. It was just the sort of present that he appreciated most.

The whole operation had to be abandoned suddenly because Marshal Konev's tank armies, charging unexpectedly towards Berlin from the south-east, threatened their base at Jüterbog.

The fortunes of war still favoured Konev's 1st Ukrainian Front after its attack across the Neisse. The 13th Army and the 5th Guards Army had broken open the second line of German defence. Even while heavy fighting continued on either side, Konev sent through his leading tank brigades to race for the River Spree between Cottbus and Spremberg. Large patches of pine forest burned fiercely from the renewed bombardments of both artillery and ground-attack Shturmoviks. These fires were dangerous for tanks which carried their fuel reserves in barrels strapped to the back. But speed was vital, because they had a chance of breaching the Spree barrier before the Fourth Panzer Army could reorganize a new line of defence. Konev's troops scented victory. There was a feeling in the 4th Guards Tank Army that 'if the Germans could not hold on to the Neisse, they can't do anything now'. Commanders carried out a weapon inspection before the assault. A young Communist was found to have a rusty weapon. 'How are you going to fire it?' the officer yelled at him. 'You should be an example to everyone, but your own weapon is dirty!'

An armoured breakthrough towards Berlin ran the risk of a German counter-thrust to its lines of communications. Konev therefore angled Zhadov's 5th Guards Army to the left towards Spremberg and the 3rd Guards Army to the right to force the Germans back on Cottbus.

That evening, when the leading brigades of the 3rd Guards Tank Army reached the Spree, General Rybalko, their army commander, who took pride in leading from the front, did not wait for bridging equipment to come up. He selected a point which looked as if it might not be too deep, then sent a tank straight into the river, which was about fifty metres wide at this point. The water rose above the tracks but no more. The tank brigade followed across in line, fording the river like cavalry. Unlike cavalry, however, they could ignore the German machine guns firing at them from the far bank. The bulk of both tank armies was able to follow on across the Spree during the night.

Konev knew that his tanks would find the lakes, marshes, watercourses and pine forests of the Lausitz region difficult going, but if they were quick, the roads to Berlin would be sparsely defended. The German Fourth Panzer Army had already committed its operational reserve in an attempt to hold the second line, while commanders in Berlin would be more preoccupied by the threat from Zhukov's armies.

Konev had come to a similar conclusion to Zhukov, that it was easier to break the enemy early in the open than later in Berlin. But he did not mention this when he spoke to Stalin that evening on the radio-telephone from his forward command post, a castle perched on a small hill with views across the top of the surrounding pine forests.

Konev had almost finished his report when Stalin suddenly interrupted him. 'With Zhukov things are not going so well yet. He is still breaking through the enemy defences.' A long pause followed, which Konev decided not to break. 'Couldn't we,' Stalin continued, 'redeploy Zhukov's mobile troops and send them against Berlin through the gap formed in the sector of your Front?' This was probably not a serious proposal, but a gambit to make Konev put forward his own plan.

'Comrade Stalin,' he replied, 'this will take too much time and will add considerable confusion . . . The situation for our Front is developing favourably, we have enough forces and we can turn both tank armies against Berlin.' Konev then said that he would advance via Zossen, which they both knew was the headquarters of OKH.

'Very good,' Stalin replied. 'I agree. Turn the tank armies towards Berlin.'

In the government quarter of Berlin during the course of 17 April, nobody really knew what to do except draft stirring declarations combined with further threats of execution. 'No German town will be declared an open city', read the order sent by Himmler to all military commanders. 'Every village and every town will be defended with all possible means. Any German who offends against this self-evident duty to the nation will lose his life as well as his honour.' He ignored the fact that the German artillery was virtually out of ammunition, tanks were already being abandoned for lack of fuel and the soldiers themselves were without food.

Nazi bureaucracy, even at the lowest levels, did not change in the face of annihilation. The little town of Woltersdorf, just south of the Reichsstrasse 1 to Berlin, found itself overrun with refugees on 17 April. Yet the local authorities still allowed just their 'non-employed [inhabitants] and those not liable for Volkssturm service' to leave, and then only if they had 'written confirmation from their host location' that shelter was available. In addition, each person had to seek permission of the Kreisabschnittsleiter, the Nazi district chief. The local spirit of resistance, however, was far from fanatical. The town's Volkssturm emergency platoon asked permission to be excused further duty.

*

Konev's forces were now less than eighty kilometres to the south-west of the OKH and OKW command centres at Zossen. Yet neither the Fourth Panzer Army nor Field Marshal Schörner's Army Group Centre had reported that the Soviet 3rd and 4th Guards Tank Armies were crossing the Spree in force and that there were no further reserves to stop them. The attention of staff officers at Zossen was fixed primarily on the struggle for the Seelow Heights.

General Heinrici had already sent the major part of his army group reserve – Steiner's III SS *Germanische* Panzer Corps – to support Busse's beleaguered Ninth Army. The 11th SS Division *Nordland* received orders at midday on 17 April to move south to Seelow. The *Nordland* consisted mainly of Danes and Norwegians but also Swedes, Finns and Estonians. Some have suggested that there was even a handful of British in its ranks, but this seems more than doubtful. Commanded by SS Brigadeführer Joachim Ziegler, it had around fifty armoured vehicles, mainly with its reconnaissance battalion and the Hermann von Salza Panzer Battalion. The bulk of the remaining manpower was with the 'Danmark' and the 'Norge' panzergrenadier regiments, and a sapper battalion. The *Nordland*, which had been evacuated from the Courland encirclement and then thrown into the heavy fighting for the Oder estuary east of Stettin, had suffered just under 15,000 casualties since the beginning of the year, with 4,500 killed or missing.

Heinrici sent another formation of foreign Waffen SS, the *Nederland* Division, even further south. Its destination was south-west of Frankfurt an der Oder and Müllrose, where it would come under the command of the V SS Mountain Corps. Relations between SS and Wehrmacht were enflamed. Himmler was furious that Heinrici should strip Steiner's SS Corps of his strongest divisions. And the *Nordland* itself, demonstrating great reluctance to serve under an army commander, did not exactly hurry to join its new formation.

Dawn on Wednesday 18 April produced a red sky along the eastern horizon. Those still fighting to cling on to the Seelow Heights were filled with foreboding. It was not long before they heard the deep, harsh noise of tank engines and churning tracks. Air attacks began soon afterwards. Shturmoviks again dive-bombed the *Nordland* column while it was still some way from the front, and the SS panzergrenadiers in the open trucks were showered with earth. Ziegler had gone on ahead to Weidling's headquarters to inform him that his vehicles had run out of fuel and that was why the division was taking so long to get to him. Weidling was furious.

Zhukov, too, was in a dangerous mood that morning. He now knew that Konev's tank armies had been allowed to swing north on Berlin. Stalin had also raised the possibility during their night-time conversation of turning Rokossovsky's 2nd Belorussian Front down towards Berlin once it crossed the Oder to the north. The *Verkhovny* had goaded him even further by offering *Stavka* advice on how to run his Front. Zhukov's orders to his army commanders that morning were uncompromising. They were to reconnoitre their front in person and report back on the exact situation. Artillery was to be moved forward to take on German strongpoints over open sights. The advance was to be accelerated and continued day and night. Once again, soldiers were to pay with their lives for the mistakes made by a proud commander under pressure from above.

After another heavy barrage and bombing raids, Zhukov's exhausted armies went back into the attack early that morning. On the right, the 47th Army attacked Wriezen. The 3rd Shock Army pushed up to the Wriezen–Seelow road, but met heavy resistance around Kunersdorf. The 5th Shock Army and 2nd Guards Tank Army managed to push across the road north of Neuhardenberg but were also halted. Chuikov's 8th Guards Army and Katukov's 1st Guards Tank Army, meanwhile, continued to hammer at the town of Seelow itself and the Friedersdorf–Dolgelin sector. Chuikov was furious that the neighbouring 69th Army on his left had hardly advanced at all. This exposed his flank dangerously. But fortunately for him, all of Busse's forces were heavily engaged already.

In fact, both of Zhukov's extreme flanks had met with little success. South of Frankfurt, the 33rd Army was still grinding down the defences of the SS *30. Januar* Division in the V SS Mountain Corps. And at the extreme northern end of the Oderbruch, the 61st Army and the 1st Polish Army had not been able to advance until Wriezen was taken.

The breakthrough came suddenly just behind Seelow on the Reich-strasse 1. At 9.40 a.m. on 18 April, Colonel Eismann at Army Group

Vistula headquarters received a message that 'leading enemy armoured groups had broken through at Diedersdorf'. They were heading for Müncheberg along the Reichstrasse 1. The infantry was running away. Twenty minutes later, on Heinrici's insistence, Eismann was ringing Colonel de Maizière at OKH to find out what had happened to the 7th Panzer Division, which he needed to secure the gap between the left of the Ninth Army and the right flank of the Third Panzer Army.

At midday Busse rang Heinrici. 'Today is the moment of crisis,' he reported. The two main thrusts were coming from south-west of Wriezen and along the Reichstrasse 1. Busse saw that his army was being broken up. The 3rd Shock Army and the 5th Shock Army were splitting open the front between Wriezen and Seelow. Half a dozen kilometres west of Seelow, near the village of Alt Rosenthal, the Germans launched a counter-attack with infantry and tanks. Major Andreev of the 248th Rifle Division in the 5th Shock Army left two of his companies to hold the thrust, while he led another company round to attack the Germans from the rear. 'His battalion liquidated 153 soldiers and officers and two tanks.'

It was a pitiless battle. At Hermersdorf, south-west of Neuhardenberg, Soviet infantry advanced past a T-34 still burning from a panzerfaust. A German soldier in a nearby foxhole screamed to them for help. A grenade dropped in the foxhole had blown off his feet and he lacked the strength to pull himself out. But the Red Army soldiers left him there, despite his cries, in revenge for the burned crew.

At 4.20 p.m., Göring, furious at the collapse of the 9th Parachute Division, rang Army Group Vistula headquarters to order that General Bräuer should be stripped of his command immediately. At 6.45 p.m., General Busse rang Heinrici. The split in his army was unavoidable. 'Which sector,' he asked, 'is more important from a command point of view, north or south?'

At 7.50 p.m., the Luftwaffe liaison officer informed the operations staff at Army Group Vistula that their aircraft had destroyed fifty-three enemy planes, forty-three tanks and another nineteen 'probables'. Somebody on the staff added two exclamation marks in pencil in the war diary to demonstrate their scepticism at these claims. The fighting was violent, but German claims of Red Army losses were highly inflated. The Nazi newspaper *Der Angriff* stated that '426 Soviet tanks' had been destroyed on that day alone. Nevertheless, Soviet casualties had indeed been much heavier than German losses. Zhukov, in his desperation to capture the Seelow Heights, had lost just over 30,000 men killed, while the Germans lost 12,000 during the battle.

German prisoners sent towards the rear were overawed by the endless columns of tanks, self-propelled guns and other tracked vehicles moving forward. 'And this is the army,' some of them thought, 'which in 1941 was supposed to have been at its last gasp.' Soviet infantrymen coming up the other side of the road would greet them with cries of '*Gitler kapuuutt!*', accompanied by a throat-cutting gesture.

One of the German prisoners was convinced that a number of the dead they passed were 'Soviet soldiers who had been crushed by their own tanks'. He also saw Russian soldiers trying out some captured panzerfausts by firing them at the wall of a half-ruined house. Others were stripping greatcoats from their own dead, and in one village, he saw a couple of soldiers taking pot shots at nesting storks. Target practice seemed compulsive even after the battle. Some of the prisoners, taken to the magnificent schloss at Neuhardenberg, were alarmed when their escort, spotting a 'superb chandelier', raised his sub-machine gun and fired a burst at it. A senior officer reprimanded him, 'but that seemed to make little impression'.

'In the town of Gusow', a detachment of the 5th Shock Army reported, 'we freed sixteen Soviet women. Soldier Tsynbaluk recognized a girl he knew from home. Her name was Tatyana Shesteryakova. The women told the soldiers of their terrible suffering during their slavery. They also mentioned that before fleeing, their ex-owner, Frau Fischke said, "For us, the Russians are worse than death."' Political departments claimed that Red Army soldiers were outraged by the 'fascist propaganda' slogans daubed on walls about defending German womanhood from the Bolsheviks.

South of Berlin, Konev had an uneasy moment on 18 April. Field Marshal Schörner, the commander-in-chief of Army Group Centre, alarmed by the breakthrough on the Spree, sent in a counter-attack near Görlitz against the flank of the 52nd Army heading for Dresden. But Schörner's failure to concentrate his forces – in his haste he sent them into the attack piecemeal – made it comparatively easy for the 52nd Army to fight them off. The 2nd Polish Army at first did not have to halt its advance. But repeated attacks over the next few days slowed them down considerably.

Konev carried on pushing the 13th Army across the Spree behind his two tank armies. All this time, Gordov's 3rd Guards Army kept the pressure on the Germans round Cottbus and Zhadov's 5th Guards Army continued to attack Spremberg, thus securing the breach. Konev also instructed his staff to assemble all the trucks they could. The leading formations of the 28th Army, arriving as reinforcements, were now across the Neisse, and he wanted to hurry them forward to support the tank forces advancing on Berlin. By the end of that day, Rybalko's 3rd Guards Tank Army had advanced thirty-five kilometres beyond the Spree, while Lelyushenko, facing less resistance, had moved forward forty-five.

In the afternoon, General Reymann, the commander of the Berlin Defence Area, had received an order to send all the Volkssturm units out of the city to the Ninth Army to strengthen a new line. Reymann was appalled that the city was to be stripped of its defences. When Goebbels, as Reich Defence Commissar for Berlin, confirmed the order, Reymann warned him that 'a defence of the capital of the Reich is now unthinkable'. Reymann had not realized that this was just what Speer and Heinrici had wanted in order to save Berlin. In the event, less than ten battalions and a few anti-aircraft guns were sent westward. They marched out of the city in the early hours of the following morning. News of this order, according to Speer, created a widespread assumption that 'Berlin would in effect be an open city'.

General Weidling, to his exasperation, found that he had another self-important visitor from Berlin. This time it was Artur Axmann, the head of the Hitler Youth. Weidling tried to persuade him that it was futile to throw fifteen- and sixteen-year-olds armed with panzerfausts into the battle. It was 'the sacrifice of children for an already doomed cause'. Axmann was prepared only to admit 'that his youngsters had not received enough training'. Despite an assurance to Weidling that he would not use them, he clearly did nothing to withdraw them from combat. An even more chilling measure of Nazi desperation that day was the beheading of thirty political prisoners in Plötzensee prison.

On the Ninth Army's northern flank, the CI Corps had retreated less on 18 April than its neighbours. But this meant that many of its regiments soon found that Soviet troops were already well to their rear. One detachment, the remains of an officer candidate regiment, sent a couple of their comrades back to headquarters that evening to find out what had happened to their rations. The two returned out of breath and shaken. 'The Russians are eating our supper right now,' they said. Nobody had any idea where the enemy had broken through and where the front line now lay. They grabbed their equipment and marched back through the darkness, bypassing a village ablaze. The billowing black clouds reflected a bright red glow from the flames.

That night, a massive katyusha strike destroyed and set light to the village of Wulkow, behind Neuhardenberg. Almost all its houses were crammed with exhausted German soldiers who had fallen asleep. The state of the burned and panic-stricken survivors was terrible. The *Nordland* reconnaissance battalion also suffered a katyusha strike. They lost more men in a few moments than in all the bitter fighting round Stettin a few weeks earlier.

On 19 April, the Ninth Army began to split up in three main directions, as General Busse had feared. The Red Army's capture of Wriezen and the 3rd Shock Army's advance further westward on to the plateau behind Neuhardenberg forced CI Corps back towards Eberswalde and the countryside north of Berlin. Weidling's LVI Panzer Corps in the centre began to withdraw due west into Berlin. And on the right, the XI SS Panzer Corps began to withdraw south-westwards towards Fürstenwalde. The *Kurmark* Division had less than a dozen Panther tanks left.

That day, the 1st Guards Tank Army and Chuikov's 8th Guards Army pushed on from Seelow along Reichsstrasse 1 towards the key town of Müncheberg. The remains of the 9th Parachute Division, which had rallied the day before, fled in panic again, shouting, '*Der Iwan kommt.*' The reconnaissance battalion of the SS *Nordland* Division, which had finally reached the front, rounded up some of the paratroopers, gave them ammunition and brought them back into the battle in a temporarily successful counter-attack.

The retreat along Reichstrasse 1 and for quite a distance on either side soon collapsed into chaos and misery. 'Are you the last?' everyone asked. And the reply always seemed to be, 'The Russians are right behind us.' Soldiers of all arms and services were mixed up together, Wehrmacht and Waffen SS alike. The most exhausted flopped down under a tree and stretched out their legs. The local population, hearing that the front had collapsed, swamped the roads to seek shelter in Berlin. Soldiers passed refugees with carts halted by a broken axle or wheel, often hindering military traffic. Officers stood in their Kübelwagen vehicles to shout at the unfortunates to push their obstruction off the road or to order a group of resting soldiers to do it. In the retreat, officers found that they had to draw their pistol more and more often to have their orders obeyed.

The Feldgendarmerie and SS groups continued to search for deserters. No records were kept of the roadside executions carried out, but anecdotal evidence suggests that on the XI SS Corps sector, many, including a number of Hitler Youth, were hanged from trees on the flimsiest of proof. This was nothing short of murder. Soviet sources claim that 25,000 German soldiers and officers were summarily executed for cowardice in 1945. This figure is almost certainly too high, but it was unlikely to have been lower than 10,000.

Executions by the SS were even more unforgivable since word was being passed round SS formations that they were to pull back 'with orders to reassemble in Schleswig-Holstein' near the Danish border, which was not exactly the best place from which to fight the Russians. They did not appear to know that the British Second Army had reached the Elbe at Lauenburg that day, just south-east of Hamburg.

The 19th of April was another beautiful spring day, providing Soviet aviation with perfect visibility. Every time Shturmoviks came over, strafing and bombing, the road emptied as people threw themselves in the ditches. Women and girls from nearby villages, terrified of the Red Army, begged groups of soldiers to take them with them: '*Nehmt uns mit, nehmt uns bitte, bitte mit!*' Yet some people living quite close to the front seemed incapable of appreciating the scale of the impending disaster. A Herr Saalborn wrote to the bürgermeister of Woltersdorf on 19 April, demanding confirmation that, in accordance with Article 15 of the *Reichsleitungsgesetz* (the version of 1 September 1939), he would get back his bicycle, which had been commandeered by the Volkssturm.

The remnants of trainee and officer candidate battalions from the CI Corps found themselves retreating 'village by village' westwards to Bernau, just north of Berlin. Most had lost nearly three-quarters of their strength. They were exhausted, hungry and thoroughly confused. As soon as they halted for a rest, everyone fell heavily asleep and their officers had to kick them awake several times when it was necessary to move on. Nobody knew what was happening on either side or even in front or behind. Radios and field telephones had been abandoned. There was also no hope of re-establishing an effective front line, despite the best efforts of the more experienced officers, who grabbed any stragglers from other units and incorporated them into their own little command.

General Heinrici's attention now had to focus on the northern part of the Oder defence line between the Baltic coast and the Hohenzollern Canal at the top end of the Oderbruch. General von Manteuffel, who had been flying in a light reconnaissance aircraft over the forward areas of Rokossovsky's armies, had no difficulty spotting enemy preparations. The 2nd Belorussian Front faced a formidable task. North of Schwedt, the Oder followed two channels, with marshy ground on either side and in between. That night of 19 April, Rokossovsky reported to Stalin that the offensive would start at first light the next morning, preceded by heavy bombing raids and artillery bombardment.

Rokossovsky had had the most difficult time of all Front commanders, redeploying his troops from Danzig and the Vistula estuary. This huge logistic problem had prompted Zhukov to warn Stalin on 29 March of what was involved. 'Well, we'll have to start the operation without waiting for Rokossovsky's Front,' he had replied. 'If he's a few days late, that's not a great trouble.' Clearly, Stalin had not been worried then. But now that Rokossovsky's armies might be needed for Berlin, he was much more concerned.

17

The Führer's Last Birthday

Friday 20 April was the fourth fine day in a row. It was Adolf Hitler's fifty-sixth birthday. A beautiful day on this date used to prompt greetings between strangers in the street about 'Führer weather' and the miracle that this implied. Now only the most besotted Nazi could still hint at Hitler's supernatural power. There were still enough diehards left, however, to attempt to celebrate the event. Nazi flags were raised on ruined buildings and placards proclaimed, '*Die Kriegsstadt Berlin grüst den Führer!*'

In the past, a mass of birthday greetings flooded the Reich Chancellery on the Führer's birthday. Six years earlier, Professor Doctor Lutz Heck of the Berlin Zoological Garden had sent the Führer, 'with heartiest congratulations', an ostrich egg weighing 1,230 grams to make scrambled eggs. But in 1945, there were very few letters and parcels, and not just because the postal system had collapsed. The Berlin Zoo was also half-destroyed, with many of the animals starving.

American and British bomber forces were well aware of the date. Sirens sounded in the morning as massed squadrons approached to greet the Führer's birthday with a particularly heavy raid. It was almost a double celebration for the USAAF and RAF bomber crews. With Soviet forces approaching Berlin, this was their second-last raid on the capital of the Reich.

Göring had woken that morning at Karinhall, his country house north of Berlin, to the opening bombardment of Rokossovsky's offensive. A convoy of Luftwaffe trucks, although desperately needed for more urgent duties, was ready, loaded with his looted treasures. A motorcycle detachment would escort them south. Göring addressed the men briefly and watched them leave. The engineer officer, who had laid the explosives to blow up Karinhall, then escorted the Reichsmarschall over to where the plunger stood ready. Göring had insisted on blowing the place up himself. The explosion blasted vast clouds of dust outwards, then this over-extended monument to vanity collapsed in on itself. Göring, apparently without looking back, walked to his enormous limousine to be driven to Berlin. He needed to be at the Reich Chancellery at noon to congratulate the Führer on his birthday.

Himmler had returned to the sanatorium at Hohenlychen the night before and ordered champagne at midnight to toast the Führer's birthday. He had just arranged separate meetings with Count Folke Bernadotte of the Red Cross and Norbert Masur, the representative of the World Jewish Congress, who had been flown secretly into Tempelhof aerodrome earlier in the day. Bernadotte and Masur assumed that he wanted to discuss the possible release of prisoners, but for Himmler, the purpose was to establish a line of communication to the Western Allies. The Reichsführer SS, while still convinced of his own loyalty to Hitler, felt that he alone could replace him. He would become the leader with whom the Western Allies could negotiate. What he had to do was to convince the Jews that the Final Solution was something that both sides needed to put behind them.

Goebbels, the only leading Nazi planning to stay in Berlin with Hitler until the bitter end, broadcast a birthday speech that morning. He called on all Germans to trust blindly in the Führer, who would lead them out of their difficulties. 'I wondered whether he was mad,' wrote Ursula von Kardorff in her diary, 'or whether he was playing some sort of cold-blooded trick.'

Göring, Ribbentrop, Dönitz, Himmler, Kaltenbrunner, Speer, Keitel, Jodl and Krebs were driven to the Reich Chancellery before noon. There, they trooped through the huge rooms faced in polished marble, with doors almost to the ceiling. This quasi-cinematic monument to conspicuous power now looked tawdry in its half-wrecked state, yet it remained deeply sinister.

Many of the celebrants offering their birthday wishes that day thought that Hitler looked at least twenty years older than he was. They urged their leader to take the road to Bavaria while there was still time. Hitler stated with conviction that the Russians were about to suffer their bloodiest defeat before Berlin. Dönitz, whom Hitler had ordered to take command in the north of Germany, received an affectionate farewell. But Göring, who claimed that he would organize resistance in Bavaria, was treated in a distant manner. Hitler, Speer observed to his American interrogators less than a month later, was 'disappointed by the cowardice of Göring and the others'. He had always persuaded himself that his close followers were men of courage.

During the situation conference that day, the main question was how soon the Reich would be cut in two south of Berlin. The territory still unoccupied was diminishing every day. The British were on the Luneburg Heath, heading towards Hamburg. The Americans were on the middle Elbe, on the borders of Czechoslovakia and moving into Bavaria. The French First Army was advancing into southern Germany. To the south-east, the Red Army was west of Vienna and the Allies in Italy were moving north across the Po valley. Again the subject of the Nazi hierarchy abandoning Berlin came up. 'To the surprise of nearly everyone present,' Speer stated, 'Hitler announced that he would stay in Berlin until the last minute and only then fly to the south.' His entourage was surprised that 'discussion of evacuation had been general'. After the meeting, the rest of the leadership began to invent 'all manner of excuses' to leave Berlin on official business. Himmler, Ribbentrop and Kaltenbrunner departed in different directions. A number of the Reich Chancellery staff were detailed to leave for the Berghof the next day. 'Führer's birthday but unfortunately no mood for celebration,' Bormann noted in his diary. 'The advance party is ordered to fly to Salzburg.'

That afternoon, in the ruined Reich Chancellery garden, the Führer worked his way slowly down a line of Hitler Youth, some of whom had received the Iron Cross for attacking Soviet tanks. Hitler could not present any medals himself. To prevent his left arm shaking too obviously, he walked gripping it behind his back with his right hand. For brief moments, he could afford to release it. With what looked like the intensity of the repressed paedophile, he lingered to cup a cheek and tweak an ear, unconscious of his leering smile.

After receiving members of the close entourage that evening in the tiny sitting room in the bunker, Hitler retired to bed much earlier than usual. Eva Braun led the others up to the Reich Chancellery. With Bormann and Dr Morell among them, it was a strange and inauspicious group for a party. One of the large round tables designed by Speer was laid with food and drink. They drank champagne and made a pretence of dancing, but there was only one record for the gramophone: 'Blood-red Roses Tell You of Happiness'. According to Hitler's secretary, Traudl Junge, there was much hysterical laughter. 'It was horrible; soon I couldn't stand it and went back down to bed.'

The question of evacuation was extremely volatile. On Sunday 15 April Eva Braun had mentioned to Hitler that Dr Karl Brandt, who had been his personal surgeon, was moving his family to Thuringia. To her horror, Hitler exploded with anger, saying that he had chosen a place about to be taken by the Western Allies. That was treachery. Bormann was told to investigate the case and to interview 'Eva Braun and Dr Stumpfegger', the devoted SS surgeon who had replaced Brandt. Eva Braun described the affair as 'a really foul trick' in a letter to her best friend, Herta Ostermayr. Although physically at the centre of power, she had no understanding of National Socialist reality.

Brandt was charged next day with defeatism. Axmann was leader of the court and Brandt was condemned to death. But execution of the sentence appears to have been postponed by enemies of Bormann, including Himmler, who had at last realized that Bormann had been blackening his name at court. Brandt escaped execution by the Nazis, but was later sentenced to death by the allies.*

Brandt, a former intimate of the Obersalzburg circle, wrote a witty paper on the 'Women around Hitler' for his American captors at the 'Ashcan' interrogation centre. Hitler, he wrote, had never married because he wanted 'to keep the mystic legend alive in the hearts of the German people that so long as he remained a bachelor, there was always

---

* In October 1944, after Brandt had accused Dr Morell of providing Hitler with dangerous drugs, the dispute had been solved by making Brandt Reich Commissioner for sanitation and health. The allies later held him responsible for euthanasia killings and medical experiments on prisoners and rejected his defence that he had had no control over the establishments where this had happened.

the chance that any one of the millions of German women might possibly attain the high distinction of being at Hitler's side'. Hitler apparently even spoke of this in front of Eva Braun. In 1934, he had also announced in her presence, 'The greater the man, the more insignificant should be the woman.'

Brandt believed that the relationship between the two had an even stronger element of father–daughter than teacher–student. But whether or not he was right about this, one thing was certain. The Führer's *maîtresse sans titre* was the opposite of a Pompadour. She never schemed for or against people at the court. Yet after years of having to hide herself away like a servant to preserve the Führer myth of celibacy for Germany, it was hardly surprising that she occasionally tried to play the great lady. According to Brandt, she treated her easily led younger sister, Gretl, whom she had married to Fegelein, 'almost like a personal maid'.

The question of Hitler's sexuality has received a good deal of speculative attention recently. There can, however, be little doubt that he suppressed his homoerotic side in the interests of his image as the virile Führer. This repression explains a good deal of his manic energy and myth-making. Some members of his household insist that he never made love with Eva Braun, but her personal maid is convinced that he did, because she used pills to suppress her menstrual cycle when he arrived at the Berghof. His appalling halitosis towards the end of his life must have made him even less physically attractive than before, but Eva Braun, like several other close female friends, was clearly besotted with him. There is no proof either way, but the passionate kiss which Hitler later bestowed on her when she refused to leave the bunker for the safety of Bavaria weakens the theory that there had never been any form of sexual contact between them.

Eva Braun, like Hitler himself, had always been fascinated with the glamour of motion pictures. Movies appear to have been a major subject of conversation between them. One of the greatest frustrations of her seclusion must have been her inability to mix at state receptions with the film stars invited by Goebbels to add a touch of sophistication to the usual collection of Nazi wives. Perhaps Eva Braun saw her destiny with Hitler in terms of a cinematic finale. Her last letters are untainted by melodrama and yet she had found a magnificent role – the heroine who, after suffering years of humiliation and neglect in the shadow of the man she loves, is vindicated in an ending where her devotion is finally acknowledged.

Her furniture had been moved into a room next to Hitler's in the Reich Chancellery underworld on 15 April, and from then on she slept down there too. 'She was always immaculately turned out,' wrote Hitler's Luftwaffe aide, Nicolaus von Below. 'She was charming and obliging and she showed no weakness right up to the last moment.' The threat of being caught alive by Russian soldiers prompted her and Hitler's secretaries into pistol practice in the ruined courtyard of the Ministry of Foreign Affairs. They were proud of their prowess and challenged officers in the bunker to a competition.

'We can already hear the gunfire from the front,' Eva Braun wrote to Herta Ostermayr. 'My whole life is spent in the bunker. As you can imagine we are terribly short of sleep. But I'm so happy, especially at this moment, at being near him ... Yesterday, I telephoned Gretl probably for the last time. From today on, there's no way of getting through. But I have an unshakeable faith that all will turn out well and he is unusually full of hope.'

That morning, the ordinary women of Berlin emerged to queue for food after the air raid. The sound of artillery fire in the distance confirmed their fears that this might be their last chance to stock up. The sunshine buoyed up the spirits of many. 'Suddenly one remembers it's spring,' wrote one young woman that afternoon. 'Through the fire-blackened ruins the scent of lilac comes in waves from ownerless gardens.'

The desperation for news meant that a small crowd of people were already waiting at the kiosk when the paper boy arrived. 'Newspapers' were now no more than a single piece printed on both sides and they contained far more propaganda than information. The only useful section was the Wehrmacht daily communiqué, which, despite its evasive circumlocutions, indicated by the towns it cited how far the enemy had advanced. The mention of Müncheberg that day, seventeen kilometres west of Seelow on Reichstrasse 1, meant that the Russians had definitely broken through.

For the moment, however, the obsession with food was paramount. Rumours had reached Berlin that their fellow countrymen trapped in Silesia had been reduced to eating roots and grass. The Russians, it was said in the queue at the grocer's, would starve them too. Priorities became stark. Only things that could be eaten or drunk, or objects that could be bartered for food, were now of any use. And on this day Berliners were supposed to receive 'crisis rations', which meant some sausage or bacon, rice, dried peas, beans or lentils, some sugar and a little fat. It was the authorities' indirect acknowledgement that the city was both besieged and embattled.

With water, gas and electricity severely interrupted or cut off, Berliners suddenly faced a primitive existence. Already many of them had been reduced to cooking half-rotten potatoes over a tiny fire enclosed by three bricks on the floor of their balcony. Provident housewives began to pack suitcases with essential provisions to carry down to the cellar to survive the battle to come. And this was after eighty-three air raids since the beginning of February. The determined show of normal life, with people still travelling to bomb-blasted offices each day, ceased abruptly.

Marshal Zhukov recorded that, on that afternoon of 20 April, 'the long-range artillery of the 79th Rifle Corps of the 3rd Shock Army opened fire on Berlin'. But in fact few people in the city were aware of the fact. Zhukov seemed to have no idea that it was Hitler's birthday. He was desperate for something to show that he had attacked Berlin before Konev. The guns were firing at extreme range and only the north-eastern suburbs were affected.

When Zhukov heard for certain of Konev's tank army advancing on Berlin from the south, he sent on that evening an urgent order to Katukov and Bogdanov, the commanders of the 1st and 2nd Guards Tank Armies. He gave them 'a historic task: to break into Berlin first and to raise the banner of victory'. They were to send the best brigade from each corps to break through to an outskirt of Berlin by 4 a.m. the next day, and to report at once so that Stalin could be informed immediately and it could be announced in the press. In fact, the first of his tank brigades did not reach the outskirts until the evening of 21 April.

South-east of Berlin, meanwhile, Marshal Konev was whipping on his two tank armies across the Spreewald. His main interest was with the 3rd Guards Tank Army targeted at the southern flank of Berlin. Rybalko's leading tank corps attempted at midday to rush the town of

Baruth, just twenty kilometres south of Zossen, but failed at the first attempt. 'Comrade Rybalko,' Konev signalled, 'you are again moving like a hose. One brigade is fighting while the whole army is stuck. I order you to cross the line Baruth–Luckenwalde via a swamp using several routes in an extended battle order. Inform me on fulfilment.' The town was taken within two hours.

Lelyushenko's 4th Guards Tank Army, further to the south and west, was heading in a roughly parallel line for Jüterbog and then Potsdam. Stalin was still concerned that the Americans might suddenly advance again. The *Stavka* that day warned Zhukov, Konev and Marshal Rokossovsky of the possibility of encountering the Western Allies and passed on recognition signals. But what neither Konev nor the *Stavka* seems to have appreciated fully was that his 1st Ukrainian Front advancing from the south-east would run into Busse's Ninth Army trying to withdraw round the southern side of Berlin. Konev, like Zhukov, had become obsessed with Berlin. That night he dispatched signals to his two tank army commanders: 'Personal to Comrades Rybalko and Lelyushenko. Order you categorically to break into Berlin tonight. Report execution. Konev.'

The German retreat from the Seelow Heights during 19 and 20 April left no front line. Exhausted stragglers pulled back as best they could and improvised battle groups fought fierce little engagements wherever they were threatened. Ninth Army headquarters informed Heinrici of their '*Auffanglinien*' or 'holding lines', but they were little more than chinagraph marks on the map – a staff officer's attempt to impose a semblance of order on chaos.

Berzarin's 5th Shock Army had reached the edge of Strausberg on the evening of 19 April. To make matters worse for the retreating German forces, all roads leading westwards were blocked with increasingly panic-stricken refugees. When the T-34s reached Werneuchen airfield, the anti-aircraft defence battery depressed their 88mm guns to take on ground targets. But in all such fighting west of Berlin, 'It was clear to us soldiers,' wrote one participant, 'that this battle could not last long.'

During the morning of 19 April, the *Nordland* Division was fighting in the area north-west of Müncheberg, from where General Weidling's headquarters had just been forced to withdraw rapidly. The 'Norge' Regiment was pulling back from Pritzhagen, while the 'Danmark' to their south in the Buckow forest was mixed with Hitler Youth and remnants of the 18th Panzergrenadier Division.

Weidling ordered them to counter-attack in the Buckow forest, but this failed. The reconnaissance battalion of *Nordland* was almost surrounded and badly mauled. The Hitler Youth detachment suffered an even worse fate, cut off from the rest in a part of the forest which had caught fire. The Soviet tanks cautiously stayed out of range of the panzerfausts. 'Then the tanks began firing into the tree-tops,' Sturmmann Becker reported, 'and the splinters from above began hitting us in our positions below.'

The survivors were forced to retreat towards Strausberg along small roads through the pinewoods. Russian infantry followed rapidly along the ditches, with their tanks coming up behind to give them covering fire. The Scandinavian Waffen SS had only infantry weapons and a couple of mortars. A lone German assault gun appeared and attempted to take on the T-34s. It was destroyed immediately. But then a solitary King Tiger appeared through the trees. It blasted the two T-34s and saved the situation.

The remnants of the reconnaissance battalion reassembled in a wood near Strausberg. They bound their wounds, patched up their vehicles and cleaned their weapons. The desolate scene did not stop Sturmbannführer Saalbach from making a speech about the Führer's birthday and the meaning of the battle against Bolshevism in which they were engaged.

Obersturmbannführer Langendorf, who had been wounded, was taken back to the SS field hospital. He heard Goebbels's speech for Hitler's birthday while the surgeon was working on him. The SS surgeon muttered, 'Now we'll let them have it.' The nurses were volunteers from Holland, Flanders, Denmark and especially from Norway. One of the young Norwegian nurses, Langendorf noticed, had discovered her Waffen SS lover among the badly wounded just brought in. 'She embraced him and laid his head in her lap and stayed with him until he died from a serious head-wound.' Like all the foreign fascists and National Socialists who had volunteered for the SS, they had lost their countries and now had lost their cause. This, combined with their visceral hatred of Bolshevism, made them formidable fighters in the battle for Berlin.

During the best part of that day, the 'Danmark' and 'Norge' regiments hung on to Strausberg airfield, defending it against Katukov's tanks. Obersturmbannführer Klotz, the regimental commander of the 'Danmark', was killed when his vehicle received a direct hit. He was laid out by his men in the small chapel of a nearby cemetery. There was no time to bury him. They soon had to withdraw further, south-westwards to the Berlin autobahn ring.

The *Nordland* avoided the main roads in its withdrawal. Reichsstrasse 1 was in chaos, especially the section near Rüdersdorf, with hundreds of vehicles heading westwards, often blocked by farm carts full of refugees machine-gunned by Shturmovik ground-attack aircraft. Soldiers who had received no rations for five days broke into houses abandoned by their owners. Some were so exhausted that after eating whatever they could find, they collapsed on to a bed, their uniforms still encrusted with mud from their trenches. They then slept so long that in some cases they awoke only with the arrival of the enemy. One Hitler Youth was so exhausted that, after a long and deep sleep, he woke with a start to find that a battle had been fought all around him.

Officers tried to reimpose order at pistol point. A major halted a self-propelled flak gun transporting wounded to the rear. He ordered the driver to take it back towards the enemy. The crew told him that the barrels were shot out and useless. The major still insisted and ordered them to unload the wounded. Some Volkssturm men nearby shouted out, 'Shoot him! Shoot him!' The major backed off. An officer's authority, unless supported by the sub-machine guns of the Feldgendarmerie, carried little weight on such a retreat.

The chaos on the roads was further increased by rumour and panic. There were false cries of '*Der Iwan Kommt!*', and other occasions when Soviet tanks really did appear, having overtaken them. German soldiers claimed that a 'Seydlitz traitor' drove through the retreating troops giving out orders to pull back as far as Potsdam on the far side of Berlin. This may well be true, since the Red Army 7th Department was pushing its 'anti-fascist' prisoners to take almost any risk.

Red Army soldiers clearly felt at home fighting through the pine forest west of the capital, even if the warm weather made those still wearing a fur *ushanka* and padded jacket jealous of those already in summer uniforms. 'The closer one gets to Berlin,' one Russian noted, 'the more the area looks like the country round Moscow.' But some Red Army habits did not speed their advance. On 20 April, Müncheberg was heavily looted 'mostly by officers and men of special [i.e. tank and artillery] regiments . . . More than fifty soldiers were arrested in a day. Some were sent to rifle companies. They were stealing clothes and shoes and other things right in full view of the local population. These men explained that they were looting because they wished to send things home.'

While Weidling's LVI Panzer Corps was pushed back towards the western suburbs of Berlin, the remains of the CI Corps had withdrawn north of the city to the area of Bernau during the night of 19 April. The wounded had been abandoned by the side of the road, because there were so few vehicles left with any fuel. Many of them were apparently killed where they lay by further shelling.

Most of the troops in Bernau were trainee officers and technicians from scratch regiments. As soon as they were quartered in schools and houses, they simply collapsed and fell asleep. One group of apprentice signallers found an abandoned barracks. But in the early hours of 20 April, when the 125th Rifle Corps of the 47th Army attacked, a sergeant had to go round, kicking them awake, to force them out to defend the town. 'It was all senseless,' commented one of their commanders years later, but at the time the Wehrmacht fought on because nobody had told them that they could stop.

The fighting for Bernau, the last real defensive action before the battle for Berlin began in earnest, was chaotic and short. German officers commanding the young trainees soon realized that they could no longer prevent total disintegration. Many escaped, slipping away alone or in small groups. When the 47th Army captured Bernau, a battery of the 30th Guards Artillery Brigade fired off a victory salute aimed at Berlin. In the meantime, Bogdanov's 2nd Guards Tank Army pushed on past the north-eastern suburbs of the city, just outside the autobahn ring. Many Soviet soldiers had heard of it as a massive engineering feat, but those who had witnessed Stalinist showpieces professed disdain.

The 7th Department used more and more prisoners as agents to encourage desertion. On the 3rd Shock Army's front, five soldiers from a Volkssturm battalion were sent back to their comrades on 20 April. 'They returned the following day with almost the whole battalion.' But despite the promises of the political department, many Russian soldiers seemed to be obsessed with finding Waffen SS soldiers on whom to take revenge. '*Du SS!*' they would shout accusingly. Soldiers who laughed in astonishment were in severe danger of being shot out of hand. Some of those captured by NKVD troops and accused by SMERSH of being members of *Werwolf* were forced into confessing that they had been 'given chemical substances to poison wells and rivers'.

General Busse, with the larger half of the Ninth Army – the XI SS Panzer Corps, the V SS Mountain Corps and the garrison of Frankfurt an der Oder – soon began to withdraw south-westwards towards the Spreewald, despite orders from the Führer bunker that the line of defence on the Oder must never be abandoned.

The Führer's compulsion to launch counter-attacks for their own sake returned on the evening of 20 April, just when Zhukov and Konev were forcing their own tank army commanders to advance more rapidly. Hitler told General Krebs to launch an attack from the west of Berlin against Konev's armies to prevent encirclement. The force expected to 'hurl back' the 3rd and 4th Guards Tank Armies consisted of the *Friedrich Ludwig Jahn* Division, made up of boys in Reich Labour Service detachments, and the so-called 'Wünsdorf Panzer formation', a batch of half a dozen tanks from the training school there.

A police battalion was sent to the Strausberg area that day 'to catch deserters and execute them and shoot any soldiers found retreating without orders'. But even those detailed as executioners began to desert on their way forward. One of those who gave themselves up to the Russians told his Soviet interrogator that 'about 40,000 deserters were hiding in Berlin even before the Russian advance. Now this number is rapidly increasing.' He went on to say that the police and the Gestapo could not control the situation.

18

The Flight of the Golden Pheasants

On the morning of Saturday 21 April, just after the last Allied air raid had finished, General Reymann's headquarters on the Hohenzollerndamm swarmed with brown uniforms. Senior Nazi Party officials had rushed there to obtain the necessary authorization to leave Berlin. For once the 'Golden Pheasants' had to request permission from the army. Goebbels, as Reich Commissioner for Berlin, had ordered that 'no man capable of bearing arms may leave Berlin'. Only the headquarters for the Defence of Berlin could issue an exemption.

'The rats are leaving the sinking ship' was the inevitable reaction of Colonel von Refior, Reymann's chief of staff. Reymann and his staff officers received a fleeting satisfaction from the sight. Over 2,000 passes were signed for the Party 'armchair warriors', who had always been so ready to condemn the army for retreating. Reymann said openly that he was happy to sign them since it was better for the defence of the city to be rid of such cowards.

This idea was echoed strongly two days later by the *Werwolfsender*, Goebbels's special transmitter at Königswusterhausen, when it broadcast appeals to the '*Werwolfs* of Berlin and Brandenburg' to rise against the enemy. It claimed that all the cowards and traitors had left Berlin. 'The Führer did not flee to southern Germany. He stands in Berlin and with him are all those whom he has found worthy to fight beside him in this historic hour . . . Now, soldiers and officers of the front, you are not only waging the final and greatest decisive battle of the Reich, but by your fight you are also completing the National Socialist revolution.

Only the uncompromising revolutionary fighters have remained.' This deliberately ignored the far larger numbers of reluctant Volkssturm and conscripts forced to fight on with the threat of a noose or a firing squad.

An intensive artillery bombardment of Berlin began at 9.30 a.m., a couple of hours after the end of the last Allied air raid. Hitler's SS adjutant, Otto Günsche, reported that the Führer, a few minutes after having been woken, emerged unshaven and angry in the bunker corridor which served as an anteroom. 'What's going on?' he shouted at General Burgdorf, Colonel von Below and Günsche. 'Where's this firing coming from?'

Burgdorf answered that central Berlin was under fire from Soviet heavy artillery. 'Are the Russians already so near?' asked Hitler, clearly shaken.

General Kazakov had pushed forward his breakthrough artillery divisions and all the other heavy gun batteries with 152mm and 203mm howitzers. More messages had been daubed on the shells – 'For the rat Goebbels', 'For Stalingrad', 'For the fat belly of Göring' and 'For orphans and widows!' The gun crews were encouraged into a frenzied rate of fire by political officers. Senior artillery officers felt especially proud and made self-satisfied remarks about 'the bloody god of war', which had become an almost universal euphemism for Soviet gunnery. From that morning until 2 May, they were to fire 1.8 million shells in the assault on the city.

The casualties among women especially were heavy as they still queued in the drizzling rain, hoping for their 'crisis rations'. Mangled bodies were flung across the Hermannplatz in south-west Berlin as people queued outside the Karstadt department store. Many others were killed in the queues at the water pumps. Crossing a street turned into a dash from one insecure shelter to another. Most gave up and returned to their cellars. Some, however, took what seemed like the last opportunity to bury silver and other valuables in their garden or a nearby allotment. But the relentlessness of the bombardment and the random fall of shells soon forced the majority of the population back underground.

In the cellars and air-raid shelters distinctive subcultures had grown up during two years of heavy air raids from '*die Amis*' by day and '*die Tommys*' by night. The 'cellar tribe', as one diarist called these curious microcosms of society, produced a wide variety of characters, whether in markedly rich or poor districts. Each cellar always seemed to have at least one crashing bore, usually a Nazi trying to justify his belief in the Führer and final victory. A number of Berliners, for some reason, had suddenly started to refer to Hitler as 'that one', and it was not necessarily a term of abuse.

People clung to lucky charms or talismans. One mother brought with her the spare artificial leg of a son still trapped in the siege of Breslau. Many cellar tribes developed a particular superstition or theory of survival. For example, some believed that they would survive an almost direct hit by wrapping a towel round their head. Others were convinced that if they bent forward at the first explosion, this would prevent their lungs from tearing. Every eccentricity of German hypochondria seems to have received full expression. When the all-clear sounded after a bombing raid, cellars and shelters echoed with nervous laughter and compulsive jokes. A favourite among older, more raucous women was, 'Better a Russki on the belly than an Ami on the head.'

During the course of the day, while shattered German units and stragglers fell back, Hitler still insisted that Busse hold a line which had been disintegrating for two days. The remnants of Busse's left wing, the CI Corps, had been forced out of the Bernau area. Wolfram Kertz of the *Grossdeutschland* guard regiment was wounded near the Blumberg autobahn junction north-east of Berlin. Of the 1,000 or so men of the guard regiment, only forty reached Berlin. So much depended on '*Soldatenglück*', or 'soldier's luck'. Kertz was propped up against a church wall when Russian soldiers found him. They saw the Knight's Cross at his neck. '*Du General?*' they asked. They called up a horse-drawn cart and took him to a headquarters for interrogation. A senior officer asked him whether Hitler was still alive and what he knew about any plans for a German counter-stroke with the Americans against the Red Army.

This no doubt reflected the paranoia in the Kremlin. In fact, the Americans were still fighting the Germans everywhere, including on the Berlin axis. Their ground troops and US Air Force Mustangs were launching continual attacks against the *Scharnhorst* Division of the Twelfth Army north of Dessau. This was a response to the unexpected Luftwaffe attacks against the Elbe crossings and bridgeheads. Peter

Rettich, commanding a battalion in the *Scharnhorst*, had only fifty men left on 21 April.

In the Ninth Army's centre, the remnants of Weidling's LVI Panzer Corps were also pushed back against and across the eastern side of the Berlin autobahn ring. Corpses lay in the ditches on either side of the obvious highways. Most were the victims of Shturmovik low-level strafing attacks.

Side roads and main routes alike were encumbered by civilians with handcarts, prams and teams of farm horses. Soldiers were surrounded by civilians desperate for news of the enemy's advance, but often had no clear idea themselves. Pickets of Feldgendarmerie at each crossroads again grabbed stragglers to form scratch companies. There were also men hanged from roadside trees, with a card on their chest stating, 'I was a coward.' Soldiers sent to defend houses either side of the road were the luckiest. The inhabitants gave them food and some hot water to shave and wash in, the first for many days.

In Petershagen, a company of the *Nordland* under Sturmbannführer Lorenz, supported by a few reconnaissance vehicles, prepared to make a stand against the 8th Guards Army, but they were suddenly devastated by a massive katyusha strike. One account claims that the Soviet troops had filled the warheads with an improvised napalm. The reconnaissance vehicles apparently burst into flame and in some cases exploded. The panic-stricken survivors jumped into the vehicles left undamaged and drove off, leaving the injured, many with terrible burns, to their fate. Only Lorenz and his radio operator stayed to care for them. They loaded the ones most likely to survive on to the only remaining half-track and drove them back to the dressing station. It had been set up in a barn within a hollow next to a command post. Lorenz had 'a very bad feeling'. A few moments later the Soviet Guards artillery landed another accurate katyusha strike. Hardly anybody survived unscathed. Lorenz himself received shrapnel in the right shoulder.

Close by, Gerhard Tillery, one of the survivors of a trainee officer battalion, saw a colonel from their division outside a racing stable at Hoppegarten. 'See that you all get home safe and sound,' the colonel told the surprised soldier. 'There's no more point to any of this.' But Tillery could not follow this advice straight away. Their new scratch company was commanded by a very determined young artillery officer with no infantry experience at all. He pulled them back to Mahlsdorf, where they took up defensive positions in a cemetery. In the lull before the fighting began again, Tillery and a couple of others were sent to collect food offered by local civilians. They brought it back in a couple of milk churns. Tillery saw that there were some Volkssturm and a police battalion on their right. They all knew that it would not be long before the Russians appeared, feeling their way forward and firing mortars at any likely defensive position.

There, on the eastern side of Berlin, the German remnants of the Ninth Army faced the 5th Shock Army and Chuikov's 8th Guards Army. But then Zhukov pushed the 8th Guards Army further south towards the Spree. He wanted Chuikov and Katukov's 1st Guards Tank Army, still working closely together, to enter Berlin from the south-west. This, he hoped, would pre-empt Konev's attempt to attack Berlin from that direction. On 21 April, some of Katukov's tank brigades advanced with the infantry of 8th Guards Army and captured Erkner, just south of Rüdersdorf.

To encircle the northern flank of Berlin, Zhukov had sent the 47th Army round towards Spandau and the 2nd Guards Tank Army to Oranienburg. Pressure from Stalin prompted the signal: 'Due to the slowness of our advance, the Allies are approaching Berlin and will soon take it.' The leading tank brigades, which were supposed to have reached the city the night before, were only at the outskirts by the evening of 21 April. Zhukov refused to acknowledge that a headlong advance with tanks in such surroundings involved heavy losses. Every house by the side of the road, every allotment or garden, almost every bush could contain a Hitler Youth or Volkssturmer armed with a panzerfaust. Rifle regiments from the 3rd Shock Army and the 5th Shock Army also reached the north-eastern suburbs of Malchow and Hohenschönhausen that night.

Twenty kilometres south of Berlin in the huge underground head-quarters at Zossen there was a mood of profound anxiety. The day before, when the threat of Soviet tanks coming up from the south had arisen, General Krebs had sent off the OKH's small defence detachment in reconnaissance vehicles to investigate. At 6 a.m. on 21 April, Krebs's second aide, Captain Boldt, was woken by a telephone call. Senior Lieutenant Kränkel, commanding the defence detachment, had just seen forty Soviet tanks coming up the Baruth road towards Zossen. He was about to engage them. Boldt knew that Kränkel's light armoured vehicles stood no chance against T-34s. He informed Krebs, who rang the Reich Chancellery to ask permission to relocate the headquarters. Hitler refused. Shortly before the 11 a.m. situation conference, tank guns could be heard clearly in the distance. One staff officer observed that the Russians could reach Zossen in half an hour. Another message arrived from Kränkel. His attack had failed with heavy losses. There was nothing left to stop the enemy tanks.

General Krebs appeared from his office. 'If you're ready, gentlemen,' he said, and thus began the very last conference of German general staff officers. It was hard to keep their minds off their imminent capture by Soviet armoured forces and the prison camps which awaited them in Russia. But there was no more shooting. The tanks had halted north of Baruth because they were out of diesel. And finally, at 1 p.m., General Burgdorf rang from the Reich Chancellery. The OKH was to move its headquarters to a Luftwaffe base at Eiche near Potsdam. Their companions in the adjoining OKW bunker system were to move to the nearby tank base at Krampnitz. The decision was taken only just in time.

A larger convoy of vehicles and non-essential personnel left Zossen on a hazardous journey to the south-west and then on down to Bavaria. They knew nothing of Lelyushenko's tank brigades crossing their path ahead, but instead they were hit by one of the last Luftwaffe sorties. The German pilots misidentified their vehicles. The smaller party, meanwhile, headed for Potsdam, on a parallel route to Lelyushenko's tanks.

Late that afternoon, Soviet soldiers entered the concealed camp at Zossen with caution and amazement. The two complexes, known as Maybach I and Maybach II, lay side by side, hidden under trees and camouflage nets. It was not the mass of papers blowing about inside the low, zigzag-painted concrete buildings which surprised them, but the resident caretaker's guided tour. He led them down into a maze of galleried underground bunkers, with generators, plotting maps, banks of telephones and teleprinters. Its chief wonder was the telephone exchange, which had linked the two supreme headquarters with Wehrmacht units in the days when the Third Reich had stretched from the Volga to the Pyrenees and from the North Cape to the Sahara. Apart from the caretaker, the only defenders left were four soldiers. Three of them had surrendered immediately. The fourth could not because he was dead drunk.

A telephone suddenly rang. One of the Russian soldiers answered it. The caller was evidently a senior German officer asking what was happening. 'Ivan is here,' the soldier replied in Russian, and told him to go to hell.

Just as Krebs's staff officers were transferring with unseemly haste to the western side of Berlin, a rumour started that General Weidling had also moved his headquarters to Döberitz, just north of Potsdam. This was to lead to a black comedy two days later, when Hitler first wanted to execute Weidling for treason and cowardice, but then appointed him commander of the defence of Berlin.

Hitler took the Soviet bombardment of Berlin as a personal affront, which, considering the slogans daubed on the Soviet shells, it was intended to be. His instinctive reaction was to blame the Luftwaffe for allowing this to happen. He threatened General Koller with execution, not for the first time. The fact that the Luftwaffe had few serviceable aircraft left and even less aviation fuel did not concern him. Anger, he was convinced, lent him inspiration. The Soviet attempt to encircle the city from the north exposed their right flank. He would order a counter-attack and cut them to ribbons. He remembered from the situation map the III SS *Germanische* Corps, commanded by Obergruppenführer Felix Steiner, north-west of Eberswalde. Hitler refused to accept that Heinrici had already allocated most of its divisions to help the Ninth Army. Steiner's corps, according to Army Group Vistula headquarters, consisted of no more than 'three battalions and a few tanks'.

Hitler, oblivious of reality, began to talk about 'Army Detachment Steiner', an inflation which was grandiose even by his own standards. He argued that it could in any case be reinforced with all the units from CI Corps which had retreated north of Berlin. He even thought of Göring's Luftwaffe bodyguard at Karinhall, but they had already departed. Every soldier, sailor and airman who could be scraped together would be thrown into battle and any commander who held back his men faced execution within five hours. Hitler had always taken as gospel the remark of Frederick the Great, 'Whoever throws his last battalion into the struggle will be the winner.' It bolstered his fantasy that reckless gambling with the lives of others was the mark of greatness.

Steiner, when he received the telephone call from the Führer bunker, was dumbfounded by Hitler's order to attack. After collecting his thoughts, he rang Krebs back to remind him of the true situation, but Krebs was standing almost next to Hitler. By then it was too late. Steiner received an official order to launch a counter-attack against the right flank of the 1st Belorussian Front. He and his officers were also threatened with execution if they failed to obey. When Heinrici was informed a little later, he rang the Reich Chancellery to protest at this lunacy. Krebs told him that the decision had been made and that he could not speak to the Führer, who was too busy to talk to him.

Hitler, during the course of that night of madness, also sacked General Reymann as commander for the defence of Berlin. General Burgdorf had convinced Hitler that he was no good. And Goebbels had taken against him ever since he refused to move his headquarters into the Zoo bunker alongside his own, as Reich Commissioner for the Defence of Berlin. Reymann was made commandant of a weak division in Potsdam instead, which received the title Army Group Spree. Two replacements were considered and rejected. Hitler then chose a Colonel Käther, whose main qualification for the task was that he happened to be the chief National Socialist *Führungsoffizier*, the Nazi copy of the Soviet military commissar. Käther was promoted to major general and then lieutenant general, but the appointment was cancelled the following day. Berlin was without a commander just as the Red Army was entering the suburbs.

For Zhukov the pace of advance was still far too slow. Sunday 22 April had been the target date for capturing Berlin, yet his leading divisions were still on the periphery. On that morning he signalled to his army commanders: 'The defence of Berlin is weakly organized, but the operation of our troops is progressing very slowly.' He ordered a 'twenty-four-hour-a-day advance'. But the fact of its being Lenin's birthday still encouraged political departments to distribute more symbolic red banners to be raised over prominent buildings.

The Russians were unimpressed by the Spree. One officer described it as 'a dirty, swampy little river'. But just as Zhukov had underestimated the defensive strength of the Seelow Heights, he had also overlooked the networks of rivers, canals and lakes in this forested area of Brandenburg. It was thanks only to the great experience of reconnaissance companies in swimming attacks across rivers during the two-year advance and the bridging skills and bravery of Soviet sappers that the advance did not take longer. The 1st Guards Tank Army prepared to build a pontoon bridge across the Spree near Köpenick, even though still some way off.

The 8th Guards Army, working with the tanks, was forcing Weidling's LVI Corps back into the city without realizing it. On their right, the 5th Shock Army pushed into the eastern suburbs, and further round, the 3rd Shock Army was ordered to advance into the central northern suburbs and then down towards the centre. On its right, the 2nd Guards Tank Army was to enter the city via Siemensstadt and head for Charlottenburg. Finally, the 47th Army, after astonishing French prisoners of war in Oranienburg with their carts and bowsers towed by camels, moved further westwards to finish the encirclement of the northern half of the city.

Early that Sunday morning, General Weidling summoned his divisional commanders to discuss the situation with them. They all, with one exception, wanted to fight their way through southwards to join up with General Busse and the other two corps of the Ninth Army. The exception was Brigadeführer Ziegler of the SS *Nordland* Division, who, to Weidling's fury, made no secret of wanting to rejoin Steiner. Nobody knows whether this was prompted entirely by SS tribalism, or was also a way of pulling his Scandinavian volunteers back into an SS stronghold near the Danish border.

The *Nordland* continued to defend Mahlsdorf and the entrance to Berlin along Reichsstrasse 1. In Friedrichsfelde, one of its detachments rounded up French prisoners of war and forced them to dig trenches at gunpoint. After heavy attacks in the middle of the day, the division pulled back into Karlshorst. One of its detachments dug in beside the track for trotting races, setting up mortar positions. But it was not long before they themselves came under heavy fire, with 'Soviet shells exploding in the stands and stable-blocks'.

It was by now almost a week since soldiers had seen the last of their iron rations, which often consisted of no more than a tin of processed cheese, a *Dauerbrot*, or long-life bread, and a waterbottle full of coffee or tea. Now the best they could hope for was a tin of pork left on the shelf of an abandoned house which they stabbed open with their bayonet. They were filthy, bearded and had bloodshot eyes.

Conditions for the bulk of the Ninth Army to their south-east were even worse. Hitler's orders to hold on to the line of the Oder were senseless. The remnants of the XI SS Panzer Corps, the V SS Mountain Corps and the Frankfurt garrison began to pull back into the Spreewald from different directions. Men moved singly or in groups. There were few formed units left and hardly any capable of taking orders from Busse's headquarters. Vehicles were abandoned as they ran out of fuel along the way.

Odd detachments were left behind as a covering force, but their resistance did not last long. Reinhard Appel, one of the Hitler Youth trained at the Olympic Stadium, formed part of a group detailed to replace SS troops from the *30. Januar* Division not far from Müllrose. His life was saved by an old sergeant, highly decorated from the Eastern Front. As the Soviet soldiers advanced, Appel, in a desperate attempt to sell his life dearly, raised himself ready to throw a grenade. The sergeant grabbed his arm and prised the grenade from his grasp. He yelled at the boy that it was mad to try to be brave in a hopeless position. The Russians would just wipe out everyone in the bunker. He had a white handkerchief attached to a stick and raised his arms in surrender as the Soviet soldiers appeared with their sub-machine guns. With cries of '*Voina kaputt!*' ('the war's had it') and '*Gitler kaputt!*', the Russians rushed forward to strip the young soldiers of weapons, which they threw to one side, then grabbed their watches. The boys and the old sergeant were ordered to march eastwards towards the Oder.

Eighty kilometres to their rear, reconnaissance detachments of the 3rd Guards Tank Army had reached Königswusterhausen the evening before. It represented an advance from the Neisse of 174 kilometres in less than six days. They were separated from Chuikov's 8th Guards Army on the north bank of the Müggelsee by a network of lakes and waterways in between. The two Soviet armies and this barrier effectively meant that Busse's remaining portion of the Ninth Army was now encircled.

Marshal Konev, warned by air reconnaissance of the mass of enemy troops in the Spreewald on his right, speeded up the 28th Army's move forward in trucks. These divisions were intended to seal the gap between Gordov's 3rd Guards Army, finishing off the German forces round Cottbus, and the 3rd Guards Tank Army, pushing on to Berlin. Konev decided to reinforce Rybalko's tank army with an artillery breakthrough corps – 'a powerful hammer' – and an anti-aircraft division.

By the evening of 22 April all three of Rybalko's corps had reached the Teltow Canal, the southern rim of Berlin's perimeter defence line. The German defenders were 'completely surprised to find themselves face to face with Russian tanks'. A 3rd Guards Tank Army report, in an unusually poetic phrase, described their arrival as unexpected 'as snow in the middle of summer'.

German communications were so bad that even Army Group Vistula headquarters knew nothing of this advance. And 'no steps were taken to remove the supplies' from a large Wehrmacht ration store on the south side of the canal. 'On the contrary, even when the first Russian tank was only a few hundred metres away, the administrator refused to let rations be distributed to the Volkssturm troops on the north bank of the canal because a regulation issue certificate had not been filled out.' He set fire to the provisions instead.

The 9th Mechanized Corps had charged through Lichtenrade, the 6th Guards Tank Corps had captured Teltow and, just to its left, the 7th Guards Tank Corps had taken Stahnsdorf. Further to the west, part of Lelyushenko's 4th Guards Tank Army was ten kilometres short of Potsdam. Further out, two more of his corps were snaking round the western end of Berlin and were less than forty kilometres away from Zhukov's 47th Army coming from the north.

French prisoners in Stalag III, close to the Teltow Canal, were enjoying a moment of spring warmth when there was a rush to the barbed-wire perimeter. 'At about five in the afternoon,' one of them recorded, 'the first Russian soldier appeared. He was walking jauntily, quite erect, sub-machine gun at his waist, ready to fire. He was walking along the ditch beside the road. He did not even bother to look at our camp.' A little later, however, Soviet officers entered the camp. The Russian prisoners there were ordered to fall in. They were handed a rifle or sub-machine gun and expected to go straight into action.

Another French prisoner of war on the south-eastern side of the city happened to see 'a Hitler Youth aged thirteen or fourteen with the face of a child in spite of his helmet, in a foxhole, awkwardly gripping a panzerfaust'. The boy seemed to have no doubt that the hole in the ground would become his grave the next day.

In their rapid progress north, Konev's tank brigades had overtaken carts loaded with civilians, some of whom, on closer inspection, turned out to be German soldiers who had concealed their uniforms. Those soldiers who managed to slip westwards through the rear of Lelyushenko's 4th Guards Tank Army spread word of its advance. In addition to the three corps encircling Berlin from the west, the 5th Guards Mechanized Corps was moving towards the Elbe, ready to block any attempt by Wenck's Twelfth Army to join up with Busse's Ninth Army.

At the improvised hospital complex in the barracks near Beelitz-Heilstätten, Sister Ruth Schwarz, who had helped evacuate the sick children from Potsdam, was horrified to hear on 21 April that the Russians were already at Jüterbog. That was less than forty kilometres away. Emergency rations of chocolate, dry sausage and crispbread were distributed to the different wards. Nurses slept at least four to a room, hoping that that might protect them when the Russian soldiers came. Their 'hearts raced in fear' on news of the Soviet advance.

On 22 April, they heard that the Red Army had reached Schönefeld, just ten kilometres away. Mother Superior Elisabeth von Cleve, who had arrived with part of the staff and adult patients from Potsdam, set up an altar with candles and had hundreds of patients wheeled in for an impromptu service to provide consolation. When they sang '*Ein feste Burg ist unser Gott*', tears ran down faces. Their only hope seemed to lie in rumours that Beelitz-Heilstätten had been declared an international zone under Swiss supervision. But this evaporated the next morning when they heard that Soviet troops had reached Beelitz and were 'plundering, torching and raping'. 'I immediately took out my small nail scissors for the direst emergency,' recorded Sister Ruth Schwarz, and the nurses carried on with their work.

Soviet military authorities had their own problems in the rear areas. Groups of German officers and soldiers bypassed on the Seelow Heights were trying to slip back westwards. Desperate for food, they were ambushing the horse-drawn supply carts and even individual Red Army soldiers to get their bread bags.

Now approaching the climax of the war, NKVD rifle regiments continued to react with their usual suspicion and lack of proportion. 'On 22 April,' one regiment reported, 'a Red Army cook, Maria Mazurk-evich, met officers of a division in which she had worked previously and went with them by car. This means that she deserted. We are taking every step to find her.' This was at a time when virtually no steps were taken to stop rape or looting, or even murder.

Vasily Grossman, who was returning to the 1st Belorussian Front from Moscow, came via Zhukov's rear headquarters at Landsberg. 'Children are playing soldiers on a flat roof,' he wrote in his notebook. 'This is at the very moment when German imperialism is being finished in Berlin, and here the boys with wooden swords and clubs and long legs, and blond fringes and their hair cut short at the back of the head, are shouting, jumping, leaping and stabbing at one another . . . It's eternal. It can never be eliminated from mankind.' But this pessimistic mood did not last long. He found Brandenburg bathed in sunshine, and was struck by the dachas closer to Berlin. 'Everything,' he noted, 'is covered with flowers, tulips, lilac, apple trees, plum trees. The birds are singing: nature feels no pity for the last days of fascism.' He watched a column of ex-prisoners of war moving in carts, on foot, limping with the aid of sticks, pushing prams and wheelbarrows. They too displayed improvised national flags. 'French *poilus* have managed to keep their pipes,' he observed.

One of the signs of the fall of fascism was the accelerating breakdown of German propaganda services. On 21 April, the Transocean News Agency fell silent and so did the Reichssender Berlin. The following day, the pro-Nazi Irish nationalists at Irland-Redaktion blamed the British and Americans for reducing Europe to a Soviet zone of influence.

It was their penultimate broadcast. The transmitter at Nauen was captured two days later.

More and more Berliners had been taking the risk of listening to the BBC on the wireless and even dared to discuss its news. But power cuts were now creating a more effective censorship of foreign broadcasts than the police state had ever achieved. London had little idea of the great Soviet offensive, but its announcement that Sachsenhausen-Oranienburg concentration camp had been liberated just north of Berlin gave a good idea of Red Army progress and its intention to encircle the city. The indication of the horrors found there was also another reminder of the vengeance which Berlin faced. This did not stop most Berliners from convincing themselves that the concentration camp stories must be enemy propaganda.

Apart from broadcasts heard on battery-operated radios and a few announcements on posters about rations, most news now came by word of mouth. Rumour and fact became even more difficult to disentangle. A sense of nightmare unreality pervaded the city as it awaited its doom on that day of bright spring sunshine and heavy showers. Comparisons with its recent status as the imperial capital of occupied Europe were inescapable. Once grandiose buildings were reduced to mere façades, with the sky visible through the upper windows. And the decline from mechanized military power was underlined by the sight of German soldiers driving hay wagons drawn by small Polish horses.

The constant background of Kazakov's artillery bombardment set nerves on edge. People found that the phrase 'the thunder of guns' was not one of those bombastic clichés of war but an entirely accurate description. The sound rolled and echoed, especially in courtyards behind buildings, just like a storm. Everyone was afraid, but women had most to fear. An anonymous diarist recorded that although women in ration queues discussed every advance of the enemy, there was an unspoken agreement. 'Not a single woman talked about "it".'

'These are strange times,' she added in the large sales ledger which she used as her diary. 'One experiences history in the making, things which one day will fill the history books. But while living through it, everything dissolves into petty worries and fears. History is very tiresome. Tomorrow I'm going to look for nettles and try to find some coal.'

*

Hitler, on the other hand, had by now realized that history was all that was left to him – except that his notion of history was fatally dominated by an obsessive desire for immortality. Unlike Himmler, he did not try to change his image with concessions. If anything, his addiction to bloodshed and destruction intensified. One of the main reasons for his decision to stay on in Berlin was quite simple. The Fall of Berchtesgaden did not have quite the same ring as the Fall of Berlin. Nor did it offer the same spectacular images of smashed monuments and blazing buildings.

During the night of 21 April, Hitler had almost collapsed after ordering the Steiner counter-attack. His doctor, Morell, found him in such low spirits that he suggested an injection to revive him. Hitler went into a frenzy. He was convinced that the generals wanted to drug him with morphine and put him on a plane to Salzburg. It appears that he spent most of his days and nights in the bunker, when not in situation conferences, sitting in his room, lost in thought, often gazing at the portrait of Frederick the Great. It had become his icon.

For most of the morning of 22 April, Hitler feverishly demanded news of Steiner's attack from the north. He told General Koller, the Luftwaffe chief of staff, to send up aircraft to see if Steiner's troops had yet started to move. He contacted Himmler to ask him. The Reichsführer SS had not the slightest idea of what was going on. He and his chameleon eminence Gruppenführer Walter Schellenberg were still preoccupied with the idea of secret overtures to the Western Allies through Count Bernadotte. Himmler just made a guardedly optimistic reply, which Hitler seized upon as fact.

At the midday situation conference, however, Hitler heard for certain that Steiner had not moved. Soviet forces had also broken the perimeter defence ring in the north of the city. He began to scream and yell. The SS was betraying him now as well as the army. This rage was far worse than any of his rows with Guderian. Eventually he collapsed into an armchair, drained and weeping. He said quite openly for the first time that the war was lost. Keitel, Jodl, Krebs and Burgdorf were shaken. Hitler went on to say that because he could not die fighting, because he was too weak, he would simply shoot himself to avoid falling into the hands of the enemy. They tried to persuade him to leave for Berchtesgaden, but he had clearly made up his mind. He ordered Keitel,

Jodl and Bormann to leave for the south, but they refused. Anyone else who wanted to go could go, he told them, but he was staying in Berlin to the end. He wanted an announcement made to that effect.

Goebbels was summoned to the Reich Chancellery to help persuade him to leave, but he was the worst choice, since he was already determined to stay himself. He spoke alone with Hitler in his room for some time, trying to calm him down. When Goebbels came out, he told those waiting outside that the Führer had asked him to bring his family into the bunker. It would appear that Goebbels had told Hitler during this conversation that he and his wife, Magda, had already decided to kill their six children and then themselves.

Hitler, to the surprise of his distraught entourage, re-emerged in calmer mood. Jodl had suggested that General Wenck's Twelfth Army could be turned around from facing the Americans on the Elbe and ordered to relieve Berlin. Hitler seized on this idea. 'General Field Marshal Keitel,' wrote Jodl, 'was ordered to coordinate the actions of the Twelfth Army and the Ninth Army, which was breaking out of its encirclement.' Keitel offered to leave immediately, but Hitler insisted that he first sat down while servants brought him a meal as well as sandwiches for his journey, and half a bottle of cognac and chocolate as iron rations. Keitel then left for Wenck's headquarters and Jodl for the new OKW base at Krampnitz, north of Potsdam.

The debate over Hitler's degree of sanity or madness can never be resolved. But Colonel de Maizière, who was there on that evening of Sunday 22 April and who had observed him closely during numerous situation conferences, was convinced that 'his mental sickness consisted of a hypertrophic self-identification with the German people'. This may well explain why he felt that the population of Berlin should share his suicide. But he also seemed to experience real pleasure in casualties among his own men as well as those of the enemy. 'Losses can never be too high!' he had exclaimed to Field Marshal von Reichenau in 1942, when informed of heavy casualties in the SS *Leibstandarte Adolf Hitler*. 'They sow the seeds of future glory.'

Operation Seraglio, the evacuation to Berchtesgaden, was accelerated. A party prepared to leave early the next day. Admiral von Puttkammer, Hitler's naval aide, had been given the task of destroying all Hitler's public papers at the Berghof. Julius Schaub, Hitler's personal adjutant, who had dealt with all the papers in the Reich Chancellery and bunker, was to destroy all his private correspondence. Two of the four secretaries had already been sent southwards. Dr Morell, who was apparently trembling with fear, managed to attach himself to the party. He took with him a German Army footlocker full of Hitler's medical records.

Allied intelligence services heard far more extravagant rumours of escape from Berlin. The State Department in Washington, DC, was warned by its embassy in Madrid that 'the chiefs plan to get to Japan by way of Norway. Heinkel 177s will take them to Norway, and there, already waiting, are planes – probably Vikings – for the non-stop flight to Japan.' This was no doubt the wishful thinking of Nazis in Spain, who also talked of U-boats being provisioned to take food to Germany and perhaps to bring out Nazi leaders. 'There exist in Switzerland several hospitals where, under cover of wounds or illness, Germans are hospitalized. In reality these are important personalities to be saved.' The claim that 'camouflaged German planes continue to bring in notables [to Spain]' was, however, much closer to the truth. Pierre Laval, the former prime minister of Vichy France, was among those flown out of Germany to Barcelona in unmarked Junkers transports. Franco felt obliged to return Laval to France, but a number of Nazis obtained sanctuary.

The exodus meant that rooms in the bunker and Reich Chancellery were liberated. Major Freytag von Loringhoven, who had moved into the bunker with General Krebs, found that the ventilation system worked well. But in the tiny conference room, with fifteen to twenty people in there, the air became almost unbreathable. Hitler was the only one to sit. The others were almost asleep on their feet. The bombing and shelling began to create cracks in the walls, and dust seeped out into the air. Since smoking was strictly forbidden in the lower Führer bunker, those desperate for a cigarette had to creep up a floor to the upper bunker. Despite these inconveniences, the bunker and the Reich Chancellery cellars were 'superbly stocked' with food and alcohol. The generous supplies of drink did not contribute to clear thinking. 'In the bunker,' Colonel de Maizière noted, 'an atmosphere of disintegration reigned. One saw drunkenness and dejection, yet also men of all ranks acting in a frantic manner. Discipline had ceased to exist.' This dissipation appeared to provide a striking contrast with the Nazi notion of family values when Frau Goebbels arrived, leading her six children. And yet both contained exactly the same currents of sentimentality, self-pity and brutality.

Freytag von Loringhoven was at the bottom of the stairs when he suddenly saw Magda Goebbels descend the concrete stairs, followed by her six children. She looked '*sehr damenhaft*' – 'very ladylike'. The six children behind ranged from twelve years old down to five: Helga, Hilde, Helmut, Holde, Hedda and Heide. Their first names, all beginning with the same letter, had not been chosen like a class of warships, but to honour the place in the alphabet marked by the Führer's name. They descended the stairs like a school crocodile. Their pale faces stood out against their dark coats. Helga, the oldest, looked very sad, but she did not cry. Hitler knew and approved of the decision by Joseph and Magda Goebbels to kill their children before they killed themselves. This proof of total loyalty prompted him to present her with his own gold Nazi Party badge, which he always wore on his tunic. The arrival of the children in the bunker had a momentarily sobering effect. Everyone who saw them enter knew that they would be murdered by their parents as part of a Führerdämmerung.

After his terrible emotional storm in the early afternoon, Hitler rested in his small bunker sitting room with Eva Braun. He summoned his two remaining secretaries, Gerda Christian and Traudl Junge, his Austrian dietician, Constanze Manzialy, and Bormann's secretary, Elsa Krüger. Hitler told the women that they must prepare to leave for the Berghof like the others. Eva Braun smiled and went to him. 'You know that I am never going to leave you,' she said. 'I will stay by your side.' He pulled her head down to him and, in front of everybody, kissed her full on the lips. This act astonished all who knew him. Traudl Junge and Gerda Christian said that they would stay too. Hitler looked at them fondly. 'If only my generals had been as brave as you,' he said. He dispensed cyanide pills to them as a farewell present.

It was presumably soon after this that Eva Braun went to type a last letter to her best friend, Herta Ostermayr. This was to accompany all her jewels. One of the men about to fly south was waiting to take the package for her. She told Herta in the letter that the jewels were to be distributed according to her will. Their value would help friends and family keep their heads 'above water' in the days to come. 'Forgive me if this is a bit confused,' she wrote, 'but I am surrounded by the six children of G[oebbels] and they are not being quiet. What should I say to you? I cannot understand how it should have all come to this, but it is impossible to believe any more in a God.'

19

The Bombarded City

On 23 April, the Nazi-controlled radio station in Prague claimed that the Führer's decision to stay in the capital of the Reich gave 'the battle a European significance'. The same morning, the headline of the newspaper of the 3rd Shock Army read, 'Motherland Rejoice! We are on the streets of Berlin!' National Socialism had laid claim to an international cause, while international Communism had become unashamedly patriotic.

For the civilians of Berlin, ideological causes made little difference any more. Survival was what counted under the bombardment. Worse was to come. General Kazakov was bringing in 600mm siege guns on specially widened tracks along the line leading to the Schlesicher Bahnhof in the east of the city. Each shell weighed half a ton.

Apart from the three flak towers, one of the largest refuges in Berlin was the Anhalter Bahnhof bunker, next to the main station. Built in ferro-concrete, with three storeys above ground and two below, its walls were up to four and a half metres thick. Pine seats and tables had been provided by the authorities, as well as emergency supplies of tinned sardines, but neither lasted long when both fuel and food were in such short supply. The Anhalter bunker's great advantage was its direct link to the U-Bahn tunnels, even though the trains were not running. People could walk the five kilometres to the Nordbahnhof, without ever being exposed.

The conditions in the bunker became appalling, with up to 12,000 people crammed into 3,600 square metres. The crush was so great that nobody could have reached the lavatory even if it had been open. One woman described how she spent six days on the same step. For hygienic Germans, it was a great ordeal, but with water supplies cut, drinking water was a far higher priority. There was a pump which still worked outside the station, and young women near the entrance took the risk of running with a pail to fetch water. Many were killed, because the station was a prime target for Soviet artillery. But those who made it back alive earned eternal gratitude from those too weak to fetch it for themselves, or they bartered sips for food from those who lacked the courage to run the gauntlet themselves.

At the anti-tank barriers set up at major intersections, the Feldgendarmerie checked papers, ready to arrest and execute any deserters. In cellars, a growing trickle of German officers and soldiers began to appear in civilian clothes. 'Desertion suddenly seems quite natural, almost creditable,' a woman diarist noted on that morning of Monday 23 April. She thought of Leonidas's 300 Spartans at Thermopylae, about whom they had heard so much at school. 'Maybe here and there 300 German soldiers would behave in the same way: 3 million would not. The greater the crowd, the less the chance for schoolbook heroism. By nature, we women don't appreciate it much either. We're sensible, practical, opportunistic. We prefer men alive.'

When she went in search of coal later that morning along the S-Bahn tracks, she found that the tunnel to the south was already blocked against the Russians on the southern rim of the city. She heard from bystanders that a man accused of desertion had been hanged at the other end of the tunnel. Apparently he had been hanged with his feet not very far off the ground and some boys had been amusing themselves by twisting the corpse round and making it spin back.

On her way home she was horrified by the sight of 'soft-faced children under huge steel helmets . . . so tiny and thin in uniforms far too large for them'. She wondered why she was so outraged by 'this abuse of children', when if they had been just a few years older, she would have been far less upset. She concluded that some rule of nature, which protected the survival of the species, was being broken by throwing immature humans into battle. To take that step was 'a symptom of madness'.

*

Perhaps as a side-effect of this law linking death with sexual maturity, the arrival of the enemy at the edge of the city made young soldiers desperate to lose their virginity. Girls, well aware of the high risk of rape, preferred to give themselves to almost any German boy first than to a drunken and probably violent Soviet soldier. In the broadcasting centre of the Grossdeutscher Rundfunk on the Masurenallee, two-thirds of the 500-strong staff were young women – many little more than eighteen. There, in the last week of April, a 'real feeling of disintegration' spread, with heavy drinking and indiscriminate copulation amid the stacks of the sound archive. There was also a good deal of sexual activity between people of various ages in unlit cellars and bunkers. The aphrodisiac effect of mortal danger is hardly an unknown historical phenomenon.

A Norwegian journalist, describing the atmosphere in the city, claimed that boys and girls in uniform simply gave in 'to their impulses' in 'a hectic search for pleasure'. But this showed a lack of understanding, especially for the girls facing the prospect of rape. In any case, apart from those coupling round the Zoo bunker and in the Tiergarten's rhododendron bushes, which were just coming into flower amid the wreckage, many others simply cuddled each other in a desperate need for reassurance.

The other instinct of the moment was to hoard like a squirrel. Gerda Petersohn, a nineteen-year-old secretary with Lufthansa, was at home in Neukölln, not far from an S-Bahn station, when word spread in the neighbourhood that a Luftwaffe rations wagon was stranded on the track. Women rushed down to loot it. They plunged into boxes and crates to grab at anything. Gerda saw a woman nearby with her arms full of lavatory paper just as Russian planes attacked, strafing with machine-gun fire and dropping small bombs. Gerda rolled under a wagon. The woman with lavatory paper in her arms was killed. 'What a thing to die for,' Gerda thought. The last thing she grabbed before running back to their apartment building was a packet of pilot's emergency rations, containing Schoka-Cola and small malt tablets. These tablets were to prove very useful in an unexpected way.

There has been a dramatic account of the looting of the Karstadt department store in the Hermannplatz, where queuing shoppers had been blown to pieces during the first artillery bombardment on 21 April.

According to this story, SS troops allowed civilians to take what they wanted before they blew the place up. The explosion was said to have killed many over-eager looters. But in fact when the SS *Nordland* Division took over the store several days later, they did not want to blow it up. They needed Karstadt's twin towers as observation posts to watch the Soviet advance on Neukölln and the Tempelhof aerodrome.

Once the electricity supply failed and wirelesses ceased working, the rumour mill became the only news available. More false stories than true ran around Berlin. One claimed that Field Marshal Model had not committed suicide, he had been secretly arrested by the Gestapo. The regime's own smokescreen of lies made almost anything believable, however inaccurate.

The 7th Department of the 1st Belorussian Front launched a propaganda blitz on Berlin with air-dropped leaflets telling German soldiers that it was 'hopeless to fight on'. A Soviet prison was the only way to save their lives, which were not worth losing for the fascist government. Others were 'safe-conduct passes' to be shown to Red Army soldiers when surrendering. The department claimed success because 'almost 50 per cent of Germans who surrendered in Berlin' had one of the leaflets and showed it to their Soviet captors. Altogether ninety-five different leaflets, almost 50 million copies in all, were dropped. Others – around 1.66 million – were distributed by German civilians and soldiers who were sent back across the lines. During the Berlin operation 2,365 civilians were sent back to infiltrate the city. Also 2,130 German prisoners of war were sent back, of whom 1,845 returned bringing a further 8,340 prisoners. This tactic was deemed to be such a success that the commander of the 3rd Shock Army ordered the mass release of German prisoners of war under the supervision of political officers.

Indoctrinated former prisoners of war – '*Seydlitz-truppen*' as the German authorities termed them – were sent through the lines to Berlin with letters written to families by recently captured prisoners. Corporal Max S., for example, wrote to his parents, 'My beloved relatives. Yesterday I became a prisoner of the Russians. We had been told that Russians shoot their prisoners, but this isn't true. The Russians are treating their prisoners very well. They fed me, and warmed me up. I am feeling well. The war will end soon and I'll see you again soon, my dear ones. Don't worry about me. I am alive and healthy.' The phrasing and formulae in the letter suggest that it was dictated by a Russian officer, but even so the word-of-mouth effect of such missives was worth far more than tens of thousands of leaflets.

One leaflet dropped over the capital itself was addressed to the women of Berlin. 'Because the fascist clique is afraid of punishment, it is hoping to prolong the war. But you women have nothing to be afraid of. No one will touch you.' It then urged them to persuade German officers and soldiers to capitulate. Since the political officers must have known the trail of mass violation in the wake of the advance through German territory, this was a breathtaking reassurance, even by most standards of wartime propaganda. Soviet propagandists also organized radio broadcasts by 'women, actors, priests and professors' to reassure their listeners that they would not be harmed in any way.

A more effective message came in a 'letter from the inhabitants of Friedrichshafen to the Berlin Garrison'. 'The day after the arrival of the Red Army life returned to normal,' it read. 'Food supplies recommenced. The inhabitants of Friedrichshafen tell you not to believe the false propaganda of Goebbels about the Red Army.' The fear of starvation, above all the starvation of children, seems to have represented a greater fear for many women than the danger of rape.

Field Marshal Keitel, who had left the Führer bunker the evening before with the sandwiches, chocolate and cognac provided by a solicitous Hitler, had driven south-westwards from the capital. He was fortunate not to encounter any of Lelyushenko's tanks. Keitel headed first to the headquarters of XX Corps at Wiesenburg, only thirty kilometres short of the American bridgehead at Zerbst. General Köhler's corps consisted mainly of so-called 'Young' divisions, largely those called up for pre-military training in the Reich Labour Service. They were far from fully trained, but they certainly did not lack spirit, as General Wenck had soon found.

In the early hours of 23 April, Keitel moved to the nearby headquarters of the Twelfth Army in a forestry station. He was met by General Wenck and his chief of staff, Colonel Reichhelm. There could not have been a greater contrast between the field marshal and the general. Keitel was pompous, vain, stupid, brutal and obsequious to his Führer. Wenck, who looked young, despite his silver hair, was extremely intelligent and greatly liked by both colleagues and his soldiers. Colonel Reichhelm, his chief of staff, said of their visitor that he was 'an outstanding sergeant, but no field marshal'. This was a mild criticism. Keitel, of all the generals who sided unconditionally with Hitler, was hated as the chief 'gravedigger of the army'.

Keitel began lecturing Wenck and Reichhelm on the need for the Twelfth Army to save the Führer in Berlin. He ranted as if addressing a Nazi Party rally and waved his field marshal's baton. 'We let him talk and we let him leave,' Reichhelm said later. But Wenck already had another idea. He would indeed attack towards Berlin, as ordered, but not to save Hitler. He wanted to force open a corridor from the Elbe, to allow soldiers and civilians to escape both the senseless fighting and the Red Army. It was to be a *Rettungsaktion* – a rescue operation.

Hitler, not trusting any general, insisted that his Führer order to the Twelfth Army should be broadcast over the radio addressed to the '*Soldaten der Armee Wenck!*' It was probably the only time in history that military orders were deliberately made public in the middle of a battle. This was immediately followed by the *Werwolfsender* radio station, which announced that 'the Führer has issued orders from Berlin that units fighting [the] Americans rapidly be transferred east to defend Berlin. Sixteen divisions [are] already moving and can be expected [to] arrive [in] Berlin [at] any hour'. The whole purpose was to deceive the population of Berlin into believing that the Americans were now supporting the Germans against the Red Army. By chance, that day American air activity over the central Elbe suddenly halted. It was a huge relief for Twelfth Army soldiers.

Wenck and his staff knew that Keitel was as much of a fantasist as Hitler. Any suggestion of tackling two Soviet tank armies when they lacked battle-worthy tanks was grotesque. 'So we made up our own orders,' said Colonel Humboldt, the chief operations officer. Wenck planned to drive on Potsdam with one force while the bulk of the army would advance eastwards, south of Berlin, to join up with Busse and help his Ninth Army escape. 'We were in radio contact with Busse and knew where he was.' Only a light screen of troops would be left facing the Americans.

Detailed orders were issued rapidly, and later that day, General Wenck drove in a Kübelwagen to address the young soldiers, both those who were to attack north-eastwards towards Potsdam and those who were to attack towards Treuenbrietzen and Beelitz, where the hospital complex was threatened. 'Boys, you've got to go in once more,' Wenck told them. 'It's not about Berlin any more, it's not about the Reich any more.' Their task was to save people from the fighting and the Russians. Hans-Dietrich Genscher, a young sapper with the Twelfth Army, described their emotions as 'a feeling of loyalty, a sense of responsibility and comradeship'.

Wenck's leadership struck a powerful chord, even if reactions varied between those who believed in a humanitarian operation and those keener to take on the Russians instead of the Western Allies. 'So about turn!' wrote Peter Rettich, the battalion commander of the *Scharnhorst* Division, which had taken such a hammering from the Americans. 'And now it's quick march to the east against the Ivans.'

The other key German general in the battle for Berlin to emerge at this time was General Helmuth Weidling, the commander of the LVI Panzer Corps. Weidling looked rather like a professorial version of Erich von Stroheim, only with hair.

On the morning of 23 April, Weidling rang the Führer bunker to report. General Krebs replied 'with conspicuous coldness' and informed him that he had been condemned to death. Demonstrating a remarkable moral and physical courage, he turned up at the Führer bunker that afternoon. Hitler was clearly impressed, so much so that he decided that the man he had wanted to execute for cowardice was the man to command the defence of the Reich capital. It was, as Colonel Refior observed, a 'tragi-comedy' typical of the regime.

Weidling's LVI Panzer Corps was considerably reduced. Only fragments remained of the 9th Parachute Division. The *Müncheberg* Panzer Division was reduced to remnants, and although the 20th Panzergrenadier Division was in better shape, its commander, Major General Scholz, had committed suicide shortly after entering Berlin. Only the *Nordland* and the 18th Panzergrenadier Division remained in a relatively battle-worthy condition. Weidling decided to hold back the 18th Panzergrenadier Division in reserve for counter-attack. The other formations were distributed around the different defence sectors to act as '*Korsett-stangen*' – 'corset-stiffeners'.

The defence of the city had been organized into eight sectors, designated by the letters A to H. Each was commanded by a general or colonel, but few of them had any front experience. Inside the perimeter defence line, an inner defence ring followed the circular track of the S-Bahn city railway. The innermost area was bound by the Landwehr Canal on the south and the River Spree on the north side. The only real strongpoints were the three concrete flak towers – the Zoobunker, the Humboldthain and the Friedrichshain. They had plenty of ammunition for their 128mm and 20mm guns, as well as good communications with underground telephone cables. Their greatest problem was to be overfilled with wounded and civilians in their thousands.

Weidling found that he was supposed to defend Berlin from 1.5 million Soviet troops with around 45,000 Wehrmacht and SS troops, including his own corps, and just over 40,000 Volkssturm. Almost all the sixty tanks in the city came from his own formations. There was also supposed to be a *Panzerjagd* battalion equipped with Volkswagens, each of which was fitted with a rack for six anti-tank rockets, but nobody could find any trace of it. In the central government district, Brigadeführer Mohnke commanded over 2,000 men from his base in the Reich Chancellery.*

The most immediate threat which Weidling faced on the afternoon of 23 April was the assault on the east and south-east of the city from the 5th Shock Army, the 8th Guards Army and the 1st Guards Tank Army. That night, armoured vehicles which were still battle-worthy were ordered back to Tempelhof aerodrome to refuel. There, amid an expanse of wrecked Luftwaffe fighter planes, mainly Focke-Wulfs, the armoured vehicles filled up at a depot by the huge administration building. They received an order to prepare to counter-attack south-eastwards towards Britz. They were reinforced with a few King Tiger tanks and some Nebelwerfer rocket launchers, but the main anti-tank weapon of this force was the 'Stuka on foot', a joke name for the panzerfaust.

*

* Soviet estimates put the German strength at 180,000. This was because the Red Army included all those they took prisoner afterwards, including unarmed Volkssturm, city police, railway officials and members of the Reich Labour Service. Propaganda naturally played a part too.

After his visit to the Twelfth Army, Keitel returned to the Reich Chancellery at 3 p.m. He and Jodl went to see Hitler for the last time. On their return to the temporary OKW headquarters at Krampnitz, they heard that Russian forces were approaching from the north – this was the 47th Army – and the camp was abandoned in the early hours of the morning.

It continued to be a busy afternoon in the Führer bunker after Weidling's departure. Hitler, seizing on Keitel's report on his visit to the Twelfth Army, gave himself another injection of optimistic fantasy. A hopeless addict, he felt a renewed conviction that the Red Army could be defeated. Then Albert Speer, to everyone's surprise – and to a certain degree his own – returned to Berlin to see Hitler for the very last time. The leave-taking on Hitler's birthday had been unsatisfactory for him when surrounded by so many others. Despite changing feelings about his Führer and patron, he evidently still experienced an egotistical charge from this extraordinary friendship, which some have termed homoerotic.

Speer had driven from Hamburg, trying to avoid roads clogged with refugees, then found that his way was blocked. The Red Army had reached Nauen. He went back to a Luftwaffe airfield, where he commandeered a two-seater Focke-Wulf trainer, and then flew to Gatow airfield on the western edge of Berlin. From there, a Fieseler Storch spotter plane had brought him into the centre, landing at dusk short of the Brandenburg Gate on the east–west axis. Eva Braun, who had always adored Speer, was overjoyed to see him, partly because she had predicted that he would return. Even Bormann, who loathed Speer out of jealousy, seemed pleased to see him, and greeted him at the bottom of the stairs. Speer was probably the only person capable of persuading Hitler at this late hour to leave Berlin. For Bormann, who did not share the fascination with suicide of those around him, especially Goebbels, this was the only hope of saving his own neck.

Hitler, Speer found, was calm, like an old man resigned to death. He asked questions about Grand Admiral Dönitz and Speer sensed immediately that Hitler intended to nominate him as his successor. Hitler also asked his opinion about flying to Berchtesgaden or staying in Berlin. Speer said that he thought it would be better to end it all in Berlin rather than at his country retreat, where 'the legends would be hard to create'. Hitler seemed reassured that Speer agreed with his decision. He then discussed suicide and Eva Braun's determination to die with him.

Speer was still in the bunker on that evening of 23 April when Bormann rushed in with a signal from Göring in Bavaria. Göring had received from General Koller a third-hand account of Hitler's breakdown the day before and his pronouncement that he would stay in Berlin and shoot himself. Göring was still the legal successor, and he must have feared that Bormann, Goebbels or Himmler would stake a rival claim. He clearly did not know that Dönitz had been chosen as the unanointed heir. Göring spent over half a day discussing the situation with advisers and with General Koller, who had flown down from Berlin that morning with the inaccurate version of what had been said in the Führer bunker. He then drafted the text which was transmitted to Berlin that night. 'My Führer! – In view of your decision to remain at your post in the fortress of Berlin, do you agree that I take over, at once, the total leadership of the Reich, with full freedom of action at home and abroad, as your deputy, in accordance with your decree of 29 June 1941? If no reply is received by ten o'clock tonight, I shall take it for granted that you have lost your freedom of action, and shall consider the conditions of your decree as fulfilled, and shall act for the best interests of our country and our people. You know what I feel for you in this gravest hour of my life. Words fail me to express myself. May God protect you, and speed you quickly here in spite of all. Your loyal Hermann Göring.'

It cannot have been hard for Bormann to have roused Hitler's suspicions. A second telegram from Göring to Ribbentrop, summoning him for discussions, helped convince Hitler that this was outright treason. Bormann immediately offered to draft a reply. A stinging rebuke stripped Göring of all his responsibilities, titles and powers of command. He was, however, offered the option of retirement from all his posts on health grounds. This would save him from far graver charges. Göring had little option but to agree. Even so, on Bormann's orders, an SS guard surrounded the Berghof and Göring effectively became a prisoner. As a further humiliation, the kitchens were locked, supposedly to prevent the disgraced Reichsmarschall from poisoning himself.

After this drama, Speer visited Magda Goebbels. He found her pale from an angina attack, lying on a bed in a tiny concrete room. Goebbels would not leave them alone together for a moment. Later, when Hitler had retired about midnight, an orderly arrived with a message from Eva Braun asking Speer to visit her. She ordered champagne and cakes for the two of them and they chatted about the past: Munich, skiing holidays together and life at the Berghof. Speer had always liked Eva Braun – 'a simple Munich girl, a nobody' – whom he now admired for her 'dignity, and almost a kind of gay serenity'. The orderly returned at 3 a.m., to say that Hitler had risen again. Speer left her to make his final farewell to the man who had made him famous. It lasted only a few moments. Hitler was both brusque and distant. Speer, his former favourite, had ceased to exist in his mind.

At some time during the course of that evening, Eva Braun wrote her last letter to Gretl Fegelein, her sister. 'Hermann is not with us,' she wrote of Gretl's husband. 'He left for Nauen to gather a battalion or something of the sort.' She did not know that Fegelein's journey to reach Nauen was in fact an aborted secret meeting with Himmler which was part of the plot to make peace with the Western Allies. 'He wants to fight his way out in order to continue the resistance in Bavaria, anyway for a time.' She was clearly mistaken. Her brother-in-law had risen too far to want to be reduced to a mere partisan.

Eva Braun, practical within her unworldliness, then proceeded to concentrate on business matters. She wanted Gretl to destroy all her private correspondence. 'On no account must Heise's bills be found.' Heise was her dressmaker and she did not want the public to know how extravagant she had been at the Führer's expense. Once again, she was concerned with the disposal of her jewellery. 'My diamond watch is unfortunately being repaired,' she wrote. Gretl was to track down SS Unterscharführer Stegemann, who had apparently arranged to have it repaired by a watchmaker, almost certainly Jewish, 'evacuated' from Oranienburg concentration camp in one of the last death marches.

20

False Hopes

Frightened Berliners could not resist believing Goebbels when he promised that Wenck's army was coming to save them. They were also encouraged to believe in the rumour that the Americans were joining in the battle against the Russians. Many heard aircraft fly over the city during the night of 23 April without dropping bombs. These planes, they told each other, must have been American, and perhaps they were dropping paratroops. But the two US Airborne divisions had never emplaned.

Just about the only troops coming to Berlin at this time were neither American nor German, but French. At 4 a.m. on Tuesday 24 April, Brigadeführer Krukenberg was woken in the SS training camp near Neustrelitz, where remnants of the 'Charlemagne' Division had been based since the Pomeranian disaster. The telephone call was from Army Group Vistula headquarters. Evidently, General Weidling had informed Heinrici that he insisted on removing Brigadeführer Ziegler from command of the *Nordland*. Krukenberg was told that he was to move to Berlin immediately. No reason was given. He was simply told to report to Gruppenführer Fegelein in the Reich Chancellery. The staff officer also advised him to take an escort, as he might have trouble getting through to Berlin.

Henri Fenet, the surviving battalion commander, was woken immediately and he roused his men. Krukenberg was dressed in the long grey leather greatcoat of a Waffen SS general when he addressed the assembled officers and men. He asked for volunteers to accompany him to Berlin. Apparently, the vast majority wanted to go. Krukenberg and Fenet chose ninety, because that was all that the vehicles available could carry. Many were officers, including the divisional chaplain, Monsignor Count Mayol de Lupé. After the war, Krukenberg claimed that none of them were National Socialists. This may well have been true in the strict sense of the term, but French fascism was probably closer to Nazism than to the Italian or Spanish varieties. In any case, these volunteers ready to die in the ruins of the Third Reich were all fanatical anti-Bolsheviks, whether they believed in New Europe or '*vieille France*'.

The volunteers selected filled their pockets and haversacks with ammunition and took the battalion's remaining panzerfausts. At 8.30 a.m., as they formed up by the road to climb into their vehicles, they suddenly saw the Reichsführer SS driving himself in an open Mercedes. Himmler passed right through them without even acknowledging his troops. He had no guards and no escort. Only several years later did Krukenberg realize that Himmler must have been returning to his retreat at Hohenlychen from Lübeck. He had met Count Bernadotte, the Swedish Red Cross representative, the night before.

The column of two armoured personnel carriers and three heavily laden trucks set off for Berlin. They had heard that Soviet tanks had already reached Oranienburg, so Krukenberg decided to take a more westerly route. It was not going to be easy to reach Berlin. Everyone was going in the other direction, whether formed detachments, stragglers, refugees or foreign workers. Many Wehrmacht soldiers jeered at the 'Charlemagne' volunteers, telling them that they were headed in the wrong direction. Some tapped their temples to indicate that they were crazy. Others shouted that the war was as good as over. They even encountered the signals detachment of the *Nordland* Division. Its commander claimed that he had received orders to move to Schleswig-Holstein. Krukenberg, having been out of touch, had no way of verifying this. Also he knew nothing of the row between Ziegler and Weidling.

After a strafing attack by a Soviet fighter, which killed one man, and on hearing artillery fire in the middle distance, Krukenberg directed the vehicles along small roads which he had known as an officer in Berlin before the war. Taking advantage of the pine forests, which hid them from enemy aviation, they came closer to the city. The route, however, became increasingly difficult with barricades and blown bridges, so

Krukenberg ordered the trucks to return to Neustrelitz. He retained the two armoured personnel carriers, but the vast majority of the French volunteers had to continue on foot for another twenty kilometres.

They reached the area of the Reichssportfeld, next to the Olympic stadium, at 10 p.m. The exhausted men discovered a Luftwaffe supply store, but most of them drank a special pilot's cocoa laced with benzedrine. Few managed to sleep. Krukenberg, accompanied by his adjutant, Captain Pachur, then set out across an apparently deserted Berlin to report to Fegelein in the Reich Chancellery. A rumour spread among the French volunteers that Hitler himself was coming out to review them there.

Their more direct chief, Himmler, who had driven past that morning, had finally crossed his Rubicon. The 'faithful Heinrich', as Himmler had been known with amusement at the Führer's court, was doomed as a conspirator. He had little talent for plotting and lacked conviction for his cause. His only advantage was that Hitler never imagined that the Reichsführer, who had proudly invented the SS motto, 'My honour is loyalty', would turn out a traitor.

According to Speer, Himmler was still furious over Hitler's order to strip the Waffen SS divisions in Hungary of their armband titles. Yet if Hitler had summoned him to his side or given some indication that he appreciated him above Martin Bormann, then his eyes would have filled with tears and he would have renewed his pledge of devotion to the Führer on the spot. As a result he was paralysed by indecision. Yet Himmler's greatest miscalculation, in his attempt to open negotiations with the enemy, was his belief that he was vital to the Western Allies, 'since he alone could maintain order'.

At the first two meetings with Count Bernadotte, Himmler had not dared take the conversation beyond the release of concentration camp prisoners. 'The Reichsführer is no longer in touch with reality,' Bernadotte had told Schellenberg after the meeting which followed Hitler's birthday. Himmler refused to follow the advice of Schellenberg, who urged him to depose or even murder the man to whom he had been so faithful.

Schellenberg managed to persuade Himmler not to return to the bunker to see Hitler on 22 April after they had heard from Fegelein of the Führer's frenzy that afternoon. Schellenberg was afraid that the moment his chief saw the Führer again, his resolve would weaken. Himmler offered his SS guard battalion for the defence of Berlin through an intermediary. Hitler accepted immediately and showed on the map where the battalion should be deployed, in the Tiergarten close to the Reich Chancellery. He also gave orders for the important prisoners – the *Prominenten* – to be moved so that they could be slaughtered at the moment of defeat.

On the night of 23 April, Himmler and Schellenberg met Bernadotte at Lübeck. Himmler, aware now of Hitler's determination to kill himself in Berlin, was finally resolved to take his place and start negotiations in earnest. He now formally requested Bernadotte to approach the Western Allies on his behalf to arrange a cease-fire on the Western Front. He promised that all Scandinavian prisoners would be sent to Sweden. It was typical of Himmler's strange relationship with reality that his immediate preoccupation was whether he should bow to General Eisenhower or shake hands when meeting him.

For the last Jews left in captivity in Berlin, the coming of the Red Army signified either the end to a dozen years of nightmare or execution at the last moment. Hans Oskar Löwenstein, who had been arrested in Potsdam, was taken to the Schulstrasse transit camp, based on Berlin's Jewish hospital in the northern district of Wedding. Around 600 of them packed into two floors were fed on potato peelings and raw beetroot, with a little *Wassersuppe* or 'water soup'. Among them were many half-Jews like Löwenstein himself, termed '*Mischlinge*' by the Nazis. There were also members of the privileged category of Jews protected by the Nazis, the *Schutzjuden*, who included, for example, those who had organized the Berlin Olympic Games. Foreign Jews of neutral nationality still held there, particularly South Americans, had been kept alive by relatives at home sending coffee beans to the SS administration.

The camp commander, SS Obersturmbannführer Doberke, had received the order to shoot all his prisoners, but he was clearly nervous. A spokesman from the prisoners approached him with a simple deal. 'The war is over,' he told Doberke. 'If you save our lives, we will save yours.' The prisoners then prepared a huge form, signed by them all, saying that Obersturmbannführer Doberke had saved their lives. Two hours after the form had been taken from them, they saw that the gates were open and the SS guards had disappeared. But liberation did not prove such a joyous occasion. Soviet soldiers raped the Jewish girls and women in the camp, not knowing that they had been persecuted by the Nazis.

While Soviet armies were advancing into Berlin they were cheered by 'a real International' of 'Soviet, French, British, American and Norwegian prisoners of war', together with women and girls who had been taken to Germany as slave labourers, all coming in the other direction. Marshal Konev, reaching Berlin from the south, was impressed to see that they walked in the ruts made by tank tracks, knowing that these at least would be clear of mines.

Grossman, arriving from the east, also saw 'hundreds of bearded Russian peasants with women and children'. He noted 'an expression of grim despair on these faces of bearded "uncles" and devout village elders. These are *starosty* [village leaders appointed by the Germans] and police villains who had run all the way to Berlin and now have no choice but to be "liberated".'

'An old woman is walking away from Berlin,' Grossman jotted in his notebook. 'She is wearing a little shawl over her head, looking exactly as if she were on a pilgrimage, a pilgrim in the vast spaces of Russia. She's holding an umbrella on her shoulder, with a huge aluminium saucepan hanging from its handle.'

Although Hitler still could not fully accept the idea of transferring troops from the Western Front to face the Red Army, Keitel and Jodl acknowledged that there was now no alternative. The Wehrmacht operations staff issued orders accordingly. Stalin's suspicions, combined with the Soviet policy of revenge, had become something of a self-fulfilling prophecy.

Stalin was also preoccupied with his *bête noire* of Poland. He had absolutely no intention of backing down over the composition of the provisional government. As far as he was concerned, the matter was self-evident, and the wishes of the Polish people counted for nothing. 'The Soviet Union,' he wrote to President Truman on 24 April, 'has a right to make efforts that there should exist in Poland a government friendly towards the Soviet Union.' This of course meant completely under Soviet control. 'It is also necessary to take into account the fact that Poland borders with the Soviet Union, which cannot be said of Great Britain and the United States.' With Berlin now virtually surrounded, and the Western Allies boxed out, Stalin saw no reason to be emollient. Despite all the earlier Soviet accusations against the US Air Force, there was no hint of apology when two American aircraft were attacked and one of them destroyed that afternoon by six Soviet fighters.

Stalin was still keeping the pressure on his two marshals by stimulating their rivalry. From dawn on 23 April, the boundary between Zhukov's 1st Belorussian Front and Konev's 1st Ukrainian Front was extended from Lübben, but now it turned northwards to the centre of Berlin. Konev's right-hand boundary ran all the way up to the Anhalter Bahnhof. Rybalko's tank corps at Mariendorf, on the Teltow Canal, was exactly five kilometres south of it. Zhukov had no idea that Rybalko's army had reached Berlin until late on 23 April, when a liaison officer from Katukov's 1st Guards Tank Army, approaching from the east, made contact. Zhukov was appalled.

Since reaching the Teltow Canal on the evening of 22 April, Rybalko's three corps had been given a day to prepare for an all-out assault across it. The concrete banks of the canal and the defended warehouses on the northern side appeared a formidable barrier. And although the Volkssturm detachments opposite were hardly worthy opponents for the 3rd Guards Tank Army, they had been 'corset-stiffened' with the 18th and 20th Panzergrenadier Divisions. The breakthrough artillery formations had been ordered forward two days before, but there was such a jam of vehicles on the Zossen road, including horse-drawn supply carts, that progress was slow. If the Luftwaffe had still had any serviceable aircraft, the route would have presented a perfect target. Luchinsky's 48th Guards Rifle Division arrived in time to prepare to seize bridgeheads across the canal, and the artillery was hurried into place. This was no easy matter. Nearly 3,000 guns and heavy mortars needed to be positioned on the evening of 23 April. This was a concentration of 650 pieces per kilometre of front, including 152mm and 203mm howitzers.

At 6.20 a.m. on 24 April, the bombardment started on the Teltow Canal. It was an even more massive concentration of fire than on the

Neisse or the Vistula crossings. Konev arrived at Rybalko's command post when it had almost finished. From the flat roof of an eight-storey office block, a clutch of 1st Ukrainian Front commanders watched the heavy artillery demolishing the buildings across the canal and wave after wave of bombers from their supporting aviation army. The infantry began to cross in collapsible assault craft and wooden rowing boats. By 7 a.m. the first rifle battalions were across, establishing a bridgehead. Soon after midday the first pontoon bridges were in place and tanks began to go over.

The pressure on the south-eastern corner of Berlin's defences was already great before the Teltow Canal crossing. By dawn on 23 April, some of Chuikov's rifle units managed south of Köpenick to cross both the Spree and the Dahme to Falkenberg. They had discovered a variety of craft, from rowing sculls to pleasure launches. During the day and the following night, Chuikov's guards rifle divisions and Katukov's leading tank brigades advanced up towards Britz and Neukölln. The 28th Guards Rifle Corps claimed that civilians were so frightened and subservient 'they were licking [our] boots'. And in the early hours of 24 April, a corps of the 5th Shock Army, assisted by gunboats of the Dneper flotilla, crossed the Spree further north to Treptow Park.

At first light on 24 April, almost all the rest of Weidling's corps, which had refuelled the night before at Tempelhof aerodrome, put in counter-attacks against this double threat. Even though the remaining King Tigers of the *Nordland* 'Hermann von Salza' Heavy Panzer Battalion knocked out several Stalin tanks, the enemy forces were overwhelming. 'In the course of three hours,' wrote the divisional commander of the 5th Shock Army, 'the SS made six attacks but were forced to retreat each time, leaving the ground littered with corpses in black uniforms. Panthers and Ferdinands were burning. By midday, our division was able to advance again. They secured the whole of Treptow Park and in the dusk we reached the [S-Bahn] ring railroad.' 'It was,' wrote a participant on the German side, 'a bloody, bitter fight, without mercy.' It was also a conflict without scruples. Soviet troops were told by political officers that 'Vlasov and his men are taking part' in the battle for Berlin. This was totally untrue. They were almost all down in the area of Prague by then.

*

While Konev's tank armies were forcing the line of the Teltow Canal, his rear flanks came under threat. From the west, Wenck's troops were advancing towards Treuenbrietzen and Beelitz, while on his right, the Ninth Army was trying to break out of its encirclement in the forests south-east of Berlin.

General Luchinsky had already started to turn part of his 28th Army eastwards to face the Ninth Army, roughly along the line of the Berlin – Cottbus autobahn. And the *Stavka*, having done little to deal with the isolated Ninth Army, now at last reacted quickly. Marshal Novikov, the head of Red Army aviation, was ordered to oversee the concentration of the 2nd, 16th and 18th Air Armies against these 80,000 German troops moving through the forests. What the Soviet commanders did not yet know was whether they would try to fight their way back into Berlin, or attempt to break out westwards to join up with General Wenck's Twelfth Army.

The worst fears of the nurses in the hospital complex at Beelitz-Heilstätten were realized on the morning of 24 April. Suddenly, the ground began to vibrate as the noise of tank engines and tracks grew. One of Lelyushenko's tank columns, having apparently forced the Swiss Red Cross representatives aside, rolled right into the compound. Tank crews armed with sub-machine guns stormed the first block. For the moment, they were interested only in watches and shouted, '*Uri! Uri!*' But then news arrived of rape, looting and random killing in Beelitz itself. The nurses and adult patients steeled themselves for the worst. The children from the Potsdam hospital had little idea of what was going on.

The nurses did not know that they were about to be rescued by Wenck's young soldiers. Hitler, on the other hand, was now convinced that he and Berlin would be saved by Wenck's army. Steiner's so-called army detachment was hardly mentioned any more in the Führer bunker. The loyal Grand Admiral Dönitz signalled that in answer to Hitler's appeal, he was sending all available sailors to help in the fight for Germany's fate in Berlin. The plan to deliver them by crash-landing Junkers 52s in the centre of the city showed as little regard for reality as it did for the lives of his sailors.

Clearly few people in the bunker expected anyone to get through, to judge by the surprise caused by Brigadeführer Krukenberg's arrival at midnight. When he was eventually taken to see General Krebs, whom he had known in 1943 with Army Group Centre, Krebs admitted his amazement openly. He told him that over the last forty-eight hours, large numbers of officers and units had been ordered to Berlin. 'You're the only one who has made it.'

The Führer bunker, for all the efforts and expense that had gone into its construction, lacked proper signalling facilities. As a result, Major Freytag von Loringhoven and Captain Boldt had only one method of establishing the extent of the Red Army's advance ready for the Führer's situation conferences. They rang civilian apartments around the periphery of the city whose numbers they found in the Berlin directory. If the inhabitants answered, they asked if they had seen any sign of advancing troops. And if a Russian voice replied, usually with a string of exuberant swearwords, then the conclusion was self-evident. For the European situation, they secretly obtained the latest Reuters reports from Heinz Lorenz, Hitler's chief press secretary. Freytag von Loringhoven suddenly found that everyone who had ignored them in the bunker on their arrival now became pleasant in order to have access to the only source of reasonably reliable information.

Most of the occupants of the bunker did not have anything to do. They sat around drinking and loitered in the corridors discussing whether suicide was better by gun or by cyanide. It seemed generally assumed that hardly anybody was going to leave the bunker alive. Although cool and damp, conditions in the bunker were still infinitely better than in any other cellar or air-raid shelter in Berlin. The occupants had water and electric light from generators, and there was no shortage of food and drink. The kitchens up in the Reich Chancellery were still serviceable and constant meals of stew were served.

Berliners now referred to their city as the '*Reichsscheiterhaufen*' – the 'Reich's funeral pyre'. Civilians were already suffering casualties in the street-fighting and house-clearing. Captain Ratenko, an officer from Tula in Bogdanov's 2nd Guards Tank Army, knocked at a cellar door in Reinickendorf, a district in the north-west. Nobody opened it, so he kicked it in. There was a burst of sub-machine-gun fire and he was killed. The soldiers from the 2nd Guards Tank Army who were with him started firing through the door and the windows. They killed the gunman, apparently a young Wehrmacht officer in civilian clothes, but also a woman and a child. 'The building was then surrounded by our men and burned down,' the report stated.

SMERSH took an immediate interest in the question of concealed Wehrmacht officers. It set up a special hunting group, with a bloodhound who had been a Nazi Party member since 1927. He promised to find officers for them, no doubt in exchange for his own life. Altogether they took twenty, including a colonel. 'Another officer killed his wife then committed suicide when SMERSH knocked at his door,' the report stated.

Red Army soldiers decided to use the telephone network, but for amusement rather than information. While searching apartments, they would often stop to ring numbers in Berlin at random. Whenever a German voice answered, they would announce their presence in unmistakable Russian tones. This 'surprised the Berliners immensely', a political officer wrote. It was also not long before the political department of the 5th Shock Army began to report on 'abnormal phenomena', which covered everything from looting to injuries from drunken driving, and 'immoral phenomena'.

Many of the true *frontoviki* behaved well. When a detachment of sappers from the 3rd Shock Army entered an apartment, a 'small babushka' told them that her daughter was ill in bed. She was almost certainly trying to protect her from rape, but the sappers did not seem to realize this. They just gave them some food and moved on. Other *frontoviki*, however, could be pitiless. This has been described as the effect of the 'impersonal violence of war itself' and a compulsion to treat women as 'substitutes for the defeat of an enemy'. One historian noted that Soviet troops unleashed a wave of violence which then passed fairly rapidly, but the process often began again as soon as a new unit moved in.

On 24 April, the 3rd Shock Army used its 5th Artillery Breakthrough Division on one narrow sector where the Germans had resisted bitterly. The heavy guns destroyed seventeen houses, killing 120 defenders. The Soviet attackers claimed that in four of these houses, Germans had put out white flags of surrender and then fired again later. This became a frequent event in the fighting. Some soldiers, especially the Volkssturm, wanted to surrender and surreptitiously waved a white handkerchief, but more fanatical elements still fought on.

The Germans mounted a counter-attack with three assault guns, but this was apparently thwarted by the heroism of reconnaissance soldier Shulzhenok. Shulzhenok, having retrieved three panzerfausts, took up position in a ruined house. A German shell exploded close to him, deafening him and covering him with debris. This did not stop him from engaging the assault guns as they approached. He set the first one on fire and damaged the second. The third withdrew hurriedly. He was made a Hero of the Soviet Union for this action, but on the following day he 'was killed by a terrorist in civilian clothes'. In the conditions of the time, this could mean an ill-equipped member of the Volkssturm, but the Soviet view of terrorists was little different from the Wehrmacht definition during Operation Barbarossa.

Not far behind these events, the writer Vasily Grossman stopped his jeep in the Weissensee district of north-east Berlin on the axis of the 3rd Shock Army. In a moment the jeep was surrounded by boys asking for sweets and staring curiously at the map open on his knees. Grossman was surprised by their daring. He really wanted to look around. 'What contradicts our idea of Berlin as a military barracks are the masses of gardens and allotments in blossom,' he noted. 'A great thunder of artillery in the sky. In the moments of silence one can hear birds.'

The dawn of 25 April, as Krukenberg left the battered Reich Chancellery, was cold with a clear sky. West Berlin was still strangely quiet and empty. At Weidling's headquarters on the Hohenzollerndamm, security was lax. Only pay-books were required as identity by the sentries. Weidling told him how his badly mauled panzer corps was split up to stiffen Hitler Youth detachments and badly armed Volkssturm units, none of which could be expected to fight fiercely. Krukenberg was to take over Defence Sector C in the south-east of Berlin, including the 11th SS Panzergrenadier *Nordland* Division. He received the impression that Ziegler, who was being relieved of command of the *Nordland*, was accused of not holding his men together.

Accounts of Ziegler's dismissal vary considerably. Weidling's chief of staff, Colonel Refior, believed that 'Ziegler had secret orders from Himmler ordering him to pull back to Schleswig-Holstein', and this was why he was arrested. Ziegler certainly seemed to be one of the few SS commanders who saw the pointlessness of fighting on. Shortly before his removal, Ziegler had given Hauptsturmführer Pehrsson leave to go to the Swedish Embassy to find out whether its officials would refuse to offer help to the remaining Swedes to return home.

One eyewitness claims that Ziegler was arrested late that morning at his headquarters on the Hasenheidestrasse just north of Tempelhof aerodrome by an unknown SS Brigadeführer. He was backed by an escort with machine pistols who sealed the approaches to divisional headquarters. Ziegler was escorted out to the vehicle. He saluted his astonished officers standing at the entrance and presented his compliments to them: '*Meine Herren, alles Gute!*' He was driven away under arrest to the Reich Chancellery. 'What the hell's going on?' one of the officers, Sturmbannführer Vollmer, exclaimed. 'Are we now without a commander?' Krukenberg, in his account, depicts an entirely normal handover of command, with Ziegler driving off on his own to the Reich Chancellery.

In any case, the interregnum did not last long. Shortly after midday, Krukenberg arrived, followed a little later by Fenet's men from the 'Charlemagne' battalion. Krukenberg was shaken to learn that the 'Norge' and 'Danmark' Panzergrenadier Regiments now amounted between them to little more than a battalion. The wounded, taken to the dressing station in a storage cellar on the Hermannplatz, were unlikely to feel in safe hands. They were 'laid on a blood-smeared table as if it were a butcher's block'.

The last remaining German bridgehead south of the Teltow Canal at Britz was being abandoned in a panic just as Krukenberg reached his new command. The remnants of his 'Norge' and 'Danmark' regiments were waiting impatiently by the canal for motor transport, which was having difficulty getting to them through the rubble-blocked streets. Just as the trucks finally arrived, a cry of alarm was heard: '*Panzer durchgebrochen!*' This cry prompted a surge of 'tank fright' even among hardened veterans and a chaotic rush for the vehicles, which presented an easy target for the two T-34s that had broken through. The trucks that got away even had men clinging on to the outsides.

As they escaped north up the Hermannstrasse, they saw scrawled on a house wall 'SS traitors extending the war!' There was no doubt in their minds as to the culprits: 'German Communists at work. Were we going to have to fight against the enemy within as well?'

Soon Soviet tanks were also attacking the remains of the *Müncheberg* Panzer Division on Tempelhof aerodrome amid the wrecked fuselages of Focke-Wulf fighters. The aircraft's Red Army nickname of a 'frame' at last seemed entirely accurate. The boom and crack of artillery and tank fire, punctuated by screaming salvoes of katyushas, extended right up to the *Nordland* command post. Krukenberg was lightly wounded in the face by a shell splinter.

With Neukölln heavily penetrated by Soviet combat groups, Krukenberg prepared a fall-back position round the Hermannplatz. The twin towers of the Karstadt department store provided excellent observation posts for watching the advance of four Soviet armies – the 5th Shock Army from Treptow Park, the 8th Guards Army and the 1st Guards Tank Army from Neukölln and Konev's 3rd Guards Tank Army from Mariendorf.

Krukenberg positioned half of the French under Fenet on the other side of the Hermannplatz with their panzerfausts to prepare for a Soviet tank attack. Fenet had over 100 Hitler Youth attached to his group. They were instructed to fire their panzerfausts only at close range and only at the turret. The Waffen SS believed that it was better to aim for the turret, as a direct hit there would disable the crew.

During that evening and night, the French under Fenet accounted for fourteen Soviet tanks. A determined show of resistance could take the Soviets by surprise and hold them back. By the Halensee bridge at the western end of the Kurfürstendamm, three young men from a Reich Labour Service battalion armed with a single machine gun managed to beat back all attacks for forty-eight hours.

The battle for Tempelhof aerodrome was to continue for another day, with Soviet artillery and katyusha rocket launchers blasting the administrative buildings. Inside, the corridors echoed with the screams of the wounded and were filled with smoke and the smell of burning chemicals. 'The silence which followed the end of a bombardment was a prelude to the roar of engines and rattle of tracks which announced a new tank attack.'

*

As Weidling's battered corps retreated towards the centre on that afternoon of 25 April, Hitler insisted to their commander, who had been summoned to the Führer bunker, that things would change for the better. 'The situation must improve,' he told Weidling. 'From the south-west the Twelfth Army of General Wenck will come to Berlin and, together with the Ninth Army, will deliver a crushing blow to the enemy. The troops commanded by Schörner will come from the south. These blows should change the situation to our advantage.' To underline the disaster along the whole Eastern Front, General von Manteuffel had just reported that Rokossovsky's 2nd Belorussian Front had shattered his defence lines south of Stettin. Major General Dethleffsen of the OKW command staff also had to visit the Führer bunker that day and found 'a self-deception bordering on hypnosis'.

That evening, Krukenberg was warned by General Krebs that the *Nordland* would be pulled back the next day to defence sector 'Z' (for Zentrum). This was directed from the air ministry on the Wilhelm-strasse, a block north of Gestapo headquarters. Krukenberg, when he went back to make contact, found the cellars full of unsupervised Luftwaffe personnel doing nothing. He went up to the state opera house on the Unter den Linden, a few hundred metres down from the abandoned Soviet embassy. It was where Dekanozov had returned just after dawn on 22 June 1942 after hearing from Ribbentrop of the Wehrmacht's invasion of the Soviet Union. Now, the Unter den Linden was empty as far as the eye could see. Krukenberg set up his own headquarters in the cellars of the opera house. A huge, throne-like armchair from the former royal box provided him with the opportunity to snatch a couple of hours' sleep in comfort. They were left in compara-tive peace by the enemy. No U-2 biplanes dropping small bombs appeared over their sector that night.

With the fall of Berlin imminent, SHAEF headquarters at Rheims forwarded a request to the *Stavka* in Moscow that day. 'General Eisen-hower desires to send a minimum of twenty-three Allied accredited war correspondents to Berlin following the capture of the city by the Red Army. He wishes to send more than that number if at all possible since, as he states, "the fall of Berlin will be one of the world's greatest news events".' There was no reply from the Kremlin. Stalin clearly did not want any journalists in Berlin, particularly the uncontrollable western variety. He was, however, to be troubled by them from a totally unexpected direction.

During that day the main Nazi broadcasting station, Deutschlandsender, fell silent, but the date of 25 April became known for an event which was soon flashed around the world. At Torgau on the Elbe, leading elements of Major General Vladimir Rusakov's 58th Guards Rifle Division met up with US soldiers from the 69th Division. Nazi Germany was cut in half. Signals flashed up both chains of command – to Bradley, then Eisenhower at SHAEF, and to Konev, then General Antonov at the *Stavka*. Heads of state were immediately informed and then Stalin and Truman exchanged telegrams agreeing on the announcement of the event. Eisenhower's first reaction was to send in the journalists, a decision he soon had cause to regret.

General Gleb Vladimirovich Baklanov, the commander of the 34th Corps, ordered the preparation of a typical Soviet banquet. The political department provided huge lengths of red material to decorate tables and podiums. Large portraits of Stalin were erected and rather smaller ones of Truman improvised, along with some interesting variations on the stars and stripes. Plenty of alcohol was laid on, and all the most attractive women soldiers in the 5th Guards Army were sent forward to Torgau in fresh uniforms.

General Baklanov was prepared for the usual round of Soviet toasts to victory, to peace and friendship between nations and the eternal destruction of the fascist beast. He was unprepared, however, for a group of boisterous American journalists keen to put a real swing into the celebrations. Red Army soldiers also obtained a good ration of vodka, so security was not quite as effective as usual.

Halfway through the proceedings, when Russian officers were dancing 'with the pretty Russian women soldiers', Andrew Tully of the *Boston Traveller* 'remarked jokingly' to Virginia Irwin of the *St Louis Post Dispatch*, 'Let's keep going to Berlin.' 'OK,' she said. They slipped away from the party and drove their jeep to the Elbe, where they showed the Russian soldiers operating the ferry their SHAEF identification cards. They shouted 'Jeep!' and made swimming motions. Rather bewildered sentries, who had received no instructions on the subject, let them drive on to the ferry and sent it across the river.

The two journalists had a map which reached as far as Luckenwalde. Fearing that they might be 'summarily treated as spies' on such a fluid front, they stole one of the improvised American flags which the Russians had erected at Torgau and tied it to the side of the jeep. Whenever they were flagged down by a suspicious sentry or a traffic controller, they yelled 'Amerikansky!' with an amiable grin. 'Keep smiling,' Tully told Virginia Irwin.

They reached Berlin before nightfall and there they met Major Kovalesky, a young man with snow-white hair. They communicated through halting French. Kovalesky was at first suspicious, but was then convinced when they said, '*Nous sommes correspondents de guerre. Nous voulons aller [à] Berlin.*' The unfortunate Kovalesky, having no idea that their trip was unauthorized and that he might be held accountable later, took them to his command post in a half-ruined house. With typical Russian hospitality, he told his orderly, 'a fierce Mongolian with a great scar on his left cheek', to provide hot water for their guests. A quarter-full bottle of eau-de-Cologne, a cracked mirror and some face powder were also brought for Virginia Irwin. He then gave orders for a banquet. The table was lit by candles on upturned milk bottles, spring flowers were placed in a jar and the celebration began, with smoked salmon, black Russian bread, mutton cooked over charcoal, 'huge masses of mashed potato with meat fat poured over them', cheese and platterfuls of Russian pastries. 'At each toast, the Russian officers stood up, clicked their heels, bowed deeply and drained tumblers of vodka. Besides vodka, there was cognac and a drink of dynamite strength the major described simply as "spirits".' After each course there were toasts 'to the late and great President Roosevelt, to Stalin, to President Truman, to Churchill, to the Red Army and to the American jeep'.

The two journalists, exhilarated by their exploit, returned to Torgau the next day. Tully described it as 'the craziest thing I have ever done'. Clearly, he had never imagined the wider consequences. The US military authorities were furious, but not as angry as the Soviet authorities. This was demonstrated by the signals which flashed between Rheims, Washington, DC, and Moscow. An exasperated Eisenhower decided that because they had entered Berlin illegally, their stories could not be published unless submitted to Moscow for censorship. When events were moving so fast, this, of course, meant that they would be well out of date by the time they could appear. Eisenhower was especially irritated because he believed that their jaunt to Berlin had wrecked the proposal to get other journalists there for the surrender. But the people who probably suffered the most were the trusting Russians who had helped and entertained Tully and Irwin. Apparently, even officers involved in the celebrations at Torgau became objects of suspicion to the NKVD in the post-war purges, because they had been in contact with capitalist foreigners.

Stalin wanted Berlin surrounded as rapidly as possible with a cordon sanitaire. This meant the urgent occupation of all the territory up to the Elbe which had been allocated as part of the future Soviet zone. Konev's armies not involved in the attack on Berlin or the fight against the Ninth and Twelfth Armies were pushed westwards. The Elbe was reached during the course of 24 and 25 April at numerous points other than Torgau. Units of the 5th Guards Army, the 32nd Guards Rifle Corps commanded by General Rodimtsev of Stalingrad fame and the 4th Guards Tank Corps also reached the river. General Baranov's 1st Guards Cavalry Corps went one further. At the special request of Stalin's cavalry chum Marshal Semyon Budenny, Konev had given him a specific task. Soviet intelligence had heard that the stallions of the Soviet Union's most important stud farm in the northern Caucasus, shipped back to Germany in 1942, were held west of the Elbe near Riesa. The guards cavalry crossed the river, located them and drove them back. It could have been a border raid across the Rio Grande.

To satisfy Stalin's impatience for details on Berlin, General Serov, the NKVD representative with the 1st Belorussian Front, provided an immensely detailed report of conditions in the city. Beria had it on Stalin's desk on 25 April. Serov observed that the destruction was far worse towards the centre of the city, where many buildings were still blazing from Soviet artillery fire. 'On the walls of many buildings one frequently sees the word "Pst" [i.e. silence] written in big letters.' Berliners apparently explained that it was an attempt by the Nazi government to suppress criticism of its military efforts at a time of crisis. Berliners were already asking questions about the new form of government to be established in the city. Yet 'out of ten Germans asked if they could act as local bürgermeister, not a single one agreed, producing different insignificant excuses,' he wrote. 'They seem to be afraid of the consequences and fear to take on the job. It is therefore necessary to select bürgermeisters from among the prisoners of war who come from Berlin held in our camps.' These, no doubt, were selected anti-fascists who had received the relevant political training.

'Interrogation of captured Volkssturm members revealed an interesting fact. When they were asked why there are no regular soldiers and officers among them, they said that they were afraid of their responsibility for what they had done in Russia. They will therefore surrender to the Americans, while the Volkssturm can surrender to the Bolsheviks because they are guilty of nothing.' Serov wasted no time putting in place cordons in and around Berlin, using the 105th, 157th and 333rd NKVD Frontier Guards Regiments.

Serov was perhaps most surprised by the state of Berlin's defences. 'No serious permanent defences have been found inside the ten- to fifteen-kilometre zone around Berlin. There are fire-trenches and gun-pits and the motorways are mined in certain sections. There are some trenches just as one comes to the city, but less in fact than any other city taken by the Red Army.' Interrogations of Volkssturm men revealed how few regular troops there were in the city, how little ammunition there was and how reluctant the Volkssturm was to fight. Serov discovered also that German anti-aircraft defence had almost ceased to function, thus allowing Red Army aviation a clear sweep over the city. All of these observations were naturally kept secret. Soviet propaganda accounts had to emphasize what a formidable foe they faced in Berlin.

Serov indicated, while avoiding any politically controversial remarks, the reason for continued German resistance. 'It became clear from interrogating prisoners and civilians that there is still a great fear of the Bolsheviks.' Beria, with interesting logic, used the need to change 'the attitude of Red Army troops towards German prisoners and the civilian population' as the basis for an overhaul of the military administration of civilian affairs. He recommended that, 'in order to create a normal atmosphere in the rear of the operational Red Army on German territory', a new deputy Front commander should be appointed for civilian affairs. Needless to say, the deputy Front commander in each case was the resident NKVD chief – Serov for the 1st Belorussian Front, General Meshik for the 1st Ukrainian Front and Tsanava for the 2nd Belorussian

Front. It should be a guiding principle 'that the deputy Front commander is at the same time a representative of the NKVD of the USSR and is responsible to the NKVD of the USSR for the work on removing enemy elements'. He did not need to add the key point. They owed no responsibility to the military chain of command, at a time when both Stalin and Beria were afraid of triumphant generals.

The need for action was justified by the fact that the Americans were already prepared to administer their zone of occupation, while the Soviet Union had done nothing. 'For your information: on the territory of west Germany, the Allies have established the position of special deputy of commander of Allied troops in charge of civilian affairs. Major General Lucius Clay, who until appointed to this position, was deputy chief of the bureau of mobilizing military resources of the USA.' Beria was evidently impressed to hear that he would have 3,000 specially trained officers serving under him, 'with economic and administrative experience'. Their Soviet counterparts, with the emphasis on NKVD control, clearly were to have very different qualifications. The report ended in the usual style: 'I request a decision. Beria.'

21

Fighting in the City

The civilians to be administered by Beria's deputies had little idea of the realities of Soviet rule. They also had more urgent preoccupations as the battle was fought out on their streets, in their apartments and even through the cellars in which they sheltered. The only benefit in the early hours of Thursday 26 April was a thunderstorm, with such heavy rain that it put out some of the fires. Strangely enough, that seemed to increase the smell of burning, not diminish it.

Civilian casualties had been heavy already. Like Napoleonic infantry, the women standing in line for food simply closed ranks after a shellburst decimated a queue. Nobody dared lose their place. Some claimed that women just wiped the blood from their ration cards and stuck it out. 'There they stand like walls,' noted a woman diarist, 'those who not so long ago dashed into bunkers the moment three fighter planes were announced over central Germany.' Women queued for a handout of butter and dry sausage, while men emerged only to line up for an issue of schnapps. It seemed to be symbolic. Women were concerned with the immediacy of survival while men needed escape from the consequences of their war.

The failure of mains water meant more dangerous queues. Women waited in line with pails and enamel jugs at their nearest street pump, listening to the constant metallic squeaking from the rusty joint of its handle. They found that they had changed under fire. Swearwords and callous remarks which they would never have uttered before now slipped out quite naturally. 'Over and over again during these days,' the same diarist wrote, 'I've been noticing that not only my feelings, but those of almost all women towards men have changed. We are sorry for them, they seem so pathetic and lacking in strength. The weakly sex. A kind of collective disappointment among women seems to be growing under the surface. The male-dominant Nazi world glorifying the strong man is tottering, and with it the myth "man".'

The Nazi regime, which had never wanted women to be sullied by war, or indeed anything which interfered with child-rearing, now claimed in its desperation that young women were fighting alongside men. On one of the very few radio stations still on the air, there was an appeal to women and girls: 'Take up the weapons of wounded and fallen soldiers and take part in the fight. Defend your freedom, your honour and your life!' Germans who heard this appeal far from Berlin were shocked at this 'most extreme consequence of total war'. Yet only a very few young women took up weapons. Most were auxiliaries attached to the SS. A handful, however, found themselves caught up in the fighting, through either extraordinary circumstances or an ill-judged rush of romanticism. In order to stay with her lover, Ewald von Demandowsky, the actress Hildegard Knef put on uniform and joined him at Schmargendorf, defending the freight yards with his scratch company.

In the cellars of apartment blocks, the different couples from upstairs ate their food avoiding each other's eyes. It was rather like families in railway compartments on a long journey, consuming picnics in front of each other with a pretence of privacy. Yet when news came through that a barracks nearby had been abandoned, any semblance of civility disappeared. Law-abiding citizens became frenzied looters of the store-rooms. It was every man, woman and child for themselves and anything they could grab. Once outside with their boxes, spontaneous bartering began as they eyed each other's unlawful gains. There was no fixed black-market rate at that time. It depended on caprice or particular need – a loaf of bread for a bottle of schnapps, a torch battery for a block of cheese. Abandoned shops were also plundered. Folk and personal memories from Berlin in the winter of 1918 were strong. This was another generation of 'hamsters', storing food for an oncoming cata-strophe.

Starvation, however, was not the main danger. Many were simply not prepared for the shock of Russian revenge, however much propaganda they had heard. 'We had no idea what was going to happen,' the Lufthansa secretary Gerda Petersohn remembered. Relatives serving as soldiers on the Eastern Front had never mentioned what had been done to the Soviet population. And even when relentless propaganda made Berlin women aware of the danger of rape, many reassured themselves that although it must be a risk out in the countryside, here in the city it could hardly happen on an extensive scale in front of everybody.

Gerda, the nineteen-year-old who had brought back the Luftwaffe malt tablets from the looted railway wagon in Neukölln, saw a certain amount of another girl of her age who lived in the same building. She was called Carmen and had been a member of the Bund deutscher Mädel, the female equivalent of the Hitler Youth. Carmen had pin-up posters of Luftwaffe fighter aces on her bedroom wall and had wept copiously when Molders, the most famous of them all, had been killed.

On the night of 25 April, as the Red Army advanced into Neukölln, it was unusually quiet. The inhabitants of the building were sheltering in the cellar. They then felt the vibration from a tank coming down their street. Soon afterwards, a draught of fresh air which made the candles flicker told them that the door had been opened. The first Russian word they heard was '*Stoi!*' A soldier from Central Asia armed with a sub-machine gun came in and took their rings, watches and jewellery. Gerda's mother had hidden Gerda under a pile of laundry. Another young soldier came in later and indicated to Gerda's sister that he wanted her to come with him, but she put her child on her lap and looked down. The soldier told a man in the cellar to tell her to do as she was told, but the man pretended not to understand. The soldier wanted to take her into a little room adjacent to the cellar. He kept pointing, but she kept the baby on her lap and did not move. The baffled young soldier lost his nerve and left abruptly.

When the morning of 26 April came, they emerged to find that they had got off very lightly. They heard terrible stories of what had happened during the night. A butcher's daughter aged fourteen had been shot when she resisted. Gerda's sister-in-law, who lived a short distance away, had been gang-raped by soldiers and the whole family had decided to hang themselves. The parents died, but Gerda's sister-in-law was cut down by a neighbour and brought to the Petersohn apartment. They all saw the rope marks round her neck. The young woman was beside herself when she recognized her surroundings and realized that her parents had died and she had been saved.

The next night, the families in the house decided to avoid the cellar. They would all pack into one sitting room to find safety in numbers. Over twenty women and children assembled there. Frau Petersohn grabbed the chance to hide Gerda, her other daughter and her daughter-in-law under a table with a long cloth reaching almost to the floor. It was not long before Gerda heard Russian voices and then saw Red Army boots so close to the table that she could have reached out to touch them. The soldiers dragged three young women from the room. One of them was Carmen. Gerda heard her screams. She felt so strange because Carmen was screaming her name and she did not know why. The screams eventually dissolved into sobbing.

While the soldiers were still occupied with their victims, Frau Petersohn made up her mind. 'They'll be back,' she murmured to the three of them under the table. She told them to follow her and led them rapidly upstairs to the bomb-damaged top floor, where an old woman still lived. Gerda spent the night huddled on the balcony, determined to jump to her death if the Russians came for them. But their immediate worry was how to keep her sister's baby from crying. Gerda suddenly remembered the Luftwaffe malt tablets. Whenever the baby became restless, they slipped a malt tablet in her mouth. When dawn came, they saw that the baby's face was smeared with brown, but the tactic had worked.

Mornings were safe, with Soviet soldiers either sleeping off their debauches or returned to the fighting, so they crept back down to their own apartment. There, in a grotesque version of Goldilocks, they found that their beds had been used by the soldiers for their activities. The sisters also discovered their brother's Wehrmacht uniform laid out carefully on the floor and defecated upon.

Gerda sought out Carmen to try to offer some sort of sympathy, but also in the hope of discovering why she had screamed out her name again and again. The moment Carmen set eyes on her, Gerda saw a bitter hostility. Carmen's attitude immediately became clear. 'Why me and why not you?' That was why she had yelled her name. The two never spoke to each other again.

Although there appears to have been a fairly general pattern, the course of events when Soviet troops arrived was never predictable. In another district, frightened civilians heard a bang on the door of their bunker after the sound of fighting died away. Then a Red Army soldier armed with a sub-machine gun entered. '*Tag, Russki!*' he greeted them cheerily, and went away without even taking their watches. Another lot of soldiers two hours later were more aggressive. They grabbed Klaus Boeseler, a fourteen-year-old boy who was just over six foot one and had blond hair. '*Du SS!*' one of them shouted. It was more of a statement than a question. They seemed so determined to execute him that he was terrified. But the others in the cellar eventually managed to persuade the soldiers by sign language that he was in fact a schoolboy.

As a very tall boy, Boeseler was hungry the whole time. He had no compunction about slicing up a horse killed by a shell to take the meat home for his mother to preserve in vinegar. Soviet soldiers were amazed and impressed by the speed with which city-bred Berliners, who were not 'kulaks and landowners', managed to strip a dead horse to the bone. Sensing the Russian fondness for children, Boeseler took his three-year-old sister to visit a bivouac of Soviet soldiers nearby. The soldiers gave them a loaf, then added a slab of butter. The next day, they were given soup. But then he heard of cases of gang rape in the neighbourhood, so Boeseler hid his mother and a neighbour in the coal cellar for three days.

German standards of cleanliness suffered badly. Their clothes and skin felt impregnated with the dust from plaster and pulverized masonry, and there was no water to waste on washing. In fact, prudent Berliners had been boiling water to put in preserving jars, knowing that reliable drinking water would be the greatest need in the days ahead.

The few unevacuated hospitals which had remained in Berlin were so inundated with casualties that most newcomers were turned away. The situation was made even worse by the fact that wards were limited to the cellars. In the days of bombing, staff had been able to get the patients downstairs when the sirens went, but with constant artillery fire, there was no warning. One woman who went to offer her services saw chaos and 'wax-like faces wreathed in blood-stained bandages'. A French surgeon operating on fellow prisoners of war described how they had to work in a cellar on a wooden table, 'almost without antiseptic and with the instruments scarcely boiled'. There was no water to wash their surgical clothes and lighting depended on two bicycles with dynamos.

Because of the virtual impossibility of obtaining official help, many wounded soldiers and civilians were tended in the cellars of houses by mothers and girls. This was dangerous, however, because the Russians reacted to the presence of any soldier in a cellar as if the whole place were a defensive position. To avoid this, the women usually stripped the wounded of their uniforms, which they burned, and gave them spare clothes from upstairs. Another danger arose when members of the Volkssturm, on deciding to slip away home just before the Russians arrived, left behind the vast majority of their weapons and ammunition. Women who found any guns wasted no time in disposing of them. Word had got round that the Red Army was liable to execute all the inhabitants in a building where weapons were found.

The parish pump was once again the main place for exchanging information. Official news was unreliable. The *Panzerbär*, a news-sheet called the 'armoured bear' after the symbol of Berlin, claimed that towns such as Oranienburg had been retaken. Goebbels's propaganda ministry, or the '*Promi*' as Berliners called it, was reduced to distributing handbills now that the radio transmitters were in enemy hands. 'Berliner! Hold on. Wenck's army is marching to our relief. Just a few more days and Berlin will be free again.' With several Soviet armies approaching the centre of the city, fewer and fewer people were convinced by the notion of Berlin being freed by a single German army. Many, however, still clung to the idea of the Americans riding to their rescue, even though Stalin's encirclement of the city had put paid to any hope of that.

Colonel Sebelev, an engineer attached to the 2nd Guards Tank Army in Siemensstadt, in the north-west of the city, took a moment to write to his family. 'At the moment I am sitting with my officers on the fifth floor of a building, writing orders to units. Signallers and runners come and go constantly. We are moving towards the centre of Berlin. Gunfire, fires and smoke everywhere. Soldiers run from one building to another and creep through the courtyards carefully. Germans were shooting at our tanks from windows and doors, but General Bogdanov's tankists adopted a clever tactic. They are moving not in the middle of the streets, but on the pavements, and some of them are shooting with cannons and machine guns at the right side of the street and others at the left side and Germans are running away from windows and doors. In the courtyards of the houses the soldiers from the support services are handing out food from vehicles to the city's population, which is starving. The Germans have a starved and long-suffering look. Berlin is not a beautiful city, narrow streets, barricades everywhere, broken trams and vehicles. The houses are empty because everybody is in the basements. We all are happy here to know that you are already sowing grain. How happy I would be if I could sow potatoes, tomatoes, cucumbers, pumpkins and so forth. Goodbye, kisses and hugs. Your Pyotr.'

Sebelev did not mention that tactics had not been clever to begin with and losses were heavy. Zhukov's desperation for speed, which prompted him to send the two tank armies straight into the city, led to tanks driving in a line straight up the middle of a street. Even Chuikov's 8th Guards Army, proud of their street-fighting inheritance at Stalingrad, made many mistakes at first. The roles of course were completely reversed this time, with the Red Army as the attacker enjoying a huge superiority in armour and air power, and the Wehrmacht as the defender and ambusher.

The Waffen SS did not believe in standing behind the makeshift barricades erected close to street corners. They knew that these not very effective obstacles would be the first thing to be blasted by gunfire. It was all right to put riflemen at windows of the upper floors or on roofs, because tanks could not elevate their guns enough. But with the panzerfaust, they made their ambushes from basements and cellar windows. This was because the panzerfaust was very hard to fire accurately from above. The Hitler Youth copied the SS enthusiastically, and soon the Volkssturm – the ones who had seen service in the First World War and stayed at their posts – followed the same tactics. Red Army soldiers referred to the Hitler Youth and the Volkssturm as 'totals' because they were the product of 'total mobilization'. Wehrmacht officers called them the 'casserole' because they were a mixture of old meat and green vegetables.

Tank losses, especially in the 1st Guards Tank Army, prompted a rapid rethink of tactics. The first 'new tactic' was to cover each tank with sub-machine gunners who sprayed every window and aperture ahead as the vehicles advanced. But there were so many soldiers clinging to the tank that it could hardly traverse its turret. Then they went in again for festooning their vehicles with bedsprings and other metal to make the panzerfausts explode prematurely. But more and more they relied on heavy guns, especially 152mm and 203mm howitzers, to blast barricades and buildings over open sights. The 3rd Shock Army also used its anti-aircraft guns constantly against rooftops.

Infantry tactics were based largely on Chuikov's notes, evolved since Stalingrad and hurriedly updated after the storming of Poznan. He started from the precept that 'Offensive operations carried out by major formations as if in normal battle conditions stand no chance of success.' This was exactly how the two tank armies began. He rightly emphasized the need for careful reconnaissance, both the approach and the enemy's likely escape routes. Smoke or darkness should be used to cover the approach of infantry until they were within thirty metres of their objective, otherwise losses would be prohibitively high.

The assault groups of six to eight men should be backed by reinforcement groups and then by reserve groups, ready to deal with a counter-attack. The assault groups, as in Stalingrad days, were to be armed with 'grenades, sub-machine guns, daggers, and sharpened spades to be used as axes in hand-to-hand fighting'. The reinforcement groups needed to be 'heavily armed', with machine guns and anti-tank weapons. They had to have sappers equipped with explosives and pick-axes ready to blast through walls from house to house. The danger was that as soon as they opened a hole in the wall, a German soldier the other side would throw a grenade through first. But most Red Army men soon found that the panzerfausts abandoned by the Volkssturm offered the best means of 'flank progress'. The blast was enough to flatten anyone in the room beyond.

While some of the assault groups made their way from house to house on the ground, others progressed along the rooftops, and others made their way from cellar to cellar to take the panzerfaust ambushers in the side. Flame-throwers were used to terrible effect. Sappers also prepared sections of railway line with dynamite attached to it to act as shrapnel for the final attack.

The presence of civilians made no difference. The Red Army troops simply forced them out of the cellars at gunpoint and into the street, whatever the crossfire or shelling. Many Soviet officers, frustrated by the confusion, wanted to evacuate all German civilians by force, which was just what the German Sixth Army had attempted when fighting in Stalingrad. 'We didn't have time to distinguish who was who,' said one. 'Sometimes we just threw grenades into the cellars and passed on.' This was usually justified on the grounds that German officers were putting on civilian clothes and hiding with women and children. Yet civilian accounts show that any officer or soldier who wanted to hide in a cellar or shelter was forced to get rid of his weapon as well as his uniform. There were very few genuine cases of German troops hiding among civilians to strike the Red Army in the rear.

Chuikov urged a ruthless panache when house-clearing. 'Throw your grenade and follow up. You need speed, a sense of direction, great initiative and stamina because the unexpected will certainly happen. You will find yourself in a labyrinth of rooms and corridors all full of danger. Too bad. Chuck a grenade at every corner. Go forward. Fire bursts of machine-gun fire at any piece of ceiling which still remains. And when you get to the next room chuck in another grenade. Then clean it up with your sub-machine gun. Never waste a moment.'

This was all very well for experienced troops. But so many of the young officers who had graduated after short courses had no idea of how to train or to control their men in unfamiliar surroundings. And after the Oder battle and the relentless 'twenty-four-hour' advance ordered by Zhukov, most of the Soviet frontline troops were exhausted. Tiredness slowed their reactions dangerously. Mortar fuses were sometimes set incorrectly and the bomb exploded in the tube, while soldiers who tried to use German grenades often ended up disabling themselves and their comrades.

Self-inflicted casualties occurred on an even greater scale at army level. Despite the U-2 biplanes spotting for gun batteries, the artillery and katyusha batteries supporting one army often shelled another as they converged on approaching the centre. There were 'frequent cases of mutual firing at our own troops,' wrote General Luchinsky, the commander of the 28th Army supporting Rybalko's 3rd Guards Tank Army. And with all the smoke over the urban battlefield, the three different aviation armies attached to Zhukov and Konev's Fronts were frequently bombing other Red Army troops. The situation became particularly bad in the south of the city. The aviation regiments support-ing the 1st Ukrainian Front frequently attacked the 8th Guards Army. Chuikov made representations to Zhukov, demanding the withdrawal of the 'neighbours'.

The battle for Tempelhof aerodrome against the 8th Guards Army and the 1st Guards Tank Army continued through most of 26 April. When the *Müncheberg* Panzer Division counter-attacked, so few tanks were left that they had to operate singly, supported by small groups of infantry and Hitler Youth armed with panzerfausts. The survivors extricated themselves towards evening. Sturmbannführer Saalbach pulled back the remaining vehicles of the *Nordland* reconnaissance battalion to the Anhalter Bahnhof. The division's remaining armour, eight Tigers of the 'Hermann von Salza' battalion and several assault guns, was ordered to the Tiergarten.

The morning began with an intensive bombardment. 'Poor inner city,' wrote a woman diarist in Prenzlauerberg as the artillery thundered away. The shelling of the Klein Tiergarten was particularly heavy. Churned up by explosions, the park was hard to imagine as a favourite playground for children.

Chuikov and Katukov ordered their forces on towards the Belle-Allianceplatz – named after the battle of Waterloo and ironically defended by French SS – and the Anhalter Bahnhof, the marker separating the advance of the two Fronts. The rivalry with Konev's troops had become intense, though masked by jokes. 'Now we should be scared not of the enemy, but of our neighbours,' one of Chuikov's corps commanders said to Vasily Grossman. 'I've ordered that the burnt-out tanks should be used to block our neighbours from getting to the Reichstag. There's nothing more depressing in Berlin than learning about the successes of your neighbour.'

Chuikov did not take the matter so lightly. Over the next two days, he pushed his left flank across the front of the 3rd Guards Tank Army to head it off the axis which led to the Reichstag. He did not even warn Rybalko, so this almost certainly led to the slaughter of many of his own men under the artillery shells and rockets of the 1st Ukrainian Front.

*

Katyusha rockets – 'thunderbolts from the sky' – continued to be used as a psychological weapon as well as for area targets. Early on the morning of 26 April, Colonel Refior, the chief of staff of the defence of Berlin, was brusquely awoken from a snatched sleep in their headquarters on the Hohenzollerndamm by a rapid sequence of ranging shells. (The Russians called it 'framing'.) 'Old frontline hares', Refior noted, knew this to be the 'greeting' before a salvo of katyushas. And if their headquarters were now in katyusha range, it was time to move. General Weidling had already chosen the 'Bendlerblock', the old army headquarters on the Bendlerstrasse, where Colonel Count von Stauffenberg had been executed after the failure of the July plot. It possessed well-equipped air-raid shelters and was close to the Reich Chancellery, where Weidling was constantly summoned.

In the depths of the Bendlerblock, Weidling's staff had no idea whether it was day or night. They kept awake on coffee and cigarettes. Thanks to the generators, they had lighting the whole time, but the air was clammy and heavy. There they continued to deal with increasingly urgent calls for help from sector commanders, but there were no reserves.

That evening Weidling presented to Hitler his recommendations for a mass breakout from Berlin to avoid further destruction and loss of life. His plan was for the garrison, acting as Hitler's escort, to break out westwards and join up with the remains of Army Group Vistula. There would be a spearhead consisting of the remaining battle-worthy tanks, nearly forty of them, and the bulk of the combat divisions. This would be followed by the '*Führergruppe*', with Hitler and his Reich Chancellery staff, along with other '*Prominente*'. The rearguard would consist of a single reinforced division. The breakout should take place on the night of 28 April. When Weidling came to an end, Hitler shook his head. 'Your proposal is perfectly all right. But what is the point of it all? I have no intention of wandering around in the woods. I am staying here and I will fall at the head of my troops. You, for your part, will carry on with the defence.'

The futility of it all was summed up in the slogan painted on walls: 'Berlin stays German.' One of these had been crossed out and underneath was scrawled in Cyrillic, 'But I'm already here in Berlin, signed Sidorov.'

The Red Army was not merely in Berlin, it was already setting up a provisional administration to get essential services going again. Zhukov, still unaware of Beria's plan to have the NKVD running civilian affairs, had just appointed Colonel General Berzarin, the commander of the 5th Shock Army, as commandant of Berlin. Marshal Suvorov in the eighteenth century had insisted that the commander of the first army to enter a city became its commandant and the Red Army maintained the tradition. Chuikov's jealousy of his rival must have been intense.

Grossman visited Berzarin in his headquarters on 26 April. 'The commandant of Berlin,' he wrote in his notebook, 'is fat with sly, brown eyes and prematurely white hair. He is very clever, very balanced and crafty.' It was the 'creation of the world' that day. Bürgermeisters, directors of Berlin electricity, Berlin water, sewers, the U-Bahn, trams, gas supply, factory owners and public figures had been summoned. 'They all receive their appointments here in this office. Vice-directors become directors, chiefs of regional enterprises become magnates of national importance.' Grossman was fascinated by signs other than words: the 'shuffling of feet, greetings, whisperings'. Old German Communists from before the Nazis' rise to power appeared, hoping for an appointment. 'An old housepainter shows his [German Communist] Party card. He has been a Party member since 1920. Berzarin's officers show little reaction. They tell him, "Take a seat."'

Like the other Russians present, Grossman was taken aback when a bürgermeister, on being told to provide working parties to clear streets, asked, 'How much will the people be paid?' After the way Soviet citizens had been treated as slave labourers in Germany, the answer was obvious. 'Everyone here certainly seems to have a very strong idea of their rights,' observed Grossman. But German civilians received a shock the next day, 27 April, when Soviet troops rounded up 2,000 German women in the southern suburbs and marched them to Tempelhof aerodrome to clear the runways of shot-up machines. Red Army aviation wanted to be able to use it as a base within twenty-four hours.

During the withdrawal towards the centre, Sector Z, the battle intensified. Whenever Germans managed to knock out a Soviet tank with a panzerfaust, the local Soviet commander always tried to retaliate with a katyusha strike. But revenge with such an area weapon was akin to shooting hostages in response to a partisan attack.

A small panzerfaust group of the French SS were captured by Soviet troops. The French NCO claimed that they were forced labourers who had been press-ganged into uniform by the Germans when the Red Army launched its attack on the Oder. They were lucky to be believed. At that stage, Soviet troops did not know about SS tattoos.

That evening, one of the grotesque melodramas which so characterized the fall of the Third Reich took place. General Ritter von Greim, whom Hitler had summoned from Munich to take over command of the Luftwaffe from Göring, was carried into the bunker anteroom on a stretcher. He had been wounded in the leg by Soviet anti-aircraft fire. He was accompanied by his mistress, Hanna Reitsch, a test pilot and devotee of the Führer. Flying in a Fieseler Storch for the last leg of their extremely hazardous journey, they had been hit over the Grunewald. Hanna Reitsch, reaching around the wounded Greim's shoulders, had managed to land the small aircraft near the Brandenburg Gate. It was a feat requiring considerable bravery and skill. Yet that does not alter the fact that Hitler, by insisting on this symbolic handover, had nearly managed to kill the very man he wanted to promote to the supreme command of an organization which had effectively ceased to exist.

On the following day, 27 April, General Krebs followed the Nazi leaders who were deceiving the troops under his command. Although evasive on the question of negotiations, he claimed that 'the Americans could cross the ninety kilometres from the Elbe to Berlin in the shortest space of time and then everything would change for the better'.

Everyone there was obsessed with reinforcements, whatever their number or effectiveness. Mohnke was ecstatic when he told Krukenberg that a company of sailors had been flown in and had taken up position in the gardens of the Foreign Office on the Wilhelmstrasse. Krukenberg was more encouraged to hear that eight assault guns from the 503rd SS Heavy Panzer Battalion had been assigned to support the *Nordland*. Other reinforcements included a group of Latvian SS. This prompted Krukenberg to claim that soon the whole of Europe would be represented in their sector. Considering the fact that by 1945 half of the Waffen SS was not German, this was not such a remarkable fact. And when you force an international civil war upon the world, as the Communists and fascists had done between them by the unscrupulous manipulation of alternatives, then the downfall of Berlin was an unsurprising pyre for the remnants of the European extreme right.

Krukenberg's divisional headquarters were reduced to a subway carriage in the U-Bahn station Stadtmitte without any electric light and without a telephone. His men kept going only because they had stripped the grocery shops in the nearby Gendarmenmarkt. Their fighting strength now rested on the large quantities of panzerfausts from the improvised arsenal in the Reich Chancellery cellars. Short of other weapons and ammunition, the French, like many other troops, were using them in close-quarter house combat as well as in their official anti-tank role. Hauptssturmführer Pehrsson arrived with four armoured personnel carriers taken from the Red Army and two of the original half-tracks belonging to the *Nordland* to guard the Reich Chancellery. The others had been blown up as they ran out of fuel or broke down in the withdrawal from Neukölln.

In Sector Z, wounded soldiers were sent back to the dressing station set up in the cellars of the Adlon Hotel. SS soldiers were taken to another one in the Reich Chancellery cellars run by SS doctors and surgeons. There were nearly 500 wounded packed in there by the end of the battle. A bigger one, the Thomaskeller Lazarett, resembled a 'slaughterhouse'. Like the civilian hospitals, the military field hospitals lacked food and water, as well as anaesthetic.

The Soviet advance into Berlin was extremely uneven. In the north-west, the 47th Army, which had completed the encirclement of the city by meeting up with Konev's 4th Guards Tank Army, was now approaching Spandau. Its officers had no idea that the huge citadel there housed German research into the nerve gases Tabun and Sarin. It was also involved in fierce fighting on Gatow airfield, where Volkssturm and Luftwaffe cadets used the 88mm anti-aircraft guns and shot back from behind wrecked aircraft.

In the north, the 2nd Guards Tank Army had hardly advanced out of Siemensstadt, while the 3rd Shock Army had reached the northern barrier to the Tiergarten and Prenzlauerberg. The 3rd Shock Army had bypassed the immensely powerful Humboldthain flak bunker, which was left as a target for their heavy artillery and the bombers. Continuing in a clockwise direction, the 5th Shock Army, driving into the eastern districts, similarly bypassed the Friedrichshain bunker. The bulk of its strength was between the Frankfurterallee and the south bank of the Spree after its 9th Corps crossed into Treptow.

From the south, the 8th Guards Army and the 1st Guards Tank Army had reached and breached the Landwehr Canal on 27 April. This was the last major obstacle to the government district and less than two kilometres from the Reich Chancellery, even though all of Zhukov's armies were obsessed with Stalin's target of the Reichstag. In the south-west, the 3rd Guards Tank Army had just entered Charlottenburg, with a left-flanking hook through the Grunewald against the remains of the 18th Panzergrenadier Division.

Red Army troops reached Dahlem on 24 April, and the Kaiser Wilhelm Institute for Physics the next day. The fighting, with katyushas firing and tanks advancing amid the spacious villas and neat tree-lined streets, produced strange contrasts. The frontline troops were followed by the ubiquitous panje-wagons pulled by shaggy little ponies and even pack camels.

There is nothing to show that any commanders in Rybalko's army, or even Rybalko himself, had been warned of the Institute's significance, yet they must have been aware of the large force of NKVD troops and specialists who secured the complex off the Boltzmannstrasse within two days.

Since the one thing holding up Soviet attempts to replicate the Manhattan Project's research was the shortage of uranium, the importance which Stalin and Beria attached to securing research laboratories and their supplies was considerable. They also wanted German scientists capable of processing uranium. Beria's preparations for the Berlin operation had clearly been enormous. Colonel General Makhnev was in charge of the special commission. The large numbers of NKVD troops to secure the laboratories and uranium stores were directly supervised by no less a personage than General Khrulev, the chief of rear area operations for the whole of the Red Army. The chief NKVD metallurgist, General Avraami Zavenyagin, had set up a base on the edge of Berlin and scientists from the main team of researchers oversaw the movement of materials and the dismantling of laboratories.

The NKVD commission made its report. As well as all the equipment at the Kaiser Wilhelm Institute, they found '250kgs of metallic uranium; three tons of uranium oxide; twenty litres of heavy water'. The three tons of uranium oxide misdirected to Dahlem was a real windfall. There was a particular reason for speed, Beria and Malenkov reminded Stalin rather unnecessarily in a retrospective confirmation of action already carried out: the Kaiser Wilhelm Institute was 'situated in the territory of the future Allied zone'. 'Taking into account the extreme importance for the Soviet Union of all the above-mentioned equipment and materials,' they wrote, 'we request your decision on disassembling and evacuating equipment and other items from these enterprises and institutes back to the USSR.'

The State Committee for Defence accordingly authorized the 'NKVD Commission headed by Comrade Makhnev' to 'evacuate to the Soviet Union to Laboratory No. 2 of the Academy of Sciences and Special Metal Department of the NKVD all the equipment and materials and archive of the Kaiser Wilhelm Institute in Berlin'.

Makhnev's men also rounded up Professor Peter Thiessen and Dr Ludwig Bewilogua, who were flown to Moscow. But the major figures of the Kaiser Wilhelm Institute – Werner Heisenberg, Max von Laue, Gerlag von Weizsäcker and Otto Hahn, who had won the Nobel Prize for chemistry only a few months before – were beyond their grasp. They were earmarked by the British and taken back to be lodged at Farm Hall, their debriefing centre for German scientists in East Anglia.

Other less important laboratories and institutes were also stripped out and many more scientists were arrested and sent to a special holding pen in the concentration camp of Sachsenhausen. Professor Baron von Ardenne volunteered. He was persuaded by General Zavenyagin to write 'an application addressed to the Council of People's Commissars of the USSR that he wished to work with Russian physicists and place the Institute and himself at the disposal of the Soviet government'.

Beria and Kurchatov's scientists at last had some uranium to start work in earnest, and experts to process it, but the need for further supplies was desperate in their eyes. General Serov, the NKVD chief in Berlin, was ordered to concentrate on securing the uranium deposits in Czechoslovakia and, above all, in Saxony, south of Dresden. The presence of the uncompromising General George Patton's Third Army in the region must have caused the Soviet authorities considerable concern. It may also explain why they were so nervous about whether US forces would withdraw to the previously agreed occupation zones.

In Dahlem, some of Rybalko's officers visited Sister Kunigunde, the mother superior of Haus Dahlem, a maternity clinic and orphanage. She informed them that they had not hidden any German soldiers. The officers and their men behaved impeccably. In fact, the officers even warned Sister Kunigunde about the second-line troops following on behind. Their prediction proved entirely accurate, but there was no chance of escape. Nuns, young girls, old women, pregnant women and mothers who had just given birth were all raped without pity. One woman compared events in Dahlem to 'the horrors of the Middle Ages'. Others thought of the Thirty Years War.

The pattern, with soldiers flashing torches in the faces of women huddled in the bunkers to select their victims, appears to have been common to all the Soviet armies involved in the Berlin operation. This process of selection, as opposed to the immediate violence shown in East Prussia, indicates a definite change. By this stage Soviet soldiers treated German women much more as sexual spoils of war than as substitutes for the Wehrmacht on which to vent their rage.

Rape has often been defined by writers on the subject as an act of violence which has little to do with sex. But that is a definition from the victim's perspective. To understand the crime, however, one needs to see things from the perpetrator's point of view, especially in this second stage when unaggravated rape had succeeded the extreme onslaught of January and February. The soldiers concerned appear to have felt that they were satisfying a sexual need after all their time at the front. In this most soldier rapists did not demonstrate gratuitous violence, provided the woman did not resist. A third stage in the process, and even a fourth, developed in the weeks to come, as will be seen. But the basic point is that, in war, undisciplined soldiers without fear of retribution can rapidly revert to a primitive male sexuality, perhaps even the sort which biologists ascribe to a compulsion on the part of the male of the species to spread his seed as widely as possible. The difference between the incoherent violence in East Prussia and the notion of carnal booty in Berlin underlines the fact that there can be no all-embracing definition of the crime. On the other hand, it tends to suggest that there is a dark area of male sexuality which can emerge all too easily, especially in war, when there are no social and disciplinary restraints. Much also depends on the military culture of a particular national army. As the Red Army example shows, the practice of collective rape can even become a form of bonding process.

Soviet political officers still talked of 'violence under the pretext of revenge'. 'When we broke into Berlin,' the political department of the 1st Belorussian Front reported, 'some of the troops indulged in looting and violence towards civilians. Political officers tried to control this. They organized meetings devoted to such topics as "the honour and dignity of the Red Army warrior", "a looter is the worst enemy of the Red Army" and "how to understand correctly the problem of taking revenge".' But the idea of controlling their troops through political exhortation, particularly when the Party line had suddenly changed, was doomed to failure.

Germans were deeply shocked by the lack of discipline within the Red Army and the inability of officers to control their men, except in extreme cases by shooting them on the spot. All too often, women encountered total indifference or amusement that they should attempt to complain about rape. 'That? Well, it certainly hasn't done you any harm,' said one district commandant in Berlin to a group of women who had come to request protection from repeated attacks. 'Our men are all healthy.' Unfortunately, many of them were not free from disease, as women soon found to their even greater cost.

22

Fighting in the Forest

'Who would ever have thought,' noted a battalion commander of the *Scharnhorst* Division as they advanced to Beelitz, 'that it would be just a day's march from the Western Front to the Eastern Front! It says everything about our situation.'

General Wenck's XX Corps had started its attack westwards on 24 April to break through to meet the Ninth Army encircled in the forests beyond Konev's supply lines. That evening, the *Theodor Körner* Division of Reich Labour Service youths attacked General Yermakov's 5th Guards Mechanized Corps near Treuenbrietzen. On the next day, the *Scharnhorst* Division approached Beelitz. They had no idea of what lay ahead as they moved through a mixture of thick young plantations and mature, well-spaced pine forest. The operation, observed the battalion commander, 'had the character of an armed reconnaissance'. A few kilometres before Beelitz, they came upon the hospital complex at Heilstätten.

The nurses and patients, who had been looted very thoroughly the day before by Soviet troops and liberated slave labourers, heard artillery. Nobody knew where this battle was coming from. A shell hit one of the blocks. The children were taken down into the cellars. The nurses asked each other whether this could be the Americans arriving. Later, they suddenly saw German troops arriving from the west in skirmishing formation, dashing forwards from tree to tree. Two of the nurses ran outside towards them, screaming, 'Blast the Russians away!' As the battle intensified, the director of the hospital, Dr Potschka, decided to make contact with the Americans on the Elbe. The Swiss clearly could not help them.

The battle for Beelitz continued for several days. In the course of the fighting and the earlier outrages, seventy-six civilians were killed, including fifteen children. 'It was fought with great bitterness,' the battalion commander of the *Scharnhorst* wrote, 'and no prisoners were taken.' He and his men were appalled when the Soviets captured a house in which all their wounded comrades were lying in the cellar. The young soldiers – some of them were so young that civilians in Beelitz referred to them as '*Kindersoldaten*' – suffered 'tank fright' on first encountering T-34 and Stalin tanks. But within a couple of days confidence returned when four Stalin tanks were knocked out with panzerfausts. Peter Rettich, the battalion commander, hailed his young soldiers' 'fantastic acts of bravery' and their 'dedication' and then added that it was 'a crying shame and a crime to throw such boys into this all-destructive hell'.

On 28 April, the 3,000 wounded and sick children were loaded by men of the *Ulrich von Hutten* Division on to a shuttle of goods trains which took them slowly off towards Barby. There the Kinderklinik was re-established and the Americans accepted the wounded as prisoners of war. Wenck, however, had set the Twelfth Army more important missions. One was the drive up towards Potsdam with the bulk of the *Hutten* Division to open up an escape corridor. The other was to help the Ninth Army save itself.

The German troops in the huge Spree forest south-east of Berlin represented an unwieldy mixture of mangled divisions and terrified civilians fleeing the Red Army. The 80,000 men had come together from different directions and different armies. The bulk were from General Busse's Ninth Army – XI SS Panzer Corps on the Oderbruch and V SS Mountain Corps south of Frankfurt. The Frankfurt garrison, as Busse had been hoping, also managed to escape to join them. They were joined from the south by V Corps, which had formed the northern flank of the Fourth Panzer Army until cut off and forced back by Konev's drive on Berlin.*

* Soviet sources claim that Busse's force in the forest amounted to 200,000 men, with 300 tanks and 2,000 guns, a preposterous exaggeration for propaganda purposes. One detailed US Army report, however, puts the figures even lower, at around 40,000.

Busse, having consulted with General Wenck, was determined to break out due westwards through the tall pine forests south of Berlin. He would join up with the Twelfth Army, and both would withdraw to the Elbe. Busse's main problem was that his rearguard was tied down in constant battles with Zhukov's forces, and he warned Wenck that his army was 'pushing to the west like a caterpillar'. Neither he nor Wenck intended to waste any more lives by following Hitler's increasingly hysterical orders to attack up towards Berlin. Busse, shortly after midnight on 25 April, had been given authority 'to decide for himself on the best direction of attack'. From then on, he adopted a Nelsonian tactic of refusing to acknowledge most signals, although in many cases radio communications genuinely broke down.

His men and the civilians who had sought refuge with them had virtually no food left. Vehicles were kept moving until they ran out of fuel or broke down and then they were destroyed or cannibalized for spare parts. He did, however, have thirty-one tanks left – half a dozen Panthers from the *Kurmark*, the remains of General Hans von Luck's 21st Panzer Division, and around ten King Tigers from the 502nd SS Heavy Panzer Battalion. These he hoped to use as his spearhead to break through the rear of Konev's armies attacking Berlin. Their fuel tanks were topped up by siphoning from trucks abandoned by the side of the road. His remaining artillery would fire an opening barrage with their last shells, then blow up their guns.

Busse's men were encircled in the pattern of lakes and forest southeast of Fürstenwalde by troops from both the 1st Belorussian Front and Konev's 1st Ukrainian Front. On the afternoon of 25 April, Zhukov sent his forces into the attack from the north and east. They included the 3rd Army, the 2nd Guards Cavalry Corps, which was well adapted to forest fighting, the 33rd Army and the 69th Army.

Konev had realized, after studying the map, that the Germans had little choice for their breakout. They would have to cross the Berlin–Dresden autobahn south of the series of lakes starting at Teupitz. Konev reacted rapidly, albeit rather late in the day. On 25 April, Gordov's 3rd Guards Army was rushed into positions close to the Berlin–Dresden autobahn 'to block all the forest roads leading from east to west'. They chopped down tall pine trees to form tank barriers. But Gordov did not manage to occupy the southern part of his sector. And although the 28th Army reinforced the area east of Baruth as ordered, a slight gap remained between the two armies.

On the morning of 26 April, Busse's vanguard, advancing through Halbe, happened to find the weak point between the two armies. They crossed the autobahn and reached the Baruth–Zossen road, which was the supply line to Rybalko in Berlin. General Luchinsky, to avert the danger, even had to send the 50th and 96th Guards Rifle Divisions into a counter-attack 'without information about the situation'. The fighting was chaotic, but heavy bombing and strafing from the 2nd Air Army and relentless counter-attacks on the ground forced many of the Germans back across the autobahn into the Halbe forest. The panzer crews had found that their tracks did not grip on the sandy soil of the pine forest and they were forced to avoid the forest roads because of the constant air attacks.

The group that managed to cross both the autobahn and the Baruth–Zossen road was spotted by a Luftwaffe aircraft. This was reported to Army Group Vistula and to General Jodl. Hitler was furious when he heard that they were heading westwards, but he still could not believe that Busse would dare to disobey him. A signal was sent that night via Jodl. 'The Führer has ordered that concentric attacks of Ninth and Twelfth Armies must not only serve to save the Ninth Army but principally to save Berlin.' Further signals were more explicit: 'The Führer in Berlin expects that the armies will do their duty. History and the German people will despise every man who in these circumstances does not give his utmost to save the situation and the Führer.' Hitler's one-way concept of loyalty was perfectly revealed. The signal was repeated several times that night and the following day. There was no reply from the forest.

During that night and the next day, 27 April, the Germans renewed their attack along two axes: in the south from Halbe through towards Baruth, and in the north from Teupitz. In the north, several thousand Germans supported by tanks drove a wedge into the 54th Guards Rifle Division, captured Zesch am See and surrounded part of the 160th Rifle Regiment. In the south, the thrust towards Baruth encircled the 291st Guards Rifle Regiment under Lieutenant Colonel Andryushchenko in

Radeland, where they seized attics and basements and fought until rescued by the 150th Guards Rifle Regiment from Baruth. Once again, the Germans 'suffered very heavy losses'.

This is the tidy version of events – the staff officer's summary, trying to produce order out of chaos. But within the forest, in and around Halbe especially, the reality of the battle was appalling, mainly due to Soviet artillery and air bombardment.

'If the first attempts to break out through the encirclement succeeded, they were immediately destroyed by Russian aircraft and artillery,' Major Diehl, the commander of the 90th Regiment in the 35th SS Police Grenadier Division, told his interrogators when captured. 'The losses were huge. One literally could not raise one's head and I was absolutely unable to conduct the battle. All I could do was lie under a tank with my adjutant and look at the map.'

Men with chest and stomach wounds lay bleeding to death. Most of the injuries came from wood splinters, as in an eighteenth-century battle at sea. The Soviet tank crews and artillery deliberately aimed to explode their shells high in the trees. For those below there was little protection. Digging trenches in the sandy soil filled with tree roots was an impossible task, even for those who still had spades. Some men in their desperation for shelter tried to dig frantically with their helmets or rifle butts, but they could achieve little more than a shallow shell-scrape, which was no protection from the splinters.

Air and artillery bombardments in such conditions produced a panic even among experienced soldiers. When Soviet reconnaissance or ground attack aircraft appeared overhead, those German soldiers riding on the vehicle began firing at them wildly with sub-machine guns and rifles. Any wounded or exhausted men on foot who collapsed in the path of armoured vehicles or trucks were simply run over by wheels or crushed by tank tracks.

As the battle continued in that last week of April, there were few front lines in the expanse of forest. Skirmishes were deadly, with a tank suddenly surprising an enemy in enfilade down a fire-break or ride. A Tiger and a Panther, followed by half-tracks, all covered with exhausted soldiers clinging on to the outside, were fired at by a Soviet tank. Everyone tried to fire back at once in the confusion. The infantrymen on the outsides of the tanks had to jump as the turret traversed. But the Soviet tank was faster. Its next shell hit one of the half-tracks, which happened to be loaded with cans of spare fuel. It exploded in a ball of flame, setting light to the forest around.

Constant smoke from burning pine trees drifted through the forest. Although Soviet commanders denied it, their artillery and aviation regiments certainly seemed to be using phosphorous or other incendiary projectiles. Horses towing supply carts or limbers and guns were terrified and bolted easily. The smoke also greatly reduced visibility in the already gloomy light amid the tall, straight trunks like cathedral columns. There was a constant noise of men calling to each other, hoping to make contact with their group. Despite all the attempts to issue orders to recognizable formations, the different army corps had mingled into an incoherent mass, with Wehrmacht and SS trudging uneasily alongside each other. Mutual suspicion had greatly increased. The SS claimed that army officers refused to pick up their wounded, but there was little sign of SS officers doing anything for Wehrmacht soldiers, except crush them under their tracks if they were in the way. The army's resentment of the SS as an alien organization rose very close to the surface. There were apparently also SS women, armed and in black uniforms, riding on the Tiger tanks.

After the first breakout failed, groups tried to slip through in different directions. One detachment came across a Soviet artillery position which had been stormed by half-tracks the day before. They crossed the autobahn and found dead Soviet soldiers still in their foxholes. Like the other groups, they continued on through the forests towards the rendezvous round Kummersdorf, which the first breakthrough group had almost reached. After the autobahn, the most dangerous part was crossing the Baruth–Zossen road, defended by another line of Soviet rifle divisions and artillery.

On the night of 28 April, another determined attempt at a mass breakout from the Halbe area was made. In desperate fighting, the Germans managed to smash the line held by the 50th Guards Rifle Division. 'For this they paid in heavy losses,' wrote General Luchinsky. Konev, determined that the rest should be crushed, reinforced the flanks. Trees were felled across tracks leading westwards. Each rifle division set up lines of anti-tank guns hidden behind fire-breaks or tracks, as if they were engaged in a gigantic boar shoot. Rifle regiments, supported by small tank detachments, attacked into the forest east of the autobahn.

Busse's men were spread over a wide area, with large groups around Halbe, and others stretching most of the way back to Storkow, where the rearguard still held out against Zhukov's forces. The Soviet attacks were designed to break up Busse's forces into different pockets. During almost all hours of daylight, Soviet U-2 biplanes flew low over the tree-tops, trying to spot fugitive groups for the artillery and aviation to attack. Altogether, the air divisions supporting the 1st Ukrainian Front flew '2,459 attack missions and 1,683 bombing sorties'.

For the Germans in the forest, without maps or compasses, it was almost impossible to find their way. The smoke and the trees made it hard even to see the sun to estimate where west might lie. Most of the exhausted soldiers simply trudged along the sandy paths, leaderless and lost. There was great resentment against the 'gentlemen of the staff' in their clean uniforms, driven in their Kübelwagen vehicles, and apparently not picking up any of the wounded or those who had collapsed. All around crossing points of roads there was 'a patchwork quilt of corpses, grey-green corpses'. Six soldiers from the 36th SS Grenadier Division commanded by Major General Oskar Dirlewanger, infamous for his role in the suppression of both risings in Warsaw, surrendered despite the risk of execution. 'It's already been five days since we've seen an officer,' one of them said. 'We feel that the war will end very soon, and the stronger this feeling becomes, the more we don't want to die.' It was rare for the SS to surrender. As far as most of them were concerned, capture meant a 'shot in the back of the neck' or a Siberian camp.

A terrible, one-sided battle developed round the large village of Halbe during 28 and 29 April as Soviet forces attacked from the south with katyushas and artillery. Many of the young Wehrmacht soldiers were shaking with fear and 'literally shitting themselves', according to Hardi Buhl, a villager. The local inhabitants were sheltering in their cellars, and when these terrified boy soldiers sought safety there too, they gave them clothes. But SS soldiers, on realizing what was happening, tried to stop it with reprisals. Hardi Buhl was with his family in their cellar, which was packed with other families and soldiers – some forty people in all – when an SS man appeared with a panzerfaust, which he aimed at the cowering inmates. The explosion in such a confined space would have killed them all. But before he fired, a Wehrmacht soldier in the corner nearest the stairs, who had been hard to see in the gloom, shot him in the back of the neck. There were other reports of shooting between SS and Wehrmacht around Halbe, but they are hard to verify.

Another attempt to break out westwards was made from Halbe by the central group. Siegfried Jürgs, a young officer cadet with Fahnenjunker Regiment 1239, described in his diary what he saw from his position on the leading tank. Wounded, whom nobody helped, were left screaming by the side of the track. 'I never suspected that three hours later, I would be one of them.' As they attacked a Soviet blocking detachment, he had jumped down from the tank with the other infantry to take up position in the ditch. But then a mortar bomb exploded and he was pierced through the back by a large fragment of shrapnel. Another explosion left him with shrapnel in his shoulder, chest and again in his back. Jürgs was luckier than the wounded he had seen earlier. He was picked up by a truck a number of hours later, but these vehicles were overloaded with wounded and there were screams of pain from the back as they lurched and bumped in and out of potholes on the forest tracks. Those too badly wounded to be moved were left to suffer where they lay. Few had any strength left to bury the dead. At best bodies were rolled into a ditch or shell crater and some sandy soil thrown over them.

On forest tracks and roads, vehicles burned and horses lay dead in their traces, while others still twitched and thrashed in pain. The ground was littered with abandoned weapons and helmets, prams, handcarts and suitcases. Halbe itself was described by eyewitnesses as a vision of hell through war. 'Tanks rolled down the Lindenstrasse,' the seventeen-year-old Erika Menze recorded. 'They were covered with wounded soldiers. One of the wounded soldiers fell off the back of one. The following tank crushed him completely and the next tank after that drove over the large pool of blood. Of the soldier himself, there remained no trace.' Outside the bakery, the pavement was literally covered with corpses. There was no space between them. 'The heads were a yellowish grey, squashed flat, the hands a grey-black. Only wedding rings glimmered gold and silver.'

*

Fewer and fewer vehicles were left each day – several tanks, eight-wheeler armoured reconnaissance vehicles and some half-tracks. The vast majority of the soldiers were on their feet. On 29 April after dawn, the rain stopped and the sun came out a little. It was enough to get a rough idea of direction.

Survivors remember moments which seemed so unreal that they wondered afterwards if they had dreamed them in their exhaustion. Near Mückendorf, an officer cadet threw himself to the ground like the other soldiers with him when a hidden sub-machine gunner to their flank opened fire on them. They began firing back into the underbrush, unable to distinguish a target. Suddenly, two young SS women in black uniforms and armed with pistols appeared. 'Get up!' they screamed at them. 'Attack, you cowards!' At the end of what proved a very confused skirmish, there was absolutely no sign of the two 'fanatics'.

The writer Konstantin Simonov happened to be on his way to Berlin in a jeep coming up the autobahn just after the main battle. On the stretch south of Teupitz, he saw a sight that he said he would never forget. 'In that place, there was rather thick forest on both sides of the autobahn, half coniferous, half deciduous, already becoming green. A cross-cutting, not wide, led through the forest on both sides of the motorway, and one wasn't able to see its ends . . . [it was] packed with something incredible: a terrible jam of cars, trucks, tanks, armoured cars, vehicles, ambulances, all of them not only pushed closely against one another, but literally jammed over one another, overturned, standing on end, upset, breaking the surrounding trees. In this mess of metal, wood and something unidentifiable was a dreadful mash of tortured human bodies. And all this went on along the cutting, into infinity. In the surrounding forest – corpses, corpses, corpses, mixed with, I suddenly noted, ones who were still alive. There were wounded people lying on greatcoats and blankets, sitting leaning against trees, some in bandages, others still without any. There were so many of them that apparently nobody had yet managed to do anything about them.' Some even lay on the edge of the autobahn, which was half-blocked by debris and covered in oil, petrol and blood. One of the officers with him explained that this group had been 'caught by the massed fire of several regiments of heavy artillery and katyushas'.

Soviet political departments were working hard all this time to persuade survivors to surrender. A quarter of a million leaflets were dropped over the forest. Loudspeakers boomed messages pre-recorded by 'anti-fascist' German prisoners. And Soviet soldiers shouted through the trees, '*Woina kaputt. Domoi. Woina kaputt!*' – 'The war's over. Time to go home. The war's over!' Meanwhile, the political department of the 1st Ukrainian Front stiffened its men's determination with the message, 'The remains of the destroyed German hordes are wandering in the forests like wild beasts and will try to reach Berlin at any cost. But they won't pass.' Most of them did not. Close to 30,000 men lie buried in the cemetery at Halbe and every year scores more bodies are discovered out in the forest. In June 1999, the Ninth Army's Enigma machine was also found in a shallow grave beside the autobahn. Nobody knows for sure how many refugees died with the soldiers, but it could have been as many as 10,000. At least 20,000 Red Army soldiers died too. Most are buried in a cemetery on the Baruth–Zossen road, but scores of their bodies too are still being found deep in the woods.

The most astonishing part of the story is not the numbers who died or were forced to surrender, but the 25,000 soldiers and several thousand civilians who succeeded in getting through three lines of Soviet troops to reach Wenck's army round Beelitz. (Marshal Konev refused to accept that 'more than 3,000–4,000' eluded his forces.) There, between the forest and the Elbe, where safety lay with the Americans on the far bank, they were to face many more swings between hope and despair in the last days of the war.

At the time of the main battle round Halbe, Army Group Vistula headquarters decided that it must have lost all contact with General Busse. A Fieseler Storch light aircraft was sent with an officer to make contact, but this attempt failed utterly. The Ninth Army was on its own, thus confirming the collapse of Army Group Vistula as a coherent entity.

General Hasso von Manteuffel's Third Panzer Army was already doomed once Rokossovsky's 2nd Belorussian Front broke through across the lower Oder. General Heinrici gave Manteuffel permission to withdraw westwards into Mecklenburg, but deliberately avoided informing Field Marshal Keitel or General Krebs in the Führer bunker, because this was in direct defiance of Hitler's order.

Rokossovsky's advance westwards between Berlin and the Baltic forced Heinrici and his staff to abandon their headquarters at Hassleben, near Prenzlau. On their withdrawal, they passed close to Himmler's retreat of Hohenlychen. There they saw a Hitler Youth battalion with an average age of fourteen. The boys, staggering under the weight of their weapons and packs, were trying to put a brave face on it. One staff officer spoke to their commander, saying it was a crime 'to send these children against a battle-hardened enemy', but this did no good. The Third Reich, in its death throes, revealed its frenzied rage against both common sense and common humanity.

Heinrici, having given Manteuffel permission to withdraw, knew that it would not be long before he heard from the two chief 'gravediggers of the German army'. Field Marshal Keitel, on discovering what had happened, telephoned Heinrici on 29 April, accusing him of 'disobedience and unsoldierly weakness'. He told him that he was relieved of his command forthwith. Keitel tried to appoint General von Manteuffel as Heinrici's successor, but he refused. General Jodl rang not long afterwards. In his coldest manner, he also accused Heinrici of cowardice and weak, incompetent leadership. Heinrici was ordered to report to OKW's new headquarters. His aides, fearing that he would be executed or forced to commit suicide like Rommel, begged him to spin out his journey. He followed their advice and the end of the war saved him.

23

The Betrayal of the Will

During the withdrawal into the centre of Berlin, the SS execution squads went about their hangman's work with an increased urgency and cold fanaticism. Around the Kurfürstendamm, SS squads entered houses where white flags had appeared and shot down any men they found. Goebbels, terrified of the momentum of collapse, described these signs of surrender as a 'plague bacillus'. Yet General Mummert, the commander of the *Müncheberg* Panzer Division, ordered the SS and Feldgendarmerie squads out of his sector round the Anhalter Bahnhof and Potsdamerplatz. He threatened to shoot executioners on the spot.

The conditions for those involved in the fighting became progressively worse. German troops could seldom get near a water pump. They had to quench their thirst, exacerbated by the smoke and dust, with water from canals. There were also more and more cases of nervous breakdowns from the combination of exhaustion and constant artillery fire. The number of wounded in the Anhalter bunker had grown so much that young women had made a Red Cross flag, using sheets and lipsticks. This was a wasted effort. Even if the Soviet artillery observers had seen the Red Cross symbol through the smoke and masonry dust, they would not have diverted their battery fire. A bunker was a bunker. The fact that it contained civilians was irrelevant. Numbers inside were diminishing rapidly, however, as women and children escaped along the U-Bahn and S-Bahn tunnels during the night of 27 April. Troops from the 5th Shock Army and the 8th Guards Army were literally at the door.

The 5th Shock Army, advancing from the east on the north side of the Landwehr Canal, had fought back the remnants of the *Nordland* and the *Müncheberg* from Belle-Allianceplatz and carried on to the Anhalter Bahnhof. The 61st Rifle Division of the 28th Army also arrived there from a different direction. The 5th Shock Army then found the 8th Guards Army attacking from the south across the canal into their left rear flank. The commander of the 301st Rifle Division, Colonel Antonov, immediately called in his corps commander, General Rosly. They at once set off in a jeep. 'Rosly, who is usually very calm, looked worried,' wrote Antonov. 'He thought the situation over and said, "How on earth can we get them back over the Landwehr Canal? Don't let your order of battle get mixed up with the Guards. Continue advancing along the Wilhelmstrasse and the Saarlandstrasse. Storm Gestapo headquarters, the aviation ministry and the Reich Chancellery."' Antonov did not waste time, but it took Zhukov's headquarters nearly thirty hours to sort out the muddle and establish new boundaries between the different armies. Soon the majority of Konev's troops were pulled out of Berlin – 'like a nail,' they said, to emphasize their resentment at being denied the prize – and diverted towards Prague.

Also by 28 April, troops of the 3rd Shock Army, advancing from the northern districts, were in sight of the Siegessäule column in the Tiergarten. Red Army soldiers nicknamed it the 'tall woman' because of the statue of winged victory on the top. The German defenders were now reduced to a strip less than five kilometres in width and fifteen in length. It ran from Alexanderplatz in the east to Charlottenburg and the Reichssportsfeld in the west, from where Artur Axmann's Hitler Youth detachments desperately defended the bridges over the Havel. Weidling's artillery commander, Colonel Wöhlermann, gazed around in horror from the gun platform at the top of the vast concrete Zoo flak tower. 'One had a panoramic view of the burning, smouldering and smoking great city, a scene which again and again shook one to the core.' Yet General Krebs still pandered to Hitler's belief that Wenck's army was about to arrive from the south-west.

To keep resistance alive Bormann, like Goebbels and Ribbentrop, spread the false rumour of a deal with the Western Allies. 'Stand fast, fight fanatically,' he had ordered Gauleiters early in the morning of 26 April. 'We are not giving up. We are not surrendering. We sense some developments in policy abroad. Heil Hitler! Reichsleiter Bormann.' The lie was soon underlined by the reaction of Hitler and Goebbels to Himmler's attempts to seek a genuine cease-fire with the western powers.

Truman and Churchill had immediately informed the Kremlin of the approach through Count Bernadotte. 'I consider your proposed reply to Himmler . . . absolutely correct,' Stalin replied to Truman on 26 April. Nobody in the bunker had any inkling of what was afoot, and yet a general suspicion of betrayal had certainly gripped Bormann. On the night of Friday 27 April, he wrote in his diary, 'Himmler and Jodl stop the divisions that we are throwing in. *We* will fight and we will die with our Führer, to whom we will remain devoted until the grave. Many are going to act on the basis of "*higher* motives". They are sacrificing their Führer. Phooee! What swine. They have lost any honour. Our Reich Chancellery is turning into ruins. "The world is now hanging by a thread." The Allies are demanding unconditional surrender. This would mean a betrayal of the Fatherland. Fegelein has degraded himself. He tried to run away from Berlin in civilian clothes.' Bormann rapidly distanced himself from his close companion.

Hitler had suddenly noticed Hermann Fegelein's absence early in the afternoon at the situation conference. Bormann, probably from their mutual bragging in the sauna, knew of the apartment in Charlottenburg which he used for his affairs. A group of Hitler's Gestapo bodyguards were sent to bring him back. They found Fegelein, apparently drunk, with a mistress. His bags, containing money, jewels and false passports, were packed ready for departure. He insisted on ringing the bunker and demanded to speak to his sister-in-law, but Eva Braun, shocked that he too had tried to desert her beloved Führer, refused to intervene. She did not believe him when he claimed that he was only trying to leave to be with Gretl, who was about to give birth. Fegelein was brought back under close arrest. He was held in a locked room in the Reich Chancellery cellar.

On 28 April, in the middle of the afternoon, Hitler was told of a report on Stockholm radio that Himmler had been in touch with the Allies. The idea that '*der treue Heinrich*' could be attempting to make a deal seemed ludicrous, yet Hitler had begun to suspect the SS after Steiner's failure to relieve Berlin. He rang Dönitz, who spoke to Himmler. The Reichsführer SS denied it completely. But that evening, Lorenz, Hitler's press attaché, arrived with a copy of confirmation of the story from Reuters. All Hitler's resentments and suspicions exploded. He was white with anger and shock. Fegelein was interrogated, apparently by Gruppenführer Müller, the chief of the Gestapo. He admitted that he had known of Himmler's approach to Bernadotte. Freytag von Loringhoven saw Fegelein being marched upstairs under heavy SS escort. All badges of rank, his Knight's Cross and other insignia had been torn from his uniform. Fegelein's swagger had disappeared. He was executed in the Reich Chancellery garden. Hitler was now convinced that the SS had been seething with plots against him, just like the army the year before.

Hitler went straight to the bunker room where the newly promoted Marshal Ritter von Greim lay nursing his wounded leg. He ordered him to fly out of Berlin to organize Luftwaffe attacks on the Soviet tanks which had reached the Potsdamerplatz and to ensure that Himmler did not go unpunished. 'A traitor must never succeed me as Führer,' he shouted at Greim. 'You must go out to ensure that he does not!' No time was wasted. Hanna Reitsch was summoned to help Greim up the concrete staircase on his crutches. An armoured vehicle was waiting to take them to an Arado 96 trainer, specially ordered from outside and now ready for take-off near the Brandenburg Gate. Soviet soldiers from the 3rd Shock Army who had just fought their way into the Tiergarten stared in amazement as the aircraft took off before their eyes. Their immediate fear, on recovering their military reactions, was that Hitler had escaped them. But the rather tardy explosion of anti-aircraft and machine-gun fire failed to find the target. Ritter von Greim and Hanna Reitsch escaped.

This *mouvementé* night in the Führer bunker was not over. It held an even greater surprise. Adolf Hitler proceeded to marry the sister-in-law of the man he had just had executed. Goebbels had brought to Hitler's private sitting room a Herr Walter Wagner, an official of the Gau of Berlin, who had the authority to perform a civil wedding ceremony. Wagner, bemused and overawed by his responsibilities, had come from guard duty in his brown Nazi Party uniform and Volkssturm armband. Hitler was in his usual tunic. Eva Braun wore a long black silk taffeta dress, one which he had often complimented her upon. Its colour was rather suitable in the circumstances. A very nervous Wagner then had to ask both the Führer and Fräulein Braun whether they were of pure

Aryan descent and free from hereditary diseases. The proceedings took no more than a couple of minutes under the wartime formula of simple declarations. Then came the signing of the register, with Goebbels and Bormann as witnesses. Eva Braun began to write her usual name, but stopped, scratched out the 'B' and corrected the entry to '*Eva Hitler, geb[orene]. Braun.*' Hitler's signature was totally illegible, his hand was shaking so much.

The married couple emerged into the anteroom corridor which served as the bunker conference room. Generals and secretaries congratulated them. They then retired to the little sitting room for a wedding breakfast with champagne for the new Frau Hitler, as she now insisted on being called by servants. She had finally been rewarded for her loyalty in a world of betrayal. They were later joined by Bormann, Goebbels and his wife, Magda, and the two remaining secretaries, Gerda Christian and Traudl Junge. Hitler took Traudl Junge away to another room, where he dictated his political and personal testaments. She sat there in nervous excitement, expecting to hear at last a profound explanation of the great sacrifice's true purpose. But instead a stream of political clichés, delusions and recriminations poured forth. He had never wanted war. It had been forced on him by international Jewish interests. The war, 'in spite of all setbacks,' he claimed, 'will one day go down in history as the most glorious and heroic manifestation of a people's will to live'.

Grand Admiral Dönitz, the head of the Kriegsmarine, was appointed Reich President. The Army, the Luftwaffe and the SS had either failed or betrayed him. The loyal Dönitz – 'Hitlerjunge Quex' – had emerged in front of schemers. Yet Goebbels was appointed Reich Chancellor, while 'my most faithful Party comrade, Martin Bormann' became Party Chancellor as well as executor of his private will. Hitler clearly wanted to continue his policy of divide and rule from beyond the grave, even on the most spectral administration ever assembled. Perhaps the most bizarre appointment was for Gauleiter Karl Hanke to replace Himmler as Reichsführer SS. Hanke, a pre-war lover of Magda Goebbels, was still trapped in Breslau, directing his own provincial performance of enforced suicide on a city. Goebbels, meanwhile, wrote his own will. He believed it his duty – 'in the delirium of treachery which surrounds the Führer in these most critical days of the war' – to refuse Hitler's order to leave Berlin and 'stay with him unconditionally until death'. One of the copies of Hitler's testament was sent by a trusted officer to Field Marshal Schörner, the new commander-in-chief of the army. The covering letter from General Burgdorf confirmed that 'the shattering news of Himmler's treachery' was for Hitler the final blow.

The rather sedate wedding party deep in the bunker was overtaken by much wilder behaviour closer to the surface. When Traudl Junge was finally released from her typing at around 4 a.m. on Sunday 29 April, and the Führer and Frau Hitler retired, she went upstairs to find some food for the Goebbels children. The scenes which she encountered, not far from where the wounded lay in the Reich Chancellery's underground field hospital, shocked her deeply. 'An erotic fever seemed to have taken possession of everybody. Everywhere, even on the dentist's chair, I saw bodies locked in lascivious embraces. The women had discarded all modesty and were freely exposing their private parts.' SS officers who had been out searching cellars and streets for deserters to hang had also been tempting hungry and impressionable young women back to the Reich Chancellery with promises of parties and inexhaustible supplies of food and champagne. It was the apocalypse of totalitarian corruption, with the concrete submarine of the Reich Chancellery underworld providing an Existentialist theatre set for hell.

The reality for ordinary Berliners was becoming more terrible by the hour. On 28 April, Soviet troops reached the street of an anonymous woman diarist. 'I had a queasy sensation in my stomach,' she wrote. 'It reminded me of the feeling I used to have as a schoolgirl before taking a maths exam – discomfort and restlessness, and the longing for everything to be over.' From an upstairs window they watched a Soviet supply column of horse-drawn carts, with foals nuzzling up against their mothers. The street already smelled of horse dung. A field kitchen was set up in the garage opposite. There were no German civilians to be seen at all. 'Ivans' were learning to ride bicycles they had found. The sight reassured her. They seemed like big children.

When she ventured out, one of the first questions she faced was, 'Do you have a husband?' She spoke some Russian and was able to parry their 'clumsy banter'. But then she noticed them exchanging looks and she began to feel afraid. One soldier, who smelled of alcohol, followed her when she retreated down into the cellar. There, the other women sat frozen as he walked along unsteadily, flashing his torch into their faces. He persisted in his unsubtle approach and the diarist, as if leading him on, managed to escape the cellar and fled up into the sunshine of the street. Other soldiers came and stripped the civilians in the cellar of their watches, but no violence was offered. In the evening, however, once the soldiers had eaten and drunk, they began their hunt. The diarist was ambushed in the dark by three of them, who began to rape her in turn. When the second one attacked her, he was interrupted by the arrival of three other soldiers, one of them a woman, but they all just laughed at the sight, including the woman.

Finally back in her own room, she piled all the furniture against the door and retired to bed. As was probably the case for all women in Berlin who were raped at this time, she found the lack of running water in which to wash herself afterwards made things far worse. She had hardly been in bed for long when her barricade was pushed aside. A group of soldiers came in and started eating and drinking in her kitchen. A giant named Petka picked her up when she tried to slip out of the apartment. She begged him not to allow the others to rape her as well and he agreed. Early the next morning, he woke up when the company rooster crowed down in the street. He announced that he must go back on duty, then nearly crushed her fingers in a goodbye handshake, assuring her that he would be back at 7 that evening.

Many other women also 'conceded' to one soldier in the hope of protecting themselves from gang rape. Magda Wieland, a twenty-four-year-old actress, found the arrival of Russian troops in Giesebrechtstrasse, just off the Kürfurstendamm, 'the most frightening moment of the whole war'. She hid in a huge, ornately carved mahogany cupboard when they burst in. A very young soldier from Central Asia hauled her out. He was so excited at the prospect of a beautiful young blonde that he suffered from premature ejaculation. By sign language, she offered herself to him as a girlfriend if he would protect her from other Russian soldiers. He was clearly thrilled at the idea of having a blonde girlfriend, and went out to boast to his friends, but another soldier arrived and raped her brutally.

In the cellar, Ellen Goetz, a Jewish friend of Magda's who had sought shelter there when she escaped from the Lehrterstrasse prison after a heavy bombardment, was also dragged out and raped. When other Germans tried to explain to the Russians that she was Jewish and had been persecuted, they received the terse retort, '*Frau ist Frau.*' Russian officers arrived later. They themselves behaved very correctly, but they did nothing to control their men.

Giesebrechtstrasse housed a very mixed section of Berlin life. Hans Gensecke, a well-known journalist, who had been punished for hiding Jews by being made to remove corpses from bombed cellars, also lived at No. 10. So too, on the third floor of the same block, did Kaltenbrunner's mistress, who entertained him in her apartment decorated with gilded doors and silk upholstered furniture and tapestries, no doubt looted from occupied areas of Europe. Next door, No. 11, had been infamous for the presence of 'Salon Kitty', the Nazi brothel for *Prominenten.* This establishment, with sixteen young prostitutes, had been taken over earlier in the war by Heydrich and Schellenberg. It was run by the intelligence department of the SS to spy on senior officials, Wehrmacht officers and foreign ambassadors and then blackmail them. All the rooms were bugged, and soon after the capture of Berlin, the NKVD apparently examined the technology used with great interest. Next door, on the far side, Colonel General Paul von Hase, the city commandant of Berlin, had lived until his arrest and execution following the July plot.

With Hitler Youth and SS opening fire at any house which displayed a white flag, civilians found themselves crushed by the violent intransigence of both sides. The smell of decomposing corpses spread from the piles of rubble which had been buildings, and the smell of charred flesh from the blackened skeletons of burnt-out houses. But it was not these terrible scenes as much as three years of propaganda which shaped the attitude of Soviet troops. They saw Berlin as 'this grey, frightening, gloomy, misanthropic city, this bandit capital'.

Even German Communists were not spared. In Wedding, a left-wing stronghold until 1933, activists from the Jülicherstrasse went out to congratulate the Soviet officers commanding the unit to occupy their district, showing their Party cards, which they had kept hidden during twelve years of illegality. They volunteered their wives and daughters to help out with washing and cooking, but, according to a French prisoner of war, the unit's officers raped them 'that very evening'.

*

While the occupants of the Führer bunker were preoccupied with the T-34s and Stalin tanks advancing from the Potsdamerplatz and up the Wilhelmstrasse, Soviet eyes were fixed on the northern side of central Berlin. The 3rd Shock Army angled its advance through Moabit, just north-east of the Spree, to line itself up for an attack on the Reichstag.

The commander of the 150th Rifle Division, General Shatilov, thought that Goebbels himself was directing the defence of Moabit prison and that they might capture him alive. He described Moabit prison 'looking at us maliciously with its narrow windows'. (It is striking how Russians saw evil in the very buildings of Berlin, just as they had in German trees on crossing the frontier.) Moabit prison did not appear an easy task to storm. The artillery brought forward a heavy gun, but it attracted frantic firing from within the prison. The very first gun-layer was killed and so was the second, but a breach was soon blasted in the walls.

Storm groups dashed across the street and entered the courtyard. Once they were inside, the German garrison surrendered very quickly. The sappers, who had found mines near the entrance, went running in to check for explosives. Their commander remembered the heavy metallic echo as they ran up the iron stairways. Every German who came out with raised arms was closely examined, even those in private's uniform, in case they were Goebbels in disguise. Cell doors were thrown open, and the liberated prisoners came out squinting in the sunlight.

Other objectives cost far heavier casualties in a city where the streets drifted with smoke from indiscriminate shellfire. 'What a terrible price we are paying for each step to victory,' observed the editor of the military newspaper *Voin Rodiny* on a visit to the fighting in Berlin. He was killed almost seconds later by a shell explosion. Deaths so close to the end of such a long and ferocious war seemed doubly poignant. Many were moved by the death of Mikhail Shmonin, a young and greatly admired platoon commander. 'Follow me!' he had cried to his sergeant, running towards a building. He had hardly fired three shots when a heavy shell, almost certainly a Soviet one, struck the wall in front of him. The side of the house collapsed and the lieutenant, with 'pink cheeks, clear complexion and large clear eyes', was buried under the rubble.

Even if the Red Army had 'soon learned what to expect' in street- and house-fighting in Berlin, with 'fausters near barricades' and 'stone and concrete buildings turned into bunkers', it began to rely more and more on the 152mm and 203mm heavy howitzers fired at short range over open sights. Only then would the assault teams go in. But the one battleground that Soviet troops avoided if at all possible was subway tunnels and bunkers, of which there were over 1,000 in the greater Berlin area. They were extremely cautious about entering civilian air-raid shelters, convinced that German soldiers were hiding ready to ambush them, or emerge to attack them in the rear. As a result, they virtually sealed off any shelters they overran. Civilians who came to the surface were likely to be shot. There are stories, mainly the product of German paranoia, that T-34s were driven into railway tunnels to emerge behind their lines. The only genuine case of an underground tank, however, appears to be that of an unfortunate T-34 driver who failed to spot the entrance of the Alexanderplatz U-Bahn station and charged down the stairs. Stories of light artillery bumped down station stairs, step by step, and manhandled on to the tracks also owe more to folklore than to fact.

From the Moabit prison, it was only 800 metres down Alt Moabit to the Moltke bridge over the Spree. Another 600 metres beyond that stood the Reichstag, which from time to time became visible when the smoke cleared. For the 150th and the 171st Rifle Divisions, it seemed so close now, and yet they had no illusions about the dangers ahead. They knew that many of them would die before they could raise their red banners over the building chosen by Stalin as the symbol of Berlin. Their commanders, to please Comrade Stalin, wanted the building captured in time for it to be announced at the May Day celebrations in Moscow.

The advance down to the Moltke bridge began on the afternoon of 28 April. The lead battalions from the two divisions left from the same start-line, further emphasizing the race. The bridge ahead was barricaded on both sides. It was mined and protected with barbed wire and covered by machine-gun and artillery fire from both flanks. Shortly before 6 p.m., there was a deafening detonation as the Germans blew the Moltke bridge. When the smoke and dust settled, it became clear that the demolition had not been entirely successful. The bridge sagged, but was certainly passable by infantry.

Captain Neustroev, the battalion commander, ordered Sergeant Pyatnitsky to take his platoon across in a probing attack. Pyatnitsky and his men dashed over the open space which led to the bridge and managed to shelter behind the Germans' own barricade. Neustroev then called in artillery support for the crossing. It seems to have taken rather a long time for the artillery observation officers to turn up and organize their batteries, but just as the last light was fading, artillery preparation began. The heavy bombardment at close range smashed the German fire-positions, and the leading infantry platoons dashed across to fight their way into the large buildings on the Kronprinzufer and Moltkestrasse. By midnight, just as Hitler was marrying Eva Braun, they established a firm bridgehead. During the rest of the night, the bulk of the 150th and 171st Rifle Divisions crossed the Spree.

The 150th Rifle Division stormed the Ministry of the Interior, on the southern side of the Moltkestrasse. This massive building immediately became known as 'Himmler's House'. With doors and windows blocked to provide embrasures for the defenders, it proved a hard fortress to storm. Unable to bring forward gun and rocket batteries, sappers improvised individual katyusha launchers on lengths of railway line. But the basic tools of this close-quarter fighting through the morning of 29 April were grenades and sub-machine guns.

Soviet soldiers, even if afraid of dying in the last days of the battle, also wanted to impress everyone at home. As conquerors of Berlin, they saw themselves as an élite in the post-war Soviet Union. 'Greetings from the front,' wrote Vladimir Borisovich Pereverzev that day. 'Hello, my nearest and dearest ones. So far I am alive and healthy, only I am slightly drunk the whole time. But this is necessary to keep up your courage. A reasonable ration of three-star cognac will do no harm. Naturally we ourselves punish those who don't know their capacity [for drink]. Now we're tightening the circle round the centre of the city. I am just 500 metres from the Reichstag. We have already crossed the Spree and within a few days the Fritzes and the Hanses will be kaputt. They are still writing on the walls that *"Berlin bleibt deutsch"*, but we say instead, *"Alles deutsch kaputt."* And it will turn out the way we say it. I wanted to send you my photo, which was taken, but we have not had a chance to develop it. It's a pity because the photo would be very interesting: a sub-machine gun on my shoulder, a Mauser stuck into my belt, grenades at my side. There's a lot to hit Germans with. To cut a long story short we'll be in the Reichstag tomorrow. I can't send parcels [i.e. looted goods]. There's no time for it. And we front units have other things to do. You write that part of the kitchen ceiling collapsed, but that's nothing! A six-storey building collapsed on us and we had to dig our boys out. This is how we live and beat the Germans. This briefly is my news.' Pereverzev was badly wounded shortly after finishing the letter. He died on the day that victory was announced.

'Sunday 29 April,' wrote Martin Bormann in his diary. 'The second day which has started with a hurricane of fire. During the night of 28–29 April, the foreign press wrote about Himmler's offer of capitulation. The wedding of Hitler and Eva Braun. Führer dictates his political and private wills. Traitors Jodl, Himmler and the generals abandon us to the Bolsheviks. Hurricane fire again. According to the information of the enemy, the Americans have broken into Munich.'

Hitler, even though his optimism and pessimism had been surging back and forth, finally realized that all was lost. His secure radio-telephone communications had collapsed, literally, when the last balloon raising the aerial above the Führer bunker was shot down. As a result Red Army listening stations intercepted its ordinary signals traffic that day. Bormann and Krebs jointly signed a message to all commanders: 'Führer expects an unshakeable loyalty from Schörner, Wenck and others. He also expects Schörner and Wenck to save him and Berlin.' Field Marshal Schörner replied that 'the rear areas are completely disorganized. The civilian population makes it difficult to operate.' Finally, Wenck made it clear that no miracles should be expected from the Twelfth Army: 'The troops of the Army suffered great losses and there is a severe shortage of weapons.'

Those in the Führer bunker, even the loyalists, finally saw that the longer Hitler delayed his suicide the greater the number of people who would die. After the Himmler and Göring débâcles, nobody could consider a cease-fire until the Führer had killed himself. The problem was that if he waited until the Russians were at the Reich Chancellery door, then none of them would get out alive.

Freytag von Loringhoven did not want to die in such surroundings, or in such company. After the three messengers left, bearing copies of

Hitler's last testament, the idea occurred to him that, with communications down, he and Boldt could ask for permission to join up with troops outside the city. 'Herr General,' he said to General Krebs. 'I do not want to die like a rat here, I would like to return to the fighting troops.' Krebs was at first reluctant. Then he spoke to General Burgdorf. Burgdorf said that any of the remaining military aides should be allowed to leave. His assistant, Lieutenant Colonel Weiss, should go with Freytag von Loringhoven and Captain Boldt.

Hitler was approached for his approval after the midday situation conference. 'How are you going to get out of Berlin?' he asked. Freytag von Loringhoven explained their route, out of the Reich Chancellery cellars and across Berlin to the Havel, where they would find a boat. Hitler became enthused. 'You must get an electric motor boat, because that doesn't make any noise and you can get through the Russian lines.' Freytag von Loringhoven, fearing his obsession with this one detail, agreed that it was the best method but said that, if necessary, they might have to use another craft. Hitler, suddenly exhausted, shook hands limply with each one and dismissed them.

The Russians, as the *Nordland* Division knew only too well, were already very close to the Reich Chancellery. Three T-34s had charged up the Wilhelmstrasse the day before, as far as the U-Bahn station, where they were ambushed by French SS panzerfausters.

Colonel Antonov's 301st Rifle Division began its assault in earnest at dawn on 29 April, not long after the newly married couple in the Führer bunker had retired. Two of his rifle regiments attacked Gestapo headquarters on the Prinz-Albrechtstrasse, a building which had been heavily damaged in the 3 February air raid. In the now standard tactic, 203mm heavy howitzers were brought forward to blast open a breach at close range. Two battalions stormed in and hoisted a red banner, but the Soviet accounts fail to reveal the fact that after fierce fighting and heavy casualties they were forced to withdraw that evening by a ferocious Waffen SS counter-attack. The Russians had no idea whether any prisoners of the Gestapo remained alive inside. In fact, there were seven left who had been specially spared from the horrendous massacre which had taken place on the night of 23 April.

*

The *Nordland*, now under Mohnke's command from the Reich Chancellery, was 'fed from above' with further encouraging messages about the progress of Wenck's army and negotiations with the Allies. The only reinforcements Krukenberg had received were 100 elderly police officials. His men were too exhausted to care about messages from the Reich Chancellery. They were too tired even to speak. Their faces were empty. No man would wake up unless shaken vigorously. Tank hunting, one of them wrote later, had become a 'descent into hell'.

The French 'tank destroyer squads' had played a particularly effective role in the defence. They accounted for about half of the 108 tanks knocked out on the whole sector. Henri Fenet, their battalion commander, described a seventeen-year-old from Saint Nazaire, called Roger, who fought alone with his panzerfausts 'like a single soldier with a rifle'. Unterscharführer Eugène Vanlot, a twenty-year-old plumber nicknamed 'Gégène', was the highest scorer, with eight tanks. He had knocked out two T-34s in Neukölln and then destroyed another six in less than twenty-four hours. On the afternoon of 29 April, Krukenberg summoned him to the subway car in the wrecked U-Bahn station, and there, 'by the light of spluttering candle stubs', he decorated him with one of the two last Knight's Crosses to be awarded. The other recipient was Major Herzig, the commander of the 503rd SS Heavy Panzer Battalion. Mohnke presented him with his at about the same time. Fenet himself and Officer Cadet Apollot also received awards for destroying five tanks each. A Scandinavian Obersturmführer from the *Nordland* brought three bottles of looted French wine to toast the heroes.

Fenet, who had been wounded in the foot, explained that they fought on because they had only one idea in their heads: 'The Communists must be stopped.' There was no time 'for philosophizing'. Protopopov, a White Guard officer who had fought in the Russian civil war and accompanied his French comrades to Berlin, also believed that the gesture was more important than the fact. Later, the few foreign SS volunteers who survived tried to rationalize their doomed battle as the need to provide an anti-Bolshevik example for the future. Even the sacrifice of boys was justified in those circumstances.

Just to the west of the battle around the Wilhelmstrasse, Chuikov's 8th Guards Army attacked northwards across the Landwehr Canal into the

Tiergarten. Some troops swam the canal, others used improvised craft under the cover of an artillery barrage and smoke screens. One group used sewer entrances to get behind the defenders.

At the Potsdamer bridge a clever ruse was adopted. Oil-soaked rags and smoke canisters were attached to the outside of a T-34 tank. As the tank approached the bridge, these were ignited. The anti-tank guns and a dug-in Tiger tank ceased fire, because their crews thought they had scored a direct hit. But by the time they had realized what was happening, the tank was across, firing at close range. Other T-34s raced across in its wake.

Another trick was used in the early afternoon. Three German civilians emerged with a white flag from a complex of tunnels and an underground air-raid bunker on three levels. They asked if civilians would be allowed out. A political officer, Guards Major Kukharev, accompanied by a soldier interpreter and ten sub-machine gunners, went forward to negotiate with them. The three civilians led Major Kukharev to the tunnel entrance. Three German officers appeared. They offered him a blindfold and said that they should discuss things inside, but Kukharev insisted on negotiating outside. It was eventually agreed that the 1,500 civilians sheltering inside would be allowed out. After they had left, the German captain announced that the remaining members of the Wehrmacht must now fulfil the Führer's order to resist to the end. They turned to go back into the tunnel. 'But Comrade Kukharev was not so simple,' the report continued. 'This enterprising political officer took out a small pistol which he had hidden in his sleeve and killed the captain and the other two officers.' The sub-machine gunners from the 170th Guards Rifle Regiment then charged down into the bunker, and the Germans inside raised their hands in surrender. Many of them were young cadets.

The right flank of Chuikov's 8th Guards Army on the Landwehr Canal was almost opposite General Weidling's headquarters in the Bendlerblock, but the Soviet divisional commander had no idea of its importance. Weidling, knowing that the end was close, summoned his divisional commanders. He told them that the last radio communication with General Reymann in Potsdam had taken place the day before. A part of General Wenck's Twelfth Army had broken through to Ferch, just south of Potsdam, but nobody knew whether an escape route was still open. He had summoned them to discuss a breakout westwards straight down the Heerstrasse. H-Hour was to be at 10 the next night.

24

Führerdämmerung

The assault on the Reichstag was planned for dawn on 30 April. Soviet commanders were desperate to capture it in time for the May Day parade in Moscow. Yet the pressure for results came from those in the chain of command who assumed that nothing had changed, not from Stalin. It is noticeable that once the city had been completely surrounded, preventing any American access, Stalin had relaxed and made no attempt to interfere in decisions on the ground. The Reichstag, nevertheless, remained the chosen symbol for victory over the 'fascist beast', and so it was naturally the main focal point for Soviet propaganda.

A war correspondent, summoned to the headquarters of the 150th Rifle Division just a few hours before, was told to hand over his pistol. He did so, horrified that he was being sent home for some misdemeanour. But the captain who had taken it from him put his mind at rest when he came back into the room with a fresh weapon. 'The order has come through,' he said, 'that everyone going to the Reichstag must be armed with a sub-machine gun.'

Amid sporadic fire, the journalist was taken on a zigzag route to 'Himmler's House' – the Ministry of the Interior. Fighting still continued on the upper floors, as the explosions of grenades and the rattle of sub-machine guns made clear. In the basement, however, battalion cooks, with almost as much noise, were preparing breakfast for the assault groups. On the first floor, Captain Neustroev, a battalion commander about to lead the assault on the Reichstag, was trying to orientate himself. He kept glancing down at his map and then up at the grey building ahead. His regimental commander, impatient at the delay, appeared.

'There's a grey building in the way,' explained Neustroev. The regimental commander grabbed the map from him and studied their position again. 'Neustroev!' he replied in exasperation. 'That *is* the Reichstag!' The young battalion commander had not been able to imagine that their final objective could be so close.

The journalist also peered from a window. The Königsplatz outside was 'covered with flashes and fire and exploding shells and the interrupted lines of tracer bursts'. The Reichstag lay less than 400 metres beyond. 'If there had been no fighting,' he wrote, 'this distance could be crossed in a few minutes, but now it seemed impassable, covered with shell holes, railway sleepers, pieces of wire and trenches.'

The German defenders had dug a network of defences all round the Reichstag. Most daunting of all, a water obstacle ran right across the middle of the Königsplatz. This was a tunnel which had collapsed from bombing and filled with water seeping in from the Spree. It had been dug as part of exploratory work for Albert Speer's vast Volkshalle, the centrepiece of the new Nazi capital of Germania. In this devastated, 'Hieronymus Bosch landscape', practical jokers had propped up on stones the heads of caryatids blasted by Allied bombs off the Reichstag's façade.

Once breakfast was dished up, 'everyone started checking their weapons and spare magazines'. Then at 6 a.m., the first company charged out. They had 'hardly gone fifty metres when the hurricane of fire from the enemy made them lie down'. Two rather reduced battalions made a dash forward soon afterwards, but many were killed. Heavy fire was also coming from the Kroll Opera House, on the west side of the Königsplatz, as well as from the Reichstag itself. With the assault force trapped in the crossfire, another division was rapidly deployed to deal with the Kroll Opera House, but first it had to clear the buildings behind on the embankment. More self-propelled guns and tanks were also brought over the Moltke bridge during the course of the morning to support the infantry on the Königsplatz. The smoke and dust from the bombardment were so thick that the soldiers never saw the sky.

With heavy artillery and tank fire supporting them, the 150th Rifle Division battalions reached the water-filled tunnel soon after 11 a.m.

But when another huge effort was made two hours later, heavy fire came from their right rear. The German anti-aircraft guns on the top of the Zoo bunker, two kilometres away, had opened up on them. They were forced to take cover again and wait until nightfall. During the afternoon, the 171st Rifle Division continued clearing buildings of the diplomatic quarter on the north side of the Königsplatz and more self-propelled guns and tanks moved up. Some ninety guns, including 152mm and 203mm howitzers, as well as katyusha rocket launchers, fired continuously at the Reichstag. It says much for the solidity of its construction fifty years before, during the Second Reich, that it withstood such a pounding.

Another prominent building heavily bombarded that morning was Göring's air ministry on the Wilhelmstrasse. Its ferro-concrete construction also resisted well. Because of its solidity and proximity to the Reich Chancellery, it had become an assembly point for uniformed Nazi Party members pretending that they were part of the great battle. The mixture of uniforms was striking. Along with Luftwaffe and Waffen SS, there was an elderly Volkssturm officer in his Wilhelmine uniform from the First World War who appeared 'to have escaped from a waxworks museum'.

The government district was now heavily garrisoned with all the troops which had retreated into it – in all, nearly 10,000 men, including a large proportion of foreign SS. But the escape route to the west was effectively cut off. The 8th Guards Army in the southern part of the Tiergarten and the 3rd Shock Army in the north were held back only by fire from the huge Zoo flak tower. Beyond them the one remaining corps of Konev's tank troops coming from the south and Zhukov's 2nd Guards Tank Army coming from the north had occupied most of Charlottenburg. Yet even further to the west, Hitler Youth detachments still held parts of the Heerstrasse and the Pichelsdorf bridge over the Havel. They also held on at the bridge to Spandau, just over two kilometres to the north.

The French SS on the Wilhelmstrasse were so hungry on that cold and rainy morning that when somebody brought in a frightened enemy soldier, they immediately grabbed his little canvas ration bag. Their prisoner kept telling them that he was not Russian but Ukrainian and that there would be a big attack on the next day. By then the 'Charlemagne' battalion was down to less than thirty men and they had used up a large proportion of the panzerfaust reserves from the Reich Chancellery. The last few Tigers of the SS 'Hermann von Salza' battalion had, meanwhile, been withdrawn to the Tiergarten to take on the tanks supporting the 3rd Shock Army and the 8th Guards Army.

In the Führer bunker, the morning of Hitler's death was 'like any other, with officers coming and going'. Yet the atmosphere was tense and emotional. Hitler, terrified that the poison would not work, had insisted the day before that one of Dr Stumpfegger's cyanide capsules should be tested. Blondi, Hitler's adored German shepherd bitch, was the obvious candidate. His passion for the breed dated back to 1921, when he had been given one in the depths of his poverty. He did not have enough space to keep it where he was living and had to lodge the dog elsewhere, but the animal escaped to return to him. This incident appears to have contributed greatly to Hitler's obsession with unconditional loyalty. But Blondi's absolute devotion was not enough to save her, nor her four puppies, which were taken up to the Reich Chancellery garden to be killed. The Goebbels children had been playing with the large-pawed puppies only a short time before.

Apart from Himmler's betrayal, Hitler's other great preoccupation remained his fear of being taken alive by the Russians. News had come through of Mussolini's execution by partisans and how the bodies of the Duce and his mistress, Clara Petacci, had been hoisted upside down in Milan. A transcript of the radio report had been prepared in the special outsize 'Führer typeface' which saved Hitler from wearing spectacles. It was presumably Hitler who underlined in pencil the words 'hanged upside down'. Hitler was in any case determined that his own body should be burned to prevent its exhibition in Moscow. But the historical record also concerned him deeply. His bride was a willing companion in suicide, but if she had not been, he clearly would not have wanted her left alive for interrogation by his enemies. Death had been an inescapable clause in the contract.

During the night, confirmation had been received from Field Marshal Keitel that no relief could be expected. And that morning Brigadeführer Mohnke, following the intense artillery bombardment of the government quarter, warned that they had two days or less. General Weidling, who had arrived in the latter part of the morning, estimated that resistance would collapse that night due to lack of ammunition. He again asked for permission to break out of Berlin. Hitler would not give an immediate answer.

At about the time Weidling was with Hitler, Eva Hitler took Traudl Junge to her room. She presented her with the silver fox fur cape which she would clearly never wear again. Traudl Junge wondered what Hitler and his wife talked about when they were alone. They lacked the subjects of conversation of most newly married couples. She also wondered how she was to escape from the centre of Berlin in a silver fox fur cape. (Hitler's presents to Eva had certainly improved in recent years. In 1937, his Christmas present to her had been 'a book on Egyptian tombs'.)

General Weidling, meanwhile, returned to the Bendlerblock. These journeys through the shelling, dashing bent double from ruin to ruin, were exhausting for a man in his fifties. At 1 p.m., no more than an hour after his return, an SS Sturmführer, escorted by a small detachment, arrived from the Reich Chancellery. He handed over a letter. The large envelope had the eagle and swastika and 'Der Führer' embossed in gold capitals. Hitler informed Weidling that there was to be absolutely no question of capitulation. A breakout was permitted only if it were to join other combat formations. 'If they cannot be found, then the fight is to be continued in small groups in the forests' – the very forests which the Führer had refused to 'wander about in'. Weidling was elated. One of the *Nordland* reconnaissance vehicles was sent round from position to position to warn commanders to prepare. They were going to break out westwards via Charlottenburg at 10 that night.

Before lunch, Hitler summoned his personal adjutant, Sturmbannführer Otto Günsche, and gave him careful instructions on the disposal of his corpse and that of his wife. (The very detailed investigation by SMERSH during the first few days of May concluded that Hitler's chauffeur, Erich Kempka, had received orders on 29 April, the previous day, to send over jerry cans of petrol from the Reich Chancellery garage.) Hitler then had lunch with his dietician, Constanze Manzialy, and his two secretaries, Traudl Junge and Gerda Christian. Eva Hitler, who had presumably lost her appetite, did not join them. Although Hitler appeared quite calm, little conversation was attempted.

After lunch he joined his wife in her bedroom. A little later, they both appeared in the anteroom corridor, where Günsche had assembled the inner circle. Goebbels, Bormann, General Krebs, General Burgdorf and the two secretaries made their final farewells. Magda Goebbels, evidently in a disturbed state, remained in the bunker room, which she had taken over from Dr Morell. Hitler wore his usual attire of 'black trousers and a grey-green military jacket', with a white shirt and tie, which distinguished him from other Nazi Party leaders. Eva Hitler wore a dark dress with 'pink flowers on the front'. Hitler shook hands with his closest associates in a distant manner, then left them.

The lower bunker was then cleared, but instead of sepulchral silence, a loud noise of partying came from upstairs in the Reich Chancellery canteen. Rochus Misch, the SS telephonist, was ordered to ring to stop this levity, but nobody answered. Another guard was sent up to stop the festivities. Günsche and two other SS officers stood in the corridor with instructions to preserve the Führer's final privacy, but again it was broken, this time by Madga Goebbels begging to see him. She pushed past Günsche as the door was opened, but Hitler sent her away. She returned to her room sobbing.

Nobody seems to have heard the shot that Hitler fired into his own head. Not long after 3.15 p.m., his valet, Heinz Linge, followed by Günsche, Goebbels, Bormann and the recently arrived Axmann, entered Hitler's sitting room. Others peered over their shoulders before the door was shut in their faces. Günsche and Linge carried Hitler's corpse, wrapped in a Wehrmacht blanket, out into the corridor and then up the stairs to the Reich Chancellery garden. At some point, Linge managed to take his master's watch, although it did him little good because he had to get rid of it before Soviet troops took him prisoner. Eva Hitler's body – her lips were apparently puckered from the poison – was then carried up and laid next to Hitler's, not far from the bunker exit. The two corpses were then drenched in petrol from the jerry cans. Goebbels, Bormann, Krebs and Burgdorf followed to pay their last respects. They raised their arms in the Hitler salute as a burning torch of paper or rag was dropped on to the two corpses. One of the SS guards, who had been drinking with the party in the canteen, watched from a side door.

He hurried down the steps to the bunker. 'The chief's on fire,' he called to Rochus Misch. 'Do you want to come and have a look?'

The 3rd Shock Army's SMERSH detachment had received instructions the day before to start making its way towards the government district. They soon discovered that their eventual destination was Hitler's Reich Chancellery. 'The information which the intelligence people had was scarce and self-contradictory and unreliable,' wrote Yelena Rzhevskaya, the SMERSH group interpreter. A reconnaissance company had been allotted the task of taking Hitler alive, but they still did not know for certain whether he was in Berlin. The SMERSH group interrogated a 'tongue', but he was just a fifteen-year-old Hitler Youth 'with bloodshot eyes and cracked lips'. He had been shooting at them, noted Rzhevskaya, 'now he is sitting here looking around but not understanding anything. Just a boy.' They had more luck on that evening of 29 April. A nurse was caught trying to get through the lines to her mother. She had pulled off her uniform cap. The day before she had been with the wounded in the Reich Chancellery bunker. She had heard there that Hitler was 'in the basement'.

Rzhevskaya describes how their American jeep took them through barricades, which had been blasted open, and over tank ditches, partly filled with rubble and empty fuel barrels dropped by advancing tanks. 'The air thickened as we approached the centre. Anyone who was in Berlin in those days will remember that acrid, fume-laden air, dark with smoke and brick dust, and the constant feeling of grittiness on one's teeth.'

They soon had to abandon their vehicle because of the shelling and the streets blocked with rubble. Their map of the city proved of little help. Street signs had been destroyed in the shelling, so they had to ask Germans the way. Along their route they encountered signallers crawling through holes in walls, unrolling land-line cables, a hay cart bringing up forage and wounded soldiers being taken to the rear. Above them, sheets and pillowcases hung from windows in a sign of surrender. During heavy shelling, they made their way underground from cellar to cellar. 'When will this nightmare end?' German women asked her. In the street, she came across 'an elderly woman, hatless and with a prominent white armband, taking a little boy and girl across the road.

Both of them, their hair neatly combed, were also wearing white armbands. As she passed us, the woman cried out regardless of whether or not she was understood, "They are orphans. Our house has been bombed. I am taking them somewhere else. They are orphans."'

The six Goebbels children did not face the risk of becoming orphans. Their parents intended to take them with them, or, more precisely, send them on ahead.

The Goebbels children seem to have quite enjoyed the novelty of life in the bunker. The boy, Helmuth, used to pronounce on every explosion that shook the place, as if it were all a great game. 'Uncle Adolf' had spoiled them with sandwiches and cakes, all served on a tea-table with a starched, monogrammed cloth. They were even permitted to use his private bath, the only one in the bunker. But their parents had already decided on their future. On the evening of 27 April, Magda Goebbels had intercepted the recently arrived SS doctor, Helmuth Kunz, in the bunker corridor. 'She said that she needed to speak to me about something terribly important,' Kunz told his Soviet interrogators shortly after the event. 'She immediately added that the situation was such that it was most likely that she and I would have to kill her children. I agreed.'

The children were not told what had happened on that afternoon of 30 April, but they must have imagined afterwards from the overwrought state of their mother that something terrible had taken place. Amid the portentous events, nobody had thought to give them any lunch until Traudl Junge suddenly remembered them.

While the bodies still smouldered in the ruined garden upstairs, the mood of most of those in the bunker had lightened. Many began to drink heavily. Bormann's mind, however, was preoccupied with the succession and the next Nazi government. He sent a signal to Grand Admiral Dönitz at his headquarters at Plön on the Baltic coast near Kiel. This simply informed Dönitz of his appointment as the Führer's successor instead of Reichsmarschall Göring. 'Written authority is on its way. You will immediately take all such measures as the situation requires.' He avoided telling Dönitz that the Führer was dead, presumably because he had no real power base without Hitler. Worst of all, Himmler was at Plön with Dönitz, and Dönitz had not arrested him for treason. If Bormann was to stand a chance of joining the new Nazi government and dealing with Himmler, then he needed to get out of Berlin, yet Goebbels, Krebs and Burgdorf all intended to stay and commit suicide.

Among those determined not to die were the remnants of Busse's Ninth Army, trying to break through the forests south of Berlin. Some 25,000 soldiers and several thousand civilians had breached or slipped through Marshal Konev's stop-lines. Like hunted animals, they forced themselves on even though exhausted.

Some groups had already made the rendezvous of Kummersdorf, while others still tried to reach it. The day before, another attempt, with a spearhead of several tanks and civilians lined up ready behind, was broken by a sudden Soviet artillery bombardment just as they were about to attack the barrier ahead. The Soviet 530th Anti-Tank Artillery Regiment, which had been given the task of holding a road junction near Kummersdorf without infantry support, found itself almost overwhelmed by German soldiers trying to break through. 'The gun crews often had to grab their sub-machine guns and hand grenades in order to fight off attacking infantry,' the report stated. It then went on to make the exaggerated claim that the enemy 'left about 1,800 dead in front of their fire positions, nine burnt-out tanks and seven half-tracks'.

A corporal from the *Kurmark* Division watched three of the very last King Tiger tanks being abandoned and blown up because they had run out of fuel. Even the officers from Ninth Army headquarters were now on their feet, because they too had been forced to leave behind their Kübelwagen vehicles. They looked strange and conspicuous in their trousers with the broad red stripes of the general staff, yet wearing steel helmets and carrying carbines. According to the corporal, they glanced around nervously, unused to the prospect of close-quarter fighting in the forest. But the real danger still came from air attack and Soviet gunners exploding their shells high in the trees. 'We reached a clearing where one tank remained. It was already completely covered with wounded. We turned away, because the scene of other soldiers fighting each other for a place was so frightful, sad and full of suffering.' The victors clambered on top, forcing aside the badly wounded, many of whom had unbandaged stumps from limbs which had been shot off.

30–33. (*Above and below*) The Red Army fighting street by street to capture the 'lair of the fascist beast'.

34. (*Below*) Across the Moltke bridge to attack 'Himmler's House' – the Ministry of the Interior – then the Reichstag.

35. Soviet assault gun firing down a Berlin street.

36. A riddled Volkswagen by the Reich Chancellery.

37. Forces of the 1st Ukrainian Front sent to crush the Ninth Army
in pine forests south of Berlin.

38. German soldiers surrendering to the Red Army in Berlin.

39. Soviet mechanized troops having a wash in a Berlin street.

40. Cooking in the ruins.

41. Red Army meets US Army: Colonel Ivanov proposes a toast, while Major General Robert C. Macon of the 83rd Infantry Division listens.

42. German civilians escaping the Red Army cross the ruined rail bridge over the Elbe to American territory.

43. (*Left*) The end of the battle for Hans-Georg Henke, a teenage conscript.
44. (*Right*) A wounded Soviet soldier tended by a female medical assistant.

45. General Stumpff, Field Marshal Keitel and Admiral von Friedeburg arrive at Karlshorst to sign the final surrender, 9 May.

46. A Red Army soldier tries to seize a Berliner's bicycle.

47. (*Left*) Marshal Zhukov takes the victory parade on the horse which had thrown Stalin.
48. (*Right*) Zhukov watched by General K. F. Telegin, head of the political department (*left*), and General Ivan Serov, the NKVD chief (*right*).
49. (*Overleaf*) Visiting the battleground inside the Reichstag.

Another sign of disintegration was the way that men strained to their limits could explode in suspicion. That evening an argument broke out about the direction they should be taking. One man grabbed another who disagreed with him and forced him back against a tree, screaming in his face, 'You traitor, you want to lead us right into the arms of the Russians. You're from the Free Germany lot!' And before the others could stop him, he drew his pistol and shot the man he had accused through the head.

In the centre of Berlin, the intensely claustrophobic life of those trapped in bomb shelters and cellars continued. With the total collapse of a structured existence, people tried to calm themselves by creating some sort of routine. In one cellar quite close to the government district, a tailor's wife spread a napkin on her lap at precisely set times, then cut small pieces of bread and covered them with a little jam. She then distributed these to her husband, daughter and disabled son.

Many were on the edge of nervous breakdown. A young woman with a thin little son could not stop talking about her husband, a fireman who had been sent to the front. She had not seen him for two years. Her way of coping with the anxiety had been to make a list of jobs for him to do in the apartment – to replace a door handle, a window catch. But now their house had burned down in the shelling. 'The boy was making painful grimaces,' the interpreter Rzhevskaya noted while waiting for the Reich Chancellery to be captured. 'It was apparently difficult for him to put up with his mother's story for the hundredth time.'

The fear of unjustified reprisal in the chaos of the fighting made everyone afraid. Women, when they had a chance to slip back upstairs to their apartment, tore up and burned photographs of Hitler or anything else which might indicate support for the regime. They even felt obliged to destroy their most recent photographs of husbands, brothers or fiancés because they were taken in Wehrmacht uniform.

Few people had any idea of what was really happening around them in Berlin, let alone in the outside world. The Ravensbrück concentration camp for women to the north of Berlin was liberated that day by Rokossovsky's 2nd Belorussian Front. The Western Allies also discovered that Rokossovsky's headlong advance across Mecklenburg had given the Kremlin the idea of seizing Denmark. The British reacted rapidly, advancing towards Hamburg and the Baltic coast at Kiel to forestall them.

Also on 30 April, President Truman informed General Marshall of the British request that Patton's Third Army should be directed to liberate Prague before the Red Army arrived. 'Personally,' Marshall told Eisenhower, 'and aside from all logistic, tactical or strategical implications, I would be loath to hazard American lives for purely political purposes.'

The American leaders still failed to grasp the fact that the German Army was desperate to surrender to them while resisting the Red Army at all costs. Franz von Papen, who had enabled Hitler to come to power in 1933, had told his American interrogators in the third week of April that Germans were afraid that all males would be taken into slavery in the Soviet Union. They suspected that 'a secret agreement was made at Yalta whereby the Russians were promised sufficient manpower for what they considered their needs'.

The SS Sturmführer who had brought Hitler's message that morning returned at 6 p.m. to General Weidling's command post under the Bendlerblock. Weidling and his staff were finalizing their plans for the breakout that night which Hitler had authorized. The Sturmführer had brought a message ordering that all plans for a breakout were to be put aside. Weidling was to report at once to the Reich Chancellery.

When Weidling reached the Führer bunker, he was met by Goebbels, Bormann and Krebs. They took him to Hitler's room, where the couple had committed suicide, and told him that their bodies had been burned and buried in a shell crater in the garden above. Weidling was forced to swear that he would not repeat this news to anybody. The only person in the outside world who was to be informed was Stalin. An attempt would be made that night to arrange an armistice, and General Krebs would inform the Soviet commander so that he could inform the Kremlin.

A rather dazed Weidling rang Colonel Refior in the Bendlerblock headquarters soon afterwards. He said that he could not tell him what had happened but he needed various members of his staff to join him immediately, including Colonel von Dufving, his chief of staff.

*

Heavy guns continued to thunder away at the Reichstag, less than a kilometre to the north of the Reich Chancellery. Captain Neustroev, the commander of one of the assault battalions, found himself being pestered by sergeants who wanted their platoons to have the honour of being the first into the objective. Each one dreamed of raising the 3rd Shock Army's red banner over it. Everlasting Soviet glory would be attached to the deed. One banner party was formed entirely from Komsomol members. The banner party selected by the political department for Neustroev's battalion included a Georgian, picked as 'a special present to Stalin'. Certain nationalities – such as Chechens, Kalmyks and Crimean Tartars – were rigorously excluded, because it was forbidden to recommend for Hero of the Soviet Union any member of an ethnic group which had been condemned to exile.

Their divisional commander, General Shatilov, who in a moment of misplaced optimism had encouraged Front headquarters to think that the Reichstag had been taken already – the news had been flashed to Moscow – was now ordering his commanders to get a red banner on to the building at any cost. Darkness came early because of the thick smoke, and at around 6 p.m., the three rifle regiments of the 150th Rifle Division charged the building, closely supported by tanks.

The riflemen, finding that the windows and doors had been blocked or bricked up, needed the heavy guns to blast a way in for them. They eventually forced their way through to the main hall, only to discover German defenders firing down at them with panzerfausts or throwing grenades from the stone balconies above. One of the attackers, Senior Lieutenant Belyaev, vividly remembers the splattering of blood on the huge stone columns.

The casualties were terrible, but the Red Army soldiers, using the usual combination of grenade and sub-machine gun, began to fight their way up the broad staircases, firing from behind balustrades. Part of the German garrison – a mixture of sailors, SS and Hitler Youth – withdrew into the basement. The rest conducted a fighting retreat upwards and back along corridors. Fires, ignited by panzerfausts and hand grenades, started in many rooms and soon the great halls began to fill with smoke.

It was like a deadly rugby match. While the loose scrum fought in chaos, two men of the banner group tried to slip past to race for the roof with their red flag. They managed to reach the second floor before they were pinned down by machine-gun fire. The regiment claimed that a second attempt at 10.50 p.m. succeeded and the red flag flew from the cupola of the Reichstag. This version must be treated with extreme caution, since Soviet propaganda was fixated with the idea of the Reichstag being captured by 1 May.

Whatever the exact time, the 'hoisting of the Red Flag of Victory' was a superficial gesture at that stage, since even the official accounts acknowledge the ferocity of the fighting, which continued all night. As the Soviet troops fought their way upstairs, the Germans from the cellars attacked them from behind. At one point Lieutenant Klochkov saw a group of his soldiers crouched in a circle as if examining something on the floor. They all suddenly leaped back together and he saw that it was a hole. The group had just dropped grenades in unison on to the heads of unsuspecting Germans on the floor below.

In the centre of Berlin that night the flames in bombarded buildings cast strange shadows and a red glow on the otherwise dark streets. The soot and dust in the air made it almost unbreathable. From time to time there was the thunder of masonry collapsing. And to add to the terrifying effect, searchlight beams moved around above, searching a night sky in which the Luftwaffe had ceased to exist.

An exhausted group of foreign Waffen SS soldiers sought shelter in the cellars of the Hotel Continental. The place was already full of women and children who eyed the battle-worn soldiers uneasily. The manager approached them and asked if they would go instead to the air-raid shelter in the Jakobstrasse. The SS volunteers felt a bitter resentment that they who had been sacrificing their lives were now cold-shouldered. They turned and left. Fighting soldiers found themselves treated as pariahs. They were no longer brave defenders, but a danger. In hospitals, including one of the military Lazarette, nurses immediately confiscated weapons so that when the Russians arrived, they had no excuse to shoot the wounded.

The former commander of the *Nordland*, Brigadeführer Ziegler, who had been with Mohnke in the Reich Chancellery, suddenly turned up in the Air Ministry on the Wilhelmstrasse. He did not need to be told how desperate the situation was. But then, to everyone's astonishment, a platoon of just over twenty Waffen SS commanded by a Belgian arrived. They were laughing, wrote another soldier present, 'as if we had just won the war'. This group had come from a tank-hunting sortie round the Anhalter Bahnhof and claimed that it had now become 'a tank graveyard'. An extraordinary comradeship of the damned had grown up among the foreign volunteers defending the last bastion of German nationalism. A *Nordland* section in the Air Ministry contained not just Scandinavians, but also three Latvians and 'our two Ivans', who were no doubt Hiwis absorbed into the fighting ranks.

Colonel Refior in the Bendlerblock received a call from the Reich Chancellery. He was to start sending messages to the Red Army command in Berlin informing them that General Krebs wanted to arrange a time and place for negotiations.

The whole process of arranging a cease-fire on the 8th Guards Army's sector took from 10 p.m. until the early hours of the next morning, which was already 1 May. General Chuikov gave orders for Krebs's safe conduct to his headquarters, a semi-suburban house at Schulenburgring, on the west side of Tempelhof aerodrome. Chuikov had been celebrating with the writer Vsevolod Vishnevsky, the poet Dolmatovsky and the composer Blanter, who had been sent to Berlin to compose a victory hymn.

General Krebs, accompanied by Colonel von Dufving and Obersturmführer Neilandis, a Latvian acting as Dufving's interpreter, went to the front line at around 10 p.m. Krebs himself, while remaining an apostle of total resistance, had been brushing up his Russian each day in the privacy of his shaving mirror.

The German plenipotentiaries were brought into Chuikov's headquarters just before 4 a.m. Blanter, the only member of the merrymakers not in uniform, was pushed into a cupboard. Vishnevsky and Dolmatovsky, who were in uniform as war correspondents, pretended to be staff officers.

'What I am about to say,' Krebs began, 'is absolutely secret. You are the first foreigner to know that on 30 April, Adolf Hitler committed suicide.'

'We know that,' Chuikov replied in a straight lie to disconcert his opponent.

Krebs then read Hitler's political testament and a statement from

Goebbels calling for 'a satisfactory way out for the nations who have suffered most from the war'. Vishnevsky, who was sitting on Chuikov's right, took down the whole conversation in his notebook.

Chuikov then rang Marshal Zhukov at his headquarters in Strausberg and brought him up to date on developments. Zhukov immediately sent his deputy, General Sokolovsky, to Chuikov's headquarters. He did not want Chuikov, his main critic, to be able to claim that he had taken the German surrender. Zhukov then rang Stalin, who was at his dacha. General Vlasik, the chief of his security guard, answered. 'Comrade Stalin has just gone to bed,' he told Zhukov.

'Please wake him up. The matter is urgent and it cannot wait until the morning.'

When Stalin picked up the telephone a few minutes later, Zhukov told him the news of Hitler's suicide.

'Now he's had it,' Stalin commented. 'Pity we couldn't take him alive. Where's Hitler's corpse?'

'According to General Krebs, his body was burned.'

'Tell Sokolovsky no negotiations except for unconditional capitulation, with either Krebs or any others of Hitler's lot. And don't ring me until the morning if there is nothing urgent. I want to have some rest before the parade.'

Zhukov had completely forgotten that later that morning, the May Day parade would take place in Red Square. Beria had even lifted the curfew on Moscow specially for the event. Zhukov thought of the capital's garrison moving to take up position for the parade, of the Soviet leaders assembling on the Lenin mausoleum and then the march past.

Every time that Chuikov, who knew nothing of what had really happened on the German side, brought the subject to surrender, Krebs played the role of a diplomat, not a soldier. He tried to argue that the Dönitz government must first of all be recognized by the Soviet Union. Only then could Germany surrender to the Red Army and thus prevent 'the traitor' Himmler from achieving a separate agreement with the Americans and British. But Chuikov, with his strong streak of peasant cunning, recognized this tactic for what it was.

General Sokolovsky, who had joined the group facing Krebs, eventually rang Zhukov. 'They are being very tricky,' he told him. 'Krebs declares that he is not empowered to take decisions concerning unconditional surrender. According to him, only the new government headed by Dönitz can. Krebs is trying to make a truce with us. I think we should send them to the devil's grandmother if they don't agree to unconditional surrender immediately.'

'You're right, Vasily Danilovich,' Zhukov replied. 'Tell him that if Goebbels and Bormann do not agree to unconditional surrender, we'll blast Berlin into ruins.' After consultation with the *Stavka*, Zhukov set a limit of 10.15 on that morning of 1 May.

No answer was received. At twenty-five minutes past the deadline, the 1st Belorussian Front unleashed 'a hurricane of fire' on the remains of the city centre.

25

Reich Chancellery and Reichstag

The dawn of May Day in the centre of Berlin revealed exhausted Soviet soldiers sleeping on pavements up against the walls of buildings. Rzhevskaya, the interpreter awaiting the capture of the Reich Chancellery, saw one soldier sleeping in the foetus position, with a piece of broken door as a pillow. Those who had awoken were retying their foot bandages. They had no idea of Hitler's suicide the afternoon before. Some of them still called '*Gitler durak!*' – 'Hitler's a blockhead' – at any German prisoners.

The Führer's death was kept a closely guarded secret on the German side throughout the night and into the next morning, when just a few senior officers were informed. SS Brigadeführer Mohnke, taking Krukenberg into his confidence, could not forgo the crass pomposity of Nazi rhetoric. 'A blazing comet is extinguished,' he told him.

Officers awaited word of the negotiations, but the suddenly renewed storm of fire in the middle of the morning spoke for itself. General Krebs had failed to achieve a cease-fire. The Soviet commanders insisted on unconditional surrender and Goebbels had refused. The massed artillery and katyusha launchers of the 3rd Shock Army, the 8th Guards Army and the 5th Shock Army blasted away again at semi-ruined buildings.

Mohnke also told Krukenberg that morning of his fears that Soviet troops would enter the U-Bahn tunnels and come up behind the Reich Chancellery. 'As a first priority,' wrote Krukenberg, 'I sent a group of

Nordland sappers through the U-Bahn towards Potsdamerplatz.' He gives no further details nor an exact time, but this was probably the order which led to one of the most contentious incidents of the whole battle: the blowing up of the S-Bahn tunnel under the Landwehr Canal near Trebbinerstrasse.

The demolition method used by the SS engineers was almost certainly a 'hollow charge', which meant fastening their explosives to the ceiling in a large circle to blast out a chunk. This would have been the only way to penetrate such a depth of reinforced concrete with relatively small amounts of explosive. Estimates of the time – and even the date – of the explosion vary enormously, but this is probably due to the looting of watches and clocks and the confusing, perma-night existence of all those sheltering in bunkers and tunnels. The most reliable accounts point to the explosion taking place in the early morning of 2 May. This suggests either a surprisingly long-delayed charge or that the *Nordland* sapper detachment experienced considerable difficulties carrying out their task.

In any case, the explosion led to the flooding of twenty-five kilometres of S-Bahn and also U-Bahn tunnels, once the water penetrated through a connecting shaft. Estimates of casualties ranged 'between around fifty and 15,000'. A number of Berliners are convinced that the new Soviet authorities had the victims carted to a small canal harbour near the Anhalter Bahnhof and then buried under rubble. More conservative estimates, usually around the 100 mark, are based on the fact that, although there were many thousands of civilians in the tunnels, as well as several 'hospital trains', which were subway carriages packed with wounded, the water did not rise quickly since it was spreading in many different directions. Women and children running through the dark tunnels as the floodwater rose were naturally terrified. Some recount seeing exhausted and wounded soldiers slip beneath the water, as well as many who had been seeking oblivion in the bottle. This may well have been true in a few cases, yet the high casualty estimates are hard to believe. The water in most places was less than a metre and a half deep and there was plenty of time to evacuate the so-called 'hospital trains' near the Stadtmitte U-Bahn station. It is also more than likely that many of the bodies recovered were those of soldiers and civilians who had already died of their injuries in one of the underground dressing stations and been laid aside in adjoining tunnels. The floodwater would have swept bodies along and nobody would have had the time afterwards to distinguish the real cause of death. A few of the dead were almost certainly SS men. They may have ended up among the fifty or so buried in the Jewish cemetery in the Gross Hamburgerstrasse.

At the Reichstag, the fighting inside was still savage, which made rather a mockery of raising the red banner of victory before midnight on May Day. One Soviet soldier who tried to throw back a German grenade misjudged his aim. It bounced off the door lintel and exploded at his feet, blowing them off. Soldiers on both sides fought on, exhausted and thirsty, their throats and noses raw from dust and smoke. It made a Soviet officer keep thinking of the Reichstag fire in 1933, which Hitler had used to crush the German Communist Party.

The firing did not die down until the late afternoon. Germans in the cellars shouted that they wanted to negotiate with a senior officer. The young Captain Neustroev told Lieutenant Berest to pretend to be a colonel. He gave him a sheepskin coat to hide his shoulder boards and sent him forth to negotiate. Shortly afterwards, Germans began to appear from the basement, dirty and unshaven in their ragged uniforms, with their eyes flickering nervously around and 'smiling like obedient dogs'. Some 300 enemy soldiers and officers laid down their weapons. Nearly 200 had been killed. In the improvised dressing station in the basement lay another 500, although many of them had been wounded before the Reichstag was stormed.

An even more massive fortress to be reduced was the vast Zoo flak tower in the south-west corner of the Tiergarten. Although it was powerful enough to resist direct hits from 203mm howitzers, the conditions inside, with several thousand terrorized civilians, were unspeakable. There were also over a thousand wounded and sick in the field hospital section, which was well equipped.

Katukov's 1st Guards Tank Army and Chuikov's 8th Guards Army had attacked into the Tiergarten from the south across the Landwehr Canal. But the task of tackling the Zoo flak tower was left to two regiments from the 79th Guards Rifle Division. Storming it was out of the question, so on 30 April they sent German prisoners as envoys bearing an ultimatum written in pencil to the commander: 'We propose that you surrender the fortress without further fighting. We guarantee that no troops, including SS and SA men, will be executed.'

On 1 May one of the prisoners eventually returned with a reply: 'Your note was received at 11 p.m. We will capitulate [tonight] at midnight. Haller, garrison commander.' Haller was not in fact the garrison commander and the reason for the long delay was to allow them to prepare a breakout that evening.

Another fortress besieged that day was the Citadel of Spandau at the extreme north-western corner of Berlin. Architecturally, it was a good deal more distinguished than the concrete horror at the Zoo. Spandau was built in brick in 1630 on an island at the confluence of the Havel and the Spree. During the war it served as the Army Gas Defence Laboratories, but this appears to have been a camouflage for its true work.

On 30 April, the Soviet 47th Army finally came to grips with this formidable obstacle whose guns could cover both of the nearby bridges over the Havel. Hoping to avoid a full-scale assault, the army commander, General Perkhorovich, sent forward the 7th Department under Major Grishin to soften up the enemy with propaganda. Loudspeaker trucks broadcast on the hour every hour and the Germans replied with artillery fire.

The next day, 1 May, Perkhorovich ordered Major Grishin to send surrender proposals to the garrison commander. Grishin summoned his officers. 'Because this mission is so dangerous,' he told them, 'I cannot order anyone on it. I need a volunteer to accompany me.' All seven officers volunteered. Grishin told Konrad Wolf, the future East German film-maker and brother of Markus Wolf, that he could not go. There were SS officers in the fortress, and if they suspected for a moment that he was a German in Russian uniform, they would shoot him on the spot. Wolf's best friend, Vladimir Gall, was selected instead. He and Grishin emerged from the edge of the trees waving a white flag. They slowly approached a barricade built around a burnt-out Tiger tank in front of the brick bridge over the moat.

The Germans, seeing them coming, threw down a rope ladder from a balustraded stone balcony some dozen metres above the main entrance. Grishin and Gall climbed the rope ladder, which swung around wildly.

They reached the balcony and, with considerable apprehension, entered the unlit room beyond. They made out a group of officers of the Wehrmacht and the SS. The apparent commandant of the citadel was Colonel Jung and his deputy was Lieutenant Colonel Koch. Jung, with metal-rimmed spectacles, an old lined face, grey hair clipped short and the collar of his uniform loose around his neck, did not look like a professional soldier. But neither Grishin nor Gall had any idea of his true position.

Negotiations began, conducted on the Russian side almost entirely by Gall, the Jewish philologist, since Grishin spoke very little German. Koch explained that Hitler had issued an order that any officer who attempted to surrender a fortress must be shot on the spot. Unfortunately, the 47th Army had not yet heard that Hitler was now dead. Gall sensed that the SS officers especially were in a state of nervous exhaustion and were quite capable of shooting anyone down, whatever the consequences. He told them that Berlin was now almost entirely occupied, the Red Army had joined up with the Americans at Torgau on the Elbe, and further resistance would mean only a futile loss of life. If they surrendered, there would be no executions, food would be given to everyone and medical assistance provided for their wounded and sick. He made it clear that if they refused to surrender and if the Red Army had to take the fortress by storm, none of these guarantees would apply. 'We are all soldiers and we all know that a great deal of blood would be shed. And if many of our soldiers die in the process, I cannot answer for the consequences. Also, if you refuse to surrender, you will be responsible for the deaths of all your civilians here. Germany has lost so much blood that each life must surely be important for its future.'

The SS officers stared at him with total hatred. The tension was so great that he feared 'the smallest spark' would cause an explosion. On Grishin's instruction, he told them that they had until 3 p.m. to make up their minds. In deadly silence, the two officers turned and then walked back towards the light of the window. As they climbed down the rope ladder, their bodies quivering from the tension, Gall could not help fearing that an SS officer would cut the rope.

On reaching the ground, they longed to run across the open space in front of the fortress to the safety of the trees, where their comrades awaited them, but they restricted themselves to a purposeful stride. In the trees, their colleagues ran up to embrace them, but they had to explain that no answer had been given. They could only wait. The presence of SS officers and Hitler's order about shooting officers who surrendered did not encourage them.

At 47th Army headquarters, General Perkhorovich asked the same question: 'Will they surrender?'

'We don't know. We gave them until 15.00 hours, as instructed. If they agree, they have to send a representative to our front trenches.'

'Well, Comrade Gall, just in case they do surrender, make sure that you are ready in that trench.'

The tension returned as 3 p.m. approached. Nervous jokes were made about German punctuality.

'Comrade Captain!' a soldier suddenly cried. 'Look! They're coming, they're coming.'

They made out two figures on the balcony, preparing to climb down the ladder. The garrison was going to surrender. Gall told himself to act as if he were used to receiving the surrender of a fortress as a normal part of the day's work.

When the two German emissaries, Lieutenants Ebbinghaus and Brettschneider, appeared, Russian officers and soldiers rushed up to slap them on the back in congratulation. They explained to Gall that the terms of surrender were agreed, but they must be written and signed first. They were led off in triumph to 47th Army headquarters, where they saw empty bottles everywhere from May Day celebrations. A senior officer was still asleep on a mattress on the floor. On being woken, he caught sight of the two German officers and told orderlies to prepare some food for them. Major Grishin then turned up. He was told that the garrison insisted on first having the surrender details in writing. 'Typically German!' he muttered.

When the details were written and signed, the Soviet officers brought out a bottle of cognac and filled glasses for a toast. The Russians swallowed the whole lot, and when Lieutenant Brettschneider, who had eaten very little over the past week, cautiously drank only two fingers, they laughed uproariously and refilled the glasses. '*Woina kaputt!*' they cried. 'The war's packed up.'

The celebration was interrupted by the arrival of a staff colonel from 1st Belorussian Front headquarters. The situation was explained to him.

He turned to Lieutenant Ebbinghaus, the older of the two German officers, and asked how long he thought the citadel could have held out if the Red Army had bombed and shelled it heavily. 'At least a week,' Ebbinghaus said stiffly. The Russian colonel looked at him in disbelief.

'The war is over,' Major Grishin said. 'Your duty as an officer is at an end.' There was a box of Ritmeester cigars on the table and Lieutenant Ebbinghaus helped himself.

Two hours later, Grishin and Gall entered the fortress, not via the balcony but through the main gate. Russian soldiers were piling the arms of the surrendered garrison and waving the men into columns outside.

As the two officers stood watching the scene, Jung and Koch came up to them. 'We are about to say goodbye to you,' Koch said in perfect Russian. Seeing their surprised expressions, he smiled. 'Yes, I speak a little Russian. I lived in St Petersburg as a child.'

Gall suddenly thought with a rush of horror that during the negotiations Koch must have understood every word that had passed between them. Then, to his relief, he remembered that Grishin had not said anything like, 'Promise them whatever they want and we'll deal with them later.'

In the courtyard, Gall and Grishin saw pale and trembling civilians emerging from the cellars of the fortress. General Perkhorovich told Gall to tell them that they could all go home. Afterwards, a young woman wearing a turban, as many did at that time of unwashed hair, came up to him holding a baby. She thanked him for having persuaded the officers to surrender, thus avoiding a bloodbath. She then burst into tears and turned away.

This heart-warming tale of the surrender of Spandau is, however, rather spoiled by subsequent revelations. Colonel Jung and Lieutenant Colonel Koch were in fact Professor Dr Gerhard Jung and Dr Edgar Koch, the leading scientists in the development of Sarin and Tabun nerve agents. Rather than being concerned solely with defence against chemical weapons, as its name implied, the Heeresgasschutzlaboritorium's first task was 'general testing of war gases for suitability as field agents'.

A Russian lieutenant colonel with the 47th Army immediately recognized the importance of their find at Spandau and informed the general in charge of a commission of Red Army experts – they wore a cogwheel and spanner badge on their shoulder boards. The general looked forward to interviewing the two men next day, but the NKVD got to hear of the discovery and, on that evening of 1 May, NKVD officers arrived to seize Jung and Koch. The general was furious. It took the Red Army until mid-June to find where the NKVD was holding Jung and Koch and extract them. They finally flew them to Moscow in August.

Two other leading scientists, Dr Stuhldreer and Dr Schulte-Overberg, were kept under guard at Spandau and ordered to 'continue work'. Stuhldreer, who specialized in nerve gas attacks against tanks, had used the old artillery testing ground at Kummersdorf, which had been the rendezvous in the forest for the Ninth Army. They all denied any knowledge of Tabun and Sarin, and since all the batches had been destroyed as soon as the Red Army threatened Berlin, the Soviet experts could prove nothing and they did not know what questions to ask.

In the summer, Stuhldreer and Schulte-Overberg were flown to the Soviet Union. They were reunited with Jung and Koch in a special camp at Krasnogorsk. Under Professor Jung's leadership, the group refused to cooperate with the Soviet authorities. They insisted that they were prisoners of war. Other German scientists collaborating with the Soviet Union were brought in to persuade them to change their minds, but this did little good. They were not maltreated for their stand, however, and were eventually returned to Germany with one of the last batches of prisoners of war in January 1954.

South of Berlin, the remnants of the Ninth Army made a final effort to break through Konev's last barrier. The Twelfth Army had managed to hold on just long enough in the area of Beelitz to keep open an escape route to the Elbe, as well as opening a route for nearly 20,000 men from General Reymann's so-called Army Group Spree in the Potsdam area. But pressure was building up. Beelitz was shelled heavily that morning by Soviet self-propelled guns diverted down from Potsdam. Shturmovik squadrons increased their dive-bombing and strafing attacks in the area.

A Soviet rifle regiment had occupied the village of Elsholz, six kilometres south of Beelitz. It was a crucial crossing point for the exhausted German troops. Fortunately for the Germans, the sudden appearance of the last four Panthers of the *Kurmark* Division forced the

Red Army soldiers to retreat. In fact the Panthers, with virtually empty fuel tanks, had to be abandoned there, but the way ahead was clear. Many stragglers were so exhausted and malnourished that they collapsed in Elsholz. Civilians shared their food with the soldiers and cared for the wounded, carrying them to the schoolhouse, where a doctor from Berlin and a district nurse worked together as best they could. Only one SS unit had the strength to march through the village without pausing for a rest.

Fighting still flared behind them in the forests, where Konev's troops continued to hunt down both small and large groups of stragglers. That May Day morning, a brigade of the 4th Guards Tank Army was sent back into the forest 'to liquidate a large group of Germans wandering around'. The report claims that the T-34s ran into German tanks and other armoured vehicles. 'The Soviet commander got down to business immediately,' the report stated. 'In two hours the enemy lost thirteen personnel carriers, three assault guns, three tanks and fifteen trucks.' It is very hard to believe that so many vehicles were still serviceable in a single group.

Soviet troops were also attacking Beelitz itself. A group of 200 Germans, with the last Tiger tank and an assault gun, came under automatic fire south of Beelitz as they crossed asparagus fields. All they needed to do was to carry on to the woods and wade the River Nieplitz. Just beyond was the road which led to Brück and safety.

General Wenck's Twelfth Army staff had assembled every truck and vehicle in the area to transport the exhausted mass. They had set up field kitchen units, which began to feed the 25,000 men, as well as several thousand civilian refugees. 'When the soldiers reached us, they just collapsed,' said Colonel Reichhelm, Wenck's chief of staff. 'Sometimes we even had to beat them, otherwise they would not have climbed up into the trucks and would have died where they lay. It was terrible.' The formerly plump General Busse was unrecognizably thin. 'He was totally at the end of his physical strength.'

Many of those who had experienced the horror of the Halbe *Kessel* developed an anger which did not fade with the years. They blamed senior officers for continuing the battle when all was lost. 'Was it really unquestioning obedience,' wrote one survivor, 'or was it cowardice in the face of their responsibility? The officer corps with its support for

Hitler left behind a bitter aftertaste. During those last days they all tried only to save their own skin and they abandoned soldiers, civilians and children.'

This diatribe, while containing a large measure of truth, was far too sweeping, especially when one considers the efforts of the Twelfth Army to save soldiers and civilians. Even within the Ninth Army, not all was black. Another soldier recorded how, on that same day, Major Otto Christer Graf von Albedyll, who had seen the defeat of his army and the destruction of his family's estate near the Reitwein Spur, was killed trying to help a badly wounded man. 'A much loved leader', he was buried at the side of the road to Elsholz by his soldiers.

Colonel Reichhelm himself was scathing about the most flagrant case of a senior officer abandoning his own men. General Holste, the commander of the XLI Panzer Corps, had appeared at Twelfth Army headquarters between Genthin and Tangermünde at 2 a.m. 'What are you doing here, Herr General?' Reichhelm asked him in astonishment. 'Why aren't you with your troops?'

'I do not have any any more,' Holste retorted.

In fact he had abandoned them. He had departed with his wife, two cars and two of his best horses. Reichhelm said that he must speak to General Wenck immediately. He went in to wake the army commander and told him that Holste had to be arrested. But Wenck was too exhausted. Reichhelm returned. 'You can leave Hitler, because he's a criminal,' he told Holste, 'but you can't leave your soldiers.' Holste ignored him and left to continue on his way across the Elbe.

In Berlin during the afternoon an order came through from the Reich Chancellery that the last Tiger tank supporting *Nordland* was to pull back 'to be at the immediate disposal of General Mohnke'. No explanation was given. Presumably without telling Goebbels, who categorically refused any suggestion of surrender, Bormann and Mohnke had started planning their escape from Berlin. These two, who had ordered immediate execution for anybody who failed to fight to the end, had already brought civilian clothes into the bunker ready for their escape.

The renewed bombardment had made communications with Kruken-berg's detachments even more difficult. The wounded Fenet and his Frenchmen were still defending Gestapo headquarters in the Prinz-

Albrechtstrasse. The 'Danmark' was a few hundred metres east, round the Kochstrasse U-Bahn station on the Friedrichstrasse, while the 'Norge' defended their left rear round the Leipzigerstrasse and the Splittermarkt.

Goebbels, realizing that the end was now very close, summoned Kunz, the SS doctor who had agreed to help kill his six children. Goebbels was in his study in the Führer bunker talking with Naumann, the state secretary of the Propaganda Ministry. Kunz was made to wait for ten minutes, then Goebbels and Naumann got up and left him with Magda Goebbels. She told him that the Führer's death had made the decision for them. Troops would try to break out of the encirclement that night, so the whole family was to die. Kunz claimed afterwards that he tried to persuade her to send the children to the hospital and put them under the protection of the Red Cross, but she refused. 'After we had been talking for about twenty minutes,' he recounted, 'Goebbels returned to the study and said to me, "Doctor, I would be very grateful if you help my wife kill the children." ' Kunz again repeated his suggestion about saving them.

'It's impossible,' the Reichsminister for Propaganda answered. 'They are the children of Goebbels.' He left the room. Kunz stayed with Magda Goebbels, who played patience for about an hour.

A little later, Goebbels returned. 'The Russians might arrive at any moment and interfere with our plan,' his wife said. 'That's why we should hurry up doing what we have to do.'

Magda Goebbels led Kunz to their bedroom and took a syringe filled with morphine from a shelf. They then went to the children's room. The five girls and one boy were already in bed in their nightgowns, but not yet asleep. 'Children, don't be alarmed,' she told them. 'The doctor will give you a vaccination which children and soldiers now need to have.' Then she left the room. Kunz stayed and started giving them morphine injections. 'After that,' he told his SMERSH interrogators, 'I went out again to the front room and told Frau Goebbels that we had to wait about ten minutes for the children to fall asleep. I looked at my watch and saw that it was twenty minutes to nine.'

Kunz said that he could not face giving poison to the sleeping children. Madga Goebbels told him to find Stumpfegger, Hitler's personal doctor. Together with Stumpfegger, she opened the mouths of the sleeping children, put an ampoule of poison between their teeth and forced their jaws together. The oldest daughter, Helga, was found later with heavy bruising to the face. This suggests that the morphine may not have worked very well in her case and that she may have struggled with the two adults trying to force her mouth open. After the deed was done, Stumpfegger went away and Kunz went down to Goebbels's study with Magda Goebbels. Goebbels was walking about in a very nervous state.

'It's all over with the children,' she told him. 'Now we have to think about ourselves.'

'Let's be quick,' said Goebbels. 'We're short of time.'

Magda Goebbels took both the gold party badge which Hitler had given her on 27 April in token of his admiration and also her gold cigarette case inscribed 'Adolf Hitler, 29 May 1934'. Goebbels and his wife then went upstairs to the garden, accompanied by his adjutant, Günther Schwaegermann. They took two Walther pistols. Joseph and Magda Goebbels stood next to each other, a few metres from where the bodies of Hitler and his wife had been burned and then buried in a shell crater. They crunched on glass cyanide ampoules and either they shot themselves with the pistols at the same moment, or else Schwaegermann shot both of them immediately afterwards as a precautionary *coup de grâce*. The two pistols were left with the bodies, which Schwaegermann doused in petrol from jerry cans, as he had promised. He then ignited the last funeral pyre of the Third Reich.*

At 9.30 p.m., Hamburg radio station warned the German people that a grave and important announcement was about to be made. Suitably funereal music from Wagner and Bruckner's Seventh Symphony was played to prepare listeners for Grand Admiral Dönitz's address to the nation. He stated that Hitler had fallen, fighting 'at the head of his troops', and announced his succession. Very few people in Berlin heard the news because of the lack of electric current.

Bormann, meanwhile, was evidently impatient at having to wait for

---

* Some historians believe that the poison used in all cases was prussic acid, but the Soviet autopsy report on Adolf and Eva Hitler states, 'The remains of glass ampoules which had contained cyanide compound were found in the oral cavities. These were identical to those found in the mouths of Goebbels and his wife.'

the Goebbels family drama to finish. Weidling's surrender was to take place at midnight and the breakout northwards over the Spree was due to start an hour before. The personnel from the Führer bunker, including Traudl Junge, Gerda Christian and Constanze Manzialy, had been told to assemble ready for departure. Krebs and Burgdorf, who both intended to shoot themselves later, were not to be seen.

Krukenberg, who had been summoned earlier by Mohnke, encountered Artur Axmann and Ziegler, the previous commander of the *Nordland*. Mohnke asked Krukenberg whether, as the senior officer, he wished to continue the defence of the city centre. He added that General Weidling had given an order to break out of Berlin north-westwards through the Soviet encirclement, but that a cease-fire would come into effect around midnight. Krukenberg agreed to join the breakout. He and Ziegler left to rally the *Nordland* and other units in the area. Krukenberg sent one of his aides on ahead, with messages to outlying detachments to fall back. The group led by Captain Fenet, defending Gestapo headquarters on Prinz-Albrechtstrasse, heard nothing. Krukenberg's aide, who was never seen again, probably met his death before he reached them.

The scenes in the bunker were chaotic as Bormann and Mohnke tried to organize everybody into groups. In the end, they did not leave until nearly 11 p.m., two hours later than planned. The first group, led by Mohnke, set out through the cellars of the Reich Chancellery, and then followed a complicated route to the Friedrichstrasse Bahnhof. The others followed at set intervals. The most difficult part was just north of the station, where they had to cross the Spree. This could not be done under cover of darkness because the flames from bombarded buildings lit up the whole area. The first group from the Reich Chancellery, which included Mohnke and the secretaries, wisely avoided the main Weidendammer bridge. They used a metal footbridge 300 metres downstream and headed for the Charité hospital.

The *Nordland* Tiger tank and a self-propelled assault gun were to spearhead the main charge across the Weidendammer bridge. Word had spread of the breakout and many hundreds of SS, Wehrmacht soldiers and civilians had assembled. It was a gathering which Soviet troops could not fail to miss. The first mass rush, led by the Tiger tank, took place just after midnight, but although the armoured monster managed to smash through the barrier on the north side of the bridge, they soon ran into very heavy fire in the Ziegelstrasse beyond. An anti-tank round struck the Tiger and many of the civilians and soldiers in its wake were mown down. Axmann was wounded, but managed to stagger on his way. Bormann and Dr Stumpfegger were knocked over by the blast when the tank was hit, but they recovered and went on. Bormann carried the last copy of Hitler's testament, and he evidently hoped to use it to justify his claim to a position in Dönitz's government when he reached Schleswig-Holstein.

Another attack over the bridge was made soon afterwards, using a self-propelled 20mm quadruple flak gun and a half-track. This too was largely a failure. A third attempt was made at around 1 a.m., and a fourth an hour later. Bormann, Stumpfegger, Schwaegermann and Axmann kept together for a time. They followed the railway line to the Lehrterstrasse Bahnhof. There they split up. Bormann and Stumpfegger turned north-eastwards towards the Stettiner Bahnhof. Axmann went the other way, but ran into a Soviet patrol. He turned back and followed Bormann's route. Not long afterwards he came across two bodies. He identified them as Bormann and Stumpfegger, but he did not have time to discover how they had died. Martin Bormann, although not of his own volition, was the only major Nazi Party leader to have faced the bullets of the Bolshevik enemy. All the others – Hitler, Goebbels, Himmler and Göring – took their own lives.

Krukenberg had meanwhile assembled most of his French SS escort. They joined up with Ziegler and a much larger group from the *Nordland*. Krukenberg estimated that there were four or five holders of the Knight's Cross among them. They managed to cross the Spree shortly before dawn. But they came under heavy fire just a few hundred metres short of the Gesundbrunnen U-Bahn station. Ziegler was hit by a ricochet and mortally wounded. Several others in their group also fell, among them Eugène Vanlot, the young French recipient of the Knight's Cross. He died in a nearby cellar three days later.

The Soviet forces in the area had been reinforced so strongly that Krukenberg and his remaining companions had no choice but to retreat the way they had come. At the top end of the Ziegelstrasse they saw the Tiger tank which Mohnke had taken from them. There was no sign of any of its crew. One of Krukenberg's officers had spotted a joinery workshop nearby and there they discovered some overalls to disguise themselves. Krukenberg managed to make his way to Dahlem, where he hid for over a week in the apartment of friends. Eventually he had no choice but to surrender.

Zhukov, on hearing of the breakout attempts from General Kuznetsov of the 3rd Shock Army, ordered a maximum alert. He was understandably perturbed by the 'unpleasant suggestion' that senior Nazis, especially Hitler, Goebbels and Bormann, might be trying to escape. It was not hard to imagine Stalin's anger if this should happen. Soviet officers hastily rounded up men who were celebrating May Day with alcohol and women-hunts. Brigades from the 2nd Guards Tank Army were sent in pursuit and cordons hurriedly put into place. This thwarted a second attempt to break through northwards up the Schönhauserallee by Major General Bärenfänger's troops from the eastern side of the Zitadelle defence area. Bärenfänger, a devoted Nazi, committed suicide with his young wife in a side street.

Shortly before midnight, the time when Colonel Haller had promised to surrender the Zoo flak tower, the remaining tanks and half-tracks of the *Müncheberg* Panzer Division and the 18th Panzergrenadier Division set out from the Tiergarten westwards. They then pushed north-westwards towards the Olympic stadium and Spandau. Word had also spread rapidly in this case. The rumour was that Wenck's army was at Nauen, to the north-west of the city, and hospital trains were waiting there to take soldiers to Hamburg. Thousands of stragglers and civilians made their way on foot and in a variety of vehicles in the same direction. One group of around fifty came in three trucks from the Grossdeutscher Rundfunk. They included Himmler's very different younger brother, Ernst, a leading studio technician.

The Charlottenbrücke, the bridge over the Havel to the old town of Spandau, was still standing and held by Hitler Youth detachments. In heavy rain and under artillery fire from the 47th Army, the armoured vehicles charged across, followed by a ragged crowd of soldiers and civilians. The slaughter was appalling. 'There was blood everywhere and trucks were exploding,' one of the escapers recounted. A tactic was instinctively worked out. Self-propelled army flak vehicles with quadruple 20mm guns gave covering fire from the eastern bank to keep

Soviet heads down, and during this frantic firing for up to a minute, another wave of civilians and soldiers surged across to hide in the ruined houses opposite. The slow and the lame were caught in the open by Soviet guns. As well as wave after wave of people on foot, trucks, cars and motorcycles also crossed, running over bodies already crushed by the tracks of armoured vehicles. Ernst Himmler was one of the many who died on the Charlottenbrücke, either shot or trampled in the desperate rush.

Although the massacre at the bridge was horrific, the sheer weight of German numbers forced the Soviet troops back from the river bank. But Soviet machine guns in the tower of the Spandau town hall continued to cause heavy losses. Two of the Tiger tanks then shelled the Rathaus itself, and a small group from the 9th Parachute Division stormed the tower. The main force of armoured vehicles pushed on westwards towards Staaken, but most of the troops were encircled or rounded up over the next two days. Only a handful reached the Elbe and safety.

Soviet officers searched the burnt-out remains of tanks carefully on orders from Front headquarters. 'Among the crews killed,' wrote Zhukov, 'none of Hitler's entourage were found, but it was impossible to recognize what was left in the burnt-out tanks.' Nobody knows how many died in these attempts to escape Soviet captivity.

At 1.55 a.m. on 2 May, the eighteen-year-old announcer Richard Beier made the very last broadcast of the Grossdeutscher Rundfunk from its studio in the bunker on the Masurenallee. The transmitter at Tegel had been overlooked by the Russians. 'The Führer is dead,' he announced, according to his script. 'Long live the Reich!'

26

The End of the Battle

Soon after 1 a.m. on 2 May, General Chuikov had been woken yet again. Red Army signals units had picked up repeated transmissions from the German LVI Panzer Corps requesting a cease-fire. Emissaries would come under a white flag to the Potsdamer bridge. Colonel von Dufving, accompanied by two majors, appeared. He held discussions with one of Chuikov's commanders, then returned to General Weidling. Weidling surrendered with his staff at 6 a.m. and was taken to Chuikov's headquarters, where he prepared an order to the garrison to capitulate.

On that chilly dawn, the last prisoners of the Gestapo left in its Prinz-Albrechtstrasse headquarters still did not know whether they were about to be liberated by the Red Army or murdered by their captors. Pastor Reinecke was the only priest to be spared from the massacre of a week before. 'What I experienced as sadism during those last one and a half weeks,' he wrote in a letter, 'cannot be described here.'

The survivors were a mixed group. One of his cell companions was the Communist Franz Lange, who said afterwards that, despite having had nothing to do with the Church since the age of sixteen, he would never forget Reinecke's ability to find the strength to survive through silent prayer. Another was Joseph Wagner, a former Gauleiter of Silesia, who had fallen out with the regime because of his Catholicism. The Gestapo had arrested him after the July plot.

On 1 May, their cell door had been thrown open to shouts of '*Raus! Raus!*' They had been chased downstairs by the SS guards, who had killed one of their number, a Wehrmacht NCO, on the way. The remaining six were then locked in another cell, provided with food and water, next to the SS guards' own quarters. Lange heard the Sturmbannführer in charge explain to one of his men with the unique logic of the SS, 'We're sparing these ones as proof that we shot no prisoners.' During the afternoon the six survivors heard the guards preparing to pull out. By nightfall, they were left in the darkness of the building Berliners had dubbed the 'House of Horror' when it became known that prisoners were strapped in manacles diagonally across the walls of its cellars like a medieval torture chamber.

Not long after dawn on 2 May they heard voices. The flap on their cell window opened. A voice asked them in Russian for the key to open the door. 'No key,' replied Lange, the Communist, who knew a little of the language. 'We are prisoners.' The soldier went away and a few minutes later they heard the sound of axes crashing into the door. Soon it swung open. They found themselves looking into the face of a smiling young Red Army soldier.

He and his comrades took them into the SS guards' canteen to offer them food. One of their guns went off by accident, a tragically common occurrence in the Red Army. Joseph Wagner, the former Gauleiter, fell dead at Pastor Reinecke's side.

Other Red Army soldiers wasted little time upstairs. The silk panels lining the walls of Himmler's grand reception room were slashed from their battens and bundled into packs, ready for the next five-kilo parcels to be sent home.

In the Führer bunker, General Krebs and General Burgdorf had sat down side by side at some time in the early hours of that morning, drawn their Luger pistols and blown their brains out. Rochus Misch, probably the last member of the SS *Leibstandarte* to leave the building, saw them slumped together. After all the brandy they had consumed, they were fortunate not to have botched their suicide most painfully. Captain Schedle, the commander of the *Leibstandarte* guard in the Reich Chancellery, had also shot himself. A foot wound had prevented him from getting away with the Bormann party. Apart from the doctors, nurses and wounded in the cellars, the Reich Chancellery was virtually deserted when Misch crept out.

The dramatic Soviet account of storming the Reich Chancellery that morning has to be taken with a good deal of caution, especially since the vast majority of Mohnke and Krukenberg's men had taken part in the breakout the night before. Descriptions of rolling up a howitzer to the Wilhelmplatz to blast in the front doors and 'severe battles' in corridors and on the stairs were made to sound like a companion piece to the capture of the Reichstag. The red banner was taken to the roof by Major Anna Nikulina from the political department of the 9th Rifle Corps in Berzarin's 5th Shock Army. And, for good measure, 'Sergeant Gorbachov and Private Bondarev fastened a red banner over the main entrance of the Reich Chancellery.'

Of the previous night's fugitives from the Führer bunker, only the first group to leave had stayed together. Led by Brigadeführer Mohnke, it included Hitler's personal pilot, Hans Baur, the chief of his bodyguard, Hans Rattenhuber, the secretaries and Hitler's dietician, Constanze Manzialy. In the early hours of 2 May, they had been forced to hide in a cellar off the Schönhauserallee when the area was swamped with Soviet troops. They remained concealed there until that afternoon, when finally discovered by Soviet troops. Resistance was pointless. The men were arrested immediately, but the women were allowed to go.

Traudl Junge and Gerda Christian disguised themselves as men. But the striking Tyrolean Constanze Manzialy became separated from them almost immediately. One account claims that she was seized by a huge Russian infantryman and assaulted by him and his comrades. Nobody knows whether she resorted to the cyanide ampoule which Hitler had presented in a brass container to each of his staff as going-away presents. In any case, she was never seen again. Both Traudl Junge and Gerda Christian, despite alarming adventures, managed to reach the other side of the Elbe.

Many German soldiers and officers had contrived to spend their last night of freedom in breweries. Captain Finckler met his regimental commander from the 9th Parachute Division in a brewery in Prenzlauerberg, not far from where Mohnke and his group were cornered. As a farewell, the two men shared a bottle of wine with alternate swigs as there were no glasses.

In the Schultheiss brewery that morning, a young Luftwaffe flak helper asked what was going on when he heard shots. 'Come around to the back,' a comrade said to him. 'The SS are shooting themselves . . . You have to watch.' Many were foreigners in the Waffen SS. Hitler's SS adjutant, Otto Günsche, was taken prisoner there by the Red Army later in the morning. He, like Mohnke, Rattenhuber and the others, was immediately handed over to SMERSH for interrogation. Stalin wanted to discover for certain what had happened to Hitler and whether he was still alive.

The decision on 29 April to send the SMERSH department of the 3rd Shock Army to the Reich Chancellery, an objective clearly in the 5th Shock Army's sector, could only have been taken at the very highest level. Beria and Abakumov, the chief of SMERSH, appear not only to have kept Zhukov and the military authorities in the dark, but also to have side-lined Abakumov's rival, General Serov, the NKVD chief of the 1st Belorussian Front.

The SMERSH team, which had its own signals detachment, had probably been listening in to 5th Shock Army wavelengths. They arrived within minutes of the report that the objective had been attacked. General Berzarin had promised the gold star of Hero of the Soviet Union to the soldier who discovered Hitler's body, so the troops who had taken the Reich Chancellery were less than happy when SMERSH officers turned up and ordered them out. Only Berzarin's outer cordon round the complex was left in place. As an added insult to the 5th Shock Army, the counter-intelligence group had brought in a sapper detachment from the 3rd Shock Army to check the Reich Chancellery for explosives and booby traps.

Captain Shota Sulkhanishvili, who commanded these sappers, was uneasy to find that they were working with SMERSH. 'My comrades and I tried to keep as far as possible from them,' he said. 'We were afraid of them.' But SMERSH were afraid of being blown up, and they did exactly what the sappers told them until the place was thoroughly checked. In fact, the only explosives found were reserve stores of panzerfausts, ready primed in packages of three. The sappers were also amazed at the storerooms full of champagne and 'orange briquettes of bread in cellophane packs'. Sulkhanishvili, who had fought at Stalingrad, immediately thought of the frozen bread there which they had not even been able to chop with an axe. In the garden they came across two badly charred corpses which appeared to have 'shrunk in size and looked like puppets'. The sappers, having completed their task, were rapidly sent away. The SMERSH officers recognized the outsize head from caricatures in the Soviet press, and the orthopaedic boot confirmed whose body it was. Alongside, lay the body of Magda Goebbels, with the gold cigarette case and Hitler's party badge.

The SMERSH detachment, closely supervised by Lieutenant General Aleksandr Anatolievich Vadis, the chief of the SMERSH directorate with the 1st Belorussian Front, was naturally more preoccupied with finding Hitler's body. The pressure from Moscow was intense. That morning *Pravda* had declared that the announcement of Hitler's death was just a fascist trick. One can reasonably assume that such a statement was made at Stalin's instigation, or at least with his approval. The whole question of Hitler's fate had begun to assume immense political significance before the facts were clear. Marshal Zhukov, well aware of Stalin's intense interest in the matter, went to visit the Reich Chancellery that very day, even before the firing in the city had stopped. 'They did not let me go down,' Zhukov said twenty years later, when he finally learned the truth. 'It wasn't safe down there,' they had told him. He was also informed on that first visit that 'the Germans had buried all the corpses, but who buried them and where, nobody knew'. Yet Goebbels's body had not been buried. It had been found immediately on the surface. Zhukov was apparently again refused access two days later. The headquarters of the 1st Belorussian Front was informed of the discovery of Goebbels's corpse, but no more. General Telegin, the chief of the political department, urgently requested the *Stavka* in Moscow to send forensic experts.

The closest the SMERSH officers seemed to get to Hitler was going through his tunics in his room and looking at the portrait of Frederick the Great at which he used to stare. Rzhevskaya, meanwhile, had started work on Reich Chancellery documents. She discovered ten thick notebooks containing Goebbels's diaries up to July 1941. (Vadis claimed the discovery as his own.) She also found Raya, their signaller, trying on a white evening dress of Eva Braun's, but rejecting it as indecent because of the *décolletage*. The young woman soldier selected no more than a pair of her blue shoes.

In the cellars, Professor Haase and Dr Kunz continued to look after the wounded lying in the corridor. They had only a couple of nurses left. Many of the young female BdM helpers, who had come from assisting their Hitler Youth counterparts at the Reichssportsfeld, had rushed up the Wilhelmstrasse to evacuate the wounded from the cellars of the blazing Hotel Adlon. SMERSH did not disturb the hospital section at all. One of the nurses described the officers' behaviour as 'exemplary'. A senior officer even advised the women to lock their doors that night because he 'could not vouch for his soldiers'.

SMERSH officers soon began filtering their prisoners. Those selected for interrogation were escorted to the Reich Institute for the Blind, on the Oranienstrasse. But the counter-intelligence investigators refused to believe what they were told about Hitler's suicide. Vadis brought in more and more men to complete a minute search, but it was not easy underground. The electricity generator had broken down, so there was no light, except from torches, and the air in the bunker became heavy and damp without the ventilation system.

The lack of success prompted Stalin to order Beria to send another NKVD general, in theory representing the *Stavka*, to oversee the search and report back constantly. Even the officers in the SMERSH operational group were not allowed to know his name. Major Bystrov and his colleagues found themselves having to repeat every single interrogation in front of this new general. As soon as each interview was over, the general immediately went to telephone Beria on a secure line to report. The obsession with secrecy was so great that Rzhevskaya was made to sign each interview transcript with the acknowledgement that she would be guilty of betraying state security if she repeated a word of what had been said.

When the 350-strong garrison of the Zoo flak tower finally emerged, Colonel Haller apparently tipped off one of the Soviet officers that there were two generals hidden inside who hoped to slip out of Berlin. One of them had already committed suicide by the time Soviet soldiers found him on the fourth floor. They directed the writer Konstantin Simonov to him.

Simonov had just reached Berlin early on that morning of 2 May, and he found sporadic firing, mainly Soviet guns firing at buildings where the SS still refused to surrender. He described these as 'post-mortal convulsions'. In the flak tower there was no more light, so they made their way by torchlight. A lieutenant showed him the small concrete room. 'On the bunk, with his eyes open, lay the dead general, a tall man of about forty-five, with short hair and a handsome, calm face. His right hand lay alongside his body, clutching a pistol. With his left hand he held, by the shoulders, the body of a young woman lying next to him. The woman lay with her eyes closed, young and beautiful, wearing, I remember it very well, a white English blouse with short sleeves and a grey uniform skirt. The general was wearing an ironed shirt, high boots, his high-collared jacket was not buttoned. Between the general's legs stood a bottle of champagne, one-third full.' It was part of the tawdry end to what Simonov called 'the bandit glory of the former fascist empire'. He also found it fitting that the man who took the surrender of the capital of the Reich was General Chuikov, who had commanded the defence at Stalingrad. 'It seemed as if history itself had tried its best to bring this army to Berlin and make the surrender of Berlin look particularly symbolic.'

German civilians, however, were in no mood for symbolism. They covered the faces of dead soldiers with newspapers or a piece of uniform and queued at Red Army field kitchens, which began to feed them on Berzarin's orders. The fact that there was a famine in Soviet Central Asia at that time, with families reduced to cannibalism, did not influence the new policy of attempting to win over the German people. But the change in the Party line had still not filtered down.

Soviet soldiers entered the improvised field hospitals armed with sub-machine guns and prodded each man in the chest threateningly: '*Du SS?*' they asked. When one of them came to a Swedish Waffen SS volunteer with the *Nordland*, he prodded him hard in the pit of the stomach and asked the same question. The Swede claimed that he was just an ordinary Wehrmacht soldier. '*Da, da. Du SS!*' the Red Army soldier insisted. The Swede, who had destroyed his papers, including his passport, which showed that he had fought for the Finns against the Soviet Union, somehow managed a smile as if to say how ridiculous. The soldier gave up, not noticing that he was in a cold sweat. It took another six months before the NKVD discovered that members of the SS had 'their blood group tattooed on the inside of their left arm'.

In both the Alexanderplatz and the Pariserplatz, the wounded were laid in the street wrapped in blankets. German Red Cross nurses and BdM girls continued to treat them. Just to the north, Soviet guns blasted into submission a group of doomed SS still holding out in a building on the Spree. In all directions, smoke from ruins continued to deform the sky. Red Army soldiers flushed out Wehrmacht, SS, Hitler Youth and Volkssturm. They emerged from houses, cellars and subway tunnels, their faces almost black with grime and stubble. Soviet soldiers shouted, '*Hände hoch!*' and their prisoners dumped their weapons and held their hands as high as possible. A number of German civilians sidled up to Soviet officers to denounce soldiers who continued to hide.

Vasily Grossman accompanied General Berzarin to the centre of the city. He was staggered by the scale of destruction all around, wondering how much had been wrought by American and British bombers. A Jewish woman and her elderly husband approached him. They asked about the fate of Jews who had been deported. When he confirmed their worst fears, the old man burst into tears. Grossman was apparently accosted a little later by a smart German lady wearing an astrakhan coat. They conversed pleasantly. 'But surely you aren't a Jewish commissar?' she suddenly said to him.

The German officers who had signed demobilization papers for all their men so that they could avoid prison camp had wasted their time. Anybody in any sort of uniform, even firemen and railwaymen, were rounded up for the first columns to be marched eastwards.

'I had a terrible mass of impressions,' Grossman noted down. 'Fires and smoke, smoke, smoke. Huge crowds of prisoners of war. Faces are full of tragedy and the grief on many faces is not only personal suffering but also that of the citizen of a destroyed country.' The personal suffering and dread of the future were indeed great, both for the men and boys about to be marched away and for the women and girls left behind. 'Prisoners,' he jotted. 'Policemen, clerks, old men and schoolboys, almost children. Many of the men are walking with their wives, beautiful young women, some of whom are laughing and trying to cheer up their husbands. One young soldier with two children, a boy and a girl. The people around are very nice to the prisoners. Faces are sad, they give them water and bread.' In the Tiergarten, Grossman saw a wounded German soldier sitting on a bench with a girl medical assistant, hugging her. 'They don't look at anyone. The world around has ceased to exist for them. When I walk past them an hour later they are still sitting in the same position.'

'This overcast, cold and rainy day is undoubtedly the day of Germany's collapse in the smoke, among the blazing ruins, among hundreds of corpses littering the streets.' Some of the dead, he noted, had been crushed by tanks, 'squeezed out like tubes'. He saw a dead old woman, 'her head leant against the wall, sitting on a mattress near a front door with an expression of quiet and everlasting grief'. And yet a short distance away, Russians were amazed by the thoroughness of the German *hausfrau*: 'In the streets which are already quiet, the ruins are being tidied and swept. Women are sweeping pavements with brooms as if they were indoor rooms.'

Grossman must have walked round and round for most of that day. In the 'huge and powerful' Reichstag, he found Soviet soldiers 'making fires in the entrance hall, rattling their cooking pans and opening tins of condensed milk with bayonets'.

While SMERSH carried on its work in the cellars and in the Führer bunker, Grossman was allowed, like other visitors, into the gigantic reception rooms of the Reich Chancellery. In one of them, Hitler's huge metal globe of the world was crushed and broken. In another, 'a dark-skinned young Kazakh with wide cheekbones' was learning to ride a bicycle. Grossman, along, it seems, with almost every other visitor, collected a few souvenirs to take back to Moscow.

In the Zoo, where there had been heavy fighting close to the great flak tower, he found 'broken cages, the corpses of monkeys, tropical birds and bears. On the island of baboons, babies are gripping their mothers' bellies with their tiny hands.' In front of a cage with a dead gorilla, he spoke to the old attendant, who had spent the last thirty-seven years looking after the monkeys.

'Was she fierce?' Grossman asked.

'No, she just roared loudly,' the primate keeper replied. 'Humans are much fiercer.'

Grossman encountered many people that day. Released foreign labourers sang songs but also shouted curses at German soldiers. It was only later in the day, when the firing finally stopped, that 'the colossal scale of the victory' began to sink in. Spontaneous celebrations took place round 'the tall woman' – the Siegessäule victory column in the Tiergarten. 'The tanks are so covered in flowers and red banners that you can hardly see them. Gun barrels have flowers in them like trees in spring. Everyone is dancing, singing, laughing. Hundreds of coloured signal flares are fired into the air. Everyone salutes the victory with bursts from sub-machine guns, rifles and pistols.' But Grossman learned later that many of those celebrating were 'the living dead'. In their desperation for alcohol, soldiers had drunk from metal barrels containing industrial solvent which had been found nearby. They took at least three days to die.

South-west of Berlin, General Wenck's soldiers continued to transport the shattered survivors of the Ninth Army in trucks and goods trains to the Elbe. Twelfth Army soldiers hoped that they too, with the civilian refugees, would be able to cross over to the Americans during the next few days. There were over 100,000 soldiers and almost as many civilian refugees moving south of Brandenburg towards the Elbe. Increasingly strong Soviet attacks further north, especially between Havelberg and Rathenau, risked cutting them off.

On 3 May, news of events in Berlin arrived. General Wenck immediately issued an order reinstating the military salute instead of the Nazi version. 'It's over!' wrote Peter Rettich, the battalion commander with the *Scharnhorst* Division. 'Hitler is dead, expired in the Reich Chancellery. Berlin taken by the Russians. Images of the collapse pile up. It's deeply shocking but nothing can be done.' He and his few remaining men were now marching back to the Elbe and the Americans as fast as they could go. As they went through Genthin, he saw the canal full of empty bottles of schnapps. Soldiers ahead had obviously looted some store or depot. 'Signs of disintegration!' Rettich noted in his diary.

General Wenck's staff issued orders to Twelfth Army divisions for a fighting withdrawal to the river, where they would have to defend a perimeter against Soviet attack. Wenck also ordered one of his corps commanders, General Baron von Edelsheim, to negotiate with the US

Ninth Army. On 3 May, Edelsheim and his staff crossed the Elbe near Tangermünde in an amphibious vehicle and made contact with the local American commander. Surrender negotiations took place next day in the town hall of Stendal. The American commander, General William Simpson, was in a difficult position. He had to consider not just the humanitarian concerns, but also the United States's obligations to its Soviet ally, as well as the practical problem of feeding and dealing with such a huge influx. He decided to receive wounded and unarmed soldiers, but he refused Edelsheim's request to help build and repair bridges to assist the evacuation. He also refused to accept civilian refugees. They were in any case supposed to return home at the end of the war.

The next morning, 5 May, the crossing of the Elbe began in earnest at three points: the very badly damaged railway bridge between Stendal and Schönhausen; the remnants of the road bridge near Tangermünde; and the ferry at Ferchland, a dozen kilometres to the south. The survivors of the Ninth Army were given first priority. Everyone remaining on the east bank wondered how long they had left. The Twelfth Army's defensive perimeter was already being reduced under Soviet attack. It had a frontage on the river of under twenty-five kilometres long and was about eighteen kilometres deep in the middle. Soviet artillery fire started to inflict heavy casualties on civilian refugees as well as soldiers.

The feelings of Twelfth Army soldiers at this time were very mixed. They were proud of their rescue mission, loathed the Red Army, were furious with the Americans for not having advanced further and detested the Nazi regime which had betrayed its own people. It all seemed to be summed up for them on the road of refugees to Tangermünde. By the side of it a Nazi Party hoarding still proclaimed, 'It is thanks to our Führer!'

US Army detachments controlled and filtered the flow of soldiers on to the bridges, searching for SS, foreigners and civilians. Some of them relieved German soldiers of watches and medals as well as their weapons. Many German soldiers gave their steel helmets and greatcoats to women in an attempt to smuggle them over, but the majority were discovered and pulled out of the queue. Other threatened groups also tried to slip across. Soviet-born 'Hiwis' still in their Wehrmacht uniform attempted to infiltrate the queues. They knew that they faced a terrible retribution if taken by Soviet troops. There had been 9,139 Hiwis on the ration strength of the Ninth Army at the beginning of April on the Oder, but no more than 5,000 could have survived to reach the Elbe.

Soldiers of the Waffen SS heard that the Americans would hand them over to the Red Army, so they destroyed their papers and ripped off their badges. Some of the foreign Waffen SS pretended to be forced labourers. Joost van Ketel, a dentist with the SS *Nederland* Division, had managed to escape arrest when stopped by Red Army soldiers in the forest near Halbe. '*Nix SS*,' he had said. '*Russki Kamerade-Hollandia.*' He had shown a red, white and blue striped pass, and this was accepted. Ketel managed the same trick with the Americans further south near Dessau, but his German companion was caught out immediately.

General Wenck had established his headquarters in the park at Schönhausen, the seat of Prince Bismarck. The irony that it should end there of all places was plain, since it had been Bismarck's firm belief that Germany should avoid war with Russia at all costs. By 6 May, the surrounding bridgehead had been compressed to eight kilometres wide and two deep and the battalions defending the perimeter were virtually out of ammunition. Soviet tank, artillery and katyusha rocket bombardments were killing thousands of those still queuing to cross the single-track bridges. It was a question of '*Kriegsglück*' – 'the fortunes of war' – whether you were killed in the last moments. But the increased onslaught on 6 May also put the American troops filtering the refugees in danger. The US Ninth Army, anxious not to lose men to Soviet fire, withdrew them across the river and pulled back a little way from the Elbe. This presented just the opportunity the refugees needed. They surged across.

'Quite a few people who were not able to cross the Elbe killed themselves,' said Wenck's chief of staff, Colonel Reichhelm. Others tried to get across the broad, fast-flowing river using dinghies and rafts fashioned out of planks of wood or fuel cans lashed together. Colonel von Humboldt, the operations officer, remembers canoes, skiffs and every sort of craft imaginable being used. 'The real problem,' he pointed out, 'was that one person had to bring the boat back, and among people escaping, there were few volunteers.' American detachments on the far side still tried to send them back, but they would try again. General von Edelsheim claimed that American troops were given orders to shoot at boats with civilian refugees, but this is uncertain. Strong swimmers took across the end of a line of signal cable held in their teeth, then fastened it to a tree or root on the far bank. Weaker swimmers and women and children hauled their way across on these makeshift lines, but they often broke. Scores of soldiers and civilians drowned in their attempts to cross, maybe even several hundred of them.

On the morning of 7 May, the perimeter started to collapse. The last few artillery pieces of the Twelfth Army fired off their remaining shells and then blew up their guns, 'by far the hardest moment for any artilleryman', wrote Rettich. He was shocked by the disintegration of some units and took great pride in the soldierly bearing of his cadets in the *Scharnhorst* Division – 'probably the last formation of the Wehrmacht still in battle order in northern Germany'. Prior to pulling back across the river, they destroyed their last stores and vehicles. He dealt with his 'faithful Tatra jeep' by pouring a can of petrol over it and then lobbing in a hand grenade. Hundreds of abandoned horses ran around nervously. Men tried to chase them into the water in the vain hope of forcing them to swim the river. It was 'a pitiful sight'.

Rettich assembled his remaining men near the Schönhausen bridge for a farewell address about the hard road which they had travelled together. In bitter defiance of defeat, they voiced 'a thundering "*Sieg Heil*" to Germany' before they left, 'to be parted for ever'. As they crossed the twisted iron bridge, they threw their weapons, binoculars and other remaining equipment into the dark waters of the Elbe.

That afternoon, General Wenck crossed the river close to his head-quarters at Schönhausen. He and his staff had left it until the last moment. Soviet troops opened fire on his boat, wounding two NCOs, one fatally.

In Berlin, meanwhile, the search for Hitler's corpse continued without success. The bodies of the six Goebbels children were not discovered until 3 May. They were found under blankets in their three sets of bunk-beds. A dark blush lingered on their faces from the cyanide, making it look as if they were still alive and asleep. Vice-Admiral Voss, Hitler's Kriegsmarine liaison officer, was brought in by SMERSH to identify them. Voss, apparently, looked absolutely devastated when he saw them.

A strange event occurred that day when generals from the 1st Belorussian Front visited the Reich Chancellery. The body of a man with a small toothbrush moustache and diagonal fringe was found. The corpse was subsequently eliminated from the investigation because its socks were darned. The Führer, it was agreed, would not have worn darned socks. Stalin was far more concerned to hear that some ordinary soldiers had been allowed to see Goebbels's corpse. The officers responsible were punished.

The interpreter Rzhevskaya, writing about the veil of secrecy thrown over the identification of Hitler's body, emphasized that 'Stalin's system needed the presence of both external and internal enemies, and he feared the release of tension'. The double was presumably to be used as evidence of some sort of anti-Soviet plot. Even when Hitler's real body was found on the very next day, orders immediately came from the Kremlin that nobody was to breathe a word to anybody. Stalin's strategy, quite evidently, was to associate the west with Nazism by pretending that the British or Americans must be hiding him. Rumours already circulated at a high level that he had escaped through tunnels or by aeroplane with Hanna Reitsch at the last moment, and was hiding in American-occupied Bavaria. This was almost certainly the black propaganda extension of Stalin's suspicion that the Western Allies would do a deal with the Nazis behind his back.

On 5 May, the corpses of Hitler and Eva Braun were finally found after more interrogations. It was a windy day with an overcast sky. A renewed and more thorough search of the Reich Chancellery garden was made. A soldier spotted the corner of a grey blanket in the earth at the bottom of a shell crater. Two charred corpses were exhumed. The bodies of a German shepherd dog and a puppy were found in the same pit. General Vadis was immediately informed.

Before dawn the next morning, Captain Deryabin and a driver wrapped the corpses of Hitler and Eva Braun in sheets and smuggled them out past Berzarin's cordon. They drove them to the SMERSH base at Buch, on the north-east edge of Berlin. There, in a small brick clinic, Dr Faust, Colonel Kraevsky and other pathologists summoned to examine Goebbels's corpse began work on the most important remnants of the Third Reich. According to Rzhevskaya, the forensic experts were upset when ordered to maintain absolute and everlasting secrecy about their work on Hitler's corpse. Whether or not Telegin knew of its discovery is uncertain. He was in any case arrested by Beria on another charge later. But neither Berzarin nor Zhukov was informed that Hitler's body had been found. In fact Zhukov felt deeply betrayed when he finally found out two decades later.

Vadis, to be absolutely sure that they had the true corpse before he informed Beria and Stalin, ordered further checks. His men found the assistant of Hitler's dentist. She examined the jaws from Hitler's skull and confirmed that they were indeed the Führer's. She recognized the bridgework. The jaws had been specially detached for the purpose and were kept in a red satin-lined box – 'the sort used for cheap jewellery', observed Rzhevskaya. On 7 May, Vadis felt confident enough of his facts to write his report.

The death of Hitler, although it did not bring an immediate end to the war in Europe, certainly precipitated its terminal events. German forces in northern Italy and southern Austria, nearly a million men, surrendered on 2 May. Churchill wanted to dash for Fiume and secure Trieste before Tito's Yugoslav partisans seized it. The race for the Baltic coast of Schleswig-Holstein was won by the British 2nd Army's dash north of the Elbe to Lübeck and Trävemunde. Allied troops prepared to move rapidly in to liberate Denmark. Rokossovsky's 2nd Belorussian Front, now cut off from the prize of Denmark, had occupied almost all of Mecklenburg by then. His armies had, however, taken comparatively few prisoners. To Soviet fury, the remnants of Manteuffel's Third Panzer Army and General von Tippelskirch's Twenty-First Army had moved westwards to surrender to the British. These mass surrenders to the Western Allies deprived the Soviet Union of slave labour in compensation for war damage during the Wehrmacht's invasion. Just after the final surrender, Eisenhower, still unwilling to upset the Kremlin, informed the *Stavka* that all German troops, including Schörner's, would be handed over to the Red Army. This was 'accepted with great satisfaction' by Antonov.

On the afternoon of 4 May, General Admiral von Friedeburg and General Kinzel, Heinrici's former chief of staff, arrived at Field Marshal Montgomery's headquarters on Luneburg Heath to sign an instrument of surrender for all German forces in north-west Germany, Denmark and Holland. When General Bradley met Marshal Konev on 5 May, he handed him a map marking the position of every US Army division. Bradley received nothing in return, except a warning that the Americans should not meddle in Czechoslovakia. Soviet signals were unashamedly hostile, if not brutal. In San Francisco, Molotov told a shaken Edward Stettinius, the Secretary of State, that the sixteen Polish negotiators sent to discuss matters with the Soviet-controlled provisional government had been charged with the murder of 200 members of the Red Army.

Konev's 1st Ukrainian Front had received orders to turn south to take Prague. There, the Czech resistance, aided by General Vlasov's troops in a doomed turnaround, rose in revolt against Field Marshal Schörner's troops. Churchill had asked the Americans on 30 April to send in General Patton's Third Army to secure the city before the Red Army reached it, but General Marshall refused. Vienna, Berlin and Prague were all falling into Soviet hands and the whole of central Europe with them. Soviet occupation authorities in Austria had set up a provisional government without consulting the Allies. Breslau, the capital of Silesia, surrendered on 6 May after its appalling siege lasting nearly three months.

Vlasov himself had initially rejected the idea of betraying the Germans at the twelfth hour, but he stood no chance whatever he did. 'On 12 May 1945, near the town of Pilsen, Czechoslovakia,' reported the chief of the political department of the 1st Ukrainian Front, 'tankists of 25th Tank Corps captured traitor of the Motherland General Vlasov. The circumstances were as follows: one of the lieutenant colonels of the 25th Tank Corps was approached by a man from the Vlasov army with the rank of captain who stated, pointing at a car moving alone on the road towards the west, that General Vlasov was in this car. A pursuit was organized immediately and tankists from 25th Tank Corps caught the traitor.' Vlasov, who apparently attempted to hide under some blankets, was said to be found carrying an 'American passport in his name' (an item which may have been added to the list for reasons of anti-western propaganda), 'his Party card, which he had preserved, and a copy of his order to his troops to stop fighting, lay down their weapons and surrender to the Red Army'. Vlasov himself was flown from Konev's headquarters back to Moscow. There, boasts were later made of his death under terrible and prolonged torture. On 13 and 14 May, 20,000 of his men were rounded up in the region of Pilsen and sent to specially prepared camps for interrogation by SMERSH.

In the south, meanwhile, the Americans had pushed on eastwards and south-eastwards from Munich, as well as southwards into the Tyrol, but then halted on Eisenhower's orders. The French had captured Bregenz on Lake Constance. General von Saucken, with the remains of the Second Army, still held out in the Vistula delta on the edge of East Prussia. In Courland, the divisions which Guderian had wanted to bring back to defend Berlin continued to resist, despite heavy bombardment from the Soviet armies surrounding them. And the Kriegsmarine, although short of fuel, continued its evacuations by sea from the Hela Peninsula, as well as Courland and the Vistula estuary. But the most intense activity continued round Prague, with Field Marshal Schörner's Army Group Centre resisting the attack of three Soviet Fronts.

In the early hours of 7 May, General Jodl, on behalf of Dönitz and the OKW, signed an instrument of surrender at Eisenhower's headquarters at Rheims. General Susloparov, the chief Soviet liaison officer with SHAEF, signed 'on behalf of the Soviet high command'. Stalin was furious when he heard. The surrender had to be signed in Berlin and it had to be taken by the Red Army, which had borne the brunt of the fighting. To make matters more provoking for him, the Western Allies wanted to announce victory in Europe the next day, because they would not be able to prevent newspapers publishing the details. Stalin, not surprisingly, considered this premature. Despite Jodl's signature in Rheims, Schörner's army group in Czechoslovakia continued to resist fiercely, and neither General von Saucken nor the huge force still trapped in Courland had surrendered. But the crowds already gathering to celebrate in London prompted Churchill to insist on an announcement on Tuesday 8 May. Stalin, despite compromising a little, now wanted it to be made at just past midnight, the very start of 9 May, following a full surrender in Berlin.

The Soviet authorities, however, could not prevent their own troops from jumping the gun with their celebrations. Koni Wolf, with the 7th Department of the 47th Army, fiddled with wireless dials for most of the day on 8 May. He picked up the announcement in London and yelled it to his comrades. News spread fast in Berlin. Young women soldiers wasted no time in washing their clothes, while Red Army soldiers went on a frenzied hunt for alcohol. SMERSH officers shouted to Rzhevskaya to get ready for a party. Having been told that she would 'answer with [her] head' if Hitler's jaws were lost, she spent an awkward evening, pouring drinks for others with one hand, while clinging on to the fancy red box with the other. It was a wise decision to entrust the evidence to a woman that night.

For those who had been fighting up to the very last moment, the news was even more joyously received. Those attacking the Twelfth Army's perimeter round Schönhausen on the Elbe had suffered heavy casualties. Yury Gribov's battalion lost nearly half its strength on 5 May, when attacking the remnants of the *Scharnhorst* Division. Their regimental commander, a Hero of the Soviet Union, had been killed two days later, in the last skirmishes. But by the evening of 8 May, the firing had stopped. 'We celebrated victory in the forest. We all lined up in a broad clearing and did not let the division commander finish his excited speech, with bursts of firing into the sky. Our hearts were happy and tears streamed down our cheeks.' Relief was always mixed with sadness too. 'The first toast to victory,' Red Army men said. 'The second to dead friends.'

The writer Konstantin Simonov watched the final drama in Berlin. Late in the morning of 8 May, he lay on a patch of grass at Tempelhof aerodrome, which had now been cleared of wrecked German aircraft. A Soviet guard of honour 300 strong was being drilled in presenting arms again and again by 'a fat, small colonel'. Zhukov's deputy, General Sokolovsky, then arrived. Soon, the first aircraft appeared. Andrei Vyshinsky, the prosecutor at the Moscow show trials and now the deputy foreign minister, arrived with a retinue of Soviet diplomats. He was to be Zhukov's political supervisor.

An hour and a half later another Dakota landed, bringing Air Chief Marshal Tedder, Eisenhower's deputy and representative, and General Carl Spaatz, the commander of the US Air Force in Europe. Tedder, Simonov noted, was slim, young and dynamic, 'smiling frequently and somehow in a forced manner'. Sokolovsky hurried to greet him and led his party towards the guard of honour.

A third aircraft landed. Keitel, Admiral Friedeburg and General

Stumpff, representing the Luftwaffe, emerged. General Serov hurried over and escorted the Germans round the other side of the guard of honour, in case it might be thought it was there to welcome them too. Keitel insisted on leading the way. In full uniform, holding his marshal's baton in his right hand, he walked with large strides, deliberately looking straight ahead.

Smart traffic controllers, young women soldiers with berets worn on the back of the head and sub-machine guns slung across their backs, had halted all vehicles to allow the staff cars a free passage to Zhukov's new headquarters in Karlshorst. The convoy of staff cars churned up thick dust-clouds as Germans watched from side streets and crossroads. Simonov imagined their thoughts as they saw their generals on the way to sign the final surrender.

Just before midnight the representatives of the allies entered the hall 'in a two-storey building of the former canteen of the German military engineering college in Karlshorst'. General Bogdanov, the commander of the 2nd Guards Tank Army, and another Soviet general sat down by mistake on seats reserved for the German delegation. A staff officer whispered in their ears and 'they jumped up, literally as if stung by a snake' and went to sit at another table. Western pressmen and newsreel cameramen apparently 'behaved like madmen'. In their desperation for good positions, they were shoving generals aside and tried to push in behind the top table under the flags of the four allies. Eventually Marshal Zhukov sat down. Tedder was placed on his right, and General Spaatz and General de Lattre de Tassigny on his left.

The German delegation was led in. Friedeburg and Stumpff looked resigned. Keitel tried to look imperious, glancing almost contemptuously from time to time at Zhukov. Simonov guessed that a rage was boiling within him. So did Zhukov, who also noted that his face had red blotches. The surrender documents were brought to the top table. First Zhukov signed, then Tedder, then Spaatz, then General de Lattre. Keitel sat very straight in his chair, with clenched fists. He threw his head further and further backwards. Just behind him, a tall German staff officer standing to attention 'was crying without a single muscle of his face moving'.

Zhukov stood up. 'We invite the German delegation to sign the act of capitulation,' he said in Russian. The interpreter translated, but

Keitel, by an impatient gesture, signalled that he had understood and that they should bring him the papers. Zhukov, however, pointed to the end of his table. 'Tell them to come here to sign,' he said to the interpreter.

Keitel stood up and walked over. He ostentatiously removed his glove before picking up the pen. He clearly had no idea that the senior Soviet officer looking over his shoulder as he signed was Beria's representative, General Serov. Keitel put the glove back on, then returned to his place. Stumpff signed next, then Friedeburg.

'The German delegation may leave the hall,' Zhukov announced. The three men stood up. Keitel, 'his jowls hanging heavily like a bulldog's', raised his marshal's baton in salute, then turned on his heel.

As the door closed behind them, it was almost as if everybody in the room exhaled in unison. The tension relaxed instantaneously. Zhukov was smiling, so was Tedder. Everybody began to talk animatedly and shake hands. Soviet officers embraced each other in bear hugs. The party which followed went on until almost dawn, with songs and dances. Marshal Zhukov himself danced the *Russkaya* to loud cheers from his generals. From inside, they could clearly hear gunfire all over the city as officers and soldiers blasted their remaining ammunition into the night sky in celebration. The war was over.

27

Vae Victis!

Stalin saw the capture of Berlin as the Soviet Union's rightful reward, but the yield was disappointing and the waste terrible. A key target was the Reichsbank in Berlin. Serov accounted for 2,389 kilos in gold, twelve tons of silver coin and millions in banknotes from countries which had been occupied by the Axis. Yet the bulk of Nazi gold reserves had been moved westwards. Serov, however, was later accused of having also held back a certain proportion of the proceeds for the NKVD's 'operational expenses'.

The main objective was to strip Germany of all its laboratories, workshops and factories. Even the NKVD in Moscow provided a shopping list of items wanted from police forensic laboratories. The Soviet atomic programme, Operation Borodino, had the very highest priority of all, but considerable efforts were also made to track down V-2 rocket scientists, Siemens engineers and any other skilled technicians who could help the Soviet armaments industry catch up with the United States. Only a few, such as Professor Jung and his team who refused to help on nerve gas, managed to resist Soviet pressure. Most of the others enjoyed comparatively privileged conditions and the right to bring their families with them to the Soviet Union.

German scientific equipment, however, turned out to be rather less tractable than its human designers. The vast majority of items taken back to Moscow were of no use because they required an environment suitable for precision engineering and the purest raw materials. 'Socialism cannot benefit itself,' observed one of the Soviet scientists involved in stripping Berlin, 'even when it takes the whole of another country's technological infrastructure.'

Most of the programme of stripping laboratories and factories was marked by chaos and disaster. Red Army soldiers who discovered methyl alcohol drank it and shared it with their comrades. The contents of workshops were ripped out by working parties of German women, then left in the open, where they rusted. Even when finally transported back to the Soviet Union, only a small proportion was ever put to good use. Stalin's theory of industrial expropriation showed itself to be worse than futile. And this came on top of the Red Army's less than enlightened attitude towards German property in general. French prisoners of war were astonished at 'the systematic destruction of machinery in good repair which could be reused'. It was a huge dissipation of resources and condemned Soviet-occupied Germany to a backwardness from which it never recovered.

Personal looting continued to be just as wasteful as it had been in East Prussia, although it now became more exotic. Soviet generals behaved like pashas. Vasily Grossman described one of Chuikov's corps commanders during the last few days of the battle. This general had acquired 'two dachshunds (nice fellows), a parrot, a peacock and a guinea fowl which travel with him', he jotted in his notebook. 'It's all very lively at his headquarters.'

Most of a general's loot consisted of presents from subordinate commanders, who quickly grabbed the best items for their superiors when a schloss or fine house was taken. Zhukov was given a pair of Holland & Holland shotguns. They were later to form part of Abakumov's attempt to discredit him, almost certainly on Stalin's instructions. These two guns became, with that Stalinist compulsion to multiply everything in a denunciation, 'twenty unique shotguns made by Golland & Golland [*sic*]'.

At the other end of the chain of command, Red Army soldiers accumulated an interesting array of plunder. Young women soldiers were interested in assembling a trousseau 'from some Gretchen', hoping that they still might find a husband in a world short of men. Married soldiers collected cloth to send back to their wives, but also looted 'Gretchen knickers'. This sort of present confirmed the worst jealousies at home. Many Soviet wives were convinced that German women in Berlin were seducing their husbands.

Most soldiers, however, concentrated on items for rebuilding at home, despite the fact that they were too heavy for their five-kilo allowance. An officer told Simonov that his men removed panes of glass, then fastened a bit of wood on each side and bound them up with wire to send home. He recounted the scene at the Red Army post department.

'Come on, take it!' the soldier said. 'Come on, Germans smashed my house. Come on, take the parcel. If you don't, you're not the post department.'

Many sent a sack of nails. Someone brought a saw, rolled into a circle. 'You could at least have wrapped it in something,' a soldier in the post department told him.

'Come on, take it! I've no time. I've come from the front line!'

'And where's the address?'

'On the saw. Here, see?' The address was written in indelible pencil on the blade.

Other soldiers bribed German women with bread to sew their booty up in a sheet to make a parcel. It was a matter of pride to distribute gifts of distinction to family and friends at home, such as hats or watches. The obsession with watches prized them above far more valuable items. Soldiers would often wear several timepieces, with at least one on Moscow time and another on Berlin time. It was for this reason that they continued to prod civilians in the stomach with their sub-machine guns, demanding, '*Uri, uri!*' well after the surrender. And Germans would try to explain in the Soviet version of pidgin-German that their watches had already been taken: '*Uhr schon Kamerad*' – 'watch already surrender'.

Russian boys, some as young as twelve, turned up in Berlin to loot. Two of them, when arrested, admitted that they had come all the way from Vologda, well to the north of Moscow. Less surprisingly, foreign workers, in a carnival atmosphere, were responsible for a 'considerable amount of looting' in all liberated areas, a US Army report stated. 'The men head for the wine cellars, the women for the clothing shops and both gather whatever food they can on the way.' But 'much of the looting attributed to foreigners is actually being carried out by the Germans themselves'.

The German loathing and fear of forced labourers were visceral. They were horrified when the Western Allies insisted that they should be fed first. 'Even the Bishop of Munster,' Murphy wrote to the Secretary of State on 1 May, 'is quoted as referring to all displaced persons as Russians and demanding that the Allies should afford Germany protection from these "inferior peoples".' Contrary to German expectations, however, forced labourers were responsible for surprisingly little violence, when one considers how they had suffered after their deportation to Germany.

In Berlin, the feelings of the civilian population were very mixed. While embittered by the looting and rape, they were also astonished and grateful for the Red Army's major efforts to feed them. Nazi propaganda had convinced them that they would be systematically starved. General Berzarin, who went out and chatted with Germans queuing at Red Army field kitchens, soon became almost as much of a hero to Berliners as he was to his own men. His death in a drunken motorcycle accident soon afterwards provoked widespread sadness and rumours among the Germans that he had been murdered by the NKVD.

Germans were surprised by a less altruistic form of food aid. Soviet soldiers turned up with chunks of meat and told housewives to cook it for them in return for a share. Like all soldiers, they wanted 'to get their feet under a table' in a real kitchen in a real home. They always brought alcohol with them too. Everyone would drink solemnly to peace after eating, and then the soldiers would insist on a toast 'to the ladies'.

The worst mistake of the German military authorities had been their refusal to destroy alcohol stocks in the path of the Red Army's advance. This decision was based on the idea that a drunken enemy could not fight. Tragically for the female population, however, it was exactly what Red Army soldiers seemed to need to give them courage to rape as well as to celebrate the end of such a terrible war.

The round of victory celebrations did not signify an end to fear in Berlin. Many German women were raped as a part of the extended celebrations. A young Soviet scientist heard from an eighteen-year-old German girl with whom he had fallen in love that on the night of 1 May a Red Army officer had forced the muzzle of his pistol into her mouth and had kept it there throughout his attack to ensure her compliance.

Women soon learned to disappear during the 'hunting hours' of the evening. Young daughters were hidden in storage lofts for days on end.

Mothers emerged into the street to fetch water only in the early morning, when Soviet soldiers were sleeping off the alcohol from the night before. Sometimes the greatest danger came from one mother giving away the hiding place of other girls in a desperate bid to save her own daughters.

Berliners remember that, because all the windows had been blown in, you could hear the screams every night. Estimates from the two main Berlin hospitals ranged from 95,000 to 130,000 rape victims. One doctor deduced that out of approximately 100,000 women raped in Berlin, some 10,000 died as a result, mostly from suicide. The death rate was thought to be much higher among the 1.4 million who had suffered in East Prussia, Pomerania and Silesia. Altogether at least 2 million German women are thought to have been raped, and a substantial minority, if not a majority, appear to have suffered multiple rape. A friend of Ursula von Kardorff and the Soviet spy Schulze-Boysen was raped by 'twenty-three soldiers one after the other'. She had to be stitched up in hospital afterwards.

The reactions of German women to the experience of rape varied greatly. For many victims, especially protected young girls who had little idea of what was being done to them, the psychological effects could be devastating. Relationships with men became extremely difficult, often for the rest of their lives. Mothers were in general far more concerned about their children, and this priority made them surmount what they had endured. Other women, both young and adult, simply tried to blank out the experience. 'I must repress a lot in order, to some extent, to be able to live,' one woman acknowledged, when refusing to talk about the subject. Those who did not resist and managed to detach themselves from what was happening appear to have suffered much less. Some described it in terms of an 'out-of-body' experience. 'That feeling,' wrote one, 'has kept the experience from dominating the rest of my life.'

A robust cynicism of the Berlin variety also seemed to help. 'All in all,' wrote the anonymous diarist on 4 May, 'we are slowly beginning to look upon the whole business of rape with a certain humour, albeit of the grimmer kind.' They noted that the Ivans went for fatter women first of all, which provided a certain *schadenfreude*. Those who had not lost weight were usually the wives of Nazi Party functionaries and others who had profited from privileged positions.

Rape had become a collective experience – the diarist noted – and therefore it should be collectively overcome by talking among themselves. Yet men, when they returned, tried to forbid any mention of the subject, even out of their presence. Women discovered that while they had to come to terms with what had happened to them, the men in their lives often made things far worse. Those who had been present at the time were shamed at their inability to protect them. Hanna Gerlitz gave in to two drunk Soviet officers to save both her husband and herself. 'Afterwards,' she wrote, 'I had to console my husband and help restore his courage. He cried like a baby.'

Men who returned home, having evaded capture or been released early from prison camps, seem to have frozen emotionally on hearing that their wife or fiancée had been raped in their absence. (Many prisoners who had been in Soviet camps for longer periods also suffered from 'desexualization' as a result of starvation.) They found the idea of the violation of their women very hard to accept. Ursula von Kardorff heard of a young aristocrat who immediately broke off his engagement when he learned that his fiancée had been raped by five Russian soldiers. The anonymous diarist recounted to her former lover, who turned up unexpectedly, the experiences which the inhabitants of the building had survived. 'You've turned into shameless bitches,' he burst out. 'Every one of you. I can't bear to listen to these stories. You've lost all your standards, the whole lot of you!' She then gave him her diary to read, and when he found that she had written about being raped, he stared at her as though she had gone out of her mind. He left a couple of days later, saying that he was off to search for food. She never saw him again.

A daughter, mother and grandmother who were all raped together just outside Berlin consoled themselves with the idea that the man of the house had died during the war. He would have been killed trying to prevent it, they told themselves. Yet in reality few German men appear to have demonstrated what would admittedly have been a futile courage. One well-known actor, Harry Liebke, was killed by a bottle smashed over his head as he tried to save a young woman sheltering at his apartment, but he appears to have been fairly exceptional. The anonymous diarist even heard from one woman in the water-pump queue that when Red Army soldiers were dragging her from the cellar, a man who lived in the same block had said to her, 'Go along, for God's sake! You're getting us all into trouble.'

If anyone attempted to defend a woman against a Soviet attacker it was either a father or a young son trying to protect his mother. 'The thirteen-year-old Dieter Sahl,' neighbours wrote in a letter shortly after the event, 'threw himself with flailing fists at a Russian who was raping his mother in front of him. He did not succeed in anything except getting himself shot.'

Perhaps the most grotesque myth of Soviet propaganda was the notion 'that German intelligence left a great number of women in Berlin infected with venereal diseases with the purpose of infecting Red Army officers'. Another NKVD report specifically ascribed it to *Werwolf* activity. 'Some members of the underground organization, *Werwolf*, mostly girls, received from their leaders the task to harm Soviet commanders and render them unfit for duty.' Even just before the attack from the Oder, Soviet military authorities explained the increase in VD rates on the grounds that 'the enemy is prepared to use any methods to weaken us and to put our soldiers and officers out of action'.

Large numbers of women soon found that they had to queue at medical centres. It was small consolation to find so many in the same condition. One woman doctor set up a venereal diseases clinic in an air-raid shelter, with the sign 'Typhoid' written in Cyrillic outside to keep Russian soldiers away. As the film *The Third Man* illustrated, penicillin was soon the most sought-after item on the black market. The abortion rate also soared. It has been estimated that around 90 per cent of victims who became pregnant obtained abortions, although this figure appears extremely high. Many of the women who did give birth abandoned the child in the hospital, usually because they knew that their husband or fiancé would never accept its presence at home.

At times it is hard to know whether young Soviet officers suffered from cynicism or a completely blind idealism. 'The Red Army is the most advanced moral army in the world,' a senior lieutenant declared to a sapper officer. 'Our soldiers attack only an armed enemy. No matter where we are, we always set an example of humanity towards the local population and any displays of violence and looting are totally foreign to us.'

Most frontline rifle divisions demonstrated better discipline than, say, tank brigades and rear units. And a wide range of anecdotal evidence indicates that Red Army officers who were Jewish went out of their way to protect German women and girls. Yet it would appear that the majority of officers and soldiers turned a blind eye to Stalin's order of 20 April, issued through the *Stavka*, ordering all troops 'to change their attitudes towards Germans . . . and treat them better'. Significantly, the reason given for the instruction was that 'brutal treatment' provoked a stubborn resistance 'and such a situation is not convenient for us'.

A liberated French prisoner of war approached Vasily Grossman in the street on 2 May. 'Monsieur,' he said, 'I like your army and that is why it is painful for me to see how it is treating girls and women. It is going to do great harm to your propaganda.' This indeed proved to be the case. In Paris, Communist Party leaders, riding high on the crest of admiration for the Red Army, were appalled when returning prisoners of war recounted the less heroic version of events. But it still took a long time before the message began to get through to the Soviet authorities.

Many think that the Red Army was given two weeks to plunder and rape in Berlin before discipline was exerted, but it was not nearly so simple as that. On 3 August, three months after the surrender in Berlin, Zhukov had to issue even tougher regulations to control 'robbery', 'physical violence' and 'scandalous events'. All the Soviet propaganda about 'liberation from the fascist clique' was starting to backfire, especially when the wives and daughters of German Communists were treated as badly as everyone else. 'Such deeds and unsanctioned behaviour,' the order stated, 'are compromising us very badly in the eyes of German anti-fascists, particularly now that the war is over, and greatly assist fascist campaigns against the Red Army and the Soviet government.' Commanders were blamed for allowing their men to wander off unsupervised. 'Unsanctioned absences' had to cease. Sergeants and corporals were to check that their men were present every morning and every evening. Soldiers were to be issued with identity cards. Troops were not to leave Berlin without movement orders. In fact, the order contained a list of measures which any western army would have considered as normal even in barracks at home.

Articles in the international press followed the subject throughout the summer. The effect on client Communist Parties abroad, then at the height of their prestige, clearly alarmed the Kremlin. 'This scoundrel campaign,' wrote Molotov's deputy, 'is aimed to damage the very high reputation of the Red Army and to shift the responsibility for all that is happening in the occupied countries on to the Soviet Union . . . Our numerous friends all over the world need to be armed with information and facts for counter-propaganda.'

Standards of morality had indeed taken a battering, but in the circumstances there was little option. On returning to Berlin, Ursula von Kardorff saw the scenes of impoverished people bartering near the Brandenburg Gate. She was immediately reminded of a line in Brecht's *Threepenny Opera*, 'First comes food, then come morals.'

The Brandenburg Gate had become the main focus for barter and the black market at the beginning of May, when liberated prisoners of war and forced labourers traded their loot. Ursula von Kardorff found all sorts of women prostituting themselves for food or the alternative currency of cigarettes. '*Willkommen in Shanghai*,' remarked one cynic. Young women of thirty looked years older, she noticed.

The need to survive had distorted more than just morals. The anonymous diarist, a former publisher, was approached by a Soviet sailor so young that he should still have been at school. He asked her to find him a clean and decent girl who was of good character and affectionate. He would provide her with food, the usual ration being bread, herring and bacon. The writer Ernst Jünger, when a Wehrmacht officer in occupied Paris, observed that food is power. The power, of course, becomes even greater when a woman has a child to feed, as so many German soldiers found in France. In Berlin, the black-market exchange rate was based on *Zigarettenwährung* – 'cigarette currency' – so when American soldiers arrived with almost limitless cartons at their disposal, they did not need to rape.

The definition of rape had become blurred into sexual coercion. A gun or physical violence became unnecessary when women faced starvation. This could be described as the third stage in the evolution of rape in Germany in 1945. The fourth was a strange form of cohabitation in which many Soviet officers settled in with German 'occupation wives' who replaced the Soviet 'campaign wife'. Real wives back in the Soviet Union had been furious to hear of 'campaign wives', but their moral outrage knew no bounds when they heard of the new trend. The Soviet authorities were also appalled and enraged when a number of Red Army officers, intent on staying with their German mistresses, deserted once it was time to return to the Motherland.

After being approached by the young sailor, the diarist wondered whether she herself had become a whore by accepting the protection and nutritional largesse of a cultivated Russian major. Like most of his countrymen, he respected her education, while German men she knew tended to dislike women who had been to university. Yet wherever the truth lay between rape and prostitution, these pacts to obtain food and protection had thrown women back to a primitive, almost primeval state.

Ursula von Kardorff, on the other hand, foresaw that although German women had been forced to become even more resilient than German men, they would soon have to revert to stereotype on the men's return from prison camps. 'Perhaps we women,' she wrote, 'now face our hardest job in this war – to give understanding and comfort, support and courage to so many utterly defeated and desperate men.'

Germany had fought on for as long and as bitterly as it did because the idea of defeat produced 'a conviction of total catastrophe'. Germans believed that their country would be totally subjugated and that their soldiers would spend the rest of their lives as slaves in Siberia. Yet once resistance collapsed with Hitler's death, the change in German attitudes surprised Russians in Berlin. They were struck 'by the docility and discipline of the people', having half-expected the sort of ferocious partisan war which the Soviet people had mounted. Serov told Beria that the population was behaving 'with unquestioning obedience'. One of Chuikov's staff officers ascribed this to an ingrained 'respect for the powers that be'. At the same time, Red Army officers were amazed at the way so many Germans, quite unselfconsciously, produced Communist flags out of scarlet Nazi banners with the swastika cut out of the centre. Berliners referred to this turnaround as '*Heil Stalin!*'

This submissiveness, however, did not stop SMERSH and the NKVD from seeing every fugitive or incident as an example of *Werwolf* activity. Each NKVD Frontier Guards Regiment was arresting over 100 Germans a day in early May. Over half were handed over to SMERSH. Some of the worst denouncers to the Soviet authorities were former Nazis, perhaps trying to put their denunciations in before they themselves were revealed. SMERSH blackmailed former members of the Nazi Party into helping NKVD units hunt down SS and Wehrmacht officers. Squads with sniffer dogs were used to search apartments and allotment sheds, where many German deserters had so recently been hiding from SS and Feldgendarmerie detachments.

Soviet sabotage theories included the idea 'that leaders of fascist organizations are preparing mass poisonings in Berlin through selling poisoned lemonade and beer'. Children found playing with panzerfausts and abandoned weapons faced interrogation as suspected *Werwolf* members, and SMERSH was interested only in confessions. The one sign of overt defiance appears to have been a handful of Nazi posters in Lichtenberg, proclaiming, 'The Party Lives On!' There was also one striking exception to the general pattern of submission. On the night of 20 May, 'an unknown number of bandits' attacked Special NKVD camp No. 10 and liberated 466 prisoners. Major Kyuchkin, the camp commandant, was 'at a banquet' when the attack took place. Beria was furious. After the NKVD's strong criticism of senior army officers for their lack of vigilance, this incident was deeply embarrassing.

Women in Berlin just wanted to get life back to some semblance of normality. The most common sight in Berlin became the *Trümmerfrauen*, the 'rubble women', forming human chains with buckets to clear smashed buildings and salvage bricks. Many of the German men left in the city were either in hiding or had collapsed with psychosomatic illnesses as soon as the fighting was over.

Like most working parties, the women were paid at first in little more than handfuls of potatoes, yet the Berliner sense of humour did not fail. Every district was renamed. Charlottenburg had become 'Klamottenberg', which means 'heap of rubbish', Steglitz became '*steht nichts*' – 'nothing is standing' – and Lichterfelde became 'Trichterfelde' – 'the field of craters'. To a large degree this was an outward courage masking resignation and quiet despair. 'People were living with their fate,' remarked one young Berliner.

Employees and officials obeyed General Berzarin's order to return to their workplaces. SMERSH officers, using NKVD troops, cordoned off the Grossdeutscher Rundfunk building on the Masurenallee. All members of the staff were told to stand by their desks. They were deeply relieved that they had not tried to sabotage or destroy their equipment. The SMERSH officer in charge, Major Popov, who was accompanied by German Communists, treated them well. He also made sure that the troops protected the large number of young women in the building, even though this did not save them a few days later, when they were allowed to make their way home.

The German Communists brought back from the 'Moscow emigration' were totally subservient to their Soviet masters. They may have been on the winning side, but a profound sense of failure hung over them. This was because the German working class had done nothing to prevent the Nazi invasion of the Soviet Union in 1941. Their Soviet comrades did not let them forget this. Scathing remarks about the numbers of Germans who had emerged, claiming to be members of the Communist Party before 1933, provoked an angry disbelief that so few had taken up arms against the regime. The fact that the only well-known resistance to Hitler had existed in 'reactionary circles' did not improve their mood.

Beria regarded the leading Communists as 'idiots' and 'careerists'. The only one for whom he had any respect was the veteran leader, Wilhelm Pieck, a white-haired burly man with a round nose and a square head. The group being sent from Moscow to Germany met in Pieck's room before leaving. 'We had no idea what role [the German Communist] Party was to play or whether it would even be permitted,' recorded Markus Wolf, later the chief of East German intelligence in the Cold War. 'Our task was simply to support the Soviet military authorities.' He admitted that he was 'naïve enough to hope that the majority of Germans were happy to be freed from the Nazi regime and would greet the Soviet army as their liberator'.

On 27 May, a beautiful spring day, these German Communists flew over the centre of Berlin to land at Tempelhof aerodrome. They were shaken by the scenes of destruction. The city appeared to be beyond any hope of repair. Their personal feelings were also very mixed. It was a homecoming without conviction. The younger members brought up in the Soviet Union found it strange to hear German spoken on the streets. At the victory celebrations in Moscow two weeks before, Wolf had found himself thinking 'exactly as a young Russian would have done'. Yet within a couple of days of his arrival, he heard from German Communists just how the Red Army had treated the population. 'Our *frontoviki* have wrought havoc,' he wrote in his diary on 30 May. 'All women raped. Berliners have no more watches.' Goebbels's propaganda about the Red Army had created a terrible fear. 'Then came the experience, the reality, and as a result the absolute majority of Germans, especially those east of the Elbe, were very, very anti-Soviet.'

The leader of their group in Berlin was the widely loathed and despised Walther Ulbricht, a Stalinist bureaucrat well known for his tactics of denouncing rivals. Beria described him as 'a scoundrel capable of killing his father and his mother'. Wolf remembers his Saxon accent and high voice. He thought him a 'heartless' machine, whose only loyalty was to Soviet policy. Everything that came from Stalin was 'an absolute order'. Ulbricht told Wolf to abandon any hope of returning to the Soviet Union to continue his studies as an aircraft designer. He was sent to the broadcasting centre on the Masurenallee – the Grossdeutscher Rundfunk was rapidly renamed the Berliner Rundfunk – to carry out propaganda. There, Wolf found himself in charge of a programme called *A Sixth of the Earth*, devoted to the glorious industrial achievements of the Soviet Union. There was a complete ban from the Soviet authorities, represented in this case by General Vladimir Semyonov, on mentioning the three subjects about which Germans wanted to hear. These 'taboo themes' were 'rape, the fate of [German] prisoners of war and the Oder–Neisse line' – which meant the loss of Prussia, Pomerania and Silesia to Poland.

Although Soviet propaganda was now running its own programmes, the population of Berlin was ordered to hand in all wireless sets to their nearest military post. Magda Wieland remembers carrying her set to the local *kommandantur*, but as she came close, she saw the soldiers lounging outside start to look her up and down. She simply dropped the radio set in the middle of the road, turned round and ran.

Berliners, seeing campfires in their streets, shaggy Cossack ponies and even camels, tended to convince themselves that their city was occupied by 'Mongols'. This was largely a reflection of Goebbels's propaganda. The hundreds of photographs of Soviet troops in Berlin reveal only a small percentage of Central Asian origin. But weather-beaten skin, which had acquired a brown patina from sebum and dirt, and eyes narrowed from constant exposure to wind gave many soldiers an oriental appearance. One can see a similar effect in photographs of British and French soldiers at the end of the First World War. The bizarre images in Berlin streets lingered. Emaciated urchins played in the 'burnt-out tanks lying like stranded ships on the roadside'. But soon the blackened hulls were plastered with fly-posters offering dancing classes: a first, desperate attempt at economic revival from what Berliners saw as '*die Stunde Null*' – the lowest imaginable moment of their lives.

General Berzarin's main priorities were to restore the basics of life, especially essential services, such as electricity, water and then gas. Of the previous total of 33,000 hospital beds, only 8,500 could now be used. Some events were pointedly symbolic. The first Jewish religious service was held by a Red Army rabbi in the synagogue of the Jewish hospital in the Iranischestrasse on Friday 11 May. It was an understandably emotional occasion for those who had emerged from hiding or who had been saved at the last moment from execution.

Over a million people in the city were without any home at all. They continued to shelter in cellars and air-raid shelters. Smoke from cooking fires emerged from what looked like piles of rubble, as women tried to re-create something like a home-life for their children amid the ruins.

With 95 per cent of the tram system destroyed, and a large part of the U-Bahn and S-Bahn systems still under water from the explosion, to visit friends in other parts of the city required a strength which few possessed. Almost everyone felt weak from hunger, and they had to devote the majority of their energy to foraging. As soon as trains began to run, thousands clung on to the roof or the outside to reach the countryside to find food. They were known as 'hamsters', a name coined during the near-starvation of 1918, and the trains were known as the 'Hamster-express'.

Berliners, however, were still incomparably better off than their com-patriots left in East Prussia, Pomerania and Silesia. The repression in East Prussia intensified. On 5 May, Beria sent Colonel General Apollonov there to direct nine NKVD regiments and 400 SMERSH operatives. Their task was 'to secure the elimination of spies, saboteurs and other enemy elements', of whom 'over 50,000' had already been eliminated since the invasion in January. A population which had stood at 2.2 million in 1940 was reduced to 193,000 at the end of May 1945.

Bearing the brunt of Russian hatred, East Prussia suffered the most terrible fate of all the occupied areas. The land was left devastated for several years. Houses were either burned or stripped down to the most basic fittings. Even light bulbs had been taken by peasant soldiers who had no electricity at home. The farms were dead, with all the livestock slaughtered or taken to Russia. Low-lying ground reverted to swamp. But the fate of the civilians who failed to escape was worst of all. Most women and girls were marched off to the Soviet Union for forced labour 'in forests, peat bogs and canals for fifteen to sixteen hours a day'. A little over half of them died in the following two years. Of the survivors, just under half had been raped. When they were returned to the Soviet occupied zone of Germany in April 1947, most had to be sent immediately to hospitals because they were suffering from tuberculosis and venereal disease.

In Pomerania, on the other hand, the remaining German population became quite friendly with many of their Soviet occupiers. Pomeranians dreaded the rapidly approaching day when the Poles would assume control and take their revenge. Food was in very short supply, but few actually starved. The early summer at least brought its own harvest of sorrel, nettles and dandelion, although flour was in such short supply that people diluted it with ground birch bark. Soap was unobtainable, so beech ash took the place of washing powder in the laundry.

Yet it was on Polish territory that Beria, almost certainly on Stalin's orders, concentrated the greatest repressive force once East Prussia had been dealt with. While General Serov was given ten NKVD regiments for the occupation of defeated Germany, General Selivanovsky received fifteen NKVD regiments to police the supposedly allied territory of Poland. Beria also ordered 'Comrade Selivanovsky to combine the duties of representing the NKVD of the USSR and councillor at the Polish Ministry of Public Security'. This perhaps was the best indication of the truth behind Stalin's assertion at Yalta that the Soviet Union was interested in 'the creation of a mighty, free and independent Poland'.

28

The Man on the White Horse

Soviet soldiers seemed to suffer from survivor guilt without knowing it. When they thought of all their comrades who had died, it felt slightly bewildering to be one of those alive at the end. They had 'hugged each other like brothers' in relieved congratulation, but many could not sleep well for weeks after the guns had fallen silent. The unaccustomed quietness unnerved them. They also needed to digest what had happened during all those moments when they had not dared to think too much.

There was no doubt that what they had been through was the most important period not just of their own lives, but also of world history. They thought of their homes and girlfriends and wives and how they would be respected members of the community. For women soldiers, however, the prospects were far less promising. There were fewer men to go round. Those who were pregnant knew that they would have to put a brave face on it. 'So, Ninka,' a young woman soldier wrote to her friend, 'you have got a daughter, and I will have a baby and let's not be sad about not having husbands.' Most of them had their child and returned home, claiming that their husband had been killed at the front.

The war was an extraordinary experience in other ways. It had provided an exhilarating taste of freedom after the purges of 1937 and 1938. Hopes for a complete end to the terror had arisen. Fascism was defeated. Trotsky was dead. Agreements were being made with the western powers. There seemed no reason for the NKVD to be paranoid any more. But back in the Soviet Union, people had already started to realize from the sudden arrest of friends that the informer was at work again, with NKVD squads on their early-morning calls.

The nearness of death at the front had done much to remove the Stalinist conditioning of fear. Officers and soldiers had become quite outspoken, especially about their aspirations for the future. Those from rural areas wanted to do away with the collective farms. Officers, having been given primacy over the political officers in the autumn of 1942, believed that it was now time for the Soviet bureaucratic élite, the *nomenklatura*, to face similar reform. In the most cynical fashion, Stalin had encouraged rumours of this sort during the war, hinting at greater freedom while all the time intending to crush it the moment the fighting was over.

With the approach of victory, Red Army officers had indeed started to become over-confident in the eyes of SMERSH and the NKVD. And political officers had not forgotten the insults of Red Army counterparts when they had been downgraded at the time of the battle of Stalingrad. They were also extremely concerned again by soldiers' letters comparing conditions in Germany with those at home. Abakumov's SMERSH was afraid of a new 'Decembrist' mood among officers.

The Soviet authorities were acutely aware that the soldiers of the Russian army which had invaded France in 1814 compared life there with their miserable existence at home. 'At that time,' one report explained, 'the influence of French life was a progressive one because it gave Russian people the opportunity to see the cultural backwardness of Russia, Tsarist oppression and so forth. From this, the Decembrists [who attempted a liberal *coup d'état* in 1825] drew their conclusions on the need to fight Tsarist autocracy. Nowadays, it is a very different thing. Perhaps some landowner's estate is richer than some collective farm. From this, a man who is politically backward draws a conclusion in favour of a feudal economy against the socialist variety. This kind of influence is regressive. This is why a merciless fight is necessary against these attitudes.'

Political departments were also horrified by the 'anti-Soviet comments' of soldiers complaining that their families were treated badly at home. 'We don't believe that life is getting better in the rear,' one soldier is reported to have said. 'I've seen it with my own eyes.' They were also aware of how badly they had been treated themselves at the front. Some units in the Red Army came close to mutiny just before the end of the war when an instruction specified that the bodies of dead soldiers were to be stripped even of their undergarments. Only officers could be buried fully clothed. There were also apparently an increasing number of cases of unpopular officers being shot in the back by their own men.

SMERSH arrests for 'systematic anti-Soviet talk and terroristic intentions' increased dramatically during the last months of the war and just after the surrender. Even the chief of staff of an NKVD rifle battalion was arrested for having 'systematically carried out counter-revolutionary propaganda among the troops'. He had 'slandered leaders of the Party and the Soviet government' and had praised life in Germany and 'slandered the Soviet press'. A military tribunal of NKVD troops condemned him to eight years in Gulag labour camps.

The proportion of political arrests in the Red Army doubled from 1944 to 1945, a year when the Soviet Union was effectively at war for little more than four months. In that year of victory, no fewer than 135,056 Red Army soldiers and officers were condemned by military tribunals for 'counter-revolutionary crimes'. Similarly, the Military Board of the Supreme Court of the USSR condemned 123 senior officers in 1944 and 273 in 1945.

These figures also do not take into account the treatment of Red Army soldiers captured by the Germans. On 11 May 1945, Stalin ordered that each Front should organize camps for holding ex-prisoners of war and Soviet deportees. One hundred camps holding 10,000 people each were planned. Ex-prisoners were to be 'screened by NKVD, NKGB and SMERSH'. Of the eighty Red Army generals captured by the Wehrmacht, only thirty-seven survived until released by the Red Army. Eleven of them were then arrested by SMERSH and sentenced by tribunals of NKVD forces.

The entire repatriation process was not completed until 1 December 1946. 'By then 5.5 million people had returned to the USSR, of which 1,833,567 had been prisoners of war.' Over 1.5 million members of the Red Army captured by the Germans were sent either to the Gulag (339,000 of them), or to labour battalions in Siberia and the far north, which was hardly better. Civilians taken by force to Germany were 'potential enemies of the state' to be kept under NKVD watch. They were also forbidden to go within 100 kilometres of Moscow, Leningrad and Kiev, and their families remained suspect. Even as recently as 1998, declaration forms for joining a research institute in Russia still contained a section demanding whether any member of the applicant's family had been in an 'enemy prison camp'.

Stalin and his marshals paid little regard to the lives of their soldiers. The casualties for the three Fronts involved in the Berlin operation were extremely high, with 78,291 killed and 274,184 wounded. Russian historians now acknowledge that these needlessly high losses were partly due to the race to get to Berlin before the Western Allies and partly to packing so many armies into the assault on Berlin that they were bombarding each other.

The treatment of those mutilated when fighting for their country was equally heartless. The lucky ones had to queue 'long hours for artificial limbs which looked like those pieces of wood on which men who lost a leg at Borodino stumped around'. But soon the authorities in the major cities decided that they did not want their streets disfigured by limbless 'samovars'. So they were rounded up and deported. Many were sent to Belaya Zemlya in the far north as if they too were Gulag prisoners.

Anger and frustration in the Soviet Union took many forms that summer. The most appalling were vicious outbreaks of anti-Semitism. In Central Asia, Jews suddenly found themselves being attacked and beaten up in markets and schools. Local people apparently shouted, 'Wait until our boys get back from the front, then we'll kill all these Jews.' The local authorities simply termed it an 'act of hooliganism, and often [left] the crime unpunished'.

The most serious anti-Semitic outrage took place in Kiev. At the beginning of September a Jewish NKVD major was attacked in the street 'by two anti-Semites in military uniform'. They may well have been drunk. The major finally managed to draw his pistol and shot them both. Their funerals rapidly turned into a violent demonstration. The coffins were being carried through the streets when suddenly the procession headed for the recently re-established Jewish market. On that day alone nearly 100 Jews were beaten up. Five of them were killed and another thirty-six were taken to hospital seriously injured. The unrest continued to such an extent that a permanent guard had to be placed on the Jewish market. This time not just 'hooligans' were blamed. Even members of the Central Committee of the Communist Party of the Ukraine were described as 'worthy successors' of Goebbels. The following year, Grossman and Ehrenburg's 'Black Book' on the Holocaust was removed from circulation by the authorities.

It is very hard to know how deep Stalin's anti-Semitism ran or how much it was conditioned by his loathing for Trotsky. Partly as a result of Trotsky's internationalism, he certainly seemed to see Jews as part of an international network and therefore suspect. 'Cosmopolitanism' implied treachery. This reached its peak in the anti-Semitic hysteria whipped up over the 'Doctor's Plot' shortly before his death. Stalin, although a Georgian, had become something of a Russian chauvinist. Rather like other outsiders, such as Napoleon and Hitler, he wrapped himself in the national mantle. In one notorious victory speech on 24 May, he praised the Russians above all 'the nations of the Soviet Union' for their 'clear mind, stamina and firm character'. This was aimed mainly at the southern non-Russian nations, many of whom were brutally deported on his orders, leading to tens of thousands of deaths. Yet Stalin, in contrast to Hitler, was essentially a practitioner of political rather than racial genocide.

While nothing was to be allowed to detract from the 'Russian' triumph, the Party line paid tribute to one man alone: 'Our great genius and leader of troops, Comrade Stalin, to whom we owe our historic victory.' Stalin had shamelessly pushed himself to the fore whenever a battle was about to be won, and had disappeared from view during any disaster, especially one of his own making. Commanders always had to acknowledge his wisdom and guiding hand. To take any credit for themselves was extremely dangerous.

Stalin became suspicious if any Soviet citizen was lauded abroad, and he must have been even more distrustful when Zhukov was praised to the skies in the American and British press. Although Stalin was afraid of Beria's power, which he was soon to curb, he was even more concerned by the immense popularity of Zhukov and the Red Army. When Eisenhower visited the Soviet Union, Zhukov accompanied him everywhere, even flying with him to Leningrad in Eisenhower's personal aircraft. Everywhere they went, the two great commanders received a rapturous welcome. Eisenhower later invited Zhukov and his 'campaign wife', Lydia Z–ova, to visit the United States, but Stalin summoned his marshal to

Moscow immediately to spike this plan. It was clear to him that Zhukov had built a genuine rapport with the Allied commander-in-chief.

Zhukov, although aware of Beria's attempts to undermine him, did not realize that the main threat came from Stalin's jealousy. In the middle of June in Berlin, Zhukov was asked about the death of Hitler at a press conference. He was forced to admit to the world that 'we have not yet found an identified body'. Around 10 July, Stalin again rang Zhukov to ask him where the body was. To play with Zhukov in this way clearly gave him great pleasure. Zhukov, when he finally discovered the truth twenty years later from Rzhevskaya, still found it hard to accept that Stalin should have humiliated him in this way. 'I was very close to Stalin,' he insisted. 'Stalin saved me. It was Beria and Abakumov who wanted to do away with me.' Abakumov, the chief of SMERSH, may have been the driving force against Zhukov, but Stalin knew exactly what was going on and approved.

In the Soviet capital, the populace hailed Georgy Konstantinovich Zhukov as 'our St George' – the patron saint of Moscow. After the victory celebrations in Moscow on 9 May – a day of joy and relief, but also many tears – a full parade was planned to commemorate the victory on Red Square. A regiment from each Front would take part, as well as one from the Soviet navy and one from the air force. The banner which had been raised over the Reichstag would be brought back specially. It had become a sacred object already. German flags were also collected and brought back for another purpose.

Soviet marshals and generals assumed that Stalin would take the parade on 24 June. He was the supreme commander – the *Verkhovny* – supposedly responsible for the great victory. It was, however, the Russian tradition that a victory parade had to be taken on horseback.

A week before the parade, Zhukov was summoned to Stalin's dacha. Stalin asked the former cavalryman from the First World War and the civil war whether he could still manage a horse.

'I still ride from time to time,' Zhukov replied.

'So what we'll do is this,' said Stalin. 'You will take the parade and Rokossovsky will command it.'

'Thank you for this honour,' said Zhukov. 'But wouldn't it be better if you took the parade? You are the commander-in-chief and it is your privilege to take it.'

'I'm too old to take parades. You are younger. You take it.' On saying goodbye, he told Zhukov to take the parade on an Arab stallion which Marshal Budyonny would show him.

The next day, Zhukov went to the central airfield to watch drill rehearsals for the parade. There he met Stalin's son Vasily, who took him aside. 'I'm telling you this as a big secret,' Vasily said to him. 'Father had himself been preparing to take the victory parade, but a curious incident took place. Three days ago, the horse bolted in the manege because he did not use his spurs very cleverly. Father caught hold of the mane and tried to stay in the saddle, but did not manage and fell. As he fell, he injured his shoulder and head. When he stood up, he spat and said, "Let Zhukov take the parade. He's an old cavalryman."'

'And which horse was your father riding?'

'A white Arab stallion, the one on which you are taking the parade. But I beg you not to mention a word of this.' Zhukov thanked him. In the few days left, he did not waste a single opportunity to get back into the saddle and master the horse.

On the morning of the parade it was raining steadily. 'Heaven is weeping for our dead' was a common remark among Muscovites. The water dripped from the peaks of caps. All soldiers and officers had received new uniforms and medals. At three minutes before ten, Zhukov mounted the Arab stallion near the Spassky Gate of the Kremlin. He could hear the rumble of applause as the leaders of the Party and the Soviet government took their places on Lenin's mausoleum. As the clock struck the hour, he rode on to Red Square. The bands broke into Glinka's *'Slav'sya!'* ('Glory to you!') and then fell silent. An equally nervous Rokossovsky kept firm control of his black charger. His words of command were clearly heard. The climax of the parade came when 200 veterans, one after another, marched up to the mausoleum and there, at Stalin's feet, hurled the Nazi banner which they carried down to the ground. Zhukov, cheered by the crowds on his magnificent Arab charger, had little idea that Abakumov was preparing his downfall.

Zhukov's dacha was bugged. A small dinner which he gave there for close friends to celebrate the victory was recorded. Their crime was not to have made the first toast to Comrade Stalin. This led later to the torture and imprisonment of the cavalry commander General Kryukov.

His wife, the famous folk-singer Lydia Ruslanova, was sent to the Gulag when she spurned Abakumov's sinister advances. The commandant of the Gulag camp where she was sent ordered her to sing for him and his officers. She replied that she would sing only if all her comrades, the other *zeky*, were allowed to be present.

A week after the victory parade, Marshal Stalin was appointed Generalissimo 'for outstanding service in the Great Patriotic War'. This was in addition to receiving the medals of Hero of the Soviet Union, the Order of Lenin and the Order of Victory, a five-pointed platinum star set with 135 diamonds and five large rubies. The celebration banquets and the awards demonstrated a truly Tsarist disregard for the famine in Central Asia.

The following year, Abakumov's campaign of obtaining confessions under torture from colleagues of Zhukov led to the marshal's exile in the provinces, and then at his dacha. Apart from a brief period as defence minister under Khrushchev, he remained in domestic exile until 9 May 1965, the twentieth anniversary of the German surrender to him at Karlshorst. A great banquet was held in the Kremlin in the Palace of Congress. All the guests, including ministers, marshals, generals and ambassadors, rose to their feet when Leonid Brezhnev entered at the head of his retinue. At the back, Zhukov appeared. Brezhnev had invited him at the last moment. The Soviet leader must have rapidly regretted this gesture, because as soon as Zhukov was spotted, applause broke out, then cheering. Chants of 'Zhukov! Zhukov! Zhukov!' were accompanied by thumping on the table. Brezhnev was stony-faced.

Zhukov had to return to his dacha, which was still heavily bugged. Even though officially rehabilitated, he was never to appear again on a major public occasion during the nine years left to him. Yet the cruellest wound of all was the discovery that he had been tricked by Stalin over Hitler's body.

German bitterness in defeat was rooted in the emotional and intellectual confusion which surrounded the First World War and its aftermath. The idea that the world was against Germany had become something of a self-fulfilling prophecy. American and British interrogators were flabbergasted by senior Wehrmacht officers expressing an injured innocence that the Western Allies should have so misunderstood them. They were prepared to acknowledge 'mistakes', but not crimes. Any crimes were committed by the Nazis and the SS.

In a euphemism surpassing any Stalinist circumlocution, General Blumentritt referred to the Nazis' anti-Semitism as 'the mistaken developments since 1933'. 'Well-known scientists were thus lost,' he said, 'much to the detriment of our research, which in consequence declined from 1933 on.' His train of thought appears to include the idea that if the Nazis had not persecuted the Jews, then scientists like Einstein might have helped them produce better 'miracle weapons', perhaps even an atomic bomb to prevent the Bolsheviks overrunning Germany. Blumentritt, through naïve sophistry, often did not realize that he was contradicting his own attempts to distance the Wehrmacht from the Nazis. He maintained that the lack of mutiny in 1945, in contrast to the revolutionary turmoil of 1918, clearly demonstrated what a united society Germany had become under Hitler.

The interrogation of generals continually talking about the honour of a German officer revealed astonishing distortions of logic. SHAEF's joint intelligence committee attributed it to 'a perverted moral sense'. 'These generals,' stated a report based on over 300 interviews, 'approve of every act which "succeeds". Success is right. What does not succeed is wrong. It was, for example, wrong to persecute the Jews before the war since that set the Anglo-Americans against Germany. It would have been right to postpone the anti-Jewish campaign and begin it after Germany had won the war. It was wrong to bomb England in 1940. If they had refrained, Great Britain, so they believe, would have joined Hitler in the war against Russia. It was wrong to treat Russian and Polish [prisoners of war] like cattle since now they will treat Germans in the same way. It was wrong to declare war against the USA and Russia because they were together stronger than Germany. These are not isolated statements by pro-Nazi generals. They represent the prevalent thoughts among nearly all these men. That it is morally wrong to exterminate a race or massacre prisoners hardly ever occurs to them. The only horror they feel for German crimes is that they themselves may, by some monstrous injustice, be considered by the Allies to be implicated.'

Even civilians, according to another US Army report, betrayed through their automatic use of propaganda clichés how deeply their thinking had been influenced. They would, for example, instinctively refer to Allied bombing raids as '*Terrorangriffe*' (Goebbels's phrase) and not use the ordinary term of '*Luftangriffe*', or air attacks. The report described this as 'residual Nazism'. Many civilians would talk with self-pity of Germany's suffering, especially from bombing. They fell resentfully silent when reminded that it was the Luftwaffe which had invented the mass destruction of cities as a shock tactic.

There was a general evasion of responsibility for what had happened. Members of the Nazi Party claimed that they had been forced to join. Only the leadership was guilty for anything that might have happened. Ordinary Germans were not. They had been '*belogen und betrogen*' – 'deceived and betrayed'. Even German generals implied that they too had been victims of Nazism, for if Hitler had not interfered so disastrously in the way that they ran the war, then they would never have been defeated.

Not content with exculpating themselves, both civilians and generals then tried to persuade their interrogators of the rightness of Nazi Germany's view of the world. Civilians could not understand why the United States ever declared war on Germany. When told that in fact it was Germany which had declared war on the United States, they were incredulous. It contradicted their conviction that Germans were the true victims of the war.

Both officers and civilians tried to lecture their conquerors on the need for the United States and Britain to ally themselves with Germany against the common danger of '*Bolschewismus*', which they knew only too well. The fact that it was Nazi Germany's onslaught against the Soviet Union in 1941 which had brought Communism to all of central and south-east Europe – something which all the revolutions between 1917 and 1921 had completely failed to do – remained beyond their understanding. Rather as the minority Bolsheviks had managed to exploit ruthlessly the Russian conditioning to autocracy, so the Nazis had seized upon their own country's fatal tendency to confuse cause and effect. As several historians have emphasized, the country which had so desired law and order in 1933 ended up with one of the most criminal and irresponsible regimes in history. The result was that its own people, above all the women and children of East Prussia, faced a similar suffering to that which Germany had visited upon the civilians of Poland and the Soviet Union.

The new line-up in the Cold War allowed many of the old guard from the Third Reich to believe that all they had been guilty of was bad timing. Yet some three decades after the defeat, the combination of a difficult historical debate and Germany's economic miracle enabled the vast majority of Germans to face up to the nation's past. No other country with a painful legacy has done so much to recognize the truth.

The government in Bonn was also extremely vigilant to prevent any shrine to Nazism and its leader. Yet Hitler's corpse remained on the other side of the Iron Curtain long after the Stalinist campaign of disinformation, suggesting that he might have escaped to the West in the last moments of the battle. In 1970, the Kremlin finally decided to dispose of the body in absolute secrecy. The funeral rites of the Third Reich's leader were indeed macabre. Hitler's jaws, kept so carefully in the red box by Rzhevskaya during the victory celebrations in Berlin, had been retained by SMERSH, while the NKVD kept the cranium. These remnants were recently rediscovered in the former Soviet archives. The rest of the body, which had been concealed beneath a Soviet army parade-ground in Magdeburg, was exhumed at night and burned. The ashes were flushed into the town sewage system.

Hitler's corpse was not the only one which lacked an identifiable grave. Countless victims of the battle – soldiers on both sides as well as civilians – had been buried by bombs and shells. Each year around 1,000 bodies from 1945 are still being found along the Seelow Heights, in the silent pine forests south of the city and on construction sites in the new capital of a reunited Germany. The senseless slaughter which resulted from Hitler's outrageous vanity utterly belies Speer's regret that history should emphasize 'terminal events'. The incompetence, the frenzied refusal to accept reality and the inhumanity of the Nazi regime were revealed all too clearly in its passing.

References

ABBREVIATIONS

AGMPG Archiv zur Geschichte der Max-Planck-Gesellschaft, Berlin

AWS Art of War Symposium, 'From the Vistula to the Oder: Soviet Offensive Operations', Center for Land Warfare, US Army War College, 1986

BA-B Bundesarchiv, Berlin

BA-MA Bundesarchiv-Militärarchiv, Freiburg-im-Breisgau

BLHA Brandenburgisches Landeshauptarchiv, Potsdam

BZG-S Bibliothek für Zeitgeschichte (Sammlung Sterz), Stuttgart

GARF Gosudarstvenny Arkhiv Rossiiskoy Federatsii (State Archive of the Russian Federation), Moscow

HUA-CD Humboldt Universitätsarchiv (Charité Direktion), Berlin

IfZ Institut für Zeitgeschichte, Munich

IMT Trials of the Major War Criminals before the International Military Tribunal (Nuremberg)

IVMV *Istoriya vtoroi mirovoi voiny, 1939–1945*, Vol. x, Moscow, 1979

KA-FU Krigsarkivet (Försvarsstaben Utrikesavdelningen), Stockholm

LA-B Landesarchiv-Berlin

MGFA Militärgeschichtliches Forschungsamt library, Potsdam

NA National Archives II, College Park, Maryland

PRO Public Record Office, Kew

RGALI Rossiisky Gosudarstvenny Arkhiv Literatury i Iskusstva (Russian State Archive for Literature and the Arts), Moscow

References

RGASPI* Rossiisky Gosudarstvenny Arkhiv Sotsialno-Politikeskoi Istorii (Russian State Archive for Social-Political History), Moscow

RGVA Rossiisky Gosudarstvenny Voenny Arkhiv (Russian State Military Archive), Moscow

RGVA-SA† The 'Special Archive' of captured German documents in the RGVA

SHAT Service Historique de l'Armée de Terre, Vincennes

TsAMO Tsentralny Arkhiv Ministerstva Oborony (Central Archive of the Ministry of Defence), Podolsk

TsKhIDK Tsentr Khraneniya i Izucheniya Dokumentalnykh Kollektsy (Centre for the Conservation and Study of Historic Document Collections), Moscow

ViZh Voenno-istoricheskii Zhurnal

VOV Velikaya Otechestvennaya Voina (The Great Patriotic War), Moscow, 1999, Vols. III and IV

INTERVIEWS, DIARIES AND UNPUBLISHED ACCOUNTS

Shalva Yakovlevich Abuladze (captain, 8th Guards Army); Gert Becker (Berlin civilian, Steglitz); Richard Beier (newsreader, Grossdeutscher Rundfunk); Nikolai Mikhailovich Belyaev (Komsomol organizer, 150th Rifle Division, 5th Shock Army); Klaus Boeseler (Deutsche Jungvolk, Berlin); Ursula Bube, geb. Eggeling (student, Berlin); Hardi Buhl (civilian, Halbe); Henri Fenet (battalion commander, SS *Charlemagne* Division); Anatoly Pavlovich Fedoseyev (magnetron and electronics expert sent to Berlin); Edeltraud Flieller (secretary, Siemens); Generalleutnant a.D. Bernd Freiherr Freytag von Loringhoven (military assistant to General Krebs in Fuhrer bunker); Vladimir Samoilovich Gall (captain, 7th Department, 47th Army Headquarters); Hans-Dietrich Genscher (soldier, Twelfth Army); Elsa Holtzer (Berlin civilian); Oberst a.D. Hubertus Freiherr von Humboldt-Dachroeden (Ia, headquarters, Twelfth Army); Svetlana Pavlovna Kazakova, (headquarters, 1st Belorussian Front); Oberst a.D. Wolfram Kertz (captain, Grossdeutschland Wachtregiment, 309th *Berlin* Infantry Division); Major General I. F. Klochkov (senior lieutenant, 150th Rifle Division, 5th Shock Army); Ivan Varlamovich Koberidze (captain, 1st Ukrainian Front artillery); Ivan Leontievich Kovalenko (signaller, headquarters 3rd Belorussian Front); Anatoly Kubasov, (3rd Guards Tank Army);

---

* Formerly RTsKhIDNI (Rossiisky Tsentr Khraneniya i Izucheniya Dokumentov Noveishei Istorii)

† The 'Special Archive' of captured German documents comes from the 194,000 Nazi Party, Reich Chancellery, SS and Gestapo files discovered by the 59th Army of the Red Army at a castle in Lower Saxony (probably Schloss Furstenstein near Waldenburg, rather than the Schloss Althorn mentioned in some accounts)

R. W. Leon (Intelligence Corps attached to US Ninth Army CIC); Erica Lewin (Rosenstrasse survivor); Generalmajor a.D. Rudolf Lindner (Fahnenjunker Regt 1241, Division *Kurmark*); Lothar Loewe (Hitler Youth); Hans Oskar baron Löwenstein de Witt (Rosenstrasse survivor); General Ulrich de Maizière (general staff colonel, OKH); Georgy Malashkia (captain, 9th Tank Corps); Nikolai Andreevich Maltsev (lieutenant, 3rd Guards Tank Army); General Anatoly Grigorievich Merezhko (captain, headquarters 8th Guards Army); Rochus Misch (Oberscharführer, *SS Leibstandarte* in Führer bunker); Gerda Petersohn (secretary, Lufthansa, Neukölln); Oberst a.D. Günther Reichhelm (chief of staff, Twelfth Army); Frau Helga Retzke (student, Berlin-Buch); Sergei Pavlovich Revin (junior sergeant, 4th Guards Tank Army); Yelena Rzhevskaya (Kogan) (interpreter SMERSH department, 3rd Shock Army); Alexander Saunderson (captain, war crimes investigator and Jowett's aide at Nuremberg); Erich Schmidtke (Berlin Volkssturm evader); Ehrhardt Severin (civilian); Shota Shurgaya (junior lieutenant, 16th Aviation Army); Wolfgang Steinke (lieutenant, 391st Security Division, Ninth Army); Shota Sulkhanishvili (captain, 3rd Shock Army); Frau Waltraud Süssmilch (schoolgirl); Frau Marlene von Werner (civilian, Wannsee); Magda Wieland (actress); General a.D. Markus Wolf (Ulbricht Group); General a.D. Wust (lieutenant, Luftwaffe training battalion, 309th *Berlin* Infantry Division, Ninth Army).

There are also three other interviewees whose contributions must remain anonymous.

Source Notes

PREFACE

p. xxxiii 'History always emphasizes . . .', Speer interrogation, 22 May, NA 740.0011 EW/5-145

p. xxxiii German teenagers, see *Die Woche*, 8 February 2001

p. xxxiii 'with the breakthrough . . .', 9 November 1944, reprinted in *Volkssturm*, BLHA Pr. Br. Rep. 61A/363

p. xxxiv 'culmination of all the operations', RGALI 1403/1/84, p. 1

I BERLIN IN THE NEW YEAR

p. 2 'Learn Russian quickly', Klemperer, ii, 4 September 1944, p. 431

p. 2 '*Bleib übrig!*', Loewe, conversation, 9 October 2001

p. 2 'like a stage-set . . .', Kardorff, p. 153

p. 4 Schmidtke, conversation, 15 July 2000

p. 4 '*Volksgenossenschaft*', NA RG 338 B-338

p. 4 'I have such faith . . .', SHAT 7 P 128

p. 6 ratios of enemy superiority, AWS, p. 86

p. 7 'It's the greatest imposture . . .', Guderian, pp. 310-11

p. 8 'I know the war is lost', Below, p. 398

p. 8 'wishes for a successful . . .', ibid., p. 399

p. 9 rumour of Hitler's madness and Göring's flight, SHAT 7 P 128

p. 9 Goebbels dinner, Oven, p. 198

p. 9 foreign doctors, HUA-CD 2600 Charité Dir. 421-24/1 Bd x, p. 125

p. 9 'catastrophic losses', BA-MA 218, pp. 3,725-49

2 THE 'HOUSE OF CARDS' ON THE VISTULA

p. 11 6.7 million men, *IVMV*, p. 38

p. 11 'We are lost . . .', SHAT 7 P 128

p. 11 'We no longer fought . . .', Sajer, p. 382

p. 12 'You do not need . . .', TsAMO 233/2374/337, p. 64

p. 12 attack before Christmas, TsAMO 233/2374/337, p. 64

p. 12 'Mein Führer, don't believe that . . .', Freytag von Loringhoven, conversation, 4 October 1999

p. 12 'completely idiotic', Guderian, p. 315

p. 13 'weather for Russians', General Schaal debriefing, 20 February 1946, 2e Bureau, SHAT 7 P 163

p. 13 'strange winter', Stalin to Harriman, 14 December 1944, NA RG334/ Entry 309/Box 2

p. 13 'heavy rain and . . .', RGVA 38680/1/3, p. 40

p. 14 'At that time', quoted Senyavskaya, 2000, p. 174

p. 14 'The Russian infantryman' and 'First state . . .', Senyavskaya, 1995, p. 111

p. 14 'cavalrymen, artillerymen . . .', Grossman papers, RGALI 1710/3/51, p. 221

p. 14 'You will harvest . . .', RGALI 1710/3/47, p. 19

p. 15 'disconcertedness', *VOV*, iii, p. 232, n. 8

p. 15 Konstanty Rokosowski, I am most grateful to Norman Davies for supplementary information

p. 15 'Why this disgrace?', Rokossovsky, p. 297

p. 16 'I know very well . . .', Zhukov, p. 174

p. 16 'wicked little eyes . . .', Beria, p. 130

p. 16 Korsun, see Erickson, pp. 177–9

p. 17 16th Panzer Division, 21st Army, TsAMO 233/2374/337, p. 70

p. 17 'fire-storm', Colonel Liebisch, AWS, p. 617

p. 17 'Forward into the fascist lair!', *VOV*, iii, p. 236

p. 17 'Gold', Konev, p. 5

p. 18 Sochaczew, TsAMO 307/ 246791/2, pp. 225–7

p. 18 'with their tracks', TsAMO 307/ 15733/3, pp. 37–8

p. 18 'two or three hours', Grossman papers, RGALI 1710/3/51, pp. 237–8

p. 18 'because of the big advance . . .', Bormann diary, GARF 9401/2/97, pp. 32–48

p. 19 'very stupid', 'a prestige garrison', NA RG334/Entry 309/Box 2

p. 19 'to start the advance', *ViZh* 93, No. 6, pp. 30–31

p. 20 'Stalin emphasized . . .', NA RG334/Entry 309/Box 2

p. 20 'Ah, what a life . . .', RGALI 1710/3/47, p. 14

p. 21 'Our tanks move faster . . .', Grossman papers, RGALI 1710/3/51, pp. 237–8

p. 21 'ear battalion', Duffy, p. 103

p. 21 'You must stop everything!', Humboldt, conversation, 11 October 1999

p. 21 'That evening', Humboldt, conversation, 11 October 1999

p. 22 'the situation in the east . . .', GARF 9401/2/97, pp. 32–48

p. 22 'half an hour before . . .', Guderian, p. 327

p. 22 'We saw the destruction of Warsaw . . .', Klochkov, p. 28

p. 22 Warsaw population figures, *VOV*, iii, p. 240

p. 23 'a single undulating red sea . . .', Grossman, *Krasnaya Zvezda*, 9 February

3 FIRE AND SWORD AND 'NOBLE FURY'

p. 24 'Noble fury', from the patriotic anthem 'Sacred War': 'Arise vast country/arise for the mortal battle/with the dark fascist force,/with the accursed horde. /Let the noble fury/boil up like a wave,/the people's war is going on,/ the sacred war.'

p. 24 'master of military . . .', Ehrenburg, p. 100

p. 25 'Self-propelled guns . . .', Grossman papers, RGALI 1710/3/47, p. 14

p. 25 'It's impossible . . .', Ehrenburg, p. 100

p. 25 'the Jew, Ilya . . .', 16 January, BA-B R55/793, p. 9

p. 25 'There was a time', *Krasnaya Zvezda*, 25 November 1944

p. 26 'in weather . . .', General der Artillerie Felzmann, XXVII Corps, NA RG 338, D-281

p. 27 Walter Beier, Ramm, 1994, p. 164

p. 27 'the second Stalin', Kershaw, 2000, p. 406

p. 28 sixty-two raped and murdered women and young girls, Dönhoff, p. 18

p. 28 'Red Army soldiers . . .', Agranenko papers, RGALI 2217/2/17, p. 22

p. 28 'engaged in the propaganda . . .', Kopelev, p. 10

p. 29 'many Germans declare . . .', Tkatchenko to Beria, GARF 9401/2/ 94, p. 87

p. 29 'There you are, Vera', TsAMO 372/6570/76, quoted Senyavskaya, 1995, p. 99

p. 30 'personally shot . . .', Kopelev, p. 56

p. 30 'When we breed . . .', TsAMO 372/6570/78, pp. 199–203

p. 30 'Our soldiers' behaviour . . .', Agranenko papers, RGALI 2217/2/17, p. 42

p. 30 'frenzied scream', Kopelev, p. 50

p. 31 'They all lifted their skirts . . .', Maltsev, conversation, 29 October 2001

p. 31 'Our fellows were so sex-starved', Werth, p. 964

p. 31 'mass poisoning . . .', RGVA 32925/1/100, p. 58

p. 31 'Russian soldiers . . .', Bark and Gress, p. 33

p. 32 'The extreme violence . . .', *Life and Fate*, p. 241

p. 32 'deindividualize', Kon, p. 23

p. 32 'barracks eroticism', Yuri Polyakov, quoted Kon, p. 26

p. 33 'Even the trees were enemy', Kovalenko, conversation, 21 September 1999

p. 33 'Comrade Marshal', Agranenko papers, RGALI 2217/2/17, p. 22

p. 34 'How should one treat . . .', Agranenko papers, RGALI 2217/2/17, p. 26

p. 34 'disgusted by the plenty', Shcheglov, p. 299

p. 34 wirelesses, see Solzhenitsyn, 2000, p. 125

p. 34 'politically incorrect conclusions', TsAMO 372/6570/76, pp. 92–4

p. 34 'anti-Soviet quotations . . .', TsAMO 372/6570/68, p. 12

p. 35 'You cannot imagine . . .', N. Reshetnikova, 9 February, quoted Senyavskaya, 2000, pp. 180–81

p. 35 'We thought they . . .', Agranenko papers, RGALI 2217/2/17

p. 35 'tumultuous market', Solzhenitsyn, 1983, p. 67

p. 35 'direct and unmistakable . . .', Kopelev, p. 52

p. 36 'Russians are absolutely . . .', Krivenko to Beria, Leonid Reshin, '*Tovarisch Ehrenburg uproshchaet*: The Real Story of the Famous *Pravda* Article', *Novoe Vremya*, No. 8, 1994

p. 36 'They ran away . . .', quoted Senyavskaya, 2000, p. 273

p. 36 'very few Germans left . . .', Shikin to Aleksandrov, 28 January, RGASPI 17/125/320, p. 18

p. 37 'Dear Papa!' Shcheglov, p. 289

p. 37 Frische Nehrung, BA-B R55/616, p. 184

p. 37 'the passengers on the carts . . .', KA-FU, EI: 18, Vol. 6

p. 38 'The majority are women . . .', GARF 9401/2/93, p. 343

p. 38 1.5 million Soviet Jews, Merridale, p. 293

4 THE GREAT WINTER OFFENSIVE

p. 39 'The soldier is the child of the people', General Blumentritt, NA RG 338 B-338

p. 39 'Let our husbands . . .', Serov to Beria, GARF 9401/2/93, p. 334

p. 39 'Vampire!', Freytag von Loringhoven, conversation, 4 October 1999

p. 39 'The fighting will not stop . . .', KA-FU, EI: 18, Vol. 6

p. 39 'catastrophe beds', HUA-CD 2600 Charité Dir. 421–24/1 Bd x, pp. 114, 115

p. 40 'The Führer's call . . .', NA RG338, B-627

p. 40 'All the peoples . . .', SHAT 7 P 128, Direction Générale et Inspection des P.G. de l'Axe, Paris, 2 February

p. 40 'The people were predominantly . . .', NA RG338, B-627

p. 41 'security measures . . .', BA-B R55/995, p. 166

p. 41 'Their white starved faces', Kee, pp. 228–9

p. 42 'chief physical characteristics . . .', Duffy, p. 45

p. 43 'less vulnerable . . .', Grossman papers, RGALI 1710/3/51, p. 65

p. 43 seven-hour *Lagebesprechung*, Freytag von Loringhoven, conversation, 4 October 1999

p. 44 'He's not going . . .', Klochkov, p. 31

p. 44 'disciplined German prisoners', Grossman papers, RGALI 1710/3/47, p. 3

p. 44 'their merciless . . .', Chuikov, p. 91

p. 45 NKVD rifle divisions, Meshik to Beria, 27 January, GARF 9401/2/92, p. 263

p. 45 Auschwitz report by Shikin, 9 February, RGASPI 17/125/323, pp. 1–4

p. 46 'all prisoners on arrival', RGASPI 17/125/323, p. 73

p. 47 'a serious offence', Krockow, p. 45

p. 47 'Huddled shapes . . .', Libussa von Oldershausen, quoted ibid., pp. 48–9

p. 48 'in normal times', 30 January, BA-B R55/616, p. 158

p. 48 Ilse Braun, Gun, pp. 237–8

p. 48 'around 4 million . . .', 29 January, BA-B R55/616, p. 153

p. 48 7 million, 11 February, BA-B R55/616, p. 183

p. 48 8.35 million, 19 February, BA-B R55/616, p. 211. This included East Prussia, 1.635m; Danzig and West Prussia, 480,000; Pomerania, 881,000; Wartheland, 923,000; Lower Saxony, 2.955m; and Upper Saxony, 745,000

p. 48 'The Friedrichstrasse Bahnhof . . .', Menzel, p. 116

p. 49 'Dogs and Jews . . .', Löwenstein, conversation, 14 July 2000

p. 49 'infectious diseases . . .', BA-B R55/916, p. 57

p. 50 1,800 civilians and 1,200 wounded, BA-B R55/616, p. 155

p. 51 'over 6,000 Hitlerites . . .', *Wilhelm Gustloff* and Marinesco, Senyavskaya, 2000, p. 225, n. 19

p. 51 'in order to save . . .', BA-B R55/616, p. 157

p. 52 'These people . . .', BA-B R55/616

p. 52 'He is of the opinion . . .', 18 February, BA-B R55/616, p. 208

p. 52 Czech reaction, 10 March, BA-B R55/616, p. 243

p. 52 'the general staff . . .', Guderian, p. 397

p. 53 Oberst i.G. Hans Georg Eismann's account, BA-MA MSg1/976

p. 54 'that a blind man', BA-MA MSg1/976, p. 14

p. 55 'Where the German soldier . . .', BA-MA MSg1/976, p. 32

p. 55 'under these Hitlers and Himmlers', Krockow, pp. 51–4

5 THE CHARGE TO THE ODER

p. 56 'hysteria and disintegration', Kardorff, p. 281

p. 57 'Don't come back . . .', Feuersenger, p. 206

p. 57 evacuation of ministries, NA 740.0011 EW/4–2445

p. 57 executions, see Rürup (ed.), 1997, pp. 167–71

p. 58 'He was sometimes hunched . . .', Freytag von Loringhoven, conversation, 4 October 1999

p. 59 Eva Braun, Freytag von Loringhoven, conversation, 4 October 1999, and Maizière, 9 October 1999

p. 60 white tulle, Konev, pp. 38–9

p. 61 'Strength through fear', Thorwald, 1950, p. 103

p. 61 'had acted in a correct . . .', KA-FU, EI: 18, Vol. 6

p. 61 'clearly not sufficient . . .', RGVA 32891/1/123, p. 6

p. 62 Breslau refugees on foot, see Thorwald, 1950, pp. 109–13

p. 63 seventy and 100 kilometres, TsAMO 233/2307/189, p. 78

p. 63 'When you reach the Oder . . .', Zhukov, iv, p. 194

p. 63 Łódź ghetto, Grossman papers, RGALI 1710/3/49

p. 64 'Troops of the 1st Polish Army . . .', GARF 9401/2/93, p. 334

p. 64 'the German civilian', RGALI 1710/3/51, p. 227

p. 65 'Chuikov is sitting . . .', RGALI 1710/3/51, p. 229

p. 66 'Chuikov listens . . .', RGALI 1710/3/51, p. 230

p. **66** Chuikov striking officers, Mer-ezhko, conversation, 10 November 1999

p. **66** 'We marched out of a forest', Klochkov, conversation, 25 July 2000, and Klochkov, pp. 34–5

p. **67** 'Tremble with fear . . .', 8th Guards Army, TsAMO 345/5502/93, p. 412

p. **67** 'Everything is on fire . . .', RGALI 1710/3/51, p. 231

p. **68** 'full of enemy tanks', BA-MA RH 19 XV/9b, p. 172

p. **68** Tiger tanks, BA-MA MSg1/976, p. 39

p. **68** '*Tod und Strafe für Pflichtverges-senheit*', BA-MA RH 19 XV/9b, p. 193

p. **68** food for retreating troops, BA-MA RH 19 XV/9b, p. 195

p. **68** 'The Lord God . . .', BA-MA RH 19 XV/28, pp. 1–4

p. **68** 'left his town . . .', IfZ Fa 91/5, p. 1,253

p. **69** 'Captured German generals . . .', Petrov and Kobulov to Beria, 30 January, GARF 9401/2/92, pp. 283–8

p. **69** 'a stunning surprise', Zhukov, iv, p. 196

p. **70** 'Happiness in the . . .', Walter Beier, Ramm, 1994, p. 165

p. **72** '*Stalin ante portas!*', Oven, p. 229

p. **72** Wachregiment Grossdeutsch-land, Obergefreiter Harald Arndt, quoted Ramm, 1994, p. 268

p. **72** 'Our honour is called loyalty', Baumgart, quoted ibid., p. 61

p. **72** 'marked uncomradely . . .', BA-MA 332, pp. 656, 709–11

p. **73** 'enthusiasm and fanaticism', BA-B R55/1305

p. **73** 'with comradely greetings', BA-B R55/1305

p. **74** *Panzerjagd* Division, Guderian, p. 411

p. **74** '*ein absoluter Schwindel*', BA-B R55/916, p. 63

p. **74** 'political leaders', BLHA Pr. Br. Rep. 61B/20

p. **74** 'Golden Pheasant', Kardorff, p. 291

p. **75** 'Suffered from bombing', Bor-mann diary, GARF 9401/2/97, pp. 32–48

p. **75** 'Evacuation Situation', 10 Febru-ary, BA-B R55/616, p. 172

6 EAST AND WEST

p. **78** Yalta accommodation, Alan-brooke, p. 657

p. **78** 'Riviera of Hades', Gilbert, p. 1,187

p. **80** 'the systematic . . .', Agranenko papers, RGALI 2217/2/17, p. 22

p. **81** 'It is a question . . .', *Tegeran. Yalta. Potsdam. Sbornik dokumentov*, Moscow, 1970, p. 22, quoted Volko-gonov, p. 489

p. **82** fall of Budapest, see Erickson, p. 508

p. **83** prisoner reprisals, see Kershaw, 2000, p. 779

p. **83** Dresden compassionate leave, Genscher, conversation, 4 September 2000

p. **83** Rhine floodwater, Eisenhower, pp. 406–7

p. **84** 'I can handle Stalin', Murphy, p. 233

p. **85** 'outflanking the West Wall', Deane, 25 December 1944, NA RG334/ Entry 309/Box 2

p. 85 'They looked more like...', report by Shikin, RGASPI 17/125/323, pp. 35–6

p. 86 live targets and 'sport marches', *VOV*, iv, p. 180, n. 36

p. 86 SS pianist, Stanford-Tuck, Larry Forrester, *Fly for Your Life*, London, 1956

p. 86 'Everybody seems to...', Grossman papers, RGALI 1710/3/47, p. 4

p. 86 'We are beating...', quoted Shindel (ed.), p. 125

p. 87 'We are Russian...', Agranenko papers, RGALI 2217/2/17

p. 88 'insecurity as a military leader', BA-MA MSg1/976, p. 32

p. 89 'but panzer army...', BA-MA MSg1/976, p. 35

p. 89 lunch with the Japanese ambassador, Maizière, conversation, 9 October 1999

p. 89 'You must believe me...', Guderian, p. 412

p. 90 'The Reichsführer SS is man...', ibid., pp. 413–15

p. 92 'Over the city...', Oberjäger R. Christoph, quoted Ramm, 1994, p. 186

p. 93 'preserve their pitiful lives', GARF 9401/2/94, pp. 159–65

p. 93 'almost four years...', 27 February, BA-MA 485, p. 20,755

p. 93 'significant part...', Tkachenko to Beria, 28 February, GARF 9401/2/93, p. 324

p. 94 'The Führer has ordered...', 10 March, BA-B R55/616, p. 243

p. 94 'corpses of citizens...', Shvernik to Molotov, GARF 9401/2/96, pp. 255–61

p. 94 Stutthof camp, RGVA 32904/1/19

p. 95 'The Germans have not yet...', SHAT 7 P 146

p. 95 'Morale is low but discipline is strong', RGALI 1710/3/47, p. 25

7 CLEARING THE REAR AREAS

p. 96 'Halt. Military Site...', Abakumov to Beria, 15 February, GARF 9401/2/93, pp. 6–15

p. 96 57th NKVD Rifle Division, RGVA 38680/1/3, p. 4

p. 97 'a dirty runner bespattered...', Solzhenitsyn, 1974, p. 126

p. 97 'the Führer's guard battalion...', Hans Rattenhuber's interrogation by SMERSH, *Voennye Arkhivy Rossii*, No. 1, 1993, p. 355

p. 98 'I think it would...', GARF 9401/2/93, p. 15

p. 98 'indispensable', Stalin to Tedder and Bull, 15 January, NA RG334/Entry 309/Box 2

p. 99 'saboteurs and terrorists', 1 March, GARF 9401/2/93, pp. 255–9

p. 99 'criminal act of an anti-Soviet policy', Berezhkov, 1982, p. 364

p. 99 'felt that we had at last...', Kazakova, conversation, 6 November 1999

p. 99 'some of whom...', Zhukov, iv, p. 183

p. 99 Serov as 'adviser', RGVA 32925/1/100, p. 143

p. 100 'Ukrainian-German nationalists', BA-B R55/822, pp. 5–8

p. 100 'inquiry into Rokossovsky's relatives', GARF 9401/2/94, p. 61

p. 101 'the civilian pretended...', 30 March, NA RG334/Entry 309/Box 2

p. 101 'Soviet Engineer-Captain Mela-medev . . .', NA RG334/Entry 309/Box 2

p. 101 'negligence of the officer . . .', Volkov, deputy chief NKVD troops, 1st Belorussian Front, RGVA 32925/1/100, p. 205

p. 101 'in the Soviet Union . . .', Antonov to Deane, NA RG334/Entry 309/Box 2

p. 102 'secret bakeries', RGVA 32891/1/123

p. 102 'This made him suspect . . .', RGVA 32925/1/100, p. 80

p. 102 mine detection, 12 March, RGVA 32925/1/297, p. 8

p. 102 'special dogs for smelling bandits', RGVA 38680/1/12, p. 114

p. 102 'terrorists handed over . . .', 11 March, GARF 9401/2/94

p. 102 'Left in the rear . . .', RGVA 38680/1/12, p. 48

p. 103 'a German sabotage school . . .', Lieutenant General Edunov, 13 February, RGVA 32904/1/19, p. 99

p. 103 'An attentive sergeant . . .', RGVA 38686/1/21

p. 104 'that in some . . .', 18 February, 63rd Rifle Division NKVD, RGVA 38686/1/20, p. 49

p. 104 'All this leads to . . .', RGVA 38680/1/4

p. 105 pass for wounded, RGVA 38686/1/20, p. 31

p. 105 6th Guards Tank Corps, RGVA 32904/1/19

p. 105 'The Soviet military . . .', BA-B R55/1296

p. 105 'citizens of the USSR . . .', 3rd Belorussian Front, RGVA 38680/1/3, p. 255

p. 105 'Such cases . . .', Grossman papers, RGALI 1710/3/51, p. 230

p. 105 five dead and thirty-four injured, 83rd Frontier Guards Regiment, RGVA 38686/1/21, p. 45

p. 106 Rokossovsky at traffic jam, Agranenko papers, RGALI 2217/2/17, p. 31

p. 106 'mobilize all Germans . . .', RGVA 32925/1/100, p. 47

p. 106 68,680 Germans, 10 March, GARF 9401/2/93, p. 279

p. 106 'To Siberia . . .', Agranenko papers, RGALI 2217/2/17, p. 20

p. 107 'a gendarmerie', NA RG334/Entry 309/Box 2

p. 107 'hostel of repatriated Polish women', RGVA 38680/1/3, p. 104

p. 107 'suicides of Germans . . .', GARF 9401/2/94, p. 88

p. 107 'immoral event', RGVA 38686/1/26, p. 36

p. 107 'Negative phenomena . . .', Senyavskaya, 2000, p. 184, n. 27

p. 107 Ukrainian girls taken for forced labour, RGVA-SA 1382/1/62

p. 108 'On the night . . .', 'an unknown . . .', RGASPI 17/125/314

p. 109 'had sold themselves . . .', Inozemtsev, p. 204

p. 109 'German dolls', quoted Senyavskaya, 1995 p. 181

p. 110 'the honour and dignity of the Soviet girl', TsAMO 372/6570/76 and 372/6570/68

p. 110 female soldiers treated badly from 1944, Rezhevskaya, conversation, 28 October 2001

p. 110 'For example, Eva Shtul . . .', RGASPI 17/125/314, pp. 40–45

p. 110 49,500 Soviet citizens, to Aleksandrov, 20 February, RGASPI 17/125/320, p. 36

p. 110 4 million, RGASPI 17/125/314

p. 111 'What will be their status?', RGASPI 17/125/314, p. 33

p. 112 Oppeln incident, 7 March, KA-FU, EI: 18, Vol. 6

p. 112 'They were not traitors...', Solzhenitsyn, 1974, p. 240

p. 113 Over a million Hiwis, TsAMO 2/176495/378, pp. 32–3

p. 113 *'Vlasovtsy* and other...', *VOV*, iv, p. 158

p. 113 'A man from Orel...', Grossman papers, RGALI 1710/3/47, p. 1

p. 113 camp guards, RGVA 32904/1/19, pp. 274–5

p. 113 'There must be a single...', 63rd Rifle Division NKVD, RGVA 38686/1/20

p. 113 'Comrade President...', Eugene Schirinkine, 31 July, SHAT 7 P 128

p. 114 restoration of civic rights, *VOV*, iv, p. 161

p. 114 'Comrade soldiers...', RGASPI 17/125/310, p. 10

8 POMERANIA AND THE ODER BRIDGEHEADS

p. 115 'cornerstone', Duffy, p. 187

p. 116 Colonel Morgunov, *VOV*, iii, p. 252

p. 116 'The success of the advance...', Grossman papers, RGALI 1710/3/51, p. 230

p. 116 Krukenberg and SS *Charlemagne*, BA-MA MSg2/1283, and Fenet, conversation, 19 May 1999

p. 116 'Weiss is a liar...', BA-MA MSg1/976, p. 67

p. 117 'returned in the same state...', Erickson, p. 522

p. 118 'Trek orders!', Krockow, p. 61

p. 120 'I have no intention...', Boldt, p. 81, with corrections Freytag von Loringhoven, September 2001

p. 120 supply ship, report 22 March, BA-B R55/616, p. 248

p. 121 'If the birth...', Sajer, p. 541

p. 121 'The number of extraordinary...', report, 12 April, TsAMO 372/6570/68, pp. 17–20

p. 122 'absolutely impossible...', RGALI 2217/2/17, p. 42

p. 122 'too proud', RGALI 2217/2/17, p. 39

p. 122 'I had to concede', Krockow, p. 99

p. 123 'Here I hang...', ibid., p. 76

p. 123 Herr von Livonius, ibid., pp. 114–15

p. 124 'Birds are singing...', Agranenko papers, RGALI 2217/2/17, p. 42

p. 125 *'Nach Arbeit!'*, Agranenko papers, RGALI 2217/2/17, p. 41

p. 126 'to assure the Russians...', TsAMO 233/2374/337, p. 158

p. 126 'Morale is being...', TsAMO 233/2374/337, p. 124

p. 127 'looting by German...', 24 March, IfZ MA 127/2, p. 13,025

p. 127 twenty-two death sentences, TsAMO 236/2675/339, p. 65

p. 127 'Colonel General Schörner...', TsAMO 236/2675/336, p. 60

p. 128 'criminal carelessness', TsAMO 233/2374/194, p. 8

p. 128 'went off to have...', TsAMO 233/2374/194, p. 9

p. 128 'The first piece of metal . . .', quoted Senyavskaya, 2000, p. 236, n. 52

p. 128 'Livestock was slaughtered . . .', RGVA 32891/1/391, pp. 345–6

p. 129 Estonians and Ukrainians, 21st Army political department, TsAMO 236/2675/339

p. 130 'The bedroom . . .', BA-MA MSg1/976, p. 39

p. 130 'incompetent and cowardly . . .', BA-MA MSg1/976

p. 131 'Military tribunals should take . . .', 4 February, GARF 9401/2/94, p. 163

p. 131 '*1 Unteroffizier* . . .', IfZ MA 325

p. 131 'cowardice and defeatism', IfZ Fa 600, p. 14

p. 131 'The overriding priority . . .', 13 March, IfZ MA 127/2, pp. 13,031–2

p. 132 'You're the new . . .', BA-MA MSg1/976, p. 31

p. 132 'had nothing negative . . .', KA-FU, EI: 18, Vol. 6

p. 132 'twenty Feldgendarmerie . . .', KA-FU, EI: 18, Vol. 6

p. 132 'soldiers looked apathetic . . .', 16 February, KA-FU, EI: 18, Vol. 6

p. 133 artillery observation and underwater bridges, SHAT 7 P 163

p. 133 rumours of resentment, IfZ Fa 138, pp. 15, 16

p. 133 'In the whole war . . .', BA-MA MSg1/976, p. 61

p. 134 requisitioning of carts, BLHA Pr. Br. Rep. 61A/443

p. 134 'tantamount . . .', 21 February, BLHA Pr. Br. Rep. 61A/38

p. 134 'very harsh . . .', 14 March report to Dr Naumann, IfZ Fa 600, p. 14

p. 134 'The fresh air . . .', BLHA Pr. Br. Rep. 61A/16, Gauleitung Mark Brandenburg, 19 March

p. 134 '40,000 fanatical volunteers', Guderian, p. 420

p. 135 'chalk-white face', BA-MA MSg1 784, p. 2

p. 135 'that what we . . .', Schwarz, quoted Gosztony, p. 92

p. 135 'lost in his thoughts', Kempka, quoted ibid., p. 93

9 OBJECTIVE BERLIN

p. 136 'Yakov is never going . . .', Zhukov, iv, p. 215

p. 137 'independently and proudly', GARF 9401/2/93, p. 276

p. 137 'very pleased', Zhukov, iv, p. 215

p. 137 'when we were working . . .', ibid., p. 218

p. 138 'the main axis of the Allied . . .', 14 October 1944, NA RG334/Entry 309/Box 2

p. 138 meeting at Stalin's dacha, May 1942, Zaloga, pp. 13–19

p. 139 'Virus House', Dr Engel, conversation, FU Archiv, 8 October 2001

p. 139 'whoever possesses . . .', quoted TsAMO 233/2356/5804, pp. 320–21

p. 139 'There is no doubt . . .', Alanbrooke, p. 669

p. 140 'Have a Go, Joe', quoted by David Clay Large in 'Funeral in Berlin', p. 355, in Robert Cowley (ed.), *What If?*, New York, 1999

p. 140 'In view of the great progress . . .', NA RG334/Entry 309/Box 3

p. 140 'His relations with Monty . . .', 6 March, Alanbrooke, p. 669

p. 141 Tedder not consulted, NA RG 218 JCS Box 16

p. 141 'politically and psychologically . . .', Eisenhower, p. 433

p. 141 'our armies will advance . . .', 25 March, Churchill papers 20/209, Gilbert, p. 1,264

p. 142 'criminal action . . .', NA RG334/Entry 309/Box 2, Antonov correspondence

p. 143 'We owed much . . .', Eisenhower, p. 431

p. 143 'on matters that were . . .', ibid., p. 401

p. 143 'no longer . . .', Eisenhower to Marshall, 30 March, quoted ibid., p. 438

p. 145 'The German front in the west . . .', and whole conversation, Zhukov, iv, pp. 223–6

p. 145 'Stalin was given . . .', NA RG 334/Entry 309/Box 2

p. 146 'Are you aware how . . .', Konev, p. 79

p. 147 'In the event', Zhukov, iv, p. 226

p. 147 'in the shortest . . .', *VOV*, iii, p. 267

p. 147 'The *Stavka*', ibid., p. 269

p. 147 'completely coincided', ibid.

10 THE *KAMARILLA* AND THE GENERAL STAFF

p. 148 'The British are partly . . .', 16 March, KA-FU, EI: 18, Vol. 6

p. 149 'If the attempt . . .', KA-FU, EI: 18, Vol. 6

p. 150 'taking a stroll . . .', Guderian, p. 426

p. 150 'the most unsuitable man . . .', BA-MA MSg1/976, p. 78

p. 151 'Hitler was very quiet . . .', Maizière, conversation, 9 October 1999

p. 151 'This mission of his . . .', Guderian, p. 420

p. 151 'Today I am really . . .', Freytag von Loringhoven, conversation, 4 October 1999

p. 152 *'Meine Herren . . .'*, BA-MA MSg1/976, p. 99

p. 152 'ice-cold lack of emotion', BA-MA MSg1/976, p. 107

p. 152 'Hitler became paler . . .', Freytag von Loringhoven, conversation, 4 October 1999 – eyewitness accounts of this meeting vary in some details; this description is based mainly on the accounts of Guderian and Freytag von Loringhoven

p. 153 'a mixture of nervous . . .', Maizière, conversation, 9 October 1999

p. 153 'This short, bespectacled . . .', BA-MA MSg1/976, p. 70

p. 153 'We must always . . .', BA-MA MSg1/1207

p. 153 'the man who can make . . .', Heinrici papers, BA-MA MSg2/4231

p. 153 'The war's over . . .', Freytag von Loringhoven, conversation, 4 October 1999

p. 154 'Hitlerjunge Quex', BA-MA MSg1/976, p. 75

p. 154 'mutual respect . . .', BA-MA MSg1/976, p. 62

p. 155 'In the evening . . .', GARF 9401/2/97, pp. 32–48

p. 155 'on the grounds . . .', IfZ MA 127/2, p. 13,024

p. 155 'dangerous', and Italian forced labourers, see Gellately, pp. 237–8

p. 156 'eliminating all further possibility . . .', IMT, xli, pp. 430–31

p. 156 'This time you will . . .', quoted Sereny, pp. 485–6

p. 156 'I have reports that . . .', Speer interrogation, 22 May, NA 740.0011 EW/5–145

p. 157 'lose his head', Sereny, p. 491

p. 157 'impossible to deny the hope . . .', Speer interrogation, 22 May, NA 740.0011 EW/5–145

p. 157 abortion instruction, IfZ MA 127/2, pp. 13,042–3

p. 158 Speer and Kinzel, Speer interrogation, 22 May, NA 740.0011 EW/5–145

p. 158 'in our eyes . . .', BA-MA MSg1/976, p. 92

p. 159 '*Wann kommt der Russe?*', BA-MA MSg1/976, p. 76

p. 159 'a cheerful market woman . . .', BA-MA MSg1/976, p. 72

p. 160 '*Der 800,000 Mann-Plan*', IfZ MA 305

p. 160 'It was quite . . .', BA-MA MSg1/976, p. 116

p. 160 'with Dr Kaltenbrunner', GARF 9401/2/97, pp. 32–48

p. 160 Kaltenbrunner and Darius, 15 March, BA-B, R55/1394, p. 195

p. 161 'a companion in suffering', Tillery, quoted Ramm, 1994, p. 27

p. 161 'Life is like a child's . . .', Gall, conversation, 2 November 1999

p. 161 '*gemütlich*' bunker, quoted Ramm, 1994, p. 27

p. 162 'a really crazy type', Tillery, quoted ibid., p. 29

p. 163 'For once "soldier's luck" . . .', Laudan, quoted ibid., p. 52

p. 164 'Officers have two opinions . . .', TsAMO 236/2675/339, p. 63

p. 164 'To be an officer', TsAMO 236/2675/339, p. 63

11 PREPARING THE *COUP DE GRÂCE*

p. 165 'The Berlin operation . . .', TsAMO 233/2374/194, p. 29

p. 165 4,000 men each, Erickson, p. 476

p. 165 1,030,494 transferred from Gulag by 5 September 1944, GARF 1914/1/1146, p. 21

p. 166 State Defence Committee, Prikaz No. 7942 ss of 29 March, also GARF 8131/38/236, pp. 34–5

p. 166 'a dog's death for dogs', Merridale, p. 266

p. 166 'redeem their guilt . . .', Sulkhanishvili, conversation, 12 October 2000

p. 166 'soldiers who were Soviet citizens . . .', TsAMO 233/2374/194, pp. 11–13

p. 167 'Each day I spent . . .', TsAMO 233/2374/93, p. 685

p. 167 'Is it true . . .', TsAMO 233/2374/93, pp. 700–701

p. 167 'Bad supervision . . .', RGVA 38686/1/20, p. 21

p. 168 'these [curtains] must be removed . . .', 7 April, RGVA 32925/1/100, p. 174

p. 168 'Checking Fighting Fitness for Battle', RGVA 36860/1/16

p. 168 'They regarded it quite . . .', Senyavskaya, 2000, p. 236, n. 50

p. 168 'This happens . . .', RGVA 38686/1/20, p. 26

p. **168** 'One mistake . . .', Sulkhanishvili, conversation, 16 June 2001
p. **169** 'Red Army soldier . . .', Werth,
pp. 964, 965
p. **169** 'Look how the Germans . . .',
Eugene Schirinkine, 31 July, SHAT 7 P
128
p. **169** 'Our soldiers got . . .', Gall, conversation, 2 November 1999
p. **169** 'They put us in a camp . . .',
TsAMO 236/2675/267, pp. 67–8
p. **170** 'revenge score', TsAMO 233/
2374/194, p. 24
p. **170** 'There was a big slogan . . .', Kazakova, conversation, 6 November 1999
p. **171** analysis of letters, Gall, conversation, 2 November 1999
p. **171** 'Can only be used . . .', KA–FU,
EI: 18, Vol. 6
p. **171** chemical weapons, RGVA
32891/1/384, p. 19
p. **171** 'the weapons of despair', Dono-
van to Secretary of State, 1 April, NA
740.0011 EW/4–145
p. **171** 'argued for chemical warfare',
Speer interrogation, 22 May, NA
740.0011 EW/5–145
p. **172** panzerfaust trials, Belyaev, conversation, 29 July 2000

12 WAITING FOR THE ONSLAUGHT

p. **173** 'Yesterday', Major Juhlin-
Dannfel, 4 April, KA–FU, EI: 18, Vol. 6
p. **174** 'Every Bolshevik . . .', report 9
April, SHAT 7 P 102
p. **174** 'Every male . . .', report 9 April,
SHAT 7 P 102

p. **174** 'We know the plans . . .', Staats-
sekretär Dr Naumann, BA-MA RH19/
XV/9a, p. 94
p. **175** 'to that – exclusively . . .', NA
RG260 OMGUS, Stack 390 41/7/5–6
A2/S4
p. **176** 'We Germans are not a
nation . . .', Anonymous, p. 126
p. **176** 'We believe in victory . . .',
Kleine and Stimpel, p. 9
p. **176** '*Heil Hitler!*', report 2e Bureau,
21 April, SHAT 7 P 128
p. **177** 'thought to defending . . .', Halder, NA RG338 Ms P-136
p. **177** 'There are no children . . .',
BA-MA MSg1/976
p. **177** 'Evacuation . . .', Oberst i.G
Hans Refior, BA-MA MSg1/976
p. **178** 'short-sightedness, bureaucracy
. . .', Oberst i.G Hans Refior, BA-MA
MSg1/976
p. **178** '*Muttis*', Refior, BA-MA
MSg1/976
p. **178** 'a sense of duty', NA RG338 Ms
P-136
p. **179** 'masterpiece of . . .', BA-MA
MSg1/976, p. 3
p. **179** '*Arbeitsunlustig*', RGVA-SA
1367/1/218
p. **179** 'Those madmen in Berlin . . .',
BA-MA MSg1/976, p. 15
p. **179** 'The Ninth Army . . .', BA-MA
MSg1/976, p. 15
p. **180** 'The Führer once coined . . .',
Goebbels speech, 20 February, BA-B
R55/916, p. 91
p. **180** Schmidtke, conversation, 15 July
2000
p. **181** 'I swear that . . .', IfZ MA 485,
p. 20,755

p. 181 'deciphering...', 'There is an atmosphere...', KA-FU, EI: 18, Vol. 6

p. 182 Baumgart, quoted Ramm, 1994, p. 65

p. 182 *Volkshandgranate 45*, SHAT 7 P 102

p. 183 'clever eyes', BA-MA MSg1/976, p. 100

p. 183 General Bunyachenko, Fröhlich, p. 256

p. 183 'better purposes', BA-MA MSg1/976, p. 100, and BA-MA N53/76, p. 17

p. 184 200th Rifle Division, N. M. Ramanichev, 'Iz opyta peregruppirovki army pri podgotovke Berlinskoi operatsii', *ViZh*, No. 8, 1979

p. 184 'would only get...', Klochkov, p. 72

p. 184 'Some deserters seize carts from...', 7 April, RGVA 38686/1/21P.40

p. 184 355 deserters, RGVA 32891/1/120, p. 250

p. 184 'Many soldiers...', RGVA 32925/1/100, p. 184

p. 185 'barely one half...', Beria to Stalin, GARF 9401/2/95, pp. 253–68

p. 185 stragglers, 11 April, RGVA 32925/1/130, p. 240

p. 185 'Hello Papa, Mama...', quoted Shindel (ed.), pp. 158–9

p. 186 'Our advance is too slow...', TsAMO 233/2374/92, p. 331

p. 186 'Komsomolets', TsAMO 236/2675/440, pp. 6–8

p. 186 'all Communists have a duty...', TsAMO 233/2374/93, p. 652

p. 186 Artillery regiments, TsAMO 233/2374/93, p. 652

p. 186 'the local population...', TsAMO 233/2374/93, p. 695

p. 187 'a pile of stones', Inozemtsev, p. 196

p. 187 'Encircled soldiers...', RGVA 38680/1/3, p. 68

p. 187 'The aviation is...', Inozemtsev, p. 196

p. 188 'A bronze Bismarck...', ibid., p. 201

p. 188 the hospital ship *Goya*, Duffy, p. 291

p. 188 'On Ninth Army...', BA-MA RH19/XV/9a, p. 97

p. 188 'Führer expects...', BA-MA RH19/XV/9a, p. 207

p. 188 'the Führer is instinctively...', BA-MA RH19/XV/9a, p. 221

p. 189 'The concert took us...', Below, p. 409

p. 189 Hitler Youth and cyanide capsules, Sereny, p. 507

p. 189 'Order of the Day', BA-MA RH19/XV/9b, p. 34

p. 189 'There was terror...', Senyavskaya, 2000, p. 275

13 AMERICANS ON THE ELBE

p. 190 'learning English...', captured letter, Willi Klein to Lance Corporal Hans Gerl, quoted Ehrenburg, *Krasnaya Zvezda*, 25 November 1944

p. 190 'Germany had lost...', Papen interrogation, NA 740.0011 EW/4–2445

p. 191 'Alex, where are...', Bolling, quoted Ryan, p. 229

p. 191 'Bolsheviks near Vienna...', GARF 9401/2/97, pp. 32–48

p. 191 massacres in the Leipzig area, report of Captain Claude Merry, 28 April, SHAT 8 P 22

p. 192 'On the basis of findings . . .', report 8 March, NA 740.0011 EW/3–845

p. 192 'No speeding . . .', SHAT 8 P 27

p. 192 Operation Plunder, Elliott, pp. 121, 125, 143

p. 193 'Monty was very stuffy . . .', anonymous conversation, 30 December 2000

p. 193 'a life and death struggle . . .', Elliott, p. 12

p. 194 'American tankists . . .', *Krasnaya Zvezda*, 11 April, p. 3

p. 194 'conquering with cameras', NA 740.0011 EW/4–1345

p. 194 'arrange for an orderly . . .', NA 740.0011 EW/3–2745

p. 195 'there is no evidence . . .', NA 740.0011 EW/4–2345

p. 196 'The interrogation of various . . .', report of 10 April, SHAT 7 P 102

p. 196 '*Deutschland, dein* . . .', Kardorff, p. 306

p. 196 '*Khvatit*', *Krasnaya Zvezda*, 11 April, p. 3

p. 197 'were not refusing . . .', 'politically harmful', see Leonid Reshin, '*Tovarisch Ehrenburg uproshchaet*', *Novoe Vremya*, No. 8, 1994

p. 197 'by promising immunity . . .', Ehrenburg, pp. 176, 177

p. 197 'Comrade Ehrenburg Oversimplifies', '*Tovarisch Ehrenburg uproshchaet*', *Pravda*, 14 April

p. 198 'Your wife may get it . . .', Abakumov to Stalin, 29 March, quoted Reshin, *Novoe Vremya*, No. 8, 1994

p. 198 'that we should be ruthless . . .', TsAMO 233/2374/92, pp. 360–61

p. 199 'What was surprising', Soyuz veteranov zhurnalistiki, p. 447

p. 199 'In connection with . . .', GARF 9401/2/95, pp. 31–5, and Serov to Beria, 19 April, GARF 9401/2/95, p. 91

p. 199 43,000 Polish soldiers from Gulag, GARF 1914/1/1146

p. 199 '*W Sibir ili w Armiju?*', Andrzej Rey, quoted Gerhard Gnauck in 'Wie die Horden Dschingis Khans', *Die Welt*, 8 May 2001, p. 31

p. 200 'extremely rude . . .', '*der Katastrophengeneral*', interrogation 8 April of Lieutenant General von Oriola of XIII Corps, 2e Bureau, 21 April, SHAT 7 P 128

p. 201 'You're coming . . .', Reichhelm, conversation, 5 October 1999

p. 202 'along and either side . . .', unpublished MS, diary of Peter Rettich, battalion commander, *Scharnhorst* Division, Twelfth Army, Reichhelm papers

p. 202 'no other possibility but to surrender . . .', Reichhelm, conversation, 5 October 1999, and Humboldt, conversation, 11 October 1999

p. 202 'the Ninth Army has occupied . . .', SHAEF daily report on Allied Operations, SHAT 8 P 19

p. 203 'future division of Germany . . .', Eisenhower, p. 43

p. 203 'Soldiers and officers', Maizière, conversation, 9 October 1999

p. 204 'Where in the hell . . .', quoted Ryan, p. 261

p. 204 'My Führer, I congratulate you!', Trevor-Roper, pp. 89–90

p. 204 'At the moment . . .', BA-MA RH19/XV/9b, p. 34

p. **204** 'rocking like a ship', Loewe, conversation, 9 October 2001

p. **205** 'A whole world ...', Kardorff, pp. 306–7

14 EVE OF BATTLE

p. **206** 2.5 million men etc., *Sovetskaya voennaya entsiklopediya*, Vol. i, Moscow, 1990, p. 383

p. **206** medals stripped from 20th Panzergrenadier Division, *VOV*, iii, p. 272

p. **206** 'During the night ...', V. Makarevsky, '17-ya motorinzhenernaya brigada v Berlinskoi operatsii', *ViZh*, No. 4, April 1976

p. **207** 'Active Komsomol members ...', TsAMO 236/2675/440, p. 76

p. **207** 'There will be no pity', TsAMO 233/2374/92, p. 240

p. **207** 'transmitting in clear ...', TsAMO 236/2675/440, p. 192

p. **207** no sub-units allowed to use the radio, RGVA 32891/1/160

p. **207** wavelengths and codes, RGVA 32891/1/160, p. 232

p. **207** 'morally and politically unstable', TsAMO 233/2374/93, p. 454

p. **207** speaking against collective farms, TsAMO 233/2374/92, p. 314

p. **208** Heinrici order, BA-MA RH 19 XV/9b, p. 42

p. **208** 'Many wanted to be wounded ...', Kertz, conversation, 11 October 1999

p. **208** 'You can't imagine', TsAMO 236/2675/336, p. 57

p. **209** 'We have to hold ...', TsAMO 233/2374/93 p. 411

p. **209** 'almost peaceful ...', Wust, conversation, 10 October 1999

p. **209** 'rabbit-hearted', IfZ MA 127/2, p. 12,949

p. **210** 'The keys of the city ...', Vsevolod Vishnevsky, RGALI 1038/1/1804

p. **210** newspaper reports, contradiction by TASS, see *Pravda*, 25 April

p. **211** 'other matter', NA RG334/ Entry 309/Box 2

p. **211** 'Some of them shaded ...', Klochkov, p. 72

p. **211** 'Greetings from the front', Junior Lieutenant of Medical Service Abdul Aziz Babakhanov, Soyuz veteranov zhurnalistiki, p. 491

p. **212** 'The hurricane lamp is driving away darkness', Senyavskaya, 1995, p. 181

p. **213** 'tortured to death ...', TsAMO 233/2374/92, p. 314

p. **213** '*Liricheskoe*', quoted Senyavskaya, 1995, p. 101

p. **214** 'Soon we will return home ...', TsAMO 236/2675/440, p. 16

p. **214** 'It felt like a huge ...', Gall, conversation, 2 November 1999

p. **214** 'We warned all ...', Sulkhanishvili, conversation, 12 October 2000

15 ZHUKOV ON THE REITWEIN SPUR

p. **216** arrival of Zhukov, Merezhko, conversation, 10 November 1999

p. **217** 'The hands of the clock ...', Zhukov, iv, pp. 242–3

p. **217** 'A terrible thunder ...', Klochkov, p. 73

p. 218 '*Alarm! sofort . . .*', Ramm, 1994, p. 33

p. 218 'In a matter . . .', Wagner, quoted ibid., p. 200

p. 218 'In the field of view . . .', Kleine and Stimpel, p. 39

p. 218 'burning farmhouses . . .', quoted Ramm, 1994, p. 200

p. 218 'Christ, the poor . . .', Baumgart, quoted ibid., p. 67

p. 218 'shaving officers . . .', SS Kriegsberichter Heinz Heering, BA-MA MSg2/3448, p. 6

p. 219 'These men were sacrificed . . .', Obersturmführer Helmut Schwarz, quoted Ramm, 1994, p. 170

p. 219 'It seemed that not . . .', Zhukov, iv, p. 244

p. 219 'Along the whole length . . .', letter, Pyotr Mitrofanovich Sebelev, 2nd Sapper Bde, 16 April, quoted Shindel (ed.), p. 160

p. 219 'the light was so blinding . . .', Sulkhanishvili, conversation, 12 October 2000

p. 220 'producing losses', etc., TsAMO 233/2374/92, pp. 257–8

p. 221 'Maximum Alert', Schröder diary, quoted Ramm, 1994, p. 177

p. 222 'So you've underestimated . . .', Zhukov, iii, p. 245

p. 223 'His outstanding bravery . . .', BA-MA RH19/XV/24, p. 36

p. 224 'a dull, continuous . . .', BA-MA MSg1/976, p. 17

p. 224 'women and girls stood . . .', Boldt, pp. 108–9

p. 226 'not a killing field . . .', Harald Arndt, quoted Ramm, 1994, p. 270

p. 226 'We moved across terrain . . .', Sebelev, Shindel (ed.), p. 160

p. 226 'covered with the corpses . . .', Klochkov, p. 73

p. 226 'bad organization', etc., TsAMO 233/2374/92, pp. 27–30

p. 227 'in some regiments . . .', TsAMO 233/2374/92, pp. 31–2

p. 228 'became much more frequent', TsAMO 233/2374/92, p. 31

p. 228 footnote: Medical personnel, Senyavskaya, 1995, p. 124

p. 228 'How many matches were burnt?', Senyavskaya, 2000, p. 227

p. 229 'I was deeply . . .', BA-MA MSg2/1096

p. 229 'Berlin on the sixth day . . .', *VOV*, p. 270

p. 229 'Are you sure that . . .', Zhukov, iv, p. 247

p. 230 'Even when I was . . .', TsAMO 233/2374/194, pp. 47–8

p. 230 'The god of war . . .', TsAMO 233/2374/194, p. 32

p. 230 'At the fascist lair', etc., TsAMO 233/2374/194, p. 34

p. 230 13th Army observation post, Konev, p. 91

p. 231 'The assault boats were launched', TsAMO 233/2374/194, p. 35

p. 231 'We had nowhere to hide', TsAMO 233/2374/194, p. 33

p. 231 'Ivan don't shoot, we are prison', TsAMO 236/2675/336, pp. 6, 55–6

p. 232 'unbearably slow', TsAMO 233/2374/194, p. 50

p. 232 'Zhukov is not getting . . .', TsAMO TsGV/70500/2, pp. 145–9, quoted Zhukov, iv, pp. 226–7

p. 233 '[Antonov] said . . .', NA RG334/Entry 309/Box 2

16 SEELOW AND THE SPREE

p. 235 'He was wearing a long . . .', Sul-khanishvili, conversation, 12 October 2001

p. 236 'distinctly uncultured', Erick-son, p. 569

p. 236 'In the opinion of the infantry', TsAMO 233/2374/92, p. 355

p. 236 'We infantry were once . . .', Tillery, quoted Ramm, 1994, p. 35

p. 237 'completely shattered . . .', BA-MA MSg2/1096, p. 4

p. 237 'This is my artillery . . .', BA-MA MSg2/1096, p. 5

p. 237 attacks on Oder bridges, RGVA 32925/1/130, p. 259

p. 238 German pilots' suicide attacks, NA 740.0011 EW/4–2445

p. 238 *Leonidas* squadron (2./II./KG 200), BA-MA MSg2/4429, pp. 1–44

p. 239 'if the Germans . . .', TsAMO 236/2675/149, p. 258

p. 239 'How are you going to fire it?', TsAMO 233/2374/194, p. 56

p. 240 'No German town . . .', BA-MA RH19/XV/9b, p. 131

p. 240 'non-employed and those . . .', BLHA Pr. Br. Rep. 61A/443

p. 241 *Nordland* casualties, BA-MA RH 19 XV/9b, p. 62

p. 243 'Today is the moment . . .', BA-MA RH19/XV/9, p. 264

p. 243 wounded soldier at Hermers-dorf, Kleine and Stimpel, p. 35

p. 243 '426 Soviet tanks', *Der Angriff*, Nr. 92, 20 April

p. 244 'And this is the army', Kleine and Stimpel, pp. 35–6

p. 244 'In the town of Gusow . . .', TsAMO 233/2374/92, p. 356

p. 245 'a defence of the capital . . .', BA-MA MSg1/976, p. 18

p. 245 'Berlin would . . .', Speer interrogation, 22 May, NA 740.0011 EW/5–145

p. 245 'the sacrifice of children . . .', BA-MA MSg2/1096, p. 6

p. 246 'The Russians are eating . . .', Martin Kleint, quoted Ramm, 1994, p. 296

p. 246 '*Der Iwan kommt*', ibid., p. 96

p. 247 executions on Küstrin sector, Wuth, conversation, 10 October 1999

p. 247 SS to Schleswig-Holstein, BA-MA MSg2/3448, p. 6

p. 248 Saalborn to Bürgermeister of Woltersdorf, BLHA Pr. Br. Rep. 61A/443

p. 248 'Well, we'll have to start . . .', Zhukov, iv, p. 224

17 THE FÜHRER'S LAST BIRTHDAY

p. 249 'with heartiest congratulations', RGVA-SA 1355/4/11, p. 54

p. 250 'I wondered whether he was mad', Kardorff, p. 307

p. 251 'disappointed by the coward-ice . . .', Speer interrogation, 22 May, NA 740.0011 EW/5–145

p. 251 'Führer's birthday', GARF 9401/2/97, pp. 32–48

p. 252 'It was horrible . . .', Traudl Junge, quoted Sereny, p. 512

p. 252 'Eva Braun and Dr Stumpfegger', Bormann's diary, GARF 9401/2/97, pp. 32–48

p. 252 'a really foul trick', letter of 19 April, quoted Gun, p. 247

p. 252 'to keep the mystic legend . . .', Brandt paper, NA RG319/22/XE 23 11 00

p. 254 'She was always . . .', Below, pp. 407–8

p. 254 'We can already hear . . .', letter to Herta Ostermayr, quoted Gun, p. 252

p. 254 'Suddenly one remembers . . .', Friday 20 April, Anonymous, p. 9

p. 255 'the long-range artillery . . .', Zhukov, iv, p. 250

p. 255 'a historic task: to break into Berlin . . .', TsAMO 233/2307/193, p. 88

p. 256 'Comrade Rybalko', TsAMO 236/2712/359, p. 35

p. 256 recognition signals for meeting with Allied armies, TsAMO 132a/2642/38, pp. 14–15

p. 256 'Personal to Comrades . . .', quoted Erickson, p. 578

p. 256 '*Auffanglinien*', BA-MA RH19/XV/24, p. 119

p. 256 'It was clear to us . . .', BA-MA MSg1/976, p. 18

p. 257 'Then the tanks began firing . . .', quoted Ramm, 1994, p. 96

p. 257 'Now we'll let them have it', ibid., p. 97

p. 259 'The closer one gets to Berlin', Grossman papers, RGALI 1710/3/51, p. 240

p. 259 'mostly by officers and men . . .', TsAMO 233/2374/92, p. 47

p. 259 'It was all senseless', Wuth, conversation, 10 October 1999

p. 259 30th Guards Artillery Brigade, Klochkov, p. 77

p. 260 'They returned the following . . .', TsAMO 233/2374/93, p. 722

p. 260 'given chemical substances . . .', RGVA 32891/1/125, p. 289

p. 260 'hurl back', BA-MA MSg1/976, p. 20

p. 260 'to catch deserters and execute . . .', TsAMO 233/2374/93, p. 412

18 THE FLIGHT OF THE GOLDEN PHEASANTS

p. 261 'no man capable . . .', BA-MA MSg1/976, p. 17

p. 261 '*Werwolfs* of Berlin and Brandenburg', 24 April, NA RG 260 OMGUS, Stack 390 41/7/5–6 A2/S4

p. 262 'What's going on?', Günsche interrogation, quoted Bezymenski, pp. 28–9

p. 262 'For the rat Goebbels', TsAMO 233/2374/92, p. 255, and Zhukov, iv, p. 258

p. 262 'the bloody god of war', K. M. Simonov, Notebook No. 8, RGALI 1814/4/7

p. 262 1.8 million shells, Zhukov, iv, p. 255

p. 262 'cellar tribe', Anonymous, pp. 13–16

p. 263 '*Du General?*', Kertz, conversation, 10 October 1999

p. 263 *Scharnhorst* Division, Rettich war diary, Reichhelm papers

p. 264 'a very bad feeling', Lorenz, quoted Ramm, 1994, p. 98

p. 264 'See that you all get home . . .', Tillery, quoted ibid., p. 40

p. 265 'Due to the slowness ...', 21 April, TsAMO 233/2374/92, pp. 359–60

p. 267 'three battalions and a few tanks', BA-MA MSg1/976, p. 143

p. 268 'The defence of Berlin ...', TsAMO 299/17055/4, p. 305

p. 268 'twenty-four-hour-a-day ...', Zhukov, iv, p. 276

p. 269 'a dirty, swampy little river', TsAMO 233/2374/194, p. 66

p. 270 'Soviet shells exploding ...', Wallin, quoted Ramm, 1994, p. 99

p. 271 Konev's order to the 28th Army, A. Luchinsky, 'Na Berlin!', *ViZh*, No. 5, May 1965

p. 271 'completely surprised ...', NA RG 338, P–136, p. 49

p. 271 'as snow in the middle ...', TsAMO 233/2374/194, p. 78

p. 271 'At about five in the afternoon', Rocolle, 1954, p. 87

p. 272 'hearts raced in fear', DRK-Schwester Ruth Schwarz, quoted Ramm, 1994, p. 229

p. 273 German stragglers from Seelow Heights, RGVA 32925/1/130, p. 269

p. 273 'On 22 April, a Red Army cook', RGVA 32925/1/130, p. 275

p. 273 'Everything is covered with flowers ...', Grossman papers, RGALI, 1710/3/51, p. 239

p. 274 'Not a single woman ...', Anonymous, p. 21

p. 276 'General Field Marshal Keitel', extracts from notes of Jodl, TsAMO 233/2356/5804, pp. 201–3

p. 276 'his mental sickness ...', Maizière, p. 106, and conversation, 9 October 1999

p. 276 'Losses can never ...', quoted Trevor-Roper, p. 65

p. 277 'the chiefs plan to get ...', NA 740.0011 EW/3–2245

p. 277 'There exist in ...', NA RG59 740.0011 EW/4–645

p. 277 'superbly stocked', Freytag von Loringhoven, conversation, 4 October 1999

p. 277 'In the bunker', Maizière, conversation, 9 October 1999

p. 278 night of 22 April, Below, p. 411, and Traudl Junge, television interview

p. 279 'Forgive me ...', letter of 22 April, original reproduced Gun, p. 176

19 THE BOMBARDED CITY

p. 280 'the battle a European significance', diary Uffz. Heinrich V., 23 April, BZG-S

p. 280 siege guns, Zhukov, iv, p. 255

p. 281 'Desertion suddenly seems ...', Anonymous, p. 24

p. 282 'real feeling of disintegration', Beier, conversation, 9 October 2001

p. 282 'to their impulses', Kronika, pp. 98–9

p. 282 'What a thing to die for', Petersohn, conversation, 9 July 2000

p. 283 rumour of Model's arrest, NA 740.0011 EW/4–2445

p. 283 7th Department, TsAMO 233/2374/93, pp. 413, 419

p. 284 'Because the fascist clique ...', TsAMO 233/2374/93, p. 414

p. 284 'letter from the inhabitants ...', TsAMO 233/2374/93, p. 415

p. 285 'an outstanding ...', Reichhelm,

conversation, 5 October 1999, and also Humboldt, conversation, 11 October 1999

p. 285 'gravedigger of the army', NA 740.0011 EW/4–1045

p. 285 '*Soldaten der Armee Wenck!*', BA-MA MSg1/976, p. 28

p. 285 'the Führer has issued orders . . .', NA 740.0011 EW/4–2445

p. 285 'So we made up . . .', Humboldt, conversation, 11 October 1999

p. 286 'Boys, you've got . . .', Reichhelm papers, *Das Letzte Aufgebot*

p. 286 'a feeling of loyalty . . .', Genscher, conversation, 4 September 2000

p. 286 'So about turn!', Rettich diary, Reichhelm papers

p. 286 'tragi-comedy', BA-MA MSg1/976, p. 22

p. 286 state of LVI Panzer Corps, Refior, BA-MA MSg1/976, p. 24

p. 287 Berlin defence figures, Willemer, 'The German Defense of Berlin', NA RG338, P136, p. 46

p. 288 Speer's journey to Berlin, NA 740.0011 EW/5–145

p. 288 'the legends would be hard to create', Speer interrogation, 22 May, NA 740.0011 EW/5–145

p. 289 'My Führer! – In view of . . .', quoted Trevor-Roper, p. 116

p. 290 'a simple Munich girl . . .', Sereny, p. 532

p. 290 'Hermann is not with us . . .', Gun, pp. 253–4

20 FALSE HOPES

p. 291 Krukenberg account, BA-MA MSg2/1283

p. 291 SS 'Charlemagne', Fenet, conversation, 4 June 1999

p. 293 'since he alone . . .', NA 740.0011 EW/5–145

p. 293 'The Reichsführer is no longer . . .', Trevor-Roper, p. 103

p. 294 Schulstrasse transit camp, Löwenstein, conversation, 14 July 2000

p. 295 'a real International', Konev, p. 150

p. 295 'hundreds of bearded Russian . . .', RGALI 1710/3/51, p. 239

p. 295 'An old woman . . .', RGALI 1710/3/51, p. 240

p. 295 'The Soviet Union has a right . . .', NA RG218 JCS Box 15

p. 296 US aircraft attacked, Antonov correspondence, NA RG334/Entry 309/Box 2

p. 297 'they were licking [our] boots', TsAMO 233/2374/92, p. 53

p. 297 'In the course of three hours', V. S. Antonov, 'Poslednie dni voiny', *ViZh*, No. 7, July 1987

p. 297 'It was a bloody . . .', Ramm, 1994, p. 102

p. 297 'Vlasov and his men are taking part', RGALI 1710/3/51, p. 239

p. 298 Beelitz-Heilstätten, DRK-Schwester Ruth Schwarz, quoted Ramm, 1994, p. 229

p. 299 'You're the only one . . .', BA-MA MSg2/1283, p. 11

p. 299 conditions in the bunker, Freytag von Loringhoven, conversation, 4 October 1999, and Misch, 8 July 2000

p. 300 'Another officer . . .', TsAMO 233/2374/92, p. 361

p. 300 'surprised the Berliners immensely', TsAMO 233/2374/194, p. 78

p. **300** 'abnormal phenomena', TsAMO 233/2374/92, p. 362

p. **300** 'small babushka', Sulkhanishvili, conversation, 12 October 2000

p. **300** 'impersonal violence of war itself', Glenn Gray, pp. 66–7

p. **300** 'substitutes for the defeat of an enemy', Naimark, p. 70

p. **300** waves of violence, ibid., p. 83

p. **301** Shulzhenok, TsAMO 233/2374/92, p. 333

p. **301** 'What contradicts our idea . . .', Grossman papers, RGALI 1710/3/51, p. 240

p. **301** 'Ziegler had secret orders . . .', BA-MA MSg1/976, p. 24

p. **302** *Meine Herren, alles Gute!*', Roman Burghart, quoted Ramm, 1994, p. 104

p. **302** 'laid on a blood-smeared table . . .', Wallin, quoted ibid., p. 108

p. **302** Krukenberg account, BA-MA MSg2/1283

p. **302** 'SS traitors extending the war!', Wallin, quoted Ramm, 1994, p. 103

p. **303** 'The silence which followed . . .', BA-MA N65/126

p. **304** 'The situation must improve', TsAMO 233/2356/5804, pp. 201–3

p. **304** 'a self-deception bordering . . .', BA-MA N65/126, p. 165

p. **304** 'General Eisenhower desires . . .', 25 April, Reade to Antonov, NA RG334/Entry 309/Box 2

p. **305** Deutschlandsender, NA RG59 740.0011 EW/5–1045

p. **307** Tully and Irwin, NA RG334/Entry 309/Box 6

p. **307** 'On the walls . . .', Serov via Beria to Stalin, 25 April, GARF 9401/2/95, pp. 304–10

p. **308** 'the attitude of Red Army troops . . .', Beria to Stalin, GARF 9401/2/95, pp. 317–28

21 FIGHTING IN THE CITY

p. **310** 'There they stand . . .', Anonymous, p. 28

p. **311** 'Take up the weapons . . .', Diary Uffz. Heinrich V., 27 April, BZG-S

p. **312** 'We had no idea . . .', Petersohn, conversation, 9 July 2000

p. **314** *'Tag, Russki!'*, Boeseler, conversation, 7 July 2000

p. **314** 'kulaks and landowners', TsAMO 233/2374/93, p. 747

p. **314** 'wax-like faces wreathed . . .', Anonymous, p. 29

p. **315** 'almost without antiseptic . . .', Rocolle, 1954, p. 73

p. **315** Volkssturm weapons, Toscano-Korvin diary-letter, 7 July, BZG-S

p. **315** 'Berliner! Hold on . . .', BA-MA MSg1/976, p. 28

p. **315** 'At the moment I am . . .', Pyotr Mitrofanovich Sebelev, quoted Shindel (ed.), p. 161

p. **316** 'casserole', Johannes Steinhoff, quoted Steinhoff et al. (eds.), p. 245

p. **316** 'new tactic', TsAMO 233/2374/194, p. 78

p. **317** 3rd Shock Army anti-aircraft guns, Nikolai Vasiliev, 'Krasnyi tsvet pobedy', in *Vsem smertyam nazlo*, Moscow, 2000

p. **317** 'Offensive operations carried . . .', SHAT 7 P 163

p. **317** sections of railway line with dynamite, TsAMO 233/2374/194, p. 78

p. 318 'We didn't have time . . .', anonymous interview, 5 November 1999

p. 318 'frequent cases of mutual firing . . .', A. Luchinsky, 'Na Berlin!', *ViZh*, No. 5, May 1965

p. 319 'Poor inner city', Eva Reuss in Schwerin, p. 166

p. 319 'Now we should be scared . . .', RGALI 1710/3/51, p. 241

p. 320 'thunderbolts from the sky', Grossman papers, RGALI 1710/3/51, p. 240

p. 320 'Old frontline hares', BA-MA MSg1/976, p. 25

p. 320 'Your proposal is perfectly all right . . .', BA-MA MSg1/976, p. 25

p. 321 tradition of commandant of city, Konev, p. 236

p. 321 'The commandant of Berlin . . .', RGALI 1710/3/51, p. 240

p. 322 'the Americans could cross . . .', BA-MA MSg2/1283, p. 22

p. 325 Thiessen and Bewilogua, AGMPG II. Abt., Rep. 1A, A2. IA 9/-Havemann

p. 326 Haus Dahlem, Rocolle, 1992, pp. 108–9

p. 326 'the horrors of the Middle Ages', Marianne Reinold, in Bollmann et al., p. 67

p. 326 events in Dahlem, see also Naimark, p. 82

p. 327 'violence under the pretext of revenge', TsAMO 233/2374/93, p. 706

p. 327 'When we broke into Berlin', TsAMO 233/2374/93, p. 650

p. 327 'That? Well, it certainly . . .', Anonymous, p. 49

22 FIGHTING IN THE FOREST

p. 328 'Who would ever . . .', diary of Peter Rettich diary, Reichhelm papers

p. 328 'Blast the Russians away!', Ruth Schwarz, quoted Ramm, 1994, p. 231

p. 329 'It was fought . . .', Rettich diary, Reichhelm papers

p. 329 civilian casualties in Beelitz, *Beelitzer Heimatverein*, p. 18

p. 329 footnote: Soviet estimate of Busse's army, Konev, p. 181, Erickson, p. 592

p. 329 40,000 German troops in forest, NA RG 338 R-79, p. 59

p. 330 'pushing to the west like a caterpillar', quoted NA RG 338 R-79, p. 14

p. 330 'to decide for himself . . .', quoted NA RG 338 R-79, p. 19

p. 330 'to block all the forest roads leading from east to west', TsAMO 684/492483/1

p. 331 'without information about . . .', A. Luchinsky, 'Na Berlin!', *ViZh*, No. 5, May 1965

p. 331 'The Führer has ordered . . .', 'The Führer in Berlin . . .', NA RG 338 R-79, pp. 37-8

p. 332 'If the first attempts . . .', TsAMO 236/2675/267, p. 186

p. 332 wounded crushed by tank tracks, Lindner, conversation, 10 October 2001

p. 333 'For this they paid . . .', A. Luchinsky, 'Na Berlin!', *ViZh*, No. 5, May 1965

p. 334 '2,459 attack missions . . .', Konev, p. 182

p. 334 'a patchwork quilt of corpses', Baumgart, quoted Ramm, 1994, p. 70

p. **334** 'It's already been five days . . .', TsAMO 236/2675/267, p. 189

p. **335** SS with panzerfaust in cellar, Buhl, conversation, 10 October 2001

p. **335** 'I never suspected . . .', Jürgs diary (8 May retrospective), quoted Ramm, 1994, pp. 159–60

p. **335** 'Tanks rolled down . . .', quoted Ramm, 1995, p. 25

p. **336** 'Get up!', Kleint, quoted Ramm, 1994, p. 306

p. **336** 'In that place, there was . . .', K. M. Simonov, Notebook No. 9, RGALI, 1814/4/8, p. 80

p. **337** 'The remains of the destroyed . . .', TsAMO 233/2374/194, p. 76

p. **337** 'more than 3,000–4,000', Konev, pp. 181–2

p. **337** Fieseler Storch from Army Group Vistula, Eismann, BA-MA MSg1/976, p. 138

p. **338** 'to send these children . . .', BA-MA MSg1/976, p. 143

p. **338** 'disobedience and unsoldierly weakness', BA-MA MSg1/976, p. 143

23 THE BETRAYAL OF THE WILL

p. **340** 61st Rifle Division, A. Luchinsky, 'Na Berlin!', *ViZh*, No. 5, May 1965

p. **340** 'Rosly, who is usually . . .', V. S. Antonov, 'Poslednie dni voiny', *ViZh*, No. 7, July 1987, and TsAMO 301sd/295514/1, p. 158

p. **340** 'One had a panoramic . . .', quoted Schultz-Naumann, p. 178

p. **340** 'Stand fast, fight fanatically', 26 April, 04.08 hours, GARF 9401/2/102, pp. 13–17

p. **341** 'I consider your proposed . . .', 26 April, NA RG218 JCS Box 15 File 94

p. **341** 'Himmler and Jodl stop . . .', GARF 9401/2/97, pp. 32–48

p. **342** Fegelein execution, Freytag von Loringhoven, conversation, 4 October 1999

p. **342** 'A traitor must . . .', quoted Trevor-Roper, p. 152

p. **343** 'in spite of all . . .', ibid., pp. 156–7

p. **344** 'An erotic fever . . .', Gun, p. 273

p. **346** 'Salon Kitty', *Salon Kitty*, see Peter Norden, Munich, 1970, and documentary film 'Meine Oma hatte einen Nazi-Puff' by Rosa von Praunheim about Kitty's grandson, Jochen Mattei

p. **346** 'this grey, frightening . . .', TsAMO 233/2374/194, p. 83

p. **346** 'that very evening', Rocolle, 1954, p. 69

p. **347** Shatilov and Goebbels, Klochkov, conversation, 25 July 2000

p. **347** 'looking at us maliciously . . .', Shatilov, 'U sten Reikhstaga', in *Vsem smertyam nazlo*, Moscow, 2000

p. **347** checking Moabit for explosives, Sulkhanishvili, conversation, 10 February 2001

p. **347** 'soon learned what to expect', TsAMO 233/2374/194, p. 78

p. **349** Reichstag assault, S. Neustroev, 'Shturm Reikhstaga', *ViZh*, No. 5, May 1960, pp. 42–5

p. **349** katyusha launchers on lengths of railway line, Belyaev, conversation, 25 July 2000

p. 349 'Greetings from the front', quoted Shindel (ed.), p. 151

p. 350 'Sunday 29 April', GARF 9401/2/97, pp. 32–48

p. 350 Signals intercepted, 29 April, TsAMO 233/2356/5804, p. 147

p. 351 'Herr General, I do not want . . .', Freytag von Loringhoven, conversation, 4 October 1999

p. 351 departure of Weiss, Freytag and Boldt, Freytag von Loringhoven, conversation, 4 October 1999

p. 351 assault on Prinz-Albrechtstrasse, V. S. Antonov, 'Poslednie dni voiny', *ViZh*, No. 7, July 1987

p. 352 'fed from above', Krukenberg, BA-MA MSg2/1283, p. 30

p. 352 empty faces, Weisz, quoted Ramm, 1994, p. 106

p. 352 'descent into hell', Bereznyak, quoted ibid., p. 115

p. 352 'like a single soldier with a rifle', Fenet, conversation, 19 May 1999

p. 352 'The Communists must be . . .', Fenet, conversation, 19 May 1999

p. 352 'But Comrade Kukharev . . .', TsAMO 233/2374/92, p. 70

24 FÜHRERDÄMMERUNG

p. 354 'The order has come through . . .', Shatilov, 'U sten Reikhstaga', in *Vsem smertyam nazlo*, Moscow, 2000

p. 355 'There's a grey building . . .', Vasily Subbotin, *How Wars End*, p. 131

p. 355 'Hieronymus Bosch landscape', Kardorff, p. 175

p. 356 bombardment of Reichstag, S.

Neustroev, 'Shturm Reikhstaga', *ViZh*, No. 5, May 1960, pp. 42–5

p. 356 'to have escaped . . .', BA-MA MSg2/3448, p. 10

p. 357 'like any other . . .', Misch, conversation, 8 July 2000

p. 357 'hanged upside down', Rzhevskaya, 1986, p. 44

p. 357 Hitler's fear of Eva Braun's capture, see R.W. Leon, *The Making of an Intelligence Officer*, London, 1994

p. 358 silver fox fur cape, Sereny, p. 538

p. 358 'a book on Egyptian tombs', RGVA-SA 1355/1/1, p. 18

p. 358 Kempka and petrol

p. 359 'black trousers and a grey-green military jacket', SMERSH protocol of investigation, Vadis to Beria, 7 May, GARF 9401/2/96, pp. 175–82

p. 359 lower bunker just before Hitler's suicide, Sereny p. 539, and Misch, conversation, 8 July 2000

p. 360 'The chief's on fire', and Linge taking watch, Misch, conversation, 8 July 2000

p. 360 'The information which . . .', Rzhevskaya, 1986, p. 36

p. 360 'The air thickened . . .', ibid., p. 31

p. 361 'She said that she needed . . .', Vadis to Beria, 7 May, GARF 9401/2/96, pp. 175–82

p. 362 'left about 1,800 dead . . .', TsAMO 236/2675/149, p. 274

p. 362 'We reached a clearing . . .', Gefreiter Martin Kleint, 30 April, quoted Ramm, 1994, p. 309

p. 363 'The boy was making painful grimaces', Rzhevskaya, 1986, p. 31

p. 364 'Personally, and aside from . . .',

Truman papers, quoted Martin Gilbert, *The Day the War Ended*, London, 1995, p. 41

p. 364 'a secret agreement . . .', NA 740.0011 EW/4–2445

p. 364 Weidling in Führer bunker, evening of 30 April, NA RG 338 R–79, p. ii

p. 365 'a special present to Stalin', Klochkov, conversation, 25 July 2000

p. 365 blood on stone columns, Belyaev, conversation, 25 July 2000

p. 366 soldiers dropping grenades simultaneously, Klochkov, conversation, 25 July 2000

p. 367 'as if we had just won . . .', Weisz, quoted Ramm, 1994, p. 120

p. 367 'What I am about to say', Vishnevsky, 'Berlin Diary', in Sevruk (ed.), pp. 162–93

p. 368 'Comrade Stalin has just gone to bed', Zhukov, iv, pp. 269–70

25 REICH CHANCELLERY AND REICHSTAG

p. 370 'A blazing comet is extinguished', BA-MA MSg2/3448, p. 15

p. 370 'As a first priority . . .', BA-MA MSg2/1283, p. 32

p. 371 'hollow charge', etc., Karen Meyer, pp. 47–83

p. 371 'between around fifty and 15,000', Amt für die Erfassung der Kriegsopfer, 28 July 1947; I am also grateful to Dietmar Arnold for his comments on the debate

p. 372 bouncing grenade, Belyaev, conversation, 25 July 2000

p. 372 'smiling like obedient dogs', Klochkov, conversation, 25 July 2000

p. 372 'We propose that you surrender . . .', TsAMO 233/2374/93, pp. 458–9

p. 373 'Because this mission . . .', Gall, conversation, 2 November 1999

p. 375 'Typically German!', Brettschneider's account, permanent exhibition, Zitadelle Spandau

p. 376 'general testing of . . .', Operation Dragon's Return, STIB, 28 January 1954, PRO DEFE 21/42, p. 4

p. 378 'to liquidate a large group . . .', TsAMO 236/2675/149, p. 276

p. 378 25,000 men, NA RG 338 R–79, p. 49

p. 378 'Was it really unquestioning . . .', Horst Haufschildt, quoted Ramm, 1994, p. 291

p. 379 'A much loved leader', ibid., p. 150

p. 379 'What are you doing here . . .', Reichhelm, conversation, 5 October 1999

p. 379 'to be at the immediate disposal . . .', BA-MA MSg2/1283, p. 34

p. 380 'After we had been talking . . .', Vadis to Beria, 7 May, GARF 9401/2/96, pp. 175–82

p. 381 'The remains of glass ampoules . . .', Vadis to Beria, 7 May, GARF 9401/2/96, pp. 175–82

p. 381 'at the head of his troops', Hamburg radio, Trevor-Roper, p. 188

p. 384 'unpleasant suggestion', Zhukov, iv, p. 272

p. 384 Bärenfänger, Le Tissier, 1999, p. 186

p. 384 Ernst Himmler, Beier, conversation, 9 October 2001

p. 384 'There was blood every-where . . .', Loewe, conversation, 9 October 2001

p. 385 'Among the crews killed . . .', Zhukov, iv, p. 272

p. 385 'The Führer is dead', Beier, conversation, 9 October 2001

26 THE END OF THE BATTLE

p. 386 'What I experienced . . .', Rürup (ed.), 1997, p. 184

p. 387 'We're sparing these . . .', Prinz-Albrecht-Gelände permanent exhibition

p. 388 'Sergeant Gorbachov . . .', V. S. Antonov, 'Poslednie dni voiny', *ViZh*, No. 7, July 1987

p. 388 fate of Constanze Manzialy, Musmanno, p. 39

p. 389 'Come around to the back', Lothar Rühl, quoted Steinhoff et al. (eds.), p. 434

p. 389 arrest of Günsche, Rzhevskaya, 1986, p. 212

p. 389 Berzarin's promise of award, Rzhevskaya, 2000, p. 286

p. 389 'My comrades and I . . .', Sul-khanishvili, conversation, 12 October 2000

p. 390 'shrunk in size . . .', Sulkhan-ishvili, conversation, 12 October 2000

p. 390 cigarette case and Hitler's badge, Vadis to Beria, 7 May, GARF 9401/2/96, pp. 175–82

p. 390 'They did not let me go down', Rzhevskaya, 2000, p. 295

p. 390 'the Germans had buried . . .', Zhukov, iv, p. 275

p. 391 'exemplary', Erna Flegel debrief by OSS, 23 November

p. 391 repeat interrogations of bunker witnesses, Rzhevskaya, conversation, 28 October 2001

p. 391 Colonel Haller, TsAMO 233/2374/93, pp. 458–9

p. 392 'post-mortal convulsions', K. M. Simonov, Notebook No. 9, RGALI 1814/4/8

p. 392 famine in Soviet Central Asia, see GARF 9401/2/95, pp. 57–62, 92–6

p. 393 'their blood group tattooed . . .', Beria to Stalin, 20 November, GARF 9401/2/100, p. 492

p. 393 denunciations, Belyaev, conversation, 25 July 2000

p. 393 'But surely you aren't . . .', RGALI 1710/3/51, p. 240

p. 393 'Prisoners', RGALI 1710/3/51, p. 242

p. 394 'They don't look at anyone . . .', RGALI 1710/3/51, p. 245

p. 394 'huge and powerful', RGALI 1710/3/51, p. 243

p. 395 'the colossal scale . . .', RGALI 1710/3/51, p. 244

p. 395 reinstating the military salute, Genscher, conversation, 4 September 2000

p. 395 'It's over!', Peter Rettich diary, 3 May, Reichhelm papers

p. 396 negotiations at Stendal, Edels-heim, BA-MA MSg1/236 and Reich-helm, NA RG 338 B-606

p. 396 'It is thanks to our Führer!', Robert Ohlendorf, quoted Ramm, 1994, p. 174

p. 397 9,139 Hiwis, NA RG 338 R-79, p. 58

p. 397 5,000 Hiwis reach the Twelfth

Army, Genscher, conversation, 4 September 2000

p. 397 '*Nix SS . . .*', Herbert Fuchs, quoted Ramm, 1994, p. 256

p. 397 'Quite a few people . . .', Reichhelm, conversation, 5 October 1999

p. 397 'The real problem', Humboldt, conversation, 11 October 1999

p. 399 'Stalin's system needed . . .', Rzhevskaya, 2000, p. 277

p. 400 'the sort used . . .', Rzhevskaya, conversation, 28 October 2001

p. 400 'accepted with great satisfaction', Eisenhower to Antonov, 10 May, NA RG334/Entry 309/Box 2

p. 401 Bradley and Konev, Bradley, p. 551

p. 401 'tankists of 25th Tank Corps . . .', Yashechkin, reported to GLAVPURKKA, RGASPI 17/125/310

p. 401 Vlasov hiding under blankets, Konev, p. 230

p. 402 'on behalf of the Soviet . . .', Eisenhower to Antonov, 8 May, NA RG334/Entry 309/Box 2

p. 403 'We celebrated victory . . .', Yuri Gribov, 'Igral nam v Brandenburge grammofon', *Stroki s velikoi voiny*, Moscow, 2000

p. 403 'The first toast to victory', Inozemtsev, p. 206

p. 403 'a fat, small colonel', K. M. Simonov Diary, Notebook No. 9, RGALI, 1814/4/8

p. 404 'in a two-storey building . . .', TsAMO 233/2356/5804, pp. 155–6

p. 404 'they jumped up . . .', K. M. Simonov Diary, Notebook No. 9, RGALI, 1814/4/8

27 VAE VICTIS!

p. 406 2,389 kilos in gold, GARF 9401/2/96, p. 15

p. 406 police forensic laboratories, RGVA 32925/1/100, p. 293

p. 406 deportation of V-2 rocket scientists, Siemens engineers etc., see PRO DEFE 41/116, and Counter Intelligence Corps NA 319/22/XE169886 and NA 319/22/XE 257685

p. 406 'Socialism cannot benefit itself', Fedoseyev notes

p. 407 'the systematic destruction . . .', report 2e Bureau, 21 April, SHAT 7 P 128

p. 407 'two dachshunds (nice fellows)', RGALI 1710/3/51, p. 241

p. 407 'twenty unique shotguns . . .', Abakumov to Stalin, 10 January 1948, 'Portrety bez retushi', *Voennye Arkhivy Rossii*, No. 1, 1993, p. 189

p. 408 'Come on, take it!', K. M. Simonov Diary, Notebook No. 8, RGALI 1814/4/7

p. 408 '*Uhr schon Kamerad*', Toscano-Korvin diary-letter, 7 July, BZG-S

p. 408 looting by Russian boys, RGVA 32925/1/121, pp. 61, 93

p. 408 'considerable amount . . .', Murphy to State Department, NA 740.0011 EW/4–2445

p. 409 'Even the Bishop of Munster', NA 740.0011 EW5–145

p. 409 Soviet officer and pistol, Zbarsky, p. 134

p. 410 mothers saving daughters, Kardorff, p. 358, and Lewin, conversation, 14 October 1999

p. 410 rape estimates, Dr Gerhard

Reichling, and Charité and Kaiserin Auguste Victoria, quoted Sander and Johr, pp. 54, 59

p. 410 'twenty-three soldiers . . .', Kardorff, p. 358

p. 410 'I must repress . . .', Frau Irene Burchert, quoted Owings, p. 147

p. 410 'That feeling . . .', Juliane Hartmann, quoted Steinhoff et al. (eds.), p. 455

p. 410 'All in all', Anonymous, p. 102

p. 411 'Afterwards, I had to . . .', Hanna Gerlitz, quoted Steinhoff et al. (eds.), p. 459

p. 411 'desexualization' of prisoners, see Frank Biess, 'The Protracted War', *GHI Bulletin*, No. 28 (Spring 2001)

p. 411 engagement broken off, Kardorff, p. 358

p. 411 'You've turned into shameless bitches', Anonymous, p. 202

p. 411 daughter, mother and grandmother raped, Frau Regina Frankenfeld, quoted Owings, p. 405

p. 412 'Go along, for God's sake! . . .', Anonymous, p. 66

p. 412 'The thirteen-year-old Dieter Sahl', Toscano-Korvin diary-letter, 7 July, BZG-S

p. 412 'that German intelligence left . . .', 16 June, RGVA 32925/1/121, p. 82

p. 412 'Some members of the underground . . .', 29 May, RGVA 32925/1/116, p. 428

p. 412 'the enemy is prepared to use . . .', 14 April, TsAMO 372/6570/68, pp. 17–20

p. 412 penicillin and births in hospital, Sander and Johr, p. 17

p. 412 'The Red Army is the most . . .',

26 April, TsAMO 233/2374/92, p. 240

p. 413 'to change their attitudes . . .', RGVA 32925/1/100, p. 296

p. 413 'Monsieur, I like your army . . .', RGALI 1710/3/51, p. 244

p. 413 'robbery', 'physical violence' and 'scandalous events', RGVA 32925/1/297, pp. 30–31

p. 414 'This scoundrel campaign . . .', 5 October, RGASPI 17/125/316, p. 81

p. 414 'First comes food . . .', Kardorff, p. 364

p. 414 'cigarette currency', Werner, conversation, 15 October 1999

p. 414 'occupation wives', Naimark, p. 93

p. 415 desertion of Red Army officers, OMGUS, NA, RG260 A2 B1 C3 Box 363

p. 415 'Perhaps we women', Kardorff, p. 341

p. 415 'a conviction of total catastrophe', Loewe, conversation, 10 October 2001

p. 415 'by the docility and discipline of the people', Zbarsky, p. 129

p. 415 'with unquestioning obedience', Beria to Stalin, GARF 9401/2/95, pp. 395–9

p. 415 'respect for the powers that be', Merezhko, conversation, 10 November 1999

p. 416 'that leaders of fascist organizations . . .', RGVA 32925/1/121, p. 89

p. 416 'The Party Lives On!', 7 May, RGVA 32925/1/121, p. 41

p. 416 'an unknown number of bandits', RGVA 38680/1/4, p. 43

p. 416 'Klamottenberg', Beier, conversation, 9 October 2001

p. 416 'People were living with their fate', Loewe, conversation, 9 October 2001

p. 416 Grossdeutscher Rundfunk, Beier, conversation, 9 October 2001

p. 417 'We had no idea what . . .', Wolf, conversation, 14 July 2000

p. 417 'naïve enough to hope . . .', Wolf, 1997, p. 47

p. 418 'Our *frontoviki* have . . .', Wolf, 1998, p. 33

p. 418 'Then came the experience . . .', Wolf, conversation, 14 July 2000

p. 418 'a scoundrel capable . . .', Beria, p. 88

p. 418 'an absolute order', Wolf, conversation, 14 July 2000

p. 418 'taboo themes', Wolf, conversation, 14 July 2000

p. 419 'burnt-out tanks . . .', Kardorff, p. 356

p. 419 Red Army rabbi, LA-B 3928

p. 419 'Hamster-express', 'Zeitung in der Zeitung', *Freie Welt*, July 1975, BA-MA MSg2/3626

p. 419 'to secure the elimination . . .', Beria to Stalin, GARF 9401/2/95, p. 374

p. 420 East Prussian population reduced to 193,000, 16 June, GARF 9401/2/96, pp. 343-4

p. 420 'in forests, peat bogs and canals . . .', Caritas report, NA RG 260 OMGUS, Stack 390 41/7/5-6

p. 420 fifteen NKVD regiments for Poland, Beria to Stalin, 22 June, GARF 9401/2/97, pp. 8-10

28 THE MAN ON THE WHITE HORSE

p. 421 'So, Ninka', TsAMO 372/6570/68, quoted Senyavskaya, 1995, p. 191

p. 422 'At that time . . .', TsAMO 372/6570/78, pp. 30-32

p. 422 'We don't believe . . .', TsAMO 233/2374/92, p. 288

p. 423 officers shot in the back in battle, Kubasov, conversation, 27 October 2001

p. 423 'systematic anti-Soviet talk . . .', RGVA 38686/1/26, p. 36

p. 423 'systematically carried out . . .', RGVA 32925/1/297, p. 28

p. 423 'counter-revolutionary crimes', GARF 9401/1a/165, pp. 181-3

p. 423 'screened by NKVD . . .', *VOV*, iv, pp. 191, n. 59, and 193, n. 65

p. 423 Red Army generals sentenced, Bezborodova, p. 15

p. 424 'long hours for artificial limbs . . .', V. Kardin, quoted Senyavskaya, 2000, p. 95

p. 424 'Wait until our boys . . .', 12 July, letter from Jews of Rubtsovsk in Altai to chairman of Council of Nationalities of the USSR, RGASPI 17/125/310, p. 47

p. 424 'by two anti-Semites . . .', RGASPI 17/125/310, p. 50

p. 425 'the nations of the Soviet Union', quoted Werth, pp. 1001-2

p. 425 'Our great genius . . .', TsAMO 233/2374/194, p. 83

p. 426 'we have not yet found . . .', 'Zeitung in der Zeitung', *Freie Welt*, July 1975, BA-MA MSg2/3626

p. 426 Stalin and Hitler's corpse, Rzhevskaya, 2000, pp. 292, 301

p. 426 'I still ride . . .', Zhukov, iv, pp. 297–8

p. 428 'for outstanding service . . .', BA-MA MSg2/3626

p. 428 'Zhukov! Zhukov! Zhukov!', Kazakova, conversation, 6 November 1999

p. 429 'the mistaken developments since 1933', Blumentritt interrogation, NA RG 338 B-338

p. 429 'a perverted moral . . .', 7 May, NA 740.0011 EW/5–1045

p. 430 'residual Nazism', SHAEF Psychological Warfare Division report, passed Murphy to State Department, NA 740.0011 EW/4–2445

Select Bibliography

Alanbrooke, Field Marshal Lord, *War Diaries 1939–1945*, London, 2001

Albrecht, Günter, and Hartwig, Wolfgang (eds.), *Ärzte: Erinnerungen, Erlebnisse, Bekentnisse*, Berlin (East), 1982

Altner, Helmut, *Totentanz Berlin: Tagebuchblätter eines Achtzhenjährigen*, Offenbach am Main, 1946

Ambrose, Stephen, *Eisenhower and Berlin: The Decision to Halt at the Elbe*, New York, 1967

Andreas-Friedrich, Ruth, *Der Schattenmann: Tagebuchaufzeichnungen 1938–1945*, Frankfurt am Main, 1983

– *Schauplatz Berlin: Tagebuchaufzeichnungen 1945–1948*, Frankfurt am Main, 1984

Annan, Noel, *Changing Enemies: The Defeat and Regeneration of Germany*, London, 1995

Anonymous, *A Woman in Berlin*, London, 1955

Antonov, V. S., 'Poslednie dni voiny', *ViZh*, No. 7, July 1987

Arnold, Dietmar, 'Die Flutung des Berliner S-Bahn Tunnels in den letzten Kriegstagen', in *Nord-Süd-Bahn: Vom Geistertunnel zur City-S-Bahn*, Berlin, 1999

Babadshanjan, A., *Hauptstoßkraft*, Berlin (East), 1981

Bacon, Edwin, *The Gulag at War: Stalin's Forced Labour System in the Light of the Archives*, London, 1994

Bark, D., and Gress, D., *A History of West Germany: From Shadow to Substance, 1945–1963*, Oxford, 1989

Bauer, Frank, Pfundt, Karen, and Le Tissier, Tony, *Der Todeskampf der Reichshaupt- stadt*, Berlin, 1994

Bauer, Magna E., *Ninth Army's Last Attack and Surrender*, Washington, DC, 1956

Beelitzer Heimatverein, *Um Beelitz harter Kampf*, Potsdam, 1999

Behrmann, Jörn, 'Grundlage Forschung im totalitären Staat', in Martin Stöhr (ed.), *Von der Verführbarkeit der Naturwissenschaft*, Frankfurt am Main, 1986

Below, Nicolaus von, *Als Hitlers Adjutant, 1937–1945*, Mainz, 1980

Berezhkov, V., *History in the Making*, Moscow, 1982

– *At Stalin's Side*, New York, 1994

Beria, Sergo, *Beria, My Father: Inside Stalin's Kremlin*, London, 2001

Bernadotte, Count Folke, *The Curtain Falls*, New York, 1945

Bezborodova, Irina, *Generale des Dritten Reiches in sowjetischer Hand, 1943–1956*, Graz/Moscow, 1998

Bezymenski, Lev, *Der Tod des Adolf Hitler: Unbekannte Dokumente aus Moskauer Archiven*, Hamburg, 1968

Bokov, F. M., 'Nastuplenie 5-i Udarnoi Armii s Magnushevskovo Platsdarma', *ViZh*, No. 1, 1974

– *Frühjahr des Sieges und der Befreiung*, Berlin (East), 1979

Boldt, Gerhard, *Die Letzten Tage der Reichskanzlei*, Hamburg, 1947

Bollmann, Erika, Baier, Eva, Fortsmann, Walther, and Reinold, Marianne, *Erinnerungen und Tatsachen – Die Kaiser-Wilhelm-Gesellschaft zur Förderung der Wissenschaften Göttingen-Berlin*, Stuttgart, 1956

Bordzilovsky, E., 'Uchastie 1-I armii Voiska Pol'skogo v Berlinskoi operatsii', *ViZh*, No. 10, October 1963

Borée, Karl Friedrich, *Frühling 45. Chronik einer Berliner Familie*, Darmstadt, 1954

Borkowski, Dieter, *Wer weiß, ob wir uns wiedersehen. Erinnerung an eine Berliner Jugend*, Berlin, 1991

Boveri, Margret, *Tage des Überlebens – Berlin 1945*, Munich, 1968

Bower, Tom, *The Paperclip Conspiracy*, London, 1987

Bradley, Omar, *A Soldier's Story*, London, 1951

Breloer, Heinrich, *Geheime Welten*, Frankfurt am Main, 1999

Bruyn, Günter de, *Zwischenbilanz. Eine Jugend in Berlin*, Frankfurt am Main, 1991

Burkert, Hans-Norbert, and Matußek, Klaus, *Zerstört – Besiegt – Befreit. Kampf um Berlin bis zur Kapitulation*, Berlin (West), 1985

Burleigh, Michael, *Germany Turns Eastwards: A study of Ostforschung in the Third Reich*, Cambridge, 1988

– *The Third Reich: A New History*, London, 2000

Busse, Theodor, 'Die letzte Schlacht der 9. Armee', *Wehrwissenschaftliche Rundschau*, 1954

Chaney, O. P., *Zhukov*, Norman, Oklahoma, 1996

Chinaryan, Ivan, 'Moi mesyats mai', in *Stroki s velikoi voiny*, Moscow, 2000

Chuikov, Vasily, *The End of the Third Reich*, London, 1967

Davies, Norman, *White Eagle, Red Star*, London, 1972
– *God's Playground: A History of Poland*, Vol. 2, London, 1981
Deane, J. R., *The Strange Alliance*, London, 1947
Delpla, François, *Hitler*, Paris, 1999
Deutschkron, Inge, *Ich trug den gelben Stern*, Cologne, 1978
Diem, Liselotte, *Fliehen oder bleiben? Dramatisches Kriegsende in Berlin*, Freiburg, 1982
Dinter, Andreas, *Berlin in Trümmern*, Berlin, 1999
Djilas, M., *Conversations with Stalin*, New York, 1962
Doenitz, Admiral Karl, *Memoirs*, Cleveland, 1958
Doernberg, Stefan, *Befreiung 1945. Ein Augenzeugenbericht*, Berlin (East), 1975
Domarus, M., *Reden und Proklamationen, 1932–1945*, Vol. ii, Würzburg, 1962
Dönhoff, Marion Gräfin, *Namen die keiner mehr nennt*, Munich, 1964
Dragunsky, David, *A Soldier's Life*, Moscow, 1977
Duffy, C., *Red Storm on the Reich*, London, 1993

Ehrenburg, Ilya, *The War 1941–1945*, New York, 1964
Eisenhower, Dwight, *Crusade in Europe*, New York, 1948
Elliott, W. A., *Esprit de Corps*, Norwich, 1996
Erickson, John, *The Road to Berlin*, London, 1999

Faizulin, A., and Dolbrovolsky, P., 'Vstyrecha na El'be', *ViZh*, No. 4, April 1979, pp. 51–3
Feis, Herbert, *The Atomic Bomb and the End of World War II*, Princeton, 1966
Fest, Joachim, *The Face of the Third Reich*, London, 1988
Feuersenger, Marianne, *Mein Kriegstagebuch: Zwischen Führerhauptquartier und Berliner Wirklichkeit*, Freiburg, 1982
Findahl, Theo, *Letzter Akt – Berlin 1939–1945*, Hamburg, 1946
Foerster, Roland G. (ed.), *Seelower Höhen 1945*, Hamburg, 1998
Fröhlich, S., *General Vlasov, Russen und Deutsche zwischen Hitler und Stalin*, Cologne, 1978

Gall, Vladimir, *Mein Weg nach Halle*, Berlin (East), 1988
Garayev, M., 'Georgi Zhukov: Life and Work After the War', in *Voennaia mysl*, Vol. 6, No. 4, 1997
Gehlen, Reinhard, *The Gehlen Memoirs*, London, 1972
Gellately, Robert, *Backing Hitler: Consent and Coercion in Nazi Germany*, Oxford, 2001
Gilbert, Martin, *Road to Victory*, London, 1986
Glantz, David (ed.), *Art of War Symposium. From the Vistula to the Oder: Soviet Offensive Operations – October 1944–March 1945*, US Army War College, 1986

Glantz, David, and House, Jonathan, *When Titans Clashed*, Kansas, 1995

Glenn Gray, J., *The Warriors: Reflections on Men in Battle*, New York, 1970

Goldhagen, Daniel, *Hitler's Willing Executioners: Ordinary Germans and the Holocaust*, New York, 1996

Gosztony, Peter, *Der Kampf um Berlin 1945, in Augenzeugenberichten*, Düsseldorf, 1970

Gribov, Yuri, 'Igral nam v Brandenburge grammofon . . .', in *Stroki s velikoi voiny*, Moscow, 2000

Gross, Leonard, *The Last Jews in Berlin*, New York, 1982

Guderian, Heinz, *Panzer Leader*, New York, 1952

Gun, Nevin E., *Eva Braun: Hitler's Mistress*, London, 1969

Henning, Eckhart, and Kazemi, Marion, *Veröffentlichungen aus dem Archiv zur Geschichte der Max-Planck-Gesellschaft*, Vol. I, Berlin (West), 1988

Herbert, Ulrich, *Hitler's Foreign Workers*, Cambridge, 1997

Hirschfeld, Gerhard, and Renz, Irina, *Besiegt und Befreit, Stimmen vom Kriegsende 1945*, Gerlingen, 1995

Inozemtsev, N., *Tsena pobedy v toi samoi voine*, Moscow, 1995

Irving, David, *Adolf Hitler: The Medical Diaries – the Private Diaries of Dr Theo Morell*, London, 1983

Isaev, S. I., 'Vekhi frontovogo puti', *ViZh*, No. 10, October 1991, pp. 22–5

Italiander, Rolf, Bauer, Arnold, and Krafft, Herbert, *Berlins Stunde Null*, Düsseldorf, 1979

Joachimsthaler, A., *The Last Days of Hitler*, London, 1996

Joachimsthaler, A. (ed.), *Er war mein chef, ans dem Nachlass der Sekretärin von Adolf Hitler, Christa Schroeder*, Munich, 1985

Kardorff, Ursula von, *Berliner Aufzeichnungen, 1942 bis 1945*, Munich, 1997

Kaskewitsch, Emanuel, *Frühling an der Oder*, Berlin (East), 1953

Kee, Robert, *A Crowd is Not Company*, London, 2000

Kehlenbeck, Paul, *Schicksal Elbe. Im Zweifrontenkrieg 1945 zwischen Heide, Harz und Havelland. Ein Bericht nach alten Tagebüchern*, Frankfurt am Main, 1993

Keiderling, Gerhard, *Gruppe Ulbricht in Berlin*, Berlin, 1993

– 'Als Befreier unsere Herzen zerbrachen: Zu den Übergriffen der Sowjetarmee in Berlin 1945', *Deutschland Archiv*, 28, 1995

Keitel, Wilhelm, *The Memoirs of Field Marshal Keitel*, London, 1965

Kempka, Erich, *Die letzten Tage mit Adolf Hitler*, Preussich-Oldendorf, 1976

Kershaw, Ian, *The Hitler Myth: Image and Reality in the Third Reich*, Oxford, 1989

– *The Nazi Dictatorship: Problems and Perspectives of Interpretation*, London, 1993

– *Hitler: 1889–1936, Hubris*, London, 1998

– *Hitler: 1936–1945, Nemesis*, London, 2000

Kershaw, Ian, and Lewin, Moshe (eds.), *Stalinism and Nazism: Dictatorships in Comparison*, Cambridge, 1998

Kireev, N., 'Primenenie tankovykh army v Vislo-Oderskoi operatsii', *ViZh*, No. 1, 1985

Kleine, Helmut, and Stimpel, Hans-Martin, *Junge Soldaten in der Mark Brandenburg 1945 – Rückerinnerungen nach einem halben Jahrhundert*, 1995 (MGFA)

Klemperer, Victor, *To the Bitter End, 1942–1945*, London, 1999

Klimov, Gregory, *The Terror Machine: The Inside Story of the Soviet Administration in Germany*, London, 1953

Klochkov, I. F., *Znamya pobedy nad Reikhstagom*, St Petersburg, 2000

Knappe, Siegfried, *Soldat*, New York, 1993

Knef, Hildegard, *The Gift Horse: Report on a Life*, New York, 1971

Knight, Amy, *Beria: Stalin's First Lieutenant*, Princeton, NJ, 1993

Kon, Igor, *Sex and Russian Society*, Bloomington, Indiana, 1993

Kondaurov, I. A., 'V 45-m my sami iskali protivnika', in *Vsem smertyam nazlo*, Moscow, 2000

Konev, I. S., *Year of Victory*, Moscow, 1984

Kopelev, Lev, *No Jail for Thought*, London, 1977

Krivosheev, G. F. (ed.), *Grif sekretnosti snyat poteri vooruzhennykh sil SSSR v voinakh, boevykh deistviyakh i voennykh konfliktakh*, Moscow, 1993

Krockow, Christian Graf von, *Die Stunde der Frauen*, Munich, 1999

Kronika, Jacob, *Der Untergang Berlins*, Hamburg, 1946

Kuznetsov V. G., and Medlinsky, V. P., 'Agoniya', *ViZh*, Nos. 6–7, June–July 1992

Ladd, Brian, *The Ghosts of Berlin*, Chicago, 1997

Lakowski, R., *Seelow 1945, Die Entscheidungsschlacht an der Oder*, Berlin, 1999

Lakowski, R., and Dorst, K., *Berlin – Frühjahr 1945*, Berlin (East), 1975

Lane, Anne, and Temperley, Howard (eds.), *The Rise and Fall of the Grand Alliance, 1941–1945*, London, 1995

Lange, Horst, in. H. D. Schäfer (ed.), *Tagebücher aus dem Zweiten Weltkrieg*, Mainz, 1979

Laufer, Jochen, '"Genossen, wie ist das Gesamtbild?" Ackermann, Ulbricht und Sobottka in Moskau im Juni 1945', *Deutschland Archiv*, 29, 1996

Lehndorf, Hans Graf von, *Ostpreußisches Tagebuch – Aufzeichnungen eines Arztes aus den Jahren 1945–1947*, Munich, 1999

Lemmer, Ernst, *Manches war doch anders: Erinnerungen eines deutschen Demokraten*, Frankfurt am Main, 1968

Leon, R. W., *The Making of an Intelligence Officer*, London, 1994

Leonhard, Wolfgang, *Child of the Revolution*, London, 1956

Le Tissier, T., *Zhukov at the Oder: The Decisive Battle for Berlin*, London, 1996
– *Race for the Reichstag*, London, 1999
– *With Our Backs to Berlin*, Stroud, 2001
Liddell-Hart, Basil, *The Other Side of the Hill*, London, 1948
Luchinsky, A., 'Na Berlin!', *ViZh*, No. 5, May 1965
Luck, Hans von, *Panzer Commander: The Memoirs of Colonel Hans von Luck*, New
    York, 1989
Lumans, Valdis, *Himmler's Auxiliaries: The Volksdeutsche Mittelstelle and the German
    National Minorities of Europe 1933–1945*, London, 1992

Mabire, Jean, *La Division Nordland*, Paris, 1982
– *Mourir à Berlin*, Paris, 1995
Machtan, Lothar, *The Hidden Hitler*, London, 2001
Mackintosh, Malcolm, *Juggernaut: The Russian Forces, 1918–1996*, London, 1967
Maizière, Ulrich de, *In der Pflicht*, Bonn, 1989
Makarevsky, V., '17-ya motorinzhenernaia brigada v Berlinskoi operatsii', *ViZh*,
    No. 4, April 1976
Meinecke, Friedrich, *Die deutsche Katastrophe*, Wiesbaden, 1947
Menzel, Matthias, *Die Stadt ohne Tod. Berliner Tagebuch 1943–5*, Berlin, 1946
Merridale, Catherine, *Night of Stone*, London, 2000
Messerschmidt, Manfred, *Was damals Recht war . . . Nationalsozialistische-Militär-
    und Strafjustiz im Vernichtungskrieg*, Essen, 1996
Meyer, Karen, 'Die Flutung des Berliner S-Bahn Tunnels in den letzten Kriegs-
    tagen', in Berliner S-Bahn-Museum, *Nord-Süd-Bahn*, Berlin, 1999
Meyer, Sibylle, and Schulze, Eva, *Wie wir das alles geschafft haben. Alleinstehende
    Frauen berichten über ihr Leben nach 1945*, Munich, 1984
Morozov, Boris, 'Mgnovenie voiny', *Stroki s velikoi voiny*, Moscow, 2000
Murphy, David, Kondraschev, Sergei, and Bailey, George, *Battleground Berlin*,
    London, 1987
Murphy, Robert, *Diplomat among Warriors*, New York, 1964
Musmanno, Michael A., *Ten Days to Die*, New York, 1950

Naimark, Norman, *The Russians in Germany: A History of the Soviet Zone of Occupa-
    tion, 1945–1949*, Cambridge, Mass., 1995
Neustroev, S. A., 'Shturm Reikhstaga', *ViZh*, No. 5, May 1960, pp. 42–5
Nikolai, Vasiliev, 'Krasnyi tsvet pobedy', in *Vsem smertyam nazlo*, Moscow, 2000
Noakes, Jeremy (ed.), *Nazism 1919–1945: A Documentary Reader*, Vol. iv, Exeter,
    1998

Oven, Wilfred von, *Mit Goebbels bis zum Ende*, Vol. ii, Buenos Aires, 1950
Overy, Richard, *Why the Allies Won*, London, 1995

– *Russia's War*, London, 1998

Owings, Alison, *Frauen: German Women Recall the Third Reich*, London, 1993

Padfield, P., *Himmler: Reichsführer SS*, London, 1990

Peredelsky, G., and Khoroshilov, G., 'Artilleriya v srazheniyakh ot Visly do Odera', *ViZh*, No. 1, 1985

Petrova, Ada, and Watson, Peter, *The Death of Hitler*, London, 1995

Pogue, Forrest C., 'The Decision to Halt on the Elbe, 1945', in Greenfield Kent (ed.), *Command Decisions*, London, 1960

Polyan, Pavel, 'Vestarbaitery: internirovannye nemtsy na sovetskikh stroikakh', *Rodina*, No. 9, 1999

Prikazy Verkhovnogo Glavnokomanduyushchego v period Velikoi Otechestvennoi voiny Sovetskogo Soyuza, Moscow, 1975

Ramanichev, N. M., 'Iz opyta peregruppirovki army pri podgotovke Berlinskoi operatsii', *ViZh*, No. 8, 1979

Ramm, Gerald, *Ein unbekannter Kamerad. Deutsche Kriegsgräberstätten zwischen Oderbruch und Spree*, Woltersdorf, 1993

– *Gott mit uns – Kriegserlebnisse aus Brandenburg und Berlin*, Woltersdorf, 1994

– *Halbe – Bericht über einen Friedhof*, Woltersdorf, 1995

Rein, Heinz, *Finale Berlin*, Frankfurt am Main, 1981

Richie, Alexandra, *Faust's Metropolis*, London, 1998

Rocolle, Pierre, *Götterdämmerung – La Prise de Berlin*, Indo-China, 1954

– *Le sac de Berlin, avril–mai 1945*, Paris, 1992

Rokossovsky, K. K., *Soldatsky dolg*, Moscow, 1968

Rubenstein, Joshua, *Tangled Loyalties: The Life and Times of Ilya Ehrenburg*, New York, 1996

Ruhl, Klaus-Jörg (ed.), *Unsere verlorenen Jahre – Frauenalltag in Kriegs- und Nachkriegszeit, 1939–1949*, Darmstadt, 1985

Runov, Boris Alexandrovich, 'Znanie nemetskogo pomoglo vzyat' v plen soten shest' nemtsev', in *Vsem smertyam nazlo*, Moscow, 2000

Rürup, Reinhard (ed.), *Berlin 1945. Eine Dokumentation*, Berlin, 1995

– *Topographie des Terrors, Gestapo, SS und Reichssicherheitshauptamt auf dem 'Prinz-Albrecht-Gelände'*, Berlin, 1997

Russian Federation, *Velikaya Otechestvennaya Voina*, Vols. iii and iv, Moscow, 1999

Ryan, Cornelius, *The Last Battle*, London, 1966

Rzheshevsky, O. A., 'The Race for Berlin', *Journal of Slavic Military Studies*, 8, September 1995

– 'Der Wettlauf nach Berlin – Ein dokumentarischer Überblick', in Foerster, *Seelower Höhen 1945*

Rzhevskaya, Yelena, *Berlin, Mai 1945*, Moscow, 1986
– *Vecherny razgovor*, St Petersburg, 2001

Sajer, Guy, *The Forgotten Soldier*, London, 1997
Sander, Helke, and Johr, Barbara (eds), *Befreier und Befreite. Krieg, Vergewaltigungen, Kinder*, Munich, 1992
Schäfer, Hans Dieter, *Berlin im Zweiten Weltkrieg, Der Untergang der Reichshauptstadt in Augenzeugenberichten*, Munich, 1985
Scheel, Klaus (ed.), *Die Befreiung Berlins 1945*, Berlin (East), 1985
Schenk, Ernst-Günther, *Ich sah Berlin sterben. Als Arzt in der Reichskanzlei*, Herford, 1970
Schmitz-Berning, Cornelia, *Vokabular des Nationalsozialismus*, Berlin, 1998
Shultz-Naumann, Joachim, *Die letzten dreißig Tage. Das Kriegstagebuch des OKW April–Mai 1945*, Munich, 1980
Schwarz, Hans, *Brennpunkt FHQ: Menschen und Maßtäbe im Führerhauptquartier*, Buenos Aires, 1950
Schwarzer, Alice, *Marion Dönhoff, Ein widerständiges Leben*, Munich, 1997
Schwerin, Kerrin Gräfin, *Frauen im Krieg – Briefe, Dokumente, Aufzeichnungen*, Berlin, 1999
Seaton, A., *The Russo-German War 1941–1945*, New York, 1972
Senyavskaya, Yelena, *1941–1945 Frontovoe pokolenie*, Moscow, 1995
– *Psikhologiya voiny v XX-m veke*, Moscow, 2000
Sereny, Gitta, *Albert Speer: His Battle with Truth*, London, 1995
Sevruk, V. (ed.), *How Wars End: Eyewitness Accounts of the Fall of Berlin*, Moscow, 1969
Shatilov, Nikolai, 'U sten Reikhstaga', in *Vsem smertyam nazlo*, Moscow, 2000
Shatunovsky, Ilya, 'I ostanetsya dobry sled', in *Vsem smertyam nazlo*, Moscow, 2000
Shcheglov, Dmitry, 'Military Council Representative', in Sevruk (ed.), *How Wars End*
Shcherbakov, B., 'Material'noe obespechenie 4-i tankovoi armii v Vislo-Oderskoi operatsii', *ViZh*, No. 6, 1979
Sherwood, Robert E., *The White House Papers of Harry L. Hopkins*, London, 1948
Shindel, Aleksandr Danilovich (ed.), *Po obe storony fronta*, Moscow, 1995
Shirer, William L., *End of a Berlin Diary*, New York, 1947
Shtemenko, S. M., *The Last Six Months*, New York, 1977
Shukman, Harold (ed.), *Stalin's Generals*, London, 1993
Sinenko, I., 'Organizatsiya i vedenie boya 164-m strelkovym polkom za Batslov pod Berlinom', *ViZh*, No. 4, April 1976
Smirnov, E., 'Deistviya 47 Gv. T. Br v peredovom otryade tankovogo korpusa', *ViZh*, No. 1, 1978
Solzhenitsyn, A., *The Gulag Archipelago*, Vol. i, New York, 1974

– *Prussian Nights* (tr. Robert Conquest), New York, 1983
– *Deux récits de guerre*, Paris, 2000
Soyuz veteranov zhurnalistiki, *'Zhivaya pamyat': Velikaya Otechestvennaya*, Vol. iii, Moscow, 1995
Spahr, W., *Zhukov: The Rise and Fall of a Great Captain*, Novato, Calif., 1993
Steinhoff, Johannes et al., *Voices from the Third Reich: An Oral History*, New York, 1994
Studnitz, Hans-Georg von, *While Berlin Burns*, London, 1964
Subbotin, Vassily, in Sevruk (ed.), *How Wars End*

Terkel, Studs, *The Good War*, London, 2001
Thorwald, Jürgen, *Es begann an der Weichsel*, Stuttgart, 1950
– *Das Ende an der Elbe*, Stuttgart, 1950
Tieke, Wilhelm, *Das Ende zwischen Oder und Elbe – Der Kampf um Berlin 1945*, Stuttgart, 1981
Trevor-Roper, Hugh, *The Last Days of Hitler*, London, 1995
Tsvetaev, E. N. (ed.), *Zhukov: Kakim my ego pomnim*, Moscow, 1988
Tully, Andrew, *Berlin – the Story of a Battle*, New York, 1963
Tumarkin, Nina, *The Living and the Dead: The Rise and Fall of the Cult of World War II in Russia*, New York, 1994

Vasiliev, Nikolay, 'Krasny tsvet pobedy', in *Vsem smertyam nazlo*, Moscow, 2000
Vermehren, Isa, *Reise durch den letzten Akt. Ein Bericht*, Hamburg, 1947
Vishnevsky, Vsevolod, 'Berlin Surrenders', in Sevruk (ed.), *How Wars End*
Volkogonov, Dmitri, *Stalin – Triumph and Tragedy*, New York, 1991

Warlimont, W., *Inside Hitler's Headquarters, 1939–1945*, London, 1964
Weidling, General Helmuth, *Der Endkampf in Berlin*, Potsdam, 1962
Weltlinger, S., *Hast du es schon vergessen? Erlebnisberichte aus der Zeit der Verfolgung*, Berlin, 1960
Werth, Alexander, *Russia at War*, London, 1964
Wolf, Markus, *Spionagechef im geheimen Krieg*, Munich, 1997
– *Die Kunst der Verstellung*, Berlin, 1998

Zaloga, Steven J., *Target America – the Soviet Union and the Strategic Arms Race, 1945–1964*, Novato, Calif., 1992
Zayas, Alfred M. de, *Nemesis at Potsdam: The Expulsion of the Germans from the East*, London, 1989
Zbarsky, Ilya, and Hutchinson, Samuel, *Lenin's Embalmers*, London, 1998
Zhukov, G. K., *Vospominaniya i razmyshleniya*, Vol. iv, Moscow, 1995
Ziemke, Earl, *The Battle for Berlin: End of the Third Reich*, London, 1969

Select Bibliography

– *The Soviets' Lost Opportunity; Berlin in February 1945*, London, 1969
– *The US Army in the Occupation of Germany 1944–1946*, Washington, DC, 1975
– *Stalingrad to Berlin: The German Defeat in the East*, Washington, DC, 1987

PUBLICATIONS

Der Angriff   *Istoricheskii Arkhiv*
Der Panzerbär   *Krasnaya Zvezda*
Freie Welt (DDR)   *Pravda*

Index